Stuart B. Philpott

PHYSICAL ANTHROPOLOGY AND ARCHEOLOGY

PHYSICAL ANTHROPOLOGY AND ARCHEOLOGY

Second Edition

Clifford J. Jolly
New York University

Fred Plog
Arizona State University

with **Joan Acocella**

Alfred A. Knopf New York

THIS IS A BORZOI BOOK
PUBLISHED BY ALFRED A. KNOPF, INC.

Second Edition
987654321

Library of Congress Cataloging in Publication Data

Jolly, Clifford J. 1939–
Physical anthropology and archeology.

1. Physical anthropology. 2. Archeology.
I. Plog, Fred, joint author. II. Title.
GN60.J65 1979 573 78-12996
ISBN 0-394-32093-X

Manufactured in the United States of America

Cover photo: M. P. Kahl/Bruce Coleman, Inc.

Photo research: Flavia Rando
Photo editor: R. Lynn Goldberg

Charts, graphs, and maps: Vantage Art, Inc.

ACKNOWLEDGMENTS

P. 71: Figure, from J. Kingdon, *East African Mammals.* Copyright © 1971 by J. Kingdon. Permission granted by the author. *P. 91:* Figure, from J. R. Napier and P. H. Napier, *A Handbook of Living Primates.* Copyright © 1967 Academic Press, Inc. Reprinted by permission. *P. 114:* Figure, (a) modified from F. A. Jenkins, ed., *Primate Locomotion.* Copyright © 1974 Academic Press, Ltd. Reprinted by permission of author and publisher; (b) courtesy of Animal Talent Scouts, Inc. from a photograph by Ralph Morse, *Life Magazine,* © Time, Inc.; (c) modified
(Continued on p. xxv following the Index)

Preface to the Second Edition

Our object in this book is to introduce the study of human physical and cultural evolution to students with little previous knowledge of biology or anthropology. Traditionally, texts have treated human biology and culture as separate subjects; physical anthropology and archeology as parallel but separate disciplines. We do not believe this is justified. The story of the evolution of human structure, behavior, and culture is one story. The characters change and the plot sometimes wanders, but certain major themes run throughout. Change and stability, adaptation, diversification, extinction—these are recurrent patterns in the evolution of the human species and human cultures. There is no point in this story where physical evolution ceases or cultural evolution begins. The two are intertwined in ongoing processes. Inevitably, as we reach the later chapters, we find that the pace of cultural evolution has so far outstripped physical change that archeological data occupy most of our attention. But physical variations have always played and will always play a significant part in human adaptation—a point we emphasize throughout.

As readers will quickly discover, the study of human evolution is a lively and growing discipline, full of unresolved controversies, disputes, and disagreements. (This is hardly surprising, given our subject matter: the human species.) We do not pretend to impartiality in these debates; to do so would be to abdicate the role of teacher for that of reporter or journalist. Rather, we have attempted to indicate the areas of debate and to present the evidence and explain methods in a way that will enable readers to evaluate the merits of our own and others' interpretations.

For the second edition we have substantially expanded our treatment of three major areas: Mendelian genetics (Chapter 2), human physical and cultural evolution from 250,000 to 40,000 B.P., the period of archaic *Homo sapiens* (Chapter 10), and complex variation in modern human populations, including the controversies over racial classifications and the inheritance of IQ (Chapter 15). Each of these now has an entire chapter to itself, instead of sharing a chapter with other material, as in the previous edition. In addition, we have incorporated significant new material on many topics throughout the book, among them inclusive fitness, the origins of language, the extinction of the neandertals and the appearance of fully modern humans, and the rise of the state. An Appendix on molecular genetics has been added. Much of the text has been rewritten; our aim has been to achieve greater clarity, simplicity, and liveliness. In particular, we have tried to depict more vividly and concretely how human beings lived at various stages of their physical and cultural evolution. Finally, a number of technical terms—especially anatomical ones—have been dropped in favor of their everyday equivalents. Technical terms that are essential for precise understanding and efficient communication have been defined in end-of-chapter glossaries to make study and review easier for students.

Producing a clear, readable text that does not gloss over new research and advanced ideas is a difficult undertaking, requiring the collective efforts of a team of professionals. The process involved a complex interaction among the authors, editors, reviewers, and illustrators, with all of those concerned investing more time in this book than would normally be the case. Clifford J. Jolly developed Chapters 2 through 8, 14, and 15; Fred Plog, Chapters 11 through 13; each contributed to Chapters 1, 9, and 10.

In particular, we would like to credit our editor, Dan Schiller, who directed and coordinated the work on the second edition, as well as Virginia Hoitsma, who did the same on the first edition. Biruta Akerbergs and Robert Frank provided drawings that reflect both the structure and the beauty of their subjects. Our sincere thanks are due to colleagues who read and commented on various parts of the text: Daniel Bates, Richard Blanton, Martin Boksenbaum, Margaret Conkey, Eric Delson, Sylvia Forman, David Frayer, Mark Harlan, Gregory Johnson, Francis Lees, Mark Leone, Michael Little, Philip Rightmire, Barbara Stark, Frederick Szalay, Paul Voninski, Charles Weitz, and Stephen Zegura. Graduate students Judy Rasson, Bruce Donaldson, Margie Green, Walter Wait, John Knoerl, Frank McManamon, and Ronald Anzalone provided valuable assistance.

Finally, we should like to thank our families for tolerating the many times when we were "too busy."

C. J. *New York, N.Y.*
F. P. *Tempe, Ariz.*

Contents

Part I Introduction to Evolutionary Theory

Part II The Primates and Their Evolution

Part III Human Physical and Cultural Evolution

Part IV Variation in Modern *Homo sapiens*

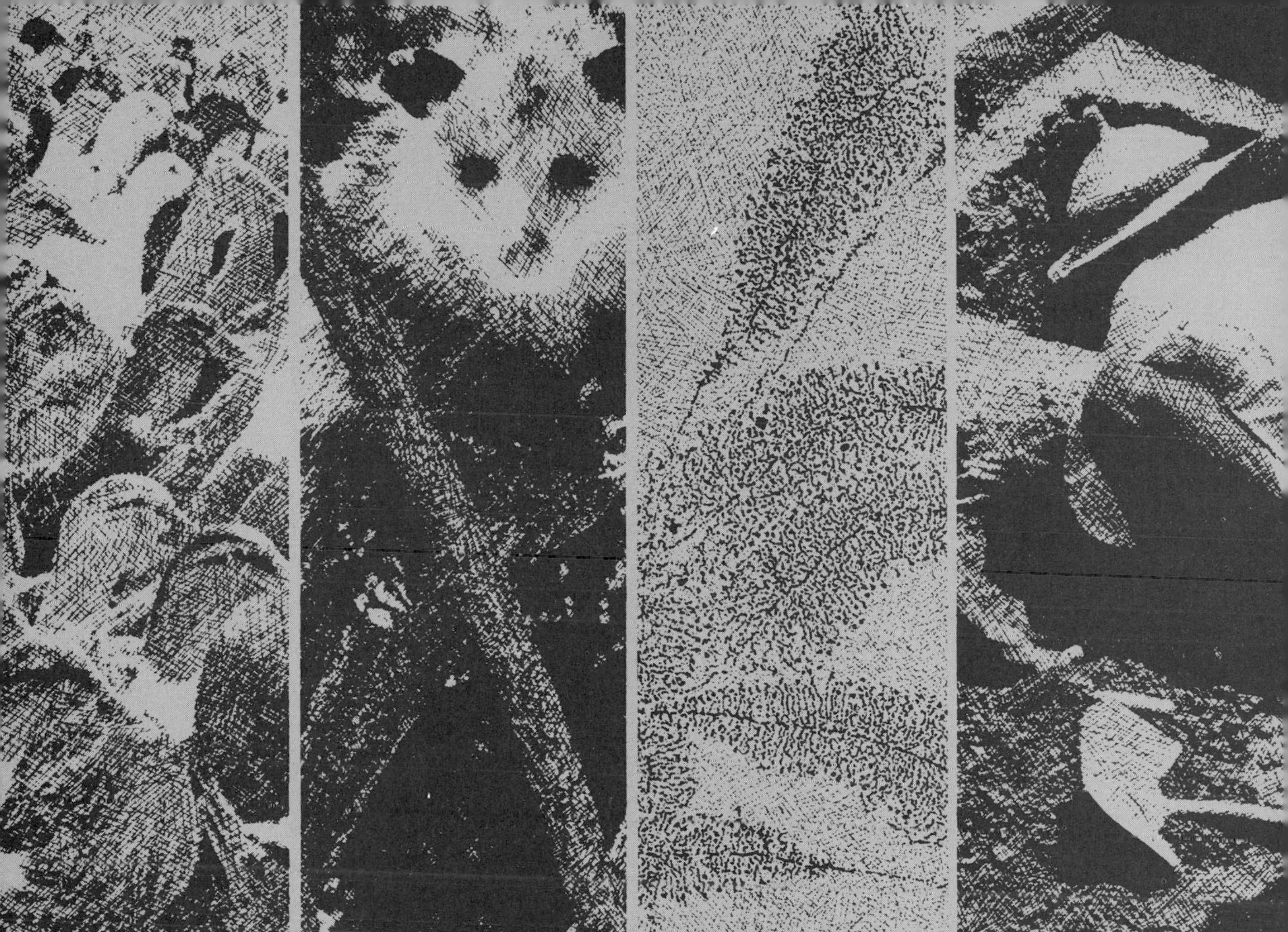

Part One

Introduction to Evolutionary Theory

Chapter One

The Evolutionary Study of Humans

All science is an effort to describe and explain natural phenomena. The aim of the discipline of anthropology is to describe and explain one particular natural phenomenon: *Homo sapiens*, the human species. Anthropology is concerned with all peoples everywhere, both those alive today and those—almost more ape than human—who lived in the distant past. And it is concerned with many aspects of their lives, from the shape of their teeth to how they get their food, build their houses, and bring up their children.

There are a number of ways to approach this vast subject. Some anthropologists explore physical variations in contemporary human populations—differences in body build, blood types, and susceptibility to various diseases. Others concentrate on the physical history of the species—studying our closest living relatives, the monkeys and apes, or retrieving and analyzing fossils, in an attempt to determine what our more primitive ancestors looked like and how they lived. Still others study the evolution of human culture, piecing together the remains of extinct societies and trying to formulate general principles as to how societies develop. Finally, others focus on contemporary cultures—the institutions, customs, beliefs, and languages of peoples throughout the world. Yet each of these studies benefits from, and sheds light on, the others. For the human pattern is a unity; what we are now is related to what we were in the distant past, and our cultures are influenced by our biological nature.

Physical anthropologists study the evolution of the human species and its place in nature among other living forms. Archeologists study human societies of the past, their ecological contexts, and the processes of cultural change that they exemplify. Much of the evidence used by both disciplines is buried, and must be painstakingly retrieved from the earth. These excavations are at Ife, Nigeria. *(Georg Gerster/Rapho/Photo Researchers)*

WHAT IS ANTHROPOLOGY?

Anthropology is not the only discipline concerned with what human beings are and how they came to be so. However, anthropologists approach these questions from a unique perspective. Psychologists, sociologists, political scientists, economists, and historians all study relations among human beings and human groups, but they are not primarily concerned with the relations between humans and the rest of the natural world. For anthropologists, on the other hand, this is where the subject begins: with the human species' place in nature, its interactions with the environment, and its relationships to other species.

Humans as Animals

Human beings are not separate from nature, or even *in* nature. Rather, we are *of* nature, one among its millions of species. Part of the task of anthropology is to view the human species in relation to the rest of the animal kingdom and identify the continuities and discontinuities between ourselves and other animals. What is it that makes us specifically human?

Like any species, humans possess a distinctive combination of physical and behavioral characteristics. We walk upright on two feet, use our hands extensively for grasping and manipulating objects, live in complex social groupings, and fashion and use many kinds of tools. Furthermore, we are capable of learning abstract theories and complex ideas and have developed a complex form of symbolic communication that we call language.

None of these characteristics, considered individually, is ours exclusively. Other animals, for example, walk upright at times. Chimpanzees, sea otters, and even some birds use simple tools in getting their food. Other species, too, have evolved complex forms of social organization (consider the bees and the ants). And almost all creatures, even the simplest, are capable of some degree of learning and of some form of communication with other members of their species. Nevertheless, the human manifestation of these characteristics is quite distinctive. For one thing, no other species has elaborated them to the extent that we have. More importantly, taken together they form an interactive complex on which our entire way of life is built. In particular, our distinctive mental qualities—our behavioral flexibility and our capacity for learning, abstraction, and symbolic communication—enable us to devise, communicate, share, and transmit to subsequent generations a great variety of ideas and behaviors. These constitute the foundation of what is known as culture.

In the broadest sense, *culture* may be defined as the system of shared meanings that people learn from their society for use in interacting with their surroundings, communicating with others, and coping with their world. This definition includes a wide range of practices, customs, beliefs, and values. By extension, it also includes human artifacts—tools, pottery, houses, machines, works of art, and so on—since they are the products of culturally transmitted skills, techniques, and traditions.

It is important to realize, however, that culture is not a single, or a static, entity. Indeed, what is most striking about human cultures is their diversity and flexibility. Each human society has developed its own distinct culture, according to its own needs and circumstances. What distinguishes our species, then, is not so much the possession of a culture as the *capacity* to evolve a great many different cultures.

Human Variability

As in any other animal species, there is considerable variation within the human species. From individual to individual there are differences in height, weight, skin color, rate of development, blood type, and innumerable other physical characteristics. Similarly, from population to population there are broad differences in average height, typical skin color, susceptibility to various diseases, and so forth. Such variation is multiplied when we add to it cultural differences. Not only does each individual have his or her own particular way of doing things, but societies too have different codes of appropriate behavior that mold the actions of their members. They also have different subsistence strategies—ways of exploiting the resources of their particular environment. A major concern of anthropology is to describe these physical and behavioral differences, especially differences among populations, and to explain them. To what extent are they determined by innate biological differences among people and to what extent by the physical or cultural environment? Can they be interpreted as adaptations, either genetic or cultural, to differing environments? Difficult as such questions are to answer, they provide the focus for much anthropological study.

Humans in Ecological Context

One of the most important manifestations of our position in nature is our dependence on the rest of nature. We, along with every other form of life, are part of a single *ecosystem*—a cycle of matter and energy that includes all living things and links them to the nonliving. All organisms depend on energy, derived ultimately from the huge atomic furnace that we call the sun; and matter, derived ultimately from the earth. To survive, each species must find a place within the ecosystem—a way of procuring the matter and energy it needs in the face of competition from other species.

In our dependence on our environment, we are no different from the lowliest bacterium or fungus. Nevertheless, our capacity for culture has put us in an unusual position within the ecosystem. This fact becomes strikingly evident when we look at our habitats and econiche. The *habitat* of a species is the area where it lives, its surroundings. Its *econiche* is its "way of making a living," as defined by what it does and by its relationships with other species—what it eats, what eats it, and so on. Most animals are limited to a few habitats and a comparatively narrow econiche. By contrast, we occupy an exceptionally broad econiche (think of the great variety of foods eaten by human beings, and the many ways in which they are procured), and live in a wide range of diverse habitats. Indeed, there are very few environments, from deserts to arctic ice sheets to tropical rain forests, where human beings have not found a way to thrive.

This extreme adaptability of our species is due largely to the refinement of one particular aspect of human culture: technology—that is, our tools and our knowledge of how to use them. Whereas other species are limited in the forms of energy they can use, technology has allowed us to transform a vast number of materials into sources of usable energy. We extract metals from the earth, for example, and fashion them into machines; then we extract fossil fuels—coal, oil, gas,—from the earth to run those machines. Of course, there are many energy resources that we share with other animals, but technology has enabled us to use even these resources in a variety of different ways. To use the energy stored in a tree, for example, other animals must drink its sap or eat its leaves and branches. Humans can not only eat the tree's products but also cut it down and use its energy in the form of fire to warm our homes and cook our food. We use the energy stored in other animals' muscles, not only by eating them, but also by harnessing them to plows or putting bits in their mouths and riding them. When a plant or animal is not well enough suited for our needs, we alter it through selective breeding to make it more useful. Even when we are using an energy resource in much the same way as other animals, technological aids allow us to exploit that resource on a grand scale. To catch a fish, a bear wades into the water and scoops one up with its paw; we send out fishing fleets to scoop them up by the thousands.

In short, technology has given us the means to funnel a vast proportion of the earth's resources of matter and energy through our own species. As a result, we have thrived. Today, we are the most widely dispersed species on the planet. Our total biomass—the total weight of the living members of the species—exceeds that of any other animal, and we are adding to it at an astonishingly rapid rate.

Yet our apparent success should not blind us to the fact that we are still dependent on the ecosystem and that its resources, no matter how ingeniously we exploit them, are still limited. The solutions that we find to our ever-increasing needs for food and energy tend to be more and more costly. Worse, they often create new environmental problems, for which we need still costlier solutions. For example, when agricultural scientists succeeded in breeding new, high-yield varieties of corn and rice, this discovery was hailed as the beginning of a "green revolution" that might put an end to human hunger. As it turned out, however, the new strains require more chemical fertilizers than their lower-yield predecessors, and are often more vulnerable to insect pests. Unfortunately, stepping up production of fertilizers and pesticides means using more petroleum—a highly limited resource—both as a raw material and to power the chemical factories. Furthermore, the high-yield strains often need elaborate irrigation, which in many areas has caused erosion and increased the salinity of the soil, making it less fertile. Cultivation of the high-yield crops also generally requires machinery for harvesting—and therefore, more money, more industrial production, and more energy. In sum, we tend to be ingenious only in the short run. Year by year, we are forced to raise the stakes; and like the Red Queen in *Through the Looking Glass* we have to run as fast as we can to stay in the same place.

Though our current dilemma is especially dramatic, involving a global ecosystem in which all humans have a stake, every human society has had to deal with resource problems, and most have done so with no more foresight than we. Indeed, all human groups are strongly influenced, both physically and culturally, by their relationship to their environment. The anthropologist studying ancient societies is often struck by the fact that new subsistence strategies must constantly be adopted to cope with ecological crises—and by how frequently such strategies fail.

Humans in an Evolutionary Context

Finally, to consider the human species as a part of nature is to consider its evolutionary relationship to other species—that is, our kinship with other animals by virtue of descent from common ancestors. Our species is related to every other living thing on earth. This is true not just in a metaphorical sense or in some vague sentimental sense, but in a strict biological sense, as two cousins are related by virtue of having the same grandparents. To some species we are of course more closely related than to others. In behavior, anatomy, and molecular structure, humans have more in common with a chimpanzee than a monkey, a monkey than a dog, a dog than a frog, a frog than a bacterium. The reason for this is that the chimpanzee is quite *literally* our closest living relative; about 14 million years ago, the ancestor of today's chimpanzees was also your ancestor and ours. Ultimately, however, *all* living things, ourselves included, are descended from the same forebears—minute organisms that lived billions of years ago in a world we would not recognize.

The diversity of the natural world is the result of *evolutionary change.* Human evolution is the sequence of biological and, eventually, cultural changes that have propelled us along our unique path and have produced the human species as we know it today. This evolutionary history and the processes that underlie it are of paramount interest to anthropologists, and merit a somewhat fuller introduction.

Evolution

Before discussing the nature of evolutionary change, let us summarize briefly the course it has taken in our species. From what we can reconstruct, the first members of the primate order (the group of mammals that includes monkeys, apes, and humans) appeared about 70 million years ago. They were small, tree-dwelling creatures somewhat like modern tree shrews. Gradually, over millions of years, these creatures gave rise to animals that were more like modern monkeys and apes that showed what we now recognize as distinctive primate trends, including relatively large brains, grasping hands and feet, and a tendency to rely more on vision than on the sense of smell. Eventually, a crucial change took place: the change from life in the trees to life on the ground. Populations of early apes living on the edge of the tropical rain forest became accustomed to foraging for food on the savanna, or grassy plain, that lay beyond the forest and eventually they remained there permanently.

However the transition occurred, we know from fossils that a close relative of the human species lived on the savannas of East and South Africa from about 5 to about 1 million B.P.[1] This creature, called *Australopithecus,* had a larger brain than any of its forest-dwelling ancestors. And unlike them, it was *bipedal*—that is, it stood and walked upright, on two feet. This was a highly significant change, since it left the hands free for all the tasks to which culture would eventually put them.

Apparently, this group developed a side-branch, for by about 2 million B.P. we find *Australopithecus* sharing the African savannas with a larger-brained cousin, recognized as our earliest truly human ancestor. However, what makes these early humans "human" is not their larger brains, but a new survival strategy. Whereas *Australopithecus,* like its ape forebears, was probably mainly vegetarian, the early humans became habitual meat eaters. (Perhaps they only scavenged at first, but it is quite possible that they learned to hunt right from the start.) Furthermore, they shared food, and the labor of food-getting, within bands. Women and children gathered vegetable foods, while the men went after meat. Finally, these early humans were

---

[1] B.P. stands for "Before Present." We will be using B.P. dates throughout this book. The "present" for all B.P. calculations is the year 1950. Thus, for example, 1000 B.P. means 950 A.D.

probably the first systematic users of stone tools, which they employed to butcher their meat. This complex of new adaptations, which probably included the crude beginnings of language as well, constituted the foundation of human culture. From this point on, culture has to be reckoned with as a major influence in the evolution of the species. Henceforth it is the brain more than any other part of the human body that changes, and those changes in the brain are primarily responses to (as well as contributors to) the man-made world of culture.

Australopithecus became extinct, but the early humans prospered. Their tools, hunting methods, and social organization became more elaborate. They learned to use fire. They built shelters and became less nomadic. Furthermore, they began to specialize—to adapt their tools to specific tasks and to adapt their hunting and food-gathering techniques to specific environments and specific seasons of the year. This enabled them to spread out and survive in new areas—Europe, Asia, and eventually North and South America and Australia—where they developed distinct cultural traditions. In time these traditions came to include not only different ways of making tools and finding food but also two less pragmatic and distinctly human pursuits: art and religion.

As more time passed, the pace of change increased. Whereas the earliest humans went on working with the same crude stone tools for about a million years, it took their descendants only a few thousand years to accomplish the first two great revolutions of human culture. Around 10,000 B.P. human beings began to find ways to make nature yield a more generous and more reliable food supply, and agriculture replaced hunting and gathering in many parts of the world. Then, around 5,000 B.P., some agricultural societies gave rise to a totally new settlement pattern—the city—and a form of political organization that is still with us today—the state.

This is a short and simple summary of a sequence of changes that stretched over millions and millions of years, and that will occupy us for the remainder of this book. Sketchy as it is, however, it gives us a glimpse of the concrete reality behind the abstract phrase "human evolution," and allows us to identify the major milestones in human evolution: the appearance of primates, the move from forest to savanna, the adoption of bipedalism, the elaboration of human culture on the basis of the hunting-and-gathering, food-sharing, and tool-making complex, the gradual development of locally adapted subsistence strategies and cultural diversity, the emergence of agriculture, and the founding of cities and states.

Evolution by Natural Selection

How did all these changes come about? Clearly, the later developments are largely a matter of cultural evolution, while the earlier ones involve not only cultural change but also biological change—even the appearance of new species. Let us consider first the causes of such biological change.

In the eighteenth and early nineteenth centuries a number of scientists recognized that species could change over time, by virtue of adapting to their environments. But they could not agree on how this change occurred. Nor, in general, did they believe that such change could actually create new species. Natural processes of evolution might produce different races or strains *within* a species, but only God could create a new species. It was not until 1859, when Charles Darwin (1809–1882) published his treatise *On the Origin of Species by Means of Natural Selection*, that the major mechanism of evolution was finally described in a way that accounted both for change within species and for the emergence of new species without divine intervention.

Darwin's Theory

Ironically, the man who was to show that species could arise without the intervention of God had been a divinity student. Biology interested him more than religion, however, and in 1831, at the age of 22, Darwin left Cambridge University for a five-year voyage on the HMS *Beagle* to study the plants and animals of South America and the Pacific Islands. His observations on this trip,

The Evolution of Evolutionary Theory

The philosophers of classical and medieval times proposed a variety of theories as to how life first appeared on earth. By the middle of the eighteenth century, however, nearly all scientists and philosophers were agreed that however living things were created, they were created in their present form. Species were fixed and immutable—and utterly separate from one another.

This doctrine, known as the *fixity of species*, is typified in the work of the Swedish naturalist Carolus Linnaeus (Karl von Linné, 1707–1778). Linnaeus developed the first comprehensive classification system for living things. (In modified form, this system is the one generally used by biologists today—see Chapter 3.) To every known plant and animal, Linnaeus assigned a separate "species" slot. Then, on the basis of their resemblances, he grouped the species into larger categories, these categories into still larger categories, and so on. The result was a neat, rigid hierarchy in which all of nature was fixed in an orderly and static arrangement—with *Homo sapiens*, of course, at the top. At the same time, however, Linnaeus inadvertently planted the seeds of evolutionary thought by giving such names as "family" and "genus" (Latin for "stock") to his groupings and thereby intimating that perhaps those fixed and immutable species were actually descendants of the same ancestors.

Significantly, the first serious challenge to the fixity of species came from France, where an equally fixed and rigid social system was about to topple. In the mid-eighteenth century, Linnaeus's system came under attack by the French naturalist Georges Louis de Buffon (1707–1788). If every species was the product of a separate act of creation, Buffon asked, why did so many species look so much alike? And why did certain animals have anatomical structures that apparently had no function? The answer, Buffon suggested, was that "families" of similar species—mammals, for example—were descendants of a common ancestor. By adapting to different environments, these descendants had come to differ from the ancestral species (and from each other), but they still retained many of the ancestor's characteristics, some of which had since lost their function. Buffon, however, did not speculate as to the exact biological mechanics of evolution. This was left to his student, Jean Baptiste de Lamarck.

A botanist-turned-zoologist, Lamarck (1744–1829) argued that, contrary to current opinion, the earth was extremely old and that over the ages natural processes had produced gradual change both in the surface of the planet and in living things. Powered by a "will" toward complexity, organisms were constantly changing physiologically during their lifetimes in order to cope better with their environment. These acquired changes were then passed on to their offspring, so that in time the species as a whole changed. The giraffe's long neck, for example, could be explained as the result of many generations of ancestral giraffes stretching their necks to reach the leaves of tall trees and transmitting this acquired trait to their offspring.

Some scientists found Lamarck's theory intriguing, especially since it could explain a rather bewildering phenomenon occurring at that time: year by year, work crews building canals or digging quarries were uncovering the bones of strange, primitive-looking animals, often arranged in successive layers. Perhaps, as Lamarck suggested, these were the evolutionary ancestors of modern animals. Still, Lamarck's ideas (especially his notion of "will") were so bizarre and so dangerous to accepted religous teachings that they were generally dismissed. Furthermore, the paleontologist Georges Cuvier (1736–1832), one of the most highly respected scientists in Europe, had proposed a theory that could account for those mysterious animal bones without threat to religious doctrine. According to Cuvier's theory, called *catastrophism*, the planet had been shaken, at periodic intervals, by sudden and violent worldwide catastrophes, of which the Great Flood described in Genesis was only the latest example. With each catastrophe, almost all living things had been destroyed—a circumstance that explained the successive geological layers and their strange fossil contents. Then, after the cataclysm, the planet was repopulated by the few survivors, perhaps with the help of some newly created species. So great was Cuvier's influence and so plausible was his theory—consistent both with religion and with the empirical evidence—that it cut off all speculation about evolution among biologists of the day.

In fact, it was geology rather than biology that provided the major stimulus for the development of evolutionary theory. In the late eighteenth century, the English geologist James Hutton (1726–1797) had proposed that ancient rocks had been built up just like any sediments—by slow accumulation through natural processes. This idea, as we have seen, was picked up by Lamarck, and later it was carried further by an English surveyor, William Smith (1769–1839). In the course of his work on canal construction, Smith had noted that not only the layers of ancient rock but also their fossil contents seemed to represent a natural and gradual succession. Contrary to Cuvier's theory, there was often no sharp break between the fossils of one layer and those of the next. Rather, the fossils formed a smooth, continuous series, increasingly like modern species as one moved from the lower layers to the higher.

In the 1830's, these ideas were revived by a geologist named Charles Lyell (1797–1875) who used them to mount an attack on Cuvier's catastrophism. The earth, Lyell argued in his *Principles of Geology,* had an immensely long history. During this time, imperceptibly slow geological processes such as erosion and earth movements had produced continuous change in the earth's surface. Where there was now a plain, mountains had once stood. Where there was dry canyon, a river had once flowed. Century by century, slow changes had cut and molded the planet's crust into its present form. There had been no catastrophes—only a gradual accumulation of natural change.

As the first volume of Lyell's book came off the press, Charles Darwin, 22 years old and bored with his theological studies, was trying to convince his father to let him leave Cambridge. Darwin had no quarrel with religion. (Though an ardent naturalist, he believed firmly in the divine creation of species.) But he had heard that the captain of the *H.M.S. Beagle,* a small surveying ship headed for the South Seas, was willing to offer free passage to any young man who would come along as an unpaid naturalist. This trip seemed much more attractive than another term at Cambridge. Darwin's father relented, though he was annoyed at his son's shiftlessness. (Darwin had already abandoned medical studies before taking up theology.) As Darwin boarded the *Beagle* in 1831, one of his former teachers presented him with some shipboard reading: the first volume of Lyell's book.

Darwin read the book with great interest—he had the second volume sent to him en route—and as the ship travelled slowly around South America, he saw much to support Lyell's theories. On the west coast, for example, he saw beaches that had been lifted high above the shore by recent earthquakes. Here, without catastrophe, was a small but significant change in the earth's surface. Might not the Andes, looming in the distance, have been thrust up by a long succession of such changes? Other ob-

Charles Darwin and his eldest son, William. This photograph was taken in 1842, five years after the return of the *Beagle* to England. (*Courtesy, American Museum of Natural History*)

and vegetation were essentially identical. What, then, were the "different ends" for which the 13 species were modified?

Soon afterward Darwin returned to England, but the problem of the finches—and of certain Galapagos plant species that also differed in minute ways—continued to haunt him. A few years later, he came across the now-famous *Essay on the Principle of Population* by Thomas Robert Malthus, an English clergyman, economist, and mathematician. In what was then a novel argument, Malthus wrote that all populations increase faster than their food supplies. The result is a fierce "struggle for existence," with starvation limiting the population to a size that the food resources can support.

Slowly, in Darwin's mind, the pieces fell together. What if species adapted not just to their broad environment—the climate, the local diseases, and other circumstances that they shared with other species—but also to their own special environmental "slot," or econiche—the specific things, such as food and living space, for which they had to compete in order to stay alive? As an experienced naturalist, he knew that within any given population of organisms there was considerable physical variation. If this or that variation gave certain members of a population an edge in their competition with their fellows, then these individuals would live longer and produce more offspring. The offspring, inheriting the beneficial variation, would in turn produce more offspring, and so on, until the variation became the norm for the group. In this way, the species would change, possibly producing a new species.

The finches that Darwin observed in the Galapagos provide a classic illustration of this process. The differences in the beaks of the various species are related to differences in their diets. Those that eat seeds have strong, stubby beaks, suitable for cracking and crushing. The species that eat insects have beaks that vary in size, depending on the favored insect. Another species—one that feeds on the nectar of cactus flowers—has a thin, pointed beak, suitable for drawing out the nectar. Clearly, what happened was that a small population of finches—perhaps only a single mating pair—was at some point blown over to the Galapagos from the mainland. As their descendants multiplied in isolation, competing with one another for food, certain variations allowed some individuals to take advantage of new, uncontested food supplies. As a result, separate populations evolved and flourished, transmitting their special traits to their descendants and eventually creating a set of distinct species. (Such diversification did not occur among mainland finches because there the econiches that were vacant in the Galapagos were already occupied by other species of birds.)

Darwin realized that this mechanism could explain not only the 13 species of Galapagos finches but also the countless varieties of plant and animal species that populated the earth. From age to age in every species, certain individuals had possessed unusual traits that conferred some special advantage, allowing them either to move into unoccupied econiches or to cope better with some change (e.g., climate, food, predators) in their existing econiche. These favored individuals had been the most successful in the struggle to survive and reproduce, and so had eventually given rise to new species. Thus it was this simple process of "natural selection"—and not divine creation—servations suggested that a similar process of gradual change might have taken place in animal and plant species, just as Buffon and Lamarck had claimed years before and as Lyell too seemed at times to suggest. Examining fossil deposits in Argentina, Darwin recognized animals that closely resembled the armadillos of the area. Might not the modern armadillos be evolutionary descendants of ancient ones? As the *Beagle* slowly sailed down the east coast of South America and up the west coast, Darwin also noted gradual changes in the birds from one region to the next. Might they not be the descendants of a common ancestor—"cousins" that, as Buffon had proposed, differed from one another because they had adapted to different environments?

This last line of thought became ever more compelling once the ship arrived at the Galapagos, a group of about fifteen desolate little islands off the coast of Ecuador. On the separate islands, Darwin counted 13 previously unclassified species of finches, differing from one another and from the mainland finches in such features as the size and shape of their beaks. Was it likely that each of them was the product of a separate act of creation? That the Creator, having produced the mainland finches, designed 13 more species, with slightly differing beaks, specifically for the barren Galapagos? More likely, though extremely unorthodox, was the thought, as Darwin later expressed it, that "one species had been taken and modified for different ends." Darwin was staring the mechanism of evolution in the face, but he did not yet see it. For even if he admitted the possibility (and he did) of the finches evolving from a single ancestor, this did not solve the problem. As conceptualized by Buffon and Lamarck, the evolution of different species from a common ancestor was the result of adaptation to different environments. But the Galapagos finches—even those that were confined to one or two islands—shared the same environment; climate that accounted for the origin of species.

Darwin did not rush out to publish his discovery. On the contrary, he mulled it over for another twenty years. Day by day, he wandered the fields around his country house, collecting fresh evidence and gradually adding pages to his growing treatise. Then, in 1858, a young man named Alfred Russel Wallace sent Darwin a scientific paper he had written, asking for Darwin's opinion of it. Wallace too had travelled extensively as a naturalist. He too had been struck by Malthus's essay. And, in the paper that he sent to Darwin, he too had come to the conclusion that species evolved through natural selection. (Unlike Darwin, he had written up his theory in two days.) Roused from his leisurely studies, Darwin arranged with Wallace that an excerpt from his own writings, together with Wallace's paper, be presented at an important scientific meeting that same year. The following year, Darwin published the long treatise on which he had been working for twenty-one years: *On the Origin of Species by Means of Natural Selection, or the Preservation of Favoured Races in the Struggle of Life.*

The *Beagle* near the southern tip of South America. (*Courtesy, American Museum of Natural History*)

along with 20 years of further biological studies in England, convinced him that new species arose not through individual acts of divine will but rather through a "blind" and utterly mechanical process.

Darwin understood that all species of plants and animals tend to produce more offspring than the environment can support, leading to intense competition for living space, resources, and mates. Only a favored few manage to reproduce successfully. In addition, Darwin noted that individual members of species differ from one another physically. In a given population, for example, some animals may have thicker fur or longer limbs than other animals. And these variations may be either *adaptive* or *maladaptive*—that is, they can either increase or decrease an animal's chances of success in the struggle to reproduce, depending on the nature of the demands placed on the species by its environment. (Heavy fur, for example, could mean a longer life in a cold environment, whereas it might be a handicap in a warm one.) Those individuals whose peculiarities give them a competitive edge in their particular environment produce more offspring—offspring that inherit the parent's peculiarities, so that they in turn survive longer and produce more offspring. Thus, with each generation, the better adapted members of a population increase in number at the expense of less favored individuals. In the process, the species as a whole changes, becoming better adapted to its environment.

This process Darwin called *natural selection.* Its key elements are:

—Variation within populations

—Different levels of reproductive success among variant types as a result of environmental factors

—The inheritance of variation

This theory served to explain not only gradual changes within species, but also the appearance of new species. For as different populations adapted to different environments or different ways of life, they would eventually diverge to the point where they became too different in anatomy or behavior to interbreed. According to Darwin, it was this process—adaptation to different ways of life—that accounted for the great variety of species observable in nature.

Evolutionary Theory after Darwin

A major weakness of Darwin's theory was that he had no systematic explanation of how "favored" characteristics were inherited. And one was needed, for the current belief was that each individual inherited a *blend* of its parents' characteristics. If this were true, newly appearing advantageous variations would be lost by dilution with less advantageous traits, long before natural selection could act on them. To counter such objections, Darwin fell back on J. B. de Lamarck's theory (see box, page 8) of the inheritance of acquired characteristics. But by the late nineteenth century, discoveries in biology were making this argument untenable. Unknown to Darwin and the others debating this matter, a new view of heredity, one that could save the concept of natural selection, had already been discovered by a monk named Gregor Mendel (1822–1884).

In the garden of his monastery (located in what is now Czechoslovakia) Mendel spent years cross-breeding strains of peas and other plants in an effort to find out how traits were transmitted from one generation to the next. What he discovered was that biological inheritance was not an irreversible blending of parental traits. Rather, individual units of hereditary information (later called "genes") were passed from parent to offspring as discrete units, according to certain regular patterns. In one individual a gene's *effect* might be blended with the effects of other genes, or even suppressed altogether. But the gene itself remained intact, ready to be passed on to the next generation, where it might express itself and thus be exposed to natural selection. Mendel, then, provided the genetic foundation that Darwin's theory lacked. However, his work attracted no attention in the scientific community until after both he and Darwin were dead. It was not rediscovered until 1900, and its relevance to evolution was not fully appreciated until the next generation.

Another supposed problem with Darwin's theory was that it conflicted with the belief of contemporary physicists that the earth was only about 20 million years old. If, as Darwin claimed, natural selection operated gradually, acting on slight variations, how could it have produced so many species of plants and animals in only a few million years? In the first decade of the century, shortly after the rediscovery of Mendel's work, another major discovery was made: genes sometimes underwent random changes, called "mutations." These mutations could produce wholly new traits, uncharacteristic of the species—traits that were then transmitted to the offspring like any other trait. Armed with this new discovery, a number of Darwin's successors claimed that natural selection was unnecessary. Evolution proceeded not by gradual modifications but by rapid "saltations," or jumps, propelled in each case by the appearance of a new mutation.

Since that time, it has been recognized that both mutation and natural selection are essential to the evolutionary process. First, advances in geophysics proved Darwin's timescale to be realistic. In the 1920s and 1930s a group of "mathematical evolutionists," including Ronald Fisher, J. B. S. Haldane, and Sewall Wright, began building a new body of evolutionary theory based on a synthesis of Darwin's and Mendel's discoveries. First, they showed that genetic changes within a population—and hence evolutionary change—could be predicted on the basis of the patterns of inheritance discovered by Mendel. Second, they demonstrated mathematically that even slight differences in the capacity to survive and reproduce could result in considerable evolutionary change in a span of time compatible with earth history. In other words, evolution did not have to proceed by huge jumps in order to have produced the great variety of living species. Furthermore, in the same period scientists showed that the age of the earth was actually several billion years—sufficient time for natural selection to have achieved what Darwin had claimed for it.

Many discoveries have since added to our understanding of evolution. We now know, for example, that mutations can spread even if unaffected by natural selection. Most significantly, we at last understand something of the chemical nature of genes and the process by which cells "read" and carry out the genetic instructions. These matters are explained in Chapters 2 and 3 and in the Appendix.

Cultural Evolution

Not only anatomy but also learned behaviors, values, and ways of thinking—in short, culture—have changed in the course of human evolution. Is it possible to extend the concepts of biological evolution in such a way as to help account for the evolution of cultures? Many anthropologists feel that an imperfect but nevertheless very useful analogy exists between the two forms of change, and that in certain respects biological evolution can serve as a model for understanding the somewhat vaguer process of cultural evolution.

Such a connection would seem logical, for culture and biology are, to a large degree, parts of a single continuum. After all, our capacity for culture is based on physical structures, notably our large brains and nimble hands. Conversely, it was the elaboration of human culture—the development of language, toolmaking, cooperative food-procurement strategies, and so forth—that provided the selective pressure for the refinement of our brains and hands. This reciprocal development may be seen, in broad terms, as part of a single adaptive process. Complex brains have clearly proved advantageous for the human species, at least so far. And with the help of these brains, our species has created various cultures that are themselves adaptive, in the sense that they allow us to respond to the challenges of our physical surroundings, neighboring groups, and other environmental factors.

The capacity for culture, then, is not an inborn "program" for a set of specific behaviors, such as the spider's web-spinning. Rather it is the ability to create complex systems of behavior in response to circumstances. As these circumstances vary, so do cultures. While there are certain elements common to all human cultures, the variety is very great. And on the whole, this variety seems to be adaptive. That is, in general, people seem to do things that make sense in their environment.

The adaptive nature of cultural variety may be viewed as the result of a process similar to natural selection. Just as there is physical variation in every group of organisms, so there is behavioral variation in every human group. No two individuals think or speak exactly alike; no two hunt, plow, raise children, or conduct business in exactly the same way. Thus there is always a certain amount of built-in cultural variety, and human beings deliberately add to it. Although conformity is usually the path of least resistance, people like to experiment with new ways of doing things. Furthermore, people make mistakes, unintentionally deviating from established patterns. Every society, then, has its own steady supply of cultural "mutations."

The vast majority of these innovations end up in the attic or on the rubbish heap and are quickly forgotten. However, on occasion someone develops a better way of doing something. If he prospers (or if his prestige is such that other people begin to copy him), the innovation will gain popularity, and the tradition it replaces will become extinct or marginal—as hunting, horseback riding, and the use of kerosene lamps have in our society, for example. The innovation may then spread to other cultures as well. Or, if it is very beneficial, the group that takes it up may grow in population, press against its boundaries, acquire new territory, and force the inhabitants of this territory to accept the new way of life. Indeed, the innovation may be a direct means of displacing other groups, as firearms and horses were for the Spanish conquistadors in South America.

In other cases, changes in the physical or social environment (such as a drought or an invasion) may actually force people to seek new ways of doing things. Those solutions that prove adaptive, and the people who adopt them, survive; those solutions that prove less adaptive are forgotten, along with their adherents. What we see, then, is something akin to the pattern that Darwin described: variations that help individuals to get along better in their particular environment are transmitted to more people than are less useful variations. Consequently, the former survive, the latter vanish, and the culture changes.

Like all analogies, this analogy between biological and cultural selection has its limitations. For one thing, the two processes involve very different means of transmission. Biological variations can be transmitted only to offspring, who are limited in number, whereas cultural innovations can be conveyed to unrelated people as well as to offspring. Indeed, through the mass media, a single person can now transmit a new idea to thousands, even millions, of people whom he never sees.

A second limitation on the analogy has to do with sources of variation. Mutation, the source of genetic variation, is a random, accidental occurrence. An organism cannot will genetic change, no matter how beneficial the change might be. Cultural innovations, on the other hand, are sometimes very consciously and deliberately introduced. (Consider, for example, space flight, or the United States Constitution.) Because of this difference, some people have argued that comparisons between biological and cultural evolution distort and dehumanize cultural change. Nevertheless, while human beings may introduce a new idea with all the purposefulness in the world, it is ultimately the environment—the social, cultural, and physical context—that determines what will happen to this idea. Man proposes; the environment disposes. The pioneers of the industrial revolution did not know that they were paving the way for the atomic bomb, any more than the pioneers of the agricultural revolution knew they were laying the foundation for cities, states, and civilization. Thus despite the initial elements of human choice and human ingenuity, cultural evolution is, in the long run, almost as blind as biological evolution.

In sum, there are a few points at which the comparison between biological and cultural evolution is imperfect, but the analogy is nevertheless a useful one. In both cases we see human beings responding, wittingly or unwittingly, to the demands placed on them by their world and changing by virtue of these responses.

THE PRACTICE OF ANTHROPOLOGY

The study of the entire human species in its past and present forms is an ambitious undertaking. No single anthropologist can straddle the whole field, particularly nowadays, with data accumulating almost continuously. Within the field, therefore, specialized disciplines have arisen, each with its own particular emphasis, approach, and methods:

1. *Physical anthropology:* the study of the physical evolution of *Homo sapiens* and of physical variations in contemporary human populations
2. *Archeology:* the study of now-extinct cultures and of the processes of cultural evolution
3. *Cultural anthropology:* the study of variations among human cultures of the present and the historic past
4. *Linguistic anthropology:* the study of how human languages are structured and how they develop.

The first two subfields are the province of this book. Let us look more closely at the types of inquiry that they involve.

Physical Anthropology

The physical anthropologist is a biologist who studies the human species, past and present, as a biological phenomenon. To obtain evidence of extinct human forms, some physical anthropologists do what many people think of as the essence of anthropology: they go out and look for fossils. However, in many cases the physical anthropologist simply analyzes fossils that have been retrieved by paleontologists and other experts. Physical anthropology—indeed, anthropology as a whole—is a highly cross-disciplinary field, depending heavily on evidence provided by geologists, paleontologists, botanists, zoologists, geneticists, biochemists, physicists, and geographers.

Romantic as it may seem, the excavation of fossils is simply a preliminary, for a fossil, once found, has to be interpreted. What creature did the bones belong to? When did it live? How did it live? How is it related to our species? To answer such questions, physical anthropologists make a close study both of human anatomy and of the anatomy of our close living relatives among the nonhuman primates—especially the monkeys and apes. Comparative anatomy, including the comparative study of protein structures in humans and other animals, is our chief key to understanding evolutionary relationships among living and extinct species.

Primatologist Jane Goodall has lived among and studied the chimpanzees at Gombe Stream National Park in Tanzania for many years. Such studies of the living primates can give us clues to how our primate ancestors may have lived and behaved. *(Hugo van Lawick/©National Geographic Society)*

Another major concern of physical anthropology is the ecology and social organization of the living primates. Anthropologists try to identify the adaptive patterns characteristic of various primate species—the ways in which their behavior and anatomy are clearly adaptations to particular habitats and econiches. Then, using such patterns as a guide, they can reconstruct to some degree the way of life of fossil species.

As for our species in its present form, physical anthropologists describe and try to account for the similarities and differences among contemporary peoples. Description, of course, involves going to the field and observing different human populations—how tall they grow, how long they live, what diseases they contract, what their blood types are, and so forth. Populations differ considerably in these respects, and physical anthropologists try to explain these differences—just as they try to explain the traits of fossils and of living primates—in keeping with evolutionary theory. That is, they try to account for them as consequences of natural selection, whereby the genes of a population shift in response to demands made by the environment, and of other evolutionary processes. In order to do this, physical anthropologists must have a thorough knowledge of genetics. They must also study people's environments—the available food, the climate, the local insects, the cultural demands—as carefully as they study the people themselves.

Archeology

To describe the extinct cultures of the past and the processes involved in their development, archeologists too must collect evidence. Their interest, however, is not so much in human or prehuman fossils as in cultural evidence—signs of ancient peoples' institutions, customs, and behavior. This includes anything made by our ancestors: clay pots, fish hooks, hearths, beads, burial urns, tools. It also includes our ancestors' garbage—the stone flakes left behind by their toolmakers, the piles of animal bones left over after their meals. Finally, the archeologist must also collect environmental evidence—clues as to the climate, plants and animals, and water resources of the area.

At the excavation of a prehistoric site in Ethiopia, archeologists painstakingly record their finds in words and photographs. The grid is used for precise location of artifacts or fossils as they are unearthed. *(Georg Gerster/Rapho/Photo Researchers)*

Again, the collection of evidence is simply a preliminary—and one that may be handled in collaboration with other specialists. The archeologist's central task is interpreting the evidence. By studying the cultural remains, and piecing them together with the environmental evidence and the anatomical evidence provided by physical anthropology, archeologists try to understand the lives that people led in ancient societies—how large their populations were, how they procured their food, how they dealt with one another and with neighboring groups, whether they had class distinctions, how they buried their dead, what they thought about the world they lived in. By gaining insights into individual groups, archeologists gradually reconstruct prehistory—the major events of the many thousands of years during which our ancient peoples had no form of writing with which to record the concerns and events of their lives. Furthermore, they try to describe general processes of cultural evolution—how, for example, agriculture transforms human societies or why cities and states arise.

Such interpretation often requires the careful analysis of an immense amount of data. (Both physical anthropologists and archeologists have begun using computers to help them store and sort information.) However, it also requires imagination. Archeologists must make educated guesses as to dates. They must try to determine which tools were used for which tasks. They must look at the remains of ancient houses and figure out what it might mean, in terms of social organization, that a group built long lodges with rows of hearths rather than individual houses with individual hearths. Above all, they must ask themselves *why*. If the evidence indicates that the people practiced magic or farming or trade, then how did they come to do so, and what advantages did the practice confer? Just as the physical anthropologist often interprets fossils by analogy with living primates, archeologists often interpret cultural remains by analogy with contemporary nonindustrial societies. If, for example, the remains indicate that the group practiced cannibalism, the archeologist may look to modern cannibal tribes for possible reasons. Whatever guides archeologists use, however, the emphasis in interpretation is on cultural developments as *responses*, whether to the physical environment or to influence and competition from neighboring peoples, or to pressures supplied by the group's own internal dynamics.

In the following chapters we will look at the account that physical anthropologists and archeologists have put together so far. We turn first to the subject of genetics, the biological basis of evolution.

Summary

Anthropology is the study of the human species as a part of the natural world. It is a broad, multidisciplinary field, including several specialized subfields and drawing frequently on the contributions of other disciplines as well.

Physical anthropologists study our similarities and dissimilarities to other animal species (especially our closest relatives, the monkeys and apes) and analyze the fossils of our ancestors. In this way they attempt to reconstruct the evolutionary history of our species and the ways in which it has adapted to its changing environments. They also study physical variation in the human species today, among individuals and among populations, and try to relate such variation to environmental and evolutionary forces.

Other anthropologists study human cultures and the principles that govern their development. *Cultural anthropologists* concentrate on the diversity of modern cultures, *archeologists* on reconstructing and explaining those of the past. Both attempt to see human societies in an ecological context, and interpret their distinctive features as responses to the challenges of their environments, physical as well as cultural.

Anthropologists are particularly interested in human *evolution*—the sequence of physical and cultural changes that have made us what we are today. The key insight into the process of biological evolution was provided by Charles Darwin's theory of *natural selection*. Darwin realized that more organisms are born than the environment can support; only a minority succeed in reproducing. Thus within each species there is constant competition. There is also great variation within natural populations. Some individuals have traits that are particularly *adaptive* to their environments—traits that give them an advantage in the struggle to survive and reproduce. Since such individuals are likely to produce the most offspring, the advantageous trait will become more common with each generation. Thus the species as a whole will change over a period of time, becoming better adapted to its environment. As populations adapt to new or changing environments, new biological species may eventually be produced.

Darwin lacked an adequate theory of how variation could be inherited. This was provided when the work of Gregor Mendel was rediscovered early in this century. Mendel had shown how individual units of hereditary information (later called genes) were passed from generation to generation according to simple laws. Darwin's and Mendel's contributions were synthesized by the mathematical geneticists, who proved that even small differences among individuals could produce, in the time provided by the earth's history, evolutionary changes large enough to account for the observed diversity of the natural world.

This body of evolutionary theory allows us to trace the biological changes that gradually transformed our early primate ancestors of 70 million years ago—small, tree-dwelling creatures—into fully modern humans, who first appeared about 40,000 years ago. The result of this process, *Homo sapiens*, is distinguished by several traits. Humans walk upright, use their hands for manipulation, live in complex social groups, make and use many tools, can learn abstract ideas, and have devised an elaborate form of symbolic communication called language. While not individually unique, these traits have been highly elaborated in our species. Moreover, they form an interactive complex that gives us the capacity to create and participate in *cultures*—bodies of ideas and behaviors that are shared by groups of human beings and transmitted to subsequent generations.

Many anthropologists believe that an analogy can be drawn between biological evolution and the processes of cultural change. Cultures too exhibit variation in ideas and practices. Those that are useful tend to spread, whereas those that prove less advantageous may eventually die out or become marginal. It is the environment that ultimately determines which behaviors are beneficial. The comparison is not perfect—cultural innovations, unlike biological mutations, can spread rapidly to many unrelated individuals. Moreover, intention and conscious choice play a role in their creation and spread. Nevertheless, this analogy provides a useful model for cultural evolution.

Our capacity for elaborate culture has made us a highly successful species. Today we live in a wide range of *habitats*, and occupy an exceptionally broad *econiche* (our way of making a living in relation to other species and the natural environment). We are nevertheless still part of, and dependent on, the *ecosystem*—the cycle of matter and energy in which all creatures participate. Our means of exploiting the natural world are becoming increasingly costly and dangerous. It remains to be seen whether we can surmount the current ecological crisis, or whether our society (or even our species) is fated for extinction.

Glossary

adaptation the process of adjustment of a species to a specific environment; or, a particular trait that makes a species more suited to and successful in its environment

adaptive increasing the likelihood of survival for an individual or a species

archeology the study of extinct cultures and of the processes of cultural evolution

Australopithecus a close relative of the human species that lived from about 5.5–1 million B.P. (see Chapter 8)

bipedal walking on two feet (see Chapter 5)

cultural anthropology the study of variations among human cultures of the present and the recent past

culture the system of shared meanings that people learn from their society for use in interacting with their surroundings, communicating with others, and coping with their world

econiche a species' way of life in relation to other species—what it eats, what preys on it, etc.

ecosystem a cycle of matter and energy that includes all living things, their interaction with each other and with the environment

evolution gradual change in a species over a period of time (for a more technical definition of *biological evolution,* see Chapter 2)

gene an individual unit of hereditary information (see Chapter 2)

habitat the area in which a species lives; its surroundings

Homo sapiens the human species

linguistic anthropology the study of how human languages are structured and how they developed historically

maladaptive decreasing the likelihood of survival for an individual or a species

mutation a random change in a gene that produces a new trait (see Chapter 2)

natural selection the process by which the best-adapted members of a population increase in number at the expense of less favored individuals

physical anthropology the study of the biological evolution of *Homo sapiens* and of physical variations in contemporary human populations

Suggested Readings

APPLEMAN, P. (ED.) 1970
Darwin. New York: Norton. A comprehensive collection of extracts, not only from Darwin himself, but also from contemporary critics and supporters and from workers who built upon Darwinian foundations.

COMMONER, B. 1971
The Closing Circle. New York: Knopf. An exceptionally interesting and lucid analysis of our present environmental crisis, how it came about, and what we must do for our future.

EISELEY, L. 1958
Darwin's Century: Evolution and the Men Who Discovered It. New York: Doubleday. A most entertaining and scholarly account of the intellectual climate preceding and surrounding the publication of Darwin's works on evolution.

FAGAN, B. 1975
In the Beginning: An Introduction to Archaeology. Boston: Little, Brown. A highly readable introduction to the theory, method, and practice of archeology.

HOLE, F., AND HEIZER, R. 1973
An Introduction to Prehistoric Archaeology. 3rd ed. New York: Holt, Rinehart and Winston. A more advanced and comprehensive introduction to the field.

ROSENZWEIG, M. L. 1974
And Replenish the Earth: The Evolution, Consequences, and Prevention of Overpopulation. New York: Harper and Row. An entertaining and thought-provoking account of evolution and the human predicament.

WATSON, P. J., LeBLANC, S., AND REDMAN, C. L. 1971
Explanation in Archaeology. New York: Columbia University Press. An advanced but readable discussion of some of the more recent archeological theories and methods.

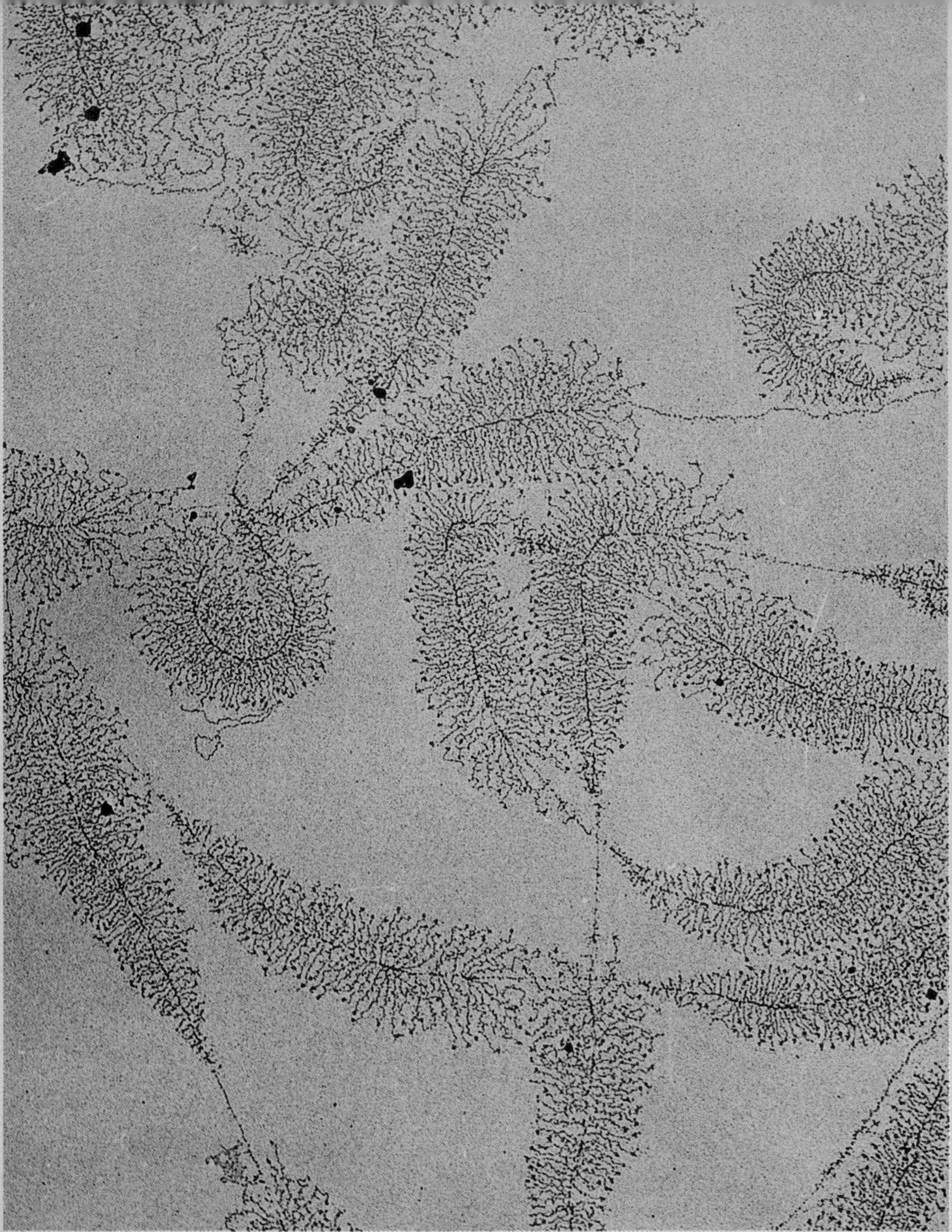

Chapter Two

The Principles of Inheritance

The theme of this book is the evolutionary history of the human species. In the following chapters we shall trace the gradual emergence of our species from simpler, more primitive forms of life. This story is pieced together from many kinds of evidence—the shape of bones, the behavior of living primates, the structure of complex molecules, and the artifacts of ancient man. The evidence, however, does not speak for itself. To read its message, we need a key—a body of theory, a set of scientific laws that enable us to make sense out of particular observations. That key is evolutionary theory.

We have already glanced briefly at evolutionary theory and the milestones in its development: Darwin's principle of evolution by natural selection, the rediscovery of Mendel's laws, the formulation of mathematical genetics. These elements have been unified to create what is known as the *synthetic theory of evolution.* The resultant body of theory is not complete; it too is still evolving, and some intriguing questions remain. Nevertheless, the main outlines of the evolutionary process are clear. We can now account for the emergence of our species—indeed, of all species—in terms of the basic properties of all living things.

As we saw in Chapter 1, human beings are descended from small furry primates that climbed and clambered in the trees. The distance between such a creature and modern *Homo sapiens* is enormous. Yet the processes by which this change took place are the very same biological processes that we see going on around us every day. We are all familiar with the fact that when organisms reproduce, their offspring resemble them to a large degree. If they are human, for example, the offspring, like the parents, will have two eyes, two ears, two rows of teeth, and so forth. But in another sense the child will be a unique product. His eyes may be darker, or his ears smaller, or his teeth more crooked than those of one or the other parent. In other words, the result of reproduction is a general *sameness* with a component of *variability.*

It is this result, repeated millions of times over millions of generations, that has produced the phenomenon we call evolution. The variability—worked on, generation after generation, by natural selection—has produced the vast accumulation of tiny changes that slowly transformed those early tree-dwelling primates into modern humans. Yet the element of sameness has preserved the family resemblance that links us to those first primates, and indeed, to every plant and animal that lives or has ever lived—for, as we saw in Chapter 1, all living things are ultimately related through descent from the same one-celled organisms. Indeed, on the chemical level, we can still see our close kinship even with bacteria; many of them extract energy from food in exactly the same way we do, using very similar molecules.

Thus the foundation of evolution—and of the unity of life itself—is the transmission of traits, with slight variation, from one generation to the next. The study of this process is called *genetics.* In the present chapter we shall examine the basic laws of genetics—how traits are passed from parent to offspring and how variation is

All living cells carry a set of chemically coded blueprints that control most of their activities. This remarkable electron micrograph shows the hereditary material itself. The long strands are molecules of DNA, which encode the genetic instructions. The shorter threads growing at right angles to the DNA are molecules of RNA, being manufactured to carry out the instructions within the cell. *(Irene Piscopo Rodgers/Phillips Electronic Instruments, Inc.)*

produced. Then, in Chapter 3, we shall discuss how the laws of genetics apply to populations; and in Chapter 4 we shall see how they govern evolutionary change.

REPRODUCTION AND THE DEVELOPMENT OF ORGANISMS

The study of genetics logically begins with the process of reproduction. Reproduction is inseparable from life itself; along with the capacity to respond adaptively to the environment, it is one of the two most basic properties of all living things.

Many plants and animals reproduce by simply dividing in two or shedding a part of themselves, thus producing offspring genetically identical to the parent. This is called *asexual reproduction.* However, we shall be dealing with the somewhat more complicated mechanism of *sexual reproduction,* which commonly requires two parents. This process involves two sex cells, or *gametes*—a *sperm* produced by the male and an ovum or *egg* produced by the female. After mating has taken place, these cells fuse to produce a *zygote,* or fertilized egg, which then gradually develops into an organism similar to its parents. Let us examine briefly this process of development as it takes place in mammals such as *Homo sapiens.*

Once fertilization has taken place, the zygote begins almost immediately to reproduce itself by cell division. First the one cell splits into two, then the two into four, and so forth. Soon the single-celled zygote has transformed itself into a raspberry-shaped cluster of hundreds of cells. It quickly becomes apparent that not all the cells are behaving in the same way. They have begun to *differentiate*—to mass themselves into different groupings, or tissues, that will ultimately perform different functions—as nerves, gut, skin, and so on. Gradually, organs—combinations of tissues arranged in shapes that enable them to cooperate in specific functional tasks—become distinguishable. As this differentiation continues, the embryo begins to take on the form distinctive of its species. In humans, for example, what was once a single cell, practically indistinguishable from the egg of a sea urchin, becomes recognizable first as a vertebrate, then as a mammal, and finally as a human being—a complex structure of highly differentiated parts. At the end of nine months, the parents' organization has been faithfully copied, and the baby is born.

Of course, development does not end at birth. The human being goes on growing for approximately twenty more years, and even after growth is completed, the process of tissue building continues. Until the moment of death, the fabric of the body is constantly being maintained and repaired; in the course of a normal human lifetime, almost every cell is replaced at least once. Indeed, insofar as we have any permanent identity as individuals, it is not as collections of molecules but as systems of information specifying the organization of molecules.

Proteins: Controllers of Life Processes

This program of development, growth, maintenance, decline, and eventual death is carried out by a remarkable set of biological molecules: the *proteins.* The human body contains at least 10,000 different kinds of proteins, each of them finely adapted, in its structure, to carrying out a particular function in development or maintenance. The structural proteins serve as raw materials for building the organism. (A major constituent of connective tissue and bone, for example, is the protein collagen.) The active proteins carry out the body's physiological responses. (The protein hemoglobin, for example, found in red blood cells, transports oxygen from the lungs to the tissues; the protein transferrin carries iron from the intestines to the tissues.) A class of proteins called *enzymes* promote and regulate the body's chemical reactions. Indeed, there is not a single bodily function that does not involve proteins. They allow us to contract our muscles, to see, hear, and smell, to build up antibodies against infection, and to convert nutrients into the energy needed to keep the body going. Above all, as we have seen, they control the development of the organism from a single cell to a complex, highly coordinated entity with millions of specialized cells. It can safely be said, then, that all life depends upon proteins.

But what controls the proteins? As we saw, each individual begins its existence as a single cell, the zygote. How, from the material in that one cell, does the growing organism manage to produce the appropriate proteins—at the appropriate times and in the appropriate amounts—to become a near facsimile of its parents?

It is clear that this immensely complex system of interacting proteins cannot be contained, ready-made, in the zygote, which is a much simpler structure. Yet the *information* necessary for the system to develop must be there. Since the zygote is formed by the joining of sperm and egg, it is equally clear that these parental sex cells must be the carriers of the hereditary information. We also know that this information is contained in a specific part of each parental cell: the nucleus.

The *nucleus* (pl. *nuclei*) is a large, membrane-bound structure present in all cells of higher organisms, at least when they are first formed. (Some lose their nuclei later.) The nucleus is the cell's control center; it contains the instructions for all of the cell's functions. What is more, the nucleus of each cell contains *all* the information needed to build the complete organism. In reproduction, the nuclei of the two parental gametes carry the genetic message as to how the new organism is to develop. As the nuclei of the sperm and egg fuse during fertilization, instructions from the father combine with those from the mother, eventually producing a new individual that resembles both parents.

Chromosomes and Genes: Blueprints for Proteins

The hereditary information is not randomly scattered through the nucleus but is neatly packaged in a set of coiled, threadlike structures called *chromosomes.* The number and shape of the chromosomes are more or less constant in all members of a species. A cabbage, for example, has 18 chromosomes, a frog 26, a plum 48, a goldfish 94, a human being 46 in each body cell. With the exception of the sex cells (which we shall discuss more fully later in this chapter), every cell in the organism receives exactly the same set of chromosomes—a duplicate of the original set contained in the zygote. As that primal cell and its descendants divide again and again, the entire chromosome set is copied over and over and passed along to each new cell.

The full complement of chromosomes is called a *diploid* set, because it consists of matching pairs of chromosomes—in humans, 23 pairs.[1] This is so because half of the zygote's chromosome set is contributed by the sperm and half by the egg. Each chromosome contributed by one of the parents has a matching, or *homologous,* chromosome—one carrying the same kind of hereditary information—in the set contributed by the other parent. The gametes carry a *haploid* chromosome set—only one chromosome of each type. (If this were not the case, the number of chromosomes would double with every generation.)

Encoded on these threadlike bodies is the information specifying what proteins the organism will produce. The instruction for each protein (or part of a complex protein) has its own fixed location, or *locus* (pl. *loci*), on a particular chromosome. For example, along the length of a given chromosome we might find the locus for an enzyme that helps to determine eye color next to the locus for another that influences stature, and next to that, the locus for one that helps break down sugar, and so on. The same loci, in the same order, would also appear on the homologous chromosome, derived from the other parent.

But what, exactly, is *at* the loci? What form does the hereditary material actually take? We now have a fairly clear answer to these questions. The chromosomes are made up chiefly of long strands of *deoxyribonucleic acid,* or *DNA,* a complex organic molecule. The chemical structure of the DNA molecules constitutes a coded message specifying the structure of all the proteins the body will manufacture during its lifetime—and,

[1] In males, one of the pairs contains chromosomes that do *not* match. This lack of symmetry is due to the sex chromosomes, as we shall see later in the chapter.

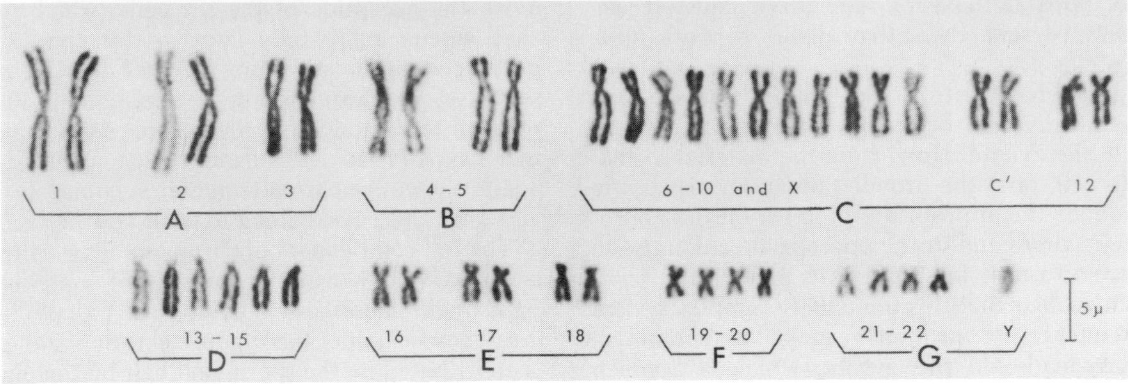

A complete (diploid) set of normal human chromosomes. The chromosomes are photographed during cell division; the photograph is then cut up and the individual chromosomes are identified, labeled, and arranged in homologous pairs in a standardized sequence. This arrangement is called a *karyotype.* Notice the unpaired X and Y chromosomes, indicating that these chromosomes belong to a male; females have a pair of X chromosomes. (The chromosomes are double-stranded because each has already duplicated itself as part of the process of cell division.) *(Courtesy of Carolina Biological Supply Company)*

quite probably, the rate at which they will be produced. That segment of a DNA molecule that codes for a single protein (or part of a complex protein) is called a *gene.*[2] Throughout the life of the organism, cells are constantly "decoding" the instructions carried by the genes and producing the proteins called for. And all these instructions, for a lifetime's worth of proteins, are contained in the zygote. (The process by which the DNA instructions are copied and decoded is explained in the Appendix, pages 408–411.)

Since the genes determine which proteins the cells can make, and since the proteins control the development and maintenance of the organism, we can say in a general way that the genes determine how the organism will use the materials from its environment to develop and maintain itself. However, there is another side to the picture. Active proteins must work with the materials that the environment supplies them, and therefore the quality of the environment influences the way in which they can work. Thus the development of every organism is influenced by two factors: (1) that organism's particular set of genetic instructions, called its *genotype,* and (2) the environment in which those instructions are carried out. The susceptibility to environmental influence of a particular trait may be anything from 0 to perhaps 100 percent, depending on the trait.

[2] Strictly speaking, a segment of DNA that codes for a protein is a structural gene. Other segments of DNA apparently serve as regulator genes, turning the structural genes on and off and so controlling the time and rate at which various proteins are produced.

THE SOURCES OF PHENOTYPIC VARIABILITY

The result of the developmental process, the functioning organism, can be described in terms of many different traits—its stature, its weight, its hair color, its blood groups, its behavior, and so on. The sum total of the individual organism's observable characteristics is called its *phenotype.* Within a given population, there is a broad similarity of phenotypes. If you look around a classroom, for example, you will probably see that everyone in it has two legs, two arms, a neck with a head on top of it, and so forth. However, as the classroom group will demonstrate, phenotypic traits also vary considerably within populations. We know that the sources of this variability are genotype and environment. But it is often difficult to unravel the ways in which these two factors interact to determine a given trait.

The Role of the Environment

It is common for environmental influences to enhance or suppress or in some way modify the effect of the genotype. For example, some people put on fat easily and lose it with difficulty. Others eat heartily yet remain slim. Since such tendencies run in families, it is very likely that genes are involved, but it would be an oversimplification to say that there are genes that "make you fat" or "keep you slim." A person with a tendency to obesity who diets carefully may well carry less fat than a "naturally" thin person who consistently overeats. Similarly, a physically active man whose genes call for a lightly muscled build may end up stronger than an inactive man whose genes call for a heavily muscled build. And no amount of innate musical ability is likely to make a great musician of a child who never has the opportunity to hear a musical instrument. In other words, the genotype may *predispose* the person to develop a certain trait, but whether or not that trait actually develops—and to what degree—depends heavily on environmental influence.

Environmental influence operates even on the cellular level. As we saw earlier, all body cells in an organism inherit the same chromosome set and hence the same DNA instructions. Yet very shortly after conception the cells begin to differentiate. They take on different functions, collect in different tissues, and produce different proteins. Clearly, each cell is reading off only a *part* of the genetic code contained within its nucleus. Why the cells should do this, and what determines the instructions they will read, is still not fully understood. It seems, however, that a major factor is the cell's position in the organism. Through some subtle interaction with the sister cells in its immediate environment, each cell receives the message as to which part of the genetic instructions it should decode and carry out.

The Influence of Genotype

Even apart from environmental influence, however, the genetic determination of a trait is not simple. As noted earlier, almost every locus[3] is represented *twice* in the genotype—once on the chromosome inherited from the mother and once on the chromosome inherited from the father. The gene occupying that locus often exists in a number of different forms, called *alleles,* that code for slightly different products. For example, the transferrin locus on a human chromosome may be occupied by any of some 20 alleles (the exact number is uncertain), each of which codes for a different form of this protein. The same is true of the corresponding locus on the homologous chromosome—it too might be occupied by any of the possible alleles.

If the two alleles at a particular locus on homologous chromosomes are identical—that is, if they both code for the same protein, or for functionally indistinguishable forms of a protein—the individual is said to be *homozygous* at that locus. If they are different, and so code for slightly different proteins, the individual is *heterozygous.* The way any particular gene affects the phenotype depends on which of its alleles are present and whether the individual is heterozygous or homozygous at that locus. To add to the complexity, the expression of the alleles may well be influenced by alleles at other loci. The phenotype, then, is the result not just of gene products interacting with environmental influences; the products of the genes themselves also interact in complex ways. How all these factors together shape the phenotype varies greatly from trait to trait, as we shall see in the following sections.

Genotype and Phenotype: A Simple Case

We have said that genes are the blueprints for the manufacture of proteins; but when we study the phenotypic expression of a particular gene, we can rarely observe directly the specific pro-

[3] The exceptions, as we shall see, are those on the sex chromosomes in the male.

tein for which it codes. What we usually see, rather, is some secondary physical effect, to which the protein in question is only one contributor—usually along with many other proteins and environmental factors. For example, we know that there is a "freckling" locus in humans, which may be occupied by either of two alleles. One causes the pigment melanin in the skin to clump, producing freckles; the other produces an even distribution of pigment, with no freckles. However, we do not know what proteins these alleles code for to influence the distribution of pigment in this way. Moreover, the effects of these alleles are clearly modified by other genes, which determine the *amount* of pigment produced, and by the environment—exposure to sunlight stimulates the production of pigment and thus of freckles in those bearing the "freckling" allele.

There are cases, however, in which we *can* actually observe the protein that a particular allele codes for. In such instances, where we are dealing directly with the primary gene product itself, there is little or no opportunity for the intervention of environmental factors. Transferrin—the iron-transporting protein mentioned earlier—is such a direct gene product. Of the numerous alleles that can occupy the transferrin locus, the two most common are *C* and *D*. Most people are homozygous for *C*—that is, they carry this *C* allele at the transferrin locus on both chromosomes. Their transferrin genotype is thus *CC*. Some people, however, are heterozygous for the two alleles: *CD*. And very rarely we find someone who is homozygous for the *D* allele: *DD*. As mentioned earlier, each of these two alleles codes for a slightly different form of the transferrin protein. Thus an individual whose genotype is *CC* will have the C protein in his veins, while a *DD* individual will make only the D protein. The *CD* heterozygote will have both forms of transferrin in roughly equal amounts. Since all three phenotypes seem to perform their physiological function with equal efficiency, no one is likely to be aware of which they possess without laboratory testing. This is a case where we are able to observe an aspect of the phenotype that is very close to the gene level—so close that the relationship between genotype and phenotype is uncomplicated by environmental influence.

Codominance

When an individual is homozygous at a particular locus—that is, when both homologous chromosomes carry the identical allele—the genetic instructions are uncomplicated. When an individual is heterozygous at a particular locus, however, that individual is carrying two different alleles, and thus two different genetic instructions. One possible result is that the phenotype will reflect the influence of *both* alleles. The heterozygote, therefore, is phenotypically different from both homozygotes. This phenomenon is called *codominance*. The transferrin example we have just discussed is an instance of codominance—the *CD* heterozygotes show the effect of both the *C* allele (coding for type C protein) and the *D* allele (coding for type D protein).

Dominant and Recessive Traits

Sometimes, however, *only one* of the alleles is fully expressed in the observable phenotype of heterozygotes. In such a case, the trait that is expressed is said to be *dominant*, while the one that is suppressed is said to be *recessive*. An example of a recessive trait is albinism, an abnormal condition in which the body fails to produce melanin (the skin pigment mentioned earlier in connection with freckles). Albinos have white hair, pink skin, and pink eyes. (The eyes and skin are pink because there is no pigment to mask the color of the blood in the capillaries.) The normal allele at this locus codes for the production of melanin; the albinism allele codes for no pigment production. Thus a heterozygote will have melanin in his skin because of the presence of the normal allele; he will be phenotypically normal. Only people who are homozygous for the abnormal allele will have the albino phenotype.

This example suggests an important point. Though it is very common to speak of dominant and recessive alleles, this usage is misleading. It is really more accurate to speak of dominant and recessive traits. The alleles themselves do not directly affect one another; each operates quite independently of its partner. It is the *effect* of a particular allele that may hide or mask the effect of another allele, so that the heterozygotes seem to show the effect of only one allele.

Many traits exhibit such dominance relationships. Freckled skin, for example, is dominant to unfreckled; people who inherit one allele for each (i.e., heterozygotes) will have as many freckles as people who are homozygous for the "freckling" allele. Similarly, in the ABO blood group system, types A and B are both dominant to O; *AA* and *AO* individuals will both have type A blood, and *BB* and *BO* individuals will both have type B blood. Only *OO* individuals will have type O blood. (Since alleles *A* and *B* are co-dominant, an *AB* heterozygote will have type AB blood.)

Polygenic Traits

The traits we have considered so far are *monogenic*—that is, they are influenced by genes at only one locus. Considerably more complicated but equally important are *polygenic* traits—those that are influenced by genes at more than one locus. Let us look, for example, at human stature.

Although very simple to measure, and a much more familiar aspect of the phenotype than transferrin or blood group type, stature (height) is a far more complex phenotypic characteristic. For one thing, it is made up of the combined lengths of many body segments—head, trunk, pelvis, leg, foot. Furthermore, each of these segments consists of several different tissues—bone, cartilage, and so forth. The rate at which these tissues grow varies from tissue to tissue and from segment to segment. How, from this multiplicity of variables, can we isolate the genes responsible for stature? At this point, we cannot. We presume that the regulators of stature are enzymes that control the rate at which bone and cartilage are added at each of the growth points, and determine when this process will cease. Therefore we can say that the genes controlling stature are those that produce these particular enzymes. We have little idea, though, how such proteins work, how they affect one another, or how many are involved—beyond the fact that there are probably many of them.

The fact that it is a polygenic trait is not the only complication with stature. Another is the environment, which here again plays an important role. Such factors as illness, nutrition, and even emotional stress can influence the rate of growth and therefore help to determine adult height.

Such examples should be kept in mind as we turn to the subject of evolution. For whereas the principles of genetics and of evolution were worked out initially on the basis of simple traits like transferrin and blood groups, many of the traits that we shall see changing in the course of human evolution are anything but simple. In fact, the most critical traits in the human species' divergence from its ape ancestors—the proportion of the limbs, and the shape and size of the teeth and of the brain—are traits that, like stature, are influenced by genes at a number of different loci as well as by the environment.

Complex Products of Single Genes

While a single trait such as height may have a complex genetic basis, the converse is also true: single genes may have many phenotypic consequences. Albinism again provides a good example. In homozygotes, as we saw, the abnormal alleles have only one direct consequence: the body produces no melanin. However, the indirect consequences are many. To begin with the obvious, the lack of melanin prevents the expression of the genes that control the *amount* of pigment in various parts of the body. Albinos, like everyone else, carry genes that code for a certain color of eyes, hair, and skin. Since the proteins have no melanin to work with, however, these instructions are never carried out. It is for this reason that a "black" (African) albino is as light-skinned as a "white" (European) one.

The lack of melanin has other consequences as well. In normally pigmented people, melanin protects the eyes and skin from the harmful ef-

A single gene causes albinism, a condition in which the body manufactures no melanin. Melanin is the pigment that gives human skin its normal color. In the absence of melanin, the genes that control the *amount* of pigmentation have nothing to influence. Thus an African albino is as light as a European one. *(Norman R. Lightfoot/Photo Researchers)*

fects of the sun's ultraviolet rays. Because they lack such protection, albinos generally squint and have poor vision. They sunburn very easily and have a high incidence of skin cancer. Moreover, albinism has emotional and social ramifications: in societies where albinos are considered strange-looking, the albino will probably have a harder time living a normal life, making friends, and finding a spouse. (This last factor undoubtedly accounts for the generally low incidence of albinism.) In short, a single gene may have a great many effects.

Sex Determination

Another area in which an apparently limited amount of genetic information has far-reaching phenotypic consequences is the determination of sex. Among the 46 chromosomes carried by human body cells, there is one pair of *sex chromosomes.* Unlike other chromosomes, which always occur in homologous pairs, there are two quite different kinds of sex chromosomes: *X chromosomes,* which contain a good deal of hereditary information, and *Y chromosomes,* which seem to specify little apart from gender. Normally, a zygote that carries two X chromosomes will develop into a female, while a zygote that bears an X and a Y will develop into a male.

This critical difference in development seems to be controlled by the Y chromosome. We do not know how many genes this chromosome carries—though they are probably very few—or how they operate. We do know that approximately seven weeks after conception, a crucial change takes place in the primitive gonad, or sex gland, of the embryo. If the Y chromosome is absent, the gonad develops into an ovary; if the Y chromosome is present, the gonad develops into a testis. Presumably, then, the Y chromosome codes for proteins that cause the gonad to become a testis rather than an ovary.

This one differentiation has massive consequences. Ovaries and testes produce different sorts of hormones—chemical messengers—and these in turn determine a far-reaching program of physiological development that we think of as distinctly male or female. While the individual is still in the womb, the hormones elicit the development of male or female genitals. Years later, in puberty, the same hormones call forth the secondary sexual characteristics. In humans, these include breast development and menstruation in the female, facial hair and a deeper voice in the male, and in both sexes, the development of pubic hair and the maturation of the reproductive organs to the point of fertility. Moreover, the sex hormones have an impact not only on physiology but also on behavior—at least in nonhuman animals, and probably in humans as well.

Mutation: The Source of New Variability

A high degree of variation seems to be the rule for natural populations. In typical human populations, for example, multiple alleles exist at appreciable frequencies for some 30 percent of all loci. Such variation—the raw material on which evolution works—is ultimately due to the process of mutation.

A *mutation* is a random change in a gene. As we saw, every cell in an organism contains an identical set of DNA instructions. Thus, the body's DNA must copy itself millions upon millions of times in the course of a lifetime. The copying process (explained in the Appendix) is highly efficient but not entirely foolproof. Every so often a mistake is made, and the genetic instructions are changed. If that particular stretch of DNA is then translated into a protein, the protein may be rather different from what was originally called for. More important, if the mutant DNA is in a cell that develops into sperm or egg, it stands a chance of being passed to a zygote. If so, it will be duplicated and decoded as part of the "regular" instructions of that new individual and, quite possibly, passed along to yet another generation. Thus a new gene is introduced into the population.

Often this process is not detectable, since in most mutations only a tiny part of the DNA sequence is altered. In such cases it is quite possible that the change will make no difference in the protein that is produced, or that it will change the protein in a way that is unimportant to its functioning. Hence many such mutations are probably *neutral.* That is, they have no noticeable effect on the phenotype of the organism and do not affect its survival.

Some mutations, on the other hand, are considerably more drastic. Long stretches of DNA can be lost or duplicated, altering large numbers of genes. When this happens, the change is not only noticeable; it is probably fatal as well. However, even minor mutations, if they are not neutral, are usually harmful. This is to be expected. If one opened up a smoothly operating piece of machinery and made some random change in it—adding a part or removing or altering one of the existing parts—it is most improbable that the machine would benefit from this change. Likewise, the genetic makeup of a species is a finely tuned, highly intricate network of interacting parts that has evolved into a state of balance over many thousands of centuries, and random changes in its parts are not likely to improve its operation.

In the rare case, however, a mutant gene *is* advantageous. But it must be stressed that mutation is totally random with regard to the needs of an organism. For example, bombarding a population of fruit flies with X-rays will increase the rate of mutation, but it will not produce a high percentage of mutations carrying resistance to radiation sickness.

THE BASIC PRINCIPLES OF HEREDITY

So far, we have looked at the way the individual's phenotype is produced by the interaction between genotype and environment. We shall now examine how the genotype itself is formed. As we saw earlier, every human being begins as a zygote, created by the fusion of sperm and egg. All the genetic information that will go to make up the new individual is contained in the two gametes—half in the sperm and half in the egg. Thus the genotype of the new individual depends entirely on which of the parents' genes are contained in those two particular gametes. This critical sorting takes place as the gametes are formed.

Meiosis and Gamete Formation

We mentioned earlier that the sex cells—the female eggs and the male sperm—constitute the one major exception to the rule that human cells carry 46 chromosomes apiece. When the body produces sex cells, the full, or diploid, set of 46 chromosomes is reduced to a half, or haploid, set of 23. This splitting of the chromosome set in order to convert diploid body cells into haploid sex cells is part of a special form of cell division called *meiosis.*

In human beings, meiosis takes place in the testes of males and the ovaries of females. Briefly, what happens is as follows. In the nucleus of the body cells, as we saw earlier, the 46 chromosomes are organized into 23 pairs of homologous chromosomes. During meiosis, the homologous chromosomes travel to opposite ends of the nucleus, and the nucleus divides down the middle. The cell itself then divides, producing two haploid cells, each of which contains a nucleus with one chromosome from each of the 23 original pairs. It is from these haploid cells that the gametes are derived (Figure 2-1).

How the male's gamete meets up with the female's gamete so that fertilization can take place depends on the species of the organism. In human beings, as with other mammals, the mechanism is, of course, sexual intercourse. What is important for our purposes is that in fertilization, the haploid chromosome set in the sperm combines with the haploid set in the egg, and the diploid condition is restored. Furthermore, each chromosome, having been separated from its original homologous chromosome during meiosis, finds a new homologous chromosome among the set contributed by the other parent. Thus we once again have a cell with a full complement of paired chromosomes. This cell, however, is a new organism, with a wholly new genotype.

Figure 2-1. A diagram of meiosis. The process actually consists of two divisions. Prior to the first division, the chromosomes duplicate themselves, becoming double-stranded. Reshuffling of the chromosomes and crossing over take place during the first meiotic division; during the second division, the double-stranded chromosomes divide to produce four haploid cells, from which the gametes are derived. (The process as depicted here is characteristic of sperm production. The production of egg cells differs slightly in detail, but is identical as far as its genetic implications are concerned.)

Genetic Variability in Gametes

The genetic information that we inherit from our parents consists of genes at thousands of different loci. The average human is estimated to be heterozygous—that is, to have two different alleles—at some 7 to 12 percent of those loci. It is the reshuffling of these different alleles into new combinations during meiosis that accounts for the genetic uniqueness of each individual.

The Independent Assortment of Chromosomes

The first important principle governing this process is that *during the formation of the gametes, chromosomes assort independently of one*

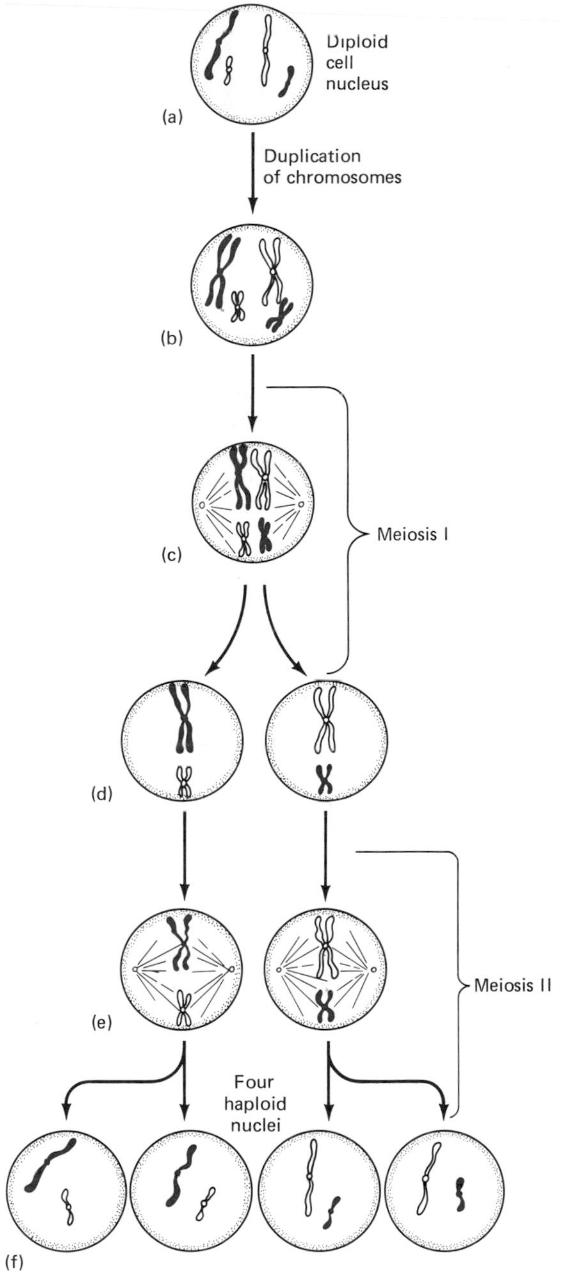

another. In meiosis, as we saw, cells containing 23 chromosomes inherited from the mother and 23 inherited from the father give rise to sex cells with 23 chromosomes each. This does not mean, however, that all the maternally derived chromosomes end up in one gamete and all the paternally derived chromosomes in the other. On the contrary, the chromosomes are distributed without regard to their origin. Every gamete gets one chromosome from each of the homologous pairs, but whether that chromosome is the one contributed by the mother or by the father is completely a matter of chance.

This fact has extremely important consequences for the transmission of genes. For if the chromosomes are reshuffled every time meiosis takes place, then the genes lying on different chromosomes are also reshuffled. As a result, combinations of traits that appeared in one generation may give way to very different combinations of traits in the next generation.

Let us assume, for simplicity, that there is a single locus for hair color, and that it can be occupied by either of two different alleles, one for dark hair (*D*), the other for light (*d*). Similarly, we will assume that eye color is governed by a single locus that is occupied by two alleles, brown (*B*) or blue (*b*).[4] Since they lie on different chromosomes, they can combine differently in every new gamete. Thus a person who is heterozygous at each of these two loci (*Bb Dd*) could produce gametes with any of four different genotypes for this pair of traits: *BD*, *Bd*, *bD*, or *bd*.

We can see that the independent assortment of chromosomes makes for great variety among

---

[4] For convenience, we are here treating multiple allele systems as if each involved only two alleles. There are in fact several alleles that determine the amount of pigment in the iris of the eye and thus whether eyes will be blue, gray, green, brown, or black. Similarly, there are a number of alleles for the brown pigment that determines whether hair will be blond, black, or any of several intermediate shades of brown. In addition, there is a pair of alleles at a separate locus that codes for red pigmentation, which may combine with various shades of blond or brown hair to create additional hues.

the gametes and thus for very great variety among the zygote genotypes that can result from the union of those gametes. Our example, after all, considers the combinations that can be formed by only 2 chromosomes, whereas, in fact, every time gametes are produced, 23 different chromosomes are sorted independently. What this means is that there are at least 2^{23}, or more than 8 million, possible ways in which the chromosomes can combine to form a single gamete. Consequently, there are at least $2^{23} \times 2^{23}$ (or about 70 trillion) different kinds of possible zygotes that can be produced by the mating of a given man and a given woman.

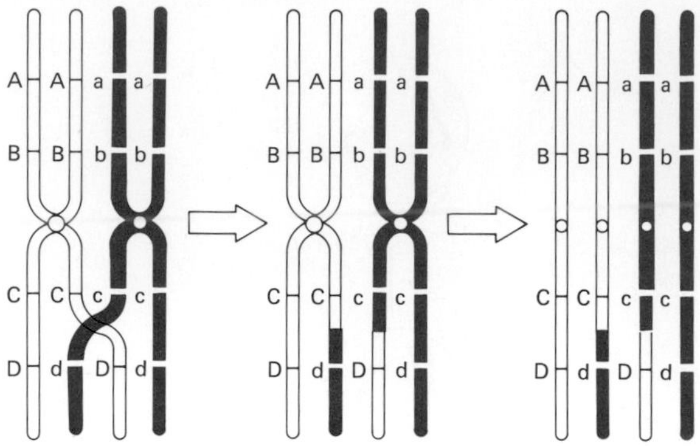

Figure 2-2. **Crossing over during the first meiotic division. The double-stranded homologous chromosomes lie side by side prior to parting company and entering the two daughter cells. Breaks occur in corresponding locations on adjacent strands of the two chromosomes, and segments are exchanged. The diagram shows each chromosome carrying four loci (in actuality, the number would be vastly greater). The two homologous chromosomes carry different alleles at all four loci: *A, B, C, D,* and *a, b, c, d.* After crossing over and the subsequent second meiotic division, there will be four combinations of alleles in the resulting haploid gametes: *A, B, C, d* and *a, b, c, D,* in addition to the original two combinations.**

Linked Genes and Crossing Over

While genes on separate chromosomes sort themselves independently into gametes, *linked genes*—that is, genes located on the same chromosome—generally do not. Remember that what we call a gene is actually a short stretch of chromosomal DNA. Thus genes located on the same chromosome are segments of the same physical entity. Where it goes, they go—together. Thus the second principle governing the relationship among genes is that *linked genes tend to be sorted into the same gametes and therefore to be inherited together.* In fruit flies, for example, the locus for red versus purple eyes is situated on the same chromosome as the locus for long versus short legs. Thus any gamete formed by a particular fruit fly will probably contain either its mother's genes for eye color and leg length or its father's genes for these traits—but not its mother's eyes and its father's legs, or vice versa.

The genes that occupy a particular chromosome, however, do not always remain linked in this way, and so do not always sort together. By the process called *crossing over,* homologous chromosomes often trade genetic information with one another (Figure 2-2). Crossing over takes place during meiosis. Before the pairs of homologous chromosomes separate, the members of one pair will break at the same point along their length and exchange the broken-off portions. Then they separate, and each chromosome, carrying some of its "partner's" genetic instructions in place of its own, becomes part of a gamete. Thus even linked genes stand a chance of being reshuffled during meiosis.

However, unlike unlinked genes, the reassortment of linked genes is not random. Crossing over is less likely among genes that are close together on the same chromosome than among genes that are farther apart. Therefore, the more closely linked two genes are, the more likely it is that an individual will transmit them to his offspring in the same combination as he received them from one of his parents. Genes whose loci are on the same chromosome but very far apart are reassorted almost randomly. (The fact that

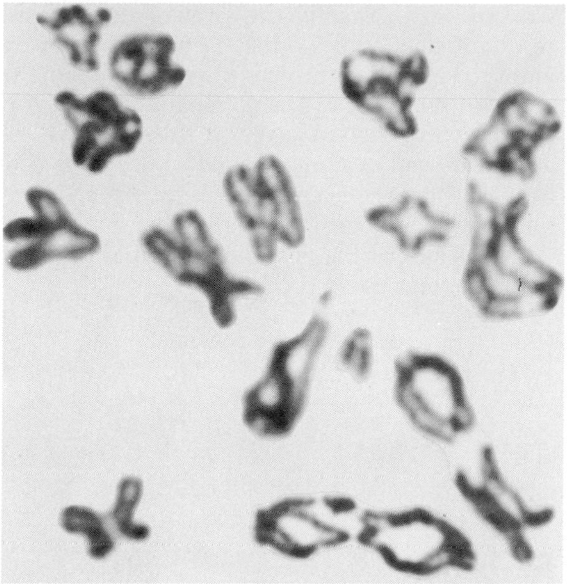

During meiosis, crossing over occurs frequently (compare Figure 2-2). In fact, it is not uncommon to find two or more points of crossing over, or *chiasmata,* on a single pair of homologous chromosomes. *(Courtesy of Dr. Georgiana Jagiello)*

the relative frequency of crossing over between any two linked genes is an indicator of how close together they lie has made it possible for geneticists actually to map the position of individual loci on the chromosome.)

Crossing over vastly increases the variability of gametes. As we saw earlier, the independent assortment of chromosomes means that a gamete produced by a human being can contain any one of at least 2^{23} possible combinations of chromosomes. Because of crossing over, however, it is clear that the number is really much higher. For crossing over seems to occur at almost every meiosis, and every human chromosome has anywhere from 1,000 to 100,000 genes between which it can take place. A reasonable estimate is that the average human being can turn out gametes with 80^{23} (60 million trillion trillion trillion) different combinations of genetic information. With this many possibilities, the same combination is extremely unlikely to appear in any two gametes produced by the same person—much less in two gametes produced by two different people. Hence the variation in human genotypes is effectively infinite.

Zygote Genotypes

How can we determine what possible genotypes will be produced by the fusion of the parental gametes? If we know the parents' genotypes at a particular locus, we can easily deduce what kinds of gametes they could produce and hence what possible genotypes the offspring might have.

Monogenic Traits

Let us take as an example of a set of monogenic traits the transferrin proteins that we discussed earlier. The mother, we will assume, is homozygous *DD.* Thus, when her homologous chromosomes split up into separate gametes, each gamete will carry the *D* allele. By the same token, if the father is homozygous *CC,* his gametes will invariably carry the *C* allele. Consequently, reproduction by these two parents will always involve a *C*-bearing sperm meeting a *D*-bearing egg, resulting in a zygote with the genotype *CD* for that locus.

Such calculations are easily done by using a simple table. To make such a table, you first draw a grid. Over the horizontal line at the top, you list the possible types of gametes the father could produce for the locus in question, writing one gamete type over each box. Next to the vertical line at the left you list the possible gamete types the mother could produce. Then in each box in the grid you write the genotype that would result if the male and female gametes corresponding to that box combined. This will give you *all the possible genotypes that could result, at the locus in question, from the mating of those two individuals.*

As an example, let us look at a slightly more complicated situation: the mating of two individuals who are both heterozygous (*CD*) at the transferrin locus:

		Father's gametes	
		C	*D*
Mother's gametes	*C*	*CC*	*CD*
	D	*DC*	*DD*

From this cross, then, we could get three possible genotypes: *CC*, *CD*,[5] and *DD*. And each of these, as we saw earlier in the chapter, will result in a slightly different transferrin phenotype.

Such a table tells us not only the possible genotypes of the zygotes but also the ***probability*** of the occurrence of each. By counting the number of boxes in which each genotype appears, we get the probability ratios. In the table above, for example, *CC* appears in one box, *CD* (or *DC*) in two boxes, and *DD* in one box. Therefore, the probabilities of these three genotypes (and for their corresponding phenotypes) are 0.25, 0.5, and 0.25, respectively.

This does not mean, however, that whenever two heterozygotes produce four children, there will invariably be two heterozygotes and one of each kind of homozygote. The ratios we arrived at are the most ***likely*** ones, but they will be borne out consistently only in very large samples. Four is far too small a sample to be statistically valuable. Similarly, in tossing a coin, we can predict an equal number of heads and tails over a long series of tosses. But a short series of tosses is unlikely to bear out the prediction exactly. If we toss the coin only four times, a 3:1 or even a 4:0 ratio would not be particularly surprising, whereas 300 heads in 400 tosses would be astonishing.

The Influence of Dominance

When a mating involves dominant and recessive traits, the genotypes and their probabilities are worked out in exactly the same way. Only the resultant phenotypes differ. Let us take, for example, the gene for brown (*B*) versus blue (*b*) eye color, in which brown is dominant to blue. Any person who is heterozygous at this locus will be as brown-eyed as a brown-eyed homozygote. But because he or she carries the blue-eyed gene, blue eyes could turn up in the next generation.

Let us look at the possible genotypes that two heterozygotes could produce:

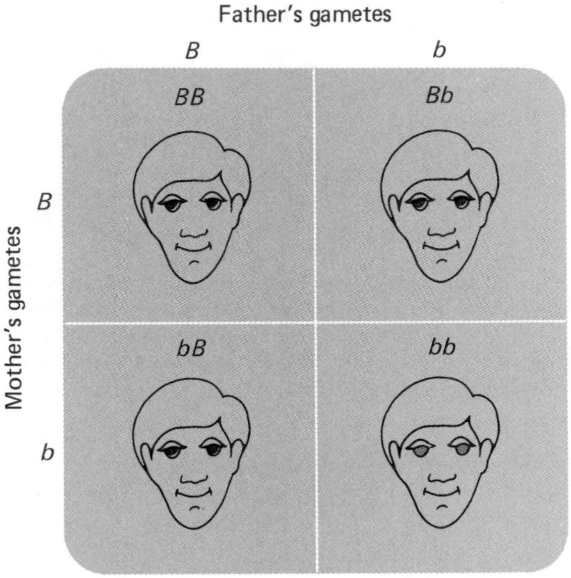

As with the transferrin example, the genotype probability ratio would be 1(***BB***):2(***Bb***):1(***bb***). However, because the brown-eyed trait is dominant to the blue, the heterozygous offspring, like their parents, would be brown-eyed. Only the homozygous recessive (***bb***) would be blue-eyed. Therefore, the probability ratio for phenotype is 3:1—three brown-eyed offspring (either ***BB*** or ***Bb***) for every blue-eyed offspring (***bb***).

To see how the same sort of analysis can be applied to several loci at one time, we can look at the traits of eye color and hair color, which we discussed previously in connection with gamete formation. If two people, both of them heterozygous for each of these traits (***Bb Dd***), were to mate, they could produce the following genotypes:

[5] *DC* and *CD* are the same genotype. It makes no difference, either in genotype or in phenotype, which allele is inherited from which parent.

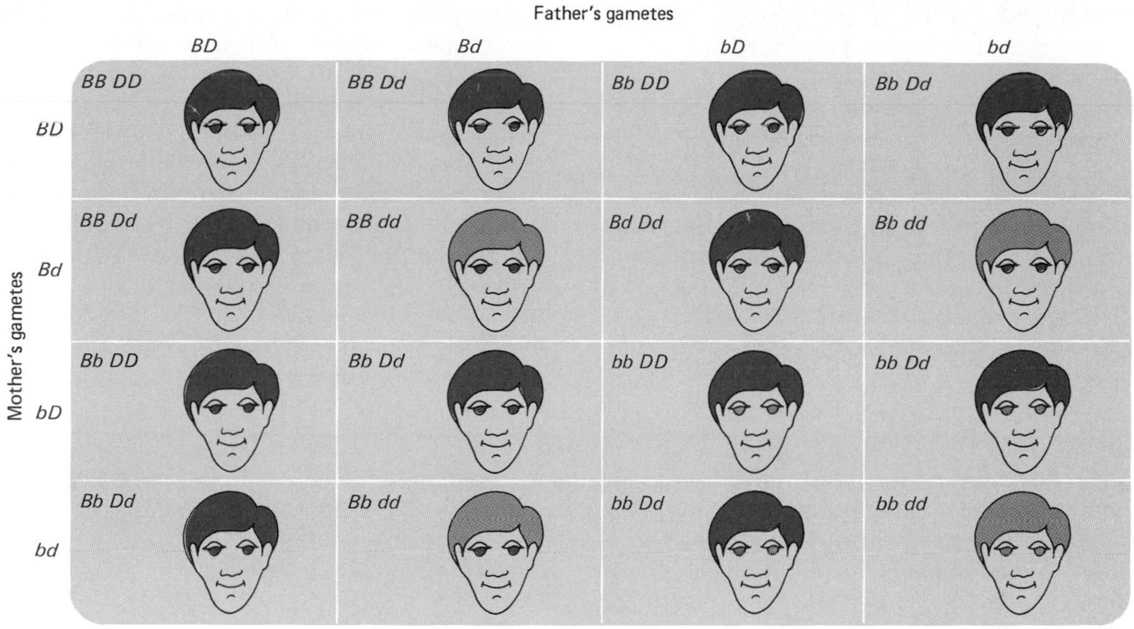

As the figure shows, such a mating could result in offspring with any of nine different genotypes for these two loci, resulting in four distinct phenotypes. (Again, the number and probability ratio of the phenotypes differ from those of the genotypes because of dominance. The probability ratios of the genotypes and phenotypes are listed in Table 2-1.)

TABLE 2-1. Genotypes and Phenotypes Resulting from the Mating of Parents Who Are Heterozygous at Two Loci

GENOTYPE	PROBABILITY RATIO OF GENOTYPE	PHENOTYPE		PROBABILITY RATIO OF PHENOTYPE
bb dd	1	light hair	light eyes	1
BB dd	1	black hair	light eyes	3
Bb dd	2	black hair	light eyes	
bb Dd	2	light hair	dark eyes	3
bb DD	1	light hair	dark eyes	
BB DD	1	black hair	dark eyes	9
Bb DD	2	black hair	dark eyes	
Bb Dd	4	black hair	dark eyes	
BB Dd	2	black hair	dark eyes	

Sex-Linked Traits

The tiny Y chromosome carries very little genetic information apart from the sex determinants. The X chromosome, on the other hand, carries a considerable number of different loci. Female mammals, because they carry two X chromosomes, may be either homozygous or heterozygous for any one of these genes. But males, as we saw, carry only one X chromosome, with no corresponding loci on the Y chromosome; their phenotypes will therefore reflect the genes on the X chromosome just as if they were homozygous.

This peculiarity of the *sex-linked genes* (that is, those genes, apart from the sex-determining ones, that are located on the sex chromosomes) becomes very significant when harmful recessive alleles are in question. Heterozygosity provides potent protection against such alleles. As long as the individual carries a normal allele in addition to the dangerous recessive one, he or she will be phenotypically normal. With regard to sex-linked genes, females still have the same protection, but males do not, for they carry only one X chromosome. Whatever genes are present on that chromosome will be expressed.

Figure 2-3. The inheritance of hemophilia among the descendants of Queen Victoria, who was a carrier of this sex-linked condition. About half the sons of carrier females are affected, and half the daughters become carriers themselves, though they do not suffer from the disease.

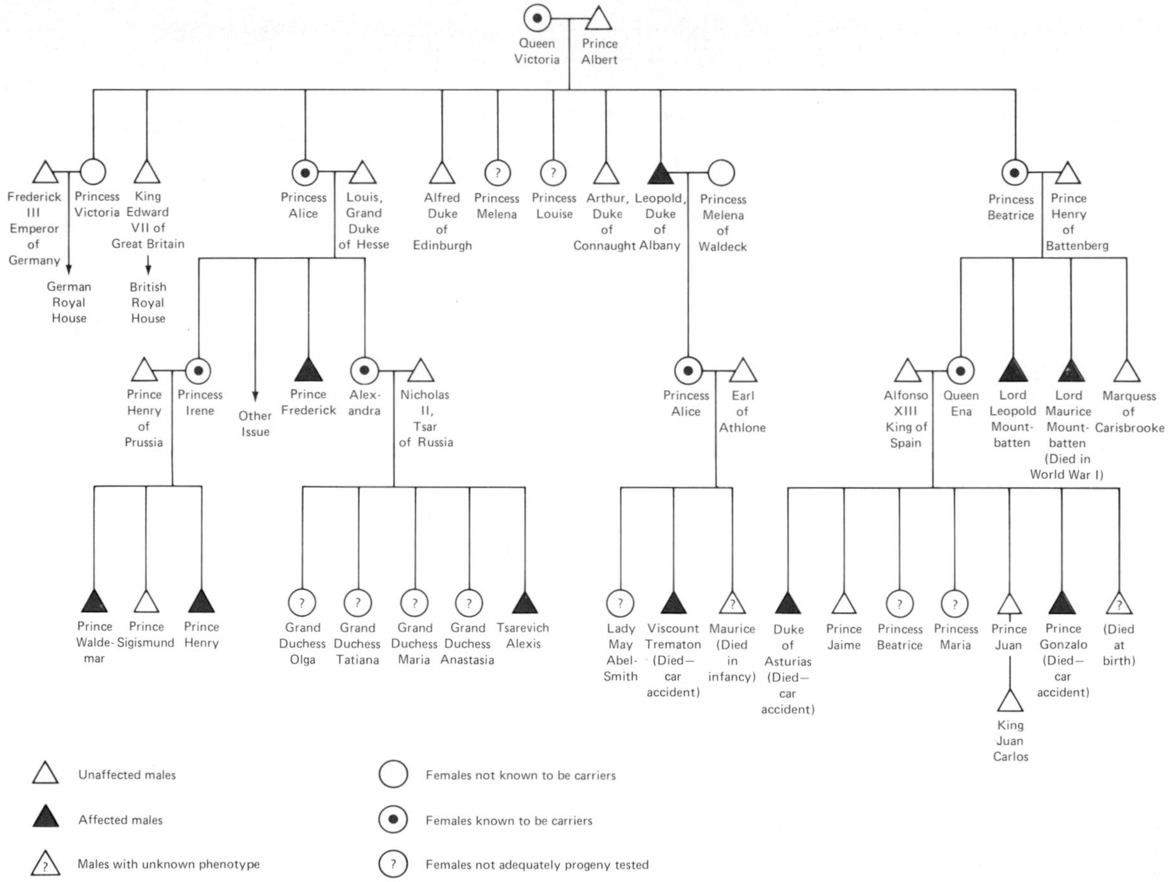

Let us take, for example, the gene for color blindness, which is on the X chromosome. If a woman carries the abnormal allele coding for red-green color blindness, along with the normal allele, she will have normal color vision, since the normal allele is dominant. But all of her sons stand a 50-50 chance of inheriting from her the X chromosome with the abnormal allele. If they do, they will be color-blind, since this will be their *only* allele at that locus. Her daughters, on the other hand, run no risk of being color-blind as long as their father has normal color vision (thus transmitting to them an X chromosome bearing the normal allele). Nevertheless, they still have a 50-50 chance of *carrying* the recessive allele and transmitting it to their own sons.

A classic case of a sex-linked trait is the hemophilia that has been passed down through the royal families of Europe for the last century. Hemophilia is a disorder in which the blood fails to clot normally, so that a hemophiliac can bleed to death from even a minor cut. The allele that causes hemophilia, like that for color blindness, is a recessive allele carried on the X chromosome. The mutant gene probably first appeared in England's Queen Victoria.[6] She herself, being heterozygous, did not have the disease. But she transmitted the allele to one of her sons—Duke Leopold, who died at the age of thirty-one—and to at least two of her daughters. And these three children, along with their descendants, carried the gene, through marriage, into most of the royal families of Europe (Figure 2-3). Juan Carlos, the present king of Spain, is the great-great-grandson of Queen Victoria, and his grandmother, Queen Ena of Spain, was a heterozygote; but his father escaped the allele, and thus so did he.

Queen Victoria with her grandchildren. A *carrier* of the hemophilia allele, she did not herself suffer from the abnormal condition, but passed it on to many of her descendants (see Figure 2-3). (*The Bettmann Archive*)

Polygenic Traits

The genes that govern polygenic traits are inherited in exactly the same way as those for monogenic traits. The only difference is that several loci interact to produce the phenotype. Therefore, there are more possible gamete genotypes and, consequently, more possible phenotypes.

Let us assume, as a hypothetical example, that pigmentation in a certain type of fish is determined by two loci, each of which has a "pigment-contributing" allele and a "non–pigment-contributing" allele:

	Locus *A*	Locus *B*
Pigment-contributing alleles	***A***	***B***
Non–pigment-contributing alleles	*A*	*B*

[6] The allele may have originated in one of the cells from which her own gametes were formed, or on an X chromosome in one of her parents' sex cells. Or, it could have originated several generations earlier and been passed down in the female line, without being expressed.

TABLE 2-2. Genotypes and Phenotypes for Pigmentation Controlled by Two Loci, Each with Two Alleles

GENOTYPE	NUMBER OF CONTRIBUTING ALLELES	PHENOTYPE
AABB	0	white
AABB, AA**B**B	1	light
AABB, **A**A**B**B, AA**BB**	2	medium
AABB, **A**A**BB**	3	dark
AABB	4	black

The phenotype—the coloration of the fish—depends on how many "contributing" alleles it receives from its parents' gametes. An individual could carry any number of "contributing" alleles up to four, and therefore could have any one of five degrees of coloration (Table 2-2).

Let us imagine that a white fish (genotype *AABB*) breeds with a black fish (genotype ***AABB***). The only kind of gamete that the white fish can produce is *AB*—two noncontributing alleles. And the only kind of gamete that the black fish can produce is ***AB***—two contributing alleles. Therefore, all their offspring will have two contributing alleles, and their coloration will be medium (***A****A****B****B*).

What happens if two of these medium-colored

Figure 2-4. The genotypes and phenotypes (pigmentation) that could result from the mating of parents each of which is heterozygous at two pigment-producing loci.

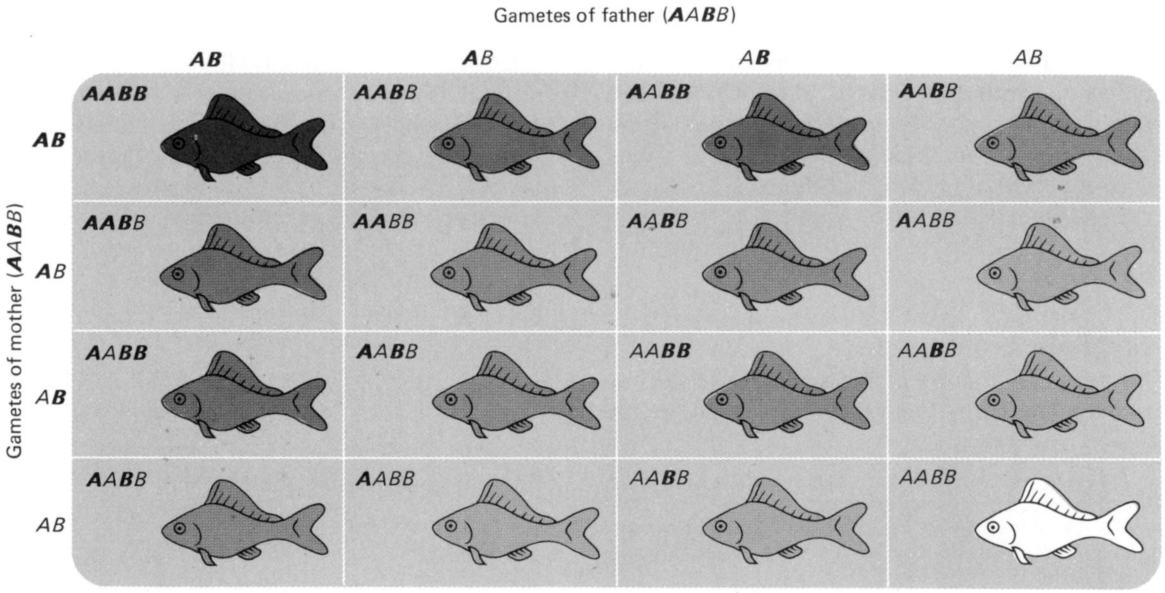

fish mate? The results are shown in Figure 2-4.[7] As you can see, any one of the five possible phenotypes could result from this mating. However, of all the sixteen ways that these parents' gametes could combine, only one way will yield the white phenotype, and only one will yield the black, whereas each of the intermediate types (light, medium, and dark) can be produced in several ways. The intermediate types, in other words, are more probable than the extreme types. By counting the number of squares producing each phenotype, we come up with a probability ratio of 1:4:6:4:1. Thus, while it is possible that the offspring will be as white or as black as their homozygous grandparents, it is much more likely that they will be intermediate. The same may be said of the transmission of polygenic traits in general: it tends to produce intermediate phenotypes.

This tendency becomes all the more striking as

[7] If you compare this table to the one that we made earlier in this chapter for blond versus black hair and light versus dark eyes, you will see that the pattern of the genotypes is exactly the same—as it should be, since both charts represent the mating of two individuals who are both heterozygous at two loci. The pattern of phenotypes, however, is different, since the earlier table concerned two traits, each controlled by one locus, whereas this table concerns one trait controlled by two loci, which produce a combined phenotypic effect.

Figure 2-5. Assuming that skin color is determined by pairs of alleles at five separate loci, this diagram represents the range of phenotypes that might result from the marriage of two individuals who are both heterozygous at all five loci. The height of each column represents the relative probability that an offspring produced by this mating will exhibit that particular phenotype. The darkest and lightest phenotypes are least likely. The most likely is an intermediate phenotype, produced by the possession of five contributing and five noncontributing genes.

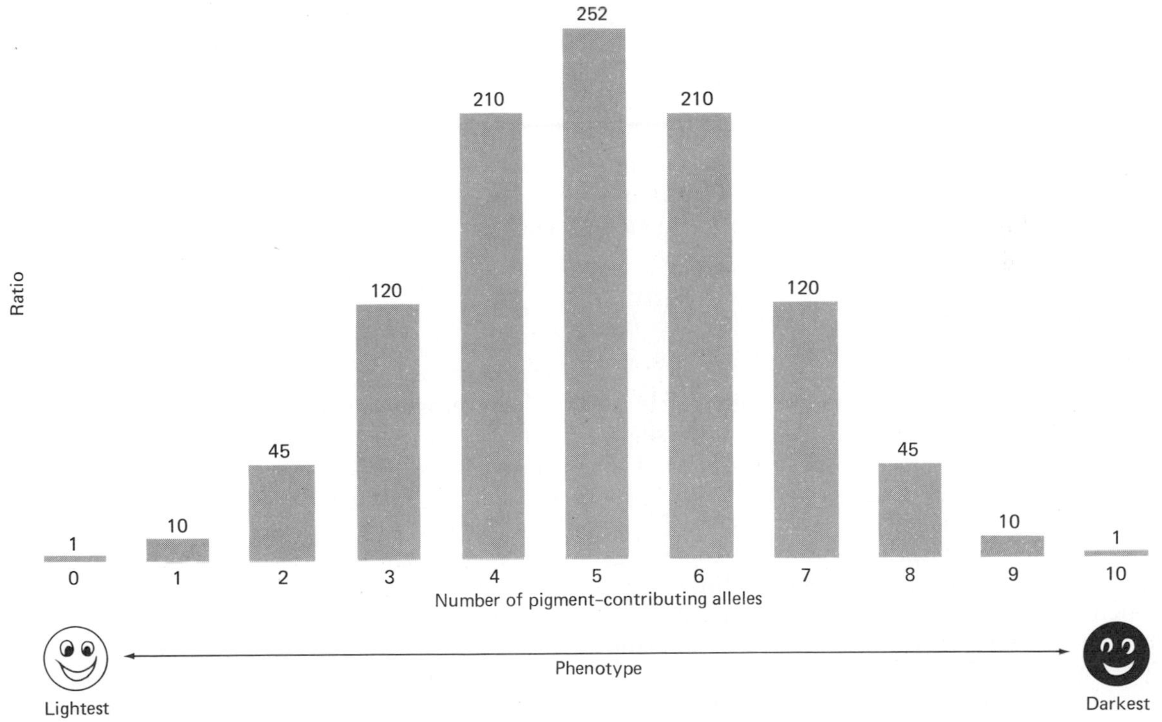

the number of loci controlling the trait increases. In the preceding example, only two loci were involved. Let us consider a more complex trait: human skin color, which is thought to be determined by four to six different loci. If we assume that five loci are involved, and imagine a mating comparable to that in the last example—that is, with each parent heterozygous at all of them—the probability of the different grades of skin color would be as shown in Figure 2-5. We can readily see that as the number of genes controlling a trait increases, the probability of the extreme type decreases. In the case of the fish, it was 1 in 16; here it is only 1 in 1,024.

The Particulate Nature of Genes

It is important to note, in the preceding examples, that extreme types, although they become less likely as the trait becomes more complex, are nevertheless still possible. This is true because of the *particulate nature of genes*—the fact that they are inherited as discrete units. However they are expressed (or not expressed) in one generation, they are still passed along unchanged to the next generation. As a result, two gray fish (if they are heterozygous) can still produce a black fish, and two brown-eyed parents (if they are heterozygous) can produce a blue-eyed child. The effects of a gene may be masked by dominance or blurred by the effects of other genes, but the gene remains, ready to express itself in a new individual when the conditions allow.

The demonstration, in Mendel's experiments, of the particulate nature of genes was of crucial importance to evolutionary theory. As we saw in Chapter 1, inheritance had previously been viewed as a process whereby the parents' traits were blended to produce the offspring's traits, like the mixing of black and white paint to produce gray. If this were true, no recombination could occur. All offspring would be intermediate between their parents, and within a few generations all members of a population would look alike—a vast gray middle. Furthermore, new variants arising through mutation would disappear, by dilution, long before evolutionary processes could go to work on them.

Particulate inheritance, on the other hand, by allowing new genes and less common genes to survive, allows for the continuous recombination of traits. Thus it ensures that variation is not lost but instead remains available as the raw material for the evolutionary processes.

Families, however, cannot illustrate these processes. It is through families, of course, that genes are handed down, but it is only in populations—groups of organisms sharing pools of genes that persist as distinct entities over long periods—that we can see not only the rules of genetics but also how evolution works within and through those rules. To populations, then, we turn in the next chapter.

Summary

The basis of evolution—and of the unity of life itself—is the transmission of traits, with slight variation, from one generation to the next. The study of this process is called *genetics*.

Sexual reproduction involves two sex cells, or *gametes*—the male *sperm* and the female *egg*. These fuse to produce a *zygote*, or fertilized egg, which gradually develops into an organism similar to its parents. This development does not stop at birth, for the body tissues are constantly maintained and repaired until death.

This program of development and maintenance is carried out largely by a set of organic molecules called the *proteins*. The human body contains at least 10,000 different proteins, each of which plays a specific part in the development and maintenance of the individual. What proteins the body can make (and to some extent when it will make them and at what rate) is determined by hereditary information packaged in the *chromosomes:* coiled, threadlike structures found in the nuclei of the parental gametes.

Half of the zygote's chromosomes are contributed by the sperm and half by the egg. The full complement of chromosomes is called a *diploid set;* the half sets carried by the gametes are known as *haploid sets.* Each chromosome contributed by one parent has a *homologous* chromosome carrying the same kind of hereditary information in the set transmitted by the other parent. Humans have 22 of these chromosome pairs, plus the sex chromosomes—two X chromosomes in females, an X and a Y in males.

The chromosomes are composed chiefly of long strands of *DNA* (deoxyribonucleic acid), a complex organic molecule. That part of a DNA molecule that codes for the manufacture of a single protein, or part of a complex protein, is called a *gene.* Each gene occupies a fixed place, or *locus,* on a particular chromosome.

The development of every organism depends upon two factors—its particular set of genetic instructions, called its *genotype,* and the environment in which these instructions are carried out. Environmental influences typically modify the effect of the genotype, which may do no more than predispose the individual to develop a certain trait to a certain degree. Some traits are extremely susceptible to environmental influence, some not at all. The sum total of the organism's observable traits is called its *phenotype.*

A gene occupying a given locus often exists in a number of forms, known as *alleles,* that code for slightly different forms of the same protein. If the two alleles at a particular locus are identical, the individual is *homozygous* at that locus. If they are different, the individual is *heterozygous.* When an individual is heterozygous at a particular locus, the phenotype may reflect the influence of both alleles. Traits governed by such alleles are called *codominant.* Sometimes only one of the alleles is expressed in the phenotype. In this case, the expressed trait is *dominant;* the suppressed trait is *recessive.* Dominant traits are expressed identically in heterozygotes and homozygotes; recessive traits are expressed only in homozygotes. Traits that are influenced by genes at only one locus are called *monogenic;* those that depend upon genes at more than one locus are called *polygenic.*

A single gene sometimes has multiple phenotypic consequences. An example is sex determination. The human body has one pair of nonhomologous *sex chromosomes. X chromosomes* contain a good deal of hereditary information; *Y chromosomes* appear to specify little other than gender. A zygote that carries two X chromosomes develops into a female; an XY zygote develops into a male. This single difference leads to the far-reaching programs of development that we think of as distinctly male or female.

High degrees of variation are typical of natural populations. Such variations are ultimately due to mutations. A *mutation* is a random change in a gene caused by an alteration in its DNA structure. Many mutations are neutral or harmful; in rare cases, they are advantageous.

The genotype of the new individual depends upon what combination of the parents' genes are contained in each of the gametes that produced it. The critical reshuffling of parental genes occurs during the process of *meiosis,* in which a diploid body cell containing 23 pairs of chromosomes divides into two haploid sex cells, each of which contains one chromosome from each of these original pairs. At fertilization, the haploid set in the sperm combines with the haploid set in the egg, producing a new diploid set. The result is a genotypically distinct organism.

Several factors increase genetic variability. One is the principle that during the formation of the gametes, chromosomes assort independently of one another. *Linked genes,* which are located on the same chromosome, tend to be inherited together. Often, however, *crossing over* takes place during meiosis, and homologous chromosomes trade genetic information with one another. This process further increases genetic variability.

The X chromosome carries a considerable number of genes. Males carry only one X chromosome, with no corresponding loci on the Y chromosome. Their phenotypes will thus reflect the influence of *sex-linked genes* on the X chromosome. This peculiarity of the sex-linked genes becomes significant when harmful recessive traits such as those for color blindness and hemophilia are involved. Females are less likely to display such traits, since they may be heterozygous for them, but such females still have a 50 percent chance of transmitting the trait to their sons.

The genes that govern polygenic traits are inherited in the same way as those that determine monogenic traits. Since several loci are involved, more genotypes and phenotypes are possible. Extreme types become less likely as the trait becomes more complex, but because genes are transmitted as discrete units, such types may still occur. It is for this reason that variation is not lost, but remains available for evolutionary processes to work on.

Glossary

alleles variant forms of a gene, any of which can occupy a particular locus

chromosomes coiled, threadlike structures in the nucleus that contain the hereditary information

codominant traits traits that reflect the phenotypic effect of both alleles in heterozygotes

crossing over the process by which homologous chromosomes trade genetic information with one another, greatly increasing genetic variability

development the process by which a fertilized egg (zygote) grows into a complete organism

diploid set the full complement of chromosomes received from mother and father

DNA (deoxyribonucleic acid) the complex organic molecule that encodes the genetic information

dominant trait a trait that reflects the influence of only one allele in heterozygotes; thus, a trait that is identically expressed in heterozygotes and homozygotes

egg the gamete produced by the female

enzymes proteins that promote and regulate chemical processes within the body

gametes the sex cells (sperm and egg)

gene in general, the unit of heredity determining a particular trait; in molecular terms, the segment of a DNA molecule that codes for a single protein or one part of a complex protein

genetics the study of the transmission of traits from one generation to the next

genotype the genetic makeup of an organism

haploid set the half set of chromosomes carried by each gamete

heterozygous having two different alleles at the corresponding loci of homologous chromosomes

homologous chromosomes a pair of chromosomes, each of which carries the same kind of hereditary information; one member of the pair is contributed by each parent

homozygous having two identical alleles at the corresponding loci of homologous chromosomes

linked genes genes that lie on the same chromosome, so that they tend to be inherited together

locus the position of a particular gene on a chromosome

meiosis the process of cell division in which haploid sex cells are produced from diploid body cells

monogenic trait a trait that is influenced by genes at only one locus

mutation a random change in a gene caused by an alteration of its DNA structure

nucleus the cell's control center, and the location of the genetic information

phenotype the sum total of an individual's observable characteristics

polygenic trait a phenotypic characteristic that is influenced by genes at more than one locus

proteins a class of molecules largely responsible for the development and maintenance of the organism

recessive trait a trait that is expressed only in homozygotes

reproduction the process in which an organism produces offspring similar to itself

sex chromosomes (X and Y) the chromosomes that determine the organism's genetic sex; in mammals, XX individuals are female, XY male

sex-linked genes genes on the sex chromosomes (mainly the X), that affect traits other than gender

sperm the gamete produced by the male

synthetic theory of evolution the evolutionary theory synthesized from the work of Darwin, Mendel, and the mathematical geneticists of this century

zygote the fertilized egg, produced by fusion of a sperm with an egg, from which a new organism develops

Suggested Readings

HARTL, D. L. 1977
Our Uncertain Heritage: Genetics and Human Diversity. Philadelphia: Lippincott. An excellent recent introduction to this subject.

MCKUSICK, V. A. 1969
Human Genetics. 2nd ed. Englewood Cliffs, N.J.: Prentice-Hall. A succinct and authoritative coverage of all major aspects of human genetics.

NASS, G. 1970
The Molecules of Life. New York: McGraw-Hill. Background on biochemistry and molecular genetics.

STURTEVANT, A. H. 1965
A History of Genetics. New York: Harper & Row. From Mendel to molecular genetics—an engaging account by a scientist who has himself made many important contributions to the field.

Chapter Three

The Genetic Bases of Evolution

In the last chapter, we saw how genes, working in environmental context, determine the phenotype of the individual, and how they are combined and passed from one generation to the next. These aspects of genetics are fundamental to the evolutionary process; but individuals, pairs of mates, and sets of offspring are not units within which evolution can be observed. Within a generation or two, their genes have been dispersed and mingled with those of other families. To study evolutionary change over time, geneticists must work with a wider unit: a group within which genes are handed down through the generations but that retains its recognizable genetic identity, distinct from that of other groups. Such a group is called a *Mendelian population.*

POPULATIONS AND VARIABILITY

Simply defined, a *Mendelian population* is a group of organisms in which each member is more likely to mate with another member than with an outsider. It is thus a group within which a single body of genes is usually transmitted. The combined genes of the population can be imagined as a *gene pool,* from which the genotype of each new individual and each new generation is drawn. Whatever degree of variation there is within the gene pool will be expressed as phenotypic variability among members of the population.

As Darwin realized, every natural population exhibits considerable variability, at least part of which is under genetic control. It is this variability that provides the raw material for the evolutionary process. Thus population genetics—the study of gene and genotype frequencies within gene pools over time—is essential for understanding evolutionary change. (*Ylla/Rapho/Photo Researchers*)

The Hierarchy of Mendelian Populations

The concept of the Mendelian population is hierarchical; large Mendelian populations often include smaller ones. The most inclusive is the *biological species,* which can be defined as a group of interbreeding populations that is reproductively isolated from other such groups (Mayr, 1963). Because members of different species in their natural habitat never meet, or do not mate when they meet, or produce offspring that cannot survive or cannot reproduce, there can be no exchange of genes. The gene pool of each species thus remains a completely discrete unit.

A species, then, can be regarded as the largest possible Mendelian population. As this definition suggests, species often include smaller Mendelian populations. The populations within a species *do* exchange genes by interbreeding. Such gene flow is generally limited, however, by geographical barriers, such as rivers or mountain chains, that restrict contact (and therefore mating) between members of neighboring populations. Major geographical populations frequently include still smaller, socially defined populations. Most primates, for example, live throughout the year in permanent groups, and mating usually occurs within this social unit. This, too, is a Mendelian population with its own gene pool. The smallest Mendelian population of a species—one that is not further subdivided in any way—is called a *deme.* It usually consists of individuals that inhabit the same limited geographical area—a particular patch of forest, for example.

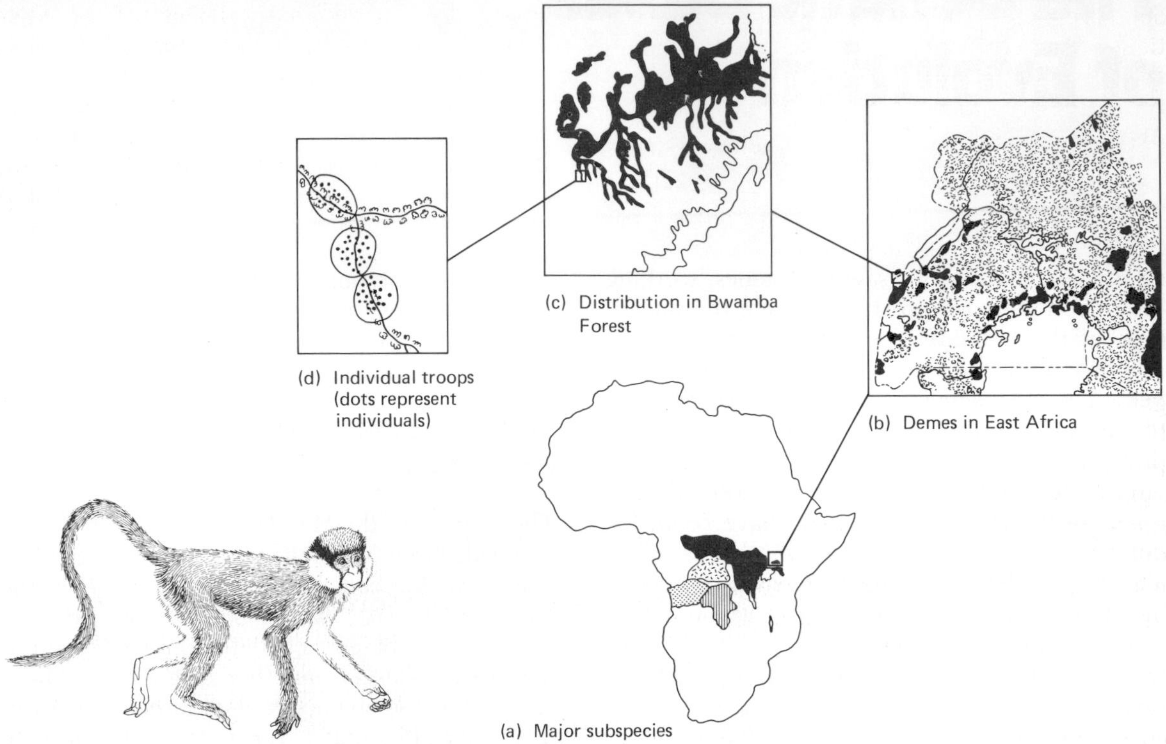

Figure 3-1. The population structure of the redtail monkey, *Cercopithecus ascanius*. Within the range of one subspecies (b), separate demes inhabit patches of forest. One, in the Bwamba Forest (c), includes many troops, each with its own home range (d). *(Robert Frank/Data from Kingdon, 1971)*

Phenotypic Variability in Population

No matter how large the population, each individual in it is unique. Ultimately, all phenotypic variation within a population derives from the same sources: varied genotypes and varied environmental influences. In practice, however, it is useful to distinguish two categories of phenotypic variation in populations: discontinuous variation and continuous variation.

Discontinuous Variation

Discontinuous variation is phenotypic variation that divides the population into discrete groups, without intermediates. The human ABO blood types, for example, represent discontinuous variation. The population can be divided into four distinct phenotypic categories: blood types A, B, AB, and O. The same is true of the transferrin types discussed in the preceding chapter. Like transferrin and blood types, most discontinuously variable traits are monogenic—they are determined by alleles at a single locus.

Discontinuous variation within a population is described in terms of phenotype frequencies. The frequencies are expressed as decimal fractions, which together add up to 1. The following, for example, are the frequencies of the four blood types among blacks in the United States:

Type A	0.27	(or 27 percent)
Type B	0.21	(or 21 percent)
Type O	0.48	(or 48 percent)
Type AB	0.04	(or 4 percent)
Total	1.00	(or 100 percent)

Such frequencies allow us to compare populations with regard to a particular trait. We can say, for example, that whereas the frequency of type A blood in American blacks is 0.27, among American whites it is 0.41.

Continuous Variation

Continuous variation expresses itself as a smooth gradient between two extremes. Let us take human stature, for example. The adult members of a population do not fall into distinct categories—small, medium, large, and extra-large, like pajamas. Rather, they show a very gradual progression from very tall to very short. The same is true of weight, skin color, intelligence, or speed in running the 100-meter dash. Individuals differ from one another only by degrees, and the number of steps in the progression is limited only by the accuracy of the measuring instrument.

The distribution of a continuously variable trait—the way it is spread in a population—usually approaches the form of a bell-shaped curve, with many individuals clustered around the middle and progressively fewer individuals toward the extremes. (Curves of this sort are shown in Figure 3-4.) The distribution is described in terms of the mean (that is, the average) and the standard deviation (a measure of the spread of the curve). These same statistics can be used to compare different populations with regard to continuously variable traits.

As we saw in the last chapter, continuous variation typically involves polygenic traits, in which the effects of genes at a number of different loci produce not just two or three phenotypes but a great many. Furthermore, with many polygenic traits, the environment also exerts an influence on the development of the phenotype. Environmental factors, by increasing the amount of phenotypic variation still further, smooth out the steps, making the distribution, for all practical purposes, continuous. Many of the traits that are most important in human evolution are of this kind.

By using phenotypic frequencies for discontinuous variation, along with such statistical measures as mean and standard deviation for continuously variable traits, we can describe the characteristics of a population and compare it with other populations. We can, in other words, describe the *collective phenotype* of a population at a given time. It is the changes in this collective phenotype over a period of many generations that we call evolution.

Gene Frequency

Just as the phenotype of an individual is partly determined by the genes that he or she carries, so the collective phenotype of a population is partly determined by its gene pool. The predominance of type A blood in a population, for example, will be due in large part to the predominance of the *A* allele, in relation to the *B* and *O* alleles, in the population's gene pool.

To describe the makeup of a gene pool, geneticists use the concept of *gene frequency.* The frequency of a particular gene is simply its abundance relative to all of its alleles in the population. For an example, let us look again at the transferrin locus. Suppose that a population of one hundred people possesses only the *C* and *D* alleles for transferrin. Of the hundred, eighty people are *CC* homozygotes, fifteen are *CD* heterozygotes, and five are *DD* homozygotes. We know that there are 200 transferrin genes in this population—2 per person—and we can easily find out how many of these 200 are *C*s and how many are *D*s by adding up the number of *C*s and *D*s in each genotype group:

	C genes	*D* genes
80 *CC*	160	—
15 *CD*	15	15
5 *DD*	—	10
Total 100	175	25

Like the frequencies of discontinuously variable traits, gene frequencies are expressed as decimal fractions. The fractions are obtained by dividing the total number of each allele by the total number of all the alleles at that locus.

Frequency of *C* genes: 175/200 = 0.875 (or 87.5 percent)
Frequency of *D* genes: 25/200 = 0.125 (or 12.5 percent)

However many alleles there are in the population, their frequencies (like the phenotype frequencies) always add up to 1, or 100 percent.

GENOTYPE FREQUENCY

If we can determine gene frequencies at many loci for a particular population, we can describe its gene pool in some detail. However, in order to describe its collective phenotype, what we need to know is not so much the gene frequencies as the *genotype frequencies:* the proportion of different genotypes in the population.

Suppose, for example, that we want to know how many members of a given population will have sickle-cell anemia, a genetically transmitted blood disorder that usually results in early death. The condition, we know, is caused by a recessive gene (*S*). People who are homozygous for that allele (*SS*) have sickle-cell anemia, whereas heterozygotes (*AS*) are phenotypically normal, aside from a slight anemia. Let us say that in a population of 400 people the frequency of the *S* gene is 0.01. Then, out of the population's 800 genes for that locus, we know that 8 are abnormal. But this still does not tell us how many members of the population will have the disease. After all, those 8 recessive alleles might end up in 8 heterozygotes, with the result that the population would have *no* sickle-cell anemics. Or they might all be carried by homozygotes, in which case there would be 4 sickle-cell anemics. Moreover, their distribution in the current generation does not tell us where they will be in the next generation. As meiosis and recombination shuffle the alleles and deal them out to the offspring, the genotype frequencies may change significantly.

Is there any pattern in the relationship between gene frequencies and genotype frequencies? There is, in fact, a predictable relationship, stated in the Hardy-Weinberg formula—the cornerstone of population genetics.

Predicting Genotype Frequency: The Hardy-Weinberg Formula

In 1908, the British mathematician G. H. Hardy and the German biologist W. Weinberg independently hit upon a simple formula that enables us, under certain conditions, to predict a population's genotype frequencies from its gene frequencies. The formula predicts that if p and q are the frequencies of the alleles *A* and *B* in the population, then the frequencies of the genotypes *AA*, *AB*, and *BB* will be p^2, 2 pq, and q^2 respectively.

The simplest way to derive this formula is to imagine a pool of male gametes and a pool of female gametes, each reflecting the gene frequencies p and q. Let us suppose that p = 0.2 and q = 0.8. Every fertilization represents the combination of a male gamete and a female gamete, each drawn at random from its respective pool. Since 20 percent (0.2) of the male gametes in the pool are *A*-bearing, the chance of drawing an *A*-bearing male gamete is 0.2. Similarly, the chance of drawing an *A*-bearing female gamete is also 0.2. The probability of an *AA* genotype being formed is found by multiplying these individual probabilities: 0.2 × 0.2 = 0.04 (that is, $p \times p = p^2$). The likelihoods of other combinations can be worked out in the same way. The probability of the *BB* genotype is 0.8 × 0.8 = 0.64 (that is, $q \times q = q^2$). The probability of the *AB* genotype is 0.2 × 0.8 = 0.16, and the probability of the *BA* genotype is 0.8 × 0.2 = 0.16. Since *A* and *B* can be combined in two ways, we must add the two probabilities together to get the total probability of the heterozygote: 0.16 + 0.16 = 0.32 (that is, pq + qp = 2pq). As with all frequencies, their combined total is 1 (0.04 + 0.64 + 0.32 = 1.00).

The same results can be obtained by using a table:

Female Gametes

Male Gametes		0.2*A*	0.8*B*
	0.2*A*	0.04*AA*	0.16*AB*
	0.8*B*	0.16*BA*	0.64*BB*

Deviations from the Hardy-Weinberg Ratios

The Hardy-Weinberg formula provides an estimate of the genotype frequencies resulting from random mating in a population. Like Mendelian ratios, however, Hardy-Weinberg ratios are a statistical abstraction. They represent the ideal—an ideal that is seldom if ever realized in any actual population. In fact, the genotype ratios observed in real populations almost always deviate to some extent from Hardy-Weinberg predictions. But it is those very deviations that are interesting, and that often tell us about evolutionary processes in the population that could not be detected or studied in any other way. Indeed, it is precisely because the Hardy-Weinberg formula allows us to spot such deviations, and to analyze their probable causes, that the formula is so valuable to geneticists.

Suppose that we pick a sample of animals from a population, look at their genotype frequencies, and find deviations from the Hardy-Weinberg predictions. These deviations may be due to three causes:

1. Our sample is too small and/or too unrepresentative.
2. Certain genotypes are being removed from the population through the action of selective forces before they can be counted.
3. The conditions of the Hardy-Weinberg law are being violated in this population.

We shall consider each of these possibilities in turn.

Sampling Error

The most common source of observed deviation—and the least interesting from an evolutionary point of view—is the fact that all real populations are finite. Because of their statistical nature, however, Hardy-Weinberg ratios will in theory only be realized exactly in an infinite population. Any actual population, no matter how large, represents only a sample of the possible genotypes that *could* be drawn from the gene pool. And just as twenty throws of a coin are unlikely to result in *exactly* ten heads and ten tails, so any sample of genotypes is unlikely to reflect Hardy-Weinberg ratios exactly. The smaller the population, the smaller the sample, and the greater the deviation from Hardy-Weinberg predictions; there are simply too few "draws" from the gene pool for the probabilities to be accurately expressed.

Exactly the same principle applies if we survey a population by examining a sample of its members. A limited sample, even from a very large population, cannot be expected to show Hardy-Weinberg proportions. But as we shall see, other factors, which are of evolutionary importance, can also cause deviation from Hardy-Weinberg ratios. So it is important to know, in any particular case, how much of the observed deviation can be written off to simple sampling error. Again, this is a question that can be answered only in terms of probabilities. Given the size of the sample, we can use statistical tests to calculate how much deviation is *likely* to be due to sampling error alone. This does not mean, of course, that any deviation above that amount is definitely due to other causes. Nevertheless, if the difference between the observed deviation and the probable sampling error is too great, we generally assume that some other factor is at work.

Presurvey Mortality

One such factor is *presurvey mortality.* Remember that the Hardy-Weinberg formula predicts the frequency with which individuals of specific genotypes will be *conceived.* But between the moment of conception and the time the survey is taken, certain genotypes may have a greater likelihood than others of being removed from the population through death. This process can begin immediately after conception; spontaneous abortion (miscarriage) often ends the existence of fetuses with genetically inherited abnormalities. Or presurvey mortality can take the form of death in infancy or early life. For example, hemophiliacs, as we saw in the last chapter, have a very high mortality rate at all ages, since they can bleed to death from minor wounds. As a result, any population—and especially its older age groups—is bound to show fewer hemophilia genotypes (the unpaired hemophilia allele, *h*, as it appears in males) than predicted by the Hardy-Weinberg ratios. Such differential mortality is a form of natural selection—which will shortly be discussed in greater detail.

Nonrandom Mating

As we saw earlier, one of the conditions necessary for the expression of the Hardy-Weinberg ratios is random mating for the gene in question. The genes must mix freely, without the carrier of any one genotype being more or less likely to mate with carriers of other particular genotypes. However, mating is seldom entirely random among either humans or other animals. Though *nonrandom mating* cannot by itself change the gene frequencies in a population, it can have considerable effect on its genotype frequencies.

Inbreeding and Outbreeding One form of nonrandom mating is *inbreeding:* regular mating among relatives. Inbreeding raises the frequency of homozygous genotypes in the population and proportionately decreases the frequency of heterozygotes. It is for this reason that incest is likely to produce offspring with genetically inherited abnormalities. Such abnormalities, as we have seen, are often due to recessive genes and therefore are expressed only in homozygotes. Hence any mating pattern that tends to produce more homozygotes also tends to produce more genetic defects. *Outbreeding,* the avoidance of mating among relatives, has the opposite effect. In either case, the genotypes of the population will deviate significantly from Hardy-Weinberg predictions.

Assortative Mating A third, and related, form of nonrandom mating is *assortative mating,* whereby individuals either choose or avoid prospective mates on the basis of shared attributes. For example, red-haired people, according to the statistics, tend to avoid one another as mates (negative assortative mating). The result is the same as with outbreeding—that is, more heterozygotes and fewer homozygotes than would be expected—but only for the gene causing red hair. On the other hand, human beings tend to choose mates of similar height and of similar intelligence (positive assortative mating). We can assume, then, that whatever genes lie behind these

Figure 3-2. **A pedigree illustrating homozygosity as the result of inbreeding. Cousins B and C have each inherited a rare recessive gene from their grandfather (A). Their marriage produces a homozygote (D) as well as a heterozygote. B's sister E, also a carrier, marries an unrelated person and produces a heterozygous carrier but no homozygous children.**

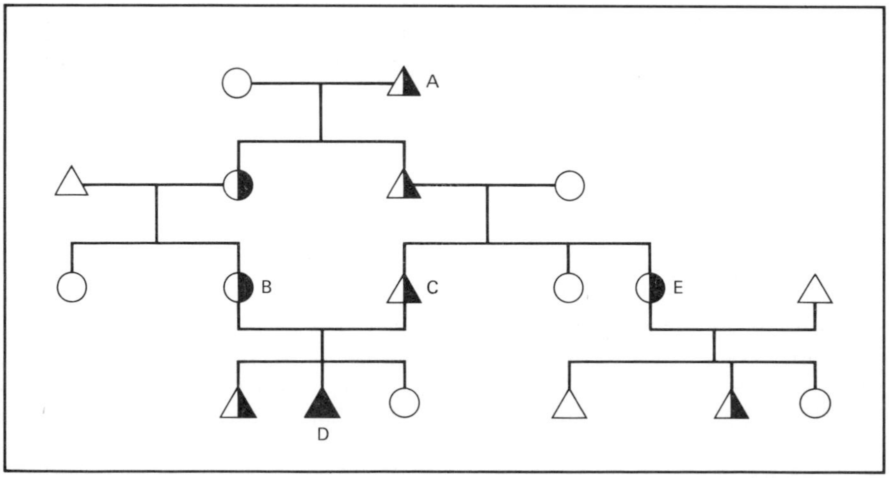

complex, polygenic traits, more people are homozygous for them than we would expect by chance. Thus, the population shows more extreme types, and a flatter distribution curve for these traits, than would be the case if mating were entirely random.

Subdivision of a Population An effect similar to that of inbreeding can be produced if, instead of randomly mating, the population *subdivides*, organizing itself into lower-level Mendelian populations within the larger one. In this case, instead of being equally likely to mate with any population member of the opposite sex, each individual is more likely to mate with a member of his or her own subgroup, be it a village, a troop, a religion, or whatever.

The effect of such subdivision on gene frequencies can be illustrated by an actual case. A research team (see box on pages 74–75) tested a population of Ethiopian baboons for blood types. Three phenotypes—types A, AB, and B—were found. (These baboons, unlike humans, have no *O* alleles.) These phenotypes were easily translated into genotypes: *AA*, *AB*, and *BB*. And once all the baboons were tested, the genotypes could in turn be translated into gene frequencies.

As shown in Table 3-1, the genotype frequencies observed in the population as a whole were not at all close to estimates based on the Hardy-Weinberg formula. There were far too few heterozygotes. However, the data tell a different story if we take into account that this population was subdivided into two different troops, with different gene frequencies. Within each of the troops, as Table 3-1 indicates, the genotype frequencies were consistent with Hardy-Weinberg predictions. It is only when the two troops are lumped together that we get the apparent excess of homozygotes.

This case illustrates a principle of considerable evolutionary importance—namely, that if a large, randomly breeding population breaks up into smaller breeding units, and these subunits develop different gene frequencies, the population as a whole will begin to produce a higher proportion of homozygotes. If the fish discussed in the last chapter, for example, were part of a population that subdivided into a number of smaller breeding groups, we would begin to get more white fish (*AABB*) and black fish (*AABB*) and proportionately fewer intermediate types.

Why should an increase in such rare homozygous genotypes be of evolutionary importance? And why, for that matter, should the smaller breeding units within a population come to differ

TABLE 3-1. The Effects of Subdivision of a Population on Genotype Frequencies

POPULATION	GENE FREQUENCIES		GENOTYPES PREDICTED BY HARDY-WEINBERG FORMULA (NUMBERS)				OBSERVED PHENOTYPES (= GENOTYPES) (NUMBERS)			
	A-gene	*B*-gene	*A*	*AB*	*B*	Total	A	AB	B	Total
Troops 1 and 2 Combined	0.23	0.77	9.3	61.5	101.2	172	15	50	107	172
Troop 1	0.04	0.96	0.1	5.8	76.1	82	0	6	76	82
Troop 2	0.41	0.59	15.3	43.5	31.2	90	15	44	31	90

Because the two troops do not interbreed freely, they are able to maintain distinct gene pools that differ markedly in gene frequencies. One result of this subdivision is that the two troops, taken together, produce more homozygotes than would be the case if they constituted a single undivided population. (Compare the predicted genotypes for the combined troops with the totals actually observed.) Note that the actual genotypes of the two troops, *taken individually*, conform very closely to the predicted Hardy-Weinberg ratios.

in gene frequency? These are questions that we take up in the following section, where we consider the forces acting upon the gene frequencies of populations.

FACTORS AFFECTING GENE FREQUENCY

So far we have been examining how genotype frequencies in populations can be predicted and why they often deviate from such predictions. In all this discussion, the gene frequencies themselves have been considered constant. But, from a genetic viewpoint, evolution is *change* in gene frequencies.

We shall now consider the forces that can cause such change and that, between periods of change, stabilize the gene pool of the population. These forces can be considered under four headings: natural selection, non-Darwinian evolution, gene flow, and mutation.

Natural Selection

Natural selection, the basis of Darwin's theory of evolution, is said to occur when certain members of a population, because they share a genotype especially well adapted to their environment, are more successful than other members in transmitting their genes to future generations. In Chapter 1 we looked at the broad outlines of this process. Let us now consider a hypothetical example. Imagine that in a population of monkeys, certain members are genetically equipped so that they are unusually fast and agile, enabling them to get to food—and away from predators—more quickly than their fellow troop members. Because of this advantage, these particular monkeys will probably live longer and therefore leave behind them more offspring than their fellows. If so, the population's gene pool in future generations will contain proportionately higher frequencies of their genes and proportionately lower frequencies of the genes of their less nimble contemporaries. As a result, such speed and agility will become more and more common in the population's collective phenotype. This, in its simplest form, is evolution by natural selection—the process whereby a population's collective phenotype comes increasingly to resemble the phenotype of those members who are reproductively most successful.

Darwinian Fitness

The success of a certain genotype, compared with that of other genotypes within the population, in transmitting its genes to future generations is called its *Darwinian fitness.* Fitness (as in the phrase "the survival of the fittest") is often mistaken to mean hardiness, aggressiveness, and the ability to beat the other fellow to the feeding trough. These qualities may *contribute* to fitness, but they do not *constitute* fitness. Mules, for example, are extremely strong, vigorous, and adaptable creatures; but they are completely sterile. Since they cannot reproduce, their fitness is zero.

The Components of Fitness Darwinian fitness, then, has to do entirely with the ability to perpetuate one's own genotype. This ability depends on many factors. Any of the following, if increased, will enhance fitness:

1. *Survival to produce offspring:* The longer an animal lives, the more time it has to produce offspring. It is in this sense that success at the feeding trough, and in the other arts of survival, contributes to fitness.
2. *Economy of energy in survival activities:* The more energy an animal spends in traveling and looking for food, the less energy it will have to compete for mates or to produce milk for infants. Thus any increase in the efficiency of its survival activities (feeding, moving with the troop, evading predators) will increase fitness.
3. *Success in attracting the most mates:* In most mammals, the reproductive capacity of the male (unlike that of the female) is limited only by the number of females he can induce to mate with him. Therefore anything that gives him an advantage in competing for mates—a

particularly dashing appearance, an ability to scare away other males—will enhance his fitness.

4. *Success in attracting the best mates:* Both sexes can increase their chances of producing hardy offspring—and therefore of having their genes transmitted to the third generation and beyond—by mating with the most fit specimens of the opposite sex.
5. *Number of offspring produced:* Other things being equal, the more offspring an animal produces, the greater its fitness.
6. *Success in rearing each offspring to maturity:* If an animal's offspring all die before reproducing, its genes die too, and therefore its fitness returns to zero. In general, then, good parents are more fit. The best overall strategy is usually some compromise between unlimited reproduction and energy spent on rearing each offspring. Exactly where the balance is struck varies from species to species.

Inclusive Fitness Traditionally, our conception of Darwinian fitness meant success in producing direct descendants, especially one's own offspring. This definition poses certain problems, however. How, for example, do we explain the fact that in many insects—including ants, termites, wasps, and bees—the workers of the group are all sterile? If evolution by natural selection molds the collective phenotype of a species in the image of its most fit members, how could it have produced—and how can it go on producing—these creatures, which, according to the traditional definition, have zero fitness?

Recently the traditional definition of fitness has been extended by the concept of *inclusive fitness,* which in large part answers these objections. Inclusive fitness is success in promoting the survival of one's own genotype—whether by producing offspring *or* by helping other relatives to survive and produce offspring. In general, the individual's best strategy for perpetuating its genotype is to produce as many and as healthy offspring as possible. However, offspring are not the only ones who carry genes identical by descent to one's own. Genetically, every individual is as closely related to its parents and its full siblings as to its own offspring. (Parents, full siblings, and offspring are all theoretically identical to the individual in half of their genes.) Therefore, although it cannot *produce* these other relatives, anything that it can do to aid in their survival and reproduction will enhance its own fitness every bit as much as will helping the survival of its own offspring. The cause of one's own fitness can also be promoted by taking an "interest" in more distant relatives—grandchildren, nieces, nephews, and half-siblings, one-fourth of whose genes are theoretically identical to one's own.

With the help of this broader notion of fitness, we can understand the evolution of the sterile worker insects, who spend their whole lives raising their nieces and nephews. Natural selection operates on all traits that have a genetic basis—on behavior as well as on anatomy. Behaviors that enhance fitness are those that are perpetuated. According to the traditional definition of fitness, the extreme altruism of the worker bees would be very puzzling; but as a demonstration of inclusive fitness, it is quite understandable. So too are other examples of altruism, such as risking one's life to save a sibling or other relative—an act often seen among the social primates, although it runs utterly counter to the traditional notion of fitness.

Detecting Differential Fitness in Action How do we observe natural selection at work? The fact that an *individual* has higher than average or lower than average reproductive success cannot automatically be attributed to natural selection. In order for high or low fitness to have evolutionary significance—in order for it to be an example of natural selection—it must, first, be related to the genes that the individual carries. Second, it must be part of a pattern; the gene or set of genes responsible must be one that *regularly* confers higher or lower fitness on its carriers.

Let us imagine, for example, that a twenty-year-old man who has no offspring is hit by a truck and killed, or crippled in such a way that he can never reproduce. If the accident is the fault of the truck driver's carelessness or a slippery road, then the man's zero fitness has nothing to do with natural selection. If, however, the man did not notice the truck because of a genetically inherited defect in hearing or vision—or could not react in time because of slow reflexes or poor coordination—then this failure in fitness does have evolutionary meaning. Indeed, it would be a good example of the process whereby selective agents in the environment "weed out" less adaptive genes from the gene pool by reducing their carriers' chances of reproducing.

To determine whether a phenotypic trait existing within a population is having any evolutionary impact, we must accumulate a sample of individuals who bear this trait and then try to determine whether their reproductive success is, on the average, significantly different from that of other phenotypes. This is usually done one trait at a time. We try to see, for instance, whether people of blood group A are more fit than those of blood groups B, AB, and O. (They are not.) Or, in a case of continuous variation, we try to determine which segment of the distribution is most fit.

Patterns of Selection

As we have seen, differences in fitness provide a powerful mechanism for evolutionary change—natural selection. As the fittest individuals stock future generations with their descendants, the makeup of the gene pool changes, and so does the collective phenotype of the population. However, natural selection can also be a powerful mechanism for stability. Whether it works for change or stability depends, as we shall see, on *whether the population's phenotypic norm is its most fit type.*

Directional Selection

When natural selection causes change in a population's gene frequencies, it is called *directional selection.* We have already discussed a hypothetical example of directional selection—the case of the nimble monkeys. Since most populations are well adapted to their environments, we rarely see directional selection at work except when the environment changes. The simplest cases to observe are those in which environmental change makes a rare allele—one that had existed within an almost homogeneous population at a very low frequency—suddenly advantageous. This turn of events can be illustrated by the classic case of the peppered moth, *Biston betularia.*

In the early nineteenth century, most of the peppered moths in England were light gray. This coloring enhanced their fitness, for it made them almost invisible when they rested on the lichen-covered bark of trees and therefore reduced their chances of being spotted and eaten by birds. Now and then a black form appeared as a result of a rare mutation in a single gene. But the black mutants did not last long. Highly visible against the lightly colored bark, they were quickly picked off by the birds.

However, as England entered the Industrial Revolution, the moths' environment changed. Soot from factories gradually covered the bark of trees in industrial areas, and consequently the fitness values of the black and gray forms were reversed. Against the blackened trees, the gray form was now conspicuous and the black form was camouflaged. Therefore, while the gray moths were being eaten by birds, the black moths lived on to produce more black moths, so that within a few decades almost all of the peppered moths in industrial areas were black. (In rural areas the gray moth remained the norm.) In other words, as the fitness values of the two forms were reversed by a change in their environment, so too were their frequencies changed by natural selection. (And it now happens that they may be reversed again. With recent controls against pollution, the trees are becoming less black, and the frequency of gray moths in proportion to black is increasing.)

The crucial component of fitness in this case was survival; more black moths than gray moths survived to transmit the genes for their coloring. But natural selection can work just as well on each of the other aspects of fitness described previously. Any genetically determined trait that in any way affects the reproductive efficiency of

Black and gray peppered moths (*Biston betularia*). When airborne soot darkened the bark of trees in industrial areas, the light gray moth became conspicuous against the dark background. Black moths, protected from predation by their coloration, eventually became the predominant form. *(M. W. F. Tweedie/Rapho/Photo Researchers)*

some members of the population is subject to evolution by natural selection.

Dominance and Directional Selection In the case of the peppered moth, the "black" gene took over very quickly. This was due in part to the great difference in fitness between the black and gray forms. The greater the fitness differential, the more intense the selection, and hence the faster the rate of replacement.

However, the rapidity of the change also had a great deal to do with the fact that the "black" allele was dominant. Dominance and recessivity have an immense impact on the rate of replacement in directional selection. Remember that natural selection operates only through differences in *phenotype*. An individual may carry an extremely advantageous allele, but unless that allele is expressed, it will have no effect on fitness and natural selection cannot go to work on it. Because the allele for black moths was dominant, natural selection did not have to wait for the extremely rare (q^2) occurrence of a black homozygote. The heterozygotes, whose occurrence was much more likely (2 pq), were also black. Thus the selection process could begin as soon as changing environmental conditions made the black phenotype advantageous.

When the advantageous allele is recessive, the rate of change is many times slower, in the beginning, for in this case natural selection *does* have to wait for the appearance of homozygotes. To get an idea of how greatly this can slow the rate of replacement, let us imagine that the frequency of a highly advantageous recessive allele is 0.001. According to the Hardy-Weinberg formula, the frequency of the homozygous recessive genotype will be 0.001^2, or 0.000001. In other words, if mating is random, only one out of every million individuals will manifest the fitness-enhancing trait on which the selection process must work. Of course, once selection increases the frequency of the gene, there will be more homozygotes, and the process will speed up. But when the advantageous allele is recessive, directional selection invariably gets off to a very slow start (Figure 3-3).

In view of this fact, we can now understand the importance of a population's mating patterns—whether it deviates from random mating, and if so, how. As we saw, certain mating patterns—especially inbreeding and positive assortative mating—increase the frequency of homozygotes. Thus, while these mating patterns do not in themselves change gene frequencies, they can stimulate such change by causing recessive alleles to be expressed, thereby exposing them to selection.

However, in most populations—and especially in large populations that practice outbreeding—low-frequency recessives rarely find their way into homozygous pairs. The probability is simply too low. And therefore these recessives, even if

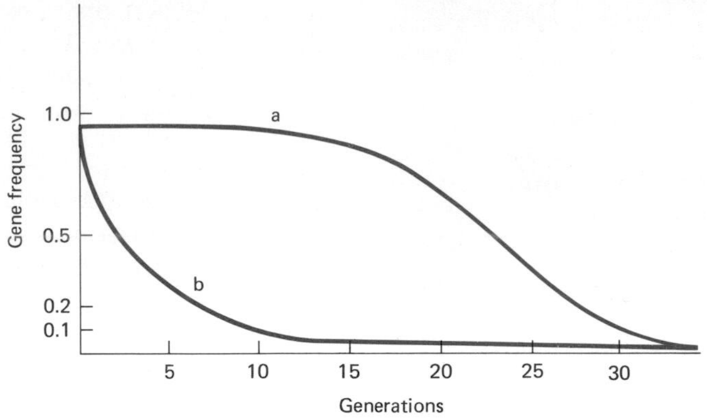

Figure 3-3. The rate of elimination of genes by natural selection: (a) selection against a dominant gene—frequency declines slowly at first, then more rapidly until the gene is lost from population; (b) selection against recessive gene—frequency drops rapidly at first, but rate slows and "residue" persists indefinitely.

they are potentially very harmful, survive in the gene pool and go on being carried, unexpressed, in heterozygotes who are phenotypically quite normal.

Selection as Compromise As we saw earlier, fitness has many components, and these in turn depend on a large number of phenotypic traits. Natural selection favors the most advantageous compromise among the various fitness-enhancing traits. In female mammals, for instance, the ability to produce offspring from an early age would improve fitness, other things being equal. But if sexual maturity comes too early, other things will *not* be equal; pregnancy could interfere with development, resulting in sickly offspring or the death of the mother. Therefore natural selection strikes a compromise between the two demands, scheduling sexual maturity late enough so as not to interfere with development but early enough to allow for a long breeding period.

Stabilizing Selection When a gene pool shows no substantial change over a considerable period of time, this does not mean that natural selection has ceased to operate. It simply means that the gene pool has arrived, by directional selection, at the most adaptive gene frequencies for the population's environment. Directional selection has given way to *stabilizing selection*—selection that operates to keep the population's gene frequencies more or less constant.

Gene-pool stability is sometimes achieved when one allele is established at close to 100 percent frequency. The homozygous genotype then becomes the population's norm. In this case, selection works only to eliminate the occasional mutant and the rare homozygous recessive emerging from the population's genetic load. This, for example, was what happened in the English peppered moth populations before the industrial soot descended on their environment; gray was the norm, and the occasional black moth was quickly weeded out.

However, stabilizing selection can also result in the long-term persistence of two or more phenotypes—a phenomenon known as balanced polymorphism.

Balanced Polymorphism It sometimes happens that a gene will be subject to two or more opposing selective trends, each favoring a different genotype. One genotype confers a particular advantage in fitness, another a different advantage. In such a case, the selective forces generally arrive at a point of equilibrium: two or more distinct phenotypes will coexist within the population, each occurring at a roughly constant frequency. This condition is called *balanced polymorphism.*

A classic illustration of balanced polymorphism is sickle-cell anemia. As we saw, people who are homozygous for the abnormal, sickle-cell allele have a very low fitness. Yet the abnormal allele persists in some populations, notably in parts of equatorial Africa, at frequencies up to 20 percent. This apparent anomaly seems to be due to an opposing selective trend, having to do with the mosquito-borne disease tropical malaria. Several studies have shown that malarial infection is more frequent and serious in individuals who are homozygous for the normal allele(*AA*) than in heterozygotes (*AS*). Thus while sickle-cell anemia is removing the abnormal allele (*S*) by picking off the abnormal homozygotes (*SS*), malaria is removing the normal allele (*A*) as it occurs in normal homozygotes (*AA*). The only ones who are relatively safe from both blights are the heterozygotes (*AS*).

When this happens—that is, when the heterozygotes are the most fit genotype—neither allele ousts the other. They both remain in the gene pool, at frequencies determined by the relative intensity of the two selective pressures. (In the case of sickle cell, for example, the *S* allele is less frequent than the *A* because the fitness of *SS* individuals is much lower than that of *AA* individuals.) The result is balanced polymorphism: a stable mix of phenotypes.

In animal species, polymorphism—the existence of multiple phenotypes within a population—is very common. Many of these polymorphisms are believed to be due, like sickle cell, to balancing selective forces. In most cases, however, the selective forces involved are unknown, and some geneticists suspect that a good deal of polymorphism may be *transient* rather than balanced: What we may be seeing is one allele in the process of replacing another, rather than two alleles coexisting at stable frequencies.

Whatever the cause, polymorphisms are an enormously important part of the genetic make-up of a species. They provide the variability upon which natural selection can work to achieve new adaptations. Without such variability, the population would have little chance of responding adaptively to new selective challenges in a changing environment and would lose its potential for adaptive evolutionary change.

Natural Selection and Polygenic Traits

Like the frequencies of monogenic traits, the distribution of a polygenic trait changes under the influence of directional selection and remains constant under the influence of stabilizing selection. If extreme genotypes at both ends of the curve have lower fitness, the two selective forces will balance each other and stabilize the distribution. This seems to occur with respect to stature in humans. The tallest and shortest people in a population have the fewest offspring, so that some "tall" and some "short" genes are lost in each generation. As a result, the distribution of phenotypes, after selection, remains relatively unchanged from one generation to the next. This process of stabilizing selection is illustrated in Figure 3-4.

If, on the other hand, one end of the distribution becomes more fit, then directional selection and evolutionary change will take place. Let us suppose, for example, that the environment changed in such a way that shortness increased fitness. The frequency of "short" genes would then increase and the frequency of "tall" genes would decrease with each successive generation. As a result, the average stature of the population would gradually decrease (Figure 3-4). Many of the long-term trends we see in mammalian evolution probably involve gradual shifts of this kind.

Non-Darwinian Evolution

Natural selection can be described as deterministic. In theory, if we know the direction and intensity of the selective forces working on a population, we can say with some certainty how the gene frequencies will change, at what rate they will change, and at what levels they will stabilize. *Non-Darwinian evolution,* on the other hand, is largely random. While it too changes gene frequencies, we cannot predict the direction of the change, and we can predict the speed of the change only in terms of probabilities. Two processes fall under the heading of non-Darwinian evolution: genetic drift and the founder effect.

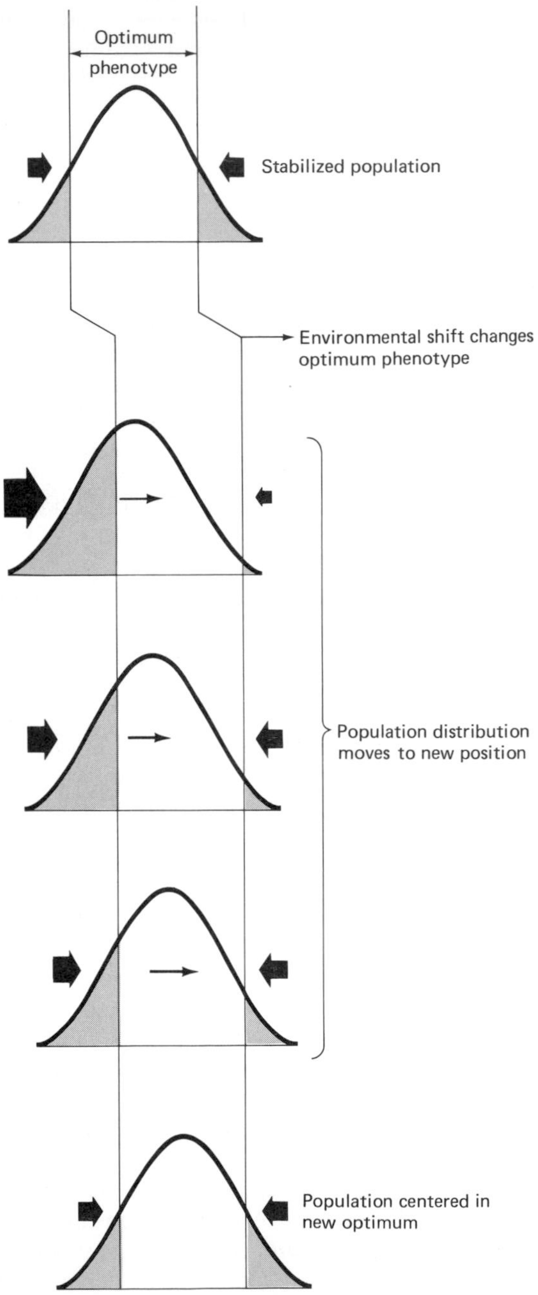

Genetic Drift

Assuming that a particular gene confers no advantage in fitness, so that selective forces cannot operate, under what circumstances can that gene totally displace its alleles? Mathematical geneticists have shown that population size is the important factor. The genes of each generation represent a *sample* drawn from the previous generation's gene pool. The smaller the population, the less likely it is that the gene frequencies of a given generation of offspring will exactly reflect those of the parental generation. In other words, gene frequencies will fluctuate from generation to generation, and the smaller the population, the wider the fluctuations will be. This phenomenon is known as *genetic drift* (Figure 3-5).

Just as a drunken bicyclist, weaving randomly down a street, will eventually hit one curb or the other, such fluctuation will eventually fix one gene at the expense of its alleles. In other words, the gradual but inevitable result of genetic drift is that one lucky gene will become established at 100 percent frequency in the population, eliminating its alleles. On the average, the smaller the population, the more rapidly genetic drift will occur. Small populations, therefore, have a tendency to lose variability and become highly homozygous. Even in large populations, one gene will replace its alleles over time, although the process will require many generations. Depending on the size of the population, we can predict the rate of genetic drift; however, we cannot predict *which* allele it will favor.

Figure 3-4. Stabilizing and directional evolution. The curves represent the distributions of a characteristic in a population. At first, the population is in equilibrium, subject to equal, opposite selective forces. A change in the environment destroys the equilibrium and exposes the population to unbalanced, directional selection. Under the influence of selection, the distribution gradually changes until it is centered upon the new optimum phenotype.

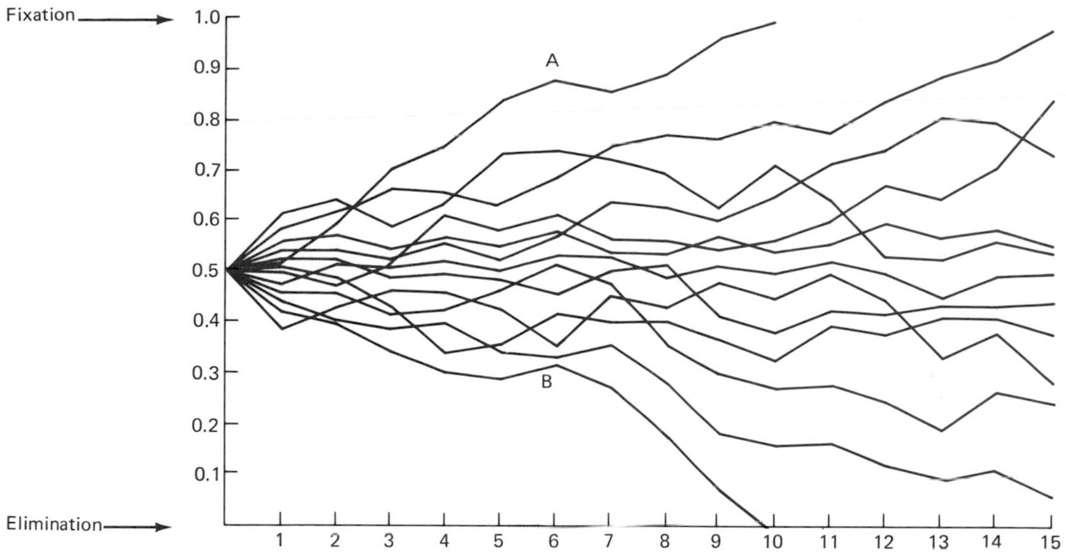

Figure 3-5. **Change in gene frequencies under the action of genetic drift in a series of populations. Each line represents the frequency of an allele in a particular population over fifteen generations. At the beginning, all populations have a frequency of 0.5. After fifteen generations, the allele has been fixed in one population (A), eliminated from another (B), and varies widely in frequency among the others.**

Having examined both natural selection and genetic drift, we can now understand why different populations within a species, or different subpopulations within a population, come to differ in their gene frequencies—a phenomenon that we observed in the case of blood groups of the Awash baboons. As long as mating patterns keep the two gene pools partially separate, genetic drift will inevitably cause their gene frequencies to wander off in somewhat different directions. If, in addition, the two subpopulations are subject to slightly different environmental pressures, then natural selection will also act on their gene pools in different ways.

The relative importance of these two factors depends on the size of the populations and on the intensity of the selective pressures to which they are subjected. The smaller a population, the more subject it is to drift. Selection, on the other hand, is not affected by population size. The role of selection depends, rather, on the extent of the difference in fitness created by the contrasting environments. If there is no significant difference—that is, if the prevalent genotype fares equally well in both habitats—then selection cannot differentiate the two populations. Divergence through drift, however, since it has nothing to do with fitness, can still occur.

The Founder Effect

A more dramatic form of non-Darwinian evolution is the *founder effect:* the loss of variability that occurs when a new population is established by a few settlers, colonists, or survivors of a catastrophe. In this case, founders' gene frequencies will inevitably differ, through sampling error, from those of their parents. For the founders will constitute only a small fraction of the original population and carry only a small sample of its gene pool. (Indeed, certain of the original population's alleles may be totally absent.) Consequently, the population that the founders produce may have gene frequencies utterly different from those of the population that produced the founders. In this case, the group phenotype may change markedly in a single generation. If a village of blue-eyed and brown-eyed people becomes overcrowded, for example, and two blue-eyed families set out over the hills to establish a new village, blue eyes will be far more common in the new village than in the old. Indeed, the new population may be uniformly blue-eyed. Or, to take an actual historical example, the blood group frequencies on the various Polynesian islands differ widely—probably because each in turn was settled by small groups of colonists from more crowded neighboring islands.

The founder effect, then, is like an extreme and sudden fluctuation in genetic drift. Or rather, genetic drift can be thought of as a mild founder effect repeated each generation. In both cases, the impact is the same: loss of variability in the population's gene pool.

Gene Flow

As we have seen, drift and natural selection tend to push Mendelian populations apart genetically. This tendency is often counteracted by *gene flow:* the transfer of genes from one population to another via migration or interbreeding. If a wolf from one pack migrates to another pack or mates with a female from another pack, then the second pack will have acquired genes from the first. Indeed, it may acquire alleles that would never have arisen among its own members. And if the two populations are very different, so that a number of new alleles are introduced into the host gene pool, then even a low rate of immigration or interbreeding can cause a large amount of evolutionary change, as we shall see shortly. Thus, while gene flow promotes homogeneity among populations, its most important effect within populations is to increase the variability on which evolutionary forces can operate.

Mutation

While gene flow allows populations to spread their variability around, the ultimate source of all variability is mutation. Mutation, then, is the final important factor affecting gene frequencies. By providing a steady flow of new alleles, it supplies the raw material for all of the processes we have just discussed. Above all, it gives natural selection its choices.

Of course, not every new allele survives to contribute to a population's variability. Many mutants do not make it beyond the first generation, and those that do persist through several generations may still be eliminated eventually. Or they may achieve a respectable frequency, in balance with other alleles. Or, as in the case of the peppered moth, they may actually replace the other alleles. Which route the mutant allele takes once it enters the gene pool depends mainly on its phenotypic effect: whether it is dominant or recessive and whether it is advantageous, harmful, or neutral. For every one that makes it, thousands are eliminated. But without the small percentage that make it, populations would, under the influence of genetic drift, quickly lose their variability.

The Establishment of a Neutral Mutation

We have seen how selection acts to weed out harmful mutations and causes beneficial ones to spread. But how can a neutral mutation—one that has no effect on the fitness of its bearer—become established in a population? Let us consider the appearance, in a single individual, of a new mutation that neither increases nor decreases fitness. The chances of this mutation's becoming established are very low indeed. Its bearer is, of course, a heterozygote. If he reproduces, only half his genotype will be transmitted to each of his offspring, and it is as likely as not that the chromosome transmitted will not include the new allele. If it does, then the allele runs the risk of elimination in the next generation.

The odds, then, are against such mutants. Very few of them persist for more than a generation or two. But evolutionary time is long, and mutation produces a steady supply of new genes. A very low but predictable proportion will, against all the odds, eventually become established as polymorphisms in the population. Human proteins, for example, show a number of variations that seem to have no phenotypic effect and that were probably introduced by this route during the long course of human evolution.

Population Structure and Gene Frequency

In evolutionary terms, the most important effect of changes in gene frequency is that they can alter the genetic structure of a Mendelian population. As we saw earlier, both genetic drift and the selective effects of slightly different environments cause populations to diverge from one another. The result is a *polytypic species*—that is, a species whose constituent populations differ in their gene frequencies and phenotypic traits.

This divergence may be particularly marked in the case of a small, marginal population of the species. Because it is small, drift will alter its gene pool more rapidly. And if its environment differs significantly from that of the other populations—if, for example, it lives where the forest meets the plains or where the plains meet the mountains—then directional selection is likely to push its gene frequencies rather far afield from the species norm.

Such a population, with its rich source of new gene combinations, is an excellent channel for evolutionary change within the species. If the population rejoins the others and feeds its genes back into the species pool, this injection of new variability will greatly intensify selection. If, on the other hand, the population remains isolated, it may simply continue diverging further and further. In the latter case, the probable result will be the appearance of a new species alongside the old.

This process, of course, does not occur in the space of a few generations. It is one of the many evolutionary patterns that emerge over hundreds or thousands of generations. These long-term patterns of evolution are the subject of our next chapter.

Summary

Evolutionary geneticists focus not on families but on *Mendelian populations:* groups of organisms in which each member is more likely to mate with another member than with an outsider. Unlike families, such groups retain their genetic identity over generations and therefore can demonstrate evolutionary change. The most inclusive Mendelian population is the *biological species,* a group of interbreeding populations that is reproductively isolated from other such groups. Species contain other, smaller Mendelian populations, the smallest of which is the *deme.*

Phenotypic variability within populations falls into two categories. *Discontinuous variation* (as in human blood groups) is usually the product of alleles at a single locus, and divides the population into discrete groups, with no intermediates; it is expressed in terms of phenotype frequencies. *Continuous variation* (as in human body weight) is generally polygenic, and expresses itself as a smooth gradient between two extremes; its distribution usually approaches the form of a bell-shaped curve, which can be described in statistical terms. Together these measures allow us to characterize a population's *collective phenotype* and the evolutionary changes therein.

The collective phenotype of a population is partially determined by the makeup of its gene pool, which is described in terms of *gene frequencies.* The frequency of a given gene is the abundance of that gene relative to all its alleles in the population. However, to account for a population's collective phenotype, we must also know its *genotype frequencies,* the proportion of different genotypes within the population. The theoretical relationship between gene frequencies and genotype frequencies is stated in the *Hardy-Weinberg* formula, which predicts that if p and q are the frequencies of the alleles *A* and *B* in the population, then the frequencies of the

AA, *AB*, and *BB* genotypes will be p^2, $2\,pq$, and q^2 respectively, under conditions of random mating. Actually, most real populations deviate from the predicted Hardy-Weinberg ratios. Such deviation may be due to *sampling error* or to *non-random mating* (inbreeding, outbreeding, assortative mating, or subdivision of the population). Alternatively, it may be due to evolutionary processes, such as differential mortality. Indeed, the major value of the Hardy-Weinberg formula is that it helps us to spot evolutionary change in action.

From a genetic viewpoint, evolution is change in the gene frequencies of a population. The major forces behind such change are natural selection, non-Darwinian evolution, gene flow, and mutation. *Natural selection* is said to occur when certain members of a population, because they share a genotype especially well adapted to their environment, are more successful than other members in transmitting their genes to future generations. The success of a certain genotype, compared with other genotypes within the population, in perpetuating its genes by passing them on to offspring is called its Darwinian fitness. Fitness depends on many factors: survival to produce offspring, economy of energy in survival activities, success in attracting the most and/or the best mates, number of offspring produced, and success in rearing each offspring to maturity. The recent concept of *inclusive fitness* expresses the insight that an organism can also enhance its fitness by promoting the survival of relatives *other than* offspring.

Natural selection can be a powerful mechanism either for change or for stability in a population, depending on whether the population's phenotypic norm is the most fit type. *Directional selection* occurs when changes in the environment lead to changes in gene frequency, at a rate determined by the strength of the selective pressure and by the dominance or recessivity of the trait in question. Selective forces can act much more quickly on dominant traits than on recessive ones. When the gene frequencies of a population have reached optimal values for a given environment, directional selection gives way to *stabilizing selection*, which operates to maintain those frequencies. This may involve the establishment of one allele at close to 100 percent frequency, or it may involve the coexistence of two or more alleles at fairly constant frequencies—a phenomenon called *balanced polymorphism*.

The changes produced by non-Darwinian evolution, including genetic drift and founder effect, are less predictable than those due to natural selection. *Genetic drift* is the result of random fluctuations in a population's gene frequencies from generation to generation. Eventually, chance will permit one gene to displace its alleles. It is through this process that separate populations and subpopulations of a species gradually come to differ in gene frequencies. *Founder effect* is the loss of variability that occurs when a new population is established by a few settlers, colonists, or survivors of a catastrophe. While non-Darwinian evolution reduces variability within a population, *gene flow*—the transfer of genes between populations through migration or interbreeding—brings in new variations from outside. At the same time, *mutation* continues to produce new genes within populations.

If genetic drift and natural selection cause a marginal population to diverge significantly from other populations of the species, this new source of variation can either give rise to a separate species or, if fed back into the species pool, can greatly intensify evolutionary change within that species.

Glossary

assortative mating selection or avoidance of prospective mates on the basis of shared attributes

biological species a group of interbreeding populations that is reproductively isolated from other such groups

collective phenotype the observable characteristics

of a population considered as a whole

deme the smallest possible Mendelian population of a species; usually a group of organisms occupying a particular geographical region

directional selection natural selection that produces change in the gene frequencies of a population

fitness success in promoting the survival of one's own genotype, either by producing offspring (Darwinian fitness) or by helping relatives to survive and produce offspring (inclusive fitness)

founder effect the loss of variability that occurs when a new population is established by a few settlers, colonists, or survivors from a larger population

gene flow the transfer of genes from one population to another by migration or interbreeding

gene frequency the abundance of a particular gene in a population relative to that of its allele or alleles

gene pool the total store of genes of a population

genetic drift change in the gene frequencies of a population over a period of time as a result of the random fluctuations in gene frequencies from generation to generation

Hardy-Weinberg formula a formula that predicts a population's genotype frequencies from its gene frequencies; if p and q are the frequencies of alleles *A* and *B* in the population, then the frequen cies of genotypes *AA*, *AB*, and *BB* will be p^2, 2 pq, and q^2 respectively, under conditions of random mating

inbreeding frequent mating among relatives

Mendelian population a group of organisms in which each member is more likely to mate with another member than with an outsider; thus a group within which a body of genes is usually transmitted

non-Darwinian evolution changes in the gene frequencies of populations that are caused by random processes, such as genetic drift and the founder effect

outbreeding the avoidance of mating among relatives

phenotypic variation differences in observable traits among members of a population; variation may be **discontinuous** (two or more discrete groups, without intermediates) or **continuous** (a smooth gradient between two extremes)

polymorphism the coexistence of two or more phenotypes within a population; if each occurs at a roughly constant frequency, due to opposing selective forces, the condition is called **balanced polymorphism**

polytypic species a species whose constituent populations differ in their gene frequencies and phenotypic traits

sampling error the difference between the theoretical gene frequencies in a population and those observed in an actual sample drawn at random from it; the smaller the sample, the larger the probable deviation

stabilizing selection natural selection that operates to keep a population's gene frequencies relatively constant

Suggested Readings

CAVALLI-SFORZA, L. L., AND BODMER, W. F. 1971
The Genetics of Human Populations. San Francisco: W. H. Freeman. A full and readable account of population genetics that does not avoid mathematical formulations, but makes them as palatable as possible for the nonmathematically inclined reader.

McKUSICK, V. A. 1969
Human Genetics. 2nd ed. Englewood Cliffs, N.J.: Prentice-Hall. A succinct and authoritative coverage of all major aspects of human genetics.

Chapter Four

Major Patterns of Evolution

In the last chapter, we concentrated on the details of the evolutionary process. We saw how reproduction merges the genes of the individual with the gene pool of the population, and how that gene pool can change from generation to generation, under the influence of natural selection and of non-Darwinian evolution. In this chapter, we look at evolution in a longer perspective. We trace the patterns that emerge as the gene pools of populations move through spans of time encompassing hundreds of thousands of generations and millions of years.

Biologists sometimes use time-lapse photography to study processes that are too slow for ordinary observation, such as the growth and flowering of a plant. To see clearly the long-term process of evolutionary change, we must speed up time in much the same way, so that generation merges with generation like the individual frames of a movie. When we adopt this perspective, populations can be seen at last in their evolutionary context—as *lineages,* or lines of descent. Over the centuries and the millennia, the lineages gradually change—flourishing, splitting, diversifying, dwindling, or becoming extinct, under the influence of evolutionary forces.

Each living species, including *Homo sapiens,* has its own unique evolutionary history. Yet, though evolutionary change is often complex and hard to trace, the forces behind it are relatively easy to understand: mutation, natural selection, gene flow, and genetic drift. The intricacy of the evolutionary record becomes even more manageable once we understand that there are patterns in long-term evolutionary change—phenomena that tend to occur again and again, even in unrelated groups of plants and animals. These patterns are the subject of the present chapter.

The common North American opossum, a species similar in structure and general appearance to mammals living 100 million years ago, is a conservative species in evolutionary terms. Well adapted to its econiche, it has been under little selective pressure for evolutionary change. Other species, however, have evolved markedly in far shorter periods of time. The human species is an example. (*Molly Adams/Rapho/Photo Researchers*)

THE NATURE OF EVOLUTIONARY CHANGE

Every species, as we have seen, has its own econiche—its way of subsisting, or "making a living," in its environment. Sometimes an environmental change opens up new opportunities for a species: a new geographical area that can be colonized, or a new potential food supply to be exploited. When this happens, the species, driven by the never-ending pressure of competition among individuals for food and living space, will respond by expanding into the new econiche. This means a change in behavior. Living in a new environment (in the trees instead of on the ground, or in grasslands instead of forest, for example), eating a different kind of food, hunting at a different time of day or in a new way—any or all of these changes may be involved. And such changes in ecology, by bringing new selective pressures to bear on the population, will generally lead to biological changes, making members of the species physically better adapted for what they are now doing. Anatomical structure, physiology, the timing of growth and development—all are under genetic control and may be modified by the selective pressures of a new way of life.

Environment, Behavior, Structure: The Evolutionary Spiral

The rapid evolutionary change in the elephant family over the past few million years provides a good example of this process. Several million years ago, the environment began to change in a way that profoundly affected the evolution of this group. The forests that had been the habitat of the ancestral elephants started to shrink and were replaced in many areas by grasslands. As we shall see in Chapters 7 and 8, these changes may have played a key role in starting a group of early apes along the path leading to humanity. The ancestral elephants too responded to the new environmental conditions. They shifted from browsing (feeding upon the leaves of trees and bushes) to grazing (feeding upon grasses and other tough vegetation). The selective pressure of this new way of life brought about corresponding changes in the elephants' anatomy. The jaws gradually became modified into efficient grinders. The entire orientation of the chewing muscles was altered. The lower tusks disappeared, and the chewing teeth evolved into massive, high-crowned grindstones that were well adapted to tough vegetation. The snout became a mobile trunk, used to gather up bundles of grass and stuff them into the mouth. Each change in the chewing apparatus was an adaptation that fitted the elephants more comfortably into their new econiche—grazing in open grassland.

Note the chain of causation in such an evolutionary change. First, the *environment* changed, opening a new opportunity to be exploited (grass eating in open country). Second, the ancestral elephants responded to the environmental challenge with a *behavioral* shift (more grazing, less browsing). And finally, their *anatomy* was modified because natural selection favored anatomical structures (big molars, mobile trunk) that could make these behaviors easier to perform.

Of course, early elephants adapted for browsing did not suddenly move into open grasslands one fine day and then wait for anatomical changes to equip them for their next meal. The process occurred in slow, small steps, driven steadily onward by *positive feedback.* This means that each change in one of the three elements—habitat, behavior, and anatomy—promoted further changes in the other two. Each small change in anatomy, for example, must have accelerated the development of new feeding habits, making the animals increasingly dependent on grazing. This in turn would have enabled them to move further into open country—where they would be subjected to stronger selective pressures toward grass-eating adaptations, and so on. The cycle would continue until a new, stable pattern of adaptation was achieved, with both behavior and anatomy fully adjusted to the most efficient exploitation of environmental conditions.

In general, then, each burst of evolutionary change represents a response to a further step in behavioral specialization, itself triggered by new environmental opportunities. Recognizing that structural evolution occurs in this way gives evolutionary biologists a method for interpreting the physical changes they observe in the fossil record. The procedure is to work backward from the structural change, asking the following questions:

1. What is the functional significance of the change?
2. What behavioral shift could have caused this change in function?
3. What environmental factors might have triggered this change in behavior?

Specialization and Generalization

A common result of evolution driven by natural selection is greater *specialization:* each species becomes better at exploiting a particular set of resources but less able to exploit other resources. In other words, its econiche narrows. Aardvarks, for example, eat little but termites and wild cucumbers; and there are species of bat that survive almost entirely on the nectar of certain flowers that open after dark. But the thrust of evolutionary change is not always in the direction of specialization. Sometimes a species becomes adapted to a very broad econiche, so that it is not heavily dependent on the exploitation of any single set of resources. On the whole, primates—the order of mammals to which the human species belongs—have tended to remain more generalized than most other mammals.

Some environments tend to encourage specialization; others are more favorable to generalists. But both specialization and generalization have their dangers as well as their advantages. Sometimes extreme specialization is the road to survival. Reptiles, for example, were once the dominant form of animal life on earth. Today, mammals dominate, and the relatively few reptile species that have managed to escape extinction are for the most part quite specialized. Having been forced by competition with mammals into relatively narrow econiches, they became so well established there that no mammal has succeeded in displacing them. Nevertheless, specialization can also mean vulnerability. Each step in specialization represents a commitment to a particular set of conditions—conditions that may not last. The more specialized a species, the less flexibility it has to meet sudden environmental changes. If and when they come, the species, previously thriving in its narrow econiche, may face rapid extinction.

The advantages and risks of generalization are exactly the opposite. The generalist's broader ecological base may give it enough flexibility to survive in the face of changing circumstances. If disease rots the fruit, it can eat leaves; if there is sudden heavy competition for the leaves, it can concentrate on insects. At the same time, however, the generalized species may be squeezed out by a number of specialists—each a little better at exploiting one part of its broad econiche.

It is well to keep in mind, however, that extinction is not a rare calamity but a very ordinary occurrence in evolutionary history. One way or another, all species eventually become extinct. This has happened to countless millions of species in the past, and there is no particular reason to think that those now living will in the long run escape the same fate.

Rates of Evolutionary Change

Evolutionary change does not hum along at an even rate. In most lineages, periods of rapid change typically alternate with long periods of *stasis*, in which the species, well adapted to its econiche and encountering little environmental change, shows little or no evolutionary development.

Such variability in the rate of evolutionary change is very striking when we compare one lineage with another. The elephants, as we have just seen, have evolved quite rapidly in the past few million years. By contrast, some species become firmly established in a stable econiche, and so change very little over much longer periods of time. A good example of such a conservative species is the common North American opossum, which is quite similar to early mammals of about 100 million years ago. During the opossum's lengthy period of stasis, evolutionary change has produced other mammals as diverse as elephants, bats, kangaroos, and whales. Extreme evolutionary conservatism does not mean that natural selection has ceased to work in a particular lineage. It simply means that most selection has been stabilizing, weeding out harmful mutations but producing little or no change. Nor is there any reason to think that such a lineage has run out of evolutionary potential. Given new ecological opportunities, it could respond as effectively as any other population—provided that it has retained the necessary variability in its gene pool.[1]

The Opportunism of Evolution

It is important to understand that evolution is merely our name for the way gene pools change in response to the selective forces brought to bear on them by the environment. Thus evolutionary change is a blind and passive phenomenon; it has no goal or purpose. This passivity accounts for the unevenness of evolution, which

[1] The contrast between the rapidly evolving elephants and the conservative opossums illustrates the fact that, in the long run, it is the intensity of selection, not the rapidity of breeding, that determines the rate of Darwinian evolution. Opossums reach maturity and start to breed within a year of birth, whereas elephants do not begin to reproduce until they are ten or more years old, and their period of gestation is about a year. Thus nearly a dozen generations of opossums can be produced in the time span of a single elephant generation. Yet the elephant has far outrun the opossum in evolutionary change.

slows or accelerates as environmental conditions stabilize or change.

Evolution is also *opportunistic*—that is, it can only make use of whatever is available, building new adaptations upon existing structures. Natural selection works on the variation that already exists within the population, favoring some traits and discriminating against others. It cannot invent totally new traits, no matter how advantageous they might be. Of course, the range of variability within the population is always being increased by new mutations. But since an individual mutation generally represents only a very small change, the potential for innovation at each step of the evolutionary process is quite limited. Thus, evolution cannot call entirely new structures into being at a single stroke; it can only modify existing ones. You may find a pig with a straight rather than a curly tail, but you are unlikely to find one with wings.

Because of this limitation on the "creativity" of evolution, the basic body plan and traces of old adaptations to former ways of life are retained as a species evolves. Its anatomy, therefore, includes both *derived* characteristics, which are the result of its own recent adaptation, and *ancestral* characteristics, which reflect the adaptations of its ancestors and which it has inherited from them. Because of the persistence of ancestral characteristics, different species, even when they have taken to very similar ways of life, never come to resemble one another in all respects. They may evolve similar derived characteristics, but the ancestral traits that they preserve usually betray their differing evolutionary histories.

The Irreversibility of Evolution

The fact that animals retain ancestral characteristics has led to the formulation of the so-called *law of the irreversibility of evolution.* This states that once it has acquired a particular specialization, a species can never revert completely to the ancestral condition. As we have just seen, natural selection can only select among existing traits. Once structures and their genetic bases have totally disappeared from a population, natural selection cannot "call them back." If surrounding conditions change in such a way that the lost ancestral trait would once again be advantageous, natural selection may modify other structures so as to produce a functional equivalent, but it is unlikely that the lost trait will return.

For example, at an early stage of evolution, the ancestor of such hoofed animals as deer and cattle became adapted for swift running. In the process, its legs and feet became elongated and slender, and the toes were reduced to two functional hooves. A foot of this kind is retained by many descendants of this lineage, including most antelopes. But in other branches of the family, such as that leading to the buffalo and its relatives, subsequent evolutionary change produced a slower-footed, heavier animal—one that needed a broader foot, adapted to bear the extra weight. In these branches, the trend toward slender feet was reversed, but the lost toes did not reappear; instead, the two remaining hooves simply became much wider.

The law of the irreversibility of evolution is extremely important. Without it, the use of ancestral traits as a basis for reconstructing evolutionary history would be impossible. Nevertheless, the law should not be interpreted too rigidly. It is true that evolutionary reversals resulting in the reappearance of a lost feature are extremely rare. Most traits, even the simplest ones, are produced by a complex of related genes. For such a reversal to occur, mutations in the population would have to reproduce the entire genetic complex—an occurrence whose probability is close to zero. On the other hand, evolutionary changes in the size and proportion of parts of the organism, which depend upon simple changes in the frequency of genes that already exist in the population, can be and often are reversed. We have an instance of this in the case of the antelope and the buffalo; the lost toes could not be restored, but the existing toes could be enlarged.

PATTERNS OF SPECIATION

So far, we have discussed evolution as if each species constituted a single homogeneous population. More often, as we saw, any one species will include a number of geographical populations, each with its own semi-isolated gene pool. Genetic drift and adaptation to the local environment inevitably cause the gene pools of such populations to become different from one another. The result is a set of diversified *subspecies:* populations whose members share certain traits with one another and not with members of other subspecies. But as long as some mating still takes place between members of the differing populations, this trend toward diversification will be counteracted by gene flow, and the subspecies will remain part of a single species. Such a species—one that includes several different subspecies—is called a *polytypic species.*

Speciation and Divergence

Given the right circumstances, however, the process of diversification may proceed beyond the appearance of subspecies and lead to the splitting off of a new species. *Speciation* is the process by which the gene pool of a species splits permanently and irreversibly, producing a new, separate species beside the old one. Then the two distinct species—the more conservative "parent" species, and the more evolved "daughter" species—pursue independent evolutionary paths. Their gene pools are isolated from each other and no longer subject to the homogenizing effects of gene flow between them. Speciation, repeated time and again, has produced the huge

Figure 4-1. Patterns of evolutionary change resulting when a population of a species is separated by a temporary barrier to gene flow. (a) Temporary isolation without speciation; (b) speciation with subsequent extinction of one of resulting species; (c) speciation with subsequent evolutionary divergence.

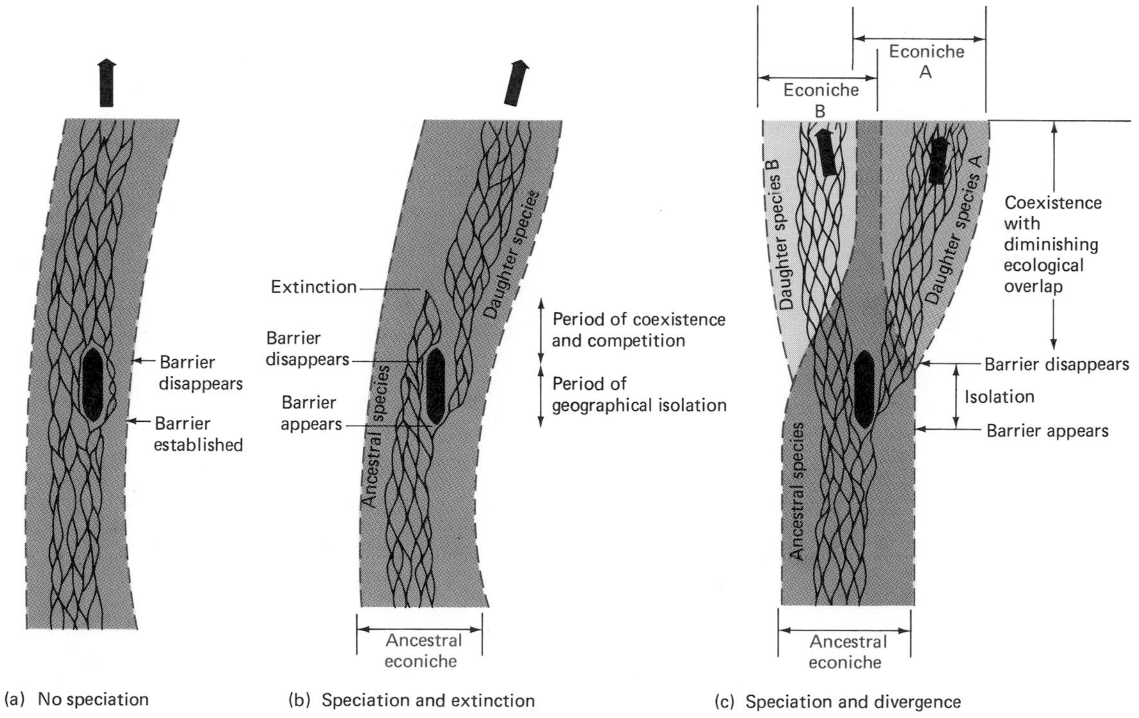

variety of animal and plant species that have succeeded one another through evolutionary time. With adaptation, it is one of the two most fundamental evolutionary processes.

Modern biologists agree that, at least in mammals,[2] speciation always involves geographical isolation at some stage. The first step is the isolation of a population from the rest of the species by a geographical barrier. The barrier may be an uncrossable river, a rising mountain chain, or a stretch of desert between the remnants of shrinking forests. Its nature is unimportant; all that matters is that it separates the two populations so that they no longer interbreed. Freed from the homogenizing effect of gene flow, the gene pools of the isolated populations diverge under the influence of genetic drift and natural selection. But at what point can we say that they have become different enough to qualify as two distinct species? The crucial test occurs if and when they meet again. If the members of the two populations recognize one another as potential mates, breed, and produce fully fit offspring, speciation has not occurred. The populations are merely separate subspecies and can continue to exchange genes. If, on the other hand, genetic *divergence* during isolation has reached the point where members of the two populations are no longer able or inclined to mate, they are now considered members of separate species (Figure 4-1).

There are instances, however, when the results of isolation are not so clear-cut. Sometimes members of the reunited populations can continue to mate with one another, but their offspring are less fit. In this case, natural selection will eventually produce either behaviors that tend to keep members of the two emerging species apart or physical markers that allow them to distinguish their own species from the other species. Among primates, which depend heavily on visual cues for recognition, closely related species that live together often have strikingly distinct color patterns, which allow the animals to tell at a glance whether an individual is of their own species, and therefore a potential mate. (See, for example, the different facial markings of the *Cercopithecus* monkeys in Figure 4-2.) Once such *isolating mechanisms* eliminate wasteful matings between the two populations, the process of speciation is completed.

The initial result of this process is two closely related species competing for the same resources and living space—that is, occupying overlapping econiches. According to circumstances, one of two things may now happen. In the first instance, one of the species may be slightly better adapted to the particular environment and may be capable of displacing the other species, which will eventually become extinct. In this case, the final outcome of the speciation process is once again a single species occupying much the same econiche as before. However, the successful species is likely to have undergone evolutionary change during the period of intense competition. Some biologists argue that most spurts of adaptive evolutionary change have been associated with speciation. Such a pattern of evolution, in which long periods of stasis are broken by short bursts of evolutionary change stimulated by speciation, is called *punctuated equilibrium.*

The second possible outcome of speciation is that the two species will continue to coexist, dividing the habitat between them by moving into slightly different econiches. Chimpanzees and gorillas, for example, evolved from a common ancestor and have managed to live side by side in the African rain forest since then by developing different feeding habits. The gorillas eat mostly the green parts of forest vegetation, while the chimpanzees feed largely on fruit; thus they avoid competition. Once divergence has occurred, the selective influence of different ecological strategies will encourage the two species to follow increasingly different adaptive paths. As a result, with the passage of time, each will also become more and more distinct from the other in anatomy—a process known as *character displacement.* The eventual result is two new species—each more specialized than the one

[2] Many new plant species are produced "instantly" from a single individual that undergoes a radical genetic change and then reproduces by self-fertilization. But most vertebrate animals cannot speciate in this way.

Figure 4-2. Faces of cercopithecoid monkeys. Such distinctive color patterns enable primates to recognize members of their own species and emphasize the gestures made in social communication. (*From Kingdon, 1971*)

from which both are descended—exploiting different econiches in the same general habitat.

Adaptive Radiation

If a single ancestral stock gives rise to many new species, and if these divergent branches survive, the result is an *adaptive radiation:* an array of related species. Obviously, a major adaptive radiation can appear only when there are a great many econiches available for occupation by the new species. Sometimes this occurs when a population of animals colonizes a new geographical area. The marsupials (opossums, kangaroos, wombats, etc.) of Australia provide an example of an adaptive radiation of this kind. When the ancestors of the present marsupials reached Australia, the absence of competing mammals allowed them to diversify in innumerable ways. Some have become tree dwellers, others live on the ground or burrow beneath it. Some are herbivores (vegetarians), others carnivores (meat eaters), still others insectivores (insect eaters).

Another important kind of adaptive radiation occurs when a particular animal stock evolves adaptations that, by a lucky chance, open up previously unusable habitats. For example, between 375 and 350 million years ago, a particular group of fishes modified the swim bladder—an organ that in most fish provides buoyancy in swimming—into a lung. They thus acquired the ability to take oxygen directly from the atmosphere. At the same time, their fins became stumpy but muscular lobes that enabled them to move about, in a limited fashion, out of the water. The lobe-fins probably lived in shallow pools in a hot and seasonably variable climate. Their unique specializations evidently enabled them to survive seasons when the water in their

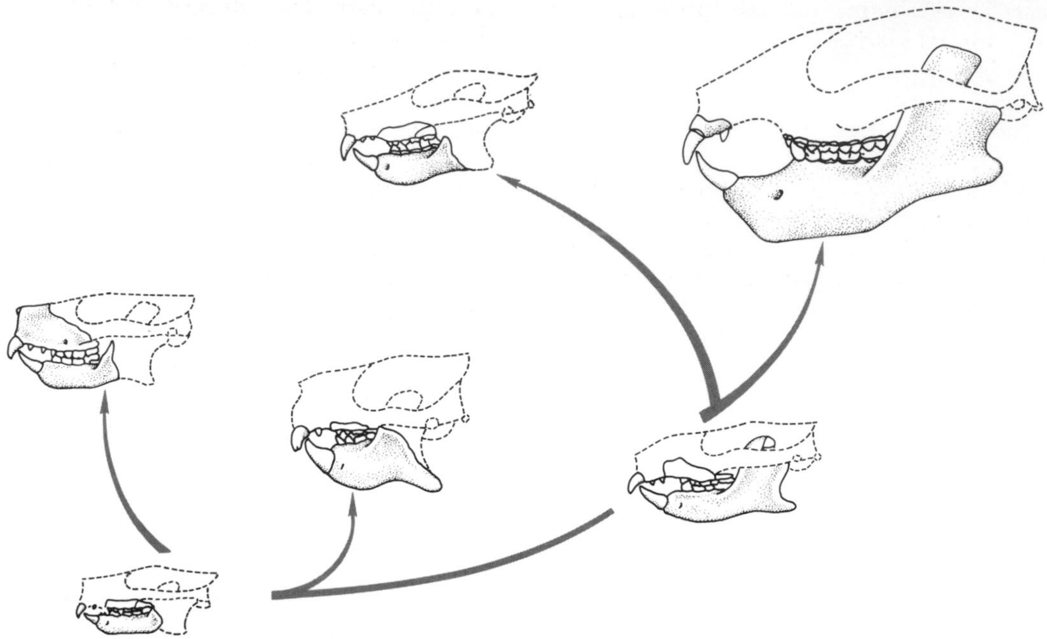

Figure 4-3. A small adaptive radiation among early primates. From an unspecialized ancestor, various more specialized forms emerge, each adapted to a different way of life. (*After Gingerich, 1977*)

pools became foul and deoxygenated or dried up altogether.

As we have seen, all specialization is a gamble, with the odds heavily in favor of extinction. The lobe-fins, however, were lucky. Their unique specializations enabled their descendants to live on land and so, eventually, to flourish in dozens of new econiches. The lobe-fins' ability to breathe air from the atmosphere and to move around on solid ground turned out to be preadaptations. A *preadaptation* is a characteristic that is originally acquired as an adaptation to a specialized econiche, but which turns out to be advantageous in a new set of circumstances as well. In the case of the lobe-fins, their lungs and their lobes formed the basis for the successive adaptive radiations of land vertebrates (amphibians, reptiles, mammals, birds), all of which have inherited their lungs and basic limb structure from their aquatic ancestor.

As we shall see, successive stages of evolution in the human ancestry seem to have been based upon such chance breakthroughs: specializations that were originally narrow, but that opened up wide new opportunities. For instance, mammals probably perfected the control of their internal temperature—the "warm-bloodedness" that distinguishes them from most reptiles—as a specialization to active insect hunting in the cool of the night. The ancestors of the primates probably first acquired their grasping hands and keen vision as a specialization to hunting in the trees. And as we shall see in Chapter 7, the development of the human family itself may have begun when a marginal population of small apes acquired the habit of standing and walking bipedally (that is, on two feet) as a specialization to the food resources of seasonal grasslands.

The successive radiations of the amphibians, reptiles, and mammals illustrate another recurrent pattern in large-scale evolution. Every time a single stock makes a significant adaptive breakthrough (such as breathing air or achieving a constant body temperature), an extensive adaptive radiation arises from this stock. After a period of flourishing and diversification, the radiation "collapses." Most of its branches become extinct, and a new radiation, often derived from an obscure sidebranch of the previous one, springs up in its place.

Convergence and Parallelism

It often happens that different species, each the product of a different adaptive radiation, will develop similar traits as a result of adapting to similar econiches. These similar traits are, however, superimposed on differing basic body plans, which each species inherits from its own particular lineage. For example, the porpoise, the shark, and the ichthyosaur (an ancient sea-living creature) were produced by three different adaptive radiations, separated from one another by millions of years. The porpoise is a mammal, the shark is a fish, the ichthyosaur was a reptile. Yet each of these species became adapted to living in the sea, and therefore each superficially resembles the others in having a strcamlined body shape. This is a trait that each lineage developed independently as a specialization for efficient swimming. When unrelated and generally dissimilar lineages evolve superficially similar forms in this way it is called *convergence.*

Convergence involves the evolution of similar adaptations in species that are otherwise very different from one another. But similar adaptations may sometimes evolve in species that are already quite similar because of a common ancestry. This phenomenon is known as *parallel-*

Figure 4-4. **Patterns of evolution in a hypothetical group of organisms. Thin black lines represent individual populations; colored outlines represent barriers to gene flow, and hence enclose biological species. The inserts depict small-scale evolutionary phenomena—diversification, speciation, extinction of single lineages. On the larger scale, the picture is of successive adaptive radiations. At time A, two radiations coexist. By time B, one has dwindled to extinction, the other has diversified. Shortly after time B, most branches of this radiation have become extinct, and by time C have been replaced by species derived from yet another radiation.**

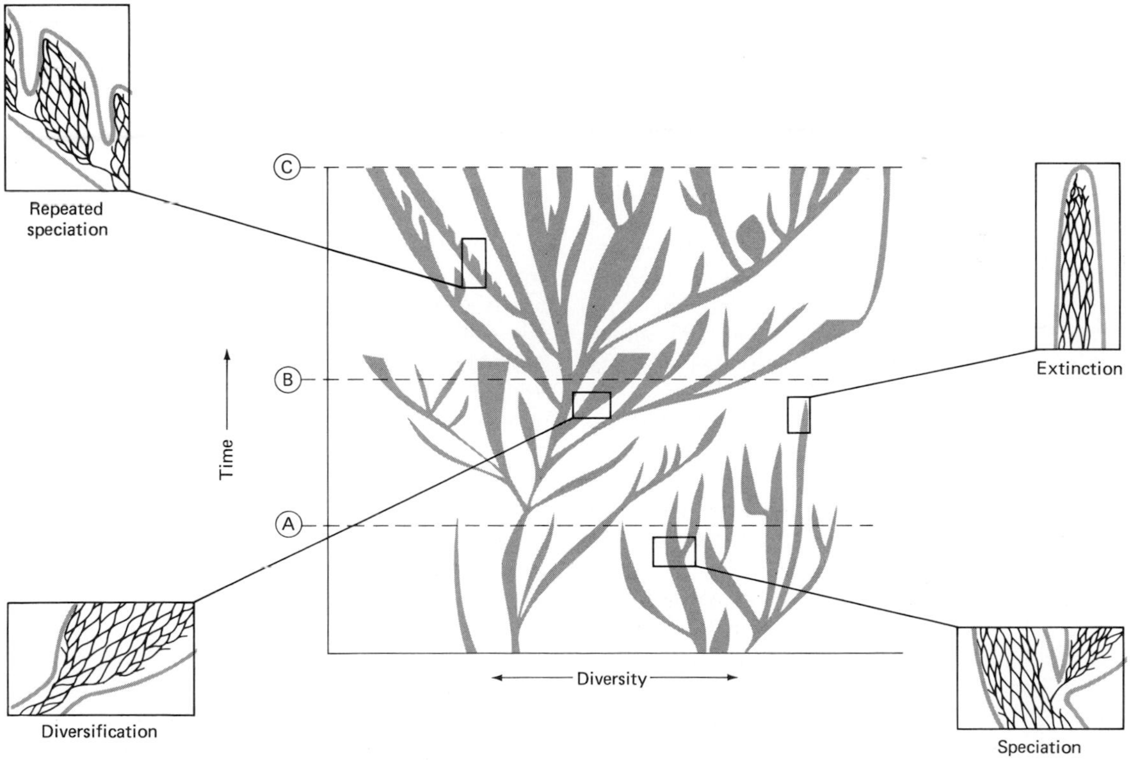

The Awash Baboon Project: A Study in Speciation

Evolutionary theory describes speciation as the gradual divergence of two gene pools, geographically isolated, to the point where the exchange of genes between them will no longer occur even if the geographical barrier disappears. This is a process that takes a considerable amount of time. Often it happens that the two populations come into contact again before speciation is complete. In such cases the mating behavior of the animals will determine whether the speciation process will continue or will be reversed by gene flow between the populations. If such a situation is found, it represents a "natural experiment" that can give invaluable insight into evolutionary processes. The baboons that live along the Awash River, 97 kilometers (60 mi.) northeast of Addis Ababa, Ethiopia, represent such a population.

Hans Kummer, a Swiss primatologist, first drew scientific attention to the Awash baboons in the early 1960s. During a survey of Ethiopian baboons, he discovered that along the Awash the range of the large, gray-brown anubis baboon adjoined that of the smaller, light gray hamadryas. And at the junction of their ranges, he found baboons that seemed to be hybrids of anubis and hamadryas, although they were generally thought to be separate species that theoretically should not interbreed. Since hamadryas baboons have a "one-male group" social system, whereas anubis baboons live in multimale troops, Kummer theorized that hamadryas males sometimes "kidnapped" anubis females and adopted them into their harems, where they produced hybrid offspring. He showed in field experiments that hamadryas males will adopt anubis females released in their range. During 1967 and 1968, Kummer's student, Ueli Nagel, mapped the intergrade zone and closely observed the abnormal social behavior of the hybrids.

The case of the Awash hybrids posed interesting theoretical issues. Speciation is a key evolutionary process, but very rarely do we see it in progress in real animal populations. Were the Awash hybrids fully fertile? And if they were, did they transmit genes across anubis and hamadryas populations? If so, was the gene flow approximately equal in either direction? Such questions could be answered only by examining genetic markers in the animals' blood factors and proteins. Such studies could also throw light on behavioral problems of theoretical interest to anthropology—questions such as how often nonhuman primates change troops. Such questions could only be answered by years of intensive, uninterrupted study.

Accordingly, in consultation with Kummer, a research plan was formulated for live trapping and taking blood samples from the Awash baboons. A team was assembled under the general direction of Clifford J. Jolly. Frederick L. Brett planned and led the field expedition, and Ronald Cauble, an experienced baboon trapper, organized the capture of the animals. For nearly a year, the field team built cages, cleared tracks through the thornbush, charted the baboons' movements, and hauled traps to the trapsites. A major apprehension proved groundless as the baboons eagerly fed on the corn scattered as bait, and confidently entered the traps, undeterred by the sight and sound of fellow troop members already caught. Each trapping day, about 40 animals were trapped, tranquilized, and taken back to the improvised field laboratory. Here the team took blood, saliva, and hair samples; weighed, measured, photographed, and fingerprinted each animal; and made a cast of its upper teeth. Each animal was also marked for future identification. When the whole troop had been captured and processed, the "prisoners" were released at the trapsites. They did not seem to mind the experience; in fact, some were retrapped when they returned for another free corn ration.

In all, twelve troops, comprising 534 anubis, hamadryas, and hybrid baboons, were processed. Data and materials were shipped to laboratories in New York and London for examination. Each animal has been tabulated in a computerized record that includes, for each individual, a tooth cast, a set of fingerprints, photographs, and a detailed genetic profile. Analysis of the data is still in progress, but some findings are emerging. One is that each troop of baboons is distinctive genetically from its neighbors. Gene frequencies differ considerably, suggesting that the exchange of members is probably infrequent. Certain genetic markers are characteristic of anubis baboons, others of hamadryas. Tentatively, it is thought that, as Kummer theorized, genes are flowing from anubis to hamadryas, but very few if any in the other direction. Whether this makes them two species or one can be left to theorists to argue.

The demographic profiles of the troops—based upon size, weight, and the eruption and wear of the teeth—are also interesting. Many of the animals are quite old, suggesting a long potential life span. But there are few very young animals, far fewer than theoretically necessary to maintain the population. It is suggested that the catastrophic drought of 1972 to 1974 took its toll of the baboons as it did of humans.

Much more information remains to be extracted from the data; analysis will take years. A return trip to Ethiopia is planned, where, armed with fingerprints and genetic profiles, primatologists will attempt to renew old acquaintances and to decipher the latest chapter in the microevolutionary story of the Awash baboons.

ism. In parallelism, two related species independently take up comparable ways of life, so that they evolve in the same direction. As a result, such species often come to resemble one another more than either resembles their common ancestor. Their initial similarity is due to shared ancestral traits; but their continued similarity after many generations of evolution reflects common derived traits, called forth by adaptation to similar econiches.

The South American spider monkey (*Ateles*) and the Asian gibbon (*Hylobates*) provide a good example of parallelism. Both animals have long arms, adapted to moving about by swinging from tree limbs. Now, these two species are fairly closely related—that is, they have a relatively recent common ancestry. Yet the long-armed trait they share was *not* inherited from this ancestor but derived independently in the two lines. It can be attributed to their occupation of similar econiches—both animals find their food in the outer canopy of the forest, dangling from branches too thin for other primates to climb on.

The resemblances between animals that are due to parallelism and convergence are called *analogies.* Analogies reflect similarities of function; they are the result of adaptation to similar environments. By contrast, resemblances resulting from a common ancestor are called *homologies.* Thus the wing of a bat, the flipper of a turtle, the front leg of a frog, and the arm of a human being are all homologous. Adaptation for different functions has served to disguise their underlying relationship, but an anatomist can trace certain similarities in the arrangement of the bones, inherited from the primitive land vertebrate that was their remote common ancestor. Such similarities clearly point to the origin of these diverse species in the lineage of land vertebrates.

UNRAVELING EVOLUTIONARY RELATIONSHIPS

The outcome of the evolutionary processes of speciation, radiation, and extinction is a great array of species, some still living, others extinct and known (if at all) only from their fossil remains. Evolutionary theory tells us that all of these species are ultimately related to one another. It is one thing, however, to understand in a theoretical way that all species are related by descent and quite another thing to be able to say exactly how one particular group is related to another. Speciation has been occurring for 3½ billion years or more, ever since the origin of life on earth. The various mammalian lines alone probably began to diverge more than 100 million years ago. We have no magic key to evolutionary history, no universal genealogy in which we can look up the relationship of long-vanished creatures to one another and to us. How, then, do we go about reconstructing these ancient evolutionary events from the very incomplete evidence available to us in the present?

Constructing a Phyletic Tree

A *phyletic tree* is a branching diagram representing ideas about the evolutionary relationships of a group of species. In building a tree, each species is represented as a branch, while the forks of the tree represent speciation and subsequent divergence. The object of tree building is to recognize *clades*, or groups of species with a single common ancestor. Theoretically, what "really happened" in evolutionary history—the true pattern of evolutionary relationships within any one group—can be represented by only one tree, branching out from a single ancestor. Anthropology is concerned with reconstructing as completely as possible the pathway through the branches that leads to modern humans. But many details are still obscure, and even the broad outlines are not universally agreed upon at every stage.

The basic information used to construct the tree comes from comparing the species in question—their anatomical structures (such as limbs, teeth, and even protein molecules) as well as elements of their social behavior. Using these comparisons to draw conclusions about how the tree should be constructed is a matter of applying three general principles derived from evolutionary theory.

If we compare enough characteristics, we can eventually arrive at a reasonable estimate of overall resemblance among species. We can say, "Species A resembles species B in twenty traits, but species C in only five. Thus A is more like B than like C." Because evolving lineages tend to retain many ancestral characteristics, overall resemblance is quite a good indication of cladistic relationship—membership in a group related by common ancestry. Thus the first principle of reconstructing evolutionary relationships is:

1. Animals that share detailed resemblances are usually closely related to one another.

This general principle provides a useful guide for sorting species into broad groups of relatives. And if it were universally true, our task as evolutionary biologists would be simple. Cladistic relationships could be directly inferred from general resemblance. The more two animals resembled each other, the more recent would be their common ancestry. However, not all resemblances are of equal weight in indicating cladistic relationships. Some resemblances are due not to a recent common ancestry but to a very ancient one.

The opossum, for example, shares with humans the characteristic of having five fingers and five toes, and in this respect both species differ from the horse, which has only one toe on each foot. Does this indicate that opossums and humans are the more closely related pair of this trio of species? It does not, because the five-fingered condition represents the ancestral condition for all land vertebrates. Frogs, salamanders, crocodiles, lizards, and turtles all have five digits, and so did the common ancestor of all mammals, including humans, opossums, and horses (Figure 4-5). Thus, the fact the opossums and humans share this characteristic tells us only that these two species belong to the clade that includes all land vertebrates; it reveals nothing at all about the exact relationship of either to the horse.

On the other hand, the fact that the zebra resembles the horse in having only one functional toe *is* of phyletic significance. Reduction of the number of toes to one is a *derived* characteristic

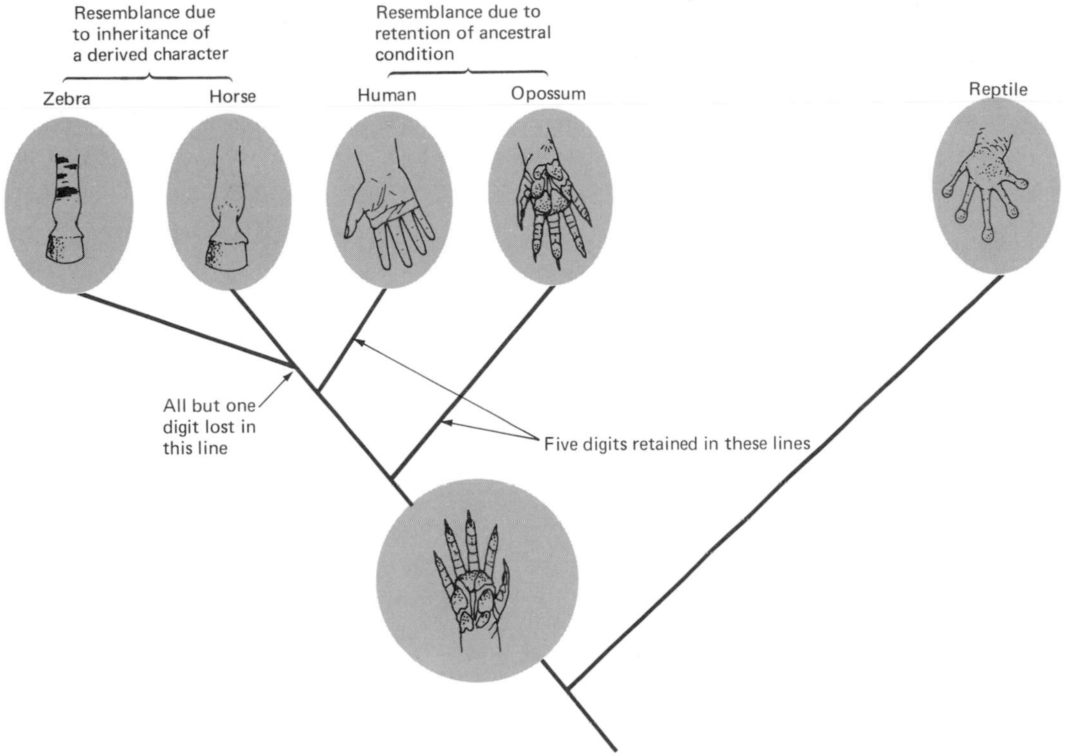

Figure 4-5. The interpretation of ancestral and derived characters in reconstructing phylogeny. Here, the problem is to deduce the phyletic relationships among the zebra, horse, human, and opossum. In practice, we would use many characters to make the decision; here, for simplicity, we consider only one character, the number of fingers. Humans are like opossums in having five fingers, but this resemblance is due to retention of the *ancestral condition,* seen also in many reptiles. It has no phyletic significance. Zebras are like horses in having only one functional finger. This is a derived condition and indicates that they share a relatively recent common ancestor.

among mammals. It is shared by the zebra and horse but not by most other mammals. It first appeared in an animal that was the common ancestor of the horse and the zebra, but that was not in the ancestry of humans or opossums. If zebras and horses shared such an ancestor, they are by definition cladistically closer to each other than to the other mammals in our comparison. Thus, we can state a second general principle for determining cladistic relationships:

2. Clades are to be recognized by the *derived* traits that their members share.

However, this second principle, like the first, requires modification. As we have seen, not all resemblances, even in derived characteristics, necessarily indicate a recent common ancestry. Different species can acquire similar characteristics through parallel or convergent evolution. Superficial convergence, such as that between dolphins and ichthyosaurs, is generally easy to recognize because other derived traits indicate the true relationships of the animals. In the dolphin, for example, the large, complex brain, "warm" blood, mammary glands, and a host of other derived features clearly indicate that this

Molecular Primate Phylogeny

Traditionally, evolutionary relationships were determined by comparing structures like teeth and bones. Now, biochemical techniques permit us to compare the genotypes of various species more directly through the analysis of proteins and nucleic acids, thus avoiding the complicating effects of environmental influences on growth and development.

The most direct measure of genetic resemblance is provided by *DNA hybridization* techniques, described in the Appendix. Another useful method involves comparing the structure of protein molecules by *sequencing.* The sequence of chemical subunits, called amino acids (see Appendix), of a particular protein chain is compared with the sequence of the same protein in another species. In this way, it was determined that the beta chain of chimpanzee hemoglobin is identical to the human, whereas the rhesus monkey shows 6 differences and the horse 25. Such data give us a picture of the genetic distances among species, which can then be used to build phyletic trees. Sequencing is a lengthy procedure, however, and biologists commonly determine the difference among proteins from different species by using the less direct techniques of immunology.

Immunological techniques make use of the fact that an animal injected with protein from another species will produce antibodies to the "foreign" protein. One classic series of experiments used the protein albumin. Albumin from human blood was injected into rabbits. After a while, the rabbits were bled. Their serum contained an antibody, anti-human-albumin (anti-HA), which, when brought into contact with human albumin, would combine with it, producing a visible reaction. Next, the anti-HA was tested against albumins from other species. With chimpanzee albumin, it reacted almost as strongly as with human albumin. With monkey albumin, the reaction was weaker, and with nonprimate albumins, it was weaker still. Because the nonhuman albumins were somewhat different in structure from the human albumin, they were less readily "recognized" by anti-HA, which had been tailored by the rabbit's immunological system specifically against *human* albumin. Thus, the strength of reaction measured the structural difference between human albumin and the albumin of the other animals. Additional experiments used anti-monkey-albumin, anti-chimpanzee-albumin, and so on. Other proteins, too, were used to check the results obtained from albumin, thus providing a picture of the overall differences and similarities among species.

The results of such techniques when applied to primates are impressively consistent, and generally agree with the conventional view of primate phylogeny. The great apes are clearly closest to us; the gibbons more distant, the Old World monkeys, New World Monkeys, and prosimians more distant still (see Figure 5-1). One surprise has been the close relationship between chimpanzees, gorillas, and humans. These three genera are a single clade, much closer to each other than to other animals. The orangutan, usually classified with the African apes, is further from them than we are. This finding rules out theories of a very ancient human lineage, independent of the apes and descended directly from monkeylike ancestors.

Some molecular biologists have gone beyond drawing trees of phyletic relationship and have attempted to derive *dates* for the branching points they depict, using proteins as a *molecular clock* for evolution. Anthropologists disagree about this use of molecular data, especially since some of the dates suggested conflict with those derived from fossil evidence. Some molecular biologists argue that genetic distance between two species will correspond to the *time* since their evolutionary divergence. According to them, human ancestry, distinct from the African apes, can be no older than 5 million years. Others consider that genetic distance will reflect the *number of generations* that have passed. They believe that the chimp-human split may be as much as 14 million years old. The discrepancy arises because the number of years per generation increased greatly during primate evolution, especially in the line leading to the apes and man.

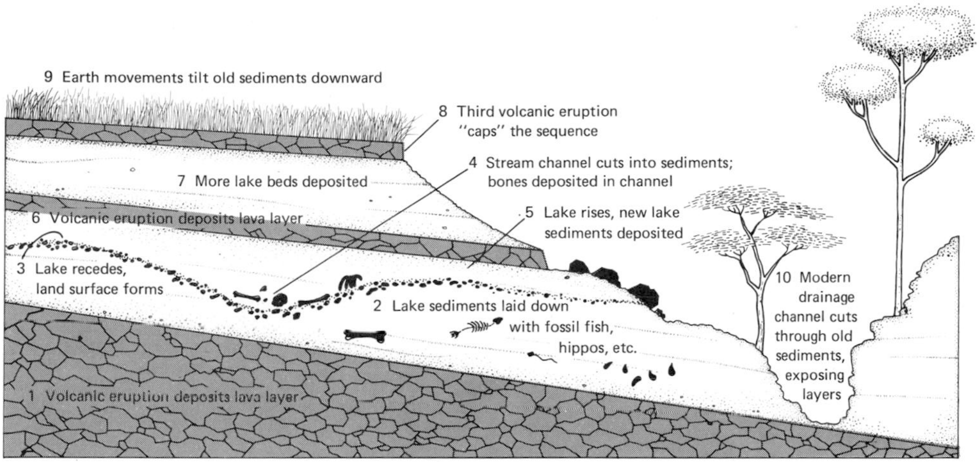

page 153 Figure 7-2: corrected figure above.

page 165 (caption): "Necrolemus" should be "Necrolemur."

page 216 Figure 9-3 (caption): "(c) modern human, African male" should be "(c) Broken Hill skull, late *Homo erectus* or early *Homo sapiens*."

page 230 Figure 9-6 (caption): "bottom right" should be "top."

page 274 Figure 11-1: label "Upper Paleolithic" should be "late Pleistocene"; label "Upper Pleistocene" should be "Upper Paleolithic."

Physical Anthropology and Archeology, second edition

Errata

page 50 Figure 3-2 (caption): "B's sister E" should be "C's sister E."

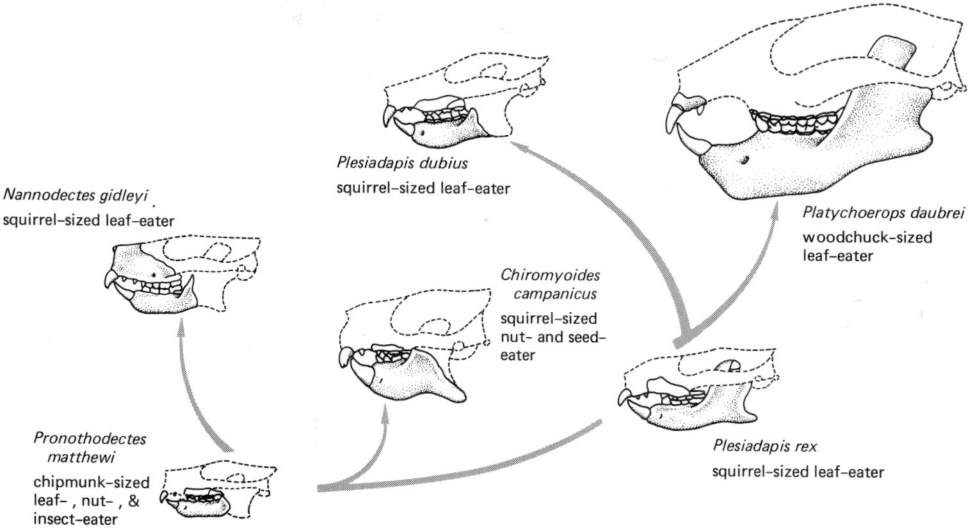

page 72 Figure 4-3: corrected figure above.

animal is related to other mammals, rather than to a reptile such as the ichthyosaur.

However, even shared derived characteristics do not always indicate close relationship. For example, the ancestor of the horse was not the only mammal to acquire a one-toed foot. The extinct *Thoatherium,* which roamed the plains of South America some 15 million years ago—long before the appearance of one-toed horses—had lost any trace of all but a single toe on each foot. Indeed, so horselike is its foot that some paleontologists were convinced *Thoatherium* was actually an ancestor of modern horses. But the structural details of its teeth and skull tell a different story. They reveal its membership in a group of extinct mammals that had a long evolutionary history in South America, and no close relationship to any group outside that continent. Although *Thoatherium*'s one-toed foot, like that of the horse, is a derived feature, it indicates convergent evolution, not common ancestry.

How, then, can we spot misleading traits, such as the foot of *Thoatherium,* and distinguish them from indications of true relationship? The answer lies once again in the nature of the evolutionary process. Since parallelisms and convergences arise as adaptations to similar ways of life, they are likely to consist of groups of related features, all functionally linked to an aspect of the animal's ecology—climbing in trees, for instance, or eating meat, or (as in the case of horses and *Thoatherium*) fast running in open country. Other characteristics not related to this adaptation will not show convergence and thus will not suggest false relationships. A conclusion about phyletic relationships, therefore, should never be based on a single feature. And if different features suggest different phyletic trees, we can distinguish the more trustworthy by asking which of them is *less* immediately related to adaptation. Thus we can derive a third general principle, which modifies the other two:

3. Shared derived characteristics that are immediately relatable to function are likely to be due to parallelism or convergence and thus are generally weak indicators of cladistic relationship.

Figure 5-1 is an example of a phyletic tree reconstructed using the three principles we have just described. It represents our concept of the evolutionary relationships in one small section of the living world—the part that includes the lemurs, monkeys, apes, and humans. These animals together constitute the living members of the order Primates. Many of our colleagues will certainly disagree with this or that detail of our tree. This is to be expected. There is no simple, foolproof formula for determining cladistic relationships. Applying general principles to particular cases requires individual judgment. It poses such questions as: Which traits are ancestral, and which are derived, in this particular group? How much similarity can reasonably be attributed to parallelism in this case? If traditional anatomy and biochemistry tell different evolutionary stories, which does one believe? In answering these questions, competent authorities often disagree, and hence they come up with slightly different phyletic trees. But, considering the immense diversity of the living world, the amount of agreement is impressive testimony to the consistency of the modern theory of evolution.

BIOLOGICAL CLASSIFICATION

Like all scientists, biologists classify the objects they study. These classifications are not an end in themselves; they are simply ways of grouping and labeling things for which a collective term is needed because they are frequently discussed as a group. The essential quality of a good classification is *usefulness.* Categories that are only rarely used are not worth remembering—or even naming.

Biologists use various schemes of classification, based on different criteria. Some are ecological (forest animals, fresh-water fish, insect-eating birds), some geographical (Australian marsupials, African apes), some chronological (Cretaceous mammals, Miocene primates). But "classification" in biology generally means the all-purpose *neo-Linnaean* classification of plants and animals (sometimes called the *natural* or *scientific* classification). This system is based on usages established over 200 years ago by the great Swedish naturalist Karl von Linné (Carolus Linnaeus).

Linnaeus established an unambiguous way of naming species, and a formal hierarchy for establishing larger categories consisting of groups of species. To Linnaeus, species were fixed and immutable; they were the building blocks of a system that reflected the orderliness of the divine Creator's plan. Linnaeus labeled each species with a Latin *binominal*[3] (double name). The domestic dog, for instance, is *Canis familiaris*. The second word (which always begins with a small letter) designates the species. The first word (with the initial letter always capitalized) is that of the *genus*. Every species belongs to a genus (plural, *genera*) that may also include other, related species. We can see from its name that the dog belongs to the genus *Canis*. So does the closely related species *Canis lupus*, the wolf. When there is no danger of confusion, the generic name may be abbreviated, with only the initial being used. Thus you may sometimes come across the form *H. sapiens* for *Homo sapiens*. (The genus initial must never be omitted, however.)

The basic building block of the neo-Linnaean classification is the biological species. A genus is a group of related species. Genera are themselves grouped into families, families into orders, and so on (see Figure 5-1 and Table 4-1). Some of the categories are obligatory—that is, they are used in the classification of all groups of animals and plants. Others are used only as needed, when a large and complex group has to be sorted out. Each category, or *taxon* (plural, *taxa*), includes one or more taxa of the next rank down. The names of some taxa have standard endings. It is important to distinguish these, for words differing only in their ending may refer to very different groups of organisms. For example, Hominidae (a family) is a much more restricted group than Hominoidea (a superfamily).

Two related conventions are used in assigning biological names, especially to species. One is that the *earliest name validly used for a group (but no earlier than the 1758 edition of Linnaeus' classification) is the valid name for that group.* For instance, *Equus caballus*, the name assigned by Linnaeus himself, is the valid name of the domestic horse. The other rule is that the earliest use of a name is the *only* valid one. After Linnaeus' use, *Equus caballus* may not be used as a name for any animal but the horse.

Given the basic structure of the Linnaean system, how does one decide which species to group in a single genus, which genera in a family, and so on? Since Darwin's day, biologists have retained the form of the Linnaean classification, but they base their categories on the modern theory of evolution. Most biologists believe that taxa should be defined *phyletically*. That is, a genus should be a group of species all descended from a single ancestral species, a family should include closely related genera, and so on. Because species often retain ancestral traits, such groups of relatives will share many characteristics. Consequently, such a phyletic classification will be the most useful grouping for a variety of purposes.

Most biologists, however, also make some concession to overall anatomical resemblance in their classifications. For instance, in Figure 5-1, the genera *Pan* (the chimpanzees) and *Gorilla* (the gorilla) are obviously phyletically closer to *Homo* (humans) than to *Pongo* (the orangutan). Yet chimpanzees and gorillas are commonly classified not with humans in the family Hominidae but with orangutans in the family Pongidae. Most anthropologists retain this classification because of the radically new *derived* traits that evolved in the human lineage after it diverged from the African apes. They find it convenient to have a category (Pongidae) that includes all apes but excludes *Homo*. Other biologists insist on a more strictly cladistic classification, and put chimpanzees and gorillas in Hominidae. Both schemes are compatible with the phyletic tree shown in Figure 5-1. The choice between them depends upon preference—what one considers the most useful grouping—not upon interpretation of the evolutionary evidence.

A final problem concerns the definition of taxa. The species, as we saw, has an unambiguous bio-

[3] Frequently (but incorrectly) called "binomial."

TABLE 4-1. The Neo-Linnaean Classification of the Human Species

TAXON	FULL NAME	ABBREVIATED OR COMMON NAME	INCLUDES
Species	*Homo sapiens*	*H. sapiens*	Modern and late prehistoric humans
Genus	*Homo*	humans	Human species, living and extinct
Family	Hominidae	hominids	Humans, australopiths, ramapiths (?)
Superfamily	Hominoidea	hominoids	Hominids, apes (pongids and hylobatids)
Infraorder	Catarrhini	catarrhines	Hominids, apes, Old World monkeys
Suborder	Anthropoidea	anthropoids, higher primates	Catarrhines, platyrrhines (New World monkeys)
Order	Primates	primates	Anthropoids and prosimians (lemurs, tarsiers, and extinct relatives)
Infraclass	Eutheria	placental mammals	Primates, rodents, etc. (mammals nourishing unborn young in uterus through placenta)
Subclass	Theria	therians	Placentals and marsupials (mammals bearing fetal young—not eggs)
Class	Mammalia	mammals	Animals with body hair and mammary glands

logical definition: it is the largest population whose members can exchange genes by interbreeding. But other taxa have no such definition rooted in observable behavior; they are merely clusters of related species, genera, and so on. How wide a group of species, then, should be included in a genus? How many families should constitute an order? There are no clear-cut answers to these questions. Genera, families, and orders are defined as broadly as is convenient to the scientists using them. Their inclusiveness is a matter of judgment or even taste, not of proof. Inevitably, therefore, not all investigators will agree on these matters, and different experts set up their schemes in slightly different ways. Some taxonomists, known collectively as "splitters," favor relatively narrow taxa; they divide each order into many families, each family into many genera. Others, known as "lumpers," use a small number of broader categories. For example, the gorilla is usually given its own genus (*Gorilla*), but there are biologists who prefer to regard it as merely another species of the genus *Pan*, along with the chimpanzee. The only real constraint on such decisions is a very general one: that taxa should be roughly equivalent in diversity throughout a major group. Each family within the order Primates, for instance, should be approximately as diverse as families of rodents or carnivores.

Summary

Populations of organisms evolve through mutation, natural selection, gene flow, and genetic drift. Seen in the perspective of thousands of generations, successive populations merge into lines of descent, or *lineages*.

Evolution occurs through a spiraling process. Changes in the population's environment lead to changes in behavior, which, through natural selection, lead to changes in anatomy. This process occurs gradually, with each type of change reinforcing the others, through *positive feedback*. The result of evolutionary change is typically greater *specialization:* a narrowing of the species' econiche. However, some species remain generalized, adapted to a broad econiche. Generalists are less expert than specialists at exploiting one particular type of resource, but they are more flexible in the face of environmental change.

Evolution is simply the name we give to the changes that gene pools undergo over time. Evolutionary change is a blind process, directed largely by external forces of selection. It does not represent the species' striving toward some definite goal. Thus the rate of evolutionary change varies greatly, depending on environmental conditions. Within a single lineage, periods of rapid evolutionary change, spurred by changes in the environment, generally alternate with periods of *stasis,* during which stability in the environment maintains stability in the gene pool. Unevenness in the rate of evolution is still more striking when we compare different lineages. Some species have evolved quite rapidly; others, well adapted to stable econiches, have changed little over many millions of years.

Evolution is opportunistic—that is, it can only build upon existing structures, but cannot create new structures from scratch. Finally, evolution is also, to some extent, irreversible—that is, once a species has acquired a particular specialization, it rarely reverts completely to the ancestral condition. However, natural selection may produce a functional equivalent of the lost trait.

A *polytypic species* is one in which semi-isolated populations have evolved in somewhat different directions through genetic drift and adaptation to local environments. As long as there is some interbreeding between the populations, they remain *subspecies* of the same species. However, if a population becomes genuinely isolated and gene flow ceases, the result may be *speciation.* That is, natural selection and drift, without the counteracting effects of gene flow, may cause the gene pool of the isolated population to split off permanently and irrevocably from the rest of the species, creating a new species beside the old.

Speciation can lead to one of two consequences: (1) The species that is better adapted to the environment displaces the other species, which becomes extinct. (2) The two related species coexist by exploiting separate econiches within the same habitat. They then live side by side as separate species, each more specialized than the original species. As they adapt to their separate econiches, they tend to become more distinct from one another anatomically—a phenomenon called *character displacement.*

Repeated speciation from a single ancestral stock, with survival of the derived branches, produces an *adaptive radiation*—a wide array of related species, each adapted to its own particular way of life. Some radiations arise when new geographical areas are colonized, others when the ancestral stock develops a *preadaptation* that opens up a variety of new econiches. (A preadaptation is a trait that originally evolves as an adaptation to a particular environment, and that by chance proves valuable in quite different circumstances at a later time.) Most adaptive radiations eventually "collapse," leaving only a few species to become the basis of new radiations.

It often happens that two species will acquire similar traits independently as a result of adapting to similar econiches. If the two species are of different lineages, this similarity of derived characteristics is called *convergence.* If they are initially somewhat similar through close relationship, it is called *parallelism.* Resemblances between species that are due to convergence and parallelism are called *analogies.* Those due to common ancestry are called *homologies.*

To depict evolutionary history and to distinguish separate *clades,* or groups of species related through common ancestry, anthropologists construct branching diagrams called *phyletic trees.* Such trees are based upon comparisons of structure and behavior in different species. Judgments about cladistic relationships are based on the following principles: (1) Animals that share detailed resemblances are usually closely related to one another. (2) Clades are to be recognized by the *derived* traits that they share. (3) Shared derived characteristics that are immediately relatable to function may be due to parallelism or convergence, and are thus weak indicators of cladistic relationship.

Species of plants and animals are usually grouped according to the *neo-Linnaean* classification system, which arranges species in a hierarchy of categories called *taxa.* Closely related species are grouped into genera, related genera into families, families into orders, and so on. Each species is labeled with a Latin *binominal,* consisting of the name of the genus followed by the name of the species. Taxa are generally determined chiefly on the basis of cladistic relationship, though anatomical resemblance may also be taken into account in some cases.

Glossary

adaptive radiation an array of related species occupying different econiches

analogy a resemblance between animals that is due to parallelism or convergence rather than common ancestry

binominal a Latin "double name," consisting of the genus and species designations for a particular animal or plant, in the neo-Linnaean classification system (e.g., *Homo sapiens*)

character displacement the process by which two closely related species occupying overlapping ranges minimize their competition by evolving in different directions

clade a group of species with a single common ancestor

convergence the evolution of superficially similar traits by unrelated lineages as a result of adaptation to similar ways of life

feedback (positive) the process by which an evolutionary change acts to promote even greater change in the same direction

genus (pl. genera) a taxon in the neo-Linnaean classification system, consisting of a group of closely related species

homology a resemblance between animals due to inheritance from a common ancestor

irreversibility of evolution the principle that once a species has evolved a certain trait, it can never revert entirely to its ancestral condition

isolating mechanism a characteristic that prevents interbreeding between members of closely related species

lineage a series of populations in direct line of descent

neo-Linnaean classification the system of categorizing plants and animals based on usages established by Carolus Linnaeus

order a taxon in the neo-Linnaean classification system, consisting of a group of related genera

parallelism the evolution of two related species in the same direction so that they come to resemble each other more than their common ancestor

phyletic tree a branching diagram representing the evolutionary relationships of a group of species

polytypic species a species that includes several physically distinctive populations

preadaptation a trait that is first acquired as an adaptation to a specific environment, but that turns out to be generally advantageous under new circumstances

punctuated equilibrium a model of evolutionary change in which long periods of stasis alternate with briefer periods of rapid evolution stimulated by speciation

speciation the process by which the gene pool of a species splits permanently and irreversibly to produce one or more new species

stabilizing selection natural selection that does not produce evolutionary change in the population

stasis a phase during which a species is undergoing little or no evolutionary change

subspecies a major division of a species, whose members share certain traits that differentiate them from the rest of the species

taxon (pl. taxa) the general term for any neo-Linnaean category (species, genus, family, etc.)

Suggested Readings

GOULD, S. J. 1977
Ever Since Darwin: Reflections in Natural History. New York: Norton. A series of thought-provoking essays on evolution and evolutionary theory.

MAYR, E. 1963
Animal Species and Evolution. Cambridge: Harvard University Press. An authoritative and comprehensive account of variation among and between species, with an emphasis on polytypy and the process of speciation.

SIMPSON, G. G. 1961
Principles of Animal Taxonomy. New York: Columbia University Press. An exposition of the principles of classification still accepted by the majority of animal taxonomists.

Part Two

The Primates and Their Evolution

Chapter Five

The Living Primates

In the last two decades, an increasing number of wild primates have had to live with uninvited guests: human investigators who suddenly appear in their habitat, position themselves quietly in trees or on the ground, and proceed to follow the group day after day, patiently observing its movements and actions. Jane Goodall has spent nearly twenty years among the chimpanzees of the Gombe Stream Reserve in Tanzania; George Schaller lived for a year with gorillas in Central Africa; a colony of monkeys on Japan's Kyushu Island has been continuously studied by a team of investigators since 1953.

This expansion of field research[1] has contributed considerably to the recent growth of primatology—the study of primates—as a distinct and fruitful branch of science. Primatology is a multidisciplinary field; it brings together the behavioral data collected in field and laboratory, the findings of comparative anatomy and physiology, and the results of biochemical studies of molecular structure.

Although the major concern of anthropology is with only one primate, the human species, information that primatologists have gathered about nonhuman primates is indispensable to the anthropologist. In the first place, it allows us to determine more precisely the unique characteristics of our own species. For instance, primatology has recently informed us that chimpanzees, like humans, use tools, though only in a very limited fashion. Therefore we can no longer characterize *Homo sapiens* by its mere use of tools, as scientists once did, but rather by its skillful and extensive use of them and by its dependence on them. This discovery has stimulated anthropologists to define more carefully the distinctive qualities of human tool use. Primatology, in other words, allows us to see what the human species is and does that makes it unlike other primate species. If the business of anthropology is to describe and explain the evolution of human traits, primatology helps us to say exactly what those traits are.

Second, primatology helps anthropologists reconstruct the traits of our ancestors, long extinct. Living primates often retain ancestral characteristics in their anatomy and behavior. We can use these, together with fossil evidence, to form a picture of earlier stages of primate evolution. However, we must bear in mind that all living primate species have evolutionary histories as long as ours, and each evolving lineage has acquired its own specializations and adaptations. No modern primate is totally primitive—a "living fossil" that resembles an ancestral form in every way. The tarsier, for instance, has a very primitive brain, and this helps us to understand brain organization in ancient primates of 50 million years ago. But it also possesses a highly specialized leg and foot that have no counterpart in any stage of human ancestry. So we must always try to discriminate carefully between derived traits and ancient ancestral ones. The latter are our precious clues to evolutionary history.

Derived characteristics, however, can be equally revealing in their own way. We know that whenever two evolving animal species develop a certain anatomical characteristic independently, they do so because they share some

[1] Field research is the observation of animals as they range freely in their natural habitats.

A young vervet monkey "mothers" an infant. Among the most common and widespread of African monkeys, vervets are semiarboreal inhabitants of woodland areas. Like many primates, they are omnivorous, with a diet that includes fruit, leaves, insects, and tree gum. *(Donald Pater son/Photo Researchers)*

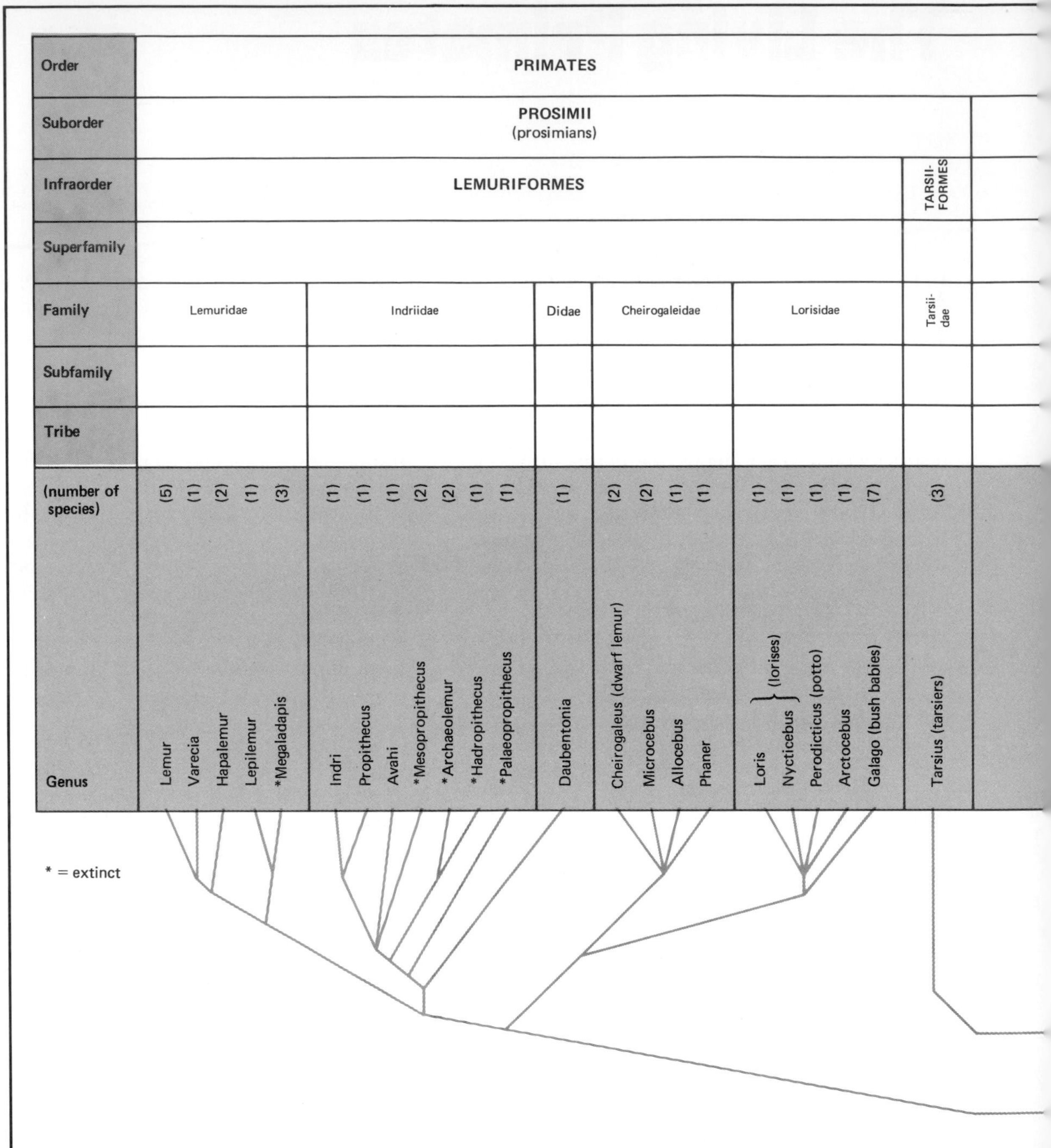

Figure 5-1. Phyletic tree (left) and classification (above) of recent primate genera (including living forms and recently extinct Malagasy lemurs). Note the standard endings of superfamilies, families, and subfamilies, and how they are formed from generic names. Classification conforms closely to phylogeny, but there are some deviations, such as the classification of *Pan* and *Gorilla* in Pongidae.

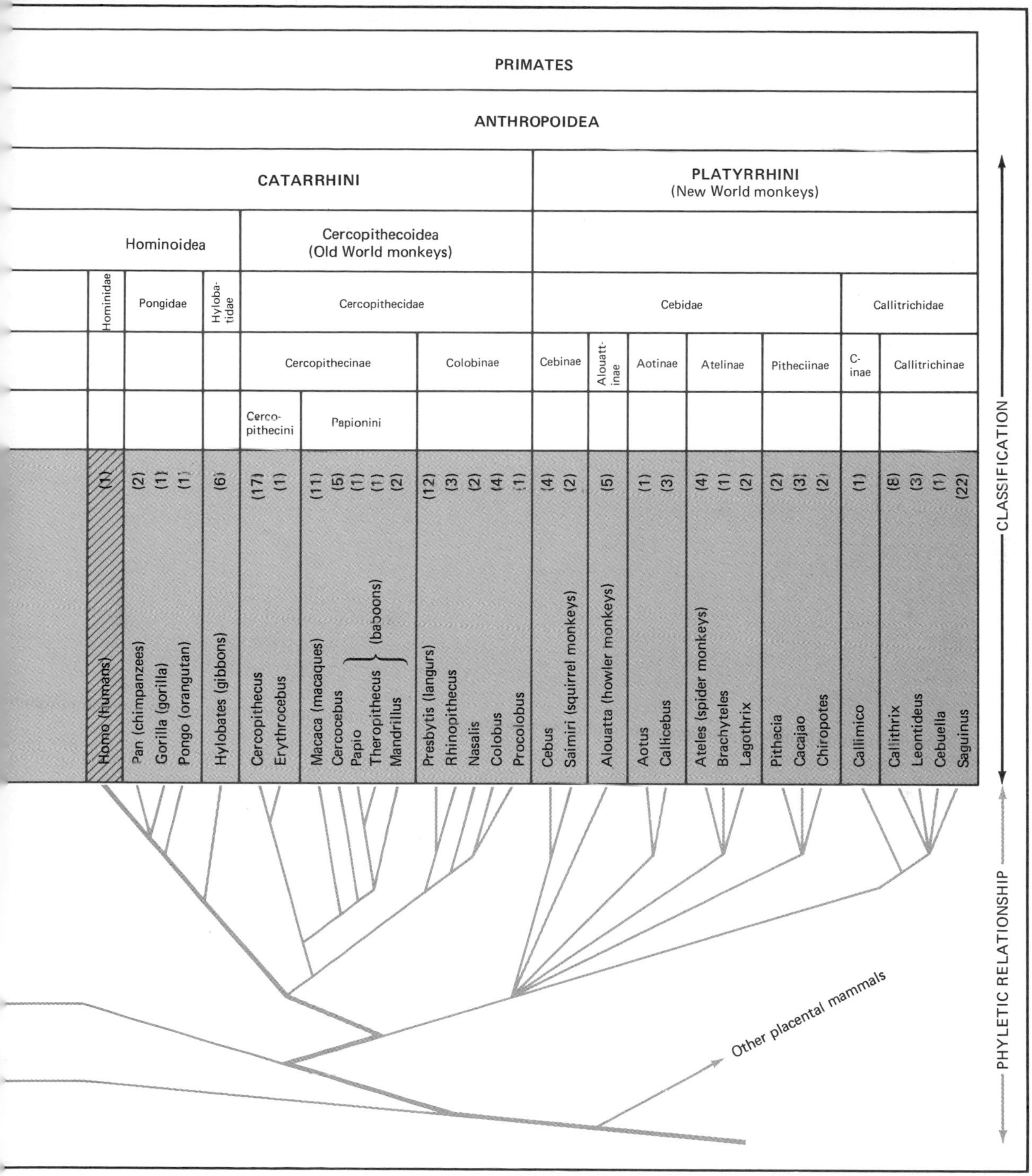
PRIMATES
ANTHROPOIDEA
CATARRHINI
PLATYRRHINI
(New World monkeys)
Hominoidea
Cercopithecoidea
(Old World monkeys)
Hominidae
Pongidae
Hyloba-
tidae
Cercopithecidae
Cebidae
Callitrichidae
Cercopithecinae
Colobinae
Cebinae
Alouatt-
inae
Aotinae
Atelinae
Pitheciinae
C-
inae
Callitrichinae
Cerco-
pithecini
Papionini
Homo (humans) (1)
Pan (chimpanzees) (2)
Gorilla (gorilla) (1)
Pongo (orangutan) (1)
Hylobates (gibbons) (6)
Cercopithecus (17)
Erythrocebus (1)
Macaca (macaques) (11)
Cercocebus (5)
Papio (1)
Theropithecus (1)
Mandrillus (2)
(baboons)
Presbytis (langurs) (12)
Rhinopithecus (3)
Nasalis (2)
Colobus (4)
Procolobus (1)
Cebus (4)
Saimiri (squirrel monkeys) (2)
Alouatta (howler monkeys) (5)
Aotus (1)
Callicebus (3)
Ateles (spider monkeys) (4)
Brachyteles (1)
Lagothrix (2)
Pithecia (2)
Cacajao (3)
Chiropotes (2)
Callimico (1)
Callithrix (8)
Leontideus (3)
Cebuella (1)
Saguinus (22)
CLASSIFICATION
PHYLETIC RELATIONSHIP
Other placental mammals

behavior for which the structure in question is adapted. Using this principle, it is often possible to deduce the behavior of extinct species, known only from fossil remains, by studying the behavior of living animals with similar anatomical adaptations. Anthropologists are particularly alert for such instances of parallelism or convergence between fossil and living animals. The third use of primatology, therefore, is that it supplies us with analogies for interpreting the features seen in fossils. In this way we have obtained much of our insight into the behavior of the ancestors of the human lineage.

In Chapters 7, 8, and 9, we shall look more closely at fossils and the information they have yielded. In the present chapter and in the next, we shall concentrate on the living primates and their various adaptive patterns.

THEMES OF PRIMATE ADAPTATION

A primate (pronounced prý-mate) is a member of the order Primates (pronounced pry-máy-tees), one of the eighteen or so major groupings into which living mammals are divided. (There are also about fifteen extinct orders.) With twelve families, Primates is neither the smallest nor the largest order. Like other taxa in a modern classification system, Primates is defined phyletically—that is to say, it is a group of species related by descent from a common ancestor. From that ancestor, the primates have inherited a set of shared derived traits that indicate their kinship to one another. For example, in all primates the bones of the capsule that encloses the middle ear are arranged in a distinctive way, and all primates show certain unique similarities in the structure of their protein molecules (see box, page 78.

There are also a number of more obvious features, which, although not seen in all primates and sometimes seen in nonprimates, are nevertheless typical of primates in general and are related to the ways of life characteristic of the order. Some of these features are ancestral characteristics, inherited from the primitive nonprimate ancestor of the order. Retained by the primates and lost by members of other orders, they have become distinctively primate features. These ancestral characteristics include

—A five-fingered hand and a five-toed foot. (The primates have not modified their limbs into flippers, wings, or hooves as have some mammals of other orders.)

—A rather unspecialized dentition (set of teeth), suitable for processing a wide variety of foods.

Other distinctively primate characteristics are derived features. Some of these probably evolved in the ancestral primate stock and were retained by the diverging lineages. Others were developed independently, through parallel evolution, in the various lineages. These derived features include the following:

1. The development of grasping hands and feet, with fingers and toes equipped with nails. These hands and feet can grip the branch of a tree by encircling it, rather than by digging claws into the surface.
2. A tendency to make vision the dominant sense and to reduce the importance of the other senses, especially smell. This tendency leads to specialization of the eyes for acute vision and to enlargement of the visual areas of the brain.
3. A tendency to use the hand as an exploratory organ rather than simply as an aid in locomotion. When primates want to investigate something, they reach and grab for it with their hands, rather than literally poking their noses into it and grabbing it with their muzzles and teeth.
4. A tendency to reduce the number of offspring in a litter and to increase the time the young are dependent upon the mother. This is the period during which most learning takes place.
5. A tendency to increase the relative size of the brain, especially those parts associated with

the "higher functions" of learning and association.

6. A tendency to increase the length of the individual's life span, especially the period of immaturity.
7. A tendency to live in permanent groups consisting of individuals of all ages and both sexes.

The first three characteristics in this list probably originated as adaptations to a particular specialized econiche—stalking and grabbing insects in the small branches of the forest canopy or the undergrowth (Cartmill, 1972). If the ancestor of all living primates did occupy such an econiche, this way of life established these three characteristics as basic attributes of the order.

The last four characteristics (numbers 4–7 in the list) are also related to one another. As an order, primates have specialized in rearing rather few offspring but rearing them very carefully. During the long period of immaturity, the young primate learns from its parents and other group members, acquiring social skills and techniques for dealing with the environment. The large and complex brain can be seen as an adaptation to acquiring and using this store of learning.

A reproductive strategy involving long immaturity is best suited, as we shall see, to the stable environment of the tropical rain forest, and therefore strongly suggests that this was the habitat in which the ancestral primates lived.

PRIMATE HABITATS

According to evolutionary theory, the diversity of a group such as the primates is, in large part, the result of adaptation to different environments, each with its own challenges and opportunities. Thus, to understand the diversity of the primates, one must be familiar with the habitats in which they live.

Figure 5-2. Primate realms and habitats. Each of the three major realms (South and Central America, Madagascar, Africa-Asia) includes a variety of habitats, and each has its own distinctive primate fauna. No families crosscut the realms in their distribution. *(After J. R. Napier and P. H. Napier, 1967)*

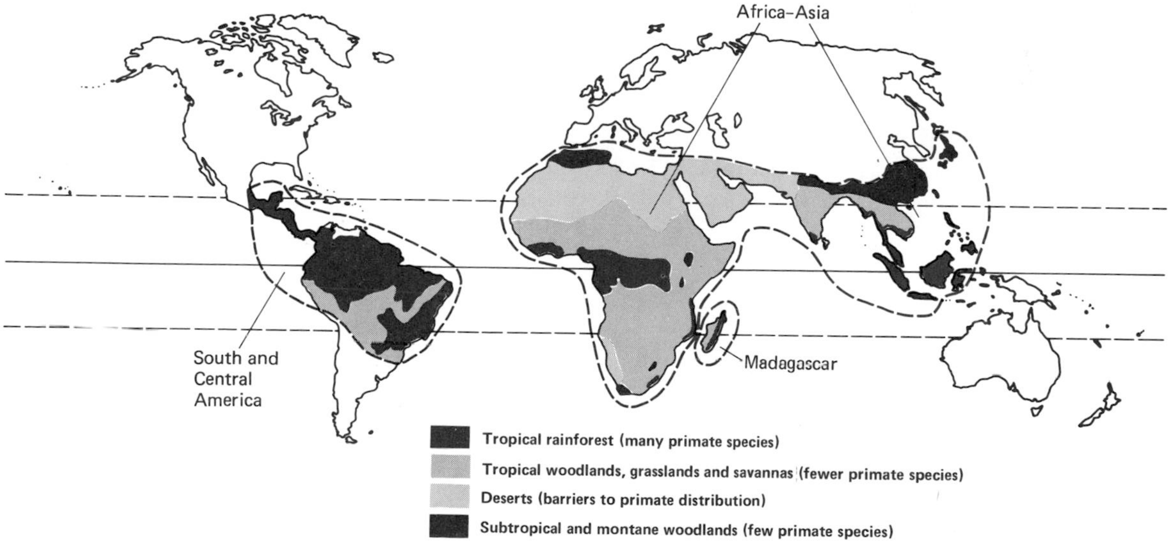

As we have just seen, the ancestral primates probably lived in the tropical rain forest. And to a large extent the primates have remained a tropical group. The great majority of primate species are still found in the zone between the northern and southern tropics (see Figure 5-2). The range of the primates is divided by deep water barriers into three distinct regions: South and Central America, Africa-Asia, and Madagascar. Each of these regions has a distinctive primate fauna:[2] in South and Central America, the platyrrhines, or New World monkeys; in Africa-Asia, the lorises, tarsiers, Old World monkeys, and anthropoid apes; and in Madagascar, the lemurs. *Homo sapiens* is the only primate common to all three regions, and his arrival in America and Madagascar is comparatively recent.

Each of these three regions includes a variety of habitats, differing in climate and vegetation. Each habitat makes different demands upon its inhabitants and thus favors different behaviors and physical adaptations. The evolutionary line leading to *Homo sapiens* has apparently, at different stages, adapted first to one and then to another of these various habitats, and this progression has had a profound influence upon the direction human evolution has taken.

Many of these habitats, and the ecological opportunities they present, can be found in all three major geographical regions. Each of the three has grasslands, for example, and each includes rain forests. This has resulted in a good deal of parallel evolution among their various primate faunas. Thus each region has leaf-eating primates as well as insect eaters and fruit eaters. And both Africa-Asia and Madagascar are, or were, the home of primates that independently forsook the trees for life on the ground.

We will examine two of the most important primate habitats: the tropical rain forests and the grasslands.

Tropical Rain Forests

Tropical rain forests are the primate heartland, containing the most numerous and diverse primate species.

The climate of the equatorial rain forest is

[2] The *fauna* of a region or of a period of time consists of the animals of that region or period considered as a whole. Similarly, *flora* means the plants of a region or period taken as a whole.

Figure 5-3. Diagrammatic profile of major habitats of nonhuman primates. (a) tropical rainforest—several major layers, little ground cover; (b) swamp forest—dense growth on waterlogged ground within rainforest; (c) woodland—deciduous, low-canopy trees, lush ground cover; (d) gallery forest—taller, evergreen trees along a waterway in woodland or steppe; (e) dry savanna or steppe—scattered trees and shrubs, short grass. (*Robert Frank*)

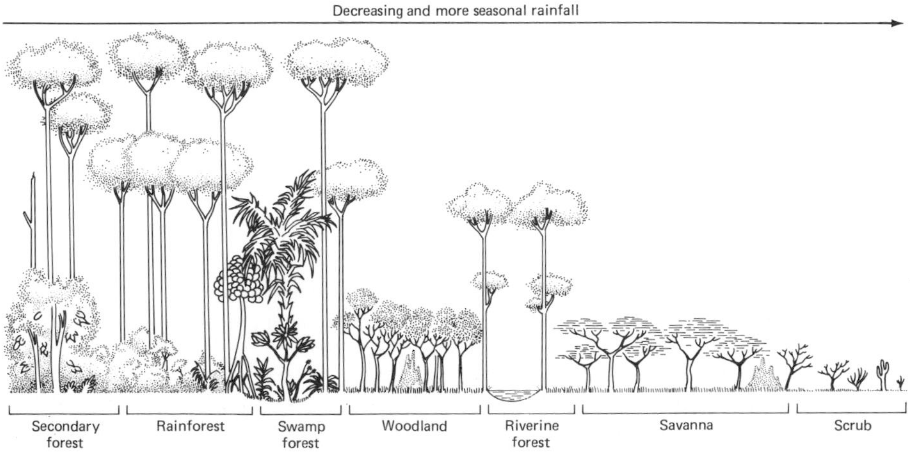

An African tropical evergreen forest. This vegetation type is dominated by trees and vines and is the habitat of most primate species. *(Carl Frank/Rapho/Photo Researchers)*

nearly always hot and humid, though it is not particularly sunny. Although there are peaks in rainfall, there is always sufficient moisture for year-round plant growth. Trees are the dominant life form, and the crowns of the rain forest trees form a closed canopy of leaves through which very little sunshine can reach the lower layers. Because so little light penetrates the canopy, the ground vegetation in a mature forest is typically sparse and unproductive.

It is in the sun-drenched canopy that most food for primates and other animals grows. Hence, the best living in a tropical rain forest is generally to be made by climbing animals that can reach the canopy. Many rain forest primates spend their whole lives in the swaying world of the treetops. Others prefer the tangled growth of shrubs and leafy plants that springs up when the canopy is broken by the fall of a giant tree. Still others inhabit the low, dense forest that grows in swampy areas. Compared with other habitats, the tropical rain forest provides a large number of distinct but rather narrow econiches for primates and other animals. In the almost unchanging climate of the rain forest, there are some insects hatching, some trees fruiting, and some new leaves bursting throughout the year. Rain forest animals can thus afford to become ecological specialists, each one concentrating on a comparatively narrow range of resources—such as insects, fruits, or young leaves—that are more or less continuously available all year long.

Rain Forest Habitat and Reproductive Strategy

The relative lack of seasonal variation in the rain forest affects the reproductive strategy of its inhabitants. In the rain forest, there is no pronounced lean season (like winter in a northern woodland) during which food supplies decrease dramatically and the animal population, especially of small mammals, drastically declines. Nor is there a "spring" when resources abruptly increase and populations are rapidly swelled by a new crop of young animals. Thus, animal numbers in the rain forest tend to remain fairly stable the year round.

In such a habitat, it would be of little advantage to produce many, fast-growing young. The territory is already fully occupied by adult animals, with little food or living space to spare for a new crop. A more advantageous adaptation is to produce few offspring but rear them carefully, so that they are well prepared to compete for the places of adults that die. In this way, though the total number of offspring is smaller, the chance of producing successful offspring—offspring that live long enough so that they themselves can reproduce—is increased.

As we saw earlier, this combination of fewer offspring and prolonged immaturity is characteristic of the primate order in general. The early primates probably developed this reproductive strategy as an adaptation to life in the rain forest, and their descendants have carried it with them as they moved out of the rain forest and into new habitats.

Tropical Grasslands

The tropical rain forest zone is flanked north and south by *tropical grasslands.* There is less rainfall here than in the forests, and it is more seasonal, occurring almost entirely during one or two sharply defined rainy seasons each year. As a result, the tree cover is less dense, allowing light to penetrate to the ground and nourish grasses and other low-growing vegetation.

Tree growth in these tropical grasslands varies with the type of soil and the amount of rain. In the drier areas, the trees are relatively sparse and grow chiefly along the banks of rivers and

Savanna country in the Ngorongoro Crater, Tanzania. Scattered trees dot the open grassland and line the seasonal watercourses. In the middle distance is a stretch of woodland. This area supports baboons, vervet monkeys, and a great variety of grazing animals, as well as the carnivores that prey on them. *(Bruce Coleman, Inc.)*

streams. Thorny scrub and short, wiry grasses dominate the vegetation. In the rainier areas, tree growth is sometimes vigorous enough to form *woodlands*, which have a closed canopy (though it is neither so tall nor so continuous as that of the rain forest). Another widespread vegetation type in many areas is grassland with scattered trees, called *savanna*.

Vegetation in the tropical grasslands changes with the changing seasons. When the rains come, they stimulate an explosion of vigorous growth. Trees and shrubs put out new leaves, grasses and other ground plants throw up new shoots, and for a short time all is green and bushy. During the dry season, most of the trees lose their leaves and the grassy plants dry into a natural hay that is cropped by grazing animals. Then, eventually, the rainy season returns, reviving the greenery once again.

The typical inhabitants of these zones are not tree-climbing primates, as in the rain forest, but grazing and browsing animals—antelopes, zebras, elephants, and the like—along with the carnivores that prey upon the grazing herds. Nevertheless, some primate species, such as the common baboons, do inhabit them, and these primates have modified their survival strategies to cope with the environment. Because of the seasonal variability, each food resource becomes available for only a few weeks or months at a time and then disappears. Grassland primates are therefore forced to exploit a much wider spectrum of resources than their relatives in the rain forest, switching from one to another with the changing seasons. This means that they must be able to move on the ground between feeding places; and when the trees offer little food, they must be able to feed on the ground as well.

Water too can be a problem. Outside of the rain forest, primates cannot rely on dripping rain and juicy fruit to supply moisture. Foods that grow in the savanna are generally less juicy than those in the rain forest, and water is relatively scarce. Except during the rainy season, therefore, thirsty primates must often trek to water holes or riverbanks to drink, and they must adapt to the risk of meeting the predators that often lurk in such places.

As we shall see, the move from the rain forest to the new challenges of the tropical grasslands was probably an important influence in the evolution of the human lineage.

PRIMATE DIVERSITY

In this section, we shall be concerned mainly with primate ecology—the relationship of each species to its habitat and the way in which its behavior is adapted to exploit that habitat. The order Primates includes about thirty living genera and well over one hundred living species, each with its own unique way of life. It is convenient to treat the living primates family by family. Readers will find it useful to refer to Figure 5-1 as they go. We shall start with the human family and its closest relatives, and then move on to more distant and less familiar primates. In this way, our more distant primate relatives may seem less strange. Furthermore, by taking the primates in this sequence, we hope to avoid the common pitfall of regarding the living primates as if they were merely steps on an evolutionary ladder—the humble prosimians at the bottom, the noble human species at the top.

The Family Hominidae

The human family, Hominidae, includes only one living genus, *Homo*, with a single living species, *Homo sapiens*. Unlike other primates, *Homo sapiens* is worldwide in distribution, inhabiting all major climatic and vegetational zones, and relying extensively upon tools, weapons, and shelters—in a word, upon technology—to control the environment. Human behavior is to a large extent governed by rules and customs that are systematically arranged, codified, and deliberately transmitted from generation to generation through the use of a flexible symbolic communication system called language. The immense variety of modern human societies and cultures is founded upon these few general traits.

Physically, *Homo sapiens* is most distinctive at the extremities—the huge brain and its globular case overshadowing the comparatively weak face and jaws, and the pelvis and hindlimb (thigh, leg, and foot) adapted for habitual upright posture and bipedalism. In later chapters we shall examine each of these traits more closely, in an evolutionary context.

The Family Pongidae

Our closest living relatives are the members of the family Pongidae, also called the "great apes": the chimpanzees (genus *Pan*), the gorilla (genus *Gorilla*), and the orangutan (genus *Pongo*). However, as the phyletic tree in Figure 5-1 indicates, the family Pongidae is not really a true clade. The African apes—the chimpanzees and the gorilla—are closely related to one another and to *Homo sapiens,* while the Asian orangutan is more distantly related to these three. The nineteenth-century naturalist Thomas Henry Huxley suspected the close relationship between the human species and the African apes on the basis of comparative anatomy, and his suspicion has since been strikingly confirmed by the evidence of protein structure. No matter what protein is chosen for comparison, gorillas and chimpanzees consistently show much greater resemblance to the human species than do any other primates. There can no longer be any reasonable doubt that our common ancestry with the African apes is much more recent than our common ancestry with any other primate. Cladistically, we are the third genus of African ape. Although our latest common ancestor with an African ape certainly did not exactly resemble a chimpanzee or a gorilla, the ancestral characteristics that these modern apes retain are good clues to what such an ancestor must have been like.

The Chimpanzee

There are two closely related species of chimpanzee: the common chimpanzee, *Pan troglodytes,* and the pygmy chimpanzee, *Pan paniscus.* The range of the common chimpanzee extends across tropical Africa (Figure 5-4). South of the Congo River, it is replaced by the smaller pygmy chimpanzee. In the following account we will concentrate on the common chimpanzee, which has been much more extensively studied.

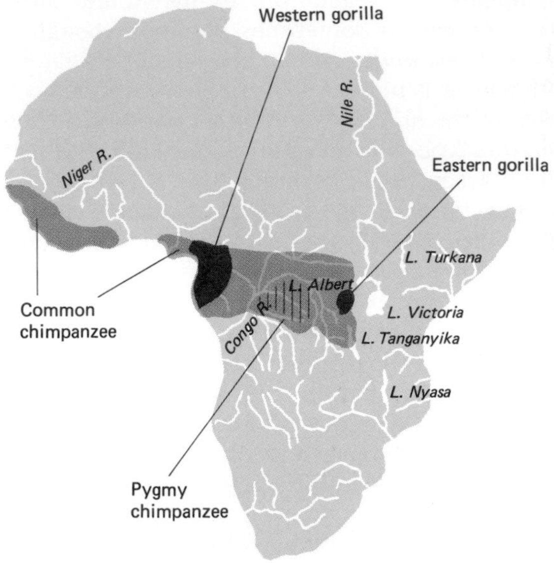

Figure 5-4. Both chimpanzees and gorillas are primarily rain forest dwellers, though some chimpanzee populations inhabit woodland environments. This map shows the ranges of the two genera, along with some of the localities in which major primatological studies have been carried out.

Most chimpanzees live in the tropical rain forest, and it is in this habitat that the densest populations are to be found. Chimps are adaptable, however, and some populations live in tropical woodlands, where there is a distinct dry season. Though they are in some ways atypical, these woodland chimpanzees hold a special interest for anthropologists, for they are facing challenges similar to those encountered by the earliest hominids when they left the rain forests for life in more open country. Most of the longer studies, such as Goodall's, have been carried out on woodland rather than rain forest populations.

Like other nonhuman primates, forest chimpanzees spend most of their day feeding. Their food consists chiefly of forest fruits, although they also eat leaves, stems, and insects. Much of their time is spent in the trees, but they are quite at home on the ground and use beaten tracks through the undergrowth to travel from one feeding area to another. Although chimpanzees can walk quite well bipedally, they use this form of locomotion only occasionally and for short distances. Their normal way of moving on the ground is knuckle-walking—that is, walking quadrupedally on the soles of their feet and the knuckles of their hands.

Social Behavior In the forest, an observer may meet chimpanzees in groups of thirty or forty, especially when they are gathered on a large fruit-bearing tree such as a wild fig. At other times, they split up into smaller groups, which may be all male, all female, or mixed. Kinship seems to form the basis of some of these parties, which consist of a group of siblings, or a mother with her grown offspring and perhaps their infants as well. But these associations tend to be quite fluid—a given chimpanzee may spend the morning with one group of foraging companions and the afternoon with another group.

The fact that chimpanzee groups join, split up, and rejoin while foraging at first led observers to believe that chimpanzee society was entirely "open." But there is now considerable evidence that the chimpanzees of an area—the "local population"—form a relatively permanent and stable troop and have a clear sense of community, treating outsiders with suspicion or even hostility. Male chimpanzees have been seen to kill (and partially eat) the babies of strange female chimpanzees that entered the group's territory. And, in recent years, members of Goodall's team have observed several murderous attacks by groups of adult males on individual chimpanzees of a smaller neighboring community. It may be that competition for living space and food resources lies at the root of these incidents; over a period of years, most of the members of the smaller group seem to have been killed off and their territory taken over by the attackers' group.

One of the most spectacular aspects of chimpanzee group behavior is their vocal display, which begins with a series of loud, low hoots, becoming a crescendo of maniacal screams, often accompanied by the waving of vegetation or kicking or drumming upon tree trunks. This communal uproar seems to occur in situations of intense group excitement, but its function is not entirely clear. It may serve to advertise the group's presence in an area and warn off other chimpanzees. (This seems to be its function, too, when directed against intruding humans. To be the object of such a chorus is one of the more interesting experiences of the African forest.)

At other times, this vocal display may serve to gather scattered members of the group to a bonanza of fruit discovered by a foraging band. Cooperative behavior of this kind is an efficient way of exploiting fruiting trees in the forest. Each tree fruits abundantly, but only for a short time, and is likely to be quite far from other fruit-bearing trees. Thus it would be of no advantage for a small foraging band to keep to itself the discovery of a tree heavy with ripe fruit. The fruit would rot and fall before the small group could ever eat it all. On the other hand, advertising the find would be positively advantageous, so long as other group members returned the favor when they made a similar discovery. Thus, although chimpanzees, unlike humans, do not collect food and bring it back to a base to share, they seem to have acquired, as an adaptation to the rain forest habitat, a foraging strategy akin to true food sharing—a trait believed to be crucial in the early evolution of humans.

Chimpanzees also cooperate in hunting and share the meat they catch. While the staple of the chimpanzees' diet is fruit, from time to time they will stalk small animals, such as young baboons and monkeys. And they do so in a quiet, efficient, and cooperative manner that is impressively different from their usually noisy foraging and feeding patterns. Goodall relates a striking example of a pincer movement that was apparently arranged without any oral communication:

> I was watching four red colobus monkeys resting in a tall, leafless tree when suddenly a young

> chimpanzee climbed into a neighboring tree. He sat close enough to one of the monkeys to attract its attention, yet not close enough to scare it away. Meanwhile another young chimpanzee bounded up the tree in which the monkey was sitting, ran with incredible speed along the branch, leaped at the colobus, caught it with its hands, and presumably broke its neck (1963, p. 307).

In other cases, a group of chimpanzees, usually adult males, will surround the victim on the ground and silently close in for the kill.

The normal chimpanzee feeding strategy of individual foraging offers little opportunity or incentive for food sharing (though mothers will often permit infants to take food from their mouths). Where meat is concerned, however, sharing is very much the rule rather than the exception. One observer has commented that "no chimpanzee at Gombe has ever been observed to capture and privately consume a mammal, however small, if other adult chimpanzees were present" (Teleki, 1973, p. 40).

But though meat is invariably shared, it is not necessarily shared by all the animals present. The kill belongs to the hunter, and he distributes pieces of it to individuals of his own choosing—usually in response to their solicitations. Goodall describes a typical scene: "The others in the group show respect. They sit as close to the male as they can, watching the meat with longing eyes, holding out their hands palm uppermost in a begging gesture" (1963, p. 307). Unauthorized grabbing, though sometimes tolerated, is relatively rare, and fighting virtually nonexistent. Interestingly, the pattern of sharing seems to be largely independent of the troop's normal dominance hierarchy. High-ranking males have been observed begging from subordinate animals—and sometimes coming away empty-handed.

Tool Use In their food-sharing behavior, which is an integral part of their adaptive strategy, chimpanzees are more humanlike than any other primate. They also show other striking resemblances to humans. They kiss and embrace and pat one another affectionately. They scratch their heads when they are bewildered. They squeeze fruit to find out whether it is ripe. They laugh. In their early years they play tug-of-war with sticks, and they chase and tickle one another very much like human children. But few aspects of chimpanzee behavior are so distinctly humanlike as their use of objects from their environment.

Like humans, but unlike most other primates, young chimpanzees often play by manipulating objects: leaves, twigs, and bits of grass. In adults, this behavior is extended into the occasional use of such objects as tools or weapons. Captive chimpanzees (quite justifiably, in our view) often throw turf, rocks, and feces at human visitors and may pick up sticks to use as improvised clubs. The use of sticks for threatening and fighting has also been seen in the wild, and when a field researcher placed a stuffed leopard in the path of one group of chimpanzees, they clubbed it furiously.

Chimpanzees also use natural objects as simple tools; for example, they employ stones as hammers to break open nuts too tough for their teeth. More remarkably, they have also been observed to fashion crude implements for specific purposes. In other words, chimpanzees not only use bits of their environment to solve problems but actually *modify* these objects. They make "sponges" to extract water from inaccessible spots: when rainwater collects in a tree hollow too small to drink from, the thirsty chimpanzee will chew some leaves into a wad, dip the wad into the water, and then suck the water from it. The most striking example of chimpanzee technology, however, is their use of "termiting sticks." Termites are a much-prized food among chimpanzees. To extract these insects from their underground nests, the animals fashion special probes. They select a thin twig about 1 foot long and, if necessary, trim off its leaves. Then they carry the stick to the termite mound and poke it into one of the tunnels. After a few moments, they withdraw it, lick off whatever termites are clinging to it, and reinsert the stick into the tunnel.

There is no doubt that these behaviors represent more than random, spur-of-the-moment im-

A chimpanzee female (center) and her adult daughter (right) use simple tools fashioned from grass stems to "fish" for termites. Infants gradually learn the technique by watching and imitating their elders. *(Hugo van Lawick/© National Geographic Society)*

pulses. Termiting sticks are simple implements, but they are carefully fashioned, to a set and regular pattern. Moreover, chimps have been observed making a termiting stick first, and only then, equipped with the necessary tool, going in search of a suitable mound. This raises the intriguing possibility that some element of forethought and conscious planning may be involved in such behaviors—though we cannot be certain of this.

It is fairly clear, too, that these tool-using techniques are learned skills. Though the tendency to employ bits of the environment as tools is evidently built into chimpanzee biology in a way that is not true of the other nonhuman primates (except possibly the orangutan), particular techniques such as termiting seem to be passed from generation to generation by imitation and learning. Young chimpanzees watch their elders termiting, and almost immediately they are making their own crude probes and pushing them into the termite tunnels. Among humans, most techniques are transmitted in just this way, even in societies where textbooks and laboratory manuals are used.

In the face of such evidence, it would be hard to deny that something similar to human culture may exist among chimpanzees. Toolmaking and the transmission of skills by learning can no longer be considered distinctive of our species. To be sure, tool use, food sharing, and hunting are relatively minor components of chimpanzee behavior. Unimportant as these behaviors may be to the chimpanzee, however, they are extremely important to the anthropologist. Their existence among the chimpanzees indicates that they may have been part of the life style of the common ancestor of chimpanzees and humans before the ancestral hominids left the rain forest. Evidently these ancestral behaviors remained rudimentary in the chimpanzee line, whereas in our line they were increasingly elaborated.

Woodland Chimpanzees: An Analogue for Early Hominids As we saw earlier, some chimpanzees live in the dry, seasonal woodlands—the same habitat into which the earliest hominids (members of the family Hominidae) moved when they left the rain forest. It is this coincidence that makes these populations particularly interesting. Presumably, by comparing the behavior of woodland chimpanzees with that of their more typical rain forest relatives, we can get some idea of the adjustments the earliest hominids had to make in meeting the challenges of open country life.

Such a comparative study has recently been carried out in the Kaskati Basin, Tanzania, by a team led by Akira Suzuki. These researchers found that the Kaskati chimpanzees differed from the rain forest populations in two major respects: (1) the size of their range and (2) their diet. Whenever possible, the Kaskati chimpanzees fed in the forests bordering riverbanks; but to find enough food, they had to exploit wide areas of more open woodland as well. In doing so, they ranged over an area ten times as large as that used by comparable groups of forest chimpanzees.

No increase in meat eating or tool use was seen among the woodland populations (though they may have eaten more ants and termites). The most striking and obvious dietary difference between the woodland and forest chimpanzees was in the *consistency* of the food that they ate. While most forest fruits are pulpy and fleshy, the seeds of savanna trees and grasses, which were the dry season staple of the savanna chimpanzees, tend to be small, hard, and tough. They are, however, surprisingly nutritious—high in proteins, fats, and starches. As we shall see, the distinctive teeth and jaws of the early hominids—and possibly also their adoption of habitual bipedalism—are most plausibly interpreted as adaptations to just such a diet.

The Gorilla

The second genus of African apes, *Gorilla*, contains only one species, *Gorilla gorilla*, the largest of the living primates. The gorilla is to be found only within the African rain forest. Though it eats some fruit, the green parts of forest plants—leaves, pith, stems, and shoots—constitute its basic diet. In its lush habitat, the gorilla is literally surrounded by this food; the problem is not to find it but to pack in enough, since it is bulky and low in nutritional content.

Gorillas tend to live in small groups—usually including only one fully adult male, with a few females and young. Unlike the chimpanzee, the gorilla does not have to engage in social interaction—foraging parties, food-alert calls—to find enough to eat. Indeed, with its rather stolid and reserved nature, the gorilla is quite the opposite of the noisy, excitable, and sociable chimpanzee. Among gorillas, social interaction of all kinds is infrequent and low key. According to Schaller, who spent a year among the gorillas of Central Africa, "gorillas tend to have an extremely placid nature which is not easily aroused to excitement. They give the impression of being stoic . . . and introverted" (1964, pp. 118–119). Periodically an adult male will produce the celebrated chest-thumping display, but only after continued provocation by rival males or by such irritants as camera-carrying tourists.

The gorilla is much less of a climber than the chimpanzee and spends most of its time sitting or knuckle-walking on the ground. Virtually the only occasion for bipedalism is the chest-thumping display. Tool use has not been reported in wild gorillas. Unlike the chimpanzee, the gorilla shows marked *sexual dimorphism*—that is, differences between male and female; female gorillas are about half the weight of males.

The Orangutan

The third genus of the family Pongidae (and the genus for which the family was named) is *Pongo*. Like *Gorilla* and *Homo*, this genus includes only one living species: the orangutan, *Pongo pygmaeus*, of Sumatra and Borneo. Because of the destruction of its habitat and the collection of animals for zoos, the orangutan is rapidly disappearing in the wild.

With its shaggy reddish fur, the orangutan is strikingly different in appearance from the African apes. It is also much more arboreal than either the chimpanzee or the gorilla and dwells only in the forest, where it feeds on both fruit and leaves. The orangutan has been called a "four-handed climber," and the description is apt, because its legs and feet are as flexible and mobile as its hands and arms. Curiously for a higher primate, it is apparently solitary, except for mothers with young.

Recent experiments have shown that the orangutan's persistence and skill in improvising and using simple tools, at least in captivity, is every bit as impressive as the chimpanzee's. This discovery suggests that the trait of "handiness" may be considerably more ancient than is usually assumed. It may have existed in the ancestral apes even before the *Pongo* line diverged from that of the African apes and man.

The Family Hylobatidae: The Gibbons

The family Hylobatidae contains only one genus, *Hylobates*, a successful group of small, active, arboreal apes commonly known as the gibbons. There are six species, all found in Southeast Asia. Gibbons are forest animals, ranging from the temperate forests of the Himalayas and southern China to the rain forests of Java and Sumatra. Their most striking characteristic is their powerful, elongated arms. These are the anatomical basis for their most spectacular behavior, *brachiation*—moving about by swinging from the

A young orangutan, calling, shows the expressive mobility of the face characteristic of all higher primates but most highly developed in hominoids. (*Toni Angermayer/Rapho/Photo Researchers*)

The long arms, powerful hands, and great flexibility of the hip, knee, and ankle are well shown in this picture of a resting orangutan. Note also the wide span between the big toe and the other toes in the animal's left foot. (*Russ Kine/Rapho/Photo Researchers*)

A gibbon (*Hylobates lar*) feeds from a small twig while hanging by one arm. The gibbon's adaptations for hanging in this way enable it to exploit food resources in the outer canopy of the forest that are not easily accessible to other primates. *(Courtesy, D. J. Chivers)*

branches of trees, supporting the body weight by hands and arms alone. The gibbons' long arms also permit them to feed comfortably while suspended in the small twigs found in the outer canopy of the forest trees, where they eat fruit and young leaves.

Gibbons have an interesting form of social organization. A mated pair holds a small patch of forest as a territory, guarding it jealously from all other adult gibbons of the same species and ejecting their own offspring as they become mature. The whooping of gibbons proclaiming their territories is one of the distinctive sounds of the Malaysian forest.

The Family Cercopithecidae: The Old World Monkeys

The three families that we have just discussed—Hominidae, Pongidae, and Hylobatidae—form a related group: the superfamily Hominoidea. The next family to be considered, Cercopithecidae, constitutes its own superfamily, Cercopithecoidea. These are the monkeys (as opposed to the apes) of Asia and Africa; they are also called the Old World monkeys. By any standards, they are a most successful group. They number twelve genera and sixty-one species, and exploit a variety of adaptive niches in habitats ranging from the Cape of Good Hope to Japan, and from the steaming African rain forest to the snowy Himalayas. (By contrast, the five living genera of hominoids[3] number only eleven species among them and, apart from humans and a few chimpanzee populations, are confined to the rain forest.)

Varied as they are in external appearance, the Old World monkeys share certain features that distinguish them from the hominoids. Hominoids lack an external tail, and, though their limb proportions vary, all of them share the basic shape of the trunk: broad-chested, with the rib cage flattened from front to back. The Old World monkeys, by contrast, have tails, and a trunk shaped more like a dog's than a human's: long and narrow from side to side, but deep from front to back. When they move on all fours, as they usually do, the Old World monkeys rest upon the palms of their hands or on their finger pads, not on their knuckles. While most Old World monkeys are agile climbers, they are less specialized in this direction than the apes. Their teeth, too, are quite distinctive. All Old World monkeys, but no hominoids, have molars with pairs of cusps connected by crests. The basic body plan

---

[3] The *hominoids* are the members of the superfamily Hominoidea. Note the difference (marked, unfortunately, by only one letter) between the hominoids on the one hand and the hominids, members of the family Hominidae, on the other hand. The former includes all the apes and hominids; the latter only human beings and our immediate ancestors. (See Figure 5-1 and Table 4-1.)

of the Old World monkeys has proved readily adaptable to life on the ground, and several lineages have left the forests to exploit ground resources in the grasslands and woodlands.

Genetic and protein studies show that all Old World monkeys are closely related to one another, and that their adaptive radiation was relatively recent compared with that of the hominids. Within the family, however, are two rather distinct subfamilies:

1. The Colobinae: These are mainly arboreal monkeys with stomachs specialized for digesting leaves.
2. The Cercopithecinae: This is a diverse subfamily containing a wide variety of forms. They are a highly adaptable and omnivorous group of animals, feeding on fruits, leaves, insects, and a variety of other foods. Although they lack the digestive specializations of the Colobinae, they have cheek pouches that can be filled with food to be carried off and eaten at leisure.

The Cercopithecinae include the macaques (genus *Macaca*) of Asia, the guenons (genus *Cercopithecus*) and the mangabeys (genus *Cercocebus*) of the African forest, and the patas (genus *Erythrocebus*), an African monkey that has become adapted to grasslands. The remaining three genera of Cercopithecinae are all baboons—the most interesting group from the point of view of human evolution.

The Baboons

The mandrills (genus *Mandrillus*), the common baboons (genus *Papio*), and the geladas (genus *Theropithecus*) are three closely related, large African monkeys, collectively known as baboons. All three have powerful projecting muzzles that give them a superficially doglike appearance.

The mandrills live in tropical rain forests, where they forage both in the trees and on the ground. The common baboons, while they prefer wooded savannas, live in a variety of habitats, from forest edge to semidesert scrub, and inhabit most of Africa south of the Sahara. The geladas live only in treeless grasslands in the highlands of Ethiopia. Having adapted to life outside the rain forest, the common and gelada baboons, like the savanna chimpanzees, are interesting to compare with early hominids, who evidently made the same transition. Moreover, it appears that the ancestral baboons competed with the early hominids in the savannas and thus probably influenced the direction of human evolution.

The *Papio* baboons have been the subject of a number of field studies. These have demonstrated the extreme versatility of the group and the way in which its behaviors enable it to survive the unique challenges of the savanna.

Most *Papio* baboons live in troops that number up to one hundred animals, including members of both sexes and all ages. While the troop is in open country, it generally moves as a compact group, its members keeping in touch by a murmuring of low grunts. However, troops of baboons that live in less open habitats, and are therefore less vulnerable to attack by predators, often seem to split up into smaller parties for foraging, much as chimpanzees do.

Each day the baboon troop leaves the trees or rock ledges where it has slept and forages until dusk, pausing now and then for rest and play in the heat of the day. Nothing edible is ignored by foraging baboons. They have been seen to eat fruits, grass stems and roots, seeds, nuts, ants, and, on the seashore, mussels and crabs. Quite often baboons will catch and eat small animals, such as lambs, hares, and guinea fowl. Among baboons, as among chimpanzees, meat catching seems to be primarily an activity of adult males. Unlike chimpanzees, however, baboons do not share meat—or any other food, for that matter. Each animal, even newly weaned juveniles, forages for itself.

Baboons, like most monkeys and apes, are extremely protective toward their young. DeVore, who studied baboons in Kenya, reports: "It is scarcely possible to overemphasize the significance of the newborn baboon. It becomes the center of interest, absorbing the attention of the entire troop. From the moment the birth is discovered, the mother is continuously surrounded by the other baboons, who walk beside her and sit as close as possible when she rests." Both males and females will play with, carry, and protect infants and juveniles, not only their own offspring but any young member of the group. Indeed, adult males will usually go on protecting a young baboon for about six months after its mother, occupied with a new offspring, has ceased to look after it. An adult male with an infant in its arms is virtually immune to attack by other males—an impressive show of deference in view of the normally quarrelsome nature of the baboons.

Defense against predators often poses a problem to baboon troops as they forage in open country, away from trees that might offer refuge, or pass through dense bushes on their way to drink at a stream or river. In such dangerous situations, females and infants stay near the center, close to the powerful adult males. These animals—twice as large as females and armed with huge, saberlike canine teeth—will sometimes boldly attack large cats, such as leopards. In many cases attack is unnecessary. For, when confronted by a predator, a baboon will utter a characteristic roaring bark and open its jaws as wide as possible, flashing its formidable canines at the opponent. This display generally makes a profound impression, often causing predators to back off cautiously and depart.

The gelada baboon is the lone survivor of a group that up to a few hundred thousand years ago was widespread and successful in Africa. Some of its fossil cousins were as large as gorillas. Unlike the versatile common baboon, the gelada is a specialist, foraging exclusively on the ground and feeding mostly on grass roots, rhizomes, and

A large herd of gelada baboons (*Theropithecus gelada*) forages in the short grass of the Ethiopian mountains. Although social organization is of the one-male-group type, the groups mingle as they forage. (*Wrangham/Anthro-Photo*)

stems, as well as on insects and small animals. Although its distribution is now limited, its population density, where it occurs, is much higher than that of common baboons. Huge herds of geladas graze on the short turf, their hands busily working as they delicately pluck at the grass. As we shall see, some of the anatomical specializations that the gelada has developed in adaptation to its special diet and open country way of life help us to interpret the fossils of early hominids.

Infraorder Platyrrhini: The New World Monkeys

As can be seen in Figure 5-1, the apes and Old World monkeys together constitute a single infraorder called Catarrhini. The New World monkeys—that is, the monkeys of South and Central America—are allocated to a separate infraorder, Platyrrhini, expressing their evolutionary distance from the Old World group.

Superficially, many of the New World monkeys look very much like Old World monkeys, but various anatomical features of skull and teeth set them apart from all catarrhines as a more primitive group. Some New World monkeys—though by no means all—have a strong *prehensile* (that is, grasping) tail that acts as a kind of fifth hand and is used mainly to support the animal as it hangs to feed in the canopy. No catarrhine has this. Studies of blood proteins support the idea that the New World monkeys form a clade apart from the catarrhines.

New World monkeys are found only in tropical rain forests. They constitute an extensive and ancient adaptive radiation occupying a wide variety of econiches within the forest. The tiny marmosets and tamarins (family Callitrichidae) are squirrel-like insect eaters, for example, while the bulky spider monkeys (genus *Ateles*) and howler monkeys (genus *Alouatta*) are fruit and leaf eaters. Diverse as they are, however, the New World monkeys never gave rise to ground-living, savanna-dwelling species comparable to the baboons.

The New World monkeys are a fascinating group. To the student of human evolution, their major significance is that their radiation has in some respects paralleled that of the catarrhines. A good example, that of the spider monkey and the gibbon, has already been mentioned in Chapter 4. Like the gibbon, the spider monkey has long, slender arms, from which it frequently swings beneath branches. And, like the gibbon, it is mainly a fruit eater and dangles while plucking its food in the forest canopy. Because of such parallelism, the behavior of the more primitive New World monkeys can often help us to reconstruct, by analogy, stages through which catarrhines passed long ago, which are now represented only by fossils.

A family of marmosets (*Callithrix*) showing the father carrying his twin offspring. Twin births and paternal care are the rule among the marmosets, the smallest of the anthropoid primates. The sharp, pointed front teeth reflect the marmoset's insectivorous diet. (*San Diego Zoo*)

Suborder Prosimii

In spite of their diversity, all the primates we have described so far are readily recognized as

The Lemurs of Madagascar

The ancestors of the lemurs of Madagascar (families Lemuridae, Indriidae, Daubentoniidae, and Cheirogaleidae) seem to have arrived on the island sometime between 70 and 35 million years ago. Their journey was presumably quite accidental; a few animals or a pregnant female probably rafted from Africa or Asia on pieces of floating vegetation. As we saw in Chapter 4, a group of animals that colonize a "new" geographical area will often give rise to an extensive adaptive radiation, and that is precisely what happened in this case. Proliferating in isolation, they produced a great variety of species adapted to diverse ways of life. They ranged from rat-sized nocturnal insectivores to bulky herbivores the size of chimpanzees.

Among the most primitive of the Madagascar lemurs are the dwarf lemurs and mouse lemurs of the family Cheirogaleidae. These are small, mainly insectivorous animals whose large eyes betray their nocturnal habits. *Microcebus,* the mouse lemur, is the smallest of the living primates. Both mouse lemurs and dwarf lemurs share a trait that is unique to them among primates: each year during the dry season, when little food is to be found, they go through a quiet phase when their metabolic rate slows drastically and they live on stored fat.

The extinct lemur *Megaladapis.* (*Courtesy, American Museum of Natural History*)

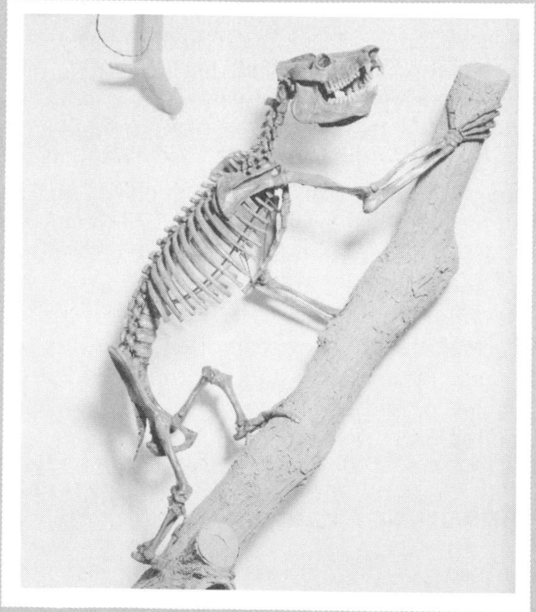

Unlike the prosimians of Asia and Africa, the lemurs of Madagascar faced no competition from anthropoid primates, for monkeys and apes did not cross the Mozambique channel. As a result, the adaptive radiation produced forms that filled the same econiches that monkeys and apes occupied on the mainland. The members of the genus *Lemur,* for instance, are active, diurnal, mainly fruit-eating tree-dwellers that live in groups with a complex social structure. In these respects, they parallel many of the monkeys and apes. As with the *Cercopithecus* monkeys of Africa, the numerous species of *Lemur* are distinguished by brightly colored patterns in the fur.

By contrast, the members of the genera *Indri* and *Propithecus* are leaf eaters, rather like the colobine monkeys of Africa and Asia. (Both *Indri* and *Propithecus* are remarkable for their ability to make tremendous leaps from tree to tree.) Others, now extinct, adapted to life on the ground, and thus evolved in much the same direction as the baboons. One of these, *Hadropithecus,* shows striking parallelisms with the gelada as well as with early hominids.

Perhaps the most fascinating parallelism, however, is that revealed by the limb bones of the extinct lemur *Palaeopropithecus.* This animal, about the size of a pygmy chimpanzee, was evidently quite unlike any living prosimian in its locomotor habits. Its limb skeleton can be matched bone for bone with that of the orangutan or gibbon, and there is little doubt that like these apes and the spider monkey, *Palaeopropithecus* was a brachiator that swung from its arms beneath branches to feed and move about. This provides a striking instance of how parallel evolution can produce similarities in animals that are only distantly related.

Other special adaptations among the lemurs have no parallel among the primates. The members of the genus *Megaladapis,* for example, were bulky lethargic tree-climbers that must

A modern lemur of Madagascar (not yet extinct). *(Roy Pinney/Photo Researchers)*

have looked like giant koala bears. Another member of the Lemuriformes, the aye-aye (genus *Daubentonia*), bears very little resemblance to any other member of the animal kingdom. A cat-sized nocturnal animal covered with rather untidy-looking dark fur, the aye-aye feeds largely on wood-boring insect larvae, which it apparently locates in their tunnels by its acute sense of hearing. Breaking open the wood with its powerful chisel-like incisors, it probes for the larvae with its extremely long, thin third finger.

Unfortunately, the lemur fauna of Madagascar is now pitifully depleted. When human beings first arrived on the island from Indonesia about 1000 years ago, they found the lemurs easy prey. Soon all the more vulnerable species—the larger ones and the terrestrially adapted ones—became extinct. We now know about these magnificent animals only from remains preserved in swamps and garbage pits. Sadly, the surviving lemurs are threatened with a similar fate, as human beings hunt them for food and destroy their forest habitat.

relatives of man. Their large, rounded braincases, with close-set eyes that face directly forward from above the nose; their immobile, rounded ears, set close to the side of the head; and their mobile, expressive faces—all are features that give them an unmistakably humanlike appearance. This similarity and the phyletic relationship that underlies it are expressed by grouping catarrhines and platyrrhines together into the suborder Anthropoidea.

The members of the remaining families of living primates, grouped into the suborder Prosimii, are much less obviously humanlike. Most have smaller, flatter braincases, above which extend pointed, mobile ears. A pointed muzzle projects from between the eyes and is in most cases tipped by a moist *rhinarium:* a wet, naked patch of skin like a dog's nose. The whole look of the face reminds one more of a fox or a small cat than of a human being. In these features, the prosimians are more primitive—more like the ancestral, nonprimate mammal—than are the monkeys and apes. Below the neck, however, the prosimians clearly betray their primate affinities, with hands and feet adapted for climbing by grasping.

On the whole, the prosimians have changed little from the early primates of 50 million years ago. They are interesting to anthropologists partly because they show ancestral features that help us understand the very early stages of primate evolution. On the other hand, the prosimians also represent an interesting adaptive radiation in their own right. Their basic body plan has proved remarkably versatile and has given rise to a great variety of specially adapted types.

The living prosimians fall into two distinct clades, ranked as infraorders: Tarsiiformes and Lemuriformes.

Infraorder Tarsiiformes

The tarsier (family Tarsiidae, genus *Tarsius*) of Borneo and the Philippines is the sole survivor of the infraorder Tarsiiformes, once a widespread and successful group. In most features, such as its teeth and brain, it is quite primitive. It has, however, acquired two extreme specializations that now totally dominate its anatomy. One is its enormously enlarged eyes, used for locating its insect prey in the late dusk. The other is the great elongation of its hindlimb, especially in the ankle region. (Indeed, it derives its name from the tarsal bones of the ankle.) This is an adaptation to hopping and leaping from branch to branch when hunting.

Tarsier (*Tarsius*). Both the adult and young tarsier show the long ankle (tarsus) that gives the animal its name. Its long legs are flexed, ready to hop. Its huge eyes reflect its nocturnal habits. Two of the toes bear claws, used to groom the fur. *(San Diego Zoo)*

Infraorder Lemuriformes

As a group, the Lemuriformes are clearly distinguished from other living primates, including the tarsier, by a number of shared anatomical features. All have retained a moist rhinarium and well-developed organs of smell. Most also retain tactile whiskers on the face. These specialized, stiff hairs, highly sensitive to touch, can help an animal with weak sight or nocturnal[4] habits to get around in the forest canopy and undergrowth. They are rudimentary in other primates. The Lemuriformes also share two features used for grooming the fur: a claw on the second toe of the foot and a comblike specialization of the lower front teeth. Finally, all share a kind of placental membrane that is basically different from that of other primates. Apart from the tooth comb, which is a derived feature indicating the relatedness of the group, most of these features are ancestral characteristics. There is little doubt that the Lemuriformes have an independent evolutionary history going back to the earliest days of the primate order.

The Lemuriformes fall into two groups, with two very different evolutionary histories. The lemurs of Madagascar (see box) represent an extensive adaptive radiation that has evolved without competition from other primates. The lorisids (family Lorisidae) include the pottos and galagos (bush babies) of the African mainland and the lorises of tropical Asia. These are small tree dwellers that have evolved in a narrow econiche alongside the monkeys and apes that dominate the primate faunas of those regions. All are nocturnal animals that subsist on a mixed diet of fruit, tree gum, and small animals. By specializing in night hunting, they, like the tarsier, have filled an econiche left vacant by the strictly diurnal apes and Old World monkeys that share their habitat. Some hunt by stealthy, slow climbing; others are leapers, and pounce on their prey.

Lorisids are more solitary in their habits than is typical for primates. This independence may be related to their hunting tactics, which would not be easy to carry out in a group. All the nocturnal, solitary lorisids seem to keep in touch with their neighbors by leaving traces of scent along the arboreal pathways that they travel. Some have special scent glands that they use for this purpose; others use urine.

The object of this chapter has been to convey something of the great diversity of behavioral adaptations among the primates. Several general points should have emerged. First, it should now be clear that one cannot really speak of "the ape," "the monkey," or "the lemur." Each of

[4] A *nocturnal* animal is one that is active by night, in contrast to *diurnal* animals, which are active by day.

these groups represents one or more major adaptive radiations that have produced a wide array of special adaptive types. Second, these separate radiations have produced many instances of parallel evolution. Thus we can speak of adaptive types—such as "leaf eater," "brachiator," and so on—that cut across taxonomic boundaries. And we can recognize the distinctive anatomical features that arise from these various specialized types of behavior. Third, as we have hinted, some of these adaptive types are of particular relevance to the interpretation of human evolution.

In the following chapter, we shall focus on the relationship between structure and function in the various adaptive types seen among the primates. We will see how specific traits—characteristics of the skeleton, the muscles, the teeth, and even the social behavior of different primates—can be interpreted in the light of their ecological strategies, feeding habits, habitat preferences, postures, gaits, and so on.

Summary

Along with approximately 200 other species, the human species belongs to the order Primates. The study of the other primates is useful in understanding human evolution, for it allows us to define the qualities of our own species more precisely. Furthermore, the primitive features of nonhuman primates give us hints as to the behavior and anatomy of our prehuman ancestors, while their derived characteristics help us to interpret, by analogy, anatomical traits of fossil primates.

As an order, the primates are distinguished by a cluster of anatomical and behavioral characteristics. Two of these—five-fingered hands and five-toed feet, and a relatively unspecialized dentition—are ancestral features, retained from the nonprimate ancestor of the order. Other primate trademarks are derived characteristics, developed either by the ancestral primates or independently, through parallel evolution, by separate early lineages. These characteristics include:

1. Grasping hands and feet, with nails rather than claws.
2. A tendency to make vision the dominant sense and to reduce the importance of the other senses, especially smell.
3. A tendency to use the hand as an exploratory organ rather than solely for locomotion.
4. A tendency to reduce the number of offspring in a litter and to increase their period of dependency.
5. A tendency to increase the relative size of the brain, especially those parts involved with learning and association.
6. A tendency to increase the life span of the individual.
7. A tendency to live in permanent groups including individuals of all ages and both sexes.

The first three items on this list are thought to be adaptations to climbing; the last four are facets of a distinctive reproductive strategy.

The primates inhabit three major geographical regions: Africa-Asia, South and Central America, and Madagascar. Most live either in tropical rain forests or grasslands. The rain forest was probably the primates' ancestral home; their adaptations to climbing and their reproductive strategy were adaptive responses to the rain forest's lush tree growth and its unchanging climate, respectively. The grassland environment, with fewer trees and a seasonally variable climate, demands flexibility in feeding patterns and an ability to move easily on the ground—features that are found in all primate species (including the human) that have ventured out of the forest.

In the family Pongidae, we find our closest living primate relatives: the orangutan, the gorilla, and the chimpanzee. Of these, the chimpanzee is most closely related and most similar to humans. Primarily forest dwellers, chimpanzees subsist mainly on fruit. They live in troops of about thirty or forty, though they are often dispersed into smaller groups. From an anthropological point of view, a striking feature of the chimpanzee is that it shows, in very rudimentary form, several behaviors that were crucial to human evolution: tool use, hunting, and the sharing of meat.

The family Hylobatidae includes the gibbons. These small arboreal apes are remarkable for their elongated arms, a specialization for brachiation in their tropical forest habitat.

The family Cercopithecidae (Old World monkeys) includes the monkeys of Africa and Asia, which differ from the apes discussed above in a number of distinct physical characteristics. Most interesting anthropologically are the baboons, which, like the ancestors of the human species, made the transition from rain forest to savanna living.

The infraorder Platyrrhini (New World monkeys), though superficially similar to the Old World monkeys, constitute a separate and generally more primitive clade. However, their radiation has in some respects paralleled that of the Old World monkeys, and therefore their behavior helps us to reconstruct by analogy early stages in the evolution of the Old World group.

The Prosimii, less humanlike than the other primates, constitute a suborder apart from monkeys, apes, and humans. In their basic body plan some have changed little from the primitive primates of 50 million years ago and therefore they give us helpful insights into the early stages of primate evolution. Nevertheless, some forms, especially among the infraorder Lemuriformes, show close parallelisms with monkeys and apes.

Glossary

Anthropoidea a suborder of Primates that includes the monkeys and apes

bipedal standing and moving on two legs

brachiation a form of locomotion used by some primates in which the body is supported by the arms alone as the animal swings hand over hand

Catarrhini the infraorder that includes the apes and Old World monkeys

grassland a vegetation zone flanking the rain forests; its climate is more seasonal and tree cover less dense

Hominidae the family that includes humans; its members are commonly referred to as **hominids**

Hominoidea a superfamily consisting of the great apes, gibbons, and humans; commonly called **hominoids**

Homo the hominid genus that includes extinct human species (***H. habilis*** and ***H. erectus***) and modern humans (***H. sapiens***)

Homo sapiens the only living hominid species; in addition to modern humans, it includes neandertals and other archaic forms

Pan the genus of chimpanzees, consisting of two species, ***Pan troglodytes*** (the common chimpanzee) and ***Pan paniscus*** (the pygmy chimpanzee)

Papio the genus of common baboons, a group of Old World monkeys

Platyrrhini the infraorder of New World monkeys

Pongidae the family of great apes, including the chimpanzees, the gorilla, and the orangutan, as well as extinct species

prehensile tail a grasping tail that some New World monkeys have developed; used for support while hanging in the trees

Prosimii a suborder of Primates that includes primitive forms such as the lemurs, tarsiers, lorises, pottos, and galagos; its members are known as **prosimians**

rain forest a tropical vegetation zone marked by a hot, humid climate with little seasonal variation and a dense tree cover; the original primate habitat

rhinarium a patch of skin on the muzzle of an animal. The prosimians have a moist rhinarium, like a dog's nose, as part of their olfactory apparatus

savanna grassland with scattered trees

woodland grassland with extensive tree cover

Suggested Readings

ALTMANN, S. A., AND ALTMANN, J. 1971
Baboon Ecology: African Field Research. Chicago: University of Chicago Press. A classic example of the way in which field data are collected and analyzed.

DeVORE, I., AND EIMERL, S. 1965
The Primates. New York: Time-Life Books. An elementary introduction to the Primate order, with fine pictorial essays.

HRDY, S. B. 1977
The Langurs of Abu: Female and Male Strategies of Reproduction. Cambridge: Harvard University Press. A primatologist's account of her fieldwork and its findings.

NAPIER, J. R., AND NAPIER, P. H. 1967
A Handbook of Living Primates. New York: Academic Press. An authoritative and systematic presentation of the Primate order, genus by genus.

SCHALLER, G. B. 1964
The Year of the Gorilla. Chicago: University of Chicago Press. The account of a classic field study.

VAN LAWICK-GOODALL, J. 1967
My Friends the Wild Chimpanzees. Washington, D.C.: National Geographic Society.

——— 1971
In the Shadow of Man. Boston: Houghton Mifflin. Charming and well-illustrated accounts of the author's years among a band of East African chimpanzees.

Chapter Six

Primate Adaptations

The living primates have adopted a great variety of ecological strategies—ways of making a living in forests, woodlands, and savannas. We believe that some of their ways of life are quite similar to stages through which the human evolutionary line passed. Others represent different adaptations that help, by contrast, to define the human life style more exactly.

As we shall see in Chapter 7, primate fossils help us reconstruct the evolutionary history of the human lineage. Although fossils do not give us direct evidence about behavior and way of life, they do tell us something of the anatomy of extinct primates. Moreover, the geological setting in which the fossils are found can indicate the habitat in which the animals lived. Thus we have two kinds of evidence about fossil animals: anatomical evidence and ecological evidence. How do we deduce their behavior from this evidence? By studying the adaptive patterns of the living primates.

In living primates, we can examine all three factors—anatomy, habitat, and behavior—as an interactive complex. We can trace the functional links between anatomical features, behavioral traits, and ecological strategy. We can see, for example, how the gibbon is physically adapted for hanging from branches, and how its environment makes this behavior advantageous. Establishing such connections is the aim of this chapter. We can then extend them to extinct animals, using what we know about a fossil species' anatomy and habitat to draw conclusions about its probable behavior and ecological strategy. We tackle this task in Chapter 7, where we take up the study of fossil primates.

This picture illustrates the mobility of the spider monkey's elbow, wrist, and shoulders, and its habit of suspending the body from above by the hands. In this characteristic, the spider monkey *(Ateles)* most closely approximates the gibbons of the Old World. However, its prehensile tail, used as a fifth limb, is a platyrrhine peculiarity. *(T. S. Satyan/Black Star)*

Each section of this chapter deals with one of four functional systems:

1. The locomotor system: how the animal moves and positions itself in space
2. The feeding system: how and what the animal eats
3. The information system: how the animal receives information about its environment and processes that information
4. Social behavior: how the animal interacts with its fellows

Each of these systems, as the list indicates, is related to a particular aspect of survival. However, we must never lose sight of the fact that every animal is an integrated whole, made up of many parts that influence and interact with one another. What an animal learns is intimately related to its social interactions; its way of finding food is closely bound up with its ways of receiving information from its surroundings; and so on. Thus the division into four separate systems should be regarded only as an analytical convenience.

THE LOCOMOTOR SYSTEM

The locomotor system includes the anatomical structures associated with posture and locomotion—that is, the way an animal holds its body and moves about. The structures involved in these activities are the bones, joints, and muscles of the limbs and trunk. Thus, in any animal, the demands of posture and locomotion will be reflected most clearly in these parts of the anatomy. Lcomotor habits are, needless to say, a fundamental aspect of the ecological strategy of any species. And, in the history of primate evolution, such locomotor adaptations have been especially important. Almost every major adaptive radiation within the primate order has involved changes in locomotor patterns that opened up a new array of econiches.

Locomotor Repertoires and Locomotor Profiles

Compared with most other mammals, primates have a very wide repertoire of locomotor activities. If you watch a group of monkeys for any length of time, chances are that within an hour or so you will see them sit, stand, walk, run on all fours (quadrupedally); stand on two feet (bipedally); climb vertical trunks and branches; hang by one, two, three, or four limbs; swing by one or two arms; jump, hop, and leap. This wide locomotor repertoire is directly related, of course, to living in trees, especially in the tangled branches of the canopy.

Although most primates share this locomotor versatility, primate species vary widely in the degree to which they use and depend upon these different gaits and postures. Some species specialize in bipedal leaping, others in brachiating; still other species move mostly in the quadrupedal position. Thus we can say that, although locomotor repertoires of all primate species—the range of gaits and postures they use—are generally wide and rather similar to one another, their locomotor profiles—the relative importance of each of these various ways of moving—are quite different.

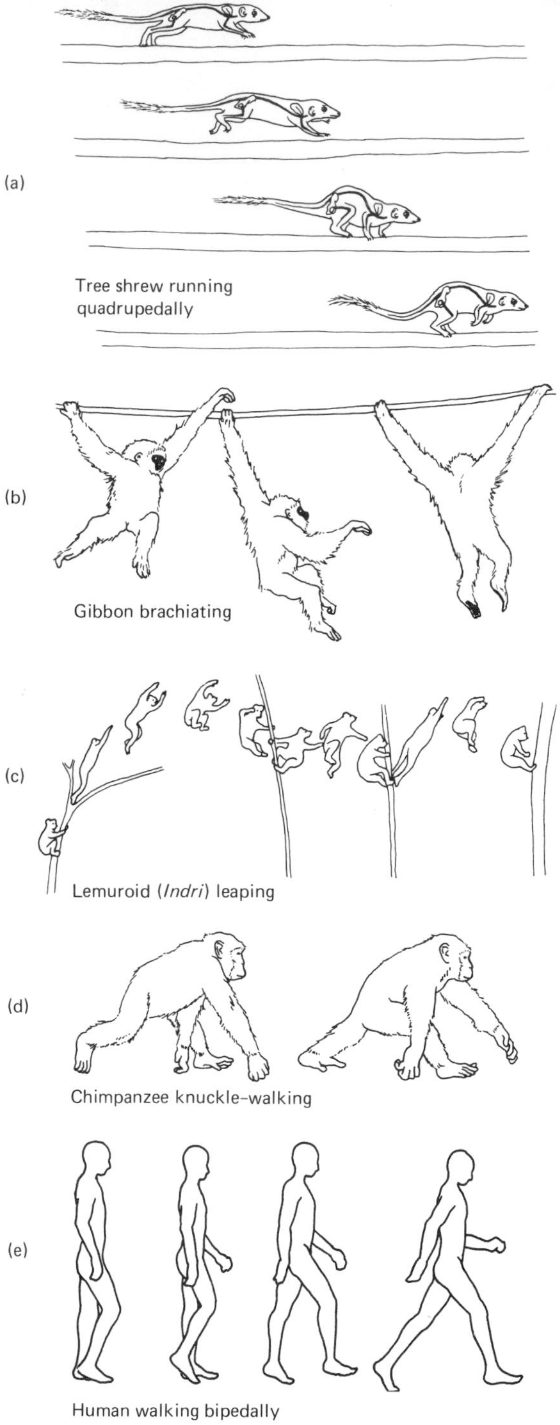

Figure 6-1. Primate locomotion. (a) branch running (arboreal quadrapedalism—tree shrew; (b) brachiation—gibbon; (c) leaping from one vertical support to another—*Indri*, a lemuriform primate; (d) knuckle-walking quadrapedalism—chimpanzee; (e) bipedalism—human being. *Biruta Akerbergs, after (a) F. A. Jenkins, 1974; (b) Ralph Morse and Animal Talent Scouts, Inc.; (c) J. R. Napier and A. C. Walker, 1967; (d) M. Hildebrand, 1968)*

Locomotion and Natural Selection

However an animal moves, it must be able to do so efficiently. Some of the penalties for locomotor inefficiency are quite obvious. Falling 100 feet from a forest tree or tripping over the toes while running away from a leopard would subtract substantially from Darwinian fitness. A more subtle but equally serious disadvantage of locomotor inefficiency would be the waste of energy in the everyday round of traveling and feeding. Field studies suggest that many wild primates operate on a very tight "energy budget," at least at some times of the year. That is to say, the amount of energy in the form of food that can be gathered and processed only just balances the cost in energy expended in traveling to find it, collecting it, and digesting it. The animal that expends the least energy in such activities will have the most left over to use in competing for mates or producing milk for young—or simply to store in the form of fat against future shortages.

Fitness is thus enhanced not only by the ability to move quickly and deftly but also by the ability to move with the least expenditure of energy. Consequently, natural selection will favor anatomical modifications that increase these locomotor virtues. Gibbons can brachiate efficiently because natural selection has endowed them with long fingers to hook over the branches. The quadrupedal baboons can run on the ground without tripping because natural selection has endowed them with short fingers and toes. And natural selection continually maintains the fit between the anatomy and locomotor profile of a species because the saving of energy that results is highly adaptive.

However, it should be emphasized again that evolution is opportunistic. Natural selection can only work on the variation at hand; it cannot design new structures from scratch. Any structure that has undergone evolutionary change will reflect old adaptations as well as new ones. Gorillas, for example, have become terrestrial quadrupeds, but their limbs and trunk still show characteristics inherited from their brachiating ancestors. Thus, to understand an animal's locomotor structures and behavior, we must take into account the stages through which it passed in the course of its evolution.

Primate Locomotor Adaptations

Fortunately, among the living primates we can observe a variety of locomotor adaptations, some more primitive, others more highly derived. In Figure 6-2, on p.116, typical primates are arranged in a series, each representing a stage of adaptation on which later stages are built. It is important to note that this diagram is *not* an evolutionary tree. The animals pictured in it are all modern. They are there simply as models, to suggest very approximately what the ancestral forms of these locomotor types may have looked like.

The diagram may look forbiddingly complex, but if you study it carefully, you will see that it tells a single story: the branching off of variations from the main theme of arboreal quadrupedalism. Starting at the top with *Ptilocercus* and moving down to *Saimiri* is the main line of generalized arboreal quadrupeds with broad locomotor repertoires. Branching off from this line are a number of pathways of specialization, each emphasizing a particular activity (leaping, brachiation, terrestrial quadrupedalism) from the arboreal quadrupeds' repertoires. Our concern is with the sequence marked by the arrows. This, we believe, is the series of locomotor stages leading to hominid bipedalism. For the purpose of describing these stages, we will look at how they are exemplified in the animal "models" pictured in Figure 6-2.

Stage 1: Primitive Arboreal Mammal—the Tree Shrew

The pen-tailed tree shrew (*Ptilocercus*), seen at the top of Figure 6-2, retains many features of the primitive mammalian form from which the primates are derived. It is a small, agile mammal that climbs, leaps, and scampers quadrupedally among the branches of the forest. It has a long and mobile back that, together with the muscular hindlimbs, provides most of the motive power in locomotion. It also has a tail that helps it

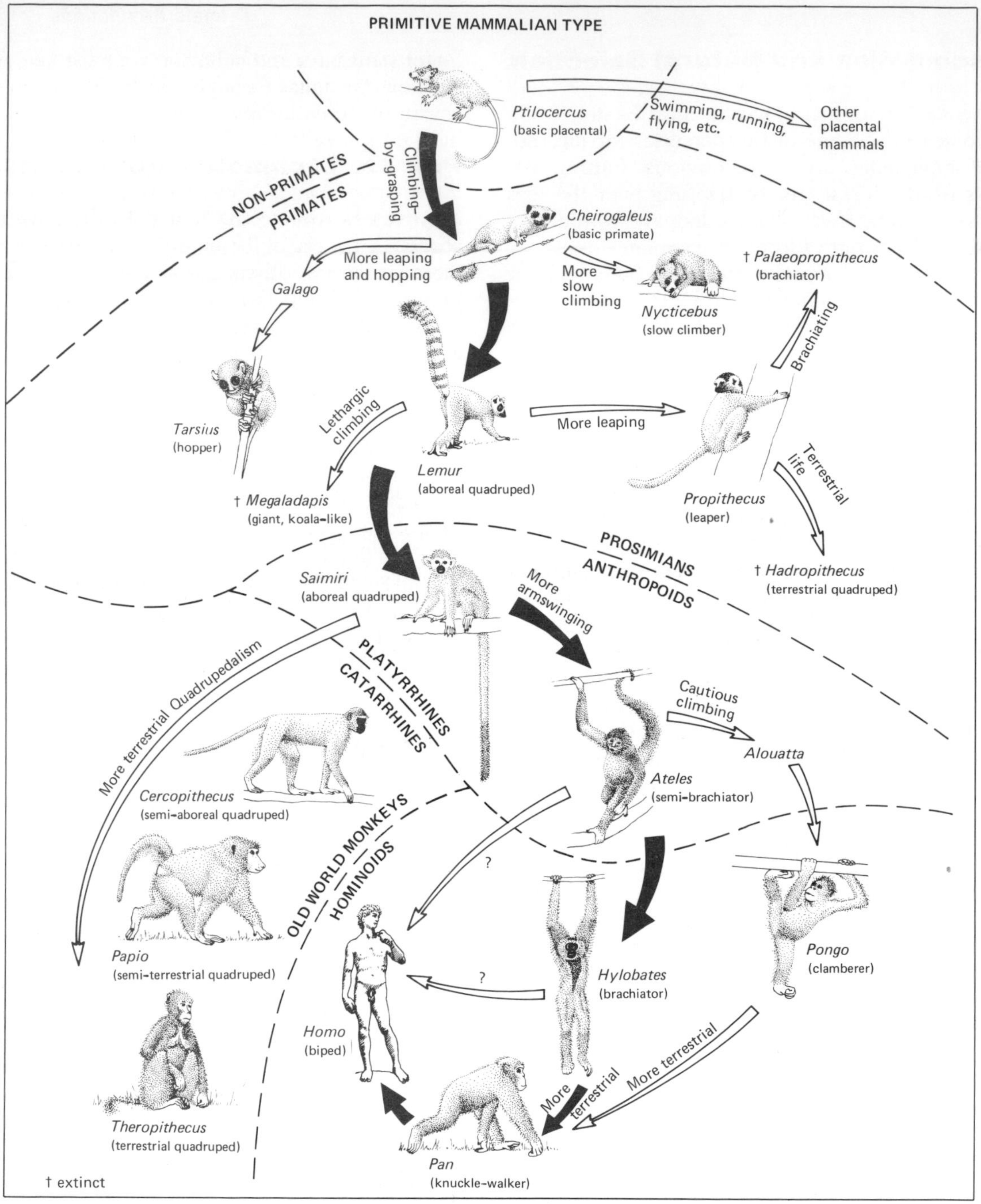

Figure 6-2. Major locomotor types among the primates. The "pathways" represent series of structural types that could give rise to each other. They do not represent real evolutionary lines, since all the animals represented are still alive or are recently extinct. The pathway by which human bipedalism probably arose is indicated by the large arrows. Note that the platyrrhine types include good "structural ancestors" for the major catarrhine types. (*Biruta Akerbergs*)

maintain balance when it runs along branches. The forelimb is somewhat shorter than the hindlimb and is used for exploration and manipulation as well as locomotion; it has a wide range of movement in all directions. The bones of the forearm are linked by mobile joints that allow it freedom of rotation. Both the hands and the feet have five clawed digits.

The tree shrew represents the kind of body plan that probably was ancestral to living placental[1] mammals, from whales to bats. In many of these mammalian lineages, the basic body plan has been greatly modified, with many bones "lost" or fused together, sacrificing locomotor flexibility for the sake of efficiency in a few specialized locomotor activities. (The rhinoceros, for example, has retained only three toes, the horse just one, while the whale has lost the entire hindlimb.) Among primates, the modifications of the primitive mammalian form have been comparatively small. In becoming tree-climbing specialists, primates have retained and improved upon the primitive ability to move the limbs, especially the forelimb, in all directions, and to use the forelimb to pull the body upward in climbing as well as to push it forward in quadrupedal walking and running.

Stage 2: Primitive Primate—the Dwarf Lemur

The primitive primate form is illustrated by the dwarf lemur (*Cheirogaleus*) of Madagascar. Although its general body form is very close to the primitive mammalian shape seen in the tree shrew, the hands and feet show the basic primate adaptation to *climbing by grasping.* This adaptation enables the animal to move freely and securely among small twigs and branches. The thumb and big toe are mobile and can be moved away from the other digits so that the hands and feet can encircle a branch. Flattened nails and finger pads have replaced claws on most digits.

An unspecialized primate form like the dwarf lemur, which can leap, run, and climb, could have given rise to the variety of more specialized locomotor types seen in the prosimians, including hoppers, such as the tarsiers, and slow climbers, such as the lorises. It is unlikely, however, that such specialized types played a part in our direct ancestry. Rather, our lineage probably progressed from the primitive primate form through an unspecialized quadrupedal type, such as the lemur.

Stage 3: Arboreal Quadrupeds—the Lemur and Squirrel Monkey

The ring-tailed lemur (*Lemur*) is predominantly a quadruped, with a locomotor profile similar to that of the dwarf lemur: its limbs are adapted to leaping, quadrupedal running, and climbing. It has retained the mobility of the shoulder, forearm, and wrist found in the more primitive forms. It is bigger, however, and has limbs that are relatively longer in proportion to its body size—necessary for a larger animal if it is to leap and climb as efficiently as a smaller one. These changed proportions can be seen as a further commitment to and specialization for life in the trees.

A very similar pattern is seen also in the primitive anthropoids, represented by the South American squirrel monkey (*Saimiri*). The squirrel monkey, in turn, represents a basic type that could easily have given rise to other locomotor types seen among monkeys and apes. Old World monkeys, for instance, have retained much the same general body form. Those that have become terrestrial have kept the same basic quadrupedal form and habits; they have made comparatively minor modifications in adapting to life on the ground.

Stage 4: Semi-brachiator—the Spider Monkey

The South American spider monkey (*Ateles*) represents an opposite trend—toward less quadrupedalism and more use of the forelimbs in suspension. The spider monkey can still move on

[1] Placental mammals nourish their unborn young through the placenta in the uterus. Marsupials, such as the kangaroo, by contrast, bear young that are relatively undeveloped, and suckle them for a long period—often in a pouch.

four feet and often does. But, whereas the more generalized arboreal quadrupeds swing beneath the branches only occasionally, the spider monkey favors brachiation as much as running and climbing. It also hangs from its arms while feeding.

This emphasis on suspension has produced a broadening of the chest, a shortening of the back, and a modification of the shape of the shoulder blade—for suspending the body weight, rather than supporting it from underneath. The arms and fingers are lengthened, the wrist, elbow, and shoulder more mobile than those of quadrupeds.

Stage 5: Classic Brachiator—the Gibbon

These features are carried still further in the gibbons (*Hylobates*), the classic brachiators. Gibbons never run quadrupedally along branches. Their habitual ways of moving are climbing (using all four limbs), running bipedally on the tops of branches, and—above all—swinging beneath the branches. The bones and muscles of the shoulder and forelimb are adapted to hanging. The arm is very long, with slender bones and powerful muscles. The hand is hooklike, with long, curved bones in the palm and fingers. The trunk is broader than it is deep. The tail, no longer used in balancing, has been lost.

A trend toward hanging beneath branches, rather than running quadrupedally on the top of them, has been acquired independently, through parallel evolution, in several different primate lineages. As we have seen, the gibbon, orangutan, and spider monkey—all of different families—are brachiators; so too were an apelike fossil primate, *Oreopithecus*, and the extinct lemur *Palaeopropithecus*. The advantage of this way of moving is that it allows comparatively large animals to feed safely among branches too small for them to balance upon—particularly in the outer canopy, where most fruit and new leaves grow. However, extreme adaptation for suspension by the arms has its costs as well. Most importantly, it effectively eliminates conventional quadrupedal locomotion from the animal's repertoire. In the specialized brachiator, the back is too short, the arms too long, and the joints too highly adapted for hanging to allow the animal to walk comfortably on all fours.

Stage 6: Knuckle-walking Ex-brachiator—the Chimpanzee

A species that has become quadrupedal again after passing through a brachiating stage bears in its anatomy the signs of its brachiating heritage. The chimpanzee (*Pan*) is such an animal. The brachiator structure of the trunk and limbs is retained, and the animal often hangs by its arms when it climbs in the trees to feed. On the ground, it usually moves by knuckle-walking. As adaptations to knuckle-walking, the wrist is strengthened and the knuckles are surfaced with pads of tough, hairless skin.

Why did the ancestors of chimpanzees and gorillas come down from the trees to become knuckle-walkers? We do not know for certain, but it seems likely that the answer is to be found in the nature of the African forests. The rain forests of Africa are less continuous than those of Southeast Asia and South America. At various times in the past, climatic changes have caused them to shrink and become relatively patchy, so that tree-dwelling animals must have been forced to move on the ground from one pocket of forest to another in search of food. In consequence, Africa now has fewer extreme arboreal specialists than Asia or South America; there are no pure brachiators, such as the gibbon, and no highly specialized tree dwellers, such as the sloths and kinkajous. Probably the change from brachiating to a semiterrestrial way of life in chimpanzees took place during one of the periodic shrinkages of the rain forests. It is not clear, however, just why knuckle-walking was the form of locomotion that evolved.

Stage 7: Habitual Biped—the Human Species

Homo sapiens is the only living primate characterized by *habitual bipedalism*—that is, the only one that normally stands and walks on two feet. There is some disagreement as to what locomotor type immediately preceded the bipedal hominid—a semi-brachiator, such as the spider monkey; a specialized brachiator, such as the orangutan or gibbon; or a knuckle-walking ex-brachiator, such as the chimpanzee. (We favor the last.) But there is little doubt that the hominid lineage passed through some kind of brachiating stage. The human trunk and forelimb are very similar in general shape and proportions to those of the brachiators. The human shoulder, however, has become less hunched than that of the brachiators, and the hand has been modified for manipulation rather than locomotion.

The major modifications associated with bipedalism in humans involve the lumbar vertebrae,[2] the pelvis, and especially the hindlimbs (Figure 6-3). Our hindlimb is one of our most specialized features. Other primates, as we have seen, have hindlimbs that allow them to walk upright but are better adapted for other forms of locomotion. By contrast, the human pelvis and hindlimb are specialized in such a way that they

[2] The vertebrae are the bones that compose the spinal column. The lumbar region of the spine is located in the lower back, just above the pelvis.

Figure 6-3. Comparison of *Homo sapiens* and *Pan troglodytes*. (a) skeleton of chimpanzee in bipedal position; (b) skeleton of modern human; (c) chimpanzee and human "bisected" and drawn to the same trunk length for comparison of limb proportions. It is the contrast in leg length that is largely responsible for the proportional difference between man and ape. Note also the hunched shoulders of the chimpanzee. (*Biruta Akerbergs*)

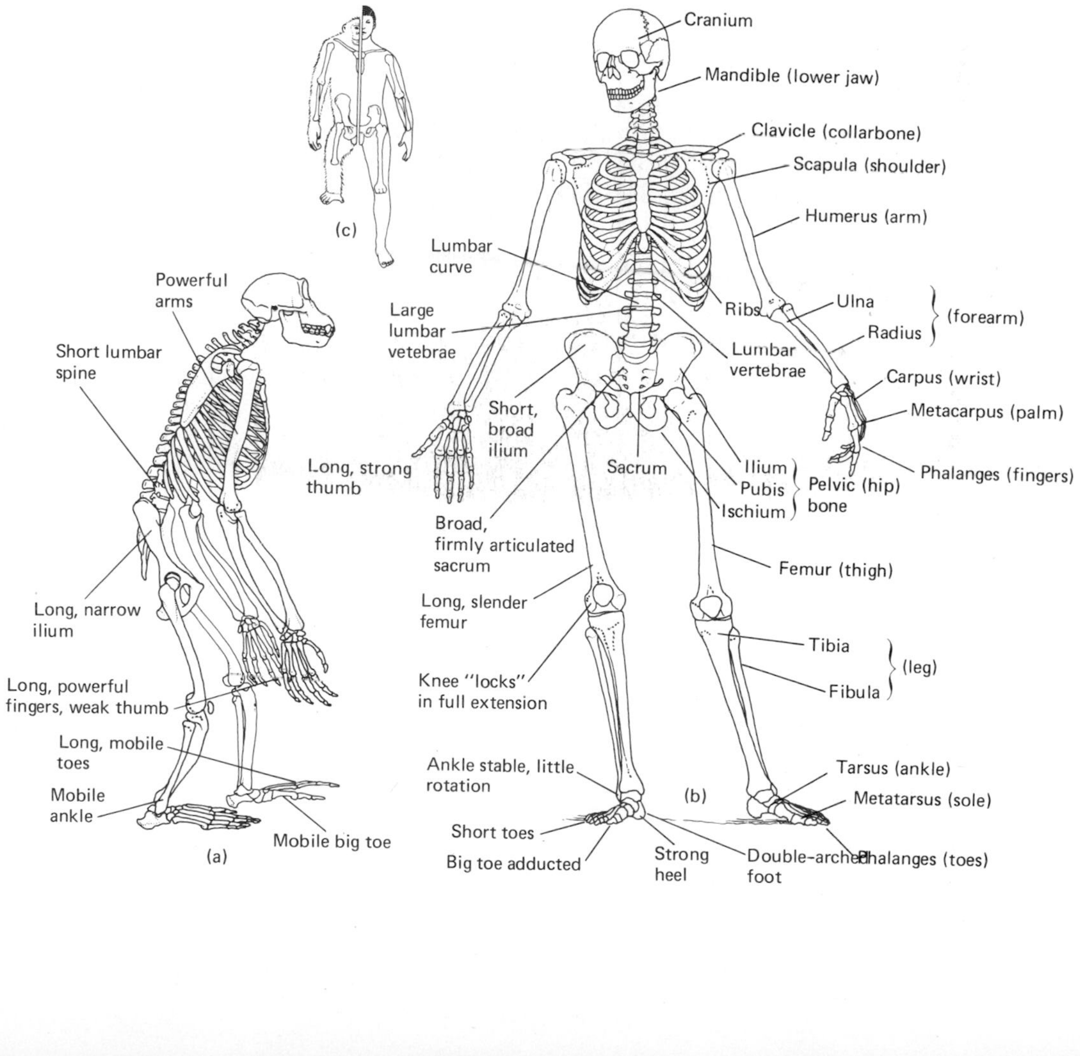

virtually rule out any form of locomotion other than bipedalism.

Most of the modifications in these anatomical structures have to do with weight distribution. In all quadrupedal walking, including knuckle-walking, the body weight is distributed between forelimbs and hindlimbs; the spine is more or less horizontal. In bipedal walking, on the other hand, the body weight is transmitted almost directly down through the nearly vertical spinal column to the pelvis, thigh, knee, lower leg, ankle, and foot. Accordingly, the bones and muscles of the lower half of the human body have developed adaptations to increased weight bearing. The lumbar vertebrae, for example, are larger and broader than those of quadrupedal primates.

Two structures deserve special comment: the foot and the pelvis. The foot, no longer used in climbing, has lost its grasping ability. The big toe has been brought into line with the long axis of the foot, and the size of the other toes has been reduced. At the same time, the foot has developed longitudinal and transverse arches that turn it into a springy dome, capable of absorbing the shock thrown upon it when the heel strikes the ground in walking.

The pelvis, which acts as a link between spine and hindlimb, shows equally important adaptations to bipedalism. The upper part of the pelvis (the ilium) is shortened. Consequently, the point where the ilium and the sacrum (the base of the vertebral column) are joined is brought closer to the acetabulum (the socket for the head of the femur, or thighbone). This more compact arrangement gives the upright body more stability than it could achieve with the elongated pelvis of the quadruped. At the same time the ilium is broadened. This ensures that, despite the shortening of the ilium, the sacrum does not obstruct the pelvic outlet, the "birth canal" through which the fetus must be delivered. The muscles around the hip joint are reorganized so that the pelvis does not tilt excessively from side to side during walking, when it is supported by only one hindlimb as the other one swings forward. The gluteus maximus, the large muscle of the buttock—used when rising into the standing position or walking over uneven ground—is increased in size and importance.

As we shall see, there is some dispute about why our ancestors developed this unique locomotor pattern. There is, however, no dispute about its enormous significance for human evolution. While the feet are doing the walking, the hands are free to carry, gather, throw, or signal. This great luxury has been one of the central factors in the elaboration of human culture.

THE FEEDING SYSTEM

An animal's feeding habits are perhaps the most basic aspect of its adaptive strategy. What it eats determines to a large extent its position in the ecosystem of which it is a part. Feeding behavior, in turn, determines how natural selection will act upon the anatomical structures used in food gathering and food processing. (Recall, for instance, the anatomical consequences of switching from browsing to grazing in the elephant lineage in Chapter 4.) Among primates, the anatomical structures that reflect most directly the animal's feeding habits are the lips, tongue, cheeks, teeth, jaws, jaw muscles, stomach, and intestines. Of these, we shall concentrate upon the teeth and jaws, which are often found as fossils, and the jaw muscles, which leave recognizable marks on bones and can thus be reconstructed from fossil evidence. The hand, which reflects the demands of both feeding and locomotion, will also be discussed in this section.

Primate Feeding Habits

Most primates are omnivorous. That is, they eat both vegetable food (usually fruit and leaves) and animal food (usually insects, sometimes meat). Adaptability in feeding habits is one of the distinctive features of the order. But all primate diets are not the same. Just as locomotor profiles vary, so do dietary profiles. There are specialized insect eaters, specialized leaf eaters, and those that eat a mixed diet based mainly upon fruit. Forest-dwelling fruit eaters feed largely on tough-skinned but juicy fruits. Species like baboons living in savannas eat a higher proportion of hard, dry fruits, like the seedpods of the acacia tree. Each of these foods makes different demands on the food-processing apparatus. Tough-skinned fruit, for example, must be opened or peeled, whereas leaves must be finely ground. Ultimately, through the action of natural selection, these demands will be reflected in the structure of the teeth, jaws, and the rest of the digestive system.

However, we must remember that primate diets always include a wide variety of foods, and only the most demanding and dominant will be reflected in tooth and jaw structure. Also, we must bear in mind that in the teeth, even more than in the locomotor system, new adaptations can be superimposed on existing plans. Each major group of primates shows common dental features that tell us more about their phyletic relationship than about their diet. Only when comparing close relatives can we confidently interpret dental differences as adaptations to the functional demands of different diets.

The Teeth, Jaws, and Chewing Muscles

The teeth can be divided into four major groups: incisors, canines, premolars, and molars (Figure 6-4). The incisors are generally used to seize food and, along with the hands, are used in its initial preparation. The canines were originally part of the seizing-holding apparatus, and still have that function in some primates. In many others, especially in monkeys like the baboon, the canines have been developed for fighting and threatening rather than for eating. The premolars and molars are used in chewing, grinding, and shear-

Figure 6-4. (a) Upper dentition of the mangabey, a fruit-eating cercopithecoid monkey. The incisors are large for biting through the rind of fruit, while the molars are relatively small. (b) A comparison of the molars of the galago, an insect eater (above) with those of the dwarf lemur, a fruit eater. Specialized insect eaters have molars with high, pointed cusps connected by sharp slicing crests in a triangular pattern. Fruit and leaf eaters have flatter, broader molars with more surface area and four cusps rather than three. ((a) *Biruta Akerbergs;* (b) *Robert Frank*)

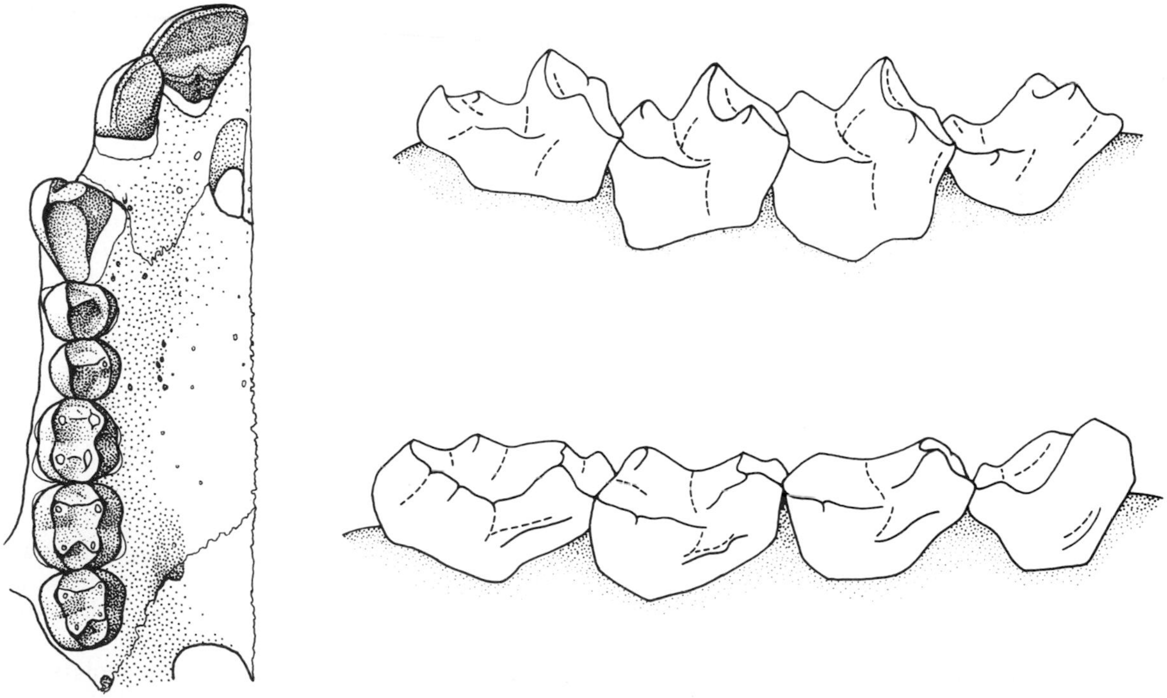

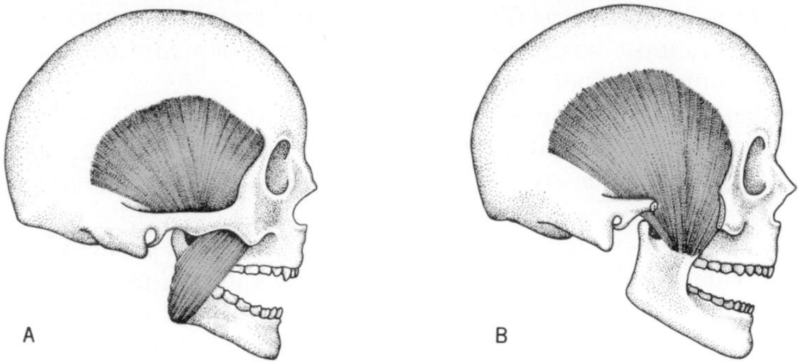

Figure 6-5. Diagram of the major masticating (chewing) muscles in humans. The masseter, shown in (a), runs from the zygomatic arch (cheekbone) to the angle of the mandible. In (b) the zygomatic arch and masseter have been removed to show the attachments of the temporal muscle to the mandible and skull wall. *(Biruta Akerbergs)*

ing the food, to break it down for swallowing. Hence they are generally stockier than the incisors and canines, and their crowns have peaks, called *cusps*, often with ridges, or *crests*, running between them.

In food processing, the lower teeth, set in the mandible (lower jaw), work against the upper teeth, set in the maxilla and premaxilla (the bones of the upper jaw). These movements of the mandible are produced by the chewing muscles (also called muscles of mastication)—the temporal muscle and the masseter muscle (Figure 6-5)—which run from the skull to the mandible. In biting with the incisors, both sides of the jaw are pulled up and slightly backward. In chewing, the mandible is swung from side to side and slightly up and down, as upper and lower molars grind across each other. (The reader can check these different movements and functions by eating an apple.)

Primate Feeding Adaptations

Just as we can distinguish locomotor types, each with its own particular adaptations of the limbs and pelvis, so we can describe dietary specializations, each associated with particular adaptations of the teeth and jaws. (Remember, though, that in doing so we are talking about differences in dietary emphasis—not *absolute* differences.)

Primates such as the tarsier that eat large numbers of insects have sharp, pointed incisors and canines for seizing their prey. Their upper molars have triangular crowns, with a pointed cusp at each corner of the triangle, and sharp crests for slicing the tough skins of insects into digestible pieces. Fruit eaters, such as the gibbon, must do less shearing but more crushing than insect eaters. Thus their molars have a fourth cusp, greater surface area, and a flatter platform for crushing. Fruit eating also requires a mechanism in the front of the mouth to bite through thick rinds. Among the monkeys and apes, habitual fruit eaters have broad, chisel-like incisors, and strong, backward-sloping temporal muscles to provide a powerful bite.

Unlike fruit, leaves are tough and difficult to digest, so they must be shredded as much as possible before swallowing. The molars of habitual leaf eaters, such as the gorilla and *Colobus* monkey, are broad, like those of the fruit eaters, but they also have sharp crests to chop the leaves to a fine pulp. The incisors tend to be comparatively small, as they are used only to pluck leaves from twigs. Since leaves are low in nutritional value relative to their bulk, the leaf eaters spend most of their day chewing. Hence their chewing muscles are thick and strong, with well-marked attachments on the jaws.

The adaptations of the grass-eating gelada are of special interest, since some of them are paralleled in the earliest hominids. The incisors are quite small, for they are not used to pluck grass; this is done by the hands. But the molars and premolars are large and high-crowned, with many complex folds of enamel. As the crowns wear down, fresh enamel edges are formed, providing a constantly self-renewing set of tiny mincing blades. This adaptation is common in grass-eating animals (such as sheep and kangaroos) but among living primates is confined to the gelada. The masseters of the gelada are powerful, and the temporals are large and set forward, in contrast to the backward-sloping temporal muscles of fruit eaters. This specialization adds power where the gelada needs it—in the crushing and grinding molars and premolars.

The Modern Human Chewing Apparatus

Finally, a word about the chewing apparatus of modern humans. Human canines, not used for fighting, are not projecting and are shaped much like incisors. The remaining teeth resemble those of apes. The molars, in particular, are very like those of a chimpanzee in shape—additional confirmation of our close kinship. Compared with the size of the body they nourish, however, the jaws, teeth, and chewing muscles of modern humans are smaller and weaker than those of apes, and the third molars ("wisdom teeth") often fail to erupt. These trends are carried to an extreme in industrialized Western people, where congenitally missing and misshapen teeth are commonplace, to the great profit of orthodontists. The weakening of the human chewing apparatus has been attributed to the use of cutting tools, grindstones, cooking, and other technological aids to take over the food-preparing functions of the teeth. According to this plausible theory, the human chewing apparatus is simply degenerating, as is the evolutionary rule for structures that have lost their functional importance.

The Hand

We have already mentioned some features of the primate hand in relation to its function in locomotion. Here we consider its other major function—manipulation. Primate hands are used for many manipulative purposes besides picking up and preparing food—for grooming the fur, digging, picking things apart, and investigating them. In other mammals, many of these tasks are performed by the snout and teeth. The primate trend, as we have seen, has been to rely more on the hand and less on the teeth and snout for investigation and manipulation.

The grasping hand, originally developed for small branch climbing, was the preadaptation that made this trend possible. In prosimians, the hand grasp remained a primitive grab: the object to be held is simply pressed against the palm by the fingers and thumb. This type of grasp, called the *power grip*, is retained in the hominoids and

A gorilla (*Gorilla gorilla*) in a zoo relieves his boredom by playing with a piece of straw. This shows the delicate precision grip between index finger and thumb characteristic of the catarrhine primates' anatomical specializations of the hand and their fine coordination between hand and eye. (*Ron Garrison/San Diego Zoo*)

An adult male gelada baboon. The deep, heavy jaws and short, dexterous fingers are adaptations to the species' diet of small-sized vegetable foods such as grass roots. The patch of bare skin on the chest is another peculiarity of the species. *(S. Nagendra/Rapho/Photo Researchers)*

monkeys, but most of them also have a *precision grip,* in which the pad of the thumb is pressed against the pad of the index finger. This grip, used for finer manipulation, is made possible by modifications of the hand that allow the pad of the thumb to be rotated so that it is opposed to the index finger. The precision grip also depends upon a more sophisticated brain. The finely tuned motor control of the hand in higher primates permits even the clumsy-looking hands of the gorilla to perform delicate manipulatory tasks.

The precision grip is used by higher primates in a variety of situations. Monkeys use it to pick apart leaf buds and bark as they search for insects. Chimpanzees use it to shape and handle their termiting sticks. But the most regular and consistent use of the precision grip in nonhuman primates is in small-object feeding—picking up morsels, such as seeds or grass blades, one by one, from the ground or from a bush or twig. All baboons are adept at this, but the gelada, the expert small-object feeder, shows special adaptations for it. In the gelada hand, the fingers are short, making it easy to bring thumb and index finger together (Figure 6-6).

THE INFORMATION SYSTEM: THE SPECIAL SENSES AND THE BRAIN

Primates, like other animals, rely on a constant flow of information from their environment. This information is gathered through the special senses—vision, smell, taste, hearing, and touch—and transmitted by the nervous system to the brain. There, it is processed, stored, and used as a basis for future actions on the part of the animal.

We have already mentioned, in Chapter 5, three distinctive trends of the primate information system. First, in gathering information, primates tend to rely heavily on a well-developed visual sense and to deemphasize the sense of smell, on which many other mammals depend for information. Second, they tend to use the hand rather than the muzzle and teeth for investigating and manipulating, with the result that the receptors for the sense of touch are localized in the hand rather than on the muzzle. Third, the primate brain is both larger and more sophisticated than that of most other mammals. Differences in the information systems of living primates concern mainly the degree to which these trends have been emphasized.

The Senses

In lemurs, the balance among the senses is more primitive. Lemurs have keen sight, with some species adapted to nocturnal vision and others to daylight. But, unlike other primates, they still rely heavily on the sense of smell. They retain a large and complex set of olfactory (scent-sensi-

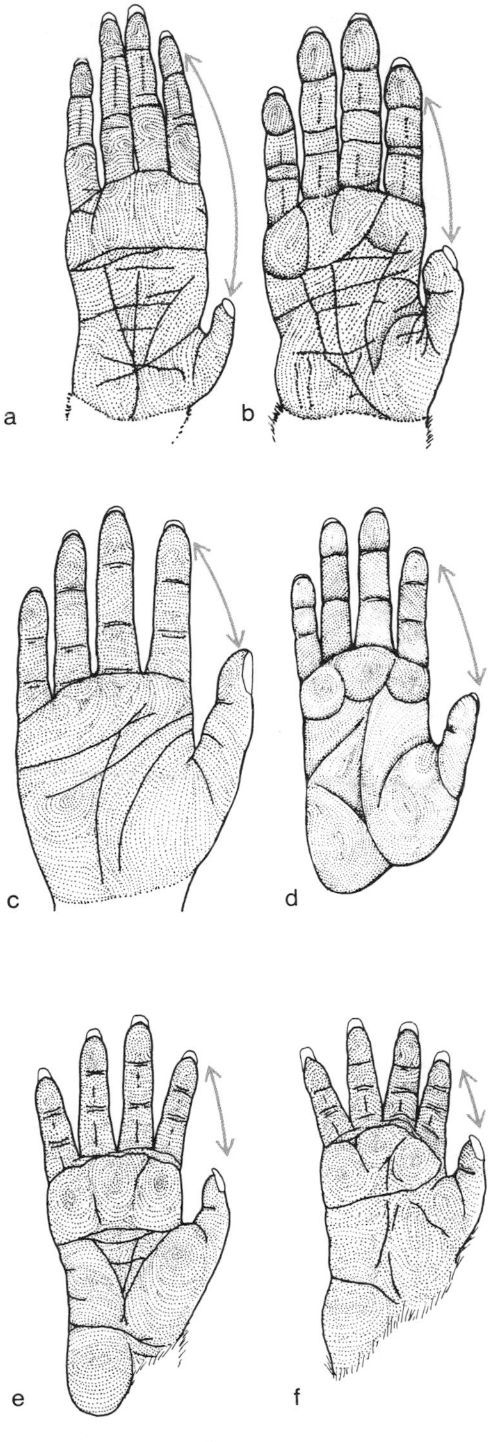

tive) membranes in the nose and, as we saw in Chapter 5, also have a moist rhinarium ("dog's nose") that enhances their sense of smell. They reach out, touch, and pick up objects with the hands, but the sense of touch is also retained in the whiskers on the muzzle.

In anthropoids, the visual sense is dominant. The olfactory apparatus is reduced in size and complexity, the nasal passages are shrunken back into the face, and the naked rhinarium has become a strip of dry, haired skin continuous with that of the face. As the nasal passages have receded, the eyes have moved to the front of the skull, looking more directly forward. At the same time, they have become more completely isolated from the region in which the powerful temporal (chewing) muscle lies (Figure 6-7, p. 126). This isolation is important for acute vision since contraction of the temporal muscle can cause minor displacement of the eyeball and thus distort the image.

The Brain

The brains of primates, compared with those of most other mammals, are large in proportion to their bodies and show extensive development of the *cerebral cortex*. This is the thick rind of "gray matter" that constitutes the outer layer of the brain and includes regions devoted to the so-called higher mental functions—memory, association, learning, reason, and so forth. In addition, the brain's proportions reflect the trends toward reliance on vision rather than smell and toward skilled use of the hand. The proportions vary, however, for not all primates manifest these trends to the same degree. In lemurs, for instance, the parts of the brain receiving and

Figure 6-6. Parallelism in the hands of hominids (a-c) and cercopithecoids (d-f). The hands of the highly arboreal orangutan (a) and Colobus monkey (d) are well adapted for climbing. Hands of semiterrestrials are shown in (b), chimpanzee, and (e) baboon, while (c), human, and (f), Gelada baboon, are hands of nonclimbers. Note that the difference in length between thumb and index fingers of (c) and (f) is less, refining the precision grip. *(Biruta Akerbergs, Robert Frank)*

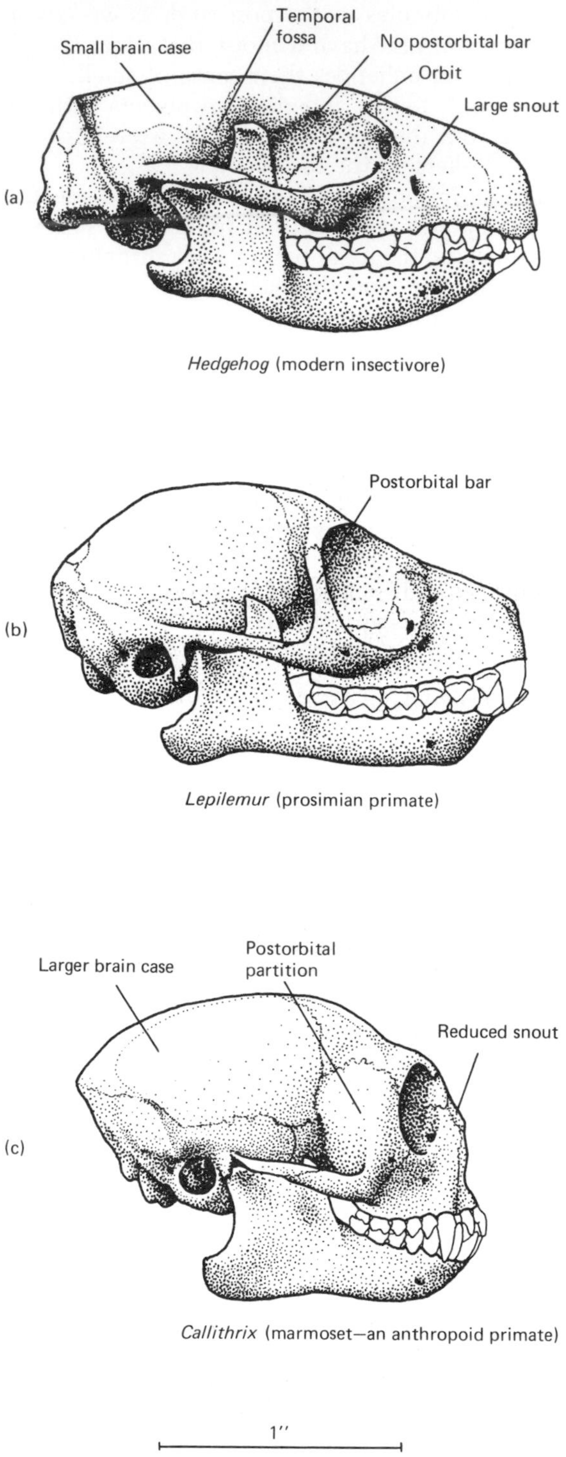

processing olfactory information are still comparatively large. In anthropoids, the areas receiving visual stimuli and information from tactile receptors in the hand are comparatively larger and more elaborate.

Development of Association Areas

While evolutionary changes in the sensory centers of the cerebral cortex are important, probably even more important are changes in those areas of the cerebral cortex that do not have an immediate simple relationship to sensory input. These are the so-called *association areas* of the brain. They are concerned with such functions as memory, storage of information, comparison of new experiences with those of the past, and the integration of information and memories from different sensory channels. When we speak of "brain" expansion as a primate trend, it is largely these areas that we are referring to, for these are the areas where most of the increase has taken place.

As Figure 6-8 indicates, the living primates represent four main grades of cortical expansion. Most primitive, as usual, are the prosimians. The Old World and New World monkeys represent the next level. The apes, especially the Pongidae, are more advanced still. Finally, the human species stands quite alone in the highest grade. As you can see in Figure 6-8, the smooth surface of the brain of a primitive prosimian contrasts strikingly with the furrowed surface of the human brain, which looks somewhat like a piece of fabric stuffed into a bottle. The human cerebral cortex has doubled back into numerous folds

Figure 6-7. Three stages in the evolution of the primate skull. The hedgehog, a nonprimate mammal, retains many primitive skull features; small braincase, large snout, and no separation of the orbit of the eye from the temporal fossa, where the temporal (chewing) muscles are located. The prosimian has a somewhat expanded braincase and a bony postorbital bar. In the anthropoid, the braincase is still larger, the snout is reduced, and the orbits face forward, protected by a complete postorbital partition. (*Biruta Akerbergs*)

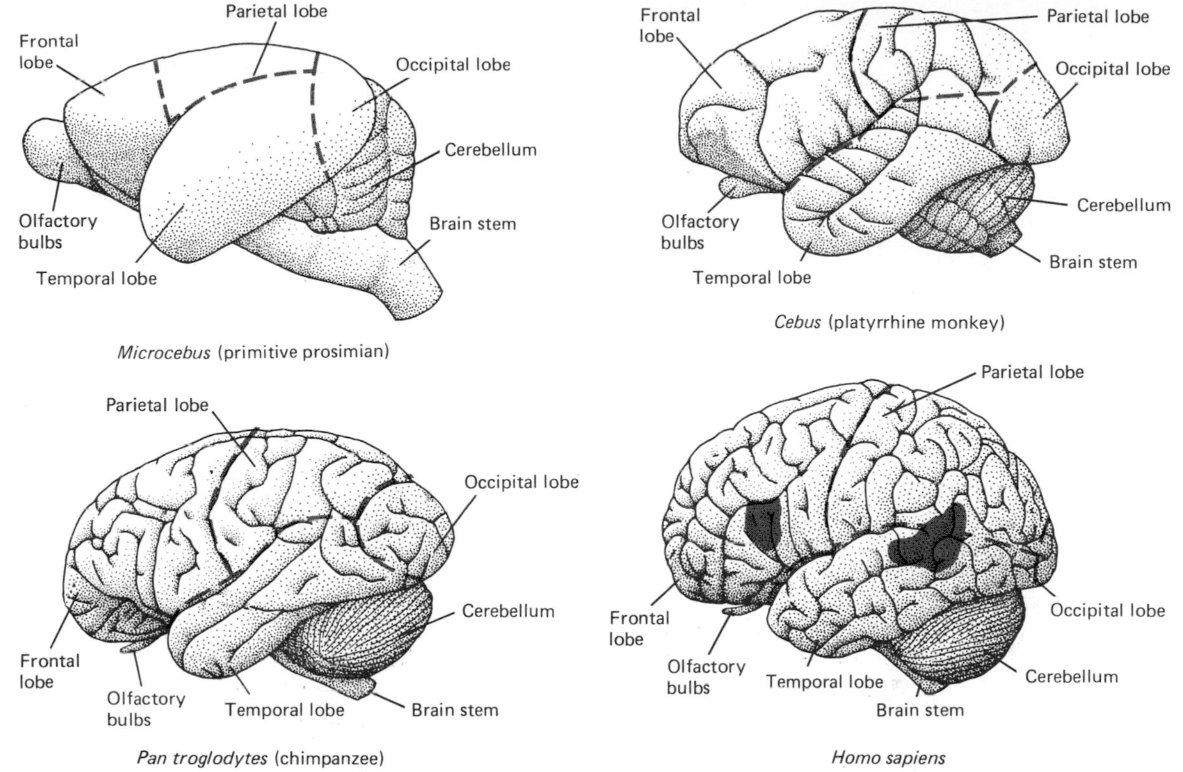

Figure 6-8. Brains of some primates (facing left), drawn to the same overall scale. Note (1) the increase in relative size and folding of the temporal, parietal, occipital, and frontal lobes, and (2) the reduction of the olfactory bulbs, concerned with receiving information about scent, in the series a–d. (*Biruta Akerbergs*)

as it has expanded relative to the volume of the deeper parts of the brain.

When the human brain is compared with those of other primates, it becomes clear that not all parts of the cerebral cortex have expanded at the same rate. There are two particular areas—the frontal association area and the parietal association area—that have expanded much more than the others. Thus it is reasonable to assume that these two parts of the brain control functions that are most characteristically human: memory, reason, imagination, speech, and so on.

Research on the human brain seems to support this assumption. In humans, the function of the frontal lobes seems to be related to the ability to focus sustained attention on a long-term goal, to screen out distracting stimuli, and to inhibit conflicting impulses. Without such control, some of the most characteristic activities of humans would be impossible—spending days in pursuit of a wounded game animal, for instance, or years in planning an advantageous business venture, or suppressing the impulse to eat food where one finds it and instead bringing it back to add to the communal pot.

Great expansion has also taken place in the parietal association area. (In Figure 6-8, compare the chimpanzee parietal lobe to the human.) This area seems to be concerned primarily with integrating information already "digested" by the primary association areas. Here, information received by one sensory pathway is linked up with memories gathered by other pathways. Both the ability to learn and use spoken language and the

Animals and Language

Anthropologists have long regarded language as a human trademark—a characteristic that truly sets our species apart from other animals. Furthermore, it is widely believed that this unique behavioral characteristic reflects certain unique mental characteristics: we alone talk because we alone have the intellectual capacity to do so. In the words of the eminent linguist Noam Chomsky, one of the major proponents of this view, language is based on "distinctive qualities of mind that are, so far as we know, unique to man" (1972:100).

While there is no denying that humans are unique in the ease with which they learn and use language, it seems that other animals share with us at least some of those "distinctive qualities of mind" that make language possible. In recent years a number of scientists have come to believe that nonhuman species—especially our close relatives the African apes—have some capacity for language. One way to test this question is to put an ape through language training. And that is what several researchers have done.

Experiments in teaching chimpanzees to *speak*—to use vocal language—have never been successful. One chimp was taught to understand about 100 words, but she herself made no attempt to speak. A second chimp, Viki, actually learned to speak in a hoarse whisper, but after three years of training she had a vocabulary of only four words: "mama," "papa," "cup," and "up." In the late sixties, two psychologists, Allen and Beatrice Gardner (1969), tried a different approach. Rather than try to make a chimpanzee do something it was not accustomed (and perhaps not equipped) to do, they would train the chimpanzee to do something that it did easily and naturally—that is, gesture. And so instead of teaching their test chimp, Washoe, to speak, they taught her American Sign Language, the standard hand signs of the deaf.

The Gardners converted their garage into a headquarters for Washoe, and there she lived for four years, surrounded by teachers who played with her during most of her waking hours, using only American Sign Language. (No spoken language was used in her presence, lest she confuse the two modes of communication.) In those four years she made astounding progress. She learned to use 130 signs, and showed that she could manipulate them creatively. For example, having learned the signal "more" to get the Gardners to resume a pillow-fight, she spontaneously used the same signal when she wanted a second helping at dinner. She also combined signals to make new words. For instance, not knowing the signal for duck, she dubbed it "water bird." In addition, Washoe learned how to combine words in grammatical order, and she seemed to have an understanding of concepts. Once, for example, she was being taught by a new assistant who was just learning American Sign Language and was having some difficulty understanding Washoe's signs. Washoe, sensing the problem, slowed down her signing to make it easier for the woman. (The woman later pointed out that there were few experiences as humiliating as having a chimpanzee deliberately slow down its language for your sake.) Washoe seemed, in other words, to understand the use and power of language.

Another chimpanzee project based on American Sign Language is that of psychologist Herbert Terrace. In playful reference to Noam Chomsky, Terrace named his test chimp Nim Chimpsky. After four years Nim had acquired a vocabulary of 128 signs and, Terrace believes, the ability to combine them spontaneously into sentences. One strikingly human skill that Nim learned was the ability to express emotions through the use of words. A hot-tempered animal, he had frequently encountered disapproval for aggressive acts such as biting. Gradually he learned, when angry, to control his impulse to bite and instead to make the sign "bite" and go on making it until his anger subsided.

American Sign Language is not the only language that has been used in such projects. At the Yerkes Regional Primate Center in Atlanta, another chimpanzee, Lana, has been taught to communicate via an electronic computer. The

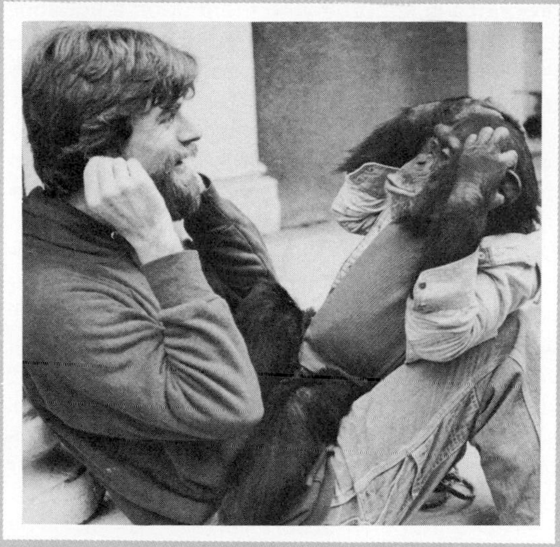

Nim Chimpsky mimics his teacher—an exercise designed to help him learn the American Sign Language, by which he communicates. *(Susan Kuklin/Photo Researchers)*

keyboard of the computer is equipped with about a hundred picture-symbols that Lana has been taught to associate with certain meanings. (Some of the symbols are stylized pictures of their meanings. For example, a circle on top of a triangle, looking something like a man's head and shoulders, represents Lana's teacher.) By pressing the keys, Lana can make the symbols line up in a row on a special display panel, and in this way she can construct sentences. Her teacher, Timothy Gill, has a corresponding keyboard. Thus, by pressing keys and reading off one another's messages, the two of them can carry on fairly lengthy conversations.

One novel aspect of Lana's language is that it is completely grammatical. The computer services all her needs—dispensing food, milk, and juice, opening the window, even playing records for her—but only if she expresses her requests grammatically, with the words in proper order and with a period at the end. (She must also express them politely. All requests must begin with "please.") The grammatical strictness of Lana's training has allowed her to explore the different meanings that words produce when combined in different ways. When Gill writes on the computer, "Tim groom Lana?" and Lana answers "yes," Gill begins parting and combing Lana's fur. This done, Gill reverses the word order, writing "Lana groom Tim?" and Lana hurries over to reverse the favor, cleaning the sleep out of Gill's eyes.

Lana has proved an extremely active learner. Like a human child, she asks the names of things and inquires how they work. One week when she was working on the preposition "in," Gill walked into the room and saw on the display panel the request "You put milk in—." She did not know the name for the milk-dispenser on her machine. Gill asked her, "What give milk?" Lana looked perplexed, and Gill pointed to the machine. She rushed to the keyboard and tapped out "Machine give milk." But apparently she was not completely satisfied with this explanation. Gill left the room briefly; when he came back, he saw on the display panel the question: "You put milk in machine?"

One of the most successful of the recent language experiments involved a female gorilla named Koko. At the age of one, Koko was borrowed from the San Francisco Zoo by Penny Patterson, a graduate student in psychology at Stanford. Patterson wanted to find out whether the achievements of chimps such as Washoe could be duplicated with a gorilla. Koko proved equal to the test. At age four she was able to use 251 different signs in a single hour, and at the age of six, she had a vocabulary of between 300 and 400 signs. After five years of training in American Sign Language, she scored between 80 and 90 (the equivalent of a 5-year-old child) on an IQ test for nonreading children.

Like Washoe, Koko combines words creatively to name new objects. A zebra she called "white tiger"; a mask, "eye hat"; a ring, "finger bracelet"; a Pinocchio doll, "elephant baby;" she is also particularly adept at expressing her feelings. Whenever Patterson was

Psychologist Penny Patterson working with Koko.
(Photo by The New York Times)

late arriving at Koko's trailer, the gorilla would sign "sad." On other mornings, when asked how she felt, she would report herself "happy" or sign "I feel good." This is the first clear instance of emotional self-awareness on the part of a nonhuman primate. Koko has also shown herself rather subtle in her emotions, and in the expression of them. Once, when asked by a reporter whether she liked Patterson or Patterson's assistant better, Koko looked first at Patterson, then at the assistant, then back at Patterson, then back at the assistant, and replied, "Bad question."

Whether this was tact or ambivalence speaking, the response seems to indicate a rather intricate reasoning process. Likewise, Lana's persistence in trying to find out where her milk came from suggests a surprising perceptiveness. Perhaps within the next few decades we will have to revise our estimate of ape intelligence. According to Duane Rumbaugh, director of the Lana project, apes have all the advanced powers of reasoning that we associate with language: "All we do in these language programs is to agree with them upon a vocabulary" (Hayes, 1977, p. 76). As for their linguistic ability, the ape-trainers contend that it differs from ours in degree but not in kind.

Nevertheless, one cannot say that these apes use "language" in a fully human sense. In the first place, unlike spoken languages, the languages that the test apes learned, American Sign Language and Lana's set of graphic symbols, were to some extent mimetic—the symbols imitated the things they stood for. We still do not know whether apes have the intellectual capacity to handle a totally open and arbitrary language such as our own. Second, there is still some question as to whether the sentences produced by the test apes were put together spontaneously or simply reproduced by rote. As Nim's trainer, Herbert Terrace, put it: "The unanswered question is: How much is expansion of the teacher's sentences and how much is real conversation?" (Rosenthal, 1977, p. 35). Third, even if ape language differs from human language only in degree, the degree is vast. While Lana, for example, may have produced some remarkable sentences, it should also be pointed out that 90 percent of her sentences consist of the following: "You give juice to Lana in cup." In short, the glimmerings of humanlike reasoning in the apes' verbalizations are intriguing, but they are also rare. Finally, it must be stressed that teaching language to an ape requires immense effort under highly artificial conditions, whereas human children learn it naturally, without training. Likewise, by dint of long training, a human being might be taught to brachiate about half as successfully as a gibbon, but baby gibbons pick up this skill automatically. This, of course, is the result of evolutionary change. Language has become as necessary for humans as brachiation is for gibbons. Selection in the human line favored a brain and a vocal tract adapted to spoken language. Among the apes, the faculties necessary for language have remained relatively undeveloped—a hint of the primitive condition from which the human adaptation evolved.

capacity for abstract thought depend on this ability to integrate information from different sensory channels.

Endocranial Casts and Brain Structure

To what degree are these differences in brain structure and function reflected in the structure of the skull? To anyone trying to interpret the fossil evidence for human evolution, this is an extremely important question. Since the brain itself does not fossilize, the skull is the only evidence we have of the brain of an extinct animal.

Given a fairly complete skull, an *endocranial cast*—a cast of the internal surface of the brain cavity—can often be made. This will give quite a good estimate of brain size and will show some of the more striking external features of the brain. We can tell, for instance, that early primates had large olfactory bulbs. Since the olfactory bulb is the receiver of "smell" information, this is additional evidence that the sense of smell has been markedly deemphasized in the course of primate evolution.

But some of the most important brain functions are products not of surface structures but of structures buried deep in the interior of the brain, or of subtle connective pathways among different structures. An endocranial cast can tell us nothing of these. For instance, the capacity to talk—to use a system of sound-symbols (words) to convey one's thoughts to another—is not located in any particular part of the cortex. Certain areas critical to speech have been identified, but they are distributed in different cortical regions. Hence, there is no way of examining the endocranial cast of a fossil skull and deducing from its convolutions whether its owner could talk.

Figure 6-9. Relative life spans and maturation rates of primates. *(After J. R. Napier and P. H. Napier, 1967)*

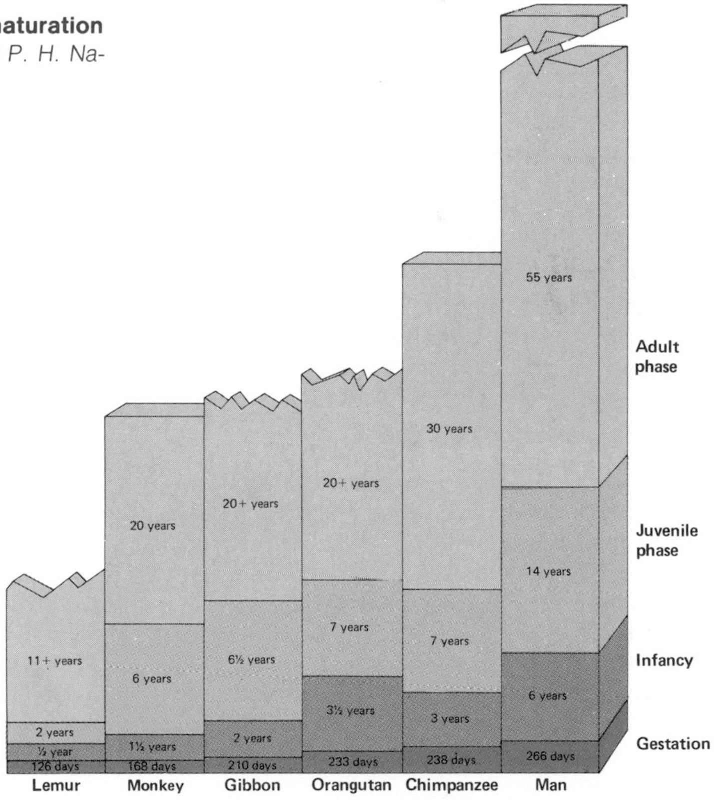

Brain Complexity and Delayed Maturation

Brain complexity in primates is related to their lengthy period of immaturity. Compared with other mammals of their size, primates spend a long time in the womb, a long time nursing, and a very long time maturing. In general, the length of the growth period in primates corresponds to the complexity of their brains (Figure 6-9). During this period of immaturity, the young primate is learning—filling the memory banks of its capacious brain with the techniques of survival, learning the behaviors and establishing the inhibitions necessary for social life. It is to this aspect of primate adaptation that we turn in the next section.

As we mentioned in Chapter 5, it is possible that primates initially embarked on a trend toward dominance of the visual sense as part of a rather narrow adaptive pattern—stalking insects in the forest canopy. Similarly, the trend toward a long period of immaturity, which is correlated with a brain capable of absorbing and integrating complex patterns of experience, probably originated as an adaptation to the rain forest. Be that as it may, this combination of traits proved to be preadaptive to many other life styles. Primates have used their sharp eyes, quick wits, and adept hands to good effect on the ground and in the savannas as well as in the trees of the forest. Ultimately, the same combination—together with a somewhat later but equally important adaptation, bipedalism—provided the major foundation upon which human culture was built.

SOCIAL BEHAVIOR

The roles that feeding, locomotion, and information gathering play in survival are fairly obvious. More subtle but equally important is the role of social behavior—the way the animals interact with members of their own species. Among mammals, the task of conceiving and nurturing offspring makes a certain amount of social behavior absolutely necessary: adults of the two sexes must come together long enough to mate, and, once the offspring is born, it must be fed and protected until it can fend and forage for itself. This, then, is the minimum possible level of social interaction—a few minutes of sexual contact and a few months (or years) of contact between mother and offspring. But, in many mammals, far more elaborate social structures have evolved from this simple base. Many have come to live in permanent groups and to use cooperative strategies to increase their chances of obtaining food or defending themselves from predators. (Animals that hunt in packs, such as wolves, or that adopt defensive formations, as do herds of musk oxen, are good examples.) Such group strategies have often opened up new food supplies or new habitats.

Among primates, this elaboration of social behavior is particularly remarkable. As an order, primates are on the whole among the most sociable of mammals. They usually live in permanent groups that include all ages and both sexes and thus involve a complex network of social ties. But the degree of sociability varies considerably from species to species. At one extreme, some prosimian species restrict direct contact to the very minimum consistent with mating and raising young. Beyond this, their social interaction is confined to olfactory messages; the animal merely leaves a "calling card" of scent to mark its territory. At the other extreme, some monkeys spend their entire lives within sight, sound, and, often, touch of other group members, immersed in a constant stream of social communication. Although scent still provides important social cues in the apes and monkeys (signaling, for instance, a female's readiness to mate), most of their communication is visual—a matter of "body language," gesture, and expression. This visual communication is aided by complex facial muscles, which allow anthropoid primates to convey shades of meaning to one another through a wide repertoire of varied and subtle facial expressions.

In their social behavior, then, as in almost everything else, the primates show immense diversity. Yet the variety of different patterns is in no way accidental. Each species' pattern of social behavior is an integral part of its general pattern of adaptation and, like the rest of the adaptive pattern, is the consequence of natural selection. Thus it seems logical to expect that the social behavior of nonhuman primate species might tell us something about the evolution of social behavior in the human species. The environments to which many living primates are adapted are often the same environments in which our earliest ancestors lived. We can reasonably assume, therefore, that in some respects their social behavior must resemble social behavior in earlier stages of the human lineage.

In order to draw such analogies, we must look more closely at the social behavior of the nonhuman primates, asking the following questions:

1. In what ways can natural selection act upon social behavior?
2. How do modern primates vary in their social organization?
3. Can we relate features of social organization to habitat and to cladistic groupings, so that we can then infer the social behavior of the early hominids from their habitats and their close cladistic relatives?

Selection and Social Behavior

The social organization of a species is its general "system" for forming and regulating living groups: how many members the group will have, and of what age and sex; who is permitted to mate with whom; who is dominant over whom; and so forth. Such a system is actually nothing more than the outcome of individual animals' responses to social situations. If, for instance, adults are intolerant of one another's presence, the species will be solitary. Or if, as in gibbons, adult males tolerate females and vice versa but both react aggressively to adult members of their own sex, social groupings will consist of heterosexual pairs.

To a large extent, such social responses are programmed by the genetic makeup of each animal. This is not to say that learning has no role in the development of social behavior. Carefully controlled laboratory experiments indicate that the social behavior typical of a species is neither totally determined by genes ("instinctive") nor totally determined by social experience ("learned"). Rather, like most phenotypic characteristics, it develops through the interaction between genetic makeup and environment. The genes determine the capacity to learn, as well as the basic behavioral responses that learning modifies. The social environment then elicits and molds these behaviors in the course of maturation.

Since it has a genetic basis, social behavior is subject to evolution by natural selection. As with feeding habits and locomotor techniques, the social behaviors that are favored are those that increase the animal's fitness by helping it to survive and reproduce. And, as social behavior evolves, so do the anatomical structures used in social interaction—manes and colored hair tufts; canine teeth to be bared in threat or used in fighting; facial muscles to convey, by changes of expression, subtler social messages. As always, the features that are retained and elaborated are those that aid in survival and reproduction.

In acting upon the social behavior of a species, natural selection operates on two levels:

—On the ecological level, through competition between individuals and populations of the same species for food and living space.

—On the reproductive level, through competition among individuals in finding mates and rearing offspring.

Social Behavior as Ecological Strategy

As with feeding behavior and locomotor behavior, natural selection will favor those social behaviors that are ecologically advantageous—those that help the group to exploit its own particular environment safely and without wasting energy. For instance, if food resources are relatively plentiful but predators constitute a threat, it might be advantageous to seek safety in numbers and live in large groups. Since such is the savanna habitat of the common baboons, we can interpret their social behavior of moving about in large troops as chiefly an ecological strategy.

If, on the other hand, the group's habitat is one in which food resources are concentrated in small and scattered patches, foraging in herds hundreds strong would be a most uneconomical way of exploiting them. At any time, most of the animals in the group would be sitting around waiting for a chance to feed. A far better technique would be to forage in small groups. We see precisely this strategy among the hamadryas baboons, who live in the dry and inhospitable semidesert regions of Ethiopia, where food resources are widely dispersed and predators scarce. Similarly, the social behavior of chimpanzees, with their fluid foraging groups and frequent signaling between groups, can be viewed as an adaptation to a particular feeding strategy in the rain forest environment, where fruit is plentiful but somewhat scattered in its distribution.

Social Behavior as Reproductive Strategy

As we saw in Chapter 1, Darwinian fitness is defined in terms of reproductive success. In large part, fitness is determined simply by the strategies an animal uses to exploit its environment efficiently and avoid predation. The better it is at staying alive and using available resources economically, the better its chances of producing a large number of successful offspring. But fitness will also be determined by the individual's success in social behavior that is directly related to reproduction—activities such as finding a mate, mating at the most fertile point in the reproductive cycle, and caring for the young.

Female Reproductive Strategy To some extent, the strategies that each sex can use to increase its reproductive success are dictated by its reproductive physiology. For the female, the number of offspring produced in a lifetime is limited by the period of time required to bear and wean each infant. In primates, as we have seen, this period is a long one. Thus, though the female primate spends most of her adult life either pregnant or nursing, she can still produce only about fifteen to twenty weaned offspring in a lifetime.

Usually a female gains no advantage in mating with many males or in competing with other females for mates—there are always enough willing males to ensure that every female becomes pregnant. But it *is* advantageous[3] for the female to be mated by the strongest and most vigorous male, for he will tend to pass on these qualities to their offspring. Moreover, in species that live in permanent groups, the consort of the most dominant male and her offspring share aspects of his privileged position. These include preferential access to scarce food resources and a position in the physical center of the troop, less exposed to attack by predators. Thus, it may be advantageous for the female to develop behaviors and anatomical structures that indicate her readiness to mate, for these signals will stimulate competition among males, with the most vigorous males presumably winning. Such signals are given off by many nonhuman female primates as they enter *estrus*, the period of sexual receptivity about the time of ovulation. In female baboons and chimpanzees, for example, the genital region becomes swollen and bright red. As if this were not signal enough, they also secrete special odors and begin approaching and presenting themselves to males.

However, in the game of reproductive success, the female's strong suit is not mating but motherhood. Her best means of ensuring that her limited number of offspring survive is to take great care of each of them, even risking injury to herself in their defense. The altruistic behaviors determined by the so-called maternal instinct are in fact the mother's way of protecting her own genes that are being carried by her offspring. Such behavior is thus an important element of Darwinian fitness—the ability to ensure that one's genes are well represented in future generations.

Male Reproductive Strategy In the case of males, reproductive strategy is not physiologically limited as it is in females. A male can father a virtually unlimited number of offspring—*pro-*

[3] Keep in mind that the term "advantageous," used in this context, refers to *evolutionary* advantage.

vided that he can compete successfully with other males in attracting and holding females.

In some species, this aspect of reproductive behavior becomes hugely exaggerated. Adapting for bluff, display, and shows of strength, the male becomes much larger than the female. He also evolves special structures that, like a peacock's tail, make him appear even bigger and more intimidating to his rivals and more impressive to potential mates. Thus sexual dimorphism is often based as much on reproductive advantage as on defense needs. However, it is not advantageous for the male to compete with his sexual rivals by fighting so fiercely as to cause exhaustion, injury, or death. The best strategy is rather to *appear* to fight fiercely, with great show and display, while in fact pulling his punches and deciding the contest without injury.

Although this strategy, which we may call "competitive begetting," is a common reproductive pattern among mammals, an alternative is possible, which we may call "nurturing." In this pattern (which is more common among birds than mammals), the male concentrates upon finding a single mate and establishing a bond with her. He then devotes his energy to helping protect and raise their offspring. Often, he feeds the mother too while she is nursing the small and helpless young. This pattern characterizes some carnivores, such as the wolf. Among primate males, both "begetters" and "nurturers" are to be found, but most species compromise by using both strategies without being highly specialized for either. As we shall see, the reproductive strategy evolved by a species seems to depend (at least partly) on ecological factors.

Modes of Social Interaction

Although reproductive strategies are important elements of the total social organization of a primate species, it is a mistake to imagine primate societies linked by bonds of continuous sexual desire. Another common misapprehension is to view primate social organization as maintained by constant fighting and violence. These notions, current a generation ago, were based upon studies of animals crowded artificially into zoo enclosures, which is like describing human social behavior on the basis of a coed penal colony. Recent field studies of wild primates have helped to correct the picture. It was found, for instance, that females spend most of their adult lives in a sexually nonreceptive state, because of pregnancy or nursing. Thus, continual sexual attraction could hardly be a major social bond. Moreover, breeding is often seasonal, and the mating season, far from being a time of social cohesiveness, is the time when the social order tends to break down under the strain of competition among males. Sex, then, does not hold primate societies together. Nor are social relationships determined by constant conflict. Field studies have shown that overt fighting is relatively rare among wild primates. Unlike caged animals, they have little time or energy to spare for such unproductive pursuits.

As it turns out, social relationships among primates are more complex, and much more subtly expressed, than was once thought. Chance (1970) has suggested that primate social interactions can be divided into two broad categories: agonistic behavior and hedonic behavior. Both types of behavior are part of the repertoire of most primate species, but they are used in different contexts.

Agonistic Behavior

Agonistic behavior (from the Greek word *agon*, meaning "contest") implies a power relationship between the actors. One animal attacks or threatens another; the latter responds by fighting, fleeing, or "submitting"—that is, making a gesture acknowledging its inferior status. Although the threat of violence is always present in agonistic encounters, very few involve an actual fight. Relationships of dominance and submissiveness are generally expressed by subtle body language—a lowered tail, a raised eyebrow, or a curl of the lip. A baboon asserting its dominance over another may do so simply by directing a hard, cold stare at the offender or "yawning" to expose its large canine teeth. The latter, in turn, will often express its submissiveness by pulling back its lips in an "appeasement grin" and screeching.

Infanticide and Fitness—a Primatological Problem

A small troop of Indian gray langurs is resting in the heat of late afternoon. Grouped together on the rocky hillside are six adult females, all nursing young infants. Several juveniles play nearby, but there is an atmosphere of tension in the group. The single adult male, about twice the size of the females, sits apart from the group, a little up the hillside, gazing into the distance. Suddenly, without warning, he charges the nearest mother. In a few loping strides he is upon her. She whirls to face him, and lunges at him, teeth bared. But the object of the male attack is not the female herself, but the infant clinging to her belly. He snatches it from her, runs off, and with a single slash of his sabrelike canines rips open its flank. By this time the other females, clasping their own infants to them, are in furious pursuit, but they are too late. The infant is mortally wounded, and after a cursory examination its mother abandons it. In spite of the females' vigilance, and their concerted efforts to protect their infants, within a few days the male has succeeded in killing them all.

Two female langurs attempt to retrieve an infant from a male who has snatched it from its mother and severely wounded it. *(Hrdy/Anthro-Photo)*

Grisly incidents such as this have now been seen frequently among Indian gray langurs, as well as, less frequently, in other monkey species that live in one-male groups. They seem invariably to follow the ousting of a resident male and a new male's takeover. While not attempting to hurt the females, the newcomer will systematically try to kill all the suckling infants, and generally succeeds in doing so. These observations provoked, among anthropologists, first incredulity, and then a series of academic fights almost as furious (though on the whole less bloody) than those among the langurs themselves. The reason for this is that the langur case brings directly into conflict two different, and partly opposed, ways of "explaining" the evolution of animal behavior. The more traditional of these approaches emphasizes the importance of behavior as an adaptation to the survival of the social group, or of the species as a whole. This viewpoint could explain, for instance, the fact that young males generally occupy vulnerable peripheral positions in a moving baboon troop by pointing out that, from the point of view of troop survival, such animals are the most expendable. (The views of the peripheral males themselves upon their "expendability" might be much different, could they be consulted.) This *group selectionist* approach is unable to find a plausible explanation for the adaptiveness of langur infanticide. Any behavior that leads to the death of infants must be "pathological"—the result of changing circumstances to which the langurs are unable to make adaptive responses. The fact that such behavior was usually reported from areas where the density of langurs was high led to the suggestion that it might be due to "tensions" caused by overcrowding—or even be a form of population control. But neither of these explanations is very satisfactory, and the observations were, on the whole, ignored until the emergence, in the 1970s, of a group of evolutionary theorists who rejected the idea of group selection in favor of an approach based upon the rigorous assessment of *individual* reproductive advantage to be gained from social acts. This school, centered mainly at Harvard University, has been interested in langur infanticide precisely because the group selectionist approach could not offer a good explanation; it was, in fact, a test case for the two conflicting approaches. In 1971, Sarah B. Hrdy of Harvard University began a study of langurs at Abu, India. This study, consisting of eleven months spent in the field over a five-year period, documented the behavior of several groups through a series of male takeovers. In each case, the new male made a determined and generally successful attempt to kill suckling infants, in spite of all kinds of subterfuges by their mothers. Using individual selectionist, rather than group selectionist theory, Hrdy was able to offer a plausible explanation for this behavior. The key observation is that the infants killed by the incoming male are not his own; his *individual* fitness would not be enhanced by their survival. On the contrary, by removing suckling infants he stimulates the females to come into estrus, mate, and bear his own offspring. The females, of course, stand to *lose* fitness, and so defend their offspring vigorously. Indeed, because the females of a group are likely to be sisters, they gain in *inclusive fitness* (see Chapter 3) by banding together in such defense. The females' strategy for protecting their fitness against infanticidal males extends to other, more subtle behaviors that might appear useless, or even bizarre, to the group selectionist. For instance, after a male takeover, even pregnant females will solicit copulations from the new male. The advantage of this behavior is, presumably, that it may establish paternal (rather than infanticidal) feelings towards her offspring when it is born. Again, females whose infants are close to weaning will abruptly deny them the breast, thereby making them far less vulnerable to attacks by the male.

Indian langurs. *(DeVore/Anthro-Photo)*

The lessons of langur society are important. They illustrate clearly how in nonhuman primate societies, as in human ones, the "interests" (in terms of fitness) of different members of society, and different age and sex classes, may often be in conflict; a conflict that may be, at times, bloody, and, to human eyes, cruel. The perfectly integrated, conflict-free utopia is as much a mirage in nonhuman primate society as it is in the society of humans. Furthermore, the case of the langurs shows how a species, in responding to the pressures of natural selection on *individual* behavior, may be trapped in a social system which, from the point of view of the species as a whole, may be less than ideal. After all, infanticide does result in a low overall success in rearing infants; if langurs were faced with competition from another species, lacking infanticide, and therefore with a greater capacity for population expansion, the result might be extinction for the infanticidal species. Here, too, there may be a lesson for humankind.

Baboons have other interesting ways of deflecting the wrath of higher-ranking individuals. Baboons have a great reverence for infants and show extreme deference toward nursing mothers—or any other troop member who happens to be holding or tending a baby baboon. It often happens that a subordinate male who has angered a dominant animal will quickly snatch up the nearest infant and cradle it maternally. This stratagem makes him quite safe from attack by higher-ranking males. Often, however, the indignant mother will try to rescue her infant, which thus becomes the object of a vigorous tug-of-war. (There is some indication in recent research that male baboons know their own offspring. One of the pieces of evidence for this conclusion is the observation that males almost always manage to choose someone else's infant when they grab a baby for self-defense.)

Interestingly, many of the signals used to

Hedonic and agonistic interaction among baboons (*Papio*). (*a*) An adult female hamadryas grooms the fur of her mate. Note the short, strong fingers of this ground-dwelling monkey. (*b*) A male hamadryas yawns in threat, showing his canine teeth. Broken teeth like these are quite common among wild baboons. (*c*) Fighting breaks out among a group of chacma baboons. The smaller animal shows its subordination by screaming and raising its tail, while the baboon seated at left grimaces, showing apprehension. (a *and* b, *Toni Angermayer/Rapho/Photo Researchers;* c, *Jen and Des Bartlett/Rapho/Photo Researchers*)

express agonistic relationships, even between members of the same sex, are derived from normal heterosexual interactions. In an agonistic encounter, "male" gestures, such as mounting another animal as if for mating, usually symbolize dominance. "Female" sexual gestures, such as presenting the rump, as if inviting copulation, symbolize subordination. These gestures, when used symbolically in an agonistic context, are often merely suggested by subtle body movement. Conversely, sexual interactions often involve agonistic elements. For example, when a young female chimpanzee is being pursued by an older male, she tends to flee, scream, and make fearful and submissive gestures, because she associates the close approach of a dominant animal with imminent attack. In such a situation, hedonic behaviors may be brought into play. By appropriate hedonic gestures, the male can assure the female that his intentions, if not honorable, are at least friendly.

Hedonic Behavior

Hedonic interactions (from the Greek root *hedon*, meaning "pleasure") involve mutuality rather than power relationships, reassurance rather than threat. Whereas the tense, hostile interactions of the agonistic mode maintain the hierarchy of power, hedonic behaviors cement society together with the bonds of relaxed friendliness.

In many primate species, the most common hedonic interaction is grooming. In the typical grooming scene, one animal sits or lies down contentedly while another animal picks through its fur bit by bit, parting it, combing it, and using fingers or teeth to remove any dirt, scruff, or parasites. Besides grooming, primates use a great variety of gestures, sounds, and postures to assure one another of friendliness and support. Significantly, many of these signals seem to be derived from the relaxed, mutually satisfying situation of "mothering." For instance, grooming is basically a maternal behavior. (Mothers groom their infants off and on all day long.) And "lip smacking," used by many monkeys and apes to express friendliness or appeasement, resembles the sound made by a suckling infant.

Field researchers have found it useful to learn this language of reassurance—and not merely for the sake of documenting primate social behavior. For example, Irven DeVore, while observing a baboon troop, once accidentally frightened an infant. Hearing the infant yelp, several adult males came charging toward DeVore. Fortunately, he had studied baboon body language and knew that, when one baboon wants to placate another, it smacks its lips loudly. This is what DeVore did, and the males, apparently satisfied by his apology, retreated.

The Bonds of Kinship

Field studies have revealed that, contrary to law-of-the-jungle notions, "friendly" (as opposed to violent or sexual) relationships are common among wild primates. As the studies were extended over five, ten, or fifteen years, and the researchers came to know which animals were born of which mothers, it became clear that in many cases "friends" were also relations. Mothers associated with their grown offspring, and ties between siblings persisted into adulthood, long after the mother died. Moreover, mother and son—and, to a lesser extent, brother and sister—generally avoid sexual contact. (Avoidance of father-daughter incest would be possible only in species where ties between parents are persistent, so that fathers know who their offspring are, and vice versa. No such species have yet been studied long enough to know whether or not fathers include their daughters in their group of mates.) Thus, simple kinship ties and the avoidance of incest are not as peculiar to humans as has often been believed. They have their roots in our primate heritage.

Patterns of Primate Social Organization

Having examined some of the elements of primate social behavior, we can now turn to the diverse forms of social organization found among primates. We will discuss a few of the more common patterns, with emphasis on their role as ecological and reproductive strategies, and their possible significance as stages in the evolution of human social behavior. We will begin with the simplest forms and go on to examine the more complex ones (Figure 6-10). This series, however, should not be interpreted as an irreversible evolutionary sequence.

The Noyau

The noyau (pronounced nwa-yó and meaning "nucleus" in French) may be the ancestral form of social organization in the primate order. Males are solitary; females are accompanied only by their immature offspring. Each adult, male or female, defends its own territory. Every male's territory overlaps that of several females, with whom he mates. This pattern is found mainly

Figure 6-10. Diagrammatic representation of different forms of primate social organization. (a) The noyau—male defends a territory against other males, overlaps range of several females. Found in many solitary prosimians; (b) Territorial pair—each territory defended and occupied by a mated pair and their immature offspring. Found in gibbons, *Callicebus;* (c) One-male group, patas type—male attached to a group of females and young, defends his position against "bachelors." Found in many monkey species, including gray langurs; (d) Multimale, multifemale troop—many members of both sexes and all ages form a coherent group. Found in baboons (except hamadryas and gelada), macaques, mangabeys, many Platyrrhini and prosimians; (e) One-male group within troop—harems of females and young cluster around adult males. Found in hamadryas baboons, geladas, mandrills.

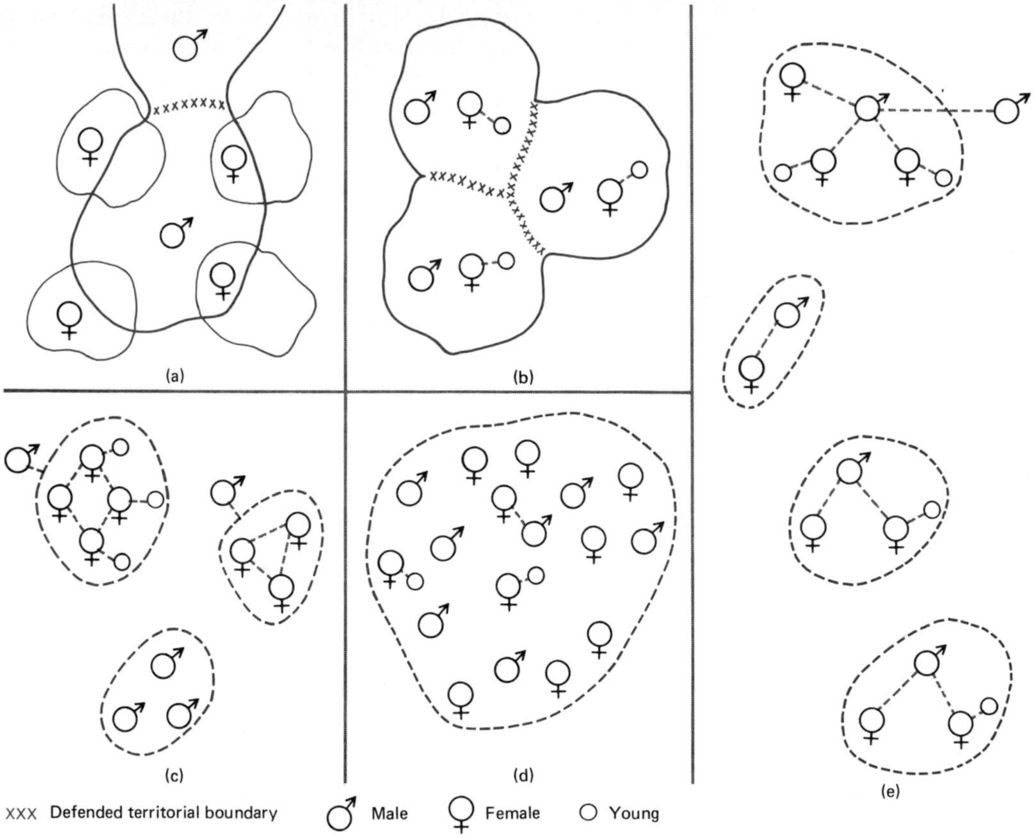

A one-male group of hamadryas baboons: a harem male (left) with his family and their group. (*Toni Angermayer/Rapho/Photo Researchers*)

among nocturnal, insectivorous prosimians, such as the bush babies and pottos, whose hunting technique would be difficult to practice in even a small group.

Territorial Pairs

In this form, a male and female live together in a small territory that they defend against other pairs. Territorial pairs are rare among primates; they are found only in a few rain forest species, including the gibbons. The advantage to the female in driving out rival females is not to preserve her mate's affections for herself but rather to preserve the territory for her own offspring—a vital consideration in the crowded rain forest. Since males and females are equally active in defending the territory, there is little sexual dimorphism in pair-organized species. In gibbons, for instance, both sexes are about the same size and have long canine teeth adapted for threatening or fighting.

The One-Male Group

In this form, the social unit is made up of adult females, their immature offspring, and a single adult male, all of whom forage and move about together. The one-male group is seen in many monkeys that live in the rain forest, as well as in the savanna-dwelling patas monkey. "Bachelor" males form troops of their own or wander independently, awaiting their chance to depose a group male and take his place. Thus, this form of social organization selects for structures in the male that enhance his fighting ability. The males are larger than the females, with long, sharp canine teeth for display and fighting. The females, who do little fighting, have canines that are not adapted for slashing or biting. In his concern with defending his position against other males, the "resident male" plays little part in the life of the group. His main interest lies outside—looking out for, and fighting off, challenges from "bachelors."

The Multimale Troop

Many primates live in groups that include more than one adult male. As examples, we may take the macaques (*Macaca*) and the baboons (*Papio*)—genera that have been thoroughly studied. These animals live in large troops, sometimes numbering a hundred or more, and consisting of several large males and many females and young. The social structure of a large multimale group may be extremely complex—an intricate network of alliances, kinships, friendships, juvenile play groups, and other subgroupings.

The relationships among the males in such a troop are governed largely by patterns of dominance and submission. One or more high-ranking animals form the core of the group. For the males, the dominance hierarchy has great impact on reproductive success. Females may dally with lower-ranking males at the beginning and end of estrus, but as ovulation becomes imminent, they are usually monopolized by the dominant males, who consequently father most of the offspring in the troop.

The multimale troop seems to be a more evolved form than the simple one-male group seen in patas, and it probably arose by a modification of the agonistic behavior of males. In a one-male species, the outcome of an encounter between adult males, if females are present, is always the defeat and flight of one of the contenders. If flight is precluded (in an enclosure, for instance), the animals will fight until one is killed or badly wounded. Among baboons, on the other hand, fights do not lead to the displacement of the losing male. Baboons have developed submissive behaviors that enable the loser to switch off the aggression of the victor. Thus the loser can continue to live in the troop so long as he expresses his subordination. The elaborate play of dominance and submission makes it possible for the lower-ranking males to remain with the troop, rather than forming bachelor troops or taking their chances as solitaries.

But why should this confer any special advantage, compared with the more rough-and-ready one-male group system? A clue may be found in the habitat of multimale species. Most multimale species live in richer savannas and woodlands. These are areas where resources are plentiful enough to permit large troops of animals to forage together. But movement on the ground is essential, and predators are numerous. The primate inhabitants of such areas therefore need a good defense strategy, and the multimale troop may be seen as that strategy. In it, the brawny bodies and powerful fighting teeth that the males originally developed for fighting among themselves can be used in cooperative defense against predators. Troops of macaques or baboons that include several large males are able to ward off and frighten all but the largest predators, and they stand a much better chance of survival than do small groups. But the multimale arrangement is not without its costs. A significant amount of energy is expended in the continual chasing, threatening, and strutting—and in the occasional fighting—necessary to maintain the dominance hierarchy.

One-Male Groups Within a Multimale Troop

The hamadryas baboons, which live in habitats where resources are scarcer, seem to have modified the multimale system to minimize this energy drain. Hamadryas baboons of the Ethiopian desert country live in multimale troops, but the structure of these troops differs from that of the savanna baboon troops. Every adult female belongs to the "harem" of an adult male. (These "harems" may include as many as ten, or as few as one female.) The group male, unlike the patas male, is the center and focus of his group. Females spend much of their day grooming his fur. Even out of the mating season, he carefully controls their movements. A female who strays more than a few yards away provokes a threat that brings her running back.

Until they find themselves a mate, bachelor males often attach themselves to the periphery of a one-male group, but they are excluded from mating by the vigilance of the harem males. Harem holders do not try to take females from one another by force; once a male-female bond is established, it is respected by other males. This arrangement, which avoids unnecessary bloodshed and saves energy, has important evolutionary implications. No longer is the male's fitness determined by his ability to fight his way up the dominance hierarchy. His reproductive success depends upon attracting and holding a large group of females. Accordingly, he has evolved a handsome cape of fur around the neck and shoulders, which probably makes him appear larger and more impressive and at the same time delightfully groomable to his mates.

This reproductive strategy, as we have mentioned, may be less costly in energy than that of savanna baboons and is thus adaptive to life in a semidesert. And because one-male groups often forage on their own, it also permits more effective exploitation of the scattered food resources to be found there. At night, one-male groups link up into troops again, and often troops themselves amalgamate into aggregations hundreds strong, taking advantage of group protection in this vulnerable period.

This system of social organization has some features that make it especially intriguing to the student of human evolution. First, it is more complex than any other system. It involves groupings at several levels—one-male group, multimale troop, multitroop sleeping aggregation—and it combines the male-male bonds of the multimale troop with the male-female bond of the one-male group. Both of these features recall the basic groupings and relationships that characterize human social organization. Second, hamadryas social organization apparently evolved in an arid habitat, where long daily ranges and flexible feeding strategies are demanded. Such, we believe, were the habitats of the early hominids.

The baboons can lend intriguing analogies for the reconstruction of early hominid behavior, but their relationship to our species is distant. We also need the information that only a closely related species can give us.

Chimpanzee Social Organization

We have already described some of the features of chimpanzee social organization in Chapter 5. Formally, a chimpanzee "local population" is a multimale troop, although its members only occasionally come together in one spot. In sharp contrast to the more rigidly ordered baboon troop, which rests and moves in formation, the members of a chimpanzee troop spend their days scattered in small, informal groups—two friends "termiting" here, a mother playing with her infant there, a "grooming group" at work over there, a foraging band off in the distance. And the animals move casually from one group to another.

Chimpanzee males recognize a rank order among themselves and are dominant to females and young. But there is little overt fighting over dominance. (In her first two years among the Gombe chimpanzees, Goodall observed only one fight among the adult males.) Rank is achieved, and occasionally expressed, not by fighting but by "charging displays." Essentially, these displays involve making as big an uproar as possible: the male hoots and howls, throws rocks and sticks (but not at the other chimpanzees), drags branches along the ground, slaps the earth with his hands, leaps into trees, and yanks their branches back and forth. The greater the uproar, the more respect he wins. One of the chimpanzees in the troop that Goodall observed vaulted quite abruptly to the highest position in the dominance hierarchy by making off with some empty kerosene cans from Goodall's tent and clanging them together on the ground in front of him as he charged forward. After a few such displays Goodall wearied of the noise and reclaimed the cans. But this inspired instance of tool use had won the animal such lofty rank that, even after he was forced to fall back on more ordinary display techniques, he was never challenged.

Actual physical combat is thus quite rare within chimpanzee local populations (though, as we saw in Chapter 5, violence between members of neighboring populations is not unknown). Nevertheless, tensions generated by the rather fluid and shifting dominance hierarchy run very strong. It has been suggested that the richness of hedonic interaction, which is such a striking feature of chimpanzee society, may actually be a kind of compensatory mechanism—a way of relieving tension and defusing potentially destructive conflict. It is certainly true that, more than any other primate, chimpanzees embrace, touch, pat, greet, groom, and reassure one another. After a show of submission, the dominant chimpanzee is likely to reach out and give the submissive one a reassuring pat. When a young chimpanzee cannot get down from a tree, he has only to whimper and another juvenile will come to rescue him. Even in breeding season, when social order tends to break down among other primates, the chimpanzees go on treating one another with remarkable affability. In estrus, a mature female will generally mate with any adult male who comes along. Goodall once observed seven males calmly waiting for their chance while an estrous female mated with each of them in turn.

Much of the hedonic behavior among the chimpanzees is probably based on kinship. The bond between mother and offspring is strong and persists long after the young one is independent and after the birth of other siblings. Siblings, brought together in the orbit of their mother, seem to develop strong ties as well. Playmates are often siblings, and foraging parties frequently consist of siblings or of a mother with her grown offspring and perhaps their infants as well. While motherhood creates powerful ties, fatherhood among the chimpanzees is nonexistent in any but a biological sense. If a particular adult male is associated with an infant in chimpanzee society, the adult is more likely to be the infant's mother's brother than its father.

As we have seen, the chimpanzees are the only nonhuman primates in which we see hints of cooperation and reciprocity in the quest for food—foraging parties calling the rest of the troop to a heavily laden fruit tree, males cooperating in the "hunt" and sharing meat when it is begged for.

The chimpanzee is also the only nonhuman primate species in which mothers have been observed giving solid food to their infants. Though these are far from the most common behaviors among the chimpanzees, they are all significant foretastes of the distinctly human characteristic of economic cooperation. Indeed, in many aspects of their social behavior—the small, flexible groups, the lasting kinship bonds, the wide repertoire of affectionate gestures—as in their tool use and imitative learning, the chimpanzees show remarkable similarities to their close relative, *Homo sapiens.*

Human Social Organization

It is clearly impossible to summarize, in a brief section, the immense variety of forms of social organization among humans. This variety itself points to a human peculiarity, namely the flexibility of our social organization. Without any significant variation in its genetic basis (or so we believe), human social organization has assumed many forms as part of the diversity of human culture. As we shall see in later chapters, this variety has been an important part of human adaptive strategy, permitting our species to occupy many different habitats.

Yet, in all this diversity, there are certain common denominators—social behaviors so nearly universal that we can think of them as basic attributes of the species. And, in most instances, these fundamental forms of human social behavior are still recognizable as variations on primate themes. Human social behavior may be distinctive, but it has many analogies with that of our closest relatives. This should come as no surprise. It is culture that is responsible for most of the differences between humans and the other primates, and culture was a relatively late arrival in our evolutionary history. The lineage leading to

Homo was social long before it was cultural. With the appearance of culture, already established social forms—forms shared with other primates—were not abandoned; they were simply modified. Hence they still reflect our primate heritage.

Summary

By understanding the connections among behavior, anatomy, and habitat in the living primates, we can discern adaptive patterns that cut across taxonomic boundaries. These patterns help us reconstruct the ecology and behavior of fossil animals from evidence of their anatomy and habitat. The adaptive patterns of the primates can be considered under four main headings: the locomotor system, the feeding system, the information system, and social behavior.

Primates in general are quite versatile in their locomotor behavior—their ways of holding and moving their bodies. Yet habitual ways of moving differ from species to species, for each species' locomotor profile is an adaptation to its own particular econiche. The locomotor profiles of living primates clearly show the correlations of anatomy, behavior, and habitat, and allow us to make educated guesses regarding the locomotor stages that led to human bipedalism. A probable sequence leads from generalized arboreal quadrupedalism, to climbing by grasping, to brachiation, to knuckle-walking, to bipedalism—each stage involving its own set of physical adaptations, traces of which are retained in the modern human. The derived features developed as adaptations to bipedalism are seen mainly in the human pelvis and hindlimb. By allowing *Homo sapiens* to use its hands for functions other than locomotion, bipedalism has greatly facilitated the development of human culture.

An animal's feeding habits largely determine its econiche, and are therefore fundamental to its adaptive strategy. In feeding as in locomotion, the primates as an order are extremely adaptable, and tend to be omnivorous. However, each species has its own dietary emphasis and, in consequence, has developed its own particular set of adaptations in the feeding apparatus. Insect eaters, fruit eaters, leaf eaters, and small-object eaters each have teeth, jaws, and jaw muscles specialized for their diets. The modern human jaw and teeth are generally rather small and weak—a reflection of our reliance on technology rather than teeth to prepare our food. The primate hand has also entered into this adaptive complex. The grasping hand—and, in higher primates, the precision grip—has permitted primates to rely on the hand for picking up and preparing food, as well as for other manipulatory tasks.

An animal's information system, consisting of the special senses and the brain, allows it to gather and process information from its environment. In general, the primate information system is distinctive in three respects: (1) elaboration of the visual sense, with corresponding deemphasis of the sense of smell; (2) shift of the tactile sense from the muzzle to the hand; and (3) enlargement and refinement of the brain. However, different primate groups vary in the degree to which they exhibit these trends. They are more pronounced in the anthropoids than in the prosimians and most pronounced of all in the human species. Especially remarkable is the great expansion of the cerebral cortex of the human brain. The two regions of the cortex that have expanded the most are the frontal association area and the parietal association areas, which are thought to be responsible for the distinctly human functions of speech, abstract thought, and the pursuit of long-term goals.

Like the primate information system, primate social behavior varies in complexity. Since social behavior is based on genetic makeup as well as on learning, it is subject to evolution by natural selection. Thus each species' pattern of social organization can be seen as a combination of ecological and reproductive strategies adapted to a given environment. These patterns vary in complexity from the noyau, to the territorial pair, to the one-male group, to the multimale troop, to the one-male group within a multimale troop.

Once thought to be based primarily on raw instincts of sex and aggression, primate social behaviors have been shown in recent years to be a much more subtle blend of agonistic behaviors, involving the regulation of power relationships, and hedonic behaviors, involving mutual gratification, often among related animals. Chimpanzees, while they maintain a dominance hierarchy, are notable for the richness of their hedonic repertoire, as well as for the strength of their kinship bonds. Human social behavior, while infinitely more diverse than that of other primate species, still shows its roots in the primate heritage.

Glossary

agonistic behavior social interaction that involves conflict and power relationships

association areas regions of the cerebral cortex concerned with information storage and integration rather than sensory input

cerebral cortex the outer layer of the brain, which includes the regions devoted to processing sensory input and to the higher mental functions

endocranial cast a cast of the internal surface of the brain cavity

estrus the period of a female animal's sexual receptivity, occurring around the time of ovulation

hedonic behavior social interaction that involves mutuality and friendliness

multimale troop a primate social group including several adult males, females, and offspring

noyau a primitive form of primate social organization in which males are solitary and females are accompanied only by their immature offspring

one-male group a primate social unit consisting of a single adult male, several adult females, and their offspring

power grip a grasp in which an object is pressed against the palm by the fingers and thumb

precision grip a grasp in which an object is held between the thumb and index finger, allowing fine manipulation

territorial pair a primate social unit in which a male and female occupy and defend an area together

Suggested Readings

CLARK, W. E. LE GROS 1971
Antecedents of Man: An Introduction to the Evolution of the Primates. New York: Quadrangle. Somewhat dated now, but still the best succinct account of primate comparative anatomy.

HRDY, S. B. 1977
The Langurs of Abu: Female and Male Strategies of Reproduction. Cambridge: Harvard University Press. A primatologist's account of her fieldwork and its findings.

JOLLY, A. 1972
The Evolution of Primate Behavior. New York: Macmillan. An account of primate natural history and adaptations, with special emphasis upon social behavior.

KUMMER, H. 1971
Primate Societies: Group Techniques of Ecological Adaptation. Chicago: Aldine. A thoughtful consideration of the determinants of primate social behavior,

with an emphasis on ecological strategies among terrestrial monkeys.

TATTERSALL, I. T., AND SUSSMAN, R. W. (EDS.) 1975
Lemur Biology. New York: Plenum. A useful collection of articles on this prosimian group.

WILSON, E. O. 1975
Sociobiology: The New Synthesis. Cambridge: Harvard University Press. A comprehensive overview of animal social behavior, providing a context for interpreting primate social organization.

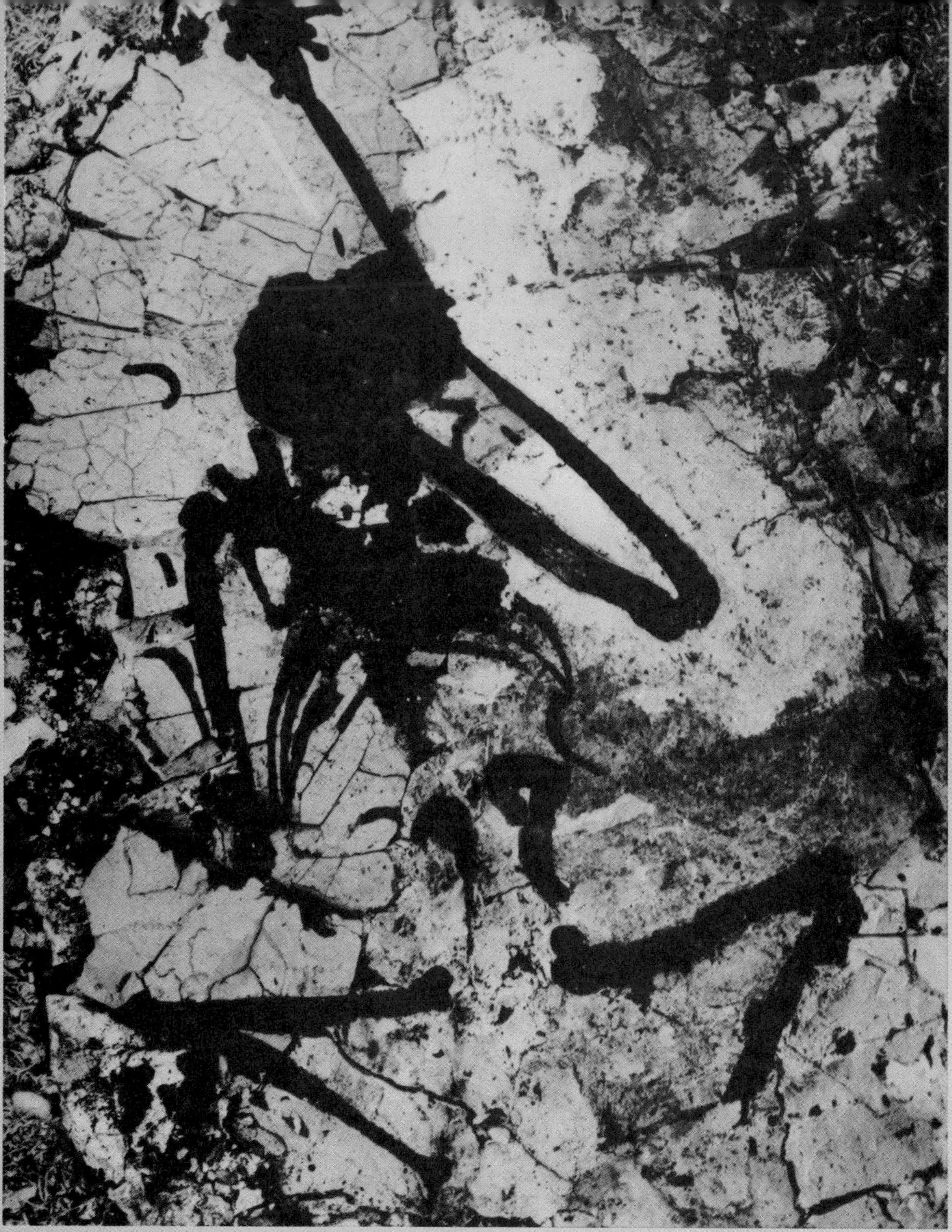

Chapter Seven

Early Primate Evolution: The Fossil Record

Seventy million years ago, when the dinosaurs still dominated the earth's dry lands, the ancestors of almost all modern mammals were beady-eyed creatures, no larger than a rat, foraging in the forest undergrowth. Unimpressive as they may have seemed, scurrying out of the path of lumbering dinosaurs, these animals eventually managed to populate much of the earth with their descendants.

Among those descendants are the primates. Through successive adaptive radiations, there arose first primitive primates, then true prosimians equipped with the grasping hands, sharper eyes, and relatively larger brain that have become the hallmarks of the primate order. Then, several million years later but still from the same stock, there emerged a group of small, monkey-like anthropoids. These in turn gave rise to a succession of apes that spread through the forests of Europe, Africa, and Asia. Eventually, certain populations of these apes began to experiment with life outside the forest, in the open savannas. There, one of these populations gradually made a number of crucial adaptations that separated it decisively from the apes. Thus the human family was founded.

How do we piece together this remote ancestry of our species? One way to reconstruct evolutionary history is through the study of fossils, interpreting them by analogy with living primates. In Chapters 5 and 6, we have examined the primate adaptive patterns that provide the analogies. Armed with this knowledge, we turn now to the fossils themselves. We will first discuss fossils in general—how they are formed, discovered, dated, and interpreted. Then we will see what the fossils tell us about the evolutionary history of the primates up to the time when the human lineage diverged.

Oreopithecus, a chimpanzee-sized fossil primate that lived about 8 million years ago. (The skeleton has been crushed flat beneath the weight of overlying deposits.) Although not a direct hominid ancestor, _Oreopithecus_ may have been bipedal; its long arms and short legs suggest that it may also have brachiated. *(Johannes Hurzeler/Natur-Historisches Museum)*

THE EVIDENCE OF FOSSILS

Occasionally, when geological conditions are favorable, the remains of an ancient animal or plant, rather than decomposing completely, may be mineralized and preserved. These relics of ancient life are called *fossils,* and they hold a very special place in evolutionary studies. There is a peculiar thrill to holding in one's hand a piece of fossil bone or a tooth and realizing that its owner—dead for 3, 4, or 40 million years—might well have been one's own direct ancestor, the carrier of a fraction, however small, of one's own genetic heritage. More scientifically, the fossil record plays a crucial role in reconstructing human evolutionary history. Studying modern primates can carry us a long way toward understanding evolutionary relationships, but there is some information that only the hard evidence of fossils can provide. For instance, comparative anatomy tells us that we share a common ancestor with the chimpanzee, and suggests what it was like—but only fossils can *show* us that com-

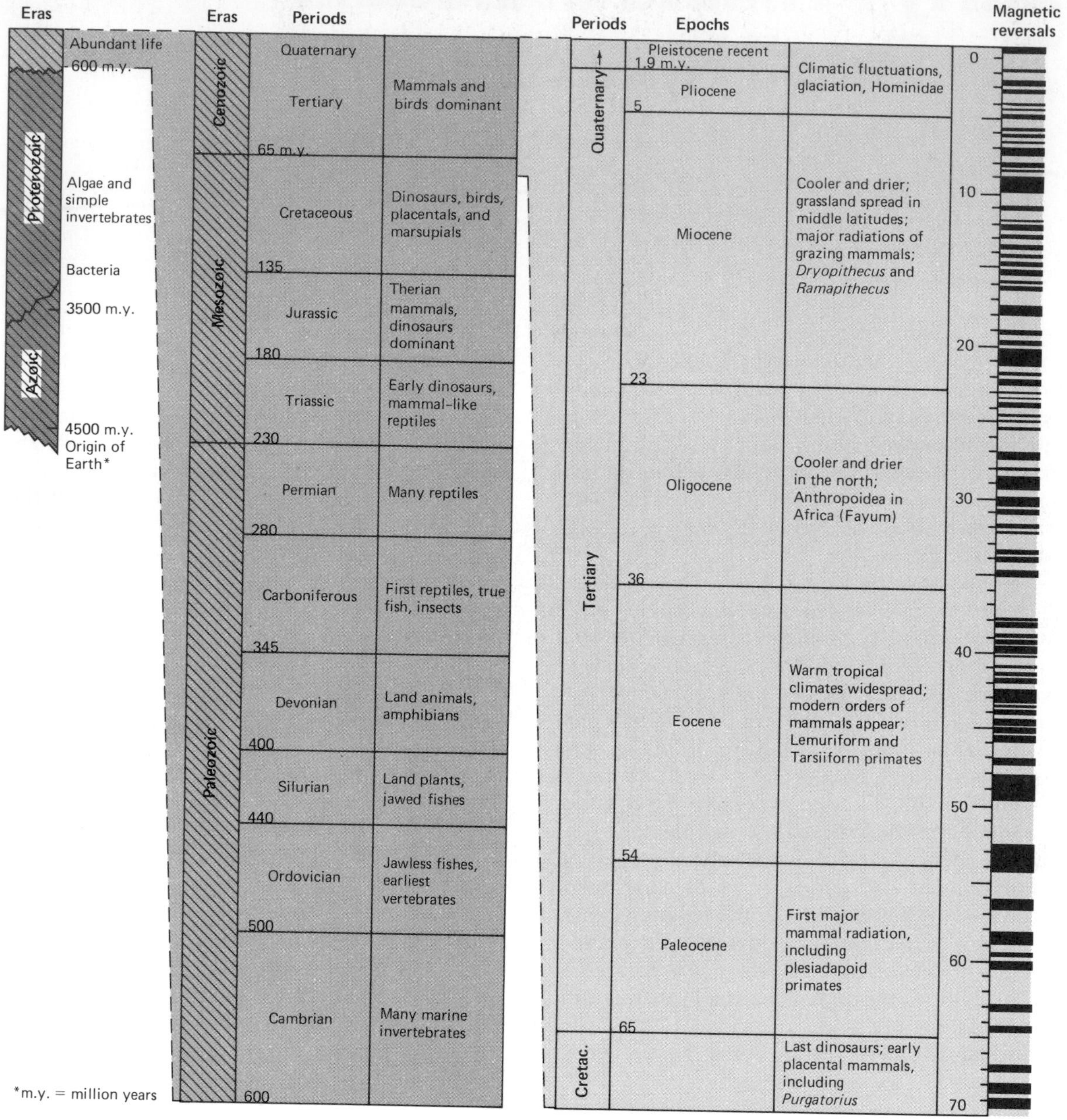

Figure 7-1. Time chart showing the geological periods, climatic changes, and major evolutionary events during the Cenozoic.

mon ancestor and tell us where and how, and most importantly, *when* it lived.

Fossils are useful in several ways. First, they provide vital information about the environment in which new adaptations emerged. The rocks in which a fossil is embedded and the other remains that are found with it supply many clues about the habitat of the fossil animal—the climate, the vegetation, the competition from other animals. Such evidence is vital, for as we have seen, the theory of evolution states that changes in the environment cause changes in behavior and anatomy through the action of natural selection. For example, paleontologists have speculated that hominids appeared when the forests shrank and grasslands expanded, opening up new econiches in the savannas. Some of the earliest hominid fossils have indeed been found in close association with grassland animals, and their geological settings bear the traces of a relatively dry seasonal climate, in which savannas would have flourished. Thus the fossil evidence supports this argument.

Sometimes, too, fossils disprove hypotheses based only on modern species. For example, human beings, compared with modern apes, have relatively small, lightly built jaws and small back teeth. Given this fact, one would never suspect that the derived features distinguishing the earliest hominids from apes included *massive* jaws and *larger* molars. Yet, when fossils of the early hominids came to light, this proved to be the case.

Finally, extinct species—including extinct side-branches of the human family—are known to us only through fossils. Without fossils, we would have no sense of the full breadth and complexity of the adaptive radiations that have arisen and declined in the course of mammalian evolution.

Fossils—Accidents in Time

Behind the public galleries of our great museums, with their careful displays of a few choice fossil specimens, are row upon row of drawers and cabinets packed with more fragmentary fossils, the raw material of the science of paleontology. Numerous as they are, however, the fossils in museum drawers represent only a tiny fraction of all the animals that have lived and died. For the fossilization of animal or plant remains is a very unlikely and rare event, occurring only when the usual process of decay is interrupted through some freak of geology.

At death, most animals are rapidly "recycled" within the ecosystem. Carnivores and scavengers chew the carcass, leaving only the most indigestible parts—the more solid parts of bones (especially jawbones) and the teeth. Gradually, these fragments decay into unrecognizable soil components. Fortunately for us, however, this process of dissolution is occasionally interrupted in such a way as to preserve parts of the animal as fossils. Nearly always, the only parts preserved are broken bones. It is extremely rare to find a complete skeleton, and there are only a few known instances of skin and other soft tissues becoming fossilized.

Burial

The chances of fossilization depend on local geological conditions. To be protected from the effects of weathering, the remains must find their way to a spot where sediments, such as silt, gravel, or sand, are being deposited. Swamps, floodplains, river deltas, lakes, and caves are all likely places for bones to find such natural burial. Preservation is most likely in places where ash from active volcanoes or rock fragments eroding from rising mountains and hills are accumulating rapidly. Thus most fossils come from geologically active times and places.

Mineralization and Preservation

Burial alone, however, is no guarantee of immortality in a museum drawer. Most buried remains are eventually broken down by bacteria and soil acids. Only under special circumstances is this process of decay interrupted, permitting fossilization. Sometimes decay is slow enough for the rock surrounding the bone to solidify, forming a natural mold. Then, as the bone slowly decays, it is replaced by fine-grained rock that gradually fills the mold, creating a stone replica of the bone—the fossil. Such fossils show only the external form of the bone. Under other conditions, dissolved minerals seeping in from the surrounding rock replace the whole bone, molecule for molecule, producing a specimen with a fine internal, as well as surface, structure.

Exposure and Collection

The discovery of fossils is as unlikely as their formation. Very rarely are fossils unearthed by deliberate digging; most of them surface without the help of science. Sometimes a contractor building a highway or excavating a gravel pit accidentally uncovers a fossil striking enough to catch his eye. Most fossils, however, are exposed by natural processes—the rock covering it is worn away by wind or water, and the fossil appears on the surface. This means that the exposure of fossils depends largely upon modern climatic conditions. Since erosion is fastest in dry "badlands," where vegetation is sparse and occasional rainstorms scour gullies into the landscape, most fossils are collected in such inhospitable places.

However, only a small fraction of these naturally exposed fossils is ever collected at all. For well-trained eyes are often needed to spot them, and there are simply too few paleontologists and anthropologists (and too little funding) to cover all the likely places. Most fossils are weathered out bit by bit until they can no longer be distinguished from the surrounding gravel and rock fragments.

Thus the formation, preservation, and recovery of fossils depends on a great many factors, past and present. Indeed, a distribution map of fossil primate sites of a given epoch tells us more about the distribution of suitable sediments, the distribution of erosion and engineering sites in modern times, and the distribution of paleontologists than it does about the range of primates in past ages.

Preservation and Reconstruction

Most fossils are damaged before discovery: gnawed by scavengers, weathered, distorted under the weight of overlying rock, or broken by engineering crews. It is important to recognize the effects of such damage. Naturally crushed skulls and bones can be misinterpreted as evidence of aggressive attacks, and bones gnawed by animals can look remarkably like man-made tools.

In the Omo Valley of Ethiopia (see box, Chapter 8), a paleontologist excavates the fossilized tusk of an extinct elephant species. Like this one, many fossils are exposed on the surface as the natural forces of erosion eat away the surrounding rock. *(Georg Gerster/Rapho/Photo Researchers)*

Nor is misinterpretation the only problem presented by damaged fossils. An incomplete or imperfect specimen inevitably tempts the paleontologist to reconstruct the missing pieces. In some cases, this is relatively straightforward—for instance, reconstructing a missing left side when the right side is preserved. But, in other cases, whole skulls have been reconstructed from a fragment of mandible or a few teeth. Such imaginative reconstruction can be useful, but anyone studying replicas of reconstructed fossils must take the reconstruction into account. The parts that represent the paleontologist's professional

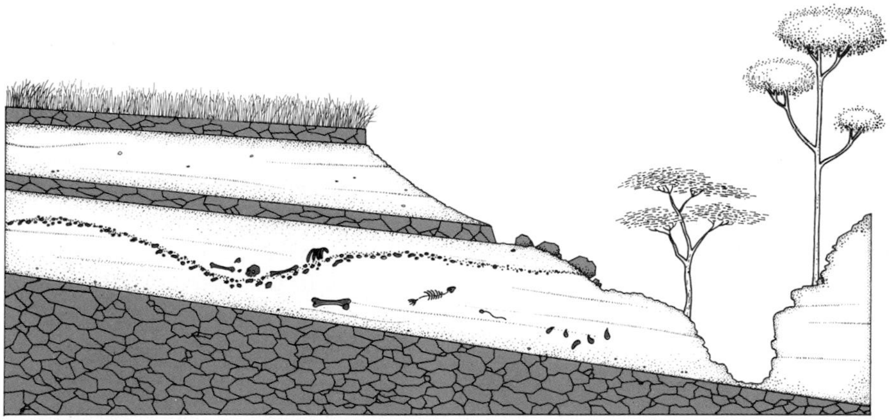

Figure 7-2. A simple stratigraphic section and the sequence of events that can be inferred from its observed features. In this case, the fossils could be "bracketed" in time if the lavas above and below were dated by the K-A method. *(Robert Frank)*

guesswork should be carefully distinguished from the parts that represent the hard facts of the fossil evidence.

Fossils, therefore, can be deceptive. To interpret them accurately, we must keep in mind that they are not like the bones of a freshly prepared skeleton. They have been shaped not only by the biology of the animal during its lifetime but also by the natural forces and accidents that have acted upon its bones since death, and by the means used to excavate, preserve, and reconstruct them.

Interpreting Fossils

The interpretation of a fossil involves consideration of many sorts of evidence—the fossil itself, the rock in which it was embedded, and the other fossils in that rock—in order to reach conclusions about the animal from which it derived. What species did the creature belong to? What are its closest relatives? Where and how did it live?

Identifying and Naming

Once a fossil has been discovered, collected, cataloged, and cleaned, the next step is to identify it. Does it belong to a known species? Or is it so different from existing specimens that it must be assigned to a "new" species—or even a new genus? How many different species are represented in a mixed bag of fossils from a particular site? This sorting requires a sharp eye for detail, good judgment, and a thorough acquaintance with fossils that have already been found. It also requires that the paleontologist keep in mind the variability that always exists within animal populations. Every individual is the product of a unique genotype and a unique life history and therefore differs in some detail from every other member of the species. In examining a fossil, the paleontologist must be able to distinguish this kind of variation—the result of normal variability *within* a species—from the kind of differences that would indicate that a *new* species had been uncovered.

In the past, paleoanthropologists did not always take this precaution and were very free with names. They would assign practically every new fossil to its own species, and often its own genus as well. More recently, paleontologists have tried, before proposing a new species name, to make sure that their material really does represent a "new" biological species, genetically isolated from all others living at the same time.

However, even the most scrupulous paleontologist must make one large exception to this rule. A population living at a particular time is not isolated genetically from its ancestors and descendants; no branching or speciation has occurred to break the genetic link between them.

Yet ancestors and descendants can be physically very different, and we need to use classification to express the differences between them. But at what point do we split them into different species? If fossils document a smooth change within a single evolving lineage, any such division is likely to be somewhat arbitrary. No matter where we draw the line, a late member of species *A* will be closer—in time, in structure, and genetically—to an early member of species *B* than to an ancestral specimen of its own species.

There is no hard and fast answer to this problem, but the patchiness of the fossil evidence often imposes a solution of sorts. It is convenient to separate forms that occur before gaps in the fossil record from their linear descendants that appear when the record is resumed—especially if noticeable change has occurred in the meantime. Somewhat ironically, therefore, classifying fossils often becomes more difficult as these convenient gaps in the record are filled by newly found specimens.

After identifying the species, the next task in the analysis of fossils is to fit that species into the natural order, by defining:

—Its *evolutionary* relationships with other species, living and extinct.

—Its *ecological* relationships with the other species among which it lived, and its way of life in general.

Determining the Evolutionary Relationships of a Fossil Species

Putting a fossil species in its proper position on the evolutionary tree is a matter of comparative anatomy, just as it is with living species. The species' traits must be described, identified as derived or ancestral, and compared with those of other species. Then its evolutionary relationships can be determined on the basis of the derived traits that it shares with other species (Chapter 4). With fossil species, we have less evidence to go on, since the muscles, guts, and other "soft" parts have long since disappeared. So have the protein molecules that are so helpful in sorting out living species. Fortunately, however, the teeth are often preserved, and their structure can be a good indicator of evolutionary relationship. The paleontologist relies heavily upon dental evidence to construct phyletic trees.

Reconstructing the Way of Life of a Fossil Species

Usually we are not content merely to determine the evolutionary relationships of a fossil species. We are also interested in its way of life: its locomotor repertoire, its habitat, its foraging and feeding habits, and its social behavior. In piecing together this picture, the anatomical structure of the fossil and the setting in which it was found are our best clues.

The Evidence of Anatomy We can never reconstruct in detail the diet and locomotor profile of an extinct animal. But we can often deduce their main features by inferring behavior from anatomy, using the analogies provided by modern primates, as described in the previous chapter. We know, for example, that *Dendropithecus*, an early African ape, resembled the living spider monkey in the shape of its trunk and arms. Hence we can guess that, like the spider monkey, *Dendropithecus* brachiated as well as ran along the branches, even though we cannot check this hypothesis by watching him swing through the Miocene forest. Similarly, the flat, low-crowned molars of *Dendropithecus* indicate that it was a fruit eater; and, from the difference between males and females in the size of the canines, we can guess that it was a social animal that lived in heterosexual troops, with males doing most of the threatening and fighting.

The Evidence of the Context Until quite recently, the very people who collected, analyzed, and restored fossils unknowingly overlooked and destroyed much valuable information. Intent upon the fossil, they tended to ignore the context in which it was found. Today, paleontologists realize that the rock in which a fossil is embedded and the other fossils with which it is found can provide as much ecological information as the fossil's anatomical structure.

The geological setting provides one set of clues. The trained field geologist can distinguish clays that settled out of still waters from sand deposited in a delta or gravels found in a riverbed. A mixture of pebbles, sand, and silt suggests occasional violent flooding rather than constantly flowing streams, and therefore indicates a climate in which rainfall was irregular and fell mostly as tropical storms. Frost, aridity, constant humidity, seasonal rainfall—all these climatic conditions leave characteristic marks on the geological setting. From such signs we can get at least a vague picture of the fossil animal's habitat and thus understand somewhat better how it lived.

Fossils of other animal species and of plants found in the same deposit help to complete the ecological picture. For instance, the earliest hominid fossils have been found with fossils of grazing animals, which indicates an open grassland habitat. By the same token, common burial with browsing and climbing animals indicates forest or woodland.

However, a word of caution is needed here. Animals that are buried together did not necessarily live together. It is very rare for land animals to be buried and fossilized where they died. Far from being an integrated group of ancient neighbors, the fossils found in a given deposit are usually a motley collection of remains with considerably different origins and histories. The silts of an African lake bed, for example, might contain the skeleton of a hippopotamus that died in its waters, bones of warthogs that inhabited the bush along the shores, and fragments of the skeletons of zebras, giraffes, and antelopes that died in the open plains but were washed into the lake by seasonal flooding.

Before we can draw conclusions about a fossil animal's habitat on the basis of fossils found in the same deposit, we have to disentangle such mixtures. This means reconstructing the processes that brought each specimen into the burial assemblage—an art that is called *taphonomy* (from the Greek *taphos*, a tomb). If a fossil bone is worn down and smoothed, for example, the taphonomist can tell that it was transported by a stream for some distance prior to burial. If the surfaces of the bone are cracked and split, it must have weathered on a land surface prior to burial. If it is fresh looking, on the other hand, or if a partial skeleton is found in articulation—that is, with the bones joined and positioned in relation to one another as they would be in life—it can be assumed that the animal was buried quite rapidly after death, probably not far from where it died. Teeth marks may identify animals killed by predators—and sometimes even tell us the likely predator. Such detective work helps the paleontologist to distinguish groups of animals that are truly associated—groups that were not only buried together but actually lived together—and thus to piece together the ecology of the extinct animal.

THE GEOLOGICAL TIME SCALE

One of the major roles of the paleontologist is to give evolution a time depth. To do this, fossils must be dated, so that the evolutionary events to which they bear witness can be seen in their true place in our planet's history. This dating is done by situating the fossil on the *geological time scale*, a timetable that divides the history of the earth into a series of epochs and periods (Figure 7-1), each of which is related to a particular set of fossil-bearing rocks. The geological time scale is based on stratigraphic relationships: relationships between different *strata*, or layers, of rock. It operates on the principle that generally speaking any given stratum, with the fossils it contains, is younger than the strata beneath it and older than those that lie above it.

This principle makes it possible to arrive only at a *relative* time scale for different rocks and their fossils. That is, we know their chronological order but not their age in years. Indeed, for many years paleontologists had only rough estimates of the actual chronology of earth's geological and evolutionary history. Today, thanks to advances in physics, various techniques can be used to calibrate the geological column, or sequence of strata, against an absolute time scale of dates in years. We now know not only the order of the epochs but also more precisely when they began and ended (Figure 7-1).

Dating Fossils

There are two broad categories of fossil-dating techniques:

—Faunal, stratigraphic, and paleomagnetic methods, which relate the rock and its fossils to other rocks whose age is known.

—Chronometric methods, which yield an age in years from the rock itself.

Faunal Correlation

This method is based on the time-honored principle that rocks containing similar fossils are probably of similar age. Thus, if the fossils in a newly discovered deposit can be matched with those from a site that is already dated, then the new finds can be assigned approximately to that same period. Faunal correlation relies heavily on certain convenient "time markers"—species that went through some obvious change, either a migration or a rapid evolutionary development, at a particular time in their history. For example, about 12 million years ago, *Hipparion*, a primitive three-toed horse, crossed the Bering Straits land bridge from North America to Siberia and spread rapidly through much of Asia and Europe. The first appearance of *Hipparion* in European and Asian deposits is useful for dating these deposits and for correlating them with American sites.

In the case of species that underwent rapid evolutionary change, all sites containing representatives of this lineage at a similar stage of evolution are likely to be roughly the same age. During the past 10 million years, the elephants have evolved rapidly, and so has the group represented by today's pigs and warthogs. Fortunately, many African sites containing hominid fossils also contain these animals, and by matching their various evolutionary stages, we are able to date the hominid-bearing deposits.

Stratigraphic Correlation

We have already mentioned the basic principle of stratigraphic relations: younger rocks, in general, overlie older ones. Thus if we can date some of the rocks at a particular site (by means of faunal evidence, for example), we can usually get at least approximate dates for adjacent layers. If one stratum is known to be about a million years old, for instance, the stratum immediately below it must be older. And if the undated deposit lies above another stratum that dates to, say, 1.6 million B.P., then we can narrow our estimate still further; we now have a maximum age as well as a minimum age for the new material.

Simple as it is in principle, such stratigraphic correlation can be quite complex in its practical applications. Unfortunately, rock formations are not always neatly stacked up one on top of another like layers in a cake. Geological forces often intervene to break or distort the sequence. It may not be easy to tell which rocks at location A correspond to which at location B, a few kilometers—or even just a few dozen meters—distant. Often a great deal of careful mapping, surveying, and walking is necessary to trace the stratigraphic pattern from one area to another.

Paleomagnetism

One of the most recent and successful dating methods involves the study of the earth's magnetic field in past eras. We now know that this magnetic field, at present oriented toward the north, has reversed its polarity at irregular intervals during geological time. (During the reversed periods, the needle of a compass would point south.) Using sensitive instruments to detect the traces of ancient magnetism in a rock, it is often possible to determine the polarity of the earth at the time the rock was formed. What makes these paleomagnetic reversals especially useful for dating is that they are worldwide—all rocks of the same age show the same polarity, no matter where they come from. By matching the pattern of magnetic reversals found in a particular sequence of rocks against the standard pattern, we can often determine the position of each successive rock stratum in the geological column. Moreover, combining paleomagnetic and radiometric analysis (see below), scientists have succeeded in dating the successive reversals back to about 5 million B.P. (Unfortunately, the accuracy of radiometric methods is not great enough to date the sequence of earlier reversals.) Thus, we now have a time-keyed standard pattern of worldwide polarity reversals extending back some 5 million years.

Radiometric Dating

By far the most useful of the chronometric dating methods is *radiometric,* or isotopic, dating. This technique not only enables us to determine the age of newly found materials but has also made it possible to calibrate much of the geological sequence established by the other methods described.

Radiometric dating is based on the fact that certain radioactive isotopes—unstable forms of fairly common elements, such as carbon and potassium—decay at a constant rate. Thus, by measuring the amount of radioactive decay that has occurred in a fossil or rock, we can calculate the number of years that have passed since it was formed. The two most important radiometric methods, *radiocarbon* (C^{14}) dating and *potassium-argon* (*K-A*) dating, are discussed in greater detail in the accompanying box. Together, they allow paleontologists to date finds that are more than 500,000 years old (potassium-argon) or less than about 50,000 years old (radiocarbon). Neither, however, can be used with accuracy for material that falls between these two time ranges—a crucial period in hominid evolution. So the search continues for a reliable radiometric dating technique to fill this gap.

EARLY PRIMATE EVOLUTION

As new fossils are uncovered and situated in their proper place on the geological time scale, we gain a clearer idea of the kinds of life that have prevailed on the earth in the various stages of its history. Paleontologists commonly divide geological time into three major *eras,* each of which was dominated by a particular group of vertebrate animals:

1. The *Paleozoic,* dominated by fish, amphibians, and primitive reptiles.
2. The *Mesozoic,* dominated by the reptiles.
3. The *Cenozoic* (in which we are living), dominated by mammals and birds.

As Figure 7-1 indicates, eras are subdivided into smaller units—*periods* and *epochs.*

The span of time on which we will focus in the remainder of this chapter is shown in the far right of Figure 7-1. It extends from the last period of the Mesozoic era, called the Cretaceous, through most of the Cenozoic era, and into the Miocene epoch, which ended some 5 million years ago. During this period, mammals, hitherto a rather minor group, expanded and diversified in a succession of adaptive radiations. In one of the earliest radiations, the first primates appeared. From this beginning we follow the path leading to our own species. As our story opens, our ancestors are tiny insect-eating creatures scurrying and squeaking in the Cretaceous underbrush; as it closes, the first members of the human family have already appeared.

Cretaceous Mammals and Primate Origins

Though the evidence is sparse, it appears that the earliest primates emerged about 70 million years ago, at the end of the Cretaceous period. The Cretaceous was the last period of the Mesozoic, the era of reptiles. During its immense span, stretching from 135 to 65 million years ago, several adaptive radiations of dinosaurs came and went, while the primitive ancestors of mammals, birds, and present-day reptiles played modest supporting roles beside them.

The late Cretaceous world was very different from today's. Continental drift was just begin-

Radiometric Dating

Radiocarbon dating makes use of the fact that the radioactive isotope C^{14} exists in the atmosphere in a more or less constant proportion. Living organisms take up C^{14} just as they do the common nonradioactive isotope C^{12} (plants do this by utilizing atmospheric CO_2, and animals by eating plants). Because living organisms are constantly exchanging carbon with the atmospheric reservoir of CO_2, the proportion of C^{14} they contain remains similar to that found in the atmosphere. When the organism dies, however, the radioisotope begins to decay and is not replenished. The result is a decline in the ratio of C^{14} to C^{12}.

Like other radioactive isotopes, C^{14} decays at a constant rate. Of any given initial amount, one half will decay into nitrogen in 5,730 years. This period is called the *half-life* of the isotope. By measuring the proportion of C^{14} remaining in a sample of organic material, and then comparing this measurement with the constant rate of decay, we can establish with some accuracy the time elapsed since the organism's death.

In taking these measurements, researchers must be extremely careful to determine that the sample has not been contaminated by later carbon. Such contamination, which can occur through weathering or handling, or from rootlets or humic acid seeping from higher levels in the soil, can be the source of appreciable error.

The margin of error is also affected by the age of the sample. Because too little C^{14} remains after about 70,000 years of radioactive decay, radiocarbon dating is effective only with materials of late Pleistocene and recent age. Within this range of time, the greatest probability of error exists in the older dates. This difference in accuracy results from the fact that although the radiocarbon method depends on C^{14} existing in the atmosphere in a constant proportion, data suggest that there have been fluctuations. By determining the radiocarbon age of the annual growth rings of long-lived trees, it is possible to correct the C^{14} scale for the last few thousand years, but this correction cannot be applied to older remains.

The *potassium-argon* (*K-A*) dating method also depends on the constant rate of decay of a radioactive isotope. It differs from the radiocarbon method in two major ways, however: it is used with much more ancient material (the *youngest* material that can be dated is about 500,000 years old), and the substances dated are not fossils or organic material but minerals found in volcanic rock.

Potassium (including K^{39}, K^{41}, and the radioisotope K^{40}) is found in many rocks. Radioactive K^{40} has an extremely long half-life: every 1.3 billion years, half the K^{40} in a mineral decays into A^{40}, an isotope of the inert gas argon. If the mineral is sufficiently dense in structure, the gas is trapped in the crystalline structure of the rock and cannot escape. If the rock is strongly heated, however (for instance, if it is reduced to a molten lava or white-hot ash in a volcanic eruption), all the accumulated argon is driven off; when the rock cools, argon again begins to accumulate. By determining the ratio of argon to potassium in such a volcanic rock, and then comparing this ratio with the disintegration rate of K^{40}, we can determine the time that has elapsed since the rock cooled. Paleontologists and archeologists can then use such determinations to date whatever fossils and artifacts are related stratigraphically to the dated layer. The Fort Ternan *Ramapithecus* fossils, for instance, were dated by this method.

Although simple in principle, the K-A dating method requires scrupulous laboratory techniques. Such care is especially important when dealing with the relatively young rocks, less than 70 million years old, of the Cenozoic period. These rocks are so young compared with the half-life of K^{40} that they have accumulated comparatively little argon, making them very difficult to date. Stringent precautions must also be observed against contamination by atmospheric argon. Furthermore, the geological history of the rock may be less straightforward than the ideal case described above. If a sample contains particles of material from an earlier eruption, for instance, its age may be overestimated. But if argon has diffused out of the rock, or a later volcanic episode has reheated the rock and driven out some of its argon, it will seem to be younger than it really is.

ning to open the Atlantic basin (see the box on page 161), and North America was still connected to Europe via a mild and temperate Greenland. South America was still quite close to Africa. In higher latitudes, the climate of the Cretaceous was much milder than today's; temperate forests clothed Antarctica, Greenland, and Alaska, while warm, shallow seas covered much of the continental surfaces of Europe, Africa, and North America.

In the Cretaceous, the plant life of the earth underwent a fundamental change, which in turn gave rise to a highly significant event in the evolution of animal life. In earlier periods, nonflowering plants (including ferns, mosses, palms, cycads, and conifers) dominated the earth's flora. During the Cretaceous, these gave way to the flowering plants (including grasses, herbs, shrubs, and trees), which underwent immense expansion and radiation.

This floral revolution seems to have set off a chain reaction of adaptive changes among animals. Many flowering plants are pollinated by insects. They advertise for this service with showy petals and pay for it in nectar. As flowering plants spread, insects multiplied in numbers and diversity. And so, in turn, did insect-eating animals. In addition, many flowering plants produce edible nuts, berries, and fruits as a bribe to enterprising animals, who then help to disperse their seeds.

Thus the new vegetation of the Cretaceous offered unique evolutionary opportunities for small, agile, and adaptable creatures. Among the vertebrates, two groups responded to the challenge. One was the feathered branch of the dinosaur clan that became the birds. The other was the mammals.

By the late Cretaceous, several major groups of primitive mammals had evolved, among them the earliest placentals and marsupials. Among the rare placental fossils from the Cretaceous is one tiny molar, which has been assigned to the genus *Purgatorius*. This is probably the earliest known primate. Judging by their teeth—and we have little else to go on—such early placental mammals, including *Purgatorius*, were mouse- to rat-sized animals that fed mainly on insects, snails, worms, and the like, possibly supplementing their diet with fruit. They probably looked much like such primitive modern mammals as the opossum or the tree shrew.

Paleocene Primates

The end of the Cretaceous, about 65 million years ago, is marked by revolutionary changes in the earth's fauna. Dinosaurs, which had dominated the earth for nearly 150 million years, died out, and the surviving reptiles slipped into the less important ecological roles they occupy today. We do not know precisely why this happened. Presumably, specialized adaptations made the dinosaurs unsuited to changing environmental conditions. The important point from our perspective is that the econiches occupied by the dinosaurs became vacant and were occupied by the mammals, which multiplied in numbers and diversity.

The surface of the earth continued to change slowly during the Paleocene epoch (65 to 54 million years ago). The two Americas were widely separated. The land bridge between North America and Europe was still present, though shrinking, as the Atlantic basin widened. The climate cooled somewhat. Mammals in general flourished—including the primates. Paleocene primate fossils have so far been found only in western North America and in western Europe, but their distribution was probably much wider, including tropical Central America and perhaps Africa. Primate fossils in Paleocene rocks consist mostly of isolated teeth, mandible fragments, and small bones from the foot. We have only a very few primate skulls from this period, all rather damaged, and a few limb bones. Incomplete as it is, however, this fossil evidence suggests that the Paleocene primates were a highly diversified group with many specialized adaptations (Table 7-1, p. 160).

Paleocene primates were quite small, ranging from the size of a tiny mouse to that of a cat. *Plesiadapis*, one of the best known, probably resembled a woodchuck (see p. 164). The limb bones that we have indicate that many Paleocene pri-

TABLE 7-1. The First Primate Radiation, Members of the Superfamily Plesiadapoidea

TAXON	DESCRIPTION	TIME	GEOGRAPHICAL DISTRIBUTION
Family Plesiadapidae 5 genera, including *Plesiadapis*	Medium-sized vegetarians with large incisors; some specialized for powerful gnawing.	Paleocene-Eocene	Europe North America
Family Carpolestidae 3 genera	Mouse- to rat-sized omnivores, with large incisors and an enlarged premolar for slicing.	Paleocene	North America
Family Paromomyidae 6 genera, including *Purgatorius*, possibly the earliest known primate	A diverse group of mouse- to rat-sized animals, including some very primitive forms. One genus with long, tweezer-like incisors.	Late Cretaceous Eocene	North America Europe
Family Picrodontidae 2 genera	Two tiny, mouse-sized animals with very specialized teeth; perhaps fed on nectar and insects.	Paleocene	North America

These earliest primates flourished during the Paleocene epoch, but some date back to the end of the Cretaceous period, more than 70 million years ago, while others lasted into the Eocene epoch. Note that several families are found in both Europe and North America, which were joined while these groups were evolving.

mates had the mobile ankles and forearms that are needed for climbing. Thus it seems that the primates had already made their crucial move into the trees. Nevertheless, they do not yet show any of the adaptations for climbing by grasping that are distinctive traits of later primates. Their fingers and toes end in sharp claws rather than in flat nails—clear evidence that they climbed like squirrels, by digging their claws into the tree bark. The skull, too, is primitive, lacking evidence of such distinctive primate traits as sharper vision and a reduced sense of smell.

In certain respects, then, the Paleocene primates were quite primitive—that is, similar to the ancestral mammal. In other respects, they were specialized. Many species, for example, had a rather specialized set of teeth, including a pair of large, protruding middle incisors separated by a sizable gap from the other teeth. They probably used these rodentlike teeth to grab insects and to snip leaves and fruits from their stalks, tasks for which later primates would use their skillful hands. However, the specializations that these primates developed are not seen in modern primates. Hence it is clear that the Paleocene primates whose fossils we have were not our direct ancestors. Rather, we can think of them as the cousins of our ancestors.

Although these early species do not yet show any evidence of distinctive primate "trends," most primatologists include them in the order because two critical derived traits—the details of

Geological Processes

Paleoanthropologists rely heavily on the techniques and concepts of geology to help them find, date, and interpret fossils and artifacts. In recent years, a major revolution has occurred in geological theory. *Plate tectonics* now provide a framework for understanding various geological phenomena such as mountain building, earthquakes, and volcanism. According to current ideas, the earth's crust consists of a series of semirigid plates floating on a layer of hot, semimolten material in the mantle below. Along one margin of each plate, new crust is formed as molten rock wells up from below and hardens. On the plate's opposite side, crust is consumed, plunging into the deeper, molten layers of the mantle. Infinitely slowly, the plates, like enormous rafts, travel across the earth's surface. The continents, consisting of less dense rock, are carried along on the plates. When a continent reaches the edge where a plate is being reabsorbed into the mantle, it may buckle, thereby forming a mountain range, or it may collide and fuse with another continental block, thrusting up mountains as it does so. New crust welling up below a continent will split it apart, first forming a deep crack, the precursor of a new ocean. Molten material, formed in the crust under the stress of plate movements, often erupts as volcanic ash, lava, and cinders.

These tectonic processes constantly renew the *relief* of the continental surface, creating new mountains, rifts, and trenches. *Erosion* attacks this relief even as it forms. Rain, frost, and plant roots detach particles from the rock surface. Propelled by wind, water, or ice, the particles scour the rock surface, eroding it further. *Glaciers* are particularly effective erosional agents. Inching their way down mountainsides, they pluck rock from the surface, crush it to an abrasive gravel, and gouge deep valleys.

Gradually, loose material from mountain peaks and hillsides finds it way into low-lying areas, blown by winds or carried by water or glaciers. Here, it accumulates as *sediment* in orderly, horizontal layers, or *strata* (singular, *stratum*). These often contain fossils. In volcanic areas, sediments frequently contain ash, and may alternate with layers of lava or pumice (volcanic rock). Such layers permit the paleontologist to use K-A dating. In time, the sediments may harden into rock under the pressure of overlying material. Sedimentary rocks become subject to uplift, contortion, and erosion in future tectonic episodes, disturbing the orderly arrangement of strata and exposing the fossils they contain. *Stratigraphy* is concerned with analyzing these processes, and deducing the chronological relationships of strata—and the fossils or artifacts they may hold.

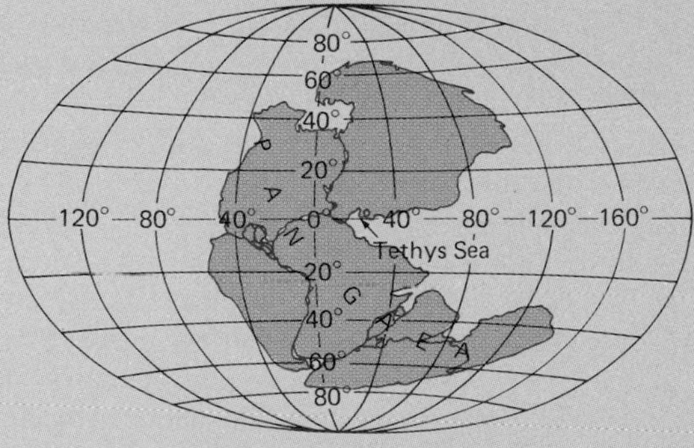

The continents 200 million B.P.

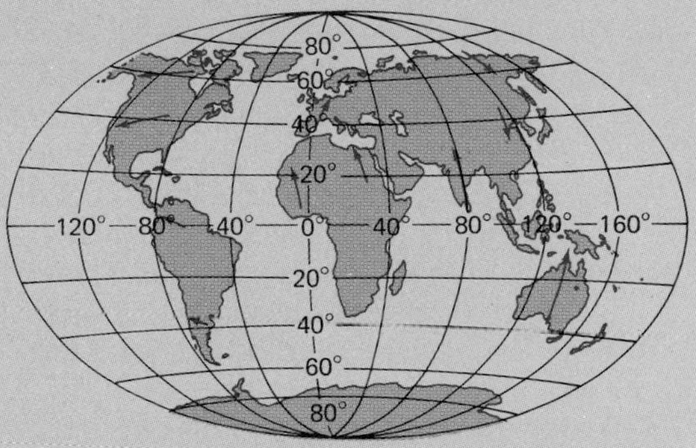

The continents today

their molar teeth and the construction of the bony capsule that encloses the middle ear—are shared with undoubted primates but not with other mammals. This is a good illustration of how apparently trivial details of anatomical structure can outweigh striking but superficial features as evidence of evolutionary relationships.

Judging by the abundance and variety of the fossil remains, the Paleocene primate radiation was immensely successful. These early primates were the equivalent, in their day, of rats, squirrels, and prairie dogs. With the evolution of true rodents in the Eocene, these rodentlike primates disappeared completely. By that time, however, another branch of the order had given rise to unmistakable "true" primates.

The New Primates of the Eocene: The First True Prosimians

The geography of the Eocene epoch (54 to 36 million years ago) was essentially similar to that of the Paleocene. The southern continents were still mainly isolated, the Atlantic basin was slowly opening (the land bridge had disappeared by 50 million B.P.), and warm, shallow seas still covered much of the continents. The climate of the Eocene was, if anything, even warmer and less seasonal than that of the Paleocene. Subtropical forests covered the plains of the American West and extended as far north as London and Paris.

Most of the Eocene primate fossils come from North America, western Europe, and Asia, though it is likely that primates also lived in Africa throughout the Eocene and reached South America by its close. Some Eocene primates are the last specialized descendants of such Paleocene forms as *Plesiadapis,* more rodentlike than primate in their adaptations. The remainder, however, are quite different. In their limb bones and skull, they show at least the beginnings of all the typical primate adaptive trends. Indeed, they are quite like modern prosimians.

The new characteristics of the Eocene fossils show a clear behavioral breakthrough—the emergence of the distinctive primate survival strategy based on the combination of sharp wits, keen eyes, and skillful hands, along with the slow, careful rearing of the young, one or two at a time.

Evidence for this new way of life is obvious throughout the anatomy of the Eocene primates. Although their brains were small and simple by standards of modern primates, they are relatively large in comparison with other Eocene mammals. Thus the primate trend toward braininess has already been established. In the eye area, the change is even more striking. In the Paleocene primates, the orbits—the bony sockets of the eyes—faced sideways and were not separated from the temporal region, with its powerful chewing muscles. By contrast, the orbits of the Eocene primates face forward, and, like those of the modern prosimians, they are protected on the side by the bony ridge of the postorbital bar (see pp. 164–165). These refinements of the visual apparatus, along with a reduction of the snout, indicate that the Eocene primates were beginning to depend at least as much on eyesight as on smell to locate food, detect danger, and keep track of one another.

Their teeth too are different. Unlike the enlarged, pincerlike front teeth seen in *Plesiadapis,* their incisors are small and unspecialized. From this we can infer that they did not need specialized teeth to manipulate fruits, seeds, and leaves—perhaps because they were using their hands for these tasks. Finally, the limb skeleton of the Eocene primates implies a thoroughgoing commitment to life in the trees, beyond that seen in the more generalized Paleocene forms. This is illustrated by the skeleton of *Notharctus* (pp. 164–165), which shows mobile, elongated fingers and toes that were clearly adapted for grasping, nails rather than claws, long hindlimbs, and a powerful mobile big toe—in short, the limbs of an active, arboreal climber and leaper, much like modern *Lemur.*

The Eocene primates, then, had clearly established the fundamental adaptive trends of the primate order. The later stages of primate evolution are largely a matter of elaborating these themes. But if the advanced primates of the Eocene are not the direct descendants of known Paleocene forms, where did they originate? As we have seen, the basic primate trends are primarily adaptations to tropical rain forests. So it seems likely that these trends first appeared in either Central American or African Paleocene primates—of which we have no fossils—that later spread north with the warming climate of the Eocene.

Diversity Among the Eocene Primates

Superimposed upon the basic prosimian body plan of the Eocene primates are a great variety of adaptations to particular life styles (Table 7-2). Some were small insect eaters, like the modern tarsier; others were larger fruit and leaf eaters, like certain of the modern lemurs of Madagascar. Some species had the large orbits typical of nocturnal primates; others clearly foraged by daylight. Many of these adaptations closely resemble those of modern prosimians, especially the lemurs. Nevertheless, only in a few cases can we trace direct phyletic relationships with later primates. The modern lemurs are probably the de-

TABLE 7-2. The "Second Wave" of Primate Evolution, the Lemuriformes and Tarsiiformes of the Eocene Epoch

TAXON	DESCRIPTION	TIME	GEOGRAPHICAL DISTRIBUTION
Infraorder Lemuriformes	The lemur branch of the prosimians.		
Superfamily Adapoidea	Early lemurs.		
Family Adapidae Several genera, including *Notharctus*	A diverse family of medium-sized lemurs; includes several robust vegetarians and some small, large-eyed (? nocturnal) forms.	Eocene-Oligocene	North America Europe
Infraorder Tarsiiformes	The tarsier branch of the prosimians.		
Family Tarsiidae Several genera	Small, tarsier-like hoppers, close to ancestry of modern *Tarsius*, but less insectivorous, more omnivorous.	Eocene-Recent	Europe Asia
Family Anaptomorphidae Several genera	American tarsier-like primates. Mostly mixed diets; some nocturnal forms. May have included ancestors of anthropoids.	Eocene-Miocene	North America Europe Asia
(Uncertain Taxonomic Status) *Pondaungia, Amphipithecus*	Two fragments, may be early anthropoids.	Eocene	Burma

Some families, but no genera, of this radiation are common to North America and Europe. This indicates that the major separation of the two land masses occurred in the Paleocene, and that distinct faunas were now evolving independently on either side of the widening Atlantic.

Primates of the Paleocene and Eocene

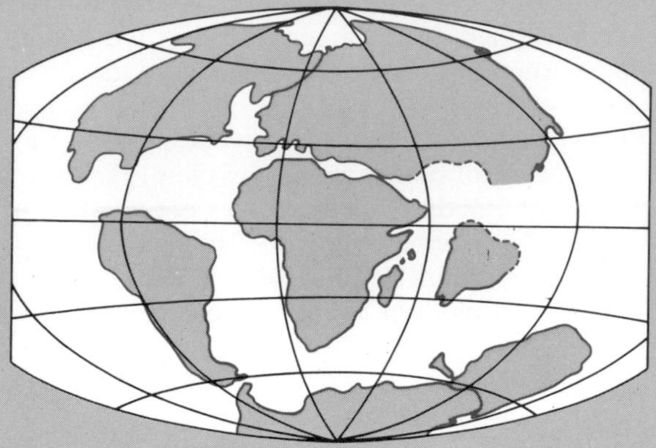

65 million years ago

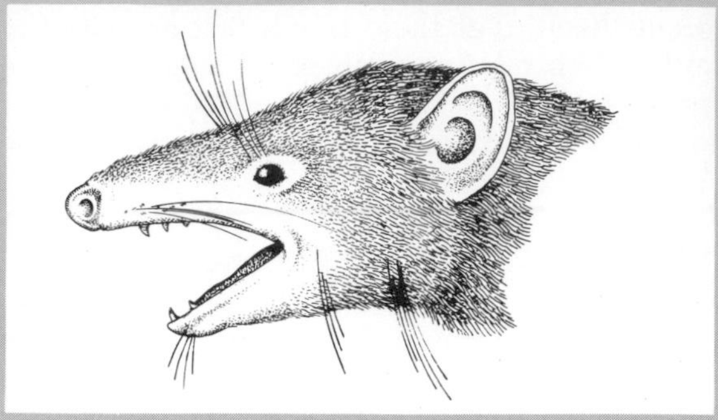

(Robert Frank)

Palaechthon, a primate of the Paleocene epoch, was an insect eater; it probably located its prey chiefly by smell, assisted by its long whiskers. Though not one of the very earliest primates, *Palaechthon* probably resembles closely the primitive primate stock. Such ancestral primate forms would have been unspecialized enough to give rise both to the more specialized plesiadapoid primates of the Paleocene and the more advanced Eocene primates.

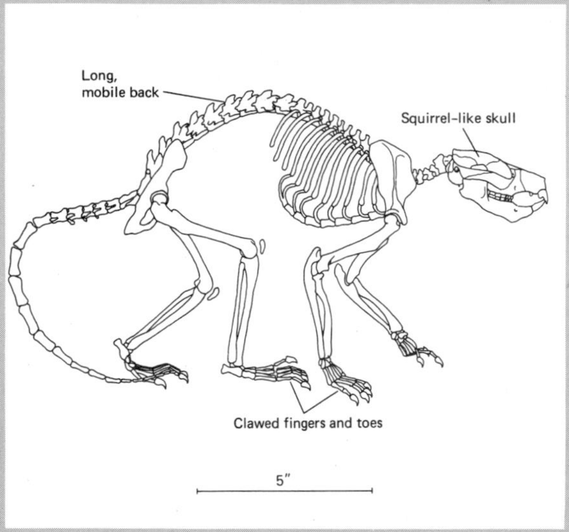

(Biruta Akerbergs, after I. Tattersall, 1970)

Many of the Paleocene primates were distinctly rodent-like. *Plesiadapis*, for example, had sharp, squirrel-like claws. It had not yet evolved the long, padded fingers and toes, adapted for climbing by grasping, that are typical of later primates. Its skull also retains a number of primitive traits, such as a comparatively small braincase and large muzzle.

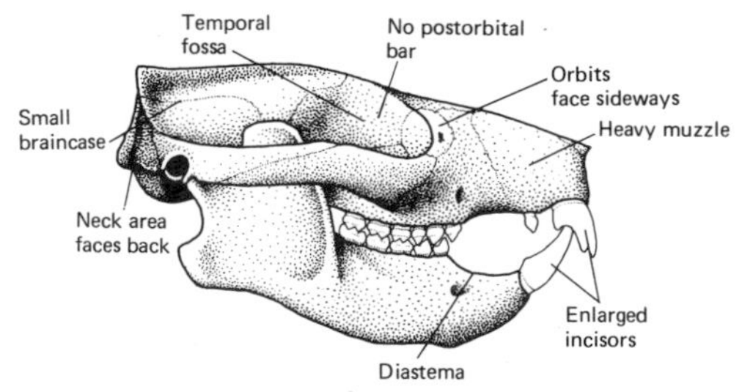

(Biruta Akerbergs, after Szalay, 1972)

(Robert Frank)

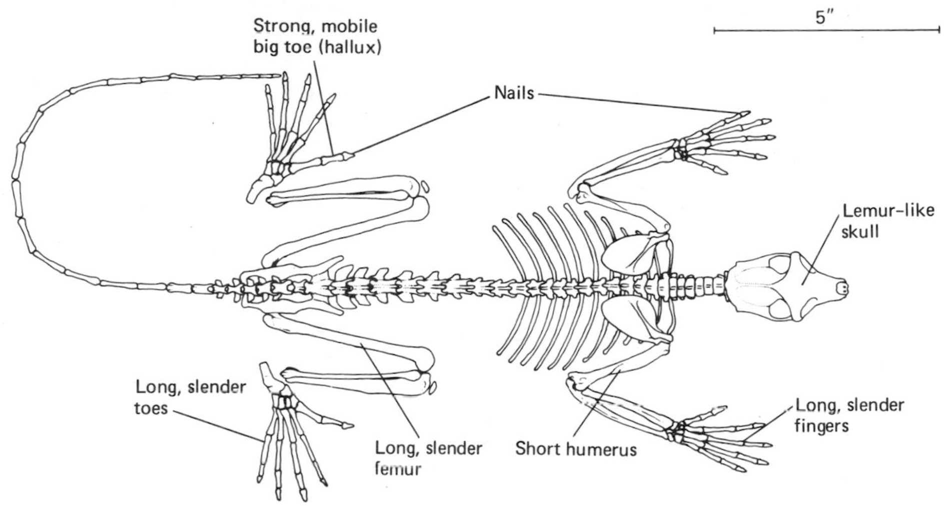

(Biruta Akerbergs, after W. K. Gregory, 1920)

(Robert Frank)

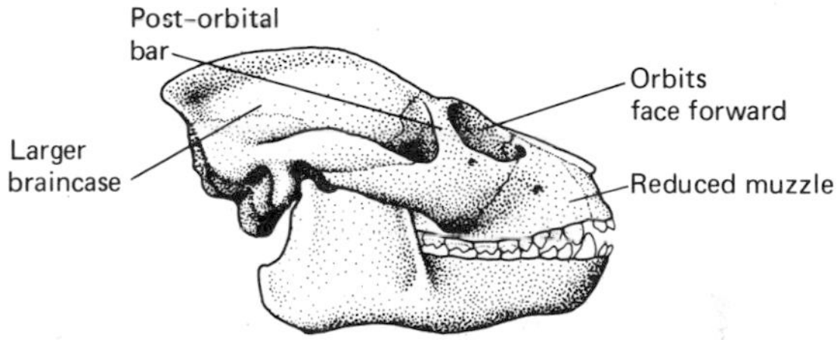

(Biruta Akerbergs)

By the Eocene, the first true prosimians had appeared. The brain case of such animals as *Notharctus* (above) and *Necrolemus*, a nocturnal, tarsier-like prosimian (left), is larger, the muzzle reduced, the eyes face forward and are partially isolated from the chewing muscles by a post orbital bar. These features suggest a greater reliance on vision rather than smell. The teeth are less specialized, and the limbs are those of a powerful climber and leaper, with long hind limbs and long, grasping fingers and toes equipped with nails rather than claws.

scendants of Eocene stocks of which we have no fossils. One particular Eocene subfamily may have been ancestral to the Anthropoidea—monkeys, apes, and humans. However, the earliest undoubted anthropoid fossils we have come from the Oligocene.

Oligocene Primates: The Anthropoid Transition

By the time the Oligocene epoch (36 to 23 million years ago) began, the earth's climate had cooled significantly, and climatic differences between the tropics and the higher latitudes had become more pronounced. The seas that still covered much of southern Europe and North America, and that had divided Europe from Asia, were shrinking, allowing faunas that had previously been separated to mix. In North America, the climate of the middle latitudes became less mild and more seasonal, and grasslands began to encroach on the subtropical forests where *Notharctus* and its relatives had lived. New World monkeys appeared for the first time in South America, presumably as immigrants from Central America. However, the focus of our study, the origin of the human lineage, lies in the Old World.

With the climatic changes of the Oligocene, primates disappear from Europe. Fortunately, just as we lose track of primates in Europe and North America, we pick up their scent again in North Africa, where fossil deposits reveal for the first time a curious mammalian fauna that had been evolving there in isolation since the earliest part of the Cenozoic. The most important site is in the Fayum, a wind-scoured depression in the Egyptian desert not far from Cairo. During the Oligocene, the Fayum was in the delta of a large river flowing from the interior of Africa to the Mediterranean. Its muddy channels and swamps abounded with fish, turtles, crocodiles, and dugongs (sea cows). Tall trees grew along the river-

Figure 7-3. Skull and reconstruction of *Aegyptopithecus*, an Oligocene primate whose fossils have been found in the Fayum, near present-day Cairo. (*Robert Frank*)

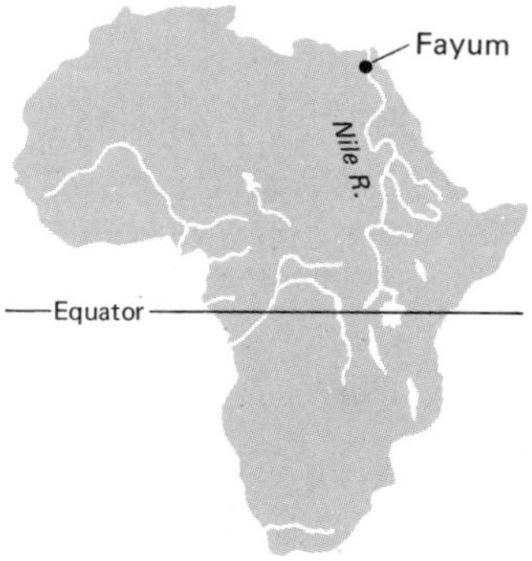

In Oligocene times the Fayum was a swampy river delta inhabited by numerous mammalian species. Its fossils give us a glimpse of the evolving primates of Africa some 30 million years ago.
Typical Fayum primates were small, omnivorous, tree-dwelling quadrupeds; *Aegyptopithecus* was about the size of a cat. All the Fayum primates show distinctly anthropoid features: smaller snout and nasal cavity, forward-facing orbits protected by a postorbital partition, unspecialized teeth, and limbs adapted to springing and climbing, like those of modern monkeys. (*Biruta Akerbergs, Robert Frank*)

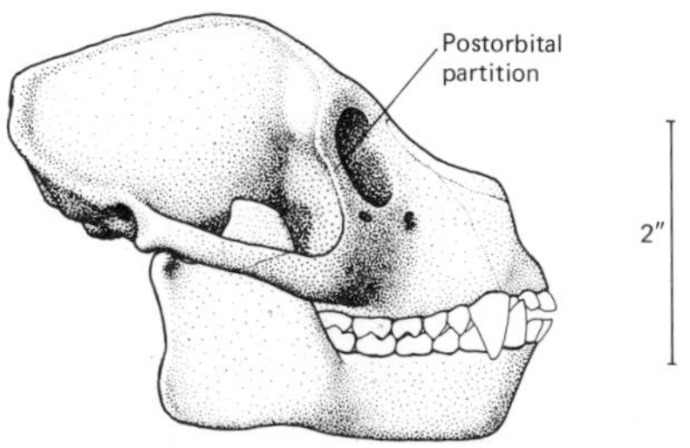

TABLE 7-3. Oligocene Primates of the Fayum

GENUS	DESCRIPTION
Propliopithecus	Medium-sized (about equal to small monkey). Perhaps ancestor of *Aegyptopithecus*.
Aegyptopithecus	Largest Fayum primate; like medium-sized monkey in size and shape.
Parapithecus and *Apidium*	Small animals (squirrel-sized) with some cercopithecoid-like features in their teeth. Perhaps ancestral to Old World monkeys. Very numerous in Fayum deposits.
Aeolopithecus	A small ape with large canines, known only from one mandible.

All these genera are catarrhines. *Propliopithecus* and *Aegyptopithecus* can be classified in the family Pongidae; the classification of the other genera is still disputed.

banks, giving way to more open country further inland.

This area supported a rich array of mammals, very different from those of the northern continents. Among them were primates quite unlike the Eocene prosimians of Europe or North America. Indeed, they were not prosimians at all but small, monkeylike anthropoids. There is little doubt that from their ranks sprang the Old World monkeys, the apes, and ultimately the human stock.

In the Fayum primates, we see the emergence of several of the characteristics that distinguish the anthropoids from the prosimians as distinct suborders. The primate trend toward precedence of the visual sense over the sense of smell has been carried beyond the prosimian level. The snout is quite small, and the nasal cavity is reduced. The orbits have moved closer together, so that they now face directly forward. The postorbital bar of the prosimians has become a complete postorbital partition, completing the protective bony socket for the eye (Figure 7-3). Recent studies of the endocranial cast of one of the Fayum primates, *Aegyptopithecus,* have shown its general shape to be anthropoid, not prosimian. And, in all the Fayum primates, the two halves of the lower jaw are firmly joined at the chin—another typical anthropoid feature.

The Fayum primates were quite small. The largest, *Aegyptopithecus,* was no bigger than a cat. Others were as small as the pygmy marmoset (page 105), which they must have resembled to some extent. All had flat-crowned teeth, which suggests that they were omnivorous, living mainly on fruit, with some leaves and insects. And all seem to have been arboreal quadrupeds. There is no evidence that the Fayum primates were adapted for brachiation, like modern apes, or for running on the ground as well as in the branches, like modern Old World monkeys. In their general appearance and locomotor habits, they probably resembled small New World monkeys like the South American howler and squirrel monkeys—highly arboreal springers and agile climbers. As suggested in Chapter 6 (Figure 6-2), such animals make good "structural ancestors" for both apes and Old World monkeys, so it is not surprising to find a similar body in these very early catarrhines.

While their advanced characteristics clearly place them among the anthropoids, the Fayum primates still retain some primitive features. The skull of *Aegyptopithecus,* for example, has a smaller braincase than that of a comparably sized modern monkey. Its snout is still quite long, and the bony opening of the ear is a simple ring—not a tube, as in modern anthropoids. Such primitive features are to be expected in the early members of a group. Thus the Fayum primates can be seen as a bridge—half-primitive, half-modern—between the Eocene prosimians, with their set of basic primate traits, and the more evolved apes and monkeys of the Miocene, in which anthropoid traits are fully developed.

Miocene Primates

The lengthy Miocene epoch (23 to 5 million years ago) was a crucial one in the story of human evolution, for by its close the first hominids had appeared.

The Miocene Environment

Shaped by the forces of geological evolution, the surface of the earth continued to change during the Miocene. The African plate, edging northward, was nudging up against Eurasia, causing volcanic activity in southern Europe, buckling the earth's crust, and thrusting up mountains in a broken chain from France to Iran. The seas between Africa and Eurasia shrank and split into separate basins. About 18 million years ago, a land bridge was established between the two continents, allowing their faunas to mix—something that had not been possible since the very early Cenozoic, some 50 million years before—and allowing anthropoid primates to move out of Africa for the first time. The Great Rift Valley systems—extending south from the Jordan Valley and the Red Sea through eastern Africa—were active, producing earth movements and volcanic activity. Further east, the Indian subcontinent was pushing against the southern edge of Asia, thrusting up mountain chains from Afghanistan to China—forerunners of the modern Himalayas. By the end of the Miocene, the continental masses and climatic belts had reached essentially their present-day configurations.

Driven by geological change, climate and vegetation also evolved during the Miocene. Early in the epoch, moist temperate forests stretched across southern Eurasia from Spain to China. The tropical rain forest belt of Africa extended from the Atlantic to the Indian Ocean. As the epoch progressed, the climate became drier. The entire Mediterranean Sea dried up. Grasslands

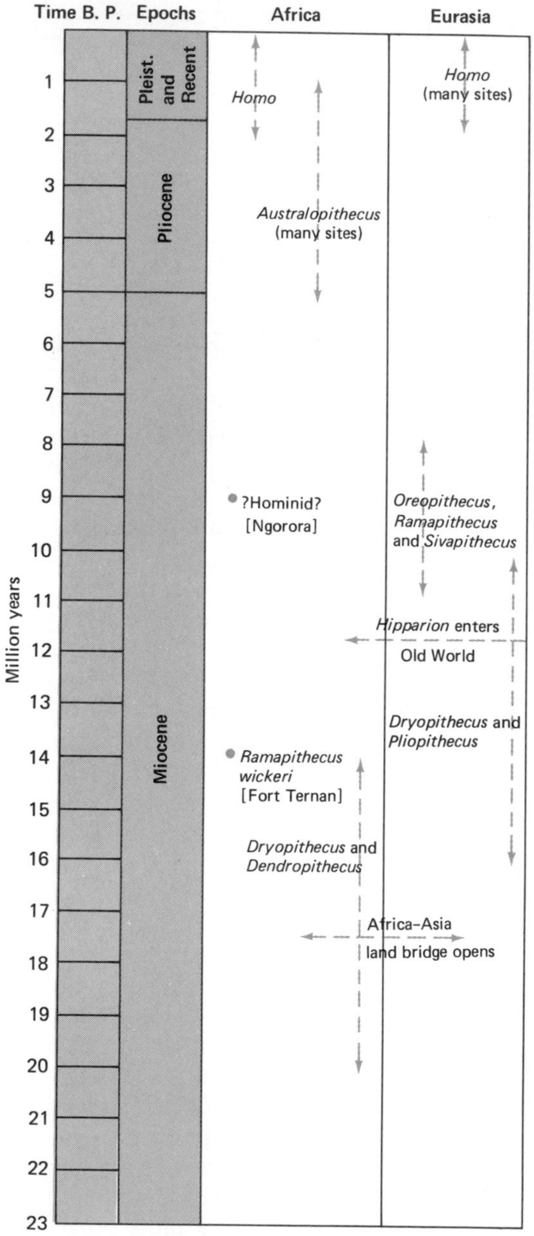

Figure 7-4. Time chart of the Miocene, Pliocene, and Pleistocene epochs.

and savannas gradually spread from the East into Europe, and the African forest belt shrank and became more broken. These changing conditions provided new challenges and new opportunities that decisively shaped the course of primate evolution in the Old World.

The Early Miocene in East Africa

The oldest Miocene primates come from sites clustered around the shores of Lake Victoria in Kenya and Uganda. They date from about 23 to 16 million years B.P. These are localities where ancient volcanoes dropped ash into shallow lakes and swamps, preserving the remains of plants and animals in fine detail.

A primatologist visiting a Kenyan forest of 20 million years ago would find the primates much more familiar than those of the Oligocene. The tiny monkeys seen in the Fayum Oligocene are gone. In their place, small lorisid prosimians, quite similar to bush babies and pottos of today, have appeared.[1] As for the anthropoid primates, they are much larger than their Oligocene forebears. The smallest are about the size of a small monkey, the largest as big as a large chimpanzee. The few skulls that we have of Miocene monkeys and apes no longer show the primitive proportions seen in Oligocene forms like *Aegyptopithecus.* The nose is reduced, and the braincase is full and rounded, as in modern apes and monkeys. Presumably, this means that they had also evolved behaviorally, becoming as flexible in their response to environmental challenges, as sophisticated in their social interactions, and as dependent upon socially mediated learning as a modern ape or monkey.

Our time-traveling primatologist would, however, notice one major difference from a modern African forest. Monkeys (Cercopithecoidea) were comparatively rare in this period. The main adaptive radiation of monkeys was yet to come, and most of the econiches that they fill today were occupied instead by a variety of apes (Hominoidea). This fact may serve to remind us that cercopithecoid monkeys are in no sense ancestral to apes or to man. Their role in the drama of human evolution has been essentially antagonistic: competing for ecological space with ancestral apes in the forest and with early hominids in the savanna.

One of the best known of these Miocene apes is *Dendropithecus* (formerly known as *Limnopithecus*). *Dendropithecus* was quite a small animal, about the size of a cat. In such features as the length and slenderness of its arms, it was intermediate between an arboreal quadruped and a specialized brachiator like the gibbon (Chapter 6). The remaining six ape species found in the early Miocene of Kenya are assigned to the genus *Dryopithecus.* Though primitive in some details, the dryopiths show unmistakable resemblances to the Pongidae and Hominidae, and most paleontologists agree that it is among this group that the common ancestor of modern apes and humans is to be found.

Dryopiths varied considerably in size. The largest species, weighing about 70 kilograms (154 lbs.) was the size of a big chimpanzee. The best known, *D. africanus,* was approximately the size of a rhesus monkey and weighed about 10 kilograms (22 lbs.). As we saw in Chapter 6, there is considerable controversy about how the hominids moved about before they made the change to bipedalism. Thus it would be of great interest to know whether the dryopiths were quadrupedal semi-brachiators, habitual brachiators, or knuckle-walkers who had passed through a brachiating stage. The limb bones we have are too fragmentary to tell us for certain. *D. africanus* seems to have been rather monkeylike in limb proportions, which would suggest that it was a semi-brachiator or a quadruped. However, some anatomists interpret the structure of its wrist bones as evidence that it had passed through a brachiating stage and was a semiterrestrial knuckle-walker, like a miniature chimpanzee.

The teeth provide other clues to dryopith behavior. Their dentition was balanced in proportion, dominated by neither back teeth nor front teeth (see p. 172). Their molars were large

[1] The origins of the lorisids, in the complete absence of prosimians from the well-known Fayum fauna, is something of a puzzle. They may be descended from immigrants that rafted to Africa from Madagascar, or they may have entered Africa by land from Asia.

TABLE 7-4. Miocene Primates of the Old World

TAXON	DESCRIPTION	APPROXIMATE TIME SPAN (MILLIONS OF YEARS B.P.)	GEOGRAPHICAL DISTRIBUTION
Suborder Anthropoidea			
Superfamily Hominoidea	The ape/human branch of the catarrhines.		
Dryopithecus	Widespread and varied group of ancestral apes.	20–10	Europe, Asia, and Africa
Gigantopithecus	A super-gorilla-sized ape; persisted into Pleistocene in China.	8–2	Asia
Pliopithecus	Small, tailed, monkey-like apes, possibly related to gibbon.	15–8	Europe
Dendropithecus		23–18	Africa
Ramapithecus, *Sivapithecus*	Perhaps earliest hominids (see text).	14–8	Europe, Asia, and Africa
Superfamily Cercopithecoidea	The monkey branch of the catarrhines.		
Several genera, Colobinae and Cercopithecinae	Colobine and cercopithecine monkeys; became commoner toward end of period, when baboons appear.	20–	Africa, Eurasia
Superfamily Oreopithecoidea			
Oreopithecus	Chimp-sized brachiator, may also have walked erect. Resemblances to hominids are probably parallelisms.	8	Europe; Africa?
Suborder Prosimii			
Superfamily Lorisoidea			
Family Lorisidae			
2 genera	Closely resemble modern pottos and galagos (bush babies).	20–18	Africa

enough to deal with leafy vegetation, while their incisors were adequate for slicing and peeling fruit. But they did not have the outsized incisors, specialized for fruit peeling, of the modern chimpanzees and orangutans, nor the high-cusped molars, specialized for leaf grinding, of the modern gorilla. All dryopiths seem to have had sexually dimorphic canines, like most modern apes and monkeys. We can imagine the males baring their long, sharp canines to keep other males in line and to protect the group against predators, while females and young took less part in agonistic encounters.

Other details of the dryopiths' way of life can be filled in by informed guesswork based on the behavior of living apes. Like chimpanzees, dryopiths probably spent most of their time in the trees searching for food, building nests, and socializing. Perhaps they also used simple tools occasionally, ate the meat of small mammals when they could catch them, and made the Miocene forests ring with shouts of discovery in the season when figs ripened. Like chimpanzees, too, dryopiths were adaptable animals. When the corridor to Eurasia opened, they spread rapidly out of Africa into the subtropical forests of the northern continents.

The Miocene Primates of Europe

Dryopithecus was evidently as much at home in the warm temperate forests of Miocene Europe as in the African rain forest. Its remains are quite frequent among the fossils that have been collected from ancient cave fillings, volcanic deposits, and lake beds in Spain, Germany, and France, dating from the period between about 15 and 8 million years ago. Along with two species of dryopiths is found a small, monkeylike ape called *Pliopithecus.* Like *Dendropithecus,* this too has been suggested as an ancestor of the gibbons.

Another Miocene hominoid of Europe has attracted attention as a possible hominid, a member of the human family. This is *Oreopithecus,* a chimpanzee-sized animal whose remains have been found in Italian lignite (brown coal) deposits dating to about 8 million years B.P. With its long arms and short legs, *Oreopithecus* was probably a brachiator. Some details of its foot and pelvis suggest that when not climbing it may have walked upright, on two feet. This fact, together with its rather short, humanlike face, have led to suggestions that *Oreopithecus* might have been a direct ancestor of the human species. But this is unlikely, since its molar teeth show structural details—extra cusps and crests—that are not seen either in ancestral hominoids, such as *Aegyptopithecus,* or in modern apes and humans. These peculiarities, which may be related to a diet of leaves, effectively rule *Oreopithecus* out of direct human ancestry. From another point of view it is interesting, however, for it shows that adaptation to at least some degree of bipedalism is not confined to tool-using humans or their direct ancestors.

Leaving the "abominable coal man" dangling from its lonely branch of the hominoid tree, we now head east in search of more likely ancestral hominids.

"Savanna Apes" of the Miocene

Adaptable as they were, the dryopiths seem to have been dependent upon the trees and their products. As savannas advanced to replace the moist forests, *Dryopithecus* disappeared from western Europe. Presumably, as the forests shrank, the dryopiths retreated with them into the Congo basin and Southeast Asia, where their descendants—the chimpanzee, gorilla, and orangutan—are still to be found. Replacing them, we find fossils whose structure indicates that offshoots of the dryopith group were beginning to pursue a new way of life—one that would eventually make them independent of the forest. The best known of these if *Ramapithecus.*

While *Dryopithecus* and other tree-dwelling apes inhabited the moist forests of Europe and tropical Africa, *Ramapithecus* was apparently adapting to more open woodlands and savannas. Its remains have been found at a variety of sites dating between 15 and 8 million years ago. Most are from eastern Europe, Turkey, northern India, and Pakistan, but an important specimen comes from the Kenyan site of Fort Ternan. The remains indicate quite a small creature, weighing about 14 kilograms (31 lbs.).

In many ways, *Ramapithecus* resembles *Dryopithecus,* its presumed ancestor. Indeed, some anthropologists believe that it falls within the expected range of variation for dryopiths and does not actually represent a new genus. However, most of those who have worked with the material at first hand believe otherwise. They feel that the distinctive features of *Ramapithecus* represent a divergent pattern of adaptation, suggesting that these animals had taken up a way of life rather different from that of their dryopith ancestors and cousins.

Ramapithecus differed from *Dryopithecus* chiefly in having larger molar teeth (relative to body size), with thick enamel, small, slender incisors and canines, a heavily-constructed palate (roof of mouth), face, and mandible. The jaw muscles were set well forward and oriented for

Primates of the Miocene

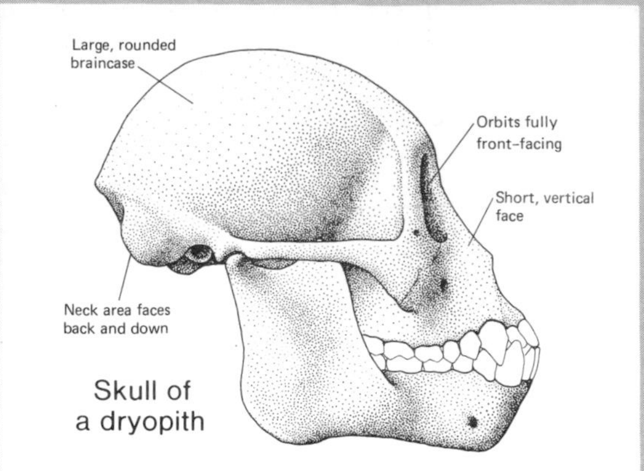

(Biruta Akerbergs, after a reconstruction by Davis and Napier)

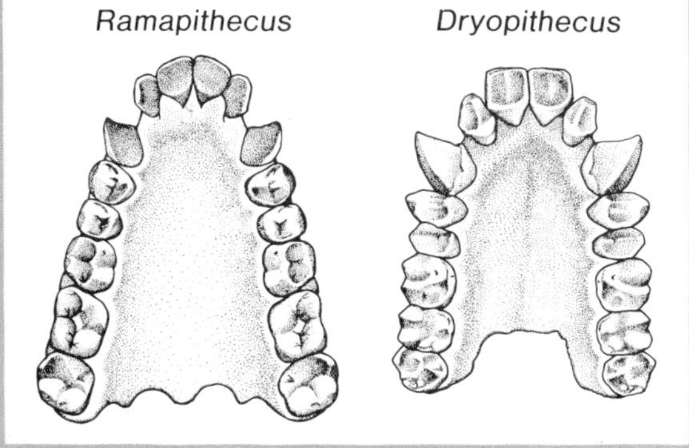

(Robert Frank)

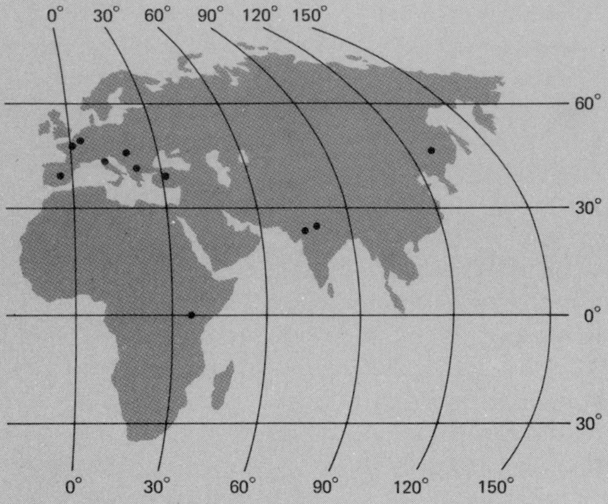

The dryopiths, which inhabited the forests of Europe and Africa during the Miocene epoch, almost certainly included the common ancestor of modern apes and humans. They were probably omnivorous and largely arboreal; some species were as large as a chimpanzee, which in many respects they must have resembled. *Dryopithecus* and its close relatives *Ramapithecus* and *Sivapithecus* have been found at many Old World sites (see map).

One of the most noteworthy is Fort Ternan in Kenya, shown in the photo. The Fort Ternan *Ramapithecus* deposits have been dated through K-A analysis of the volcanic layers that enclose them. Taphonomic studies carried out on the fossil assemblages provide evidence that *Ramapithecus* was adapting to savanna life, in contrast to its forest-dwelling dryopith cousins. A comparison between the jaws of *Ramapithecus* and *Dryopithecus* suggests the same conclusion. *Ramapithecus* had larger molars with thick enamel, small incisors, a heavy jaw, and chewing muscles oriented for great crushing power with the molars. This implies a diet of harder, drier foods typical of the savanna—roots, seeds, and so on—rather than the forest fruits that the dryopiths relied on. For this reason it is plausible to think of *Ramapithecus* as possibly the first hominid.

(© National Museums of Kenya)

maximum crushing power between the molars, rather than for slicing with the incisors.

The Adaptive Pattern of Ramapithecus No one of these characteristics alone represents a major departure from *Dryopithecus.* Taken together, however, they add up to a new adaptive complex. That is, they are part of an integrated set of features related to a specific function: more powerful chewing with the back teeth and less food preparation with the incisors (see p. 172). This probably means that *Ramapithecus* depended less on the juicy fruits of the forest and more on the harder, drier food objects found on the ground in savanna woodlands and bush.

The context in which *Ramapithecus* fossils have been found supports this hypothesis. In Pakistan and Kenya, they occur in the same sites with dryopiths, pliopiths, and other forest animals, as well as such grassland animals as giraffes and antelopes. In other words, the evidence suggests a mixed habitat of forest and woodland. However, as we saw, taphonomy can sometimes help us sort out such mingled assemblages. Taphonomic studies recently carried out at Fort Ternan strongly suggest that the grassland animals are the ones truly associated with *Ramapithecus.* Evidently, then, although *Ramapithecus* lived close to the forest edge, it foraged on the savannas, rather than in the forests as did *Dryopithecus.*

As we have seen, primates cannot make a living outside the forest unless they are able to forage on the ground as well as in the trees. If *Ramapithecus* had come to occupy such an econiche—foraging on the tougher foods of the savannas and leaving the lusher fruits of the forest to its dryopith cousins—this would explain its chewing apparatus.

Newly discovered *Ramapithecus* mandibles from Greece provide a further clue to the habitat of these animals. These specimens date from a time when grassy plains and woodlands had replaced the humid forests where dryopiths had flourished. The fossils are associated with such grassland animals as gazelles and *Hipparion,* the primitive horse. The only other primate found in a similar context is the semiterrestrial colobine monkey, *Mesopithecus,* which probably lived in the forests that grow along waterways. There is no sign of either *Dryopithecus* or *Pliopithecus.* It seems that these apes were unable to hold their own in the new environment—but *Ramapithecus* could, presumably because it was adapted to living and feeding on the ground.

Is Ramapithecus *a Hominid?* As we shall see in the next chapter, the adaptations of the chewing apparatus that distinguish these animals—jaw muscles set forward, heavily built jaws, and large back teeth—also characterize the first undoubted hominids: the australopiths of the Pliocene. This is the major reason for regarding *Ramapithecus* as a very early member of the family Hominidae.

This assignment, however, is still very tentative. In addition to the dental features mentioned, there are other derived features that characterize the later hominids—in particular, a pelvis and hindlimb adapted to walking on two legs. Whether or not *Ramapithecus* also had these features we simply cannot say. Since the limb skeleton is quite unknown, there is no evidence for or against bipedalism. (There is some material from Fort Ternan and Pakistan, but it has not yet been described.)

A second characteristic of undoubted hominids is that in both sexes the canine teeth are low-crowned and shaped rather like incisors. There is some ambiguous evidence about canine size in *Ramapithecus*—a visible socket in some of the Asian and European jaws and one preserved canine tooth from Fort Ternan. Compared with the molars, the Fort Ternan canine looks small; but this may simply be because the molars are large. Furthermore, we have no idea whether this specimen belonged to a male or a female, and therefore it tells us nothing on the question of whether both sexes had small canines. In short, we cannot settle this point with the fossils discovered to date.

But perhaps this lack of evidence is not so crucial to the hominid status of *Ramapithecus.* It is true that bipedalism and nondimorphic, incisor-shaped canines are striking derived features of later hominids. But many anthropologists are beginning to suspect that these features were not necessarily present in the *earliest* hominids, and that the first stages of hominid evolution may have been based upon a new habitat and a different feeding strategy—with bipedalism and nondimorphic canines coming later in the story. Regardless of whether *Ramapithecus* was a biped, a quadruped, or a knuckle-walker, and whether the males had large or small canines, the derived features of its chewing apparatus still make it the best middle Miocene candidate for hominid status.

More "Ground Apes"? The picture is complicated by the fact that *Ramapithecus* was evi-

Figure 7-5. The evolutionary history of the primates. (*Robert Frank*)

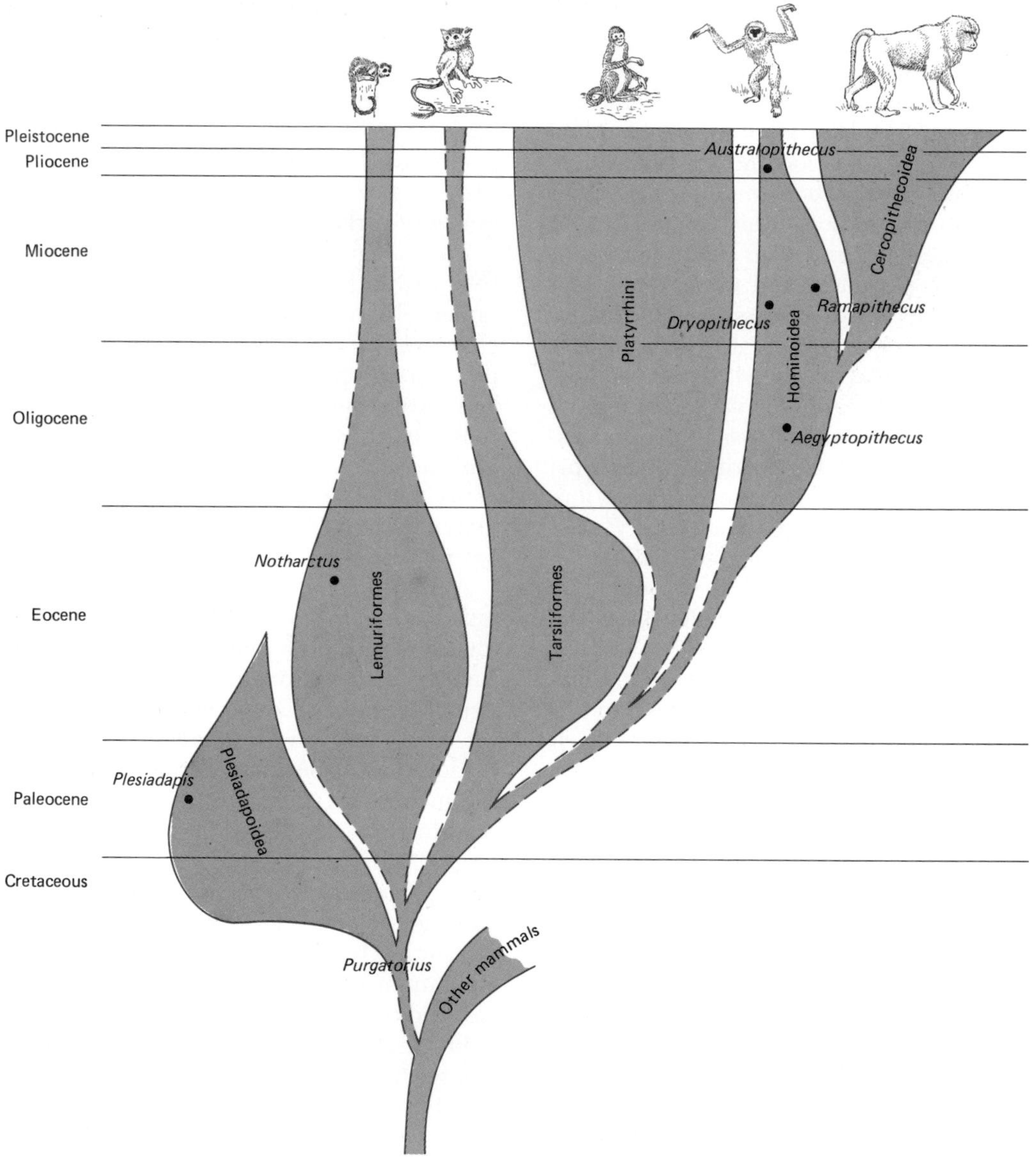

dently not the only Miocene hominoid to show hominid-like features in its jaws and teeth. The chimpanzee-sized *Sivapithecus* and the much larger *Gigantopithecus* are found with *Ramapithecus* in Europe and Asia. Like *Ramapithecus,* they had small incisors but large molar teeth with thick enamel set in short, massive jaws. Their canine teeth were short and stubby, but clearly not hominid-like—they were pointed and projecting in both sexes, and showed distinct sexual dimorphism in size. But the pattern of wear on the canines is unlike that seen in typical apes. Rather than honing to a sharp blade, the canine teeth of *Sivapithecus* and *Gigantopithecus* wore down from the tip. Perhaps this peculiar pattern of wear represents an early stage of selection for smaller, lower canines.

On the whole, *Sivapithecus* and *Gigantopithecus* are less hominid-like than *Ramapithecus,* though their chewing apparatus clearly suggests that they may have been making similar adaptations to open country life. In the case of *Gigantopithecus,* this adaptation was evidently quite successful. The genus survived at least until the late Pliocene (about 2 million years B.P.) in China, where its huge molar teeth are common among the fossils found in limestone caves. There is even an intriguing possibility—supported by historic Chinese illustrated manuscripts—that the giant apes lingered on in the remote bamboo forests of the Himalayas, eventually to give rise to stories of the Yeti, or abominable snowman.

We still have a lot to learn about these "savanna apes." We cannot be sure, for instance, whether the fossils found in Greece, Asia, and East Africa really represent a single clade or parallel, but separate and independent, attempts at colonizing the new habitat. Given the present state of our knowledge, it is probably wiser not to try to fit every fossil into a particular pongid or hominid lineage. It is better to take a wider view, namely, that in the Middle Miocene various ape populations scattered across the Old World were experimenting with life outside the closed canopy forest, and consequently were adapting to the food resources of the grassy steppes and savannas. One of these—not necessarily one represented in our present museum collections—was probably the founder of the family Hominidae, to which we belong.

Summary

Fossils are the remains of plants and animals that have been preserved and mineralized through geological accident. They provide hard evidence of extinct forms and tests of evolutionary theories based on the study of living species. Their setting can also tell us about the environment in which new adaptations emerged. By examining a fossil carefully and by comparing it with other fossils and with living species, we can often make inferences about the extinct species' evolutionary relationships and its way of life.

The *geological time scale* is a universal timetable of the earth's history. It is based on the principle that any *stratum* (layer) of rock, along with the fossils it contains, is younger than the strata beneath it. By using *faunal, stratigraphic,* and *paleomagnetic* dating methods, all of which rely on comparisons between new fossils or rocks and already dated fossils or rocks, we can situate a new fossil on the geological time scale and estimate its age. In some cases, we can also use *chronometric* methods, such as radiocarbon or potassium-argon dating, to assign a date directly.

The geological time scale is divided into three major *eras,* each dominated by a particular vertebrate group: the *Paleozoic* era, dominated by ancient fish, amphibians, and primitive reptiles; the *Mesozoic* era, by reptiles; and the *Cenozoic* era, by mammals and birds. Each era is subdivided into periods and epochs according to geological and evolutionary changes.

The last period of the Mesozoic era, the Cretaceous, witnessed a revolution in the earth's vegetation: the radiation of flowering plants. This change led in turn to changes in the earth's animal life. Insects proliferated, and so did small insect-eating vertebrates, including the earliest mammals. At the end of the Cretaceous the dinosaurs disappeared, vacating econiches that were soon filled by an extensive radiation of mammals—among them several primate species. The meager remains of these Paleocene primates, such as *Plesiadapis,* indicate that they were a diverse group of small animals, some already adapted to life in the trees. However, they do not yet show any of the distinctive primate specializations for tree living, such as the development of nails instead of claws.

By the Eocene, a sidebranch of these primitive Paleocene primates had given rise to unmistakably "true" primates, quite similar to modern prosimians. In the fossils of this group, such as *Notharctus,* we see the beginning of the distinctive primate characteristics: relatively larger brains, dependence upon vision, elongated digits for grasping, nails rather than claws—all features related to life in the forest canopy. These trends signify the emergence of a new primate adaptive strategy, the basis for a great variety of special adaptations among these Eocene prosimians.

The Oligocene primates of the North African Fayum, such as *Aegyptopithecus,* were quite different from the prosimians of Europe and North America. From their skull shape and refined visual apparatus it is clear that they belong to the Anthropoidea, or higher primates, belonging to the same group as the monkeys, the apes, and humans. Still primitive in some respects, the Fayum primates constitute a link between the Eocene prosimians and the advanced apes and monkeys that first appear in the Miocene.

Fossil Miocene anthropoids no longer have the primitive features of the Oligocene forms. They were probably as advanced behaviorally as modern apes and monkeys—as flexible in their response to environmental challenges, as sophisticated in their social interactions, and as dependent upon socially mediated learning. Apes are commoner than monkeys until the very late Miocene. Most Miocene apes fall into two main groups: the small, gibbonlike *Dendropithecus* and *Pliopithecus,* and the pongid *Dryopithecus.*

Dryopithecus probably included the common ancestor of hominids and pongids. The dryopiths were adaptable animals, with teeth less specialized and more humanlike than those of modern apes. Ten million years ago, *Dryopithecus* disappears from the fossil record. We assume that it followed the shrinking forests into central Africa and southeast Asia where its descendants, the great apes, survive today.

Oreopithecus, a European hominoid of the late Miocene, has been proposed as a possible ancestor of the human species. A much more likely candidate, however, is a group that is probably derived from *Dryopithecus* but apparently began experimenting with life outside the forest. This group is represented by *Ramapithecus* and its relatives. These genera show a new adaptive pattern: more powerful chewing with the back teeth and less food preparation with the incisors. This seems to indicate that *Ramapithecus* had abandoned the fruits of the forest to forage for the harder, drier foods of the savannas. Such dental adaptations are also found in the first undoubted hominid, *Australopithecus* of the Pliocene. Whether *Ramapithecus* should also be regarded as a hominid is disputable, but its dental features strongly suggest that the habitat and feeding strategy typical of early hominids had already been adopted by this period.

Glossary

Aegyptopithecus a cat-sized Oligocene anthropoid found in the Fayum deposits

Cenozoic the present geological era, dominated by mammals and birds

Cretaceous (135–65 million B.P.) the last period of the Mesozoic era, which saw the rise of flowering plants and early mammals

Dryopithecus a Miocene ape believed to be the common ancestor of modern apes and humans

Eocene (54–36 million B.P.) the second epoch of

the Cenozoic era, marked by development of primates resembling modern prosimians

faunal correlation dating deposits by comparing their animal remains with related fossils whose age is already known

fossils the remains of plants and animals that have been preserved and mineralized through geological accident

geological time scale a timetable that divides the earth's history into a series of periods and epochs, each of which is defined by certain geological and evolutionary events

Mesozoic the second major geological era, dominated by reptiles

Miocene (23–5 million B.P.) the fourth epoch of the Cenozoic, during which the earliest hominids appeared

Oligocene (36–23 million B.P.) the third epoch of the Cenozoic, which saw the appearance of anthropoid primates in the fossil record

Paleocene (65–54 million B.P.) the first epoch of the Cenozoic era, during which mammals became the dominant form of animal life on land

paleomagnetism residual magnetism in rocks that reveals the polarity of the earth's magnetic field at the time they were formed; useful in dating rock strata

Paleozoic the first major geological era, dominated by fish and amphibians

radiometric dating dating based on the constant rate of decay of radioactive isotopes

Ramapithecus* and *Sivapithecus Miocene hominoids that may have been early hominids

strata (sing. stratum) layers of rock, each of which is presumed to be younger than those underlying it

stratigraphic correlation dating rocks by determining their position relative to other strata whose age is known

taphonomy the study of the processes that may occur between death and fossilization; useful for interpreting fossil assemblages and reconstructing the original habitats of different fossil species found buried together

Suggested Readings

BISHOP, W. W., AND MILLER, J. A. (EDS.) 1972
Calibration of Hominoid Evolution. Buffalo: University of Toronto Press. Papers describing methods of dating and their application to primate-bearing deposits of the later Cenozoic.

SIMONS, E. L. 1972
Primate Evolution: An Introduction to Man's Place in Nature. New York: Macmillan. A leading primatologist's account of fossil primates.

SZALAY, F., AND DELSON, E. 1978
Evolutionary History of the Primates. New York: Academic Press. An authoritative, genus by genus account of fossil primates.

WILSON, J. T. (ED.) 1972
Continents Adrift. San Francisco: W. H. Freeman. A collection of articles on continental drift, including one dealing with its effects on evolution.

Chapter Eight

Australopithecus

In the previous chapter we reviewed more than 60 million years of primate history. As we saw, various apelike creatures of the late Miocene, about 8 million years ago, seem to have been adapting to open country. Some of these may be the earliest known hominids—primates that are cladistically closer to man than to living apes, such as the chimpanzee.

In this chapter our time span is narrower. We concentrate on the period stretching from the latest Miocene, about 5.5 million years ago, through the Pliocene and into the early Pleistocene, about 1 million years ago (see Figure 8-1). We are now dealing with undoubted hominids. However, new questions arise.

1. How many different kinds of hominids are there among these fossils?
2. How are the different kinds related to one another, and to *Homo sapiens*?
3. How did each fit into the ecosystem of which it was a part?

In this chapter, we attempt to answer these questions. We cannot claim, though, that our conclusions are universally accepted. From this period there are literally hundreds of hominid fossils. They span a geographical range from Africa to Java and are varied in size and structure. Our interpretation is simply one reading of this diverse evidence. Other anthropologists have differing views, and future discoveries may suggest new interpretations, as they often have in the past.

We believe that two genera of hominids, *Homo* and *Australopithecus*, can be distinguished in this period. *Homo* first appears at least 2 million years ago and probably forms a single, unbranched, evolving lineage. Although the earliest recognizable *Homo* are African, the group seems to have rapidly extended its range to tropical Asia. The members of this lineage become progressively more human in their structure and behavior. From the start, they make and use stone tools. As they evolve, and their technology becomes more elaborate, their physical structure reflects more and more strongly their dependence upon culture. We will trace the evolutionary history of the genus *Homo* in Chapters 9 through 11. The remaining Pliocene and Pleistocene hominids are, according to our view, best put into a second genus, *Australopithecus*, the subject of this chapter.

Although there are many questions still to be answered, we now have a reasonable picture of the australopiths, as members of this genus may be called. They first appear about 5.5 million years ago and seem to have been confined to Africa throughout their evolutionary history. Australopiths were bipedal, upright-walking creatures. By human standards, their brains were small and their jaws heavy, but their limbs and teeth clearly show that they were hominids. Indeed, they represent the culmination of the first phase of hominid evolution: the move from forest to open country. There they achieved a

An artist's reconstruction of a group of robust australopiths. Cousins of the human species rather than ancestors, the australopiths shared the African savannas with the earliest humans until about a million years ago, when they became extinct. *(Painting by Jay H. Matternes: Copyright Survival Anglia Ltd.)*

highly successful adaptation and survived for some 4½ million years. Early in this time span, some populations of *Australopithecus* probably gave rise to *Homo*. Other populations continued to live alongside the *Homo* line until about 1 million years ago, when the last australopiths became extinct.

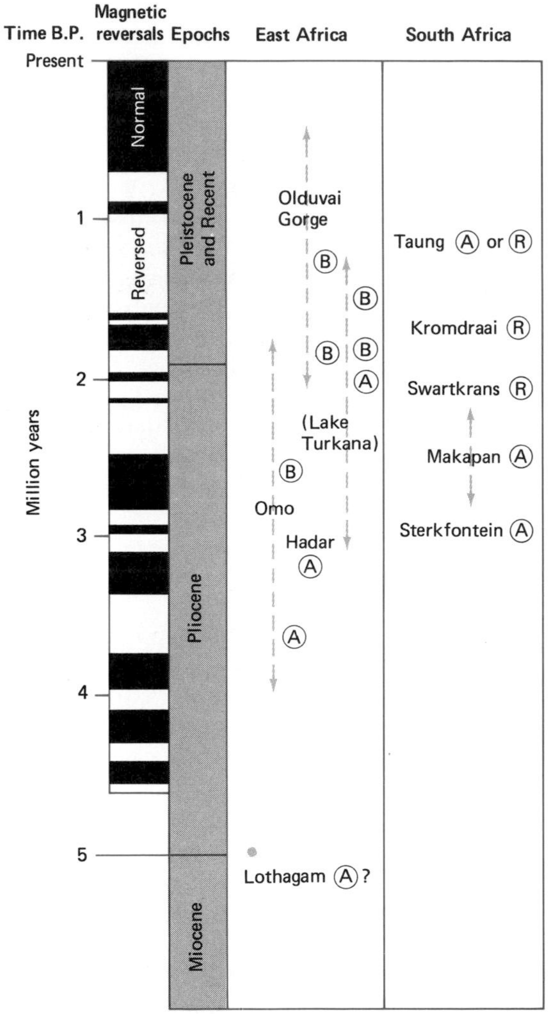

Ⓐ "Gracile" australopith (*A. africanus*)
Ⓑ "Hyper-robust" australopith (*A. boisei*)
Ⓡ "Robust" australopith (*A. robustus*)
(See text for discussion of these categories.)

Figure 8-1. Time chart of *Australopithecus* sites, correlated with magnetic reversal scale. The East African sites are mostly dated by potassium-argon; the ages of the South African sites are very approximate.

THE DISCOVERY OF *AUSTRALOPITHECUS*

Australopith fossils come from two different geographical areas and two different geological settings: limestone caverns in South Africa, and volcanic, lake, and river sediments of the East African Rift Valley.

South Africa

One day in 1924, Raymond Dart, a young anatomist at the University of the Witwatersrand, South Africa, received a box of fossil remains from a limestone quarry at a place called Taung. Among the fossils was the skull of a juvenile hominoid. With remarkable perceptiveness, Dart recognized that the skull (now known as the "Taung child") belonged to a species unknown to science, a relative of man more primitive and apelike than any previously discovered. He named it *Australopithecus africanus* (southern ape of Africa). Dart and his colleagues extended their explorations to limestone caverns near Johannesburg—Sterkfontein, Kromdraai, and Swartkrans—and to the cave of Makapan in the northern Transvaal (Figure 8-2). They were soon rewarded by the discovery of more australopith remains. Each of these sites has since produced skull fragments, some limb bones, and large numbers of teeth of australopiths, as well as quantities of remains of other animals.

In many ways, limestone caverns are ideal for fossilization. Limestone is slightly soluble in rain and soil water, so that as moisture seeps below the surface, underground caverns gradually form. Eventually, cracks appear in the overlying rock, linking the caverns to the open air. Then animal bones and other debris lying about the entrance begin to be deposited in the caves. Over the years, the lime-bearing water percolating

Professor Raymond Dart displays his "baby," the cranium from Taung that is the type specimen of *Australopithecus africanus*. (Jerry Cooke)

through the deposits finally cements them together into a solid, concretelike rock known as *breccia*, preserving bones and teeth in fine detail. As more time passes, natural erosion may remove the surrounding limestone, leaving the harder, fossil-bearing breccia exposed as a rocky mound.

In other ways, however, a limestone cave is a frustrating setting for the paleontologist. The tough breccia must be painstakingly broken down with chisels, and its fossils extracted by slowly dissolving away the matrix with acid. Worst of all, each cavern is an isolated geological entity, with no stratigraphic connections beyond its walls, and no volcanic materials that can be used in potassium-argon dating. Limestone cave deposits are therefore very difficult to date.

Dart believed that australopiths lived in the caves, and that the animal bones found there were their tools and the remains of their meals. This now seems unlikely. Connected to the surface only by narrow shafts, the caves would have been dark, dank, and inaccessible at the time they were filling. Dr. C. K. Brain (1970) has developed a more plausible theory that would account for the accumulation of bones in the caves. He observed that in the dry, windswept grassland of the Transvaal the few tall trees are often rooted in the entry shafts of underground caves. He also noted that, after making a kill, leopards like to lift the remains of their prey into a tree to secure it from hyenas. Thus, he reasoned, leopards would seek out the scattered trees, and the ground around them would become littered with bony debris, some of which would find its way down into the cave.

Brain also showed that the broken bones most commonly found in the breccia—jaws, teeth, and the tough ends of limb bones—correspond rather closely to those discarded by modern leopards. This would also account for the high proportion of baboon remains in the caves, for leopards are great baboon killers. But the taste of Pleistocene leopards must also have run to tender young australopiths. This is dramatically indicated by a juvenile skull fragment from Swartkrans, punctured by a pair of holes spaced precisely like the canine teeth in a leopard's lower jaw.

East Africa

The geological setting of the East African australopith fossils is quite different from that of the South African remains. Most come from sediments that accumulated in lakes or in the floodplains of rivers. A succession of earth movements and volcanic eruptions that began in the early Miocene have provided excellent conditions for the accumulation of such fossil-bearing sediments. In complete contrast to the South African caves, these deposits often form stratified beds that may be dozens or even hundreds of meters thick. Frequently, they extend over many square kilometers, so that relationships between individual sites can be established directly by careful stratigraphic mapping. Volcanic rock interlayered with the sediments allows us to date many of the deposits by using the potassium-argon method or by tying them to the geomagnetic reversal scale (Chapter 7).

Reconstructing Early Hominid Environments: The Omo Valley

The lower valley of the Omo River, which flows into Lake Turkana some 560 kilometers (348 mi.) southwest of Addis Ababa, Ethiopia, is one of the last corners of the old Africa. Hot, dry, and remote, its grassy plains support herds of zebra and antelope, and the lions and cheetahs that prey on them. Monkeys and bushbuck are to be found in the dense bush along the banks of the river.

The scientists who return year after year to this remote region are ecologists. The subject of their study, however, is not today's fauna; rather, it is that of three million years ago, represented by the thousands of bones that are eroding from the sediments. Since 1967, the fossil-bearing sediments of the Omo Valley have been studied by an international team under the leadership of F. Clark Howell, of Berkeley, and Yves Coppens, of Paris, enthusiastic proponents of the multidisciplinary approach to paleoanthropology.

Traditionally, the aim of paleontological field work was to gather a collection of choice fossils and to ship them back to a museum for cleaning and interpretation. But modern paleontology, with its ecological orientation, poses questions that cannot be answered in this way. We are not satisfied to know a fossil animal's structure and taxonomic relationships. We want to know something of the climate and vegetation of its habitat, what animals lived alongside it, and how its remains found their way into the deposit. The modern, multidisciplinary approach emphasizes the importance of gathering information *in the field*—and requires the cooperative efforts of a team of specialists. This was the approach used in the Omo Valley.

Before any fossil-collecting was done, the geology of the area was investigated; aerial photography, combined with a lot of footwork on the ground, gradually revealed a complex but intelligible picture. For at least the past five million years, the Omo River has carried debris from the Ethiopian highlands. As its current slows in its delta on Lake Turkana, the river drops its load of silts and sand, which have gradually accumulated and been transformed into sedimentary rock, thousands of feet thick. Periodic volcanic eruptions have interleaved layers of ash and basalt with the river and lake sediments. The whole region has been tilted by tectonic movements, setting off cycles of erosion that have exposed late Pliocene sediments and the fossils they contain. Samples sent to geochronological laboratories have established K-A dates for many of the eruptions. They form a consistent sequence between 4.1 and 1.3 million years B.P., and conveniently date the sediments that lie between them.

Within this broad framework of time, additional efforts filled in the finer details of environmental evolution. Paleobotanists have extracted and identified fossil pollens from various layers of the sediments. These indicate that the Pliocene Omo River, like today's, flowed through savanna grassland and was fringed by forest and bush. Painstaking microgeological studies have revealed the way in which the lake expanded and shrank, and the way the slow, muddy river slowly changed its course, meandering across its flood plain through a maze of boggy pools and bush-covered sandbanks. Finally, their geological context established, thousands of fossils have been carefully lifted from their matrix, cataloged, and dispatched to the laboratories of specialist paleontologists.

The fauna that the scientists have described is extraordinarily rich. There are hyenas, antelopes, wild pigs, zebras, camels, and elephants ancestral to those of today, as well as other, related forms that have become extinct—over 140 species among the mammals alone. Their diversity is also remarkable; groups like the elephants and hippopotamuses, which have only one living African representative, had two or more living side by side in the Pliocene. Hominids seem to show the same pattern. At least two taxa have provisionally been identified. One is evidently a robust australopith. The other is either a gracile australopith (*A. africanus*) or a very early human—presumably *Homo habilis* (Chapter 9). Scattered occurrences of stone tools have also been found.

This wealth of material still requires many years of study, but it is beginning to yield a multidimensional picture of animal life in the late Pliocene. At particular time horizons, fossils, pollen, and geology can be pieced together into ecological reconstructions. Animal lineages and cultural traditions can be traced through time and their evolutionary changes charted. For the first time, for instance, the gradually increasing sophistication of stone tool industries during the period from 3.0 to 1.5 million years B.P. can be charted against a firm timescale. Gradually, questions are being answered, but there is still much to be done before this fascinating region yields up all its secrets.

Such a research effort is neither easy nor inexpensive. It involves coordinating the efforts of 40 or so scientists, scattered over Africa, Europe, and Asia. It involves transporting a team of scientists, workers, and support personnel over 300 miles along dirt roads where filling stations and repair facilities are nonexistent, and maintaining them for several months in a desert where the only water is from the muddy Omo River, and all supplies must be brought in by truck. Above all, it involves a continual search for funding from foundations and other sources of support. Yet for all the difficulties, paleoanthropologists fight to expand their field work, recognizing that such projects are essential if paleoanthropology is to survive as a science. Only through such work can they raise their hypotheses about human evolution above the level of armchair speculation.

Fossil beds of the Omo Valley (*Georg Gerster/Rapho/Photo Researchers*)

The first of the East African sites to produce substantial australopith remains—Olduvai Gorge in Tanzania—consists of layer upon layer of lake beds and volcanic ashes, cut through by erosion-formed canyons that expose the successive strata. Mary and Louis Leakey spent more than twenty seasons at Olduvai, collecting stone tools and searching for hominid remains. In 1959, they were at last rewarded by the discovery of a magnificent australopith skull. Since then, many early hominid fossils have been recovered at Olduvai.

Further north, in Kenya, Richard Leakey (the son of Mary and Louis) is directing a multidisciplinary team in the investigation of some 2,600 square kilometers (1,000 sq. mi.) of Pliocene and Pleistocene sites on the eastern shore of Lake Turkana (formerly Lake Rudolf). In the past decade, Lake Turkana has yielded over 200 early hominid fossils. Both the Olduvai and Lake Tur-

Figure 8-2. ***Australopithecus*** **sites in South and East Africa.**

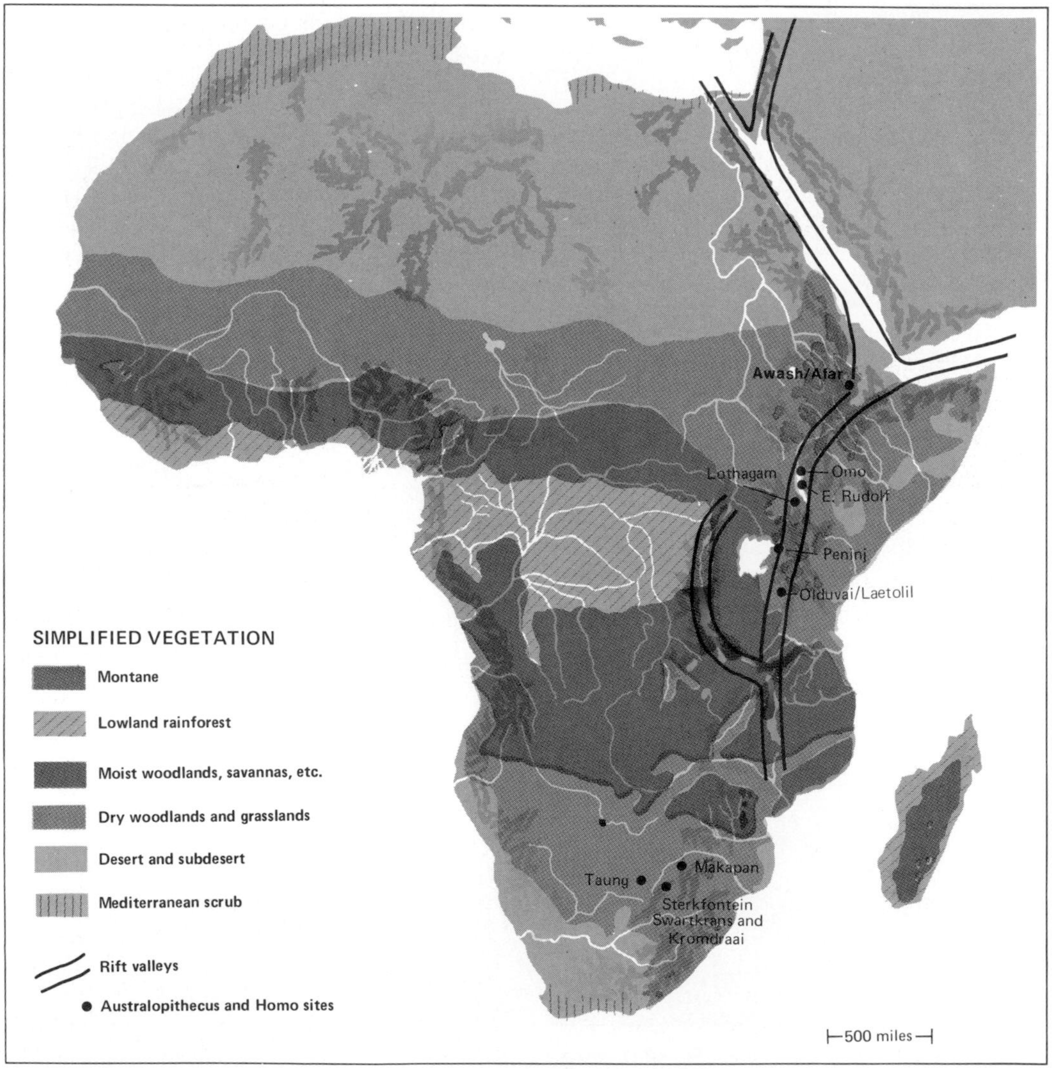

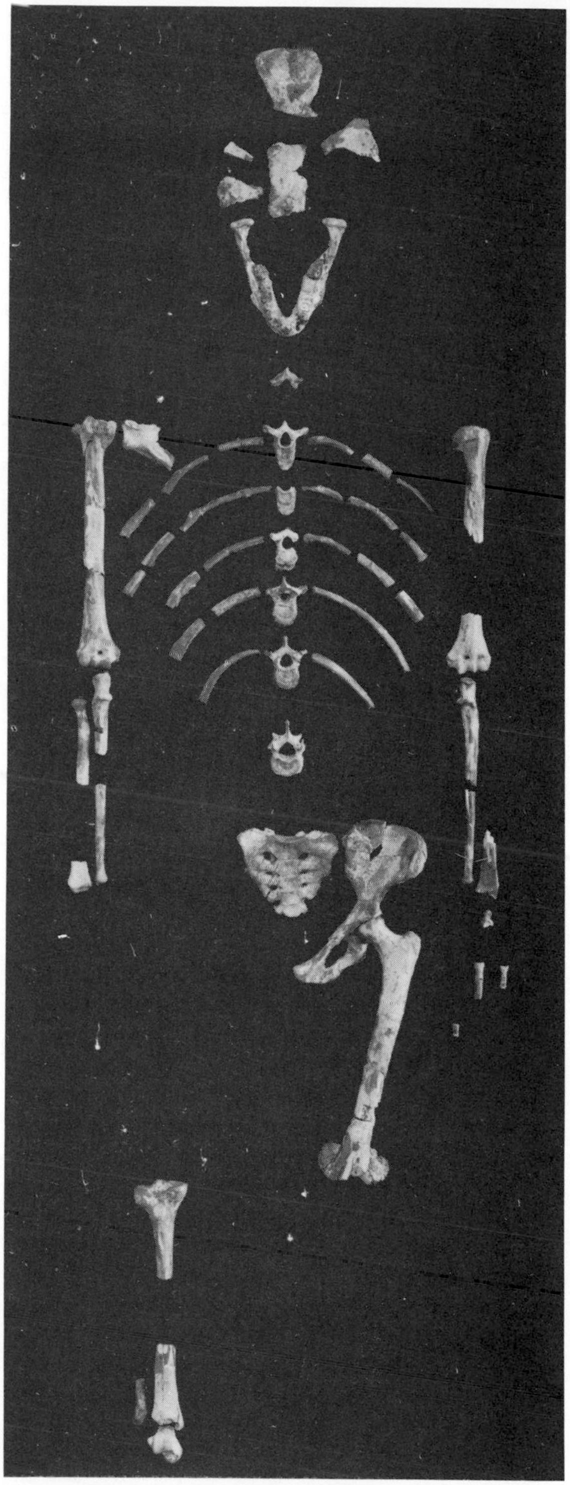

"Lucy," the most complete australopith specimen so far discovered. Originating from Hadar, Ethiopia, and nearly 3 million years old, the remains include a complete mandible, parts of the skull, ribs and vertebrae, pelvis, wrist and hand, and arms and legs. When alive, "Lucy" stood less than 1.25 meters (4 ft.) tall. *(Des Bartlett/Rapho/Photo Researchers)*

kana sites, dated by the potassium-argon method and by study of the faunal remains they contain, cover an immense span of time (Figure 8-1).

Another team, led by F. Clark Howell of Berkeley, has collected hominid fossils from the Omo River area in Ethiopia, where river sediments are sandwiched between datable volcanic layers extending back some 4 million years (see box). More recently, paleoanthropologists have turned their attention to the Afar triangle, a hot, wild, remote region of Ethiopia where the East African Rift Valley meets the rifts of the Red Sea and the Gulf of Aden in a triple junction. Comparatively little of the area has been investigated, but it clearly contains even more fossil-bearing rock than the sites farther south (Figure 8-2). One Afar site, Hadar, has proved especially rich in well-preserved hominid remains. A particularly exciting recent find from Hadar is the first relatively complete australopith skeleton. This fossil, from a diminutive female, has been named "Lucy" by its discoverers, M. Taieb and C. D. Johanson.

Additional australopith remains have been found in other locations scattered up and down the rift system. One noteworthy site is Lothagam, which has yielded a fragment of a mandible (lower jawbone) about 5½ million years old—the oldest recognizable australopith fossil discovered so far.

THE HOMINID STATUS OF *AUSTRALOPITHECUS*

The first major question posed by the australopiths was whether they were hominids or pongids. Although this is no longer a live issue, it is worthwhile considering the reasons that they were ultimately assigned to Hominidae. First, we should recall that modern classification is based not upon resemblance but upon evolutionary relationship (Chapter 4). In other words, australopiths are not classified in Hominidae just because in some respects they look like humans. (This would be a weak argument anyway, because in other ways they look like apes, and in still other ways they resemble neither.) Rather, they are classified as Hominidae because they share with *Homo sapiens,* but not with apes, certain *derived* characteristics, which show that they are clearly related to humans through an ancestor that is not shared by any ape.

These characteristics fall into two groups:

1. Modifications of the hindlimb, especially the pelvis and foot, which are related to standing and walking bipedally.
2. Modification of the shape and size of the canine tooth, so that it no longer projects as a point or blade beyond the crowns of the neighboring premolars and incisors.

The fact that *Australopithecus* shares these derived traits with humans does not mean *Australopithecus* is necessarily the direct ancestor of *Homo sapiens.* What it does mean is that *Australopithecus* and *Homo sapiens* are members of the same clade, sharing an ancestor that is not ancestral to any of the living apes.[1]

As for the negative evidence, australopiths share none of the derived features of modern apes, such as the very broad incisor teeth and the short lumbar region of the spinal column. Those characteristics in which they do resemble apes more closely than humans, such as their comparatively small brains, are primitive traits inherited from an earlier hominoid that was the ancestor of both the apes and the hominids.

Thus, the features that *Australopithecus* shares with *Homo sapiens* are important in that they show us that australopiths are hominids, close relatives of *Homo sapiens.* But they are important for another reason as well. They are part of the total adaptive pattern of *Australopithecus*—the features that these early hominids developed as they became distinct from their apelike ancestors. By looking at the physical differences between *Australopithecus* and the ancestral apes, we can form some idea of how their life styles differed.

[1] Theoretically, there is one other possibility: that the two sets of traits listed above were not inherited from a common ancestor, but evolved twice, in parallel and independently. This, however, is not very likely.

THE AUSTRALOPITH PATTERN OF ADAPTATION

Differences among the australopith fossils have led many anthropologists to divide them into different species or genera. (We will discuss some of the proposed classification schemes later in this chapter.) But diverse as the fossils are, they still permit us to form a single broad picture of the australopith pattern of adaptation. The most important elements of the pattern are:

1. A savanna habitat
2. Large back teeth and reduced canines
3. Habitual bipedalism
4. A somewhat enlarged and reorganized brain

Habitat

The habitat of a species is an important factor in shaping its way of life and its physical adaptation. Forest, woodland, and dry, open savanna—each has its own distinctive pattern of resources, and each limits the way an animal can move about and forage. Most apes, ancient and modern, live in, or on the fringes of, forests and woodlands. By contrast, fossils of *Australopithecus* are always associated with geological evidence for a rather dry, seasonal climate, not unlike that of the African savannas today. These fossils are also generally found in deposits bearing the fossil remains of grassland animals such as antelopes and horses. Moreover, the australopiths' primate associates were baboons—not forest-dwelling apes or arboreal monkeys. In short, all the evidence indicates that *Australopithecus* lived on the savanna.

Prehistoric savannas should not be imagined as treeless prairies; they were undoubtedly varied by strips of forest, woodland, and bush. But *Australopithecus* clearly lived in a habitat where moving on the ground was essential, and the trees served, at most, as a night refuge and an occasional source of food.

Since we do not have rain forest faunas among the fossils of this period, we cannot know for sure whether or not some australopiths lived there as well. However, as we shall see, certain australopith features seem best explained as adaptations to exploiting open country and the resources to be found there. This suggests that these features evolved *because* the ancestors of *Australopithecus* had left the forest and had become genetically isolated from their pongid ancestors who remained there. Thus, savanna living in itself would seem to be part of the australopith adaptive pattern.

Size and Weight

The size of *Australopithecus* can be estimated on the basis of the skeleton—particularly the pelvis, the backbone, and the bones of the leg and thigh. Some of the smallest individuals, like "Lucy" from Hadar and a specimen from Sterkfontein, probably weighed about 18 kilograms (40 lbs.) and stood less than 1.25 meters (4 ft.) tall. The largest ones probably weighed four times as much and stood well over 1.5 meters (5 ft.). Thus, the smallest australopiths weighed less than a pygmy chimpanzee, while the largest were the size of an average human.

How do we account for this great range of variation? To some extent, it reflects normal variability *within* populations. Even specimens from a single site, like Sterkfontein, vary considerably in size. Part of the variation may also be due to sexual dimorphism. Judging from modern open country primates, it is quite likely that a large male was considerably bigger than a small female—perhaps even twice as big. Geographical variation, too, probably played its part. There were undoubtedly differences of average size in different populations, just as there are in modern primates such as baboons or humans.

In themselves, the size and weight of an animal do not reveal very much about how it lives. But size and weight are extremely important for assessing the functional significance of body parts, which in turn tells us something about the animal's habits. For instance, if the teeth of one animal are larger than those of another, it is important to know whether the body mass that these teeth nourished was also proportionately larger. If it was, then no *relative* increase in tooth size has occurred, and no functional explanation need be sought. If, on the other hand, the body mass was not significantly larger, then we have to find something in the animal's way of life to account for its bigger teeth. Thus, the size and weight of *Australopithecus* are important in that they provide a frame of reference, to be kept in mind as we discuss the size of the brain and the teeth.

Brain Size and Structure

The size of the brain in various specimens of *Australopithecus* has been estimated from the capacity of the braincase. The range is between 435 and 550 cubic centimeters (26½ to 33½ cu. in.). As might be expected, the larger brains generally belong to the larger individuals. These are ape-sized brains; but relative to body size, they are larger than a chimpanzee's or a gorilla's. We know very little about relative brain size in the Miocene apes, but it is unlikely to have been greater than that of modern chimpanzees and gorillas. So we can be fairly sure that an increase in *relative* brain size was a derived feature of the australopiths.

Holloway's (1972) careful studies of the structure of endocranial casts indicate that the size increase was not a matter of simple expansion. Rather, it seems to have involved expansion of the cerebral cortex—and especially of the parietal lobe, with its association areas. We know too little as yet about the functioning of the brain, especially of the cerebral cortex, to be able to interpret this feature in more than the vaguest terms. However, in humans, parts of the parietal association cortex seem to be concerned with language production. This may mean that the australopiths had advanced further than the apes in the development of a symbolic communication system based upon sounds—the precursor of language.

Teeth, Jaws, and Feeding Habits

Perhaps the best clues to the ecology of a fossil animal are the derived characteristics of its feeding apparatus—that is, the adaptive features of jaws and teeth. In the case of *Australopithecus*, the jaws and teeth suggest adaptation to a mainly vegetarian diet gathered on the savanna.

Back Tooth Dominance

By human standards, the jaws of *Australopithecus* appear disproportionately large next to the braincase. The back of the jaw is particularly massive and holds very large molars and premolars. For many years, this feature was mistakenly thought to be a primitive trait, a holdover from a pongid ancestor. But recent work has shown that neither modern nor ancestral apes have back teeth as massive (in relation to body size) as those of *Australopithecus*. Both modern apes and *Australopithecus* have changed from the generalized condition seen in the Miocene *Dryopithecus*, but they have changed in exactly opposite directions (Figure 8-3).

The chimpanzee has retained rather small, simple molar and premolar teeth with thin enamel, but has developed broad incisors. These dental proportions can be related to its fruit-based diet. Eating fruit makes comparatively few demands on the back teeth, which are used mainly for pulping juicy fruit; but it requires large, strong incisors for piercing the tough skin of forest fruits and biting out chunks. *Australopithecus*, by contrast, had become specialized for grinding rather than biting. The thick-enameled back teeth dominate the dentition. The molars are very large, and the premolars broad and molarized—that is, their crowns have become somewhat more complex, with extra cusps to increase the grinding area. The incisors, on the other hand, are small.

Traditionally, many paleoanthropologists explained the proportions of the australopith dentition in terms of tool use. Supposedly, cutting tools took over the function of the front teeth, which then became smaller. But this explanation misses the main point. When body size is taken into account, the dental proportions of *Australopithecus* are obviously due to *expansion of the chewing teeth rather than to reduction of the incisors.* In fact, the molars of an 18-kilogram *Australopithecus* are much bigger than those of a 45-kilogram chimpanzee and are closer to those of a 90-kilogram gorilla. The australopith's incisors are not especially reduced; they are scarcely smaller than the primitive condition seen in *Dryopithecus*, although they are indeed smaller than those of the fruit-eating chimpanzee.

The shape of the jaw and the position of the muscles also reflect the dominance of the back teeth. The chewing and biting muscles—the masseters and temporals, which close the jaw and produce grinding movements—are set further forward than those of the chimpanzee. Thus, their line of action is more perpendicular to the plane on which the teeth meet (see Figure 8-3). This means that more muscular force can be exerted in crushing and grinding between the molars—the kind of movement you use to eat peanuts or sunflower seeds (Figure 8-5).

As with *Ramapithecus*, we can relate these adaptive traits to the demands of open country vegetarianism. A dentition dominated by the back teeth is ideal for seeds and other small, hard foods that require plenty of hard grinding but relatively little cutting and slicing by the incisors. Hence, this form of dentition is well suited to the kind of diet that would have been available to *Australopithecus* in the savannas—a diet based upon the tough rhizomes (rootlike underground stems) of grasses and herbs, and the hard, dry seeds of trees, shrubs, and bushes, rather than on the kind of juicy fruit to be found in the forests. This is not to say, however, that australopiths ate only seeds and similar small foods. They certainly ate a great variety of other foods to be picked up in the savanna, including, no doubt, insects, roots, and small game.

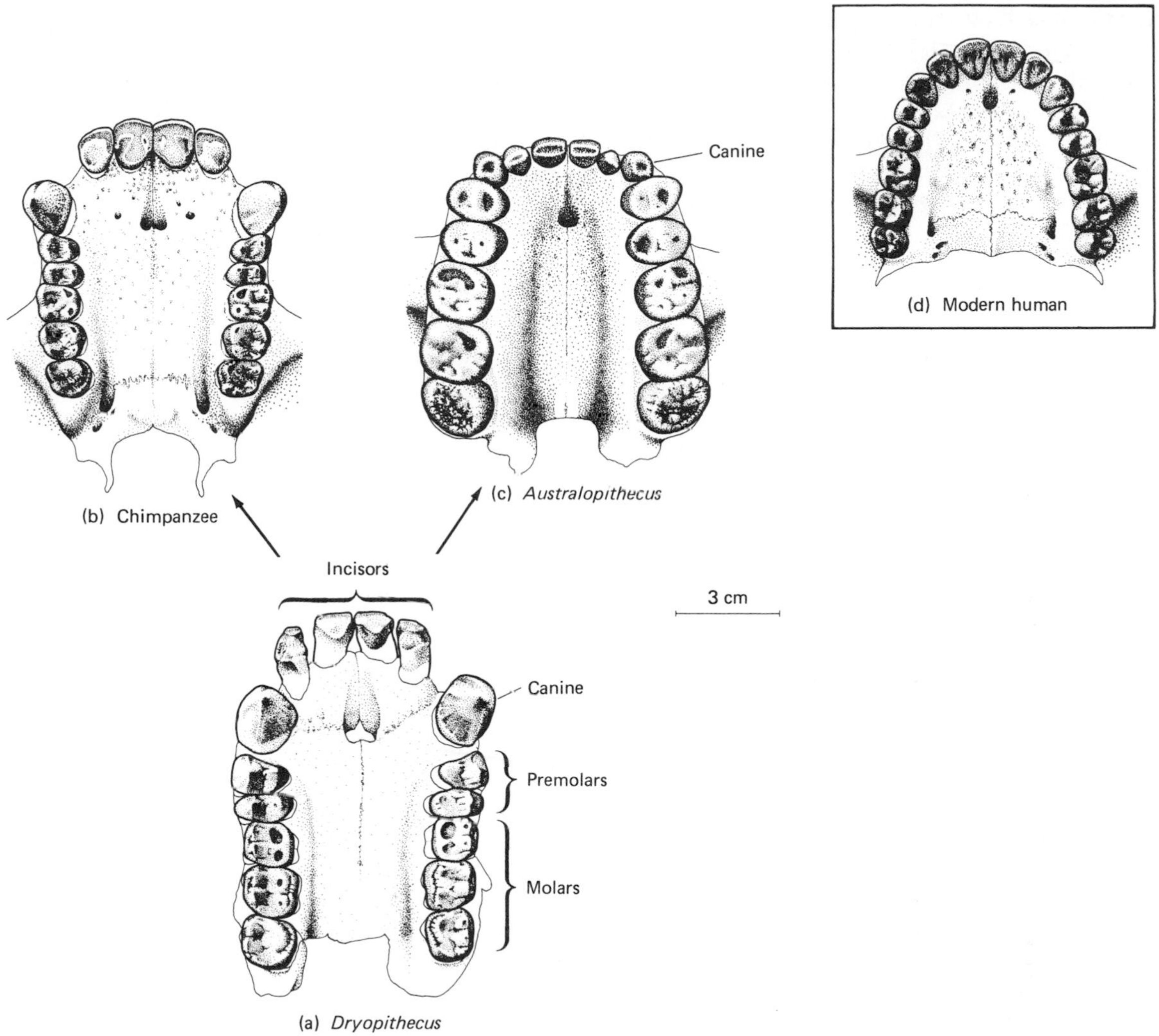

Figure 8-3. Upper teeth of hominoids: (a) *Dryopithecus major:* primitive dental proportions—moderately sized back and front teeth. (b) Chimpanzee (*Pan troglodytes*): large incisors, small back teeth. (c) *Australopithecus* (Olduvai Hominid 5): small incisors, large back teeth. (d) Modern human dentition; all teeth reduced in size. Note small canines in (c) and (d). (Biruta Akerbergs)

How Carnivorous Was *Australopithecus?*

It has been suggested that the powerful jaws of *Australopithecus* were adapted to eating scavenged meat and even bones. We find this view unconvincing. The australopiths may well have caught and eaten small mammals and birds, as chimpanzees occasionally do, and they could certainly have chewed meat with their powerful jaws. However, specialized bone and meat eaters have distinctive dental adaptations quite unlike the broad, flat molar crowns of *Australopithecus.* In fact, the shape of the jaws and teeth of *Australopithecus* is just the opposite of what one would expect in a meat eater or bone crusher. Thus, there is no *anatomical* evidence that australopiths were more carnivorous than chimpanzees. But what about *archeological* evidence—material from the sites where australopiths were found?

The most direct evidence that australopiths killed other animals comes from the South African caves. At some sites, a large number of baboon skulls show fractures that could conceivably have been caused by the blow of a club, perhaps improvised from an antelope bone. The fact that baboons would compete ecologically with an open country hominid, and also that they are one of the species occasionally eaten by chimpanzees, provides some support for this theory. However, in spite of claims that have been made, there is no good evidence that *Australopithecus* regularly killed large game animals or scavenged for marrow bones among the kills of carnivores such as lions. Most of the broken bones said to be the handiwork of *Australopithecus* are more likely to be the leavings of leopards, hyenas, and other carnivores.

Nonprojecting Canine Teeth

Like humans, all australopiths, male and female, have nonprojecting canine teeth. This is a definite departure from the primitive ancestral pattern. Male apes have long, fanglike canines, which project beyond the other teeth. When displayed, these canines are usually quite effective in scaring off predators and in arousing proper respect in fellow apes. *Australopithecus*, by contrast, has relatively small canines, intermediate in shape between a premolar and an incisor, and projecting hardly at all beyond the other teeth.

What this means, presumably, is that when australopiths fought and threatened, whether among themselves or against prowling predators, they brandished sticks and threw stones rather than biting or displaying their canines. Primitive weapon use of this kind is seen in savanna chimpanzees, and therefore it need not be considered a great departure from the ancestral condition. Yet male chimpanzees retain long, sharp canines as a backup system. Why, then, did hominids lose their fighting canines and come to depend entirely on artificial weapons?

We suspect that this development is also part of the complex associated with small-object feeding. A large male canine may be a useful weapon, but it reduces chewing efficiency. In animals with projecting canines, the pressure on the molar crowns is uneven, and this causes them to wear unevenly and wear out sooner than they would if abrasion were more evenly distributed. In the low-crowned canines of the hominids, on the other hand, the tip wears off rapidly after eruption. Thereafter the lower jaw can make freer, more horizontal movements, resulting in a flatter, less uneven pattern of wear on the molar crowns. This could be a considerable adaptive advantage to a hard chewer—particularly one with a long potential life span. Females, already enjoying the benefits of low-crowned canines, would not be subjected to this selective pressure. The result would be the evolutionary reduction of male canines until they were no more projecting than a female's.

Posture and Locomotion

As we saw in Chapter 4, some of the most distinctive features of the human pelvis, femur, leg bones, and foot can be interpreted as adaptations to habitual upright posture and bipedal locomotion. We now have good evidence that *Australopithecus* shared most of these crucial adaptations and therefore that he was a biped.

The Evidence for Australopith Bipedalism

A complete *Australopithecus* skeleton is a prize that still eludes the paleoanthropologist. Most of our knowledge of the australopith spine, pelvis, and hindlimb comes from isolated, incomplete, and often distorted specimens. The incompleteness of the bones—and the doubt that always remains when we try to reconstruct the habits of an extinct animal from its structure—leaves us with some uncertainties about the way *Australopithecus* stood and moved about. But one thing is quite certain: *Australopithecus* was a habitual

Figure 8-4. Chimpanzee (left) and *Australopithecus* (right, based upon Sterkfontein specimens) showing contrast in shape of pelvis—long and narrow in chimpanzee, short and broad in *Australopithecus.* (*Robert Frank*)

biped. The foot bones, vertebrae, pelves, and femora from Afar, Lake Turkana, and Olduvai, and from the South African sites of Sterkfontein, Makapan, and Swartkrans, make it very clear that when australopiths stood, walked, or ran, their normal pattern was to use their hindlimbs only.

The adaptations to bipedalism in *Australopithecus* can be traced from the lower back to the foot. One such characteristic is that the vertebrae of the small of the back form a distinct concavity, the *lumbar curve.* Such a curve is seen in a set of lumbar vertebrae found at Sterkfontein. Further evidence of bipedalism comes from the pelvis, which closely resembles the human pelvis in functionally important features. The ilium is short and broad, its connection with the sacrum large and firm. This fact, together with the lumbar curve, makes it clear that the habitual posture of *Australopithecus* was upright, with the trunk balanced on the pelvis and with the arms playing little or no part in bearing the body weight.

The structure of knee and foot point to the same conclusion. The australopith knee is clearly adapted for efficient weight bearing. The joint surfaces, for example, have a distinctive shape that "locks" the joint when it is fully straightened. An ankle bone (talus) from Kromdraai and a virtually complete foot from Olduvai,[2] although not identical to those of modern humans, show obvious adaptations to bipedalism. The Olduvai foot has well-developed arches. And, as in

[2] The Olduvai foot is generally attributed to *Homo habilis,* a more human hominid also apparently present at Olduvai. But since the ankle bone of this foot is quite similar to the australopith ankle bone from Kromdraai, the foot could with equal justification be attributed to *Australopithecus.*

humans, the ankle joint is formed in such a way as to allow for free up-and-down motions of the foot but very little side-to-side rotation. Similarly, the big toe of the Olduvai foot, unlike the big toe of an ape, was capable of little or no movement independent of the other toes. All in all, this is a foot that is built not for mobility in grasping and climbing but for stability and shock-absorption in carrying the body weight over hard ground. It is the foot of a terrestrial biped, not of an arboreal climber.

Some other features of the australopith limb skeleton are distinctly nonhumanlike. The iliac blade extends farther forward than in the human pelvis, and the acetabula—the sockets in which the heads of the femora rotate—face more directly to the side. The australopith ischium—the part of the pelvis projecting behind and below the hip—is comparatively long, like an ape's, rather than short and bent backward, like a human's. With the discovery of "Lucy" (see photo, page 185), we have our first clear notion of australopith limb proportions. Although a detailed analysis has not yet been published, it is clear that Lucy's femur, like that of a chimpanzee but quite unlike that of a human, was scarcely longer than her humerus (the bone of the upper arm). This combination of features suggests that, although the australopiths were undoubtedly bipeds, their bipedalism may have differed mechanically and functionally from that of humans.

Why Did Hominids Become Habitual Bipeds?

Apart from hominids, all primates that regularly move on the ground do so mostly on all fours —either knuckle-walking, like chimpanzees, or walking open-handed on the finger pads, like baboons. The adoption of bipedalism by the hominids, therefore, demands some explanation. Part of the answer might be a preadaptation in their arboreal ancestor. Some primates, especially the gibbon, have arms that are highly adapted for suspension. On the ground, these primates often walk bipedally rather than subject their arms to the compressive forces of quadrupedalism. Perhaps the prehominid ancestor was such an animal. But this explanation supposes that the prehominids were highly arboreal animals, almost certainly living in a rain forest. Such animals would be unlikely to move directly into open savanna or grassland.

More likely, the prehominids were semiterrestrial inhabitants of tropical woodlands, perhaps knuckle-walkers when on the ground but, like the chimpanzee, capable of standing and walking bipedally when circumstances called for it. The question then arises, why did the australopiths (or hominids ancestral to them) become *habitual* rather than *occasional* bipeds?

It is difficult for us to focus clearly on this problem. Being habitual bipeds ourselves, we tend to see only the advantages of two-footedness: having hands free for gesturing and for carrying food, tools, and babies; being able to see over tall grass and bushes; and so forth. But an ape would view bipedalism rather differently. Knuckle-walking quadrupedalism is a highly efficient locomotor pattern that uses energy economically and is fast when necessary. Quadrupedal knuckle-walkers are securely balanced on a broad base, with weight evenly distributed over four limbs and along the vertebral column. This system permits easy movement over rough and steep surfaces, through underbrush, and beneath branches. Moreover, when the ape has to stand or walk bipedally for a few moments, he can easily do so. And since becoming a habitual biped means losing this versatile locomotor pattern, there would have to be some overriding reason for the change. What was the reason?

One way to approach this question is to examine the situations in which quadrupedal monkeys and apes do and do not stand or walk bipedally on the ground. First, it is clear that you do not need to be bipedal to hold a helpless infant, a stick, or a large piece of food; to feed from the ground or from a shrub; or to use a stick as a prodder or tool. Apes and monkeys do all these things very satisfactorily either while sitting or while standing on two feet and one hand. Peering over tall grass, beating the chest in display, or brandishing a branch requires occasional but not habitual bipedalism, for they are activities that occupy only a tiny fraction of each day. None of these behaviors, then, would create significant selective pressure for habitual bipedalism.

Since nonhuman primates spend the greater part of each day gathering and eating food, we should examine the foraging behavior of living primates for a situation in which the animal, needing both its hands free, is forced to hold its trunk erect unsupported by its forelimbs. Bipedal walking has been seen in wild chimpanzees, for instance, when they are presented with a heap of food such as bananas or papayas. Picking up armfuls of fruit, they make off with it into the bush to feed at leisure.

But carrying food back to a home base, although it undoubtedly became important later in human evolution, was probably not a primary factor in the early appearance of bipedalism. For one thing, nonhuman primates hardly ever carry food around. There is no advantage in doing so, and most is eaten where it is found. Carrying certainly became more important in the genus *Homo* as people developed a distinctively human foraging pattern. This involved fanning out over the countryside around the base camp and bringing foodstuffs, particularly meat, back to camp to share. However, the earliest evidence we have for this kind of behavior is associated with hominids more advanced than the australopiths, and there is no reason to suppose that it was part of the initial hominid pattern.

There is, however, one feeding situation that will regularly elicit a kind of bipedalism in monkeys and apes. That is when the animal is faced with a scatter of small food objects, such as seeding grassheads in a field or berries in a bush. When this happens—and especially when other members of the group are competing for the same food—the animal will squat, crouch, or stand bipedally. This leaves both hands free for picking up food and rapidly passing it to the mouth. In other words, the erect position effectively doubles the possible rate of feeding.

It should be noted that this maneuver is advantageous only when feeding on relatively small objects. When the animal is feeding on fruit, meat, or any other large-sized foods, the rate of feeding is controlled not by the speed at which the hands work but by the speed at which chunks can be bitten off by the incisor teeth. In this situation, there is no advantage in having a second hand free; the animal can eat efficiently using one hand only.

If the food objects are not only small but scattered about, like seeding grassheads or seedpods in a thorn thicket, the rate of feeding is increased still further if the animal not only sits or stands but also *moves* bipedally. Thus the animal keeps its hands free and avoids having to drop onto all fours to shift position. Among all living primates, the gelada baboon—living, like the australopiths, in a habitat with few trees—is the expert at small-object feeding. Its diet of grassblades requires it to spend most of the day in a trunk-erect squatting position. As it feeds, it shuffles "bipedally" forward on its haunches, using both of its extremely nimble hands to pluck grass and stems.

If early hominids depended heavily on foods of this kind, the advantage of habitual bipedalism might have come to outweigh the loss of quadrupedalism. Such an interpretation of australopith foraging strategy makes sense of the unexpected combination of features seen in its hindlimb and skeleton. The features that *Australopithecus does* share with humans (the broad ilium, stable foot and knee) are adaptations to bipedal standing, slow walking, and squatting with the spinal column securely balanced upon the pelvis. Those it has *not* acquired (long legs, a short ischium) are specifically related to rapid bipedal running or walking long distances, as in pursuit of game.

This argument would still not be very convincing, however, were it not for the fact that the kinds of foods that demand two-handed gathering—seeds, nuts and berries, shoots and rhizomes—are also those that the australopith chewing apparatus was adapted to process and those, moreover, that predominate in the diet of savanna chimpanzees and baboons. Taken together, this seems to add up to quite a strong, if circumstantial, case for two-handed feeding having played an important role in the appearance of habitual bipedalism in early hominids—and also in the evolution of the dexterous, precision-gripping hominid hand.

Bipedalism and Toolmaking

Even if habitual bipedalism started as a feeding adaptation, it obviously had implications that reached far beyond this. The hands were now freed from the task of supporting the body weight, and their dexterity would have been gradually enhanced by generations of selection for nimble food gathering. This dexterity, paired with the inventiveness and mental flexibility of an animal at least as bright as a chimpanzee, would certainly be put to use in manipulative tasks, including, quite probably, the making of tools more refined and complex than any produced by modern chimpanzees. It is quite likely that *Australopithecus* used digging sticks and clubs, and perhaps employed simple stone flakes as cutting or scraping tools. Such tools would rarely be preserved or recognizable as artifacts. It is not surprising, therefore, that the direct archeological evidence for australopith toolmaking is very meager indeed.

Dart and others have claimed that many of the bone fragments found at sites such as Makapan were tools made and used by australopiths. Recent studies, however, have shown that when leopards and hyenas crunch bones, they often produce fragments that look extraordinarily like artifacts and that exactly match the types once believed to be the most characteristic tools and weapons of *Australopithecus*.

From the East African sites comes other evidence, but this too is doubtful. As we have seen, the australopiths existed from about 5.5 to about 1 million years ago. From about 3 million years ago, sites such as Hadar, Olduvai, and Lake Turkana that yield australopith remains also yield stone tools of the Oldowan culture—well-made scrapers, choppers, and cutting flakes. (The term "Oldowan" comes from Olduvai Gorge. These tools are discussed in the next chapter.) From the same sites comes evidence that these tools were used by systematic hunters to cut up large animals such as antelopes. For some anthropologists, this is sufficient proof that later australopiths were efficient hunters who made stone tools. Others have always doubted this interpretation, and such doubts have been strengthened by the discovery, at each of the sites with tools, of remains that seem to belong to true humans, members of the genus *Homo*. On the other hand, no stone tools have ever been found at sites yielding *Australopithecus* fossils alone, without *Homo*.

If two or more hominid species are found with stone tools at a particular site, archeology is no help in deciding which of them, if either, was the toolmaker. Most paleoanthropologists faced by such a situation assume, reasonably enough, that the species that is the more human in appearance is likely to be the more technologically advanced. Following this line of reasoning, we would assume that the Oldowan tools were made by *Homo*.

Of course, it is possible that *both* early *Homo* and contemporary *Australopithecus* were hunters and used stone tools of the Oldowan type. This, however, is unlikely, since it would have led to competition between them, in which case they could hardly have lived side by side, as they did, for several million years. (As we have seen in Chapter 4, no two species with overlapping ranges can occupy similar econiches for long; competition eventually eliminates one of them.) A more likely hypothesis is that the two species diverged through character displacement (Chapter 4) and coexisted by occupying separate econiches. *Homo* hunted, gathered, and made stone tools, while *Australopithecus*, remaining only a rudimentary toolmaker, simply became more highly adapted to its original econiche: open country vegetarian foraging. As we shall see in the following section, variation among australopith populations provides additional evidence of this adaptive trend.

The Social Behavior of *Australopithecus*

Since we do not have any direct evidence about australopith social behavior—and presumably never can—the following discussion is speculation. It is, however, informed speculation, for we do have indirect evidence of two kinds. There is the behavior of nonhuman, terrestrial savanna dwellers, such as the baboons, who live in a similar environment. And there is the behavior of species that are phyletically close to *Australopithecus*—chimpanzees and humans in particular.

We can probably rule out territorial pairs as the australopith form of social organization, for this pattern is seen only in rain forest species. We can very likely eliminate one-male groups as well. This pattern is not found among hominoids; moreover, since it is not very useful for defense against predators, it is atypical of open country species, with the exception of the fast-running patas monkey. It seems more plausible that the ancestral form of social organization in the australopith lineage was the multimale troop—perhaps splitting into subgroups, as chimpanzees do. If so, we can ask what modifications in this pattern might have been introduced by life on the savannas. Judging from the example of the Kaskati woodland chimpanzees (Chapter 5), the group ranges would probably have become larger, while the groups themselves would have been smaller, with a greater tendency for all group members to stay together. A reasonable estimate for australopith group size would be about thirty to forty members or perhaps slightly more.

What about the mating system? As we have seen, some open country species, such as the hamadryas baboons, have evolved one-male groups within a multimale troop. It is also suggestive that modern human social organization is, formally, of this type—though heavily modified and regulated by culturally defined rules. Did this pattern arise first among prehuman hominids? We do not know, but it seems quite possible that it evolved in the australopiths or their immediate ancestors.

DIVERSITY IN THE GENUS *AUSTRALOPITHECUS*

So far, in discussing the adaptive pattern of *Australopithecus,* we have emphasized the features common to all members of the genus. As might be expected in a group that was geographically widespread and flourished for several million years, the fossils represent several different populations, with considerable variation among them. As mentioned earlier in this chapter, some anthropologists have interpreted this variation as evidence for the existence of different species, or even different adaptive types, within the genus.

One of the more popular of such schemes was proposed by J. T. Robinson, and was based initially on the South African material. It divides the australopiths into two major adaptive types. The smaller, "gracile" (slender) type included fossils from Taung, Sterkfontein, and Makapan; the larger, heavier, "robust" type was represented at Kromdraai and Swartkrans. The robust australopith, with its relatively large cheek teeth and small incisors, was considered a specialized vegetarian. The gracile one, with more balanced dental proportions, was considered a more omnivorous creature, an active carnivore that hunted and scavenged for meat. Unfortunately, the dietary hypothesis was seized upon and exaggerated in the popular literature. Journalists with lively imaginations had a field day contrasting the poor, stupid, peaceable, clumsy, specialized robust australopith with his wily, bloodthirsty, nimble little cousin, who eventually did him in.

We believe that a less dramatic story is closer to the truth. When the full range of variation among australopiths at each of the South African sites is taken into account, the line between gracile and robust begins to blur. The "graciles" of Makapan and Sterkfontein actually include several large, robust individuals; likewise, individual specimens from Kromdraai and Swartkrans could easily fit into the gracile sample. Although there are *average* differences among australopith samples from different sites, they seem to us to represent the result of increasing specialization within a single adaptive zone rather than the result of divergent evolutionary trends.

When the East African australopiths are added to the picture, the range of variation increases still further. Some individuals are comparable to the gracile and robust forms of South Africa, others are even larger ("hyperrobust"). However, the differences involved still seem to us to represent variations on a theme, the sort of differences to be expected among individuals and populations of a lineage widely dispersed in space and time, adapting to local conditions.

Disconcerting as it may be to those who seek cut-and-dried answers, it is likely that we shall never know how many species and subspecies of australopiths are really represented in our fossil samples, or how many local populations became permanently or temporarily isolated from the main stem, fated to become extinct, or eventually to merge their genes in the common pool of the species once again. Nevertheless, a brief description of the three species that have been proposed is useful in highlighting the kind of variation found among the fossils, as well as the common adaptive trends that run through the group. It should simply be kept in mind that this three-species division is a somewhat arbitrary one, which may be used for the sake of convenience but should not be regarded as the only possible way of sorting the material.

1. *Australopithecus africanus* (the gracile type): small-sized primitive forms that are differentiated least from the ancestral pongid condition and seem to make their first appearance earlier in time.
2. *A. robustus* (the robust type): medium-sized, more evolved forms from South Africa, probably derived from *A. africanus.*
3. *A. boisei* (the hyperrobust type): large, evolved australopiths from East Africa, presumably derived from an East African form resembling *A. africanus.*

Australopithecus africanus

Sites: South Africa—Taung, Sterkfontein, Makapan
East Africa—Hadar, Lothagam (?), Lake Turkana, Olduvai (?)
Time range: approximately 5.5 to 2 million years B.P.

On the present evidence, *A. africanus* was the earliest australopith to appear. More important, it was the least differentiated from its presumed ape ancestor. As such, it shows clearly certain basic features of the australopith adaptive pattern, which are then developed more fully in the later australopiths. *A. africanus* thus offers us a number of clues to the way in which the australopiths as a group originated, as well as the evolutionary directions they subsequently took.

The primitiveness of *A. africanus* is reflected in its small size; in its face, which though deep and heavy is still quite long and projecting; and in its canines, which are still comparatively large for a hominid, though of course smaller proportionally than an ape's. (Its back teeth, by contrast, are the size of a gorilla's—larger, in proportion to body weight, than any ape's.) But these conservative traits notwithstanding, *A. africanus* fits the general australopith pattern described above. Living in open country, it shows two physical adaptations—habitual bipedalism and back tooth dominance—evolved for exploiting the kind of vegetable resources to be found there.

A. robustus and *A. boisei:* More Evolved Forms

Sites: *A. robustus:* South Africa—Kromdraai, Swartkrans
A. boisei: East Africa—Omo, Lake Turkana, Olduvai, Peninj, Chesowanja
Time range: approximately 2.5 to 1 million years B.P.

Although overlapping *A. africanus* in time range and distribution, the robust australopiths (*A. robustus* and *A. boisei*) are more evolved than the "gracile" form, from which they probably are descended. In their structure, they show australopith adaptations pushed to a higher level of specialization.

For a number of years, the geological evidence was thought to indicate that the robust australopiths lived in a wetter, lusher habitat than *A. africanus.* This is not now generally accepted. Like *A. africanus,* they appear to have been animals of dry grasslands, woodlands, and savannas. Both *A. robustus* and *A. boisei* seem to have

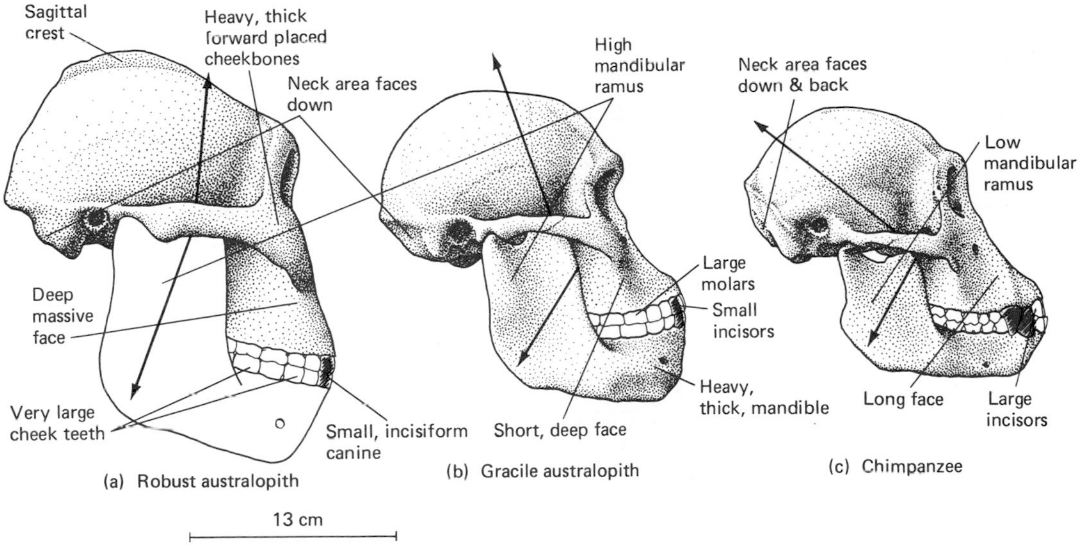

Figure 8-5. Skulls of (a) *Australopithecus boisei*, (b) *Australopithecus africanus*, and (c) *Pan troglodytes*. (a) is based upon Olduvai Hominid 5 and specimens from Lake Turkana; (b) mostly upon a Sterkfontein specimen. *(Biruta Akerbergs)*

averaged somewhat larger than *A. africanus.* A very rough estimate is that *A. robustus* was the size of a modern chimpanzee and *A. boisei* more comparable to a well-nourished human. There is evidence that sexual dimorphism was considerable, especially in *A. boisei,* where the males may have been about twice as heavy as females.

Not unexpectedly, the brains of *A. robustus* and *A. boisei* seem to have been somewhat larger than that of *A. africanus.* We have estimates of around 550 cubic centimeters (33½ cu. in.) for skulls from Olduvai, Lake Turkana, and Swartkrans. Given the larger body, this larger brain probably does not represent any increase in brain power. The shape of the braincase differs somewhat from that of *A. africanus;* the profile is less rounded and the "forehead" is flatter. It has been suggested that this difference somehow shows the robust australopiths to have been less human and less intelligent than *A. africanus.* But studies of the endocranial casts do not support this view. Moreover, the skull profile of the large, common chimpanzee differs from that of the pygmy chimpanzee in much the same way, though the bigger ape is quite as intelligent as its small relative. Hence the difference in shape between the australopith skulls probably has to do only with size and not with intelligence.

In the structure of the chewing apparatus, the robust australopiths have carried further the distinctive adaptive trends that separated *A. africanus* from the apes. Faces are even shorter, deeper, and more massive, and all the structural features associated with the large, strong chewing muscles are even more fully developed. Indeed, so large are the jaw muscles that in large full-grown individuals they meet along the skull's midline—producing, at their point of attachment, a *sagittal crest* (Figure 8-5). This is a ridge of bone that forms during the individual's lifetime in response to the powerful pull of the temporal muscles and helps to anchor them. It is seen in many adult robust australopith skulls. (It is not a unique feature of the robust australo-

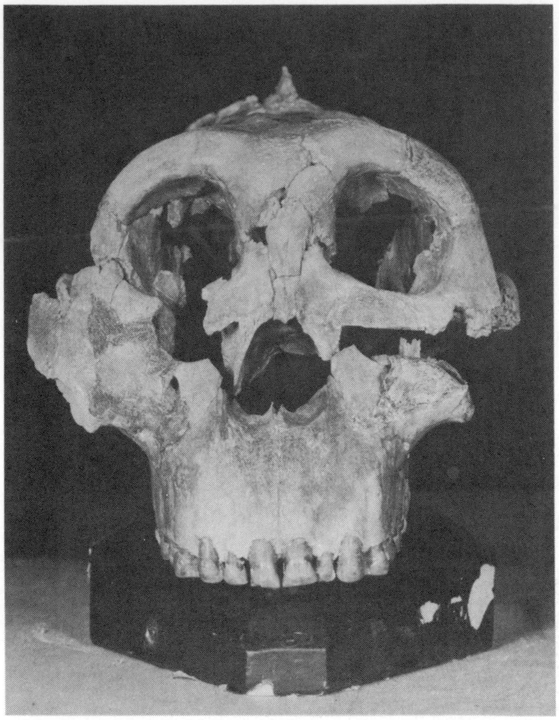

Olduvai Hominid 5, one of the most massive and complete australopith crania known, is the type specimen of *Australopithecus boisei*. The heavy, deep jaws and huge back teeth led to this young male specimen's nickname of "Nutcracker Man." *(Des Bartlett/Rapho/Photo Researchers, Inc.)*

piths, however, but is characteristic of all primates with small brains and large jaws—the gorilla, for example.)

Similarly, the tooth proportions of the later forms are highly specialized. Especially in *A. boisei*, huge back teeth overshadow the modestly sized front ones, and the tiny canines are much smaller than the first premolars just behind them. All the molars and premolars are not only larger but more complex, with additional cusps and grooves. In addition, as Wallace (1975) has shown, the robust australopiths had gone even further than *A. africanus* in freeing the side-to-side chewing motion from the interference of the projecting canine teeth. These characteristics of the teeth and jaws are not human, but they are certainly not apelike either. They are the result of the further evolution along the adaptive route taken by *A. africanus*.

It is clear that the robust australopiths were habitual bipeds, but the evidence suggests that they had advanced no further toward fully human bipedalism than *A. africanus* had. In particular, two fairly well preserved hip bones from Swartkrans seem better adapted to foraging on low vegetation than to striding long distances in the pursuit of game.

AUSTRALOPITHECUS AND *HOMO*

Contrary to a view that was once widely held, the australopiths do not represent a short-lived transitional stage between apes and man. *A. boisei* alone spans a time period in the fossil record ten times as long as that of *Homo sapiens*. They represent a stable, widespread, and successful adaptation to life on tropical savannas. Second, to regard them merely as a transitional stage—the supposed "missing link"—between ape and man is to ignore much of the fossil evidence in favor of a very narrow and human-centered version of evolution, in which all roads lead to *Homo sapiens*. Such a version may be flattering, but it is hardly realistic.

This is not to say that there were no australopiths in the ancestry of *Homo sapiens*. As mentioned at the beginning of this chapter, *Homo* is almost certainly descended from an early australopith population. But the *Homo* line probably appeared *before* the later australopiths discussed in this chapter. These australopiths show highly specialized adaptations that seem unlikely to have been present in the human ancestor. More important, many of the sites that have yielded australopith fossils have also yielded what appear to be primitive members of the genus *Homo*. In other words, all of the known populations of *A. robustus* and *A. boisei*—and some of those of *A. africanus* as well—are too late to be direct ancestors of *Homo sapiens;* they were already living side by side with early *Homo*. The

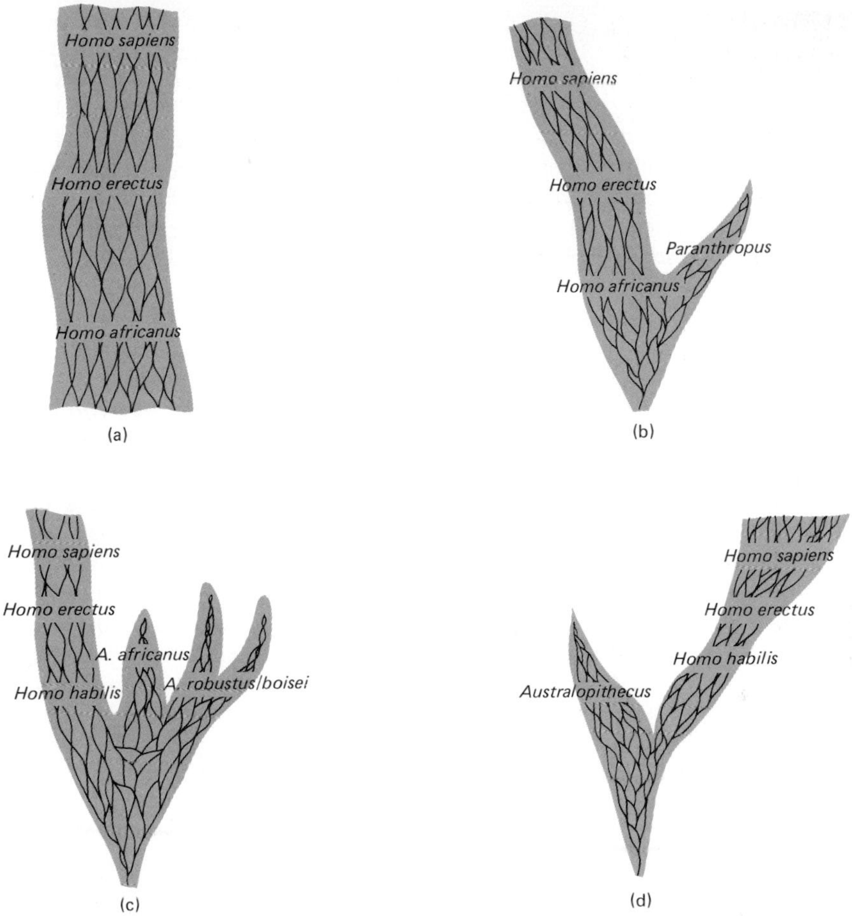

Figure 8-6. Four ways of interpreting australopith and human phylogeny: (a) The single-species view; one variable australopith species (called *Homo africanus*) is the direct ancestor of later *Homo*. (b) "Gracile" australopiths as direct human ancestors, "robust" australopiths (called *Paranthropus*) as an extinct sidebranch. (c) Gracile australopiths, robust australopiths, and humans as three or four separate species descended from an early common ancestor. (d) (The version we prefer) One highly variable australopith species; the *Homo* lineage an early offshoot from a "gracile" population of this species.

australopith ancestor of *Homo sapiens,* if there was one, was probably an earlier form of *A. africanus.*

Thus it seems that most of the australopiths, as we know them from the fossil record, were not transitional at all. Rather, they constituted an independent lineage (or perhaps several lineages) evolving alongside that of *Homo.* As for how humans and australopiths managed to coexist on the same savannas, we have already suggested a probable explanation: that they occupied separate econiches, *Homo* making stone tools, hunting, and gathering; *Australopithecus* making simpler tools and remaining a predominantly vegetarian forager. This noncompetitive arrangement continued for several million years. And then, a little more than 1 million years ago, the australopiths disappeared from the scene.

The Extinction of *Australopithecus*

Why did *Australopithecus* become extinct? We do not really know, and it is quite possible that we never will. In Africa, the disappearance of the australopiths seems to follow soon after the appearance, among populations of early humans, of a new stone-tool culture: the Acheulean (discussed in the following chapter). It seems possible, therefore (though the reader is warned that this is merely speculation), that the Acheulean industry was part of a general technological advance that may have allowed humans to nudge *Australopithecus* out of its econiche. For example, the Acheulean technology may have included ways of preparing tough vegetable foods with pounders or grindstones rather than by chewing; it may also have included the use of containers for gathering such vegetable foods more efficiently. If this were so, then these technological adaptations would have enabled the early humans to exploit the same resources that the australopiths were equipped to exploit only through physical adaptations. And technology would probably have triumphed.

Of course, it is also possible that the disappearance of the australopiths had nothing to do with competition from early *Homo*; we may never know for sure. Yet the mere fact that the australopiths became extinct does not in itself require any extraordinary explanation. Extinction is a common event in evolutionary history, and there is no reason to imagine that hominids were immune from it, especially early in their history, when physical adaptation and specialization were as important as culturally determined behavior.

Not all anthropologists accept the view that the australopith line separated from that of *Homo* and became extinct. For example, proponents of the *single species hypothesis* believe that the remains we interpret as very early *Homo*, contemporary with *Australopithecus*, are actually those of australopiths. They believe further that all australopiths made Oldowan tools, and that the human makers of the Acheulean tools evolved directly from australopiths. In this view, then, no extinction took place; the australopith lineage is continuous with that of *Homo*.

We find this a possible but less plausible interpretation, largely because we believe there is reliable evidence that primitive *Homo* did in fact exist as a separate population at the same time as the late australopiths. These early *Homo* may have been directly ancestral to the makers of the Acheulean culture and to still later humans. In any case, they at least seem to have been considerably closer to that ancestry than was any australopith. We shall follow their story in the next chapter.

Summary

The genus *Australopithecus*, first identified and named by Raymond Dart a half-century ago, is now represented by a considerable collection of fossils from South and East Africa. In South Africa, australopiths have been found in limestone caverns; these deposits are very difficult to date precisely. In East Africa, the volcanic, lake, and river sediments of the East African Rift Valley have yielded australopiths in datable strata.

Apelike in some respects, these fossils are classified as Hominidae rather than Pongidae because they share with the humans certain derived features: modifications of the hindlimb for bipedalism and reduction of the projecting canine tooth. These features indicate that *Australopithecus* was part of a clade that had already diverged from the ancestral apes and that was eventually to produce *Homo*.

The australopiths ranged from about the size of a pygmy chimpanzee to about the size of a modern human. The central elements of their adaptive pattern are (1) a savanna habitat; (2)

large back teeth and reduced canines; (3) habitual bipedalism; and (4) a somewhat enlarged and reorganized brain. In this complex, the switch from the rain forest to the savanna habitat is particularly crucial, for most of the derived features of *Australopithecus* are adaptations, direct or indirect, to the new life in the open country.

The peculiarities of the australopith feeding apparatus—the reduction of the canines, the moving forward and expansion of the chewing muscles, and especially the enlargement of the molars and premolars—seem to be adjustments for hard grinding. Such chewing would have been needed for the diet available to the australopiths on the savanna—seeds, nuts, roots, grasses, and other small, tough foods.

That *Australopithecus* was habitually bipedal (though perhaps somewhat differently from modern *Homo sapiens*) is indicated by a number of anatomical features. The vertebrae of the lower back form a concavity, called the *lumbar curve*—an adaptation to weight bearing. The pelvis and the knee have also been modified for supporting the weight of the upright body. The foot has well-developed arches for walking and has lost its adaptations to grasping.

Why should *Australopithecus* have given up the flexibility of knuckle-walking quadrupedalism for habitual bipedalism? The answer seems to lie in the resources of the savanna habitat. Small, scattered foods can be gathered most efficiently if both hands are free. Since small foods are the ones commonly found on the savanna—and since, moreover, this is the type of food to which australopith teeth and jaws seem specifically adapted—it is likely that the switch to bipedalism was at least in part an adaptation to the new dietary emphasis.

Whether the australopiths used their freed hands for extensive toolmaking as well as for feeding is a subject of debate. Many australopith sites have yielded specimens of the first stone-tool tradition, the Oldowan. Nevertheless, all these sites also include fossils of early *Homo*—more humanlike contemporaries of the later australopiths and undoubtedly the direct ancestors of modern humans. It seems logical that *Homo* specialized in stone-tool making and in hunting and gathering, while *Australopithecus* stuck to vegetarian foraging, probably using only very simple tools. Indeed, it was probably this separation of econiches that permitted the two genera to coexist in the same habitats.

Two-handed gathering of small foods, along with some crude toolmaking, probably favored the nimble precision grip that we see in the hominid hand. The demands of savanna foraging, meanwhile, probably favored development of the brain. The cranial capacity of *Australopithecus* ranged from 435 to 550 cc., relatively larger than that of modern apes. There is some evidence of expansion of the parietal lobe, which may mean that *Australopithecus* had progressed further in the direction of language. Brain expansion may also have been stimulated by a more complex social organization—perhaps involving one-male groups within a multimale troop.

For the sake of convenience, the different australopith fossils have been somewhat arbitrarily divided into three species. The earliest is *A. africanus* (5.5 to 2 million B.P.). This is the smallest and most primitive of the australopiths, with a longish face and canines that still project somewhat. Later, larger, and more evolved are the "robust" forms, *A. robustus* and *A. boisei*, both extending from about 2.5 to 1 million B. P. In these two forms we see the australopith specializations, especially those of the teeth, carried much further. The front teeth are very small, and the back teeth and chewing muscles are extremely large.

The australopiths represent a new adaptive pattern, quite distinct from that of the apes and geared to life in the open country. This pattern allowed them to survive for about 4.5 million years. During the latter part of their existence, they shared their habitat with another hominid genus, *Homo*, probably an offshoot from an earlier australopith ancestor. It is possible that the two groups eventually began to compete, with *Homo*, the more sophisticated toolmaker, eventually nudging the australopiths out of their econiche. About 1 million years ago, the australopiths became extinct, leaving the African savannas to their *Homo* cousins.

Glossary

Australopithecus an early hominid genus that flourished in Africa from 5.5 million B.P. (or earlier) to about 1 million B.P. The australopiths were bipedal and had large back teeth for chewing the tough vegetable foods of their grassland habitat. ***A. africanus*** is the earliest known species, and probably the least differentiated from the ancestral hominid. ***A. robustus*** and ***A. boisei*** were later, larger, more evolved forms, the latter contemporary with *Homo.*

lumbar curve a concavity of the vertebral column in the region of the small of the back

Pleistocene (1.9 million B.P.—present) the sixth epoch of the Cenozoic era, during which *Homo erectus* and then *Homo sapiens* appeared

Pliocene (5–1.9 million B.P.) the fifth epoch of the Cenozoic era, which saw the flourishing of the australopiths and the appearance of the earliest members of the genus *Homo*

sagittal crest a bony ridge running from front to back along the top of the skull, along the line of attachment of the temporal (chewing) muscles; found in many robust australopiths

Suggested Readings

BRACE, C. L. 1967
The Stages of Human Evolution: Human and Cultural Origins. Englewood Cliffs, N.J.: Prentice-Hall. An account of hominid evolution as seen by one of the leading protagonists of the single-species hypothesis.

CLARK, W. E. LE GROS 1976
Man-Apes or Ape-Men? Huntington, N.Y.: Krieger. One of the leading protagonists describes the discovery of australopiths and the controversy that surrounds them.

ISAAC, G., AND MCCOWN, E. 1976
Human Evolution: Louis Leakey and the East African Experience. Menlo Park, Calif.: W. A. Benjamin. A collection of papers presenting new data and interpretations of early hominid biology.

LEAKEY, R., AND LEWIN, R. 1977
Origins: What New Discoveries Reveal About the Emergence of Our Species and Its Possible Future. New York: Dutton. A finely illustrated account of hominid evolution by one of the leading figures in the field.

PILBEAM, D. R. 1972
The Ascent of Man: An Introduction to Human Evolution. New York: Macmillan. A readable and authoritative account of fossil hominids, including australopiths.

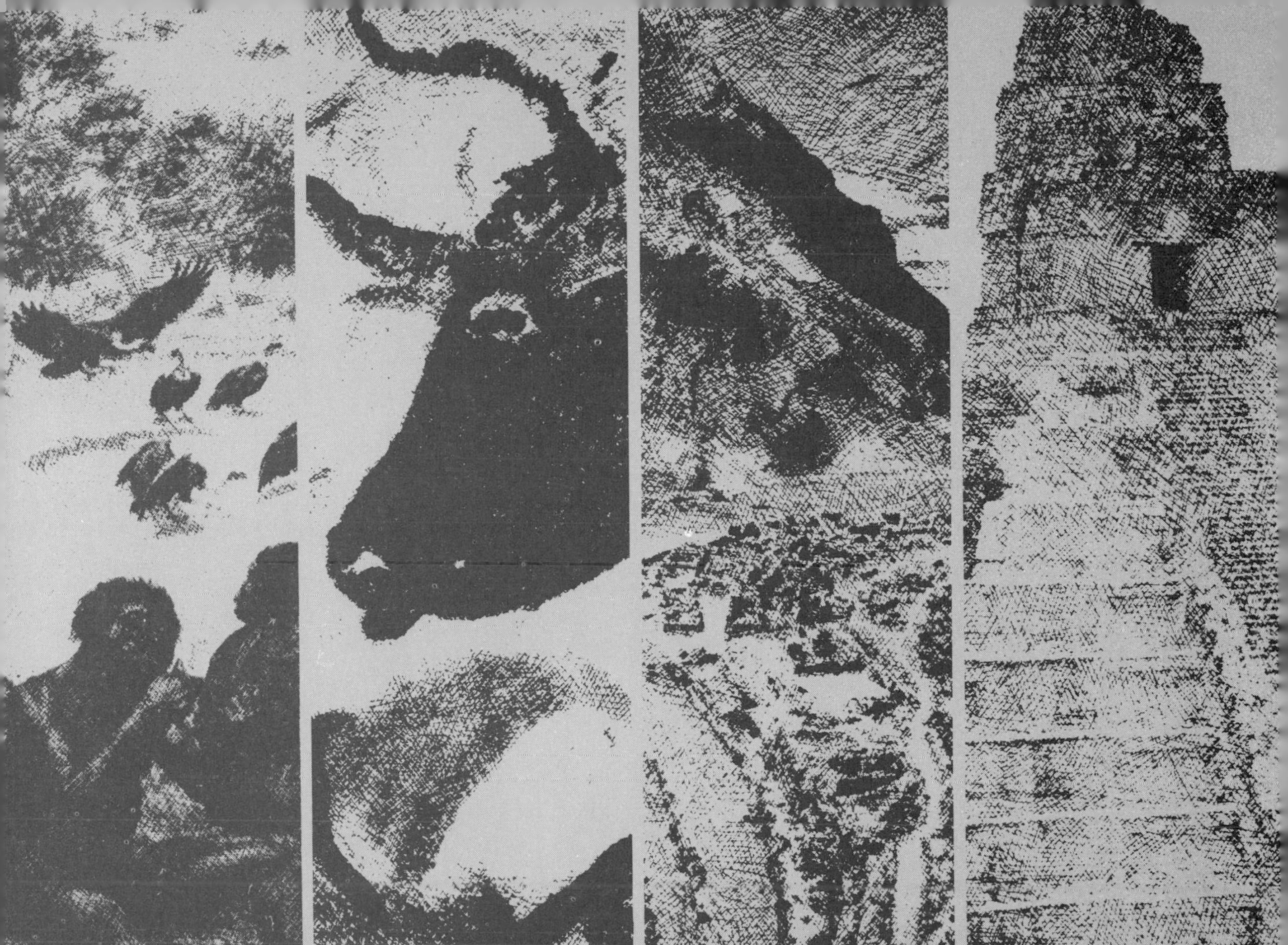

Part Three

Human Physical and Cultural Evolution

Chapter Nine

The Emergence of Cultural Essentials I: *Homo habilis* and *Homo erectus*

The year is 2 million B.P. On the shore of an African lake a troop of early hominids is camped around the bloated carcass of a hippopotamus. Breaking cobblestones one against the other, they use the sharp edges of the shattered rock to pierce the tough hide, dismember the carcass, carve the raw meat from the bones, and break the bones to extract the marrow. Slivers of pinkish flesh are torn apart by strong jaws and stout teeth. The young and the weak whine and beg, and hunks of meat pass from hand to hand. A skin bag of nuts is also passed around until all have fed. And then they lie down to sleep. Tomorrow, and perhaps for a few days after that, they will remain camped in this spot, feeding on the carcass and keeping other predators away. Then, when the meat is gone, they will move on.

This scene, reconstructed from evidence found at Lake Turkana, illustrates what was probably a fairly typical evening in the life of the earliest humans. The differences from the australopith way of life are subtle but very significant. New, distinctly human behaviors have emerged: the setting up of temporary camps, the use of stone tools, the hunting and scavenging of large game, and—most important of all—the sharing of meat and gathered vegetable foods among the members of the group. While the australopiths went on foraging, each for himself—indeed, there were probably australopiths digging up roots within a mile or two of this scene—their more human neighbors had begun to adopt a new survival strategy. And with this new strategy, the story of human evolution enters an altogether new phase.

A reconstruction of a scene from the early Pleistocene in Africa. The hominids in this picture represent the species we are calling *Homo habilis*, the first humans. Physically they are not very different from the gracile australopith who was their presumed ancestor, but their way of life shows significant innovations: food sharing, sexual division of labor, and the hunting or scavenging of large game. *(Painting by Jay H. Matternes: Copyright Survival Anglia Ltd.)*

THE DAWN OF HUMAN CULTURE

As we shift our attention from *Australopithecus* to *Homo*, the central concerns of evolutionary study change somewhat. In the first place, we are now dealing with a single evolving lineage. In previous chapters we have had to consider carefully questions of cladistic relationship—which species branched off from what primitive stock, who was ancestral to whom. In the study of the *Homo* line, speciation is a relatively minor issue. Though there are various theories as to how different populations of early *Homo* are related to modern humans, most can plausibly be seen as representing successive phases in a single evolutionary line, leading directly from the *Homo* neighbors of the australopiths to modern *Homo sapiens.*

Second, in following the progress of the *Homo* line, we must constantly take into consideration a new moving force in evolution: the force of culture. In the nonhuman primates, evolutionary change is ultimately traceable to the natural environment—climate, food resources, competitors, predators. In the human lineage, however, evolutionary change is increasingly caused not only by the demands of the natural world but also by the demands of a world that humans themselves make—the world of their culture. Once created, human culture imposed its own new selective pressures and so became a major force in physical evolution. Moreover, culture itself evolves, so that human evolution ceases to be a story of biological change alone and becomes a story of cultural change as well.

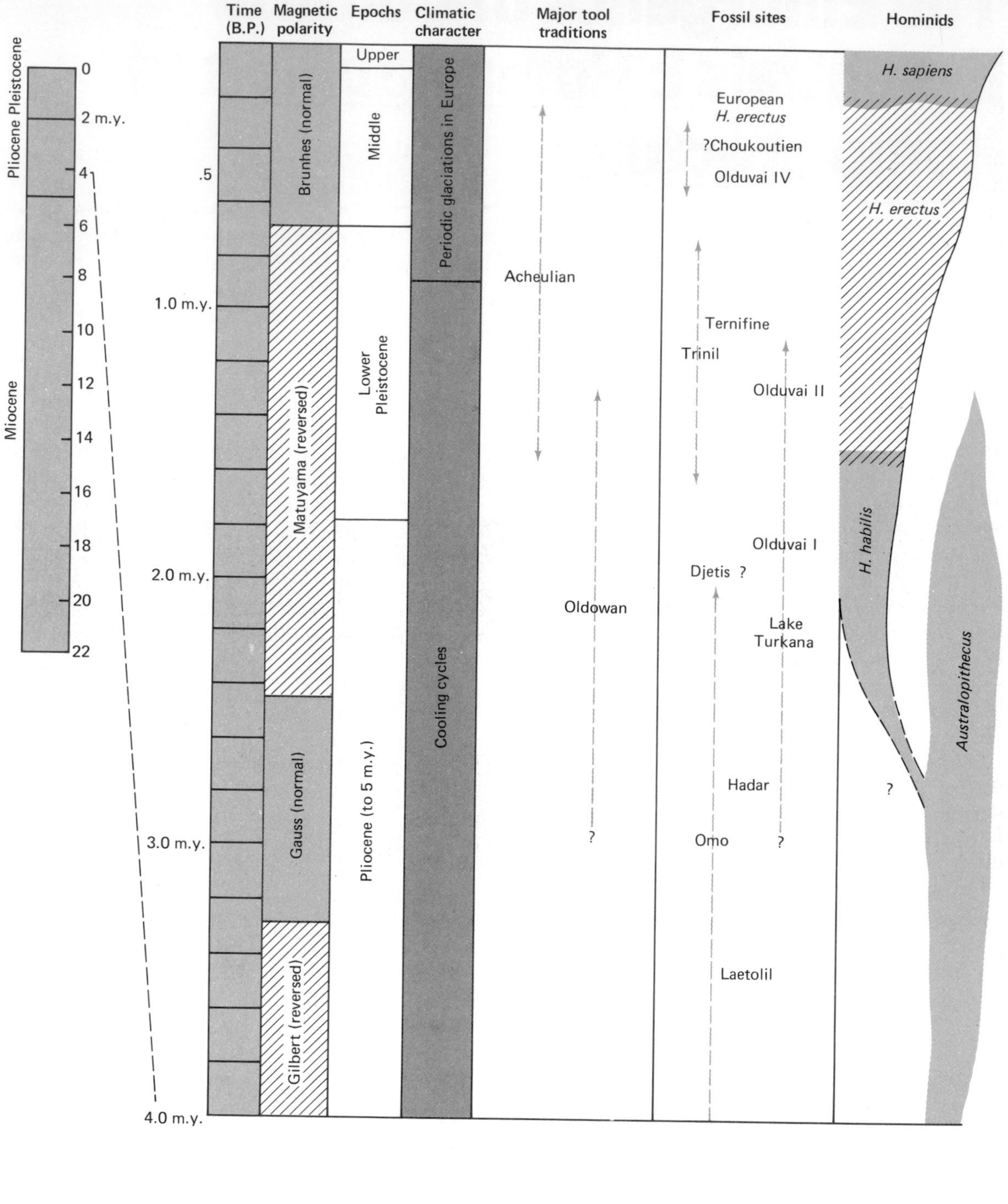

Figure 9-1. Time chart of early human evolution.

As we saw in Chapter 1, culture is an exceedingly broad concept. Nevertheless, we can isolate certain factors that are particularly central to culture as it first emerged in human evolution.

First, artifacts. Other primate species, as we have seen, can make and use simple tools. But human beings have gone far beyond that. Not only have they created a vast range of increasingly refined tools, but unlike the other primates, they have come to depend on these tools for their survival.

Second, economic division of labor. Among the nonhuman primates, chimpanzees alone share food—and then only under very special circumstances. As a general rule, every primate, once weaned, must find its own food. In human groups, on the other hand, food finding, along with other tasks essential to survival, is a cooperative effort. Members perform specialized roles according to age, sex, and ability, and the group as a whole is fed by their combined contributions. Since no individual does everything necessary for his or her own survival, each member of the group is dependent on all the others. On this principle human societies have erected an intricate structure of specialized roles, but its rock bottom was the division of the task of food finding.

Third, language. Other primates have communication systems, but these systems allow them to convey only a very limited range of meanings. Human beings, by contrast, have created an elaborate system of sound symbols by means of which they can communicate a vast range of information, including abstract thought.

A fourth essential of human culture is the ability to organize the world into patterns that have human meaning. Through myth, poetry, ritual, and religion, human beings "tame" nature and align it with society. This aspect of culture, closely associated with language, is, as far as we know, unique to human beings. It has been said that, though a chimpanzee can be taught to make a sign for water, only a human being knows the difference between drinking water and holy water.

Artifacts, division of labor, language, and the organization of experience by the mind—these are the essentials of human culture. Their development in the human lineage seems to have begun about 3 million years ago. That is when we see the first appearance of crude stone tools among hominids who were barely distinguishable from australopiths. By 40,000 years ago, our own immediate ancestors are observing rules for choosing mates, piously burying the dead and providing for their afterlife, and using a variety of tools and skills to adapt to all the major climatic zones of the Old World.

By that point, we believe, the human species is mentally as well as physically "modern." Just as it is possible to take an infant African Bushman or Australian aborigine and convert him into a westernized city dweller, so it would have been possible, we believe, to take an infant cave dweller from the late Stone Age of France or South Africa and bring him up to be a fully functional member of any human culture. While a diversity of cultures have evolved over the past 40,000 years, the intellectual equipment of the human species—the ability to use language, to manipulate tools, to reason, and to adapt—is still essentially the same. In practical terms, this means that the archeologist can interpret the culture and behavior of people who lived 5,000 years ago—or even 35,000 years ago—by analogies with the cultures and behaviors of their contemporary counterparts.

But, as we go further back in time, this assumption becomes less and less valid. In studying protohumans with brains half the size of our own, we cannot simply interpret their ecology and behavior by asking, "What would I (or a Bushman or an Australian aborigine) do in that situation?" Neither modern humans nor modern nonhuman primates provide an exact analogy for the humans of this earliest period, when both culture and the *capacity* for culture were evolving simultaneously. To try to understand them—their mentality, their social behaviors, their adaptive strategies—we must make imaginative use of everything we know about ourselves and our closest nonhuman relatives. We must also squeeze every possible drop of interpretive juice out of the remains that the early humans left behind. Fortunately, we have more than their bones and teeth to go on. For culture leaves its own remains—tools, shelters, the remains of buried campsites—in which we can dimly discern the life style of the people who made them. This archeological evidence, every bit as important as the physical evidence, is a new element that we must integrate when we turn to the study of human evolution.

Although the *Homo* line probably evolved as a single continuous lineage, species names are useful for distinguishing the different evolutionary stages. Thus, somewhat arbitrarily, anthropologists have divided the evolving *Homo* lineage into three successive species: *Homo habilis*, *Homo erectus*, and *Homo sapiens*. In the present chapter we focus on the cultural and physical development of *Homo habilis* and *Homo erectus*. In Chapter 10 we turn to *Homo sapiens*.

EARLY *HOMO*: THE PHYSICAL EVIDENCE

Homo habilis

Year by year, thanks to the painstaking work of paleontologists excavating and collecting at sites in East Africa, we are gradually obtaining a clearer picture of these earliest humans. For many years, as evidence accumulated of stone toolmaking and other "human" activities at the early African sites, it was generally accepted that the toolmakers were australopiths. Then, in 1964, Louis Leakey and a group of his colleagues described a collection of fragmentary jaws, skulls, and limb bones nearly 2 million years old, from Olduvai Gorge. They claimed that this material belonged not to an australopith but to a new species of *Homo*, which they called *Homo habilis*. The name, which means "handy man," expresses Leakey's belief that this new form, and not the contemporary australopiths, was the maker of the stone tools. Leakey claimed that *Homo habilis* differed from the australopiths in having a larger brain and less specialized, more humanlike teeth.

The material was scanty, however, and many anthropologists were unconvinced that *Homo habilis* represented a new species, let alone a different genus from *Australopithecus*. This skepticism persisted as similar remains came to light in equally old deposits at Lake Turkana (East Rudolf). Finally, in 1972, Richard Leakey recovered a now famous skull called ER 1470 (see below). The face of this remarkable specimen was deep and heavily built, like an australopith's, but the braincase was much larger than that of any australopith skull. It had a capacity of almost 800

Assembled ER 1470 skull from East Turkana, East Africa. This is the most complete skull of *Homo habilis* known. (*Courtesy, National Museum of Kenya*)

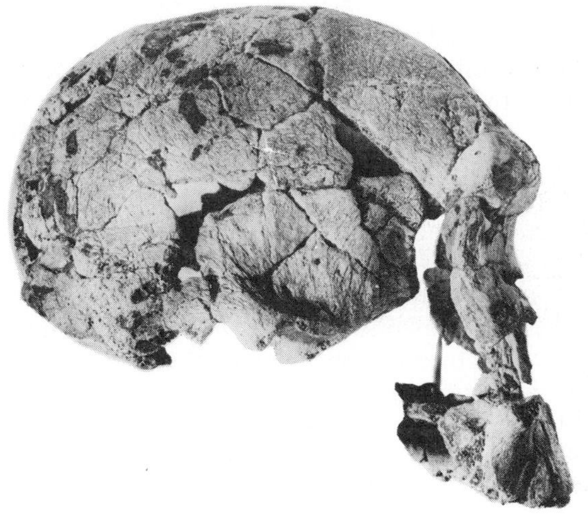

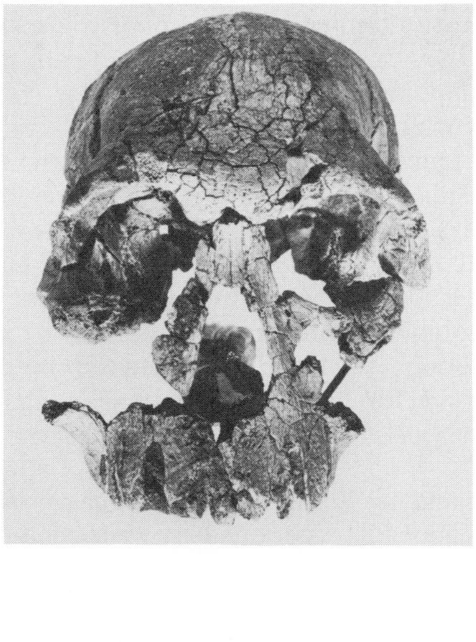

cc., compared with an estimated average of 450 cc. for *A. africanus* and 550 cc. for *A. robustus.* This skull established that there were in fact large-brained hominids living at the same time as the australopiths and thus strengthened the credentials of Louis Leakey's Olduvai *Homo habilis.* Of course, braincase size was variable in early hominids, just as it is in modern apes and humans. One could argue (and some anthropologists still do) that ER 1470 and similar specimens are simply large-brained *individuals* of a single, physically variable "australopithecine" species. But as additional specimens of the same kind are discovered, this position is becoming harder to defend. We believe that the credentials of *Homo habilis* as a distinct, large-brained species, more human in structure than contemporary australopiths, are now well established.

Of course, the fact that early humans of this kind existed does not necessarily mean that they alone made the tools found at sites like Olduvai. Perhaps both *Homo habilis* and *Australopithecus* were systematic toolmakers. This view, as we have seen, has its supporters—mainly those who believe that tool use and bipedalism are closely linked. We do not find this interpretation very likely, however. As we argued in the last chapter, if australopiths and early humans had both been stone-tool using carnivores, they would have been in close ecological competition and therefore could hardly have coexisted for nearly 2 million years. It seems more likely that *Australopithecus* remained largely a vegetarian forager and, at most, an occasional user of very simple stone tools, while *Homo habilis* adopted a different survival strategy—one that included not only the gathering of vegetable foods but also an increasing reliance on meat eating and therefore required a more elaborate stone-tool kit.

Sites and Material

As we have just seen, the most important *Homo habilis* remains come from Olduvai and Lake Turkana. The fossils that Louis Leakey uncovered in the lower levels of Olduvai date from 1.9 to 1.6 million B.P. Contemporary or slightly older deposits at Lake Turkana have yielded not only the ER 1470 skull but also a number of similar but more fragmentary specimens—skull fragments, isolated limb bones, jaws, and jaw fragments—that have been tentatively assigned to *Homo habilis.*

At Omo, early tools were found together with mandibles, part of a hominid skull, and large numbers of scattered, isolated teeth. Of these, three mandibles and many of the teeth definitely belong to a large australopith. Some of the remaining material, which is dated to around 2 million B.P. and is clearly not this robust australopith, should probably be assigned to *Homo habilis.* But without remains of the braincase, we cannot be certain.

In Hadar, the 3-million-year-old Ethiopian site that yielded the australopith skeleton "Lucy," anthropologists have discovered a number of jaws and other fossils, including an almost complete hand, along with early stone tools. These specimens have not yet been described in detail, but they seem very close in structure to the Lake Turkana fossils assigned to *Homo habilis.* Again, however, without a complete skull we cannot be sure. To complete the tally of East African material, Mary Leakey has recently reported the discovery of some jaws of apparently the same type in Laetolil, a Tanzanian site not far from Olduvai. If they are eventually assigned to *Homo,* these will be the oldest specimens of the genus yet discovered, for the site is considered to be well over 3 million years old.

In South Africa, a hominid that is probably classifiable as *Homo habilis* has been found, together with stone tools (and robust australopiths), in the cave site of Swartkrans. At Sterkfontein a similar specimen has turned up, again with stone tools, in cave deposits later than those that yielded the *A. africanus* fossils.

Finally, there are some jaws from the other side of the world: the site of Djetis, in Java. Dating from somewhere close to 2 million B.P., they have been variously assigned to an australopith, to *Homo erectus,* and to their own genus, *Meganthropus.* However, they show distinct resemblances to the *Homo habilis* jaws of East Africa. Inconclusive as they are, they are important evidence, for they tell us that by the end of the

The Leakeys at Olduvai

In 1911, a German entomologist named Wilhelm Kattwinkel, pushing his way through the bush in what is now Tanzania, suddenly found himself teetering on the edge of a canyon some 300 feet deep. He had discovered Olduvai Gorge. Inspecting it briefly, he found some interesting fossils, which he carried back to Berlin with him. These fossils, representing animals long extinct, caused considerable excitement in German scientific circles, and a research team headed by Hans Reck was sent back to the gorge to search for more. Their work was halted by World War I, and after the war Reck could not raise the money to resume it. Frustrated by his inability to get at what he guessed were the gorge's buried treasures, Reck finally wrote to Louis Leakey, a young anthropologist whom he had met a few times and who directed the anthropological museum in Nairobi, Kenya. Why, Reck suggested, didn't Leakey go and take a look at Olduvai Gorge?

Eventually Leakey did, and what he found there awed him as it would any anthropologist—a cut in the earth 25 miles long and 300 feet deep, exposing stratum after stratum of ancient rock, together with fossil animals and stone tools. Why shouldn't the walls of Olduvai also contain the remains of the toolmakers as well? The dogged search for such evidence of human prehistory, at Olduvai and other parts of East Africa, was to occupy the rest of Leakey's life, and it has occupied the lives of his wife, Mary, and of his son Richard up to the present, making Leakey the most famous name in paleoanthropology.

Louis Leakey overlooking Olduvai Gorge. (*Rapho/Photo Researchers*)

In the beginning the work was extremely difficult. Since Louis's job was in Nairobi, the Leakeys could spend only about seven weeks a year at Olduvai. The trip was expensive and arduous—a week's drive over the roughest terrain—and they had little funding, or even encouragement, from other sources. But every year they packed their digging tools, their Dalmations, and eventually their three sons into their car and made the trek to Olduvai. Once they got to the gorge, the nearest source of water was miles away, and even then it was shared with a number of wild animals. ("We never could get rid of the taste of rhino urine," Louis recalled.) By day the African sun blazed down on their heads. By night they could count as many as eleven pairs of lions' eyes shining in the darkness outside their tents. Most trying of all, however, was the fact that no hominid fossils turned up. Day after day, while the Dalmations stood guard against snakes and rhinos, the Leakeys searched the canyon, inspecting the ground inch by inch. In this way they discovered hundreds of tools, including the oldest choppers ever seen. But after twenty-eight seasons, they still had found no remains of the toolmakers.

Then, at the end of their 1959 digging season, while Louis lay ill at the camp, Mary, working in the lowest layer of the gorge, spotted a skull fragment and, above it, poking out of the dirt, two brownish molars. They were twice as broad as modern human molars, but their shape was distinctly human. She raced back to the camp and burst into the tent yelling "I've got him! I've got him!'' Louis jumped out of bed and the two of them hurried back to the site. ''I turned to look at Mary,'' Louis later recalled, ''and we almost cried for sheer joy, each seized by that terrific emotion that comes rarely in life. After all our hoping and hardship and sacrifice at last we had reached our goal.'' So as not to miss a single fragment, the Leakeys sieved tons of dirt on the slope below their find. This took them nineteen days, but at the end they had 400 fragments of what turned out to be the skull of *Australopithecus boisei.*

Fortunately, Louis Leakey possessed a flamboyant personality and an instinct for publicity. Unlike many pioneers, he had no trouble attracting the attention of the world to his discoveries. A few of his more staid colleagues disapproved of the unabashed Leakey showmanship, but it had its desired effect. Soon afterward the National Geographic Society offered to fund the Leakeys' work at Olduvai. In the next year approximately 7,000 tons of dirt were moved at Olduvai—twice as much as had been moved in the previous twenty-eight years.

Other achievements followed. In 1961, just two years after the *Australopithecus* find and at approximately the same geological level, the Leakeys' eldest son, Jonathan, discovered the first *Homo habilis* fragments. Later the discovery of *Homo erectus* in higher strata at Olduvai extended the hominid record further forward. And at Fort Ternan, Kenya, Louis and Mary discovered the oldest known *Ramapithecus* fossils, dated at 14 million B.P., thus extending the record further backward. At the same time Mary, who is an archeologist by training, worked tirelessly excavating, comparing, and cataloguing thousands of early human tools at Olduvai. In the gorge she and Louis uncovered ten living floors, including what is thought to be the remains of the oldest known man-made structure—a circle of stones 14 feet in diameter that probably served as the foundation of a hut about 1.8 million years ago.

Eventually, the Leakeys established much of the time scale for hominid evolution and stone technology in Africa. The chronology that we recognize today—from *Ramapithecus* venturing onto the savanna, to *Australopithecus* adopting bipedalism, to the offshoot *Homo habilis* becoming a hunter-gatherer and manufacturing the first stone tools, to *Homo erectus* perfecting the skills of hunting—is based in large part on Leakey finds.

In addition to carrying on their own work, the Leakeys stimulated further research by giving anthropology an aura of glamour and excitement. Louis Leakey's enthusiasm was immense, and he got others to share it. It was he who finally convinced Emperor Haile Selassie to allow anthropologists into Ethiopia, thus making the way for the Omo and Hadar finds. Convinced that the living primates were a key to human evolution, he inspired some of the most exciting field studies, such as Jane Goodall's study of the Gombe Stream Reserve chimpanzees and Dian Fossey's study of the gorillas of Rwanda. And by dint of exhausting lecture tours, he stirred up public interest, raised money for more projects, and charmed college students, drawing them into anthropology.

In his later years, despite poor health, he pursued fund-raising as single-mindedly as he had earlier pursued fossils, shuffling on two canes from lecture to lecture. Finally, in 1972, he died of a heart attack on his way to London to begin another lecture tour. The contributions of the Leakeys, however, did not end with Louis's death. Mary Leakey, one of the world's most distinguished archeologists, carries on the work at Olduvai and elsewhere, excavating, analyzing, and classifying the tools of early man. Recently, she announced the discovery of what may be the oldest known hominid footprints, dating to about 3.5 million years B.P. Richard Leakey, meanwhile, has been making a series of extraordinary finds of his own—discoveries that may have as much importance for our understanding of early human evolution as those of his parents two decades ago. Indeed, the Leakey legacy seems far from being complete.

Pliocene, humans probably occupied most of the Old World tropics.

Physical Adaptations

In physical structure, the creatures who left these fossils did not differ greatly from the primitive australopith from which they were presumably descended. Yet certain details indicate that their anatomy was adapted to a way of life more dependent on meat eating and toolmaking. As with the australopiths, the anatomical areas that provide our main clues to the way of life of *Homo habilis* are the braincase, the face and teeth, and the hindlimb.

The most distinctive feature of *Homo habilis*, compared with the australopiths, is the larger braincase. The size and presumably the complexity of the brain were correspondingly greater. As culture became a more important factor in survival, more information, and more relationships between different kinds of information, had to be processed by each individual. And if the culture of *Homo habilis* included a form of language (a question that remains unanswered), there would have been still more to remember and synthesize. The new way of life, therefore, created selective pressure for a brain that could store, combine, and manipulate ever-greater amounts of information, and the enlarged braincase of *Homo habilis* indicates that it was developing such a brain.

Unfortunately for the paleontologist who has to sort them, the teeth and jaws of *Homo habilis* are quite similar in size and proportions to those of the less specialized, earlier australopith, *A. africanus.* The back teeth are large, and the incisors are not disproportionately smaller (compared with the huge molars and premolars and the very small front teeth in the late robust australopiths). However, the molars of *Homo habilis* are said to be somewhat narrower than is typical for *A. africanus*, and in later individuals they are definitely smaller. These changes suggest that tools were now being used to do part of the molars' job of crushing and grinding foods. The incisors, on the other hand, remained large. This indicates that they had an important function, perhaps in relation to meat eating. Since humans of this time had no fires for cooking their food, they needed a substantial set of incisors for tearing tough raw meat and for gnawing it off bones.

Of the hindlimb skeleton of *Homo habilis*, we have only some isolated femora found at the same level as the ER 1470 skull in East Rudolf. These femora do not differ from those of modern humans in any feature related to movement or posture. They do, however, seem to differ in subtle ways from the femur of *Australopithecus.* The head of the femur, where it joins the pelvis, shows some changes, though the functional significance of these changes is not clear. (They may have to do not with locomotion but with the widening of the pelvis to allow for the birth of larger-headed babies.) Furthermore, whereas the shaft of the australopith femur is columnlike, the femur of *Homo habilis,* like that of modern humans, has a "waisted" shaft that tapers inward toward the middle. Unfortunately, we do not have associated arm and leg bones that would allow us to compare the limb proportions of *Homo habilis* with those of the australopiths, as represented by "Lucy." We do not know, therefore, whether *Homo habilis* had already developed the long, powerful legs, adapted to striding long distances in foraging and the pursuit of game, that are characteristic of modern humans. Our guess is that it had.

Anatomy and Culture

None of the new features seen in the *Homo habilis* fossils (with the possible exception of the enlarged braincase) constitutes, by itself, a strong case for assigning the fossils to a new genus. Together, however, they add up to a new complex of adaptations, distinct from the adaptive pattern of the australopiths. Basic to this pattern is the influence of culture, which was both cause and result of the physical changes. The development of tools, for example, made *Homo habilis* a more accomplished hunter and gatherer. Greater dependence on hunting, in turn, created selective pressure for more efficient bipedalism—and thus more successful hunting and more extensive tool use. At the same time, larger brains and more dexterous hands made possible the production of better tools, which, because they allowed *Homo habilis* to do finer and more specialized tasks, led to selection for even larger brains and more dexterous hands. Similarly, the advent of tools for preparing food—cutting meat, crushing vegetable food—allowed a reduction in the size of the teeth; and the smaller teeth encouraged even greater reliance on tool use. In other words, a new evolutionary spiral—a mutually reinforcing system—had developed. Culture had entered our ancestors' adaptive pattern, and as time went by it became an increasingly important part of the pattern.

Homo erectus

For convenience, we can consider that the boundary between *Homo habilis* and its successor, *Homo erectus,* occurs about 1.6 million B.P. But as we have suggested, there is no sharp break in the fossil record between the two forms. The placement of the species division reflects the historical accidents of discovery, rather than a period of rapid change or speciation.

Discovery and Interpretation

In the late nineteenth century, Darwin's theory of evolution was by no means widely accepted. Nor did it stand much chance of acceptance as long as there were no fossils to demonstrate that a creature intermediate between ape and man had actually lived. There was much speculation about this hypothetical creature. Ernst Heinrich Haeckel, a German zoologist and an ardent Darwinian, published a description and drawing of what he thought the "missing link" should look like, naming it *Pithecanthropus,* or "ape-man." But this too was simply guesswork, with no concrete evidence to support it. Haeckel's description, however, fired the imagination of another ardent Darwinian, a young Dutch doctor named Eugene Dubois. Dubois decided to set off in search of the ape-man's bones. He chose Java as his hunting ground, and there, after several years of searching, he in fact found what he was looking for. In 1891–1892, near the village of Trinil, he unearthed the upper part of a human skull and a human femur dating from the Middle Pleistocene.

Structurally, these fossils were somewhat different from what Dubois had expected. Many Darwinians believed that when the "missing link" was found, it would have a human head and an apelike body. Yet the flattish skull and the humanlike femur that Dubois had uncovered indicated exactly the opposite: an apelike head and a human body. To Dubois, of course, this simply enhanced the importance of his find. He christened it *Pithecanthropus,* after Haeckel's speculative creature, and added the species name *erectus* to emphasize his ape-man's upright posture.

Because of the unexpected shape of the bones, however, the scientific community (to say nothing of the public) was extremely slow to credit Dubois' find. It was not until decades later, after similar fossils had been found in other parts of the world, that *Pithecanthropus erectus* was recognized as an early human and renamed *Homo erectus.*

Sites and Material

Since Dubois's day, much additional *Homo erectus* material has been recovered. Trinil itself and other deposits in Java have yielded several more skulls and fragments, though without any tools. These, along with Dubois' finds, are dated to the first half of the Pleistocene, from about 0.8 to 1.6 million B.P. From China came the evidence that finally vindicated Dubois: an ancient cave, called Choukoutien, containing a large collection of skulls, teeth, and limb bones from some forty individuals who lived perhaps a half million years ago.[1] (Like all limestone caverns, Choukoutien is extremely difficult to locate in time.) Also in the cave were masses of animal bones, along with tools and hearths. (We will look more closely at Choukoutien later in this chapter.)

[1] Most of the Choukoutien fossils were recovered before World War II and disappeared under somewhat mysterious circumstances during the Japanese invasion of China. Fortunately, meticulous descriptions and good casts survive.

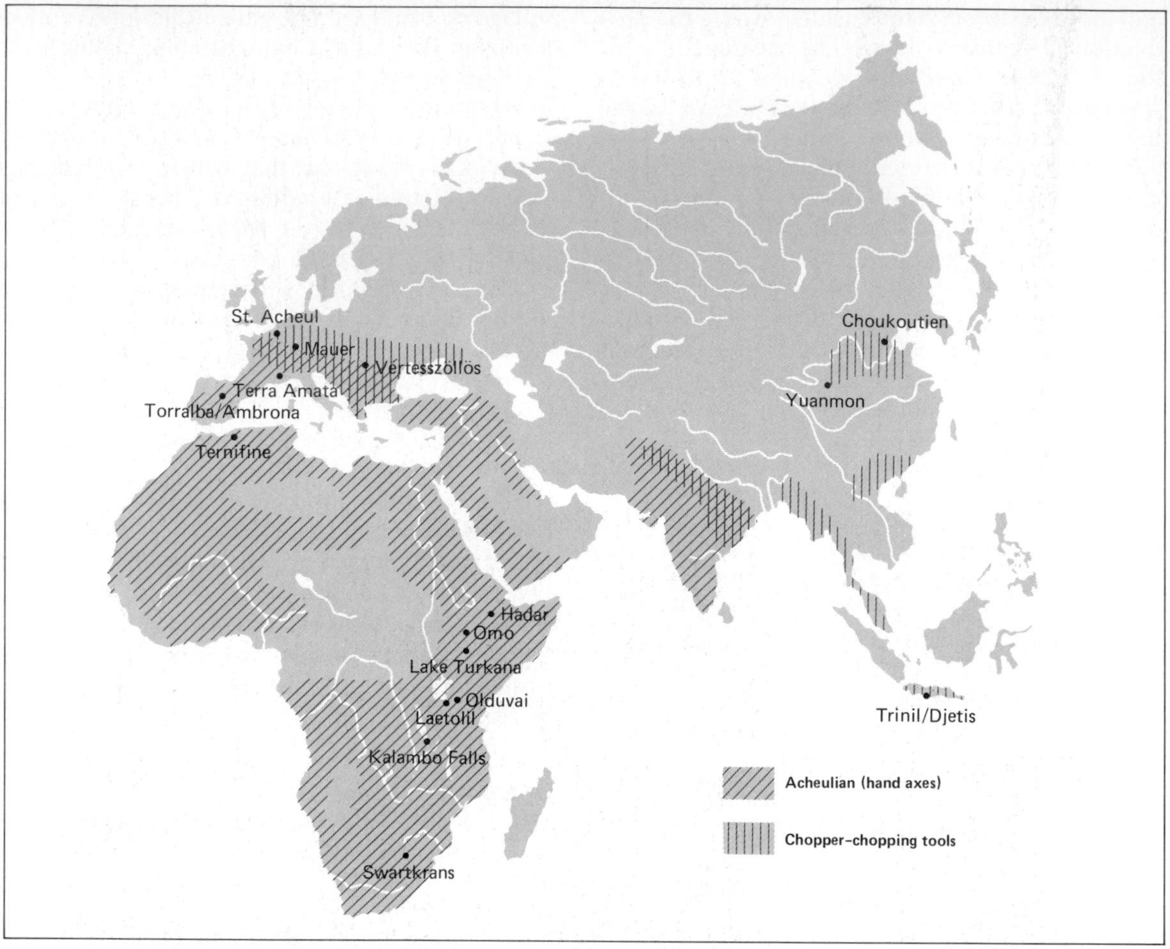

Figure 9-2. Distribution of hand-axe and chopper-tool traditions and some important contemporary fossil human sites.

In Africa, *Homo erectus* fossils have been discovered in Ternifine, near Oran in Algeria, and at Olduvai, which has yielded a massive, thick-walled skull estimated to be a little over a million years old. But the most exciting of the African *Homo erectus* finds comes, quite recently, from East Turkana. Here in 1976, Richard Leakey unearthed a *Homo erectus* skull from the same level as the remains of robust australopiths. This skull, ER 3733, is quite complete and distinctly unaustralopithecine: its braincase is even larger than that of ER 1470, and very close in shape to those of *Homo erectus* from Choukoutien. Furthermore, it is older than any other *Homo erectus* fossil; it can be dated securely at 1.6 to 1.3 million B.P. This find has pushed back the appearance of *Homo erectus* in Africa by about 0.4 million years. And whereas ER 1470, which we consider to represent *Homo habilis,* might be interpreted as an unusually large-brained australopith, the new skull is unquestionably *Homo,* thus proving that early humans did in fact live at the same time and in the same place as *Australopithecus.*

All the European *Homo erectus* fossils seem to be from a much later period. In Europe, early humans did not venture farther north than the Mediterranean basin until a million years after the appearance of *Homo erectus* in Africa. The European specimens probably date from the Middle Pleistocene, close to 400,000 years B.P. These include a stout mandible from Mauer, near Heidelberg, Germany, and an occipital bone and a few deciduous teeth ("baby" teeth) from Vértesszöllös, west of Budapest, Hungary.

Cranium ER 3733 from East Turkana, Kenya, dated about 1.6 million years B.P., and one of the most complete *Homo erectus* skulls known. This specimen is important evidence for the contemporaneity of *Homo* and *Australopithecus*. (*Courtesy, National Museum of Kenya*)

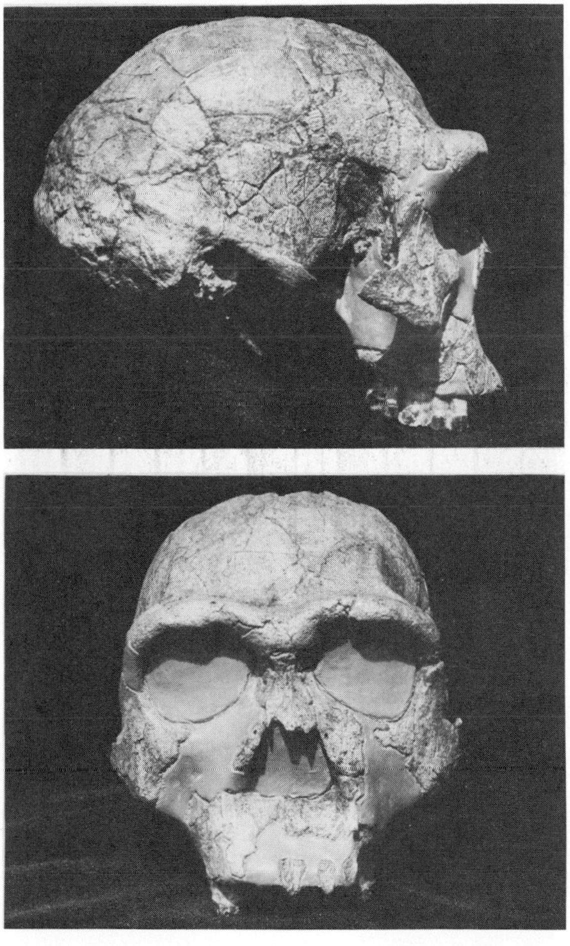

Physical Adaptations

If we mentally arrange the *Homo erectus* fossils in a rough chronological sequence and compare their structure with those of *Homo habilis,* what we see are extensions of the trend toward "adaptation for culture." In the skull, the expanding braincase comes to dominate the shrinking face. The teeth, especially the molars, are reduced in size. In fact, they overlap the upper end of the modern human range. Likewise, the structures that support the teeth and the jaw muscles become smaller and more delicate. The smaller back teeth and jaw muscles probably indicate that more and more foods were being prepared before eating—cut and pounded with tools or even, among late *Homo erectus* populations, cooked. The incisors remain large, however, indicating that they were still used for biting through tough foods like meat.

The brain, expanded already in *Homo habilis,* goes on expanding. Some of the earlier *Homo erectus* skulls, such as "Pithecanthropus IV" from Java, are as small-brained as some examples of *Homo habilis;* but later populations (such as at Choukoutien) have relatively larger, more capacious braincases. Presumably, people were becoming more "intelligent." And, as the brain gets larger, the skull fills out, becoming more convex. This is especially true of the frontal region, which rounds out as the forehead becomes wider and higher. Presumably, what occurred behind the forehead was an expansion of the frontal lobe of the brain and a consequent increase in power of concentration.

All the skull bones of *Homo erectus* are rather thick and heavy. The brow ridges, especially in large individuals, are quite massive, and the roof of the skull is remarkably thick. Indeed, in some cases, especially in earlier and presumably male skulls, it is so thickened along it midline that it looks like the keel of a boat. (This should not be confused with the sagittal crest seen in large pongids and australopiths, which acts as an attachment for the temporal muscle.)

This massive skull is a unique specialization of *Homo erectus.* It was neither inherited from *Homo habilis* nor passed on to *Homo sapiens.* What its functional significance is we do not

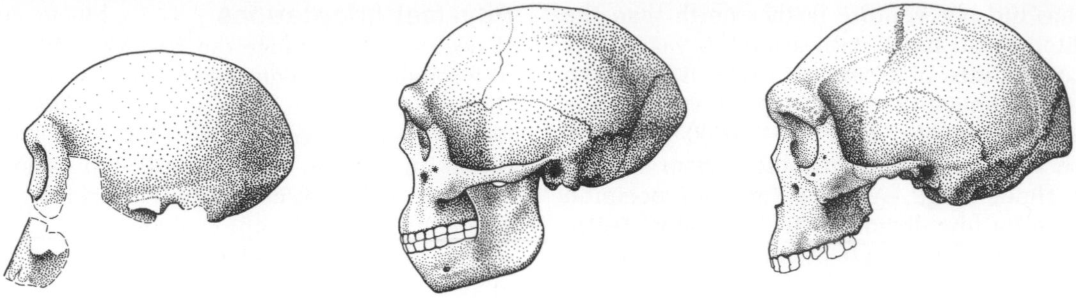

(a) *Homo habilis* (b) *Homo erectus* (c) *Homo erectus–Homo sapiens*

Figure 9-3. Lateral view of skulls of early and modern humans. (a) *Homo habilis*, based on the reconstruction of ER 1470; (b) *Homo erectus*, reconstruction of an individual from Choukoutien; (c) modern human, African male. (*Biruta Akerbergs*)

know. Heavy chewing has been suggested; however, the robust australopiths, who were much heavier chewers, and have massive faces, do not show this great thickness at the roof of the skull. One suggestion is that this bony structure served as protection against injury—a natural "helmet" for protection in fighting or the hunt. Although this interpretation seems rather quaint, recalling cartoons of cavemen with clubs, it is as good a guess as any.

The rest of the skeleton shows a few peculiarities that are rare in modern *Homo sapiens*, but overall, it is entirely modern in function. The limb bones indicate that the gait of *Homo erectus* was no different from that of *Homo sapiens*. (Ironically, the *Homo erectus* femur found by Dubois, which is so modern-looking and first gave the name "erectus" to this group, may actually be a modern bone.)

In overall body size, *Homo erectus* seems to have been somewhat larger than *Homo habilis*, although we do not have enough bones to know for sure. In both *Homo habilis* and *Homo erectus* there is considerable size range, which can probably be ascribed to sexual dimorphism as well as to the usual variation among individuals of the same sex. At Choukoutien, Ternifine, Olduvai, and Arago, there is evidence that physical difference between the sexes was much greater than in modern humans. Males seem to have been quite a bit larger than females and had heavier jaws and more massive skulls.

The Question of Geographical Variation

Despite their broad similarities, the known *Homo erectus* populations seem to show certain geographical variations. For instance, a femur and a pelvis from one of the upper layers at Olduvai indicate a population taller than the Choukoutien people, who averaged about 150 centimeters (5 ft.), judging from the femora we have. Of course, such differences may be simply the accident of small samples. On the other hand, they may well represent real geographical variations. If so, are these variations the origin of the racial differences seen in modern humans?

Carleton Coon (1962), following Franz Weidenreich, has gone so far as to suggest that *Homo erectus* evolved into *Homo sapiens* five times, as five separate, independent races. This is probably an overstatement, particularly on the basis of available material. We simply do not have enough fossils to allow us to compare different populations in the kind of fine detail necessary to prove racial differences. On the whole, the resemblances between *Homo erectus* populations are much more striking than their differences.

For example, there is a distinct resemblance between specimens from Olduvai and the more-or-less contemporary specimens from Java, thousands of kilometers away. Similarities in tooth size and other anatomical details strongly suggest that human evolution proceeded more or less at the same pace and in the same direction over a broad area of the Old World, from Africa to the East Indies.

THE HUMAN WAY OF LIFE

The early humans, as we have seen, lived in the same areas as the australopiths—in the tropical savannas. In addition to the grains, seeds, and roots that constituted the australopith diet, the savannas offered another obvious and plentiful source of food: game. A savanna can support a great deal of meat on the hoof, as much as 6 to 19 metric tons per square kilometer (17 to 54 tons per square mile)—that is, about six times as much as the Great Plains of North America before the white settlers arrived (Butzer, 1971). We believe that the early humans exploited this food resource. They were becoming hunters; and this fact had a profound influence on the course of human evolution.

Hunting

For a relatively small bipedal creature, the hunting of relatively large animals is a rather bold undertaking. As we saw in Chapter 5, chimpanzees occasionally kill small animals for food; but neither chimpanzees nor any other nonhuman primates have ever been seen killing an animal the size of an adult antelope.

Exploiting this source of food could not have been easy. For one thing, hunting such animals as antelope, boar, or zebra, armed only with clubs and simple stone implements, would have been strenuous and frequently dangerous. Flying hooves and slashing horns or tusks must surely have extracted their toll from the human hunters. The perils would have been even greater for any band hardy enough or desperate enough to tackle an elephant or a hippopotamus. Moreover, adoption of such a way of life meant a change in the role of the early human among the animals of the savanna from herbivore to predator. The old, easy, mutually beneficial relationship with antelope and other plains grazers would be gone; the appearance of a human on the scene would arouse wariness, flaring nostrils, and an uneasy shifting of position.

At the same time, the early human would be entering the competitive world of the large carnivores of the plains—lions, leopards, hyenas, cheetahs, and the great saber-toothed cats. Recent studies of such large carnivores have shown that, while each species occupies a distinct econiche, specializing in hunting a particular kind of prey at a particular time of day or night, the different species are also active competitors, the stronger stealing meat from the weaker whenever possible. Thus there is no room for the weak or inefficient in the large carnivore league; each kill must not only be brought down and dispatched, it must also be defended against other predators. This is the main reason why a small, comparatively inefficient biped, starting to adapt to life outside the forest, could not become a hunter without a long apprenticeship of adaptation to plains life—though not necessarily to hunting itself. This apprenticeship was, we believe, served by the early, foraging hominids before the *Homo* line diverged from *Australopithecus.*

But if the risks of hunting were high, so was the potential return: a new and plentiful food supply, with no competition from other hominids. And apparently this advantage was great enough to set in motion a major shift in ecological strategy.

Exactly how and when the early humans made the transition to hunting is a subject of some controversy. By the Middle Pleistocene, there is unquestionable evidence of big-game hunting. But we do not find implements that can be unambiguously identified as *killing* tools at early *Homo* sites. All we have are various disarticulated and splintered animal bones, along with stone butchering tools. These tell us that meat was eaten but not whether it was actually hunted or merely scavenged. Indeed, even the identification of Olduvai and East Turkana as butchering sites has recently been questioned (Binford, personal communication).

Some anthropologists believe that the transition was early—that it in fact formed the basis for a rapid evolutionary divergence of *Homo* from *Australopithecus.* The australopiths, like the chimpanzees, probably went on killing sprees now and then, and it is quite possible that one or two localized australopith populations turned killing into a regular pattern and began hunting larger and larger prey. This new subsistence strategy would have called forth the new adaptations on which the genus *Homo* was founded. Such an interpretation is in keeping with the current theory that evolutionary breakthroughs usually occur rapidly, and in relatively small, marginal populations.

Other anthropologists argue that in view of the lack of early evidence for systematic hunting, we must infer that this practice was not adopted until much later. According to this theory, the earliest humans (or even the australopiths) may have spent a million or so years scavenging carcasses of animals that had died naturally or been killed by other predators before they started doing the killing themselves.

Of course, it is quite possible that the truth lies somewhere in between, for hunting and scavenging are not mutually exclusive ways of life. Perhaps, like many modern-day hunter-gatherers, the early humans regularly hunted the smaller and less dangerous species, scavenged the carcasses of the larger ones, and hunted the truly formidable animals such as elephants only when prompted by opportunity or need—when they happened upon a weakened or wounded animal, for example, or when nothing else could be found.

Whatever conclusion we reach about the early evidence for hunting, it is well to bear in mind that scavenging too would have required many new skills. A lion is not easily shooed away from its dinner. Indeed, even if *Homo habilis* never hunted a single large animal but simply scavenged regularly, he would still have had to make most of the cultural advances that we associate with the rise of hunting: food sharing, sexual division of labor, cooperative labor, toolmaking, and so forth. These are as much adaptations to the eating of large animals as to hunting.

Additional research in the next few years is likely to shed new light on the subsistence practices of these early humans. At this point we can say with reasonable confidence that, from the very first, human beings were hunters in the sense that they depended heavily on meat, and that some members of each human band probably set out each day to get some, in whatever way they could—whether by hunting, or scavenging, or (most likely) some combination of the two. It is in this broader sense that we shall use the term "hunting" through much of the following discussion.

Food Gathering

The eating of large animals was an essential part of the adaptive complex of *Homo habilis.* It was this practice that allowed the first humans to find an unexploited econiche alongside the australopiths and other nonhuman primates, and so started our lineage on a new evolutionary path. Such game, however, was by no means the only source of food for early humans—nor even necessarily the most important source from a dietary point of view. The bones at the sites indicate that they also killed a variety of small animals, including rodents, bats, porcupines, pigs, birds, fish, tortoises, and snakes. More significantly, they certainly went on eating vegetable foods as well.

The archeological record probably overemphasizes meat eating, because bones are preserved far better than vegetable matter, and stone tools far better than the baskets or skin bags that would have been used for collecting foods. At Choukoutien, hackberry seeds survive as scanty evidence of the vegetarian side of the prehistoric diet. At Kalambo Falls, in Malawi, there are piles of gathered vegetable materials, including fruits. There is also much partially burned wood—probably the remains of fire-hardened wooden implements such as clubs or digging sticks. Despite improved archeological techniques, however, evidence of this sort remains scarce.

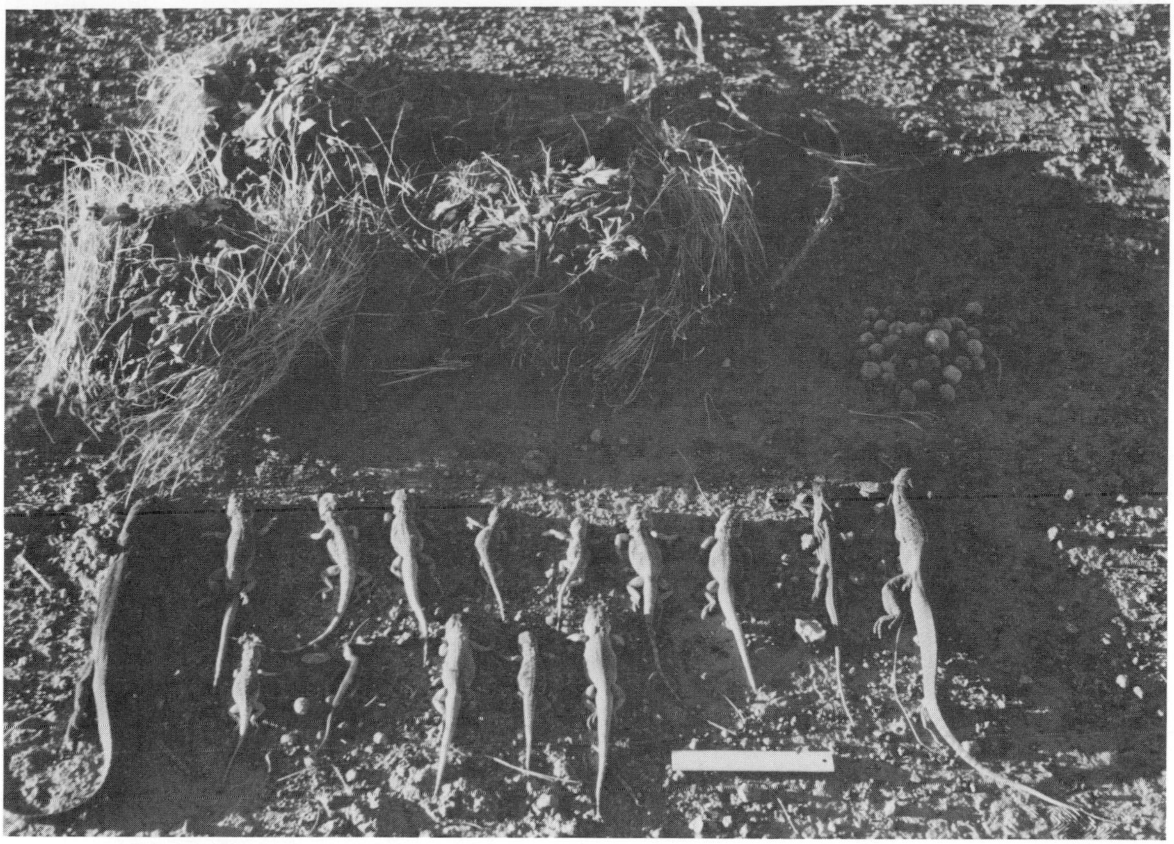

A typical day's take for a group of hunter-gatherers: nuts, lizards, and a variety of edible plants. These foods were collected by an extended family of 10 people. *(American Museum of Natural History)*

Nevertheless, we can safely assume that vegetable foods, far from being incidental, were a major component—and, when hunting was bad, the only component—of the early humans' diet. Though they had taken up hunting, the early humans retained an essentially vegetarian constitution; they could not subsist on meat alone. Even if they could have, the meat supply was too irregular to be their only staple food. The hunt is a chancy business, even for accomplished predators like lions. Many days may pass between kills. The specialized carnivores solve this problem by gorging on meat when they find it, after which they can fast until the next kill is made. This kind of feeding, however, would be quite foreign to a primate, adapted to snacking most of the day. Thus a regular supply of vegetable foods was absolutely essential.

Division of Labor by Sex

One of the most far-reaching changes that accompanied the rise of hunting and gathering was a division of work roles by sex. In other primates, social roles are of course influenced by sex, but sexual specialization rarely extends to food finding to any great extent. If all the animals are to get a balanced diet, both sexes must go after all available foods. In the beginning of their career on the savannas, hominids presumably followed

Members of a band of Kalahari Bushmen (San) set out for the day's foraging. The women carry digging sticks and collecting bags as well as their infants, while the men carry the weapons of the hunt—spear, bow, and arrows. *(De Vore/Anthro-Photo)*

the same pattern. But once early humans began to hunt systematically, food-finding roles had to be divided, because considerations of fitness greatly limited direct female participation in the hunting of big game.

As pointed out in Chapter 5, a long period of dependency in childhood characterizes the primates in general, and in no genus has this prolonged immaturity been carried as far as in *Homo*. Once culture became an integral part of the human way of life, the young had even more to learn before they could become fully functioning members of the band. Mothers usually had to look after not just one nursing infant but one or more half-grown children as well. Furthermore, human infants could not cling to their mothers, as do baby chimpanzees and baboons, since the grasping foot had been lost in the transition to bipedalism. The nursing infant now had to be carried. And when the female was not encumbered by a nursing infant, she, like other primate females, was often pregnant. Consequently females were not well suited to the role of hunter. Remember that the nurturing of offspring is the primate female's strong suit in the reproductive strategy game. No matter how skilled a hunter, a woman would have a very low fitness if she dropped or aborted her infant while chasing a gazelle. Thus the task of hunting big game passed largely to the male.

This does not mean, however, that the females and young were left to while away the day at the campsite. There were many ways in which they could contribute to the success of the hunt: mending or making weapons, serving as lookouts and beaters. But they also had an even more crucial role in the group's subsistence strategy: gathering the vegetable foods and catching the small animals (lizards and the like) on which day to day survival depended. This pattern of specialization according to sex is virtually universal among present-day hunter-gatherers, and there is little reason to doubt that its origins go all the way back to the first appearance of this subsistence strategy among early humans.

Sharing

As we saw in Chapter 6, chimpanzees share meat, but their sharing is of a very rudimentary sort. In general, the chimp who made the kill sits gobbling the meat until other chimps come to beg, whereupon he may allow them to take pieces of flesh from him. If no one came begging, however, the chimp would not go looking for dinner companions. By contrast, the sharing of food must have become much more voluntary and systematic among early humans. In order for all members of the group to get a balanced diet, the hunters would have had to butcher their kills and not only share the meat among themselves but bring most of it back to the campsite for the women and children. Similarly, women and children gathering roots, nuts, berries, seeds, fruit, and small game would have had to carry these foods to the campsite for the returning hunters to share. This pattern of mutual dependence, which represents a radical break with the simple see-and-eat pattern of modern nonhuman primates (and presumably of *Australopithecus* as well), is perhaps the most fundamental characteristic of human society.

Tools

Neither hunting nor gathering, in itself, absolutely requires tools. Digging sticks to help get at roots, for example, are certainly useful, but baboons manage without them; clubs and stone axes would surely be helpful to a hunter, but they are not essential. It is the *sharing* of food—the practice of hunting and gathering *for the group*—that makes implements indispensable: skin bags (and maybe even wooden bowls and baskets as well) to carry gathered vegetable foods, perhaps a sling to hold the baby while the hands do the gathering, stone butchering tools to cut up the carcasses of large game animals so that meat can be brought back to camp. Without such implements, a way of life based on sharing and the sexual division of labor would hardly be possible.

Stone tools were particularly important to early humans. They were stronger and sharper than any other implements that could be obtained. They were extremely useful for the tasks associated with hunting and butchering—killing animals, skinning them, cutting up the meat, cracking the marrow bones, scraping the hides. (This would have been especially true when large animals were the prey. Chimpanzees in search of meat can bash a monkey against a rock and bite through its skin. But an elephant could not be picked up and bashed against a rock, nor could its tough hide have been easily pierced by the teeth of early humans.) Stone tools could also be used to crush, chop, or pound tough vegetable foods such as roots. And they were good for digging and for chopping wood. Equally important, they could be used to *make* implements from other materials such as bone or wood.

For us, too, the stone tools are the most important—because they are usually the only ones that have come down to us. Some of the earliest implements were probably made out of bone, horn, wood, and skin, but these more perishable materials have long since disintegrated, while the stone tools have survived. Indeed, they have survived by the hundreds of thousands and are considerably more numerous than early human fossils. For whereas each early human had only one pelvis to leave to posterity, he probably made hundreds of stone tools in the course of a lifetime. The evidence indicates that the early hunters did not carry all of their tools from campsite to campsite. When they broke camp, they left their tools behind and simply made new ones as the need arose.

Stone tools, then, are our most solid evidence of the life style of *Homo habilis* and *Homo erectus.* They are so important, in fact, that when archeologists divide this stretch of prehistory into periods, they often do so by toolmaking technology. The tools made by *Homo habilis* and *Homo erectus* fall into two main groups. The earliest are those of the *pebble-chopper technology,* of which the *Oldowan* tools are the best-known examples. Later, a more advanced style of toolmaking appears: the *hand-axe technology,* commonly associated with the *Acheulean* tradition.

The Oldowan and Related Pebble-Chopper Traditions

The name Oldowan comes from Olduvai Gorge, where products of the pebble-chopper technology were first discovered by Louis and Mary Leakey. Similarly worked tools—many considerably older than the Olduvai specimens—have since been found at East Turkana in the Omo Valley, and at other sites in South Africa, North Africa, the Middle East, and even southern France. The pebble-chopper technology originated at least 3 million years ago and remained the major toolmaking method until about 1.5 million years ago.

The most characteristic tool of the Oldowan and other pebble-chopper traditions is the *chopper,* which is simply a stone chipped at one end to create a sharp edge. To make a chopper, the Pleistocene toolmaker chose a rounded stone, called the *core,* held it against a hard surface, and used another stone as a hammer to chip some flakes off one end, leaving it with a sharp edge. The typical chopper is *bifacially* worked—that is, it has flakes removed on both sides. (When a tool has flakes removed on only one side, it is said to be *unifacially* worked.) The resulting edge is surprisingly keen, far superior to nails or teeth for cutting through the skin or sinew of an animal or shaping a piece of wood. At the same time, the other end of the tool remains rounded, thus fitting comfortably into the palm of the hand.

Aside from the choppers, this technology included a limited number of other tools. The flakes chipped from the core in the process of making a chopper were often used for cutting, as

Figure 9-4. Percussion flaking is the oldest and simplest technique for making stone artifacts. It does not permit a great deal of precision in shaping a tool as indicated by the crude and very generalized characteristics of Oldowan tools. Front and side views of tool are shown. *(Biruta Akerbergs)*

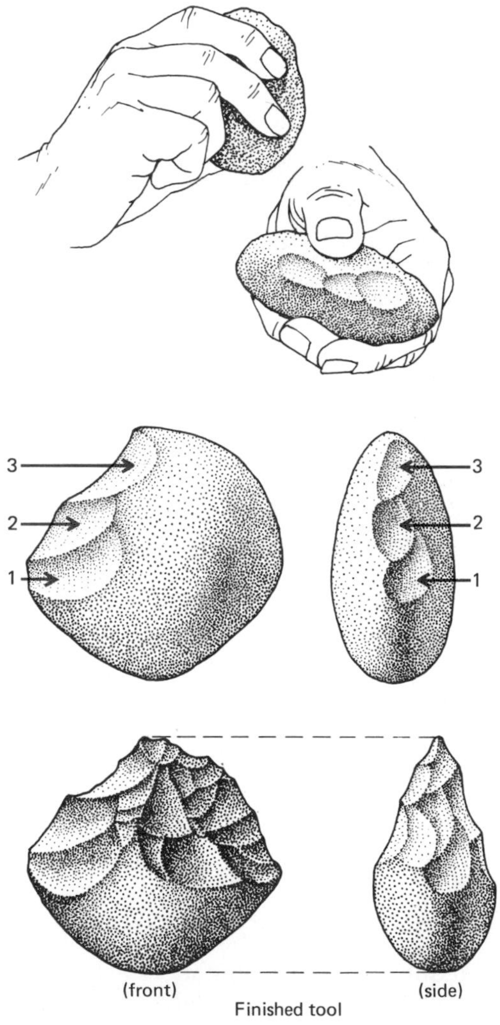

we can tell from nicks in their edges. These *flake tools,* though not as sturdy or as easy to hold as a chopper, were considerably sharper. In many assemblages, including some of the earliest, they are actually the dominant tool type. Unworked stones were sometimes used as hammers or anvils, as is indicated by signs of wear on their surfaces. Archeologists have also found pieces of stone and bone that appear to have been ground or polished and may have been used as tools. Finally, we must assume that wooden tools were plentiful as well, since wood is easier to work than either bone or stone, and since sharpened sticks are the most common tools among many present-day hunters.

In general, the Oldowan and similar tools are relatively simple and unspecialized. The very late Oldowan sites have yielded some specialized tools—such implements as scrapers and chisels, which are designed to serve a single specific purpose. But the characteristic Oldowan tools were choppers and minimally modified flakes, which, far from being specialized, were decidedly all-purpose implements. The chopper, for example, could be used to cut skins, meat, or wood; to slice meat; to work hides; to scrape and shape bone or wood into new tools; and probably to do many other things as well. It would not have been especially efficient at any one of these tasks. Its value lay in its utility for doing all of them with *some* efficiency.

Crude as the Oldowan tools were, they represent an enormous step forward in our ancestors' control of their environment. They show that the early humans had the ability not only to use an object from nature to help them do a job but also to modify that object according to a set formula, so that it could do the job better. This process requires foresight, planning, and the ability to hold in the mind an ideal pattern. That the Oldowan toolmakers had these mental qualities is revealed also in the fact that many of the tools found at Olduvai Gorge are made of stone not native to the area. Clearly, the early toolmakers realized that only certain types of stone were appropriate for making tools, and when they found the appropriate raw materials, they were willing to carry them a considerable distance for use in a future task. It is such mental qualities that led the Leakeys to conclude that the makers of the Oldowan tools were members of the human lineage and to dub them "handy men."

The Acheulean Tradition and Hand-axe Technology

The refinement of the craft of toolmaking was an extremely slow process. As we have seen, the pebble-chopper industries flourished from 2.5 to 1.2 million B.P. In other words, for over a million years the early humans went on using essentially the same tools with which they had begun. In time, however, their manual dexterity and conceptual abilities improved, and so, consequently, did their tools. About 1.6 million years ago a new style in toolmaking appeared in Africa. The new implements were more refined and more specialized. These were the products of the "second wave" of human tool manufacture, the hand-axe technology.

So little modification is required to make a pebble-chopper tool that populations in different parts of the world may have invented and reinvented this technology many times. If so, then we cannot speak of a single toolmaking tradition but only of a series of parallel traditions coexisting during the period from roughly 3 to 1.5 million years ago. With the hand-axe technology, by contrast, the pattern of manufacture is more distinctive. While we cannot be certain, it is much more likely that we are dealing with a historically transmitted body of toolmaking procedures—that is, with a tradition. This tool tradition is known as the *Acheulean.* As with the Oldowan, the name comes from the locality in which such tools were first identified, the small town of St. Acheul in northern France.

The term "Acheulean" is also commonly used, by extension, for all the populations—widely distributed in space and time—who worked in that toolmaking tradition. When we use the term in this broader way, however, and speak of "Acheulean peoples," we should not imagine that they necessarily constituted a single, completely homogeneous culture that spanned

Africa, western Europe, and the Middle East for a million and a half years. No doubt there were many variants of the Acheulean culture at different times and in different places. There was, however, enough cultural continuity and cultural interchange among groups so that people made tools in essentially the same way over a very wide area; and the pace of technological change was slow enough so that they made them that way for a very long period of time.

Acheulean tools are generally thought of as the distinctive work of *Homo erectus*, and in a very broad sense this is true. However, the pebble-chopper technology did not abruptly vanish from the toolmaking repertoire of early humans when *Homo erectus* appeared. People still made crude chopping tools when that was all they needed (as indeed many hunter-gatherers do even today). In fact, as we shall see, *Homo erectus* populations in some parts of the world continued to work almost exclusively in the pebble-chopper technology long after the appearance of the hand-axe technology. Moreover, early populations of *Homo sapiens* also made Acheulean tools. Nevertheless, the Acheulean tradition spans the period to which *Homo erectus* is assigned, and it is therefore normally identified with this species.

Acheulean tools are thinner and more elegant than Oldowan tools. Most Oldowan choppers are bifacially worked but only at one end. By contrast, the typical Acheulean tool has flakes removed not only on both sides but over most of its surface. Very little, if anything, remains of the original surface of the rock. And whereas the Oldowan chopper was completed by knocking off a few large flakes, the Acheulean tool is refined by subsequently removing many smaller flakes.

The most characteristic tool of the Acheulean tradition is the *hand axe*, a pear-shaped implement 10 to 35 centimeters (4 to 14 in.) long, with sharp edges all around and, often, a picklike point. The combination of cutting edge and pick made the hand axe a versatile tool. Another common tool is the *cleaver*, which has a straight sharp edge where a hand axe has a point. Flake tools are also common in the Acheulean. In some instances, the flakes were clearly not just the by-products of core tool manufacture but were intentionally removed from the core and then retouched. At some European sites, more than three-quarters of the tools are made from flakes.

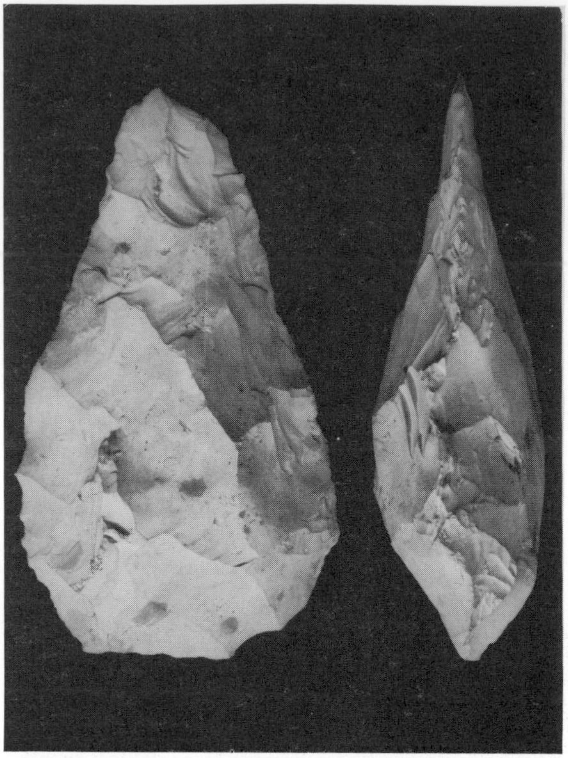

A characteristic tool of the Acheulean, a hand axe. *(Collection, Musée de l'Homme)*

These new tools reflect a number of evolutionary changes. First, the coordination of eye, brain, and hand of the toolmakers must have become more highly developed. They were now able to aim the hammer more carefully and to hold the core in different ways to produce different kinds of flakes. Perhaps even more important, they were able to carry a mental picture of the finished tool and imagine the series of blows—considerably more complex than those needed to make a pebble chopper—that would bring it into existence. They could assess the effect of each blow and direct the next one accordingly, as the tool took shape in their hands. This is evidence of a great advance in intellectual ability.

Acheulean toolmakers also tended to be even

more selective than their Oldowan predecessors in their choice of raw materials. Indeed, they had to be. With many kinds of rock, a toolmaker can get a sharp edge by knocking off a few flakes. But only with relatively few types of rock—those with a very fine, crystalline structure—can the toolmaker chip off many flakes without causing the stone to shatter. The Acheulean stone-workers clearly knew this, and chose their cores accordingly.

The later Acheulean toolmakers also developed a new method of flaking, the *soft percussion,* or *soft hammer,* technique, in which wood, bone, or antler was used instead of rock to chip flakes off the core (Figure 9-5). The use of these softer materials as hammers allowed a great deal more control over the length, width, and thickness of the flake that was removed.

These changes allowed the Acheulean toolmakers to achieve greater precision in their work. They could shape a stone to be thick or thin, rounded or straight; they could model its contours as they pleased. Consequently they were able to make many different kinds of tools. In Acheulean assemblages, to a far greater extent than in those of the Oldowan, we regularly find implements made to a variety of different patterns. One deposit at Olduvai, for example, contains eighteen different types of tools, including chisels, anvils, awls, and scrapers, in addition to the usual hand axes. Acheulean assemblages also tend to contain many more tools, simply in raw numbers, than earlier assemblages. This suggests that as the Acheulean craftsmen learned to make more specialized tools, their activities themselves became more specialized. Thus, through a circular process, their way of life became increasingly dependent on tools—a trait that aligns them with modern humans.

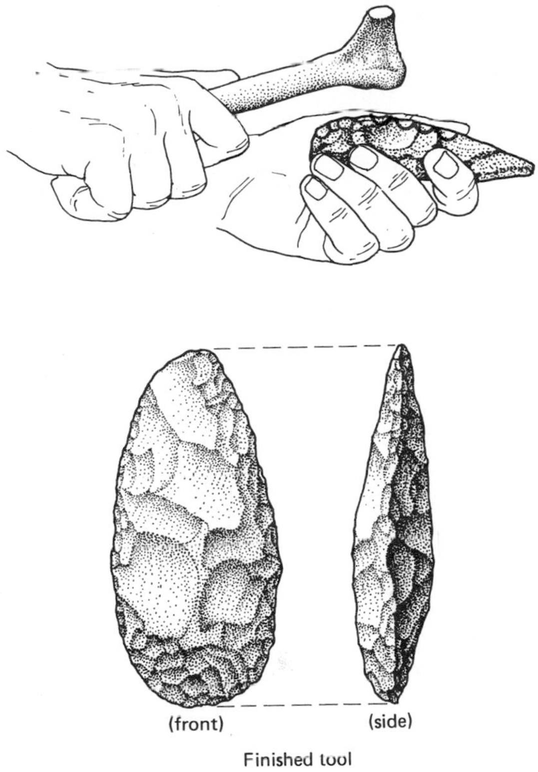

Figure 9-5. The use of a bone or wood hammer, which was softer than stone, enabled toolmakers to be more precise in sizing and shaping the flakes removed in making an artifact. This technique resulted in the creation of more refined and diverse forms of tools. (*Biruta Akerbergs*)

Geographical Variation in Toolmaking Traditions As pointed out earlier, the time spans of the pebble-chopper and hand-axe technologies overlap. In fact, the archeological evidence indicates that the toolmakers of eastern Europe and eastern Asia went on working primarily in the pebble-chopper technology for hundreds of thousands of years after the toolmakers of Africa, western Europe, and India had started to use the hand-axe technology (Figure 9-2).

The apparent coexistence of these two traditions can be explained in a number of ways. One possibility is that both pebble-chopper and hand-axe tools were being made—at different worksites, for different purposes[2]—in both areas about a half million years ago, but that we have

[2] We know this was the case in Africa, for example.

uncovered more pebble-chopper worksites in the East and hand-axe worksites in the West. More likely, however, is the possibility that we are in fact witnessing the coexistence of two different technological traditions. If so, some social barriers would have been required to maintain the distinction. This leads to some interesting speculations regarding the social organization of the early humans, which we will discuss shortly.

Acheulean Tool Kits One reason archeologists have considered the possibility that individual bands of hunter-gatherers made both Oldowan and Acheulean tools is that specialized sets of tools, called *tool kits,* have been found in certain Acheulean assemblages. Howell and Clark (1963), for example, analyzed groups of artifacts found together in different levels at three African sites and concluded that they represented at least four distinct tool kits. One has a high proportion of large cutting-edge tools, with a smaller proportion of large scraping tools and relatively few waste flakes and cores. The second tool kit has few large cutting-edge tools but a higher proportion and a great variety of small tools, as well as a high proportion of waste flakes. A third, represented only by a single collection, has a great many heavy tools—picks, scrapers, and choppers—as well as large knives. And a fourth consists almost entirely of waste products and roughly shaped material.

It is unlikely that these differing tool kits were the work of separate human groups. Rather, they appear to have been produced by the same people performing different tasks at different times. The first type seems to have involved mostly cutting, with little scraping or toolmaking. The second, with the greatest variety of tools, might have been the comprehensive "tool cabinet" of some sort of base camp. It is impossible to generalize about the third because the sample is so small. The fourth probably derives from a very temporary camp where a few tools were made.

These different tool kits constitute further evidence that the development of the specialized Acheulean tools was accompanied by an increased specialization of activities and labor. At any one time of the year, for example, one part of the band might have been occupied with scraping hides outside the shelter, another with gathering nuts and berries in the vicinity, while yet another group, off hunting for a few days, was at a temporary camp. The sites discussed in the following section support such a picture of separate places for separate functions. As we shall see, the evidence suggests that even the task of cutting up an elephant was done in stages, each performed at a different spot and probably requiring a somewhat different set of tools.

Sites and Living Floors

The emergence of complex culture in the human lineage means that we no longer have to depend solely on bones or stone tools to reconstruct the life styles of our earliest ancestors. The sites that yield the physical remains and stone tools of the early humans often yield more elaborate archeological remains as well—concrete evidence of a developing human culture. Indeed, in some deposits archeologists have uncovered full *living floors.* These are stretches of earth, buried for hundreds of thousands of years, on which early human bands once camped for periods of time, leaving behind the debris of their habitation: the hearths in which they built their fires, the shelters they erected against the wind, the tools they made, the bones of the animals they ate, and sometimes their own bones as well. On these living floors we find the clearest evidence of a way of life rooted in hunting and gathering.

Most of the living floors are rather late, and therefore they give us little help with the question of how early the hominids became systematic hunters. But they do allow us to reconstruct—still, as with the bones, using some guesswork—how the hunt was pursued and what changes a subsistence strategy based on hunting and gathering made in the lives of the people. For hunting and gathering is not merely a way of finding food; it is a whole way of living. It entails certain specific adaptations in thinking, moving about, forming social groups, dividing tasks, even mating and reproducing. Much of the remainder of this chapter will be devoted to examining the cultural changes associated with this subsistence strategy. First, let us examine three particular sites and the more obvious developments that we can read in them.

Choukoutien

Choukoutien is situated close to Peking. About half a million years ago, it was a large cave, set in a cliff of limestone, where human hunters lived through a number of seasons. The cave was a fine location for a hunting-and-gathering band. It was near water and offered an excellent view of the grazing animals on the plains below. Equally important, it gave protection from the chilly climate of northern China, and it kept the rains from putting out the hearth fires.

The hunters who occupied Choukoutien clearly recognized these advantages and were willing to fight for them. In order to move into the cave, they had to evict the animals that lived there. The bones indicate that over the years the hunters in turn moved out many times, and were replaced by saber-toothed tigers, leopards, bears, and hyenas. Eventually, however, the humans took permanent possession of the cave, and the evidence indicates that they used it—perhaps seasonally, perhaps year-round—for a very long time. In one of the hearths, the ashes form a continuous layer some 7 meters (23 ft.) thick. Choukoutien has also yielded over 100,000 stone tools of the pebble-chopper technology, fragments of over forty humans, and thousands of animal bones. Some of these animals were probably the prey of the nonhuman carnivores who periodically reclaimed the cave. But many other bones—those of the wild pig, elephant, rhino, camel, water buffalo, and horse, along with vast quantities of deer bones—are charred. Thus we know that these animals were the prey of humans—people who cooked their meat and who had a taste for venison.

All the human skulls from Choukoutien have been carefully opened through the base, presumably to extract the brain. This suggests that the Choukoutien people were not only hunters, but also cannibals—or at least headhunters. We tend to think of cannibalism as a bestial and inhuman practice, but in fact nothing better demonstrates the human status of the Choukoutien people. Among living peoples, cannibalism is rarely just a matter of nutrition. Often it is a solemn ritual act—perhaps to express family piety toward the deceased or magically to impart the deceased's spirit and qualities to the living. We may be confident that the atmosphere of Choukoutien during the cannibal meal was closer to mass than to McDonald's. Choukoutien, then, reveals humans able to compete successfully with the fierce cave animals, to survive in colder climates (thanks to the use of fire and shelter), and perhaps even to conceive of other human beings as spirit rather than simply as matter.

Terra Amata

In 1965, in a spot called Terra Amata near Nice on the French Riviera, bulldozers began clearing a piece of land to make way for a new apartment complex. Several years earlier, an ancient stone tool had been found in Terra Amata. This fact was known to Henry de Lumley, a young French anthropologist, and as the bulldozers went to work, de Lumley stationed himself nearby, to see whether anything interesting turned up. What turned up were several stone tools, clearly the work of early humans. Construction stopped and excavation began. Within five months de Lumley and his crew had dug 22 meters (72 ft.) into the ground, uncovering twenty-one different living floors, one on top of the other, dating from a period about 300,000 years ago.

Used from time to time over the course of about a century, the Terra Amata living floors contain a wealth of clues to the lives of Acheulean hunter-gatherers. For one thing, there is clear evidence that huts once stood in these spots. Each of the living floors is surrounded by an oval arrangement of stones, which probably buttressed the walls. Next to the stones are the imprints of the stakes or saplings that constituted

Archeology—Tracing Human Prehistory

Archeologists study extinct societies. Like detectives, they begin with the barest clues—scraps and marks left behind by human beings as they went about their business hundreds, thousands, or even millions of years ago. Tools are the most common class of evidence—a sharpened piece of stone once used for scraping, a sherd (that is, a broken piece of pottery), the tip of a bone splinter once used as a needle. Also very useful are the remains of prehistoric meals—charred seeds, bones split open to extract marrow, a circle of blackened stones that formed an ancient hearth. Similarly, a circle of post holes or of rocks may indicate where the walls of a house once stood. Of course, some materials are more spectacular—a beautiful vase, a statue, a massive temple or pyramid. But much of what the archeologist employs in reconstructing the past is essentially ancient garbage—things used and then tossed aside and forgotten. These materials are only a meager reflection of the family activities, hunts, tribal councils, ceremonies and markets, of which they provide evidence. Yet, when carefully analyzed, they often allow archeologists to reconstruct important evolutionary episodes and to trace the processes of cultural evolution.

The Survey

Archeologists decide to work in a particular area because they believe it will contain evidence useful in answering some question they wish to address. Once a general area is decided upon, the next step is locating sites—sites, that is, of ancient human activity. Historical documents, explorers' journals, and even legends about ancient dwelling places and migrations may direct the archeologist to a likely spot. However, the most important technique for locating prehistoric sites is the survey. A *survey* is a systematic examination of the surface of the ground in a given area. Signs of human habitation are not always visible on the surface, but frequently a few scattered artifacts or rubble from a house will alert the archeologist to buried evidence. In other cases, more subtle clues are used. Variations in soil color and overgrowth may, for example, suggest buried buildings, irrigation canals that have filled with silt, and the like. (Such variations can sometimes be identified in photographs taken from an airplane or a satellite.) When archeologists locate a site, they typically draw a map of it, collect a sample of artifacts from the surface, and make notes on its environmental setting and on the kinds of archeological materials found there.

By increasing the archeologists' knowledge of the range of sites in an area, a thorough inventory gathered by survey enables a researcher to choose sites for excavation that are most likely to yield the desired data. Some archeologists use the survey alone, without subsequent digging, as a research tool. For example, surveys are the only way to establish the boundaries of a prehistoric trade route or of a cultural or ethnic group—a group that shared a tool or ceramic tradition. By indicating the kinds of locations in which prehistoric peoples chose to settle, surveys can also provide valuable clues concerning their subsistence practices. Finally, the survey is the only method of gathering data on the distribution of people—whether, for example, they lived in large towns or small hamlets—and on patterns of prehistoric population change. Nevertheless, the major function of the survey is still to guide the archeologist in deciding where to excavate. By examining all the possible sites in the area, he or she can make an educated guess as to which is the most likely to contain abundant and interesting material. Then the digging begins.

Excavation

Excavation is the process of digging a site to recover artifacts and other buried evidence of human activity. Yet excavation is more complicated than simply digging. Many forms of valuable archeological evidence would not look at all "archeological" to the layman. Some, such as pollen samples, are so small that they can be identified only by microscopic study in the laboratory. Others, such as early stone choppers, are barely distinguishable from natural objects. Hence the archeologist needs a trained eye not to overlook or accidentally destroy the evidence. Furthermore, once an artifact has been identified, its location must be precisely noted, for the location of artifacts in relation to one another is as important in interpreting them as the nature of the artifacts themselves.

The first step in the actual excavation is to map the site and its surroundings and establish a datum, or reference, point—a point from which distances will be measured in specifying the location of finds. The datum point may be the corner of a building, a large rock, or a metal rod—anything that is visible and fairly permanent. Usually, the crew then digs one or more test pits, from which they collect data on the natural layering of the soil, the depth of archeological deposits, and the presence of architecture or other features. This information can then be used to make certain strategic decisions about how the excavation will be conducted.

1. What percentage of the site will be excavated? Large units are generally preferable, for they enhance the possibility of significant finds and minimize the danger of cave-ins. However, if the site is large or the crew small, the archeologist may decide on a sample of small pits—perhaps 3 to 5 meters (10 to 16 ft.) on a side—scattered over the area.
2. What shape pits will be dug? Sometimes, architectural features such as rooms dictate the shape (and size) of excavation units. More often, however, archeologists impose a shape on the excavation units by dividing the site into squares or rectangles and then designating that certain of these will be dug.
3. Can natural stratification be used to distinguish finds from different levels in the pit? If so, the site is ideal, for stratification marks different chronological levels. If there is no visible layering in the soil, or if the layers are too thick to be useful, the excavator must declare arbitrary levels—anywhere from approximately 5 centimeters to a meter (2 to 39 in.) in depth.
4. What kinds of materials are to be collected? In addition to artifacts, the excavator may want to collect charcoal or other material for dating, as well as seeds, pollen, and animal bones for ecological data. Each kind of material requires its own special handling.

These decisions made, a grid of squares is laid on a map of the site, with the datum point at one of the intersections. This grid allows the crew to record and map squares on the site (using the datum point as a reference) so that they will be able to record the exact location of every find. They can now dig—square by square, layer by layer. Depending on the stage of the excavation, the type of evidence being sought, and a number of other factors, the crew works with anything from power machinery to bent screwdrivers and small brushes. Artifacts are bagged and labeled according to their horizontal location in the grid and their vertical location in the soil layers. Usually, the crew makes a photographic record of each stage of the excavation process and each find so that others can see what they have done. Excavation may take a few days, months, or years. (The record for longest excavation is probably Susa, Iran, where successive teams of archeologists have been digging more or less continuously for some ninety years.)

Excavation, however, is only the beginning. There remains the task of interpreting what is excavated. The purpose of digging up ancient artifacts is to reconstruct the lives of ancient peoples—their environments, their strategies for getting food, their patterns of trade and social organization, their ways of thinking—and to describe the evolutionary processes that shaped these aspects of their lives. In later boxes we shall consider in detail the various techniques used to extract this information from archeological evidence.

the walls. In the middle of the floor, along the central axis, are large holes; these, presumably, are the marks of thick posts that supported the roof. The result would have been an oval shelter affording some protection against cold and rain. The stones indicate that the shelters ranged in size up to 6 by 15 meters (20 by 49 ft.). They could have housed bands of anywhere from fifteen to twenty-five members.

On the living floors there are shallow pits of baked earth, the hearths in which people built their fires. Next to the hearths are small piles of stones that probably acted as windbreaks. The earth around the hearths is free of litter, and one of the floors bears the clear imprints of animal skins. This, presumably, is where the band slept, either lying on or dressed in hides. The floors also contain the usual wealth of animal bones and of tools—some of them made from bones. There is a possible hint of another kind of implement as well. On one floor there is a smooth, rounded depression, perhaps made by a bowl used for holding water or for carrying nuts or berries or perhaps even for cooking.

The huts were not permanent shelters. The earth on the living floors is only very loosely compacted, indicating that they were occupied for no longer than a few days. Apparently, the people who built them—like most of the people of this time—had to move from place to place in search of food. When they had exhausted the food resources in one spot, they moved on. They probably returned to Terra Amata seasonally. From the pollen contained in the feces left in the huts, the season appears to have been spring, when game would have been plentiful in the area.

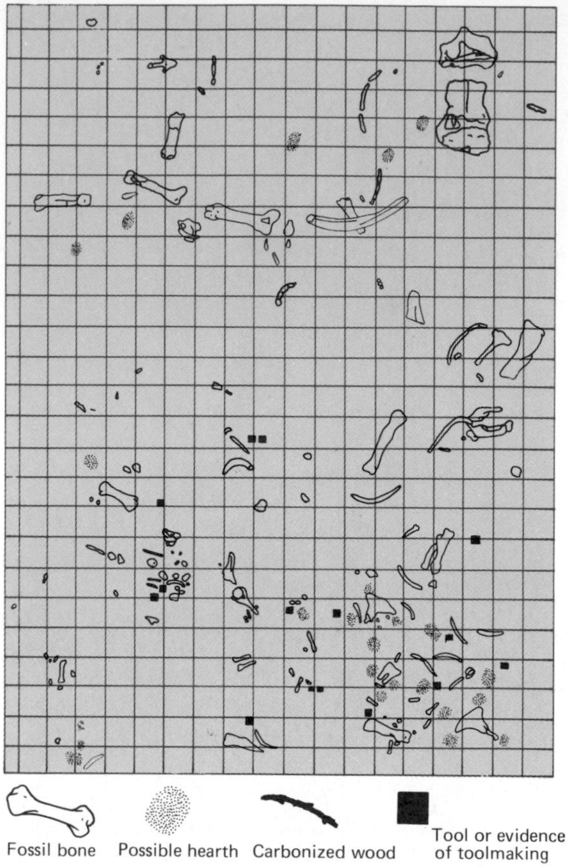

Figure 9-6. A chart of part of the Torralba/Ambrona butchering site, based upon observations and measurements made during excavation. The tusk and bones at bottom right appear to have been placed in alignment by the occupants of the site.

Torralba and Ambrona

Torralba and Ambrona, two neighboring sites in northeastern Spain, contain no human fossils and no evidence of shelters. What they do contain is the most striking evidence of the early humans' skill as hunters. Scattered over the sites are quantities of enormous elephant bones. As the condition and position of the bones indicate, these elephants were systematically hunted and butchered by bands of early humans during at least ten successive hunting seasons around 400,000 years ago.

The valley in which Torralba and Ambrona are located was probably on the path of the elephants' seasonal migrations. We can guess that different bands of hunters, knowing that a vast supply of meat would be passing this way, returned to the valley at the time of the migration and lay in wait for the elephants. Pieces of charcoal and charred wood widely dispersed over the sites suggest that the hunters set fires in the grass to drive the animals into bogs, where they could

Elephant bones unearthed at the Ambrona butchering site in Spain. *(Courtesy of F. Clark Howell)*

easily be dispatched while trapped in the mud.[3]

Once they had killed the elephants, the hunters apparently butchered them in three different stages. First they removed the most desirable sections of the carcass and carried them to a second butchering site. Here they cut the flesh into more manageable pieces and broke open the long bones to extract the marrow. Then they transported the pieces of meat to a third spot, where they seem to have cooked and eaten them, as is indicated by piles of small, charred bone fragments. It is possible that they also preserved some of the meat for future consumption—perhaps by smoking it or drying it in the sun.

Interpreting the Evidence From the Living Floors

On the basis of the evidence at such sites as Choukoutien, Terra Amata, and Torralba-Ambrona, we can make certain generalizations about the lives of *Homo erectus.*

First, as we have indicated, they had become hunters. Dining on other animals was no longer a caprice; it was a basic subsistence strategy. They may have begun their meat-eating career by scavenging, but at least by the time of late *Homo erectus* they had become cunning, systematic hunters. They knew enough to work together. They understood animal migrations and planned their own routes accordingly. They executed daring ambushes, driving herds of game into bogs. And after the kill, they went about the task of butchering with care and precision, as the three types of butchering sites at Torralba-Ambrona indicate. This sophisticated approach to hunting suggests that the intelligence of *Homo habilis* and *Homo erectus* was increasing a matter that we will explore later in this chapter.

Second, the early humans established camps—home bases from which they would depart to find food and to which they would return with their kills or with the vegetable foods they had gathered. These home bases might be permanent, as Choukoutien apparently was, or they might be temporary campsites as was Terra Amata, to which bands returned each year when the hunting was best. In either case, the existence of a home base almost certainly stimulated the growth of culture. Around the familiar hearth—in the same place, with the same people—language, ritual, complex social relationships, and refined toolmaking techniques would have had a chance to develop.

Furthermore, it should be noted that even

[3] The early hunters of East Africa apparently used the same technique. In one level at Olduvai, archeologists discovered the bones of whole herds of antelope which had obviously been driven into one spot to be killed. The four limbs of one animal were still implanted in the earth. Evidently, the hunters hacked off most of the body and left the limbs standing in the mud.

when the home bases were extremely temporary, the early humans did build shelters. They had begun to take control of their relationship with the elements—to put roofs over their heads, to pile up stones between their hearths and the prevailing winds, perhaps even to make clothing or sleeping mats out of hides. These skills permitted them to expand their territory. By 500,000 B.P., humans had moved northward from the tropics into the cooler climates of Europe and Asia. Aside from Australia, which was isolated by water, and frigid zones of Central Asia and of the Arctic and Antarctic, most of the Old World was now inhabited by humans.

Finally, as all three sites (especially Choukoutien) indicate, humans had learned to use fire and had come to depend on it. Along with shelters, fire made it possible for them to survive in the colder northern regions. Fire not only kept them warm; it also allowed them to deal on equal terms with animals much larger and fiercer than they. With fire, they turned bears out of caves and scared them away when they returned. As we saw at Torralba-Ambrona, fire allowed them to stampede herds of large animals into spots where they could be killed more easily. Eventually, fire was used to cook meat, making it more tender and increasing its nutritional value. Fire was also employed in toolmaking—to harden pieces of bone, antler, and soft wood, which could then be used as spears, as digging sticks, or as hammers for making stone tools. Moreover, the light of the campfire lengthened the working day for early humans, increasing the number of hours that could be devoted to toolmaking, story-telling, and planning marriages and alliances.

The skillful use of fire was yet another cultural development that allowed the early humans to bend nature to their own needs. What they lacked physically they had begun to supply culturally—shelter and fire to keep them warm in climates in which their naked bodies were unsuited, cunning techniques to allow them to hunt animals much larger than they. They had begun to master their environment, but at the same time to rely more and more heavily upon technology.

MENTAL AND SOCIAL DEVELOPMENT

By placing an increasingly elaborate culture between themselves and nature, our ancestors set themselves on a unique evolutionary course. Yet this course was not so unique that the forces of Darwinian evolution ceased to apply. With the early humans, as with all other animals, ecological strategy influenced physical and behavioral adaptations. Just as foraging in the savannas created selective pressures that favored the development of certain posture, dental proportions, and social habits among the australopiths, so did the adoption of hunting and gathering create new selective pressures for specific kinds of physical and behavioral adaptations in the *Homo* line. Our early ancestors depended upon hunting and gathering for well over a million years, and quite possibly for 2 or 3 million years—far longer than our more recent ancestors have spent making their living through farming or industry. This immensely long period saw the development, through natural selection, of many of the traits that we consider most distinctive of our species. In a sense, we started to become human by adapting to the hunting-and-gathering way of life. But this subsistence strategy was only the initiator of a larger and more complex cycle of changes: the changes we associate with human culture. Very soon, human beings began adapting to a cultural environment of their own creation.

We have already discussed the physical adaptations that distinguish *Homo habilis* and *Homo erectus* from their australopith forebears. Most of these can be directly related to hunting and gathering, and to the toolmaking traditions and patterns of social cooperation that developed with this way of life. The human hand became more dexterous as an adaptation to the making and using of tools. The hindlimb, answering the hunter's need to walk long distances in foraging and to run swiftly in pursuit of game, acquired its modern human structure and may have become relatively longer. As tools were used to prepare food and fire to tenderize it, the teeth, and especially the molars, became smaller.

More striking than any of these adaptations, however, is the change in the early human brain. Adaptation to culture affects many parts of the body, but it is the brain in which cultural information is stored, and on which above all cultural adaptation makes its demands. Thus as the culture of the early humans developed, their brains grew rapidly in size and complexity. The possessors of those brains began to develop a deftness of intellect and a complexity of social behavior that make them recognizably human.

Mental Development

The new way of life posed a great many challenges to the mind. First there were those of subsistence itself. The individuals who could meet such challenges were the most successful hunters and foragers; they stood the least chance of being outwitted by a wounded boar, or of forgetting the best place to find hibernating lizards during the dry season; they had the best chance of bringing back to camp enough food to keep themselves, their mates, and their offspring alive. So, by the force of natural selection, hunting and gathering resulted in increasing intelligence and mental flexibility. At the same time, other aspects of the emerging cultural complex, such as toolmaking and more complex social interaction—both cooperation and competition—strongly reinforced this trend toward braininess.

Let us consider briefly some of the specific mental qualities that culture favored.

Memory

In the first place, both hunters and gatherers needed good memories. They had to be able to learn large stretches of countryside so that they could range widely during the day and still find their way back to the base camp at night. Furthermore, they had to go through this learning process repeatedly, for the band was continually moving its camp. To return to a seasonal hunting ground such as Terra Amata, the early humans had to recall what route to take and what season was best for hunting in that particular region.

Not only the peculiarities of the terrain but also the peculiarities of various plants and animals had to be carefully studied. Early hunters could not afford to specialize in any one kind of quarry; the available game changed from place to place and from season to season, and the hunters had to go after whatever was there. Consequently, they needed to stock their memories with information on many different kinds of animals—their tracks, their habits, their migratory patterns. Knowing the precise time of year that herds of bison visited a particular valley, knowing that an elephant wounded with a spear will charge its attacker, whereas a deer will run away—such things could mean the difference between life and death. So could remembering where to find the best nut trees, which plants had edible roots, and which berries made one sick when eaten.

Success in toolmaking, which had enormous survival value for early humans, also depended heavily on memory and the ability to make more complex associations among ideas. The toolmaker had to recall not only the techniques necessary to produce a particular implement but also the best sources for the raw materials. More complex social relations, too, must have spurred the development of memory. During the period we are surveying, alliances, feuds, and relationships by blood and marriage were no doubt becoming more intricate and more important in the social life of early humans. The person who could remember friendships and enmities, favors and threats, who could distinguish a stranger from a relative, was likely to live longer, acquire better mates, produce more offspring, and, in general, have greater inclusive fitness than his more scatterbrained companions.

Concentration and Persistence

We pointed out earlier that much of the expansion of the early human brain seems to have taken place in the frontal lobe: the area that controls the ability to concentrate on one goal, screening out distractions and resisting temptations that conflict with its achievement. This ability, without which civilizations could not have been created, may well have developed as an adaptation to hunting and gathering. Hunting, for example, is an enterprise in which concentration and persistence are absolute prerequisites. Deer tracks may lead for miles and then disappear. Campsite after campsite may yield nothing but a few rabbits. When big game is finally brought down, the feast is plentiful, but simply finding it may require weeks of planning and waiting. Modern hunter-gatherers demonstrate the indispensability of such tenacity. For example, in taking on large prey such as elephants, they will often wound the animal with a spear and then follow it, hour after hour, until it collapses from exhaustion and can be killed. It is likely that early humans used similar techniques and had need of similar mental qualities.

Once again, however, we need not assume that hunting was the sole agent selecting for these traits. Gathering must have made similar demands. And toolmaking would have required the very same qualities: intense concentration on the work at hand, persistence in seeking the best kind of stone, patience in shaping the tool as carefully as possible, and perseverance through repeated failures, when the stone shattered or did not acquire the proper shape or edge.

Planning and Cooperation

Most of the animals hunted by early humans were bigger or quicker than they. To compensate for this disadvantage, the hunter had to use cunning. Knowing, for example, that an antelope trying to escape a pursuer tends to travel in an arc, the hunter could walk in a straight line, which, if properly aimed, would allow him to cut the animal off despite its speed. Such complex planning is a skill that modern humans take for granted; but it was probably through hunting that humans mastered it in the first place.

Cooperative hunting required some division of roles, which would make planning all the more necessary and all the more complicated. In plotting an ambush, for example, the hunters would have had to imagine the task as a whole and then divide it into separate roles—one person keeping watch for the animals and giving the signal, another person lighting the brushfire, and so on. Each hunter would have had to think of his own actions as part of a whole and make them dovetail with the actions of the other hunters. Again, this mental skill is something that we take for granted; children do it on ball fields every day. But it is actually a sophisticated mental operation rarely seen in any nonhuman primate.

Toolmaking, too, would have selected for the ability to formulate a plan and cooperate in its execution. Planning is of course indispensable to the conscious creation of any artifact, even the simplest implement. But cooperation would also have been valuable: one person finding the best stone and bringing it to camp, another making the tool—perhaps for a third person to use. Such cooperation would have made the most efficient use of individual skills, to the benefit of the group.

It is difficult to imagine that cooperation of this sort could have been achieved without at least some rudimentary form of language. We do not know how far the humans of this period had advanced beyond the crude and limited communication systems of the other primates, but the progress must have been substantial. (The development of speech is discussed in the following chapter.)

Sharing

We have already discussed the development of food sharing among early humans—its role in their subsistence strategy and its influence on the development of tool use. In order for this pattern to develop, the human mind had to become capable of inhibiting immediate impulses in favor of long-term goals. Hunters who made kills had to refrain from eating the meat on the spot; gatherers had to save enough vegetable foods and small game to bring back to camp.

Cooperative hunting would have given the early humans further training in the art of sharing. When present-day hunter-gatherers make a large cooperative kill, they divide the meat among themselves, and early *Homo* probably did likewise. And as sharing became the established pattern, it probably laid the foundation for reciprocity in other areas of life. The early humans, we can guess, began to think of their actions in general as they affected the group—to feel "duty" to the others and "guilt" over failing the others. In other words, the sharing of food helped to lay the foundations of conscience.

Competition and Conflict

So far in this account we have stressed cooperation and sharing. While these are comforting notions, we must also emphasize that aggression and competition—among individuals, among families, among bands—probably played an equally great role in stimulating mental development. Certainly competition would create strong selective pressures for the very same intellectual qualities we have mentioned: flexibility, concentration, persistence, memory, and even, paradoxically, cooperativeness (in forming alliances against enemies and rivals). A more complicated social life probably meant feuds as well as friendships, stealing of mates as well as exchange of mates, mutual raiding as well as cooperative hunting. In such activities, guile might be as important as strength; increasingly, it paid to be a bit smarter than one's neighbors. Politics—the art of manipulating social relationships in order to get the better of others—must have been increasingly important among these early humans, and those who proved good at it were the most likely to survive and to leave the largest number of offspring.

Mental Development and the Base Camp

The existence of base camps is itself a proof of the increasing mental organization of the early humans. It shows that they were able to organize their lives around a geographical center—a place where they could build their fires, erect their shelters, and perhaps store their tools.

At the same time, the base camps *contributed* to mental development. As we have seen, they provided a sort of nest for the growth of culture. Furthermore, by providing a place where a sick member of the group could rest and get well, and where others could bring back food to him, the base camp eased the selective pressure for physical strength alone. If the most sharp-witted hunter sprained his ankle, he might still live; his sharp wits therefore stood a better chance of being passed on to the next generation.

Social Organization

From sifting the archeological record, and from observing such modern hunter-gatherer groups as the Bushmen of the Kalahari Desert and the aborigines of Australia, we can piece together a picture of the kind of social organization that the early humans built up around the new subsistence strategy of hunting and gathering. Early humans probably lived in bands totaling less than a hundred people—most frequently about twenty-five—and consisting of men who were related to one another, their wives (who usually came from neighboring bands),[4] and their unmarried children. Leadership was determined by sex, age, and especially personal ability, but leadership roles were not formalized in such a way that some members of the band held permanent control over others. Likewise, individuals had to conform to certain rules of conduct, but these rules were usually informal understandings, not formal laws. In general, the band was held together by ties of kinship and of need. As relatives (by blood or marriage), they were loyal to one another and saw themselves as a unit; it was as a unit that they stood the best chance of survival. The corollary of this mutual loyalty and dependency is that they were probably hostile to outsiders.

The band stayed alive by moving from place to place, within a relatively large range, in search of food. During a day of food seeking, individuals or small groups dispersed to collect what edibles they could find within several square miles of the temporary base camp. The

[4] We cannot be sure, of course, whether the bands were patrilocal, as we are describing, or matrilocal, with a core of related women and their husbands from other bands. The fact that the women may have been the repository of the group's lore, customs, and traditions has led some people to suggest that the bands were woman-centered. However, most known present-day hunter-gatherer bands are patrilocal.

men hunted, and the women, carrying their infants, picked nuts and berries and dug up roots. The band could sometimes remain in one camp for several nights. Eventually, though, the food within range of the camp would be exhausted, and the band would have to move on, perhaps returning to that spot again in a few months or a year.

How did this form of social organization develop? If we look at its constituent parts, it becomes clear that they are all related, directly or indirectly, to hunting and gathering.

The Development of the Family

Like so many of the important transitions made by *Homo* during this period, the transition from a prehuman mating system to human marriage is difficult to place in time. It is likely, however, that the sexual division of labor provided the impetus for the change. In Chapter 8, we have suggested, as an educated guess, that the social system of the australopiths was a cross between that of the chimpanzees and that of the hamadryas baboons—that is, one-male mating groups within a loosely organized "local population." The adoption of hunting and gathering as a way of life would have transformed such mating groups into work associations and partnerships, with males hunting and females gathering. Once this happened, it would no longer be advantageous for each male simply to attract and hold as many mates as possible. If he were providing meat for them, he could support only a limited number; and it would pay him to choose each mate very carefully, partly for her prowess as a producer and nurturer of children, but also as a knowledgeable and efficient provider of vegetable food.

While the reduction in number of mates would, in a sense, decrease the male's Darwinian fitness, he could make up the deficit by adopting the primate female strategy of investing considerable time and energy in each child. In other words, he became more of a "nurturer" and less of a "competitive begetter" (Chapter 6). Thus, ties of mutual obligation and mutual care would come to bind the mates to one another and to their children. In other words, the one-male group would come to look something like the modern human family.

The change in mating patterns would also influence the direction of selection. At the same time that the males were selecting wives for their gathering abilities, the females would be looking for husbands who were good hunters. Such mate-choosing standards would create a powerful selective pressure in favor of physical, mental, and cultural adaptation to the new hunting-and-gathering way of life.

Changes in Reproductive Biology

Another adjustment to the new way of life was the modernization of female reproductive biology: the disappearance of estrus and the evolution of menopause.

Estrus Human beings are the only primates that have no estrus period in their sexual cycle. This feature was probably lost early in our ancestors' adaptation to hunting and gathering. As we have seen, one function of an obvious estrus in nonhuman primate groups is to stimulate males to compete for females. With the transition to hunting and gathering, however, fitness required a great deal more than vigor. The new way of life demanded intellectual and cultural abilities as well. The selective pressure in favor of these qualities, along with physical strength, was already being generated by the new system of choosing mates on the basis of economic prowess. Thus the function of estrus became obsolete.

Furthermore, by creating tension and competition among the males, estrus was actually counterproductive. With the rise of hunting and the related cultural advances, *Homo* had to develop a spirit of cooperation far beyond that seen in any of its primate cousins. Early humans had to plan together and work together for long hours; often, they had to save one another's lives. Consequently, they could no longer afford socially disruptive aphrodisiacs. Among the males there would be occasion enough for tension—disputes over distribution of meat, quarrels over desirable mates—without having the tension increased by the sight and scent of estrous females.

Menopause The disappearance of estrus no doubt made it easier for females to get along with one another as well. Once again, we should not allow the important fact of hunting to obscure the equally important fact of female roles and female associations. We have pointed out in Chapter 6 that in many nonhuman primate species the "core" of the social group consists of the adult females; they constitute the stable membership of the group, and consequently they are the custodians of much of its knowledge, which they pass on (by example) to the young. Among early humans, the passing of responsibility for food gathering to women must have made this female role of keeper-of-the-lore doubly important. We have some proof of this in another biological peculiarity of the human female: menopause.

In other primate species, females continue to reproduce until decrepitude or death overtakes them. Among humans, on the other hand, the woman loses her capacity to reproduce in vigorous middle age. Presumably, this change, like the others we have discussed, took place as an adaptation to hunting and gathering. But how was it adaptive? What possible advantage could there be in the *loss* of reproductive capacity?

If one looks at the question in terms of overall fitness, the advantage becomes clear. With the rise of culture and the division of labor, the accumulated wisdom and skills of the middle-aged female became a valuable resource. It no longer made sense, from an evolutionary point of view, for her to risk death in childbirth for the sake of an additional offspring or two. Giving birth was becoming a more dangerous undertaking. As brain size increased, so did the skull size of the fetus—while at the same time, adaptations to bipedalism had narrowed the birth canal. Thus from the standpoint of Darwinian fitness (Chapters 3 and 6), it was more advantageous to forgo additional pregnancies later in life. In this way, the female would stand a better chance of living on to instruct her children—and perhaps their children as well—in the lore of the band and the arts of survival. In this development we see a further extension of the basic primate trend favoring quality over quantity in child rearing. As human beings became increasingly dependent on culture, they devoted more and more energy to socializing and instructing each new child—even if this meant fewer children.

Social Contact Among Bands

We have no direct evidence that the early humans had any formal social organization above the level of the band—intergroup alliances, seasonal gatherings of bands in one place, and so on. Yet to account for the uniformity of tool traditions over vast stretches of territory, we must assume that there was considerable contact between bands. After all, people made hand axes in essentially the same way in a region extending from southern Africa to northern England to India. It is unlikely that they all invented the hand axe independently. Each band must have learned from its neighbors and passed the knowledge on to other neighbors.

In part, such cultural transmission was probably the result of *exogamy*, the rule requiring that the individual marry someone not of his or her own tribe. Depending on the local tradition, either the male or the female, when it was time to marry, found a mate from a neighboring tribe and went to live with that tribe. As bands met to negotiate matches, and as brides or grooms carried their own bands' traditions to the new band, cultural traits were passed from group to group.[5] Furthermore, the system created a network of ties and obligations among bands, ensuring continued contact.

We should recall, however, that the tool traditions were not completely homogeneous. As we saw, there is evidence that as the Acheulean tradition developed, a pebble-chopper technology continued to exist alongside it for thousands of years in parts of Europe and Asia. What this in-

[5] Genes were also passed from group to group. Thus the practice of exogamy would also explain the similarity of physical adaptations among populations that were widely dispersed geographically.

dicates is that although interband contact may have been the rule, there were evidently barriers to interband contact as well. To a certain extent these barriers may have been simply geographical. Rather than try to cross mountains or major rivers, bands would tend to arrange marriages and trade hunting stories with groups in their own areas. Yet in many regions groups working in different tool traditions must have lived close enough together to have had social contact. Therefore, for their tool traditions to remain separate, there must have been social barriers—language differences, traditions of conflict or avoidance—that maintained the boundary between groups. Here we may be witnessing the first stages of the genetic isolation of groups by culture as well as by physical or geographical difference.

Conscience and Social Codes

The society that we see dimly emerging from these speculations was more complex than any seen in nonhuman primates. In particular, it involved its members in cross-cutting social groups and thus subjected them to competing appeals to their loyalty. Loyalty to the family, for example, would at times conflict with loyalty to the all-male hunting group or the all-female gathering group. In a young person marrying into a different tribe, ties to the old work group and family would conflict with ties to the new. And such conflicts would create tension among individuals.

To some extent, tension must have acted as a creative force among the early humans. It would have taxed their ingenuity in manipulating social situations, and therefore it would have favored the clever over the dull-witted. Nevertheless, a society that allowed disputes to rage continually would have had a very low fitness. As we have seen, these people had to cooperate in order to survive. Hence, the existence of tensions would also favor the development of rules of conduct to prevent or settle disputes. The result would be the gradual evolution of codes of ideal behavior—codes that would answer such perennial questions as how the meat should be distributed after the hunt, who should take orders from whom in a group, and which mates were available to each person. Such codes of behavior, in turn, would favor new mental qualities—the ability to distinguish the real from the ideal, to say "I ought to" as well as "I want to," and to know the difference.

The Pace of Evolution

The evolutionary developments discussed in this chapter did not occur overnight. Indeed, to the inventive brain of the modern human, it seems almost incredible that our ancestors, having invented stone tools, did not improve upon their first simple stone tools for well over a million years—or that it took them millions of years to venture north of the Mediterranean basin.

Still, as each new cultural element appeared, the evolutionary process gained momentum. The Oldowan tradition lasted almost two million years, the Acheulean just over a million, and later traditions succeeded each other ever more rapidly. Change, having begun slowly, gradually accelerated. As new cultural demands arose, the brain, sharpened by culture, was better prepared to meet them.

Summary

With the emergence of the genus *Homo,* culture becomes a major force in human evolution. For one thing, culture imposed its own selective pressures. Moreover, culture itself evolved—slowly at first, but with increasing rapidity, so that evolution was no longer a matter of biological change alone. Four factors are central to culture as it first appears in the human lineage—production and use of artifacts, economic division of labor, language, and the ability to organize experience into meaningful patterns.

The earliest known species of *Homo* is *Homo habilis*, whose known remains date back at least as far as 2 million B.P., and perhaps beyond 3 million B.P. The most distinctive feature of *H. habilis*, compared with the australopiths, is its larger braincase, strongly suggesting a greater degree of intelligence. At the same time as *H. habilis* appears, we have evidence of a new adaptive pattern based on hunting and gathering and the making of stone tools.

Homo erectus appeared in Africa as early as 1.6 million B.P., and thus coexisted with the last australopiths. European *H. erectus* fossils are later; they date from about 400,000 B.P. *H. erectus* continues the trend toward adaptation for culture. The braincase has expanded further, and the teeth have reduced in size—probably because food was being processed more with tools and, eventually, cooked. *H. erectus* had certain unique characteristics, including a very thick skull, but its skeleton was functionally modern. Although the known *H. erectus* populations are generally quite similar, they do show some geographical variation.

Like the australopiths, the early humans lived principally in the tropical savannas. While *Australopithecus* was mainly a vegetarian forager and small-game hunter, however, *Homo* also began to hunt larger animals. This transition had a profound influence on the course of human evolution. Exactly how and when the change took place is still a subject of controversy, but there is unquestionable evidence of big-game hunting by the middle Pleistocene. Nevertheless, vegetable foods remained a major component of the early humans' diet.

One of the most far-reaching changes that accompanied the rise of hunting and gathering was a division of work roles by sex. Because humans have a long period of dependency in childhood, mothers had to look after not only nursing infants but also half-grown children. Thus, males generally hunted, while women and children gathered vegetable foods. In order for all members of the group to get a balanced diet, the sharing of food must have became voluntary and systematic—a major departure from the feeding patterns of nonhuman primates.

Hunting and the sharing of food made implements indispensable. Tools were needed to butcher game, and artifacts such as skin bags were needed to help carry gathered vegetable food to the campsite. Stone tools were particularly important to early humans. They were used for killing and skinning animals, cutting meat, crushing and pounding vegetable foods, and making implements of other materials such as bone and wood.

Stone tools are our most solid evidence of the life style of *H. habilis* and *H. erectus*. These tools fall into two main groups. The earliest are those of the *pebble-chopper technology*, of which the *Oldowan* tools, first discovered at Olduvai Gorge, are the best known examples. Similar tools have since been found at other sites in Africa, the Middle East, and southern France. The pebble-chopper technology originated at least 3 million years ago, and was predominant until about 1.5 million B.P.

In general, Oldowan and similar tools are simple and unspecialized. The characteristic tools of the Oldowan and other pebble-chopper traditions are *choppers* and *flake tools*. A chopper is a stone chipped at one end to create a sharp edge. Choppers were made from rounded stones, or *cores*, and were generally *bifacially* worked. The flakes chipped from the cores were often used as cutting tools. We must assume that wooden tools were made as well, though they have not survived.

About 1.6 million years ago, the *hand-axe technology* appeared. The pattern of manufacture is more distinctive than in the pebble-chopper technology, thus suggesting a historically transmitted body of toolmaking procedures. This tool tradition and the associated culture are known as the *Acheulean*. It is normally identified with *H. erectus*, although it persisted among early populations of *Homo sapiens* as well.

Acheulean tools are thinner and more precisely made than Oldowan tools. The typical Acheulean tool has many flakes chipped from over most of its surface, resulting in a more refined form. The characteristic tool of the Acheulean tradition is the *hand axe*, a pear-shaped implement with sharp edges all around and, often, a picklike point. Cleavers and flake tools are also common. These tools reflect more highly developed coordination of eye, brain, and hand as well as great advances in conceptual ability.

Archeological evidence indicates that the pebble-chopper technology persisted in eastern Europe and eastern Asia for hundreds of thousands of years after the hand-axe technology had been adopted in Africa, western Europe, and India. This suggests that two very different cultural traditions may have coexisted at this time. Archeologists have identified several different *tool kits*, or specialized sets of tools, in some Acheulean assemblages. These were probably used by people performing different tasks at different times.

At some sites, archeologists have uncovered *living floors*. These are places at which early humans once camped, leaving behind evidence of their habitation—hearths, shelters, tools, and bones. They allow us to reconstruct the way of life of these ancestors, and to study the cultural adaptations it required. On the basis of evidence from such sites, we can conclude that humans had become skilled hunters for whom meat eating was a basic subsistence strategy, that they had achieved a considerable degree of social cooperation, that they established home bases—permanent or temporary—where culture could develop in many dimensions, and that they had learned to use and depend upon fire.

The adoption of hunting and gathering created selective pressures for specific kinds of physical and behavioral adaptations in the *Homo* line. More and more, humans adapted to the cultural environment of their own creation. The physical adaptations that distinguish *Homo* from *Australopithecus* include smaller teeth and a larger and more complex brain. The way of life of the early humans also favored the development of certain mental qualities—memory, concentration and persistence, planning and cooperation, and sharing.

Early humans probably lived in bands of about 25 people on the average—a group of related men, their wives (who usually came from neighboring bands), and their unmarried children. In general, the band was united by ties of kinship and need. It is likely that the division of labor by sex provided the impetus for the transition from a prehuman mating system to human marriage. The new way of life also probably led to changes in female reproductive biology—the disappearance of estrus and the appearance of menopause.

Because of the uniformity of tool traditions over vast stretches of territory, we must assume that there was considerable contact between bands. Such cultural transmission was probably largely the result of *exogamy*, the practice of marrying outside one's own band. (However, tool traditions were not completely homogeneous, which implies both geographical and social barriers to intergroup contact.) The conflicting loyalties that arose from the demands of this new way of life encouraged new mental attributes—the ability to suppress immediate impulses, to work for the good of the group, and to acknowledge obligations as well as desires. In this way, human intellect and human conscience were born.

Glossary

Acheulean tradition the toolmaking tradition associated with the hand-axe technology; more broadly, the term "Acheulean" is used for the culture of human populations in the areas where this toolmaking tradition flourished

bifacially worked flaked on both sides

chopper a stone chipped at one end to create a sharp edge; typical tool of the Oldowan and other pebble-chopper traditions

core a rounded stone from which tools were made

by chipping off flakes

exogamy the practice of marrying outside one's own group

flake tools cutting tools made from the stone flakes chipped from a core

hand axe the characteristic tool of the Acheulean tradition; a pear-shaped implement with sharp edges all around and, often, a picklike point

hand-axe technology a more advanced toolmaking technology that replaced the pebble-chopper technology in Africa, western Europe, and India; it first appears about 1.6 million B.P.

Homo erectus the human species that flourished from about 1.6 million to 300,000 B.P.

Homo habilis the earliest known human species; probably the first systematic hunter-gatherer and extensive stone-tool maker

living floor a place where early human bands camped, leaving behind evidence of their habitation

Oldowan tools early stone tools from Olduvai Gorge and similar sites in East Africa; the best known examples of the pebble-chopper technology

pebble-chopper technology the oldest known stone toolmaking technology, used initially by *H. habilis* as early as 3 million B.P.; its products are relatively simple and unspecialized

soft percussion (soft hammer) a later Acheulean toolmaking technique that used wood, bone, or antler instead of rock to chip flakes from the core

tool kits specialized sets of tools found in some Acheulean assemblages

Suggested Readings

BORDAZ, J. 1970
Tools of the Old Stone Age. Garden City, N.Y.: Natural History Press. A thorough discussion of the variety of tools used by early humans and changes in techniques of manufacture.

BUTZER, K. W. 1971
Environment and Archaeology. 2nd ed. Chicago: Aldine. A comprehensive review of the aims, methods, and findings of human paleogeography.

BUTZER, K. W., AND ISAAC, G. L. (EDS.) 1975
After the Australopithecines: Stratigraphy, Ecology, and Culture Change in the Middle Pleistocene. Chicago: Aldine. A very useful collection of papers describing advances in the study of Middle Pleistocene hominids.

Chapter Ten

The Emergence of Cultural Essentials II: Archaic *Homo sapiens*

In 1960 anthropologist Ralph Solecki, excavating a cave called Shanidar in Iraq, discovered the grave of a 30-year-old man with a badly crushed skull. The remains dated from about 60,000 B.P. As usual, Solecki took soil samples from the earth around the bones and sent them off for pollen analysis, to see what they might reveal about the climate and plant life of the area at the time the man had lived. The report that he received back was fascinating. The soil sample contained not just the usual scattering of pollen grains but masses of pollen, still in clusters, along with the remains of at least eight species of flowers. These were small, brightly colored wildflowers—hollyhock, bachelor's button, grape hyacinth. They not only covered the body but also cushioned it from below. The flowers could not have grown there; the grave was in the back of the cave. Nor could they have been carried to this spot by animals. Apparently, they were placed there by human mourners as part of some ritual—perhaps bidding a final farewell to someone they cared about.

In this burial we see evidence of a new element in human evolution, a new way of behaving and looking at the world. Apparently, emotional attachments to individual human beings now outlive the individuals themselves. The burial ritual perhaps represents an attempt to grapple with death and bereavement and to express respect for the dead in a symbolic way. Perhaps the Shanidar people believed, too, that when a person dies, some nonmaterial essence survives—a spirit that deserves reverence. Certainly it would seem that they were expressing some such feeling by means of a symbolic gesture: dispatching the spirit into the afterlife on a bed of flowers.

The "flower burial" at Shanidar Cave in Iraq. *(Ralph Solecki)*

Long before Shanidar was excavated, the human fossils of the period from about 250,000 B.P. onward were assigned to the species *Homo sapiens*—the same species as ourselves. The assignment was based largely on physical evidence; though the taxonomic boundary, as usual, is blurred, these people are more modern in structure than *Homo erectus.* Yet as we have just seen, early *Homo sapiens* was modern in more ways than anatomy. Indeed, the physical changes are relatively minor compared with the behavioral changes. Yet physical development did continue, both as a cause and as a result of cultural change.

In this chapter we will explore the earliest stage in the evolution of *Homo sapiens,* extending from about 250,000 to 40,000 B.P.—the period of archaic *Homo sapiens.* We will then focus our attention on one particularly well-known and interesting population of archaic *Homo sapiens:* the neandertals, who flourished in Europe and adjacent areas of the Near East between 100,000 and 40,000 years ago. We will concentrate particularly on their culture, since cultural change has by now replaced biological adaptation as the evolutionary pacemaker in the human lineage. Finally, we will examine the fate of the neandertals and the origin of fully modern humans.

ARCHAIC *HOMO SAPIENS*

The site of Bodo D'ahr is to be found in the Awash Valley, Ethiopia, some 200 kilometers (124 mi.) south of Hadar, home of the australopith "Lucy." In 1975 the geologist Jon Kalb, codiscoverer of Hadar, came upon Acheulean hand axes and other tools eroding from a hillside. With

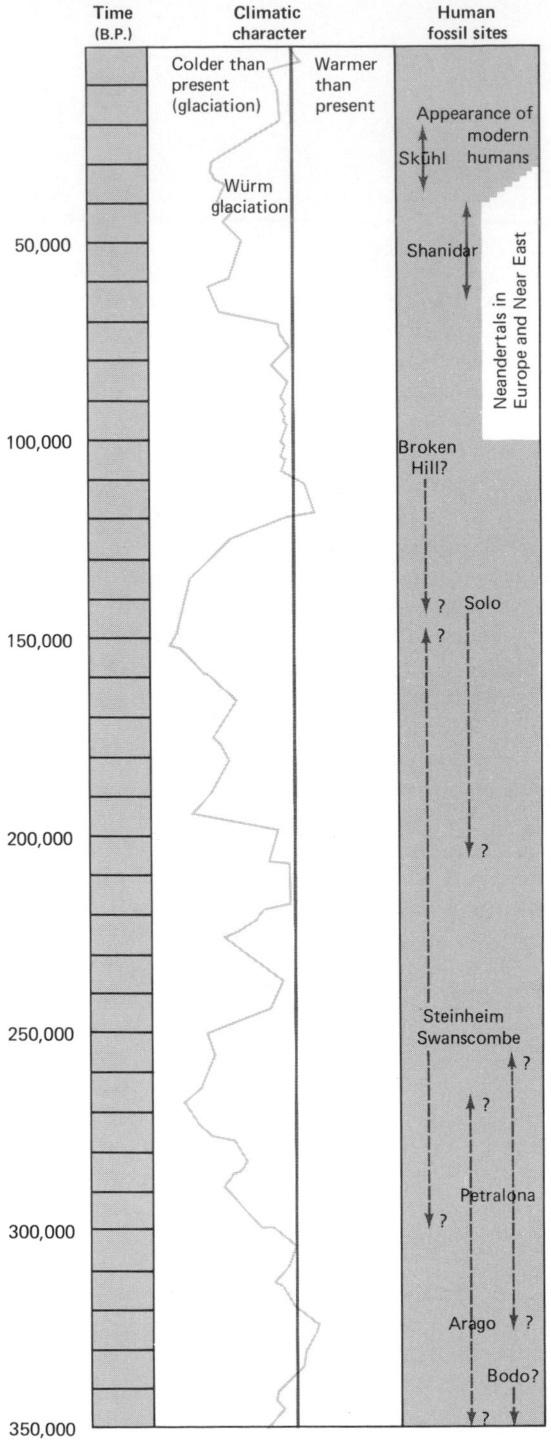

Figure 10-1. Time chart of human evolution—archaic and early modern *Homo sapiens.*

them were split and broken animal bones, suggesting that this was an early human camp and butchering site. Kalb and his associates recognized that Bodo could make an important contribution to our knowledge of Acheulean lifeways, and in the fall of 1976 excavations were begun by a team of archeologists.

As the archeologists laid out and excavated their test trenches, details of the Bodo people's life began to emerge. Evidently, they had had a taste for pork; many of the bones belonged to *Mesochoerus,* a giant, extinct relative of the warthog. The skull of one great boar was especially interesting. In the center of the massive forehead was a depressed fracture—an indentation of the bone caused by a violent blow, perhaps from a club. Was the injury caused by an encounter with man? We shall never know for sure, although we suspect it was. If so, the arm that struck the blow must have been extraordinarily powerful.

The archeological team had little hope of discovering the remains of the hunters themselves—most Acheulean butchering sites, such as Torralba-Ambrona, have yielded no human remains. But on this occasion luck was with them. A member of the expedition, casually scouting a sandy outcrop close to the excavation, came across an odd-shaped lump of rock that on closer inspection proved to be the lower half of a human face, minus the mandible. Further searching soon produced another chunk comprising the upper face, and a number of smaller fragments. At this point the remains were turned over to a team of three physical anthropologists, including one of the authors of this book, for examination and reconstruction.

We found that the two largest pieces fitted perfectly together, enabling us to look Bodo man (in this case, we feel the masculine term is justified) in the face. And an impressive face it was, long and massive, with a broad nose, heavy cheekbones, and rugged, heavy brow ridges—a face, we felt, worthy of the smiter of mesochoeruses. At this stage, we guessed that we might be dealing with a typical specimen of *Homo erectus*, comparable to the largest individuals from Java, North Africa, or Olduvai. But this opinion had to be revised when we went to work on the complicated jigsaw of silver dollar-sized cranial fragments. Gradually, the contours of the front two-thirds of the braincase were reconstructed. In spite of its ruggedness—some of the cranial bones are over 1.5 centimeters (0.6 in.) thick—the braincase is more filled out, less angular, and larger than is typical of *Homo erectus.* It became clear that Bodo man belongs to the select company of Middle Pleistocene skulls that bridge the morphological gap between *Homo erectus* and our own species, *Homo sapiens.*

The Origins of *Homo sapiens*

Bodo man and his relatives are representative of human populations that were widespread in Africa, Asia, and Europe during the late Middle and early Upper Pleistocene—roughly, from 250,000 B.P. to 40,000 B.P. As a group, they combine heavy faces, large teeth, and low-vaulted skulls—all ancestral traits reminiscent of *Homo erectus*—with a cranial capacity at least as large as that of modern peoples, and a braincase that is more rounded and less angular than that of *Homo erectus.* As we shall see, beneath this broad similarity lie a multitude of variations—individual, populational, and probably evolutionary, too. People of this general type have been assigned various names. The one we use—*archaic Homo sapiens*—was chosen to stress the fact that although they are sufficiently advanced to be assigned to our own species, they retain ancestral features indicative of their derivation from *Homo erectus.*

Although the picture is complicated by the lack of good dates from this period (which falls between the ranges of potassium-argon and carbon-14 dating) present evidence suggests that archaic *Homo sapiens* was widespread by about 250,000 years ago. Some specimens of uncertain but probably early date come from Europe—Swanscombe in England, Steinheim in Germany, Arago Cave in France, and Petralona in Greece. Others come from Africa—Kabwe (formerly Broken Hill) in Zambia, and Bodo in Ethiopia. A series of skulls from the Solo River, Java, indicates that archaic *Homo sapiens* was occupying these ancient homelands of *Homo erectus.*

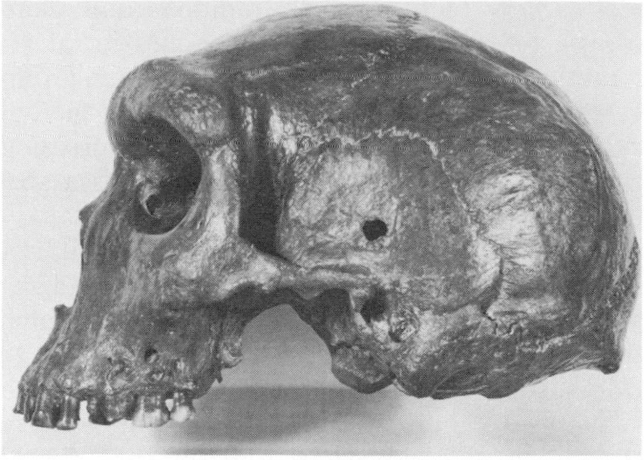

Two archaic *Homo sapiens* from Africa. The side view is of the skull from Kabwe (Broken Hill), Zambia; the front view is of the recently excavated skull from Bodo, Ethiopia (see text). Although these skulls show some similarities to *Homo erectus*, they are generally modern enough in their structure to be classified as belonging to our own species. *(Copyright, British Museum; D. L. Cramer)*

Where did *Homo sapiens* originate? As usual, we are faced with two conflicting models for the origin and spread of a new species.

According to one view, many local populations of *Homo erectus* gradually, and in parallel, evolved to the point where they crossed the arbitrary, imaginary threshold defining *Homo sa-*

piens. New technological traditions and more complex strategies of subsistence and social interaction arose and were transmitted from group to group, favoring the development of mental capacity that is crudely expressed in increasing cranial volume. At the other extreme is a scenario based on the idea that most evolutionary breakthroughs occur in comparatively small, isolated populations, which then expand and replace the more conservative stock from which they were derived. In this view, the transition to *Homo sapiens* was a local phenomenon. The "advanced" human populations—not merely technological innovations—rapidly spread and replaced their predecessors.[1] Our sample of early archaic *Homo sapiens* is too small, and its dating too uncertain, to decide between these possibilities at present. On the whole, though, we tend to favor the first alternative—widespread evolution rather than local breakthrough.

Technological Advances

Wherever a cultural context can be established, the earliest representatives of our species seem to be associated with late, sophisticated versions of the Acheulean or related contemporary toolmaking traditions. As we saw in the previous chapter, these traditions have their roots in the early Pleistocene, some 1.5 million years B.P. Early in the Upper Pleistocene, however (about 100,000 B.P.), new and significant trends in stone-tool manufacture start to appear. For one thing, the hand axes that distinguish the Acheulean become smaller and more finely made—an indication of more skill and precision in stone-working technique. Another important advance was the introduction of the *prepared core*, or *Levallois*, technique.

Workmanship: The Prepared Core Technique

The history of early toolmaking is largely a progression toward increasingly precise control of force. As we have seen, the Oldowan toolmakers simply struck one stone with another, dislodging a few sharp-edged flakes and producing a roughly shaped core. There was little control over the exact size or shape of the flakes removed, however. The Acheulean stone-workers improved on this technique by learning, essentially, to whittle. Using finer-grained rock and softer hammers, they could remove small flakes from the entire surface of the rock and thus gradually pare it down into the form they wanted. Beginning about 100,000 years ago, *knappers* (makers of stone tools) incorporated this approach into a new method, called the prepared core technique (Figure 10-2), that allowed them to produce more cutting edge in less time and from less stone, as well as a more standardized tool.

The first step of this technique was to prepare the core by trimming its edges and flaking its top surface. Then a series of small flakes were removed from one end (Blow 1 in Stage 3, Figure 10-2) to create a striking platform. Finally, by aiming a sharp blow at a well-chosen spot on the striking platform (Blow 2 in Stage 3, Figure 10-2), the knapper could remove, as a single large flake, the entire top surface of the core (Stage 4, Figure 10-2). This flake, of predetermined shape and size, and with a long cutting edge, became the tool.

Using the prepared core technique, a skillful stone-worker was able to produce about 100 centimeters (39 in.) of cutting edge from a pound of stone—about five times more than the Acheulean toolmaker and twenty times more than the Oldowan toolmaker. Since fine-grained stone was not always easy to find, and often had to be carried to the workplace, this represented a great saving in time and energy.

Aside from its efficiency, the prepared core technique reflects the gradually developing mental abilities of its users. The Acheulean toolmaker had the encouragement of watching his hand axe emerge gradually under the blows of his hammer. He could also plan the tool as he went along. By contrast, making a prepared core tool involves three entirely separate processes—preparing the core, fashioning the striking plat-

[1] These two theoretical models are discussed more fully later in this chapter, in connection with the appearance of modern *Homo sapiens*.

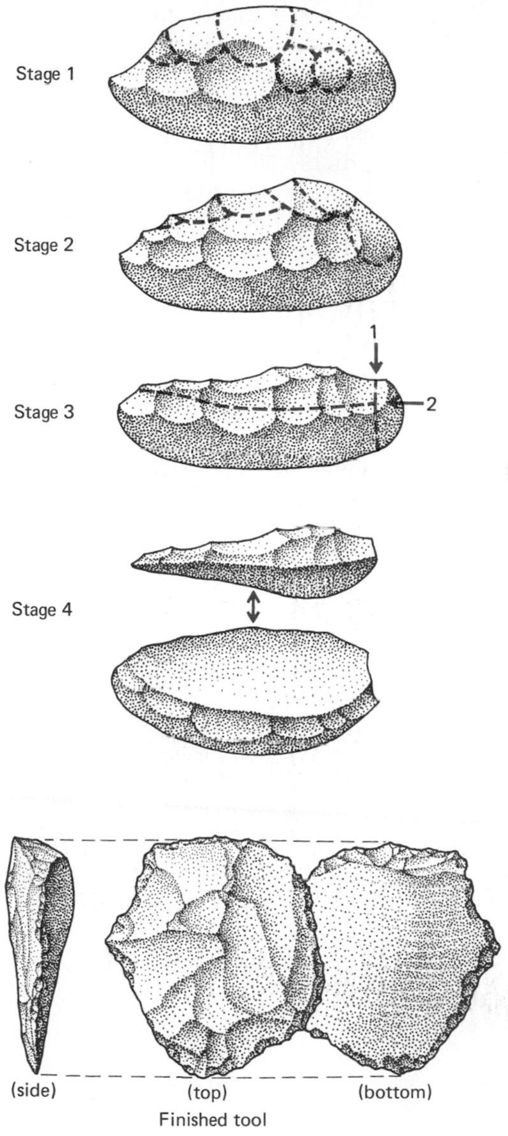

Figure 10-2. The prepared core (or Levallois) technique, which appeared about 100,000 B.P., increased the efficiency of stone tool making and the toolmaker's control of the process. In this method, the core was prepared in such a way that its entire top surface could be removed as a single flake of predetermined form. This flake became the tool. (*Biruta Akerbergs*)

form, and striking off the tool. The whole sequence has to be held in the imagination and executed in just the right order to produce the kind of flake that is wanted; nothing resembling a finished tool emerges until the final blow. Thus the knapper, like a person working all week for a Friday paycheck, got no results until the very end. To master this technique, therefore, the stone-workers of this period must have had considerable powers of visualization and concentration.

Regional Tool Traditions

Not only did new stone-working techniques appear, so did new tool traditions. Significantly, these traditions were geographically specialized—the tools were adapted to the specific requirements of different localities. For example, in the plains of southern Africa, we find the *Fauresmith* tradition. This is actually a more sophisticated form of the Acheulean, with scrapers, flake knives, and small hand axes. In central Africa, archeologists have identified another tool tradition, the *Sangoan,* which was probably created by forest dwellers. Sangoan assemblages include few hand axes; instead, the predominant tools are a planelike implement and a large, heavy pick. These were probably woodworking tools that enabled their users to exploit the resources of the tropical forests.

New Habitats, New Subsistence Strategies

The development of regional traditions such as the Fauresmith and the Sangoan represents a significant trend in human cultural evolution. Throughout the previous million years or so, cultural change had been slow. It took something over a million years for *Homo erectus* populations to spread from the tropics of Africa and Southeast Asia and, with the help of fire, to establish themselves in the temperate zones of Europe and China. By the time advanced *Homo erectus* populations were crossing the threshold to *Homo sapiens,* they were expanding their range still further, to encompass such challenging habitats as the rain forests of central Africa. Significantly, their means of adaptation was a *cultural* one. This is reflected in the appearance of tool kits adapted to specific local conditions. The general uniformity of tool types that had been so striking during the Acheulean began to break down in favor of specialization geared to local needs and resources.

Nowhere was the resourcefulness of early *Homo sapiens* more fully challenged than in temperate Europe and Asia. Throughout the middle and upper Pleistocene, Europe was subject to periodic glaciations, when ice sheets spread from the north, and harsh, tundralike conditions extended well into France, Germany, and central Europe (see box, p. 250). At each glacial advance the human population retreated, following the warm weather faunas to the south—at each glacial advance, that is, until the episode known as the *Würm*, the major glaciation preceding the present interglacial.

The Würm Glaciation

The Würm, which lasted from about 75,000 to about 11,000 B.P., was a series of relatively rapid glacial advances and retreats, with associated changes in animal and vegetable life. During much of this period, northern Europe was covered with thick sheets of ice. The rest of Europe, though not frozen, was bitterly cold. In central Europe the annual mean temperatures were below freezing; in southeastern Europe it was only slightly warmer.

This seemingly inhospitable climate could nevertheless support abundant life. In the Mediterranean areas there were forests, and in southeastern Europe there were open woodlands.

An Alpine meadow in August. The summer vegetation in many parts of Europe during the Würm glaciation would have been very similar. This cover of grasses and herbs supported large herds of grazing animals. (© *Jeanne White, from National Audubon Society/Photo Researchers*)

Parts of southeastern Europe and all of central Europe were windswept plains with a cover of hardy grasses and other herbs. These provided rich summer grazing for a large supply of game. Indeed, the carrying capacity of the northern grasslands was probably greater than that of the Mediterranean woodlands. Huge herds of large grazing animals, including wild horses, bison, mammoths, and reindeer, roamed over the chilly plains, while deer, ibex, wild cattle, and wild boars were abundant in the forest areas. These animals, in turn, provided ample prey for a number of cold-adapted carnivores—distinctive species of bear, lion, and hyena. And for the first time, human populations too were able, by adapting culturally as well as physically, to exploit the wandering herds (Butzer, 1971).

Specialization and Diversification

Between 75,000 and 40,000 B.P.—from the onset of the Würm to the appearance of modern *Homo sapiens*—humans did not make any significant additions to their territory. There was a slight expansion of range, particularly in Russia, but no new regions were opened up. Yet the nature of the habitat itself changed. The Würm glaciation transformed Europe into a variety of different climatic zones, each with its own characteristic vegetation. The diversity of habitats was greater than ever before, and the range of conditions to which people had to adapt was more extreme.

The climatic changes of the Würm seem to have accelerated the tendency of different populations to develop different ways of life. Peoples in the colder northern regions naturally came to depend more heavily on fire and shelters. The archeological evidence also suggests that these northern populations depended more upon hunting and less upon the gathering of vegetable foods than their relatives farther south. This is not surprising, since temperate areas generally have a narrower range of plant resources than more tropical areas, and even these are commonly available only during a limited season each year. In fact, most of the vegetation on the plains at the edge of the glaciers would have been tough grasses and herbage—fine grazing for animals, but not suitable for human consumption. But even within Europe, the life styles of various populations evidently began to diverge, spurred on by the increasing diversity of local climatic conditions.

Such adaptation to changing habitats and new resources demonstrates the behavioral flexibility of these early humans. One result was a wider resource base and broader econiche for the species as a whole. But the effect on individual populations was exactly contrary; each one was becoming more specialized for making use of the resources of its own particular habitat. Thus, while the species *Homo sapiens* remained undivided, the cultures of individual populations became more distinct, less able to exchange ideas and techniques.

THE NEANDERTALS AND THEIR CULTURE

One of the best known of the human populations of this time is also one of the most peripheral, and to judge from its habitat, one of the most ingenious at wresting a living from a hostile environment. This population is known as the *neandertal* peoples, originators of the Mousterian culture. In the account that follows, we shall use the neandertals to illustrate some of the characteristics we believe were typical of populations of this general stage of cultural and physical evolution.

Who Were the Neandertals?

No term in human evolution has caused more confusion than "neandertal," largely because it has been used in such a variety of different ways. Some authors, for instance, use it for all populations we call "archaic *Homo sapiens*"; others restrict it to a supposed physical type, without regard to distribution in time or space. We use the term in a limited sense: for human populations living in Europe and the adjacent parts of the Near East during the first part of the Würm glaciation and the last part of the preceding in-

Glacials and Interglacials, Pluvials and Interpluvials

The Würm glaciation was only the latest episode in a pattern of climatic change that has affected the course of primate evolution from the time the order first appeared. Climate, as we know, is the most important influence on vegetation, and vegetation is the main factor in determining what resources are available for exploitation by animals, including human beings.

In the Eocene, warm, subtropical climates extended to central Europe and North Dakota; cool temperate climatic belts probably extended nearly to the poles. Thereafter, the climate of higher latitudes grew colder and less equable, and seasonal contrasts in temperature and rainfall increased. By mid-Miocene times, Antarctica and Greenland bore icecaps; by the late Pliocene, glaciers had started to scar the higher mountains in mid-latitudes. By the middle Pleistocene, the cooling trend had culminated in *continental glaciations,* in which sheets of ice, hundreds of feet thick, blanketed much of northern Europe and North America.

During glacial episodes, frigid climates and cold-adapted vegetation expanded southward. Faunas slowly adjusted their ranges so as to follow the habitats to which they were adapted as these shifted southward. Cold, barren deserts fringed the ice sheets, but much of glacial Europe was covered by grassland and tundra that supported large herds of grazing animals—and hunters hardy enough to pursue them on the windswept steppes.

Episodes of glacial advance alternated with *interglacials* when warmer conditions and temperate forest returned from the south. Traditionally, geologists have distinguished four or five glacial advances, separated by interglacials, on the basis of terrestrial deposits. Deep-sea cores, however, which preserve a much more complete record of climatic variation, suggest that the picture of just five major glaciations in the Pleistocene of Europe and North America, separated by four lengthy interglacials, is much too simple. Many more than five glacial advances occurred, and interglacials were evidently quite short—about 10,000 years. Only the last glacial and the preceding interglacial can be clearly identified in land deposits. The record of previous glaciations is confused, for the geological deposits and fossil remains have been repeatedly disrupted by the very glacial advances for which we seek evidence.

Another notion, widespread until fairly recently, is that in the tropics—especially Africa—a series of rainy periods, or *pluvials,* alternated with *interpluvials,* and that these episodes could be directly correlated with glacial advances and retreats further north. If this were true, it would help to establish a very convenient evolutionary timetable for the Pleistocene epoch.

Unfortunately, radiometric dating, and more critical geological surveys, indicate that this neat relationship does not hold. Glacials and interglacials in the north did not correspond directly to wet and dry periods in the tropics. Africa was probably covered with a patchwork of forests, woodland, and grassland throughout human evolution, as it is today. Rainfall fluctuations probably did occur in tropical Africa, and some were undoubtedly influenced by glaciations at high latitudes. But recent evidence suggests that glaciations corresponded to drier periods south of the Sahara, rather than wetter ones, as was traditionally believed. However, neither the glacial sequence nor the pluvial sequence of the tropics is useful for dating purposes. For anthropologists, climatic changes are significant as selective influences upon the evolution of species, and especially on human physical and cultural evolution.

terglacial—roughly speaking, from 100,000 to 40,000 B.P.

Thus defined, neandertals comprise a series of populations whose remains have been recovered at sites from Spain to Afghanistan. They share certain physical characteristics and have a general cultural similarity. This does not mean, of course, that individual physical variation and local cultural traditions were lacking, as we shall see. Nor must we suppose that the neandertals were totally isolated from other archaic populations to the south and east. We can imagine a series of human populations, linked by ties of gene flow and open to the exchange of cultural innovations, extending in all directions. In concentrating upon those groups that lived in and adapted to conditions at the northerly edge of the human range, we are merely isolating a part of humanity that it is convenient to study. The boundaries we choose to draw, geographically and chronologically, are bound to be somewhat arbitrary.

Discovery and Interpretation

In 1856, three years before the publication of Darwin's *Origin of Species,* a work crew came across some ancient human bones in Neandertal, a limestone gorge in western Germany. Most scientists at this time did not believe in evolution, thus they were unwilling to consider the status of the bones in this light. A few scientists did suspect that modern humans had issued from more primitive forms—but the neandertal bones were *too* primitive. The top of the skull was too flat, the brow ridges too thick and prominent, the limb bones too stocky and heavy. "Neandertal man" seemed "brutish" to his modern examiners, and his bones were generally dismissed as neither ancient nor ancestral. The most popular theory was that they were the remains of a relatively modern but badly deformed person—perhaps a congenital idiot.

In the years that followed, similar fossils began to turn up. In fact, one had been discovered even before the German find; a primitive-looking skull, resembling the one from Neandertal, had been found on Gibraltar in 1848, but it had been generally ignored. Then, in 1886, two more neandertal skeletons were found in a cave near the Belgian town of Spy. Unlike the German and Gibraltar fossils, these bones were clearly associated with stone tools and the remains of extinct animals. Clearly, then, "Neandertal man" *was* ancient. But this did not make him ancestral to modern humans. Indeed, as more and more fossils turned up, the anthropological interpretation of them became increasingly grotesque, as if unconsciously calculated to dissociate these creatures from the human lineage. One famous paleontologist, taking the arthritic skeleton from La Chapelle-aux-Saints as representative of the group as a whole, declared that the neandertals had a permanently stooped posture, with knees bent. On the basis of the skull shape, he pronounced their intelligence to be grossly retarded, "of a purely vegetative or bestial kind." Thus arose the comic-book conception of the neandertal—a hunchbacked, grunting, lumbering brute, dragging his club behind him.

Physical Structure

Though this conception of the neandertals is very much alive today, it has been proved entirely mistaken. Examination of other, nonarthritic fossils, from a point of view less biased, has yielded a more complex and less brutish picture of these people. Good examples of the neandertals include a cannibalized skull from Monte Circeo, Italy, and the remarkably complete skeletons from the "family" graveyard at La Ferrassie, France. Other classic neandertals have been found near La Ferrassie at the sites of La Quina and Le Moustier. These fossils indicate that the neandertals, though stocky and powerfully built, were a people every bit as upright and nimble as modern humans, and probably not much less intelligent.

The specialized characteristics that distinguish the neandertals from other archaic *Homo sapiens* fossils are seen most strikingly in the face. The nose was broad but high-bridged and prominent, the orbits were high and rounded, and the cheekbones were swept back. The braincase was large and bulged at the sides, but it was still flat

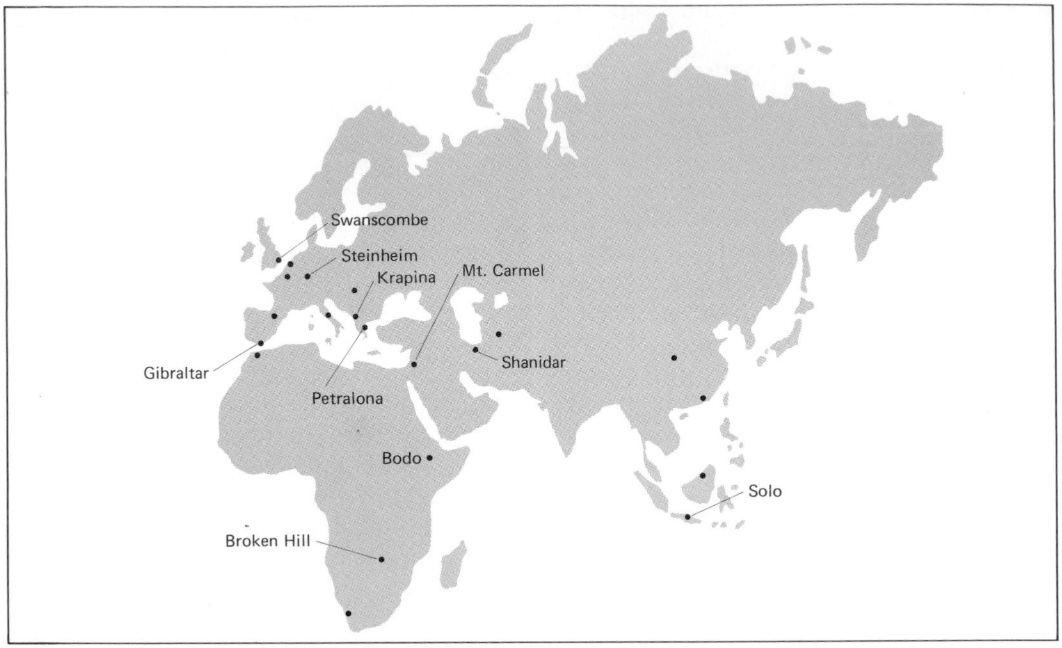

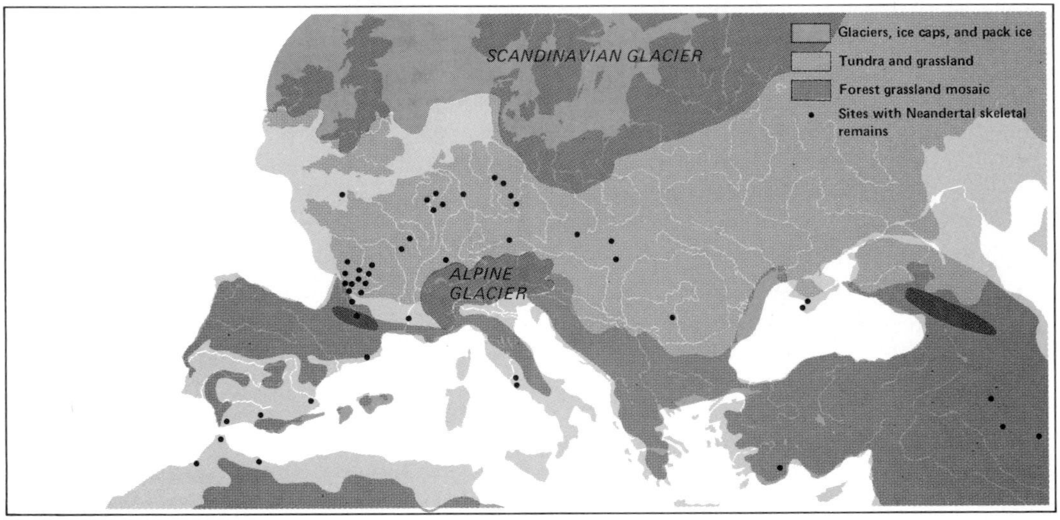

Figure 10-3. Archaic and early modern *Homo sapiens* sites. The second map shows Europe and environs during the Würm glaciation. The Würm not only made Europe colder, but created a great variety of local climatic and vegetation zones. The neandertals were able to adapt to these challenging habitats and exploit the large herds of grazing animals that roamed the plains and forests of glacial Europe. (*After Butzer, 1971*)

on top, perhaps indicating that the frontal lobe of the brain remained relatively small or was different in structure from that of modern humans. The cranial capacity of the neandertals was greater than that of earlier humans. Indeed, in some instances it was even greater than that of most modern skulls, reaching 1,600 to 1,800 cc.

The neandertals were generally short people, averaging about 150 cm. (less than 5 ft.) in height, but stocky and barrel-chested. Their leg bones were short, heavy, and somewhat bowed, with large joints indicating powerful muscles. Such characteristics seem to be neither inherited from more primitive *Homo* forms nor transitional to modern humans. Their functional significance, if any, is obscure. It has been suggested that since short, stocky bodies conserve heat best, the neandertal physique may have been an adaptation to the cold of the last glaciation.

The Mousterian Tradition

The name *Mousterian* is derived from Le Moustier, one of the earliest neandertal sites to be excavated and the one at which Mousterian tools were first identified. Like the term Acheulean, Mousterian is used in two senses. In the narrower sense, it refers to a specific group of tool styles. More broadly, it is used for the cultural tradition of which these tools are one representative—the culture of the neandertal peoples.

Mousterian Tools

In general, Mousterian tools are smaller and more elaborately crafted than Acheulean ones. Their most notable features are their precision of workmanship and their degree of specialization. These are characteristics that we have already seen in products of the Acheulean tradition, but Mousterian stone-workers carried them many steps further.

Using the prepared core technique, the Mousterian stone-workers could produce a standardized flake, a "blank" that could be finished in a variety of ways. The variety of tools increased; but this is not the variation caused by individual clumsiness or random error. On the contrary, each tool type was made to a standard pattern in a way that is eloquent testimony both to the ability of the Mousterian stone-worker to hold a pattern in the "mind's eye" and to increasingly sophisticated stone-working techniques. Typical tools, such as the Mousterian point and the large side scraper, are quite standardized and recognizable throughout the regions of Mousterian culture.

It seems likely that each of the special tools was manufactured to perform a particular set of tasks in food preparation or in manufacturing other artifacts, although in many cases we are not quite sure what that task was. Binford and Binford (1968) have identified at least a dozen different special-purpose tools in Mousterian assemblages. Among them are certain familiar items, such as choppers, scrapers, and hand axes—more refined than their Oldowan and Acheulean predecessors but clearly related to those traditions. There are also a number of new types, including

1. The *point*, a triangular implement, used primarily in hunting
2. The *burin*, a chisel-like tool, probably used for shaving wood or bone or for removing small splinters (themselves used as tools) from these materials
3. The *borer*, a small implement with a point like an icepick, used for punching holes in leather and other soft materials
4. The *drill*, another pointed tool, used for making holes in harder materials; it was employed with a rotary or twisting motion, like a modern drill bit
5. The *denticulate*, a tool with a jagged-toothed edge, used for shredding foods and wood
6. The *notch*, a tool with a deep indentation, probably used for rounding wooden objects such as spear shafts
7. The *knife*, often double-edged, used primarily for slicing.

Within this variety there is further variety, for each of these tools was made in a number of dif-

Two typical Mousterian tools—a scraper from the La Quina site, and a point from La Ferrassie. The point was a hunting weapon; it was probably used attached to a shaft to make a spear or lance. *(Collection, Musée de l'homme; Courtesy, American Museum of Natural History)*

ferent ways. Bordes (1968) has identified sixty different subtypes. For example, not only are there tools that are specifically scrapers, but there are many different kinds of scrapers—straight scrapers, convex scrapers, concave scrapers, double scrapers, single scrapers, side scrapers, transverse scrapers. Thus, while Acheulean tools were to some degree specialized for different tasks, the purposes for which Mousterian tools were made were much more narrowly defined. Toolmaking had come a very long way from the simple, poorly defined tool types of the Oldowan, and the minds that conceived these tools were recognizably much closer to our own.

Variability in Mousterian Tool Assemblages

One of the most striking features of the Mousterian tradition is the variety of tool types likely to be found in any given assemblage. But, whereas all Acheulean tool assemblages are relatively similar, Mousterian assemblages exhibit considerable variation. Bordes (1968) has classified the assemblages according to the assortment of tool types each includes and has identified five different types of assemblage. One has a large proportion of scrapers, another a large proportion of denticulates and knives. In one, the prepared core technique predominates; in another it is almost absent. (The five assemblage types and their characteristic features are listed in Table 10-1.)

It would obviously be of great interest to know what these differences signify. What was going on in this period that could have resulted in the use of five distinct types of tool assemblages? Three very different answers to this question have been proposed.

First, many archeologists once believed that

TABLE 10-1. The Five Mousterian Assemblage Types

NAME	CHARACTERISTICS
Mousterian of the Acheulean Tradition (MAT)	Some hand axes present (almost none in the other four assemblage types); early MAT has many scrapers (20–40 percent); later MAT has fewer hand axes and scrapers, many denticulates and backed knives
Typical Mousterian	Up to 50 percent side scrapers, carefully shaped points, some prepared core flake tools
Quina Mousterian	Many scrapers (50–80 percent), including styles not found in the other assemblage types; numerous notched flakes, hardly any prepared core flake tools
Ferrassie Mousterian	Similar to Quina Mousterian, but including some prepared core flake tools
Denticulate Mousterian	Many denticulates and notched flakes (35–55 percent), relatively few scrapers (5–25 percent), no backed knives; prepared core flake tools sometimes present

the various assemblages might belong to different *time periods* during the Mousterian stage. As the centuries passed, human technology evolved, and the five assemblage types represent five successive stages of its evolution. The fact that the assemblage types appear in different sequences from site to site has made some investigators doubt this theory. However, Paul Mellars (1973) has shown that there are still important overall time differences among the various assemblage types, so this hypothesis cannot be ruled out.

Second, Bordes (1968) claims that each type of assemblage represents a discrete tradition, the work of a distinct ethnic group living at roughly the same time and traveling the same areas as other groups that produced different traditions. Group after group would camp in a particular area, and each would leave its own cultural remains above those of groups who had come that way earlier.

Third, Binford and Binford (1968) argue that the five types of assemblages differ not because their makers belonged to different ethnic groups or different historical periods but because they were performing different tasks in different spots. They simply represent five separate sorts of specialized tool kits, all of which were probably made and used by every band at different times and places to do certain specific jobs. For example, every spring one group might have used a particular cave for scraping hides and shredding vegetable foods. These two tasks would have required certain tools, which the people would make, use, and leave behind. Thousands of years later, we find this assemblage, recognize its similarity to another assemblage (the remains of another season of scraping and shredding, by the same or another group, in a different cave), and group the two together as examples of a "tradition."

Clearly, this last theory need not exclude the other explanations. Populations living at different periods of time or belonging to different ethnic groups might have engaged in very different activities, which would have produced functionally different assemblages.

Each of the theories suggests an important conclusion about the Mousterian stage. If each assemblage type in fact reflects a different period of time, then the rate of change in the manufacture and use of tools was accelerating rapidly during this stage. If each represents the work of a different ethnic or cultural group, then we have the first good evidence of relatively tight social groupings, with uniform cultures, above the level of a single band. If each represents a different set

Analyzing Artifacts

Many laymen think of archeologists as people who search for and recover the artifacts of prehistoric times. But digging up artifacts is only a prelude to the less glamorous but more significant work of analysis and interpretation. Often it is only after careful study that the objects made by people long dead can yield us some insight into the way of life of their makers.

One of the most basic steps in this study is the setting up of *typologies.* Quite simply, a *type* is a group of artifacts that share certain characteristics, or *attributes,* which suggest that they were made in the same way, or used in the same way, or both. Given the very large number of whole and broken artifacts that are unearthed in excavation, and their wide range of different attributes, such classification is essential if the material is to be organized in a meaningful way.

Constructing a typology is arduous work. What seems obvious to the casual eye can be highly misleading. Suppose, for example, that an archeologist finds hundreds of fragments of pottery, including some that are red and some that are brown. It would be tempting to conclude that two different types of pottery are represented. However, if one arranged the pieces along a continuum of color, one might discover that all of the pottery was in fact of a single type, reddish-brown, with only a few distinctly red and brown pieces at the extremes. Of course, all artifacts have hundreds of attributes, some of which can only be discerned through complex physical and chemical analysis.

A researcher is often unable to discover the pattern of associated attributes that define a type until he has considered many different potential combinations. Suppose, for instance, that an archeologist has 200 pieces of chipped stone. Some appear to have been used as knives, others as scrapers; some are made of chert, others of obsidian. When these tools are sorted by function and raw material, the following breakdown is obtained:

	Chert	Obsidian
Knives	49	52
Scrapers	51	48

Thus arrayed, there seems to be no relationship between the two attributes. This is a bit surprising, for one might expect some correlation between the function of a tool and the raw material from which it is made. When a third attribute—the size of the tool—is taken into account, however, a clear pattern does in fact emerge:

	Small		*Large*	
	Chert	Obsidian	Chert	Obsidian
Knives	47	0	2	52
Scrapers	1	45	50	3

Apparently, if the stone worker was making a knife, chert was preferred for a small tool and obsidian for a large one. In making scrapers, on the other hand, obsidian was chosen for the smaller artifacts and chert used for the larger ones. Such a pattern might reflect both the characteristics of the raw material and the uses to which different tools were put in performing different tasks.

Typology, of course, is not an end in itself. Archeologists attempt to categorize tools in this way as a means of learning more about the past—to help date a site, for example, or to identify the cultural tradition of which it was a part. If we find different types of artifacts at nearby sites, it may mean that we have discovered the boundary between two traditions; if we find different types of artifacts at the same site, we may be dealing with different stages of cultural evolution. Increasingly, however, archeologists have undertaken the analysis of chipped stone and other artifacts in order to identify their function—the activities in which they were used by prehistoric peoples. A number of kinds of evidence are brought to bear in making such interpretations.

First is the overall size and shape of the artifact. Think about the tools our own society employs; clearly it would be impossible to drive a nail with a screwdriver, cut down a tree with a pair of scissors, or sew a button with a bottle opener. While the differences among various prehistoric tools are generally less clear-cut, we can usually infer that larger tools were used for heavier tasks, pointed tools for boring or drilling, sharp-edged tools for cutting, and so on. The angle of the working edge of the tool, and its location in relation to the shape of the artifact and the way it was held, are particularly important clues to its function. So too, in many cases, is the type of stone from which it was made.

Another important source of information is the wear pattern on the tool. The kinds of materials on which tools are used often leave their marks on the working edge of the implement. The degree of rounding or blunting of the edge, or the precise pattern of breakage that occurs, may indicate how hard was the material being cut or chopped or scraped. Sometimes scratches may suggest that the tool was used on wood or grass, which contain particles of silica harder than the tool itself. "Sickle sheen" helps to identify stone implements used to harvest grasses—the silica in the grasses actually polishes the edge of the stone. Fred Briuer of UCLA has used techniques borrowed from the police laboratory to show that organic residues left on the edge of a stone tool may provide clues as to whether it was used on plant or animal materials.

The context in which artifacts are recovered also provides important evidence about their use. Tools found with cut and charred bones, for instance, are likely to be butchering implements. Distinctive woodworking implements such as drills and burins (similar to our chisels) may provide help in interpreting less easily identified tools that are found with them.

Another approach that helps us to infer behavior from material culture is *experimental archeology:* archeologists actually manufacture items of prehistoric technology and use them in a variety of different activities—cutting and scraping, for example—and with a variety of different raw materials, such as bone, meat, and wood. These studies have provided fresh insights, not only into the uses to which prehistoric tools were put, but also into the processes by which they were made and the patterns of wear that might result from their use. Such information greatly increases our understanding of the ways of life of prehistoric peoples.

of tasks, then we are seeing the evolution of groups that had extremely specialized and methodical strategies for exploiting local and seasonal resources. As we shall see in the next chapter, it is likely that all these changes—increased "ethnic" and economic specialization, along with an accelerating rate of technological change—were beginning to occur during the Mousterian stage.

In any case, we see in the Mousterian tools a pattern that contrasts strongly with that of the previous technological stage. Then, only two contemporary traditions existed, and tools from sites thousands of miles apart were very similar. Now, tools and tool kits from nearby sites show marked differences, and most of the more thoroughly excavated areas have yielded assemblages of several different types.

Sedentism

Related to specialization is another tendency that becomes more evident in this period—the tendency toward *sedentism,* settling down in one place. The practice may have originated in those localities where the supply of game was fairly reliable throughout the year. One such region lies in southwestern France, where herds of large game regularly passed through a series of river valleys on their way south to their winter feeding grounds, and again on their way back for their summer grazing on the rich grasslands to the north. These seasonal migrations assured the human inhabitants a regular supply of meat, and archeologists have uncovered several sites that suggest possible year-round occupation. Here, bands of humans often lived in *rock shelters*—high-roofed, shallow caves in limestone cliffs. In several of the shelters, the people made windscreens by driving posts into the ground and stretching hides or tying branches across them. Inside the shelter were hearths for keeping warm and cooking meat.

At this stage, however, sedentism was still the exception rather than the rule. Far more numerous than the year-round sites are temporary or seasonal open-air sites, and sites with seasonally specialized tool kits. Such evidence indicates that, for the most part, humans were still living as wandering bands.

Ritual, Religion, and Human Values

Among the cultural remains of *Homo habilis* and *Homo erectus,* we find little evidence of any activity that is not directly related to survival. We see them hunting, gathering, making tools, and building shelters, all in the service of staying alive. But of nonutilitarian activities there is almost no trace. Among the remains of archaic *Homo sapiens,* on the other hand, we repeatedly find relics that seem to have symbolic rather than utilitarian value.

Humans, it seems, had begun to construct a new picture of reality. They had come to entertain beliefs, ideas that they could not confirm with their senses. They had evidently begun to believe in the supernatural—invisible forces at work in nature. Moreover, they had begun to use *ritual*—religious ceremonies involving symbolic actions and objects—to organize and control these mysterious forces. Religion had entered human evolution.

Why did religion develop as part of human culture? Numerous theories have been advanced to answer this question. Perhaps, as human intelligence increased and people became more aware of their world's complexity, they had to develop a set of beliefs to explain what they *couldn't* understand: why hunting was good last season but bad this season, why the rock slide had claimed the band's best hunter, why the sun rose and set. Perhaps, as they came to control their environment better, religion helped them expand their sense of control; if the hunting was bad and there was no practical solution for it, they could at least offer sacrifices to imagined forces that controlled the reindeer migrations. Possibly, as a higher intelligence and a more complex way of life enlarged their range of choices, religion relieved the anguish and anxiety of choosing; it chose for them, or confirmed their choices. Possibly, as they came to see a more complex world, religion reflected—and perhaps assuaged—a growing sense of awe, bewilderment, and helplessness.

To some extent, all these psychological factors probably contributed to the growth of religious faith. Furthermore, religion no doubt performed social functions as well. As we saw in Chapter 9, hunting bands, to prevent conflict from rupturing the social order, would have needed rules for conduct. In all societies, even the most complex, religion is an excellent means of teaching and reinforcing social rules.

Whatever its origin, religion was clearly established in neandertal culture. There are some signs of religious practices among late populations of *Homo erectus*—for example, the cannibalistic rites at Choukoutien. At neandertal sites, such signs are quite common. We have already seen one example: the flower burial at Shanidar. Other sites offer additional evidence.

The Bear Cult

That religion was in part a reflection of human awe and an effort to control life's dangers is suggested most strongly by the evidence of a bear cult during this period. Present-day hunters often perform solemn rites before and after a lion or bear hunt, to placate the spirit of their fierce prey. For archaic *Homo sapiens,* the cave bear seems to have been an object of similar reverence. This awesome beast weighed about 1,360 kilograms (3,000 lb.) and stood 3 meters (nearly 10 ft.) high when on its hind legs; an encounter with one was bound to make a lasting impression on anyone who survived it. In any case, the bear's remains were not treated casually. In Drachenloch, a cave in the Swiss Alps, archeologists found a large stone-lined pit sunk into the ground and sealed with a huge slab of rock. Removing the slab, they found that the chest contained seven bear skulls, neatly stacked, all facing toward the mouth of the cave. Farther back in the cave, six bear skulls stood in niches in the walls. A leg bone had been wedged behind the cheekbone of one of them. Further evidence of bear cults comes from a French cave, Regourdou. Here, underneath a slab weighing almost a ton, archeologists found another stone vault, this one containing the remains of twenty bears.

We cannot know the precise reasons why the bears' remains were stored in these painstakingly constructed tombs. Was this the hunters' idea of the burial due to a demigod? Or did they believe that they had to seal up the bear's angry spirit in a stone vault in order to prevent it from coming back to haunt the living? Whatever the motives—reverence or fear (probably both)—they must have been extremely powerful in order to induce the cave dwellers to drag a stone slab weighing a ton from wherever they found it into their cave.

Burial of the Dead

Shanidar is by no means the only known neandertal burial. At many different sites of this period, human remains repose in deliberately dug graves. Almost invariably these graves also yield objects that were purposefully placed with the body at burial. Often they contain some special object or are arranged in some special way that seems quite irrelevant to a purely functional burial. Thus while burial itself could be interpreted as a utilitarian act, the burials of this period appear to have been accompanied by ritual.

For example, in one of the earliest excavations, the cave of La Chapelle-aux-Saints in southern France, an old man was interred with a bison leg resting on his chest and with stone tools and fragmented animal bones lying at his side. In another French site, La Ferrassie, archeologists have uncovered what may be the graves of an entire family, buried together in an ancient rock shelter. In two of the graves, an adult male and female lay head to head. The male was buried with flakes of flint and bone fragments, and a stone slab had been laid over his head and shoulders. In neat parallel rows at the male's feet were the graves of two children, both about five years old. Further toward the rear of the shelter were the graves of a newborn infant (possibly stillborn), buried with three tools, and of a six-year old, again with three tools. This last grave was the most puzzling. It contained only the child's skull and his lower skeleton, placed about three feet apart. Over the skull lay a triangular stone slab, with a pattern of scooped-out holes on its underside.

In other sites too, burial was evidently ceremonial. In the cave of Teshik-Tash, in the Soviet republic of Uzbekistan, six pairs of mountain goat horns encircled the grave of a young boy. At Mount Carmel, Israel, archeologists found ten carefully buried bodies, all of which were once tightly bound in an exaggerated fetal position. Over the chest of one of the males lay the jawbones of an enormous boar.

The symbolic meaning of such details remains a mystery. Was the boar the man's most prized kill, or was the man the boar's kill? When tools were placed in a grave, was this simply a ritual offering or tribute, like the satin-lined coffins of today, or did the mourners feel that the dead would need some tools in the afterlife? Were the flowers in the grave at Shanidar placed there because they were beautiful or because the ancient inhabitants of this area, like the tribes living there now, prized them for their medicinal value? We do not know. However, it seems indisputable that such objects did have symbolic value and that they were related to a belief in the supernatural.

Ritual Cannibalism

In some instances, the neandertals evidently honored the spirits of the dead not only by according them a ceremonious burial but also by eating them. We have already examined the evidence of cannibalism at Choukoutien. In later sites, such evidence becomes more common. In the cave of Hortus in southern France and at the site of Krapina in Yugoslavia, archeologists have uncovered masses of splintered human bones—in each case, the remains of at least twenty individuals. It is clear that they were eaten by human beings. The skulls were smashed open, and the long bones were split to extract the marrow. Most tellingly, some of the bones are charred, indicating that the human meat was cooked.

Several sites have yielded isolated human skulls in which the opening at the base has been widened to extract the brain. At Monte Circeo, south of Rome, a single skull, surrounded by a circle of stones, was found on the floor of a dark and airless cave, far from the entrance. The owner of the skull had evidently been killed by a blow to the head. Again the skull was hacked open at the base. In the same chamber were three neat bundles of animal bones. These were evidently the remains of haunches of meat, presumably offered either as a token of respect or, more pragmatically, as provisions for the afterlife.

As we pointed out with regard to the skulls at Choukoutien, such cannibalism is generally interpreted as a ritual act. The symbolic elements of the eerie scene at Monte Circeo—the circle of stones, the bundles of animal bones—support this interpretation. It seems probable that, like most modern cannibals, neandertals ate the flesh of other human beings to gain some influence over their spirits—to absorb the skill and bravery of a great hunter, to capture the spirit of an enemy, or to express piety toward a dead kinsman. One can imagine a band carrying into the cave at Monte Circeo the head of their best hunter—murdered, perhaps, in a quarrel with another man. Piously they remove the brain, divide it among themselves, and eat it, perhaps to absorb his anger and thus hasten their revenge. They encircle the skull with stones to imprison his spirit, and leave behind some meat to be eaten in the afterlife, where hunting would be unpredictable. The ceremony finished, they abandon the cave and move on.

This, of course, is pure speculation. The brain might as easily have been eaten, and the provisions left, by the murderer, as an act of appeasement—to prevent the victim's spirit from returning to take revenge. But it seems likely that some such ceremony was the context of ancient *Homo*'s acts of cannibalism.

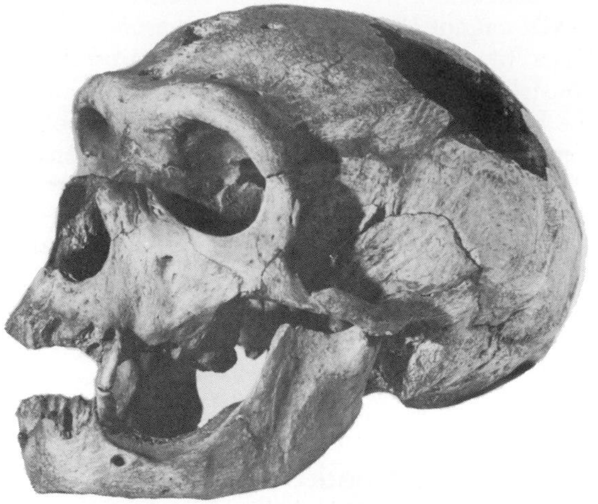

The skull of the elderly arthritic neandertal man from La Chapelle. It was the misinterpretation of this specimen that gave rise to the popular image of the neandertals as stooped, brutish, and unintelligent. The fact that this man had lost most of his teeth, in addition to being crippled by arthritis, is interesting evidence that fitness was no longer being determined entirely by physical qualities. Apparently people were willing to help keep alive individuals whose value to the group must have been largely cultural—perhaps as medicine men or sorcerers. *(Collection, Musée de l'homme)*

Treatment of the Aged and the Handicapped

A striking sign of the growing role of culture in the lives of the neandertals is the evidence that old and handicapped individuals—people who, in terms of physical abilities, were less than useful to the band—were able to survive. The old man from La Chapelle-aux-Saints, for example, was extremely arthritic. He could certainly not have earned his keep by hunting. Indeed, he probably had trouble even eating, for he had no back teeth left. For this man to survive, his fellows would not only have had to provide food for him but also to take special pains preparing it—perhaps by shredding it with tools, perhaps by prechewing it—so that he could swallow it. Similarly, one of the graves at Shanidar contained the skeleton of a man whose shoulder and right arm were deformed, possibly from birth. Despite this handicap, which probably kept him from hunting, he lived to the age of about forty—a long span for people of that era.

The survival of these two men implies that humans now valued individuals too old and decrepit to hunt or gather efficiently. For the anthropologist, the appearance of such a new value is not simply evidence for the awakening conscience of humanity or the evolution of the human soul; it is part of the evolution of a total culture. To a large extent it reflects the environmental pressures acting upon the group in question and its way of dealing with them. What are the implications of this regard for the aged and infirm?

Among nonhuman primates, as we have seen, the weak get no favors from the strong. When a chimp is too sick to forage, no food is brought to it. When a baboon is wounded, the troop does not slow its pace. With a foraging pattern in which each animal fends only for itself, and a habitat in which to be caught away from the trees at nightfall is to court death in the jaws of a leopard or hyena, there is no advantage in extending altruistic behavior to this point.

We suggested earlier that the establishment of a base camp allowed the sick and the temporarily incapacitated a safe refuge until they were able to resume their place as productive members of the group. More important, with the emergence of the human subsistence strategy of complementary hunting and gathering and the sharing of food, the survival of each hunter and gatherer became a matter of concern to the whole group. Thus the welfare of the human group favored a greater degree of altruism on the part of its members. By neandertal times, as the evidence of Shanidar and La Chapelle shows, the notion of "usefulness" had expanded still further—a one-armed man and a toothless cripple were evidently valued members of the group, although their hunting potential must have been very low. Perhaps their contribution to the hunt was not brawn but knowledge or psychic power. As senior members of the society, they may have been repositories of information about the band's hunting grounds and the behavior of their fauna. Alternately, they might have been noted medicine men or shamans, whose ability to cure the sick or to control the movements of the herds was as vital a contribution to the group's survival as the strong right arm of a younger hunter.

The growth of altruism, along with the new importance of social and cultural contributions to the group's welfare, made it possible for the physically weak to go on living and, presumably, to reproduce. Thus, more and more, fitness was being defined by cultural rather than simply physical criteria.

LANGUAGE AND SPEECH

The level of cultural and intellectual sophistication that we see among the neandertals and other populations of archaic *Homo sapiens*—their social cooperation, their ability to adapt their tools to specific environments and specific tasks, their use of symbols, their participation in ritual—would almost certainly have been impossible without some form of language. Indeed, there is almost certainly a close connection between the elaboration of language (an abstract symbolic system) and the many other evidences of increasing powers of abstract thought and conceptualization that we encounter during this period, such as the development of the prepared core technique and the appearance of religion. As we shall see, some anthropologists believe that these people could not speak with the ease of modern humans. But it is generally thought that archaic *Homo sapiens*, along with his predecessor, *Homo erectus*, used language.

How and when did our ancestors begin to speak to one another? To understand the theories as to how language evolved, we must first see what it evolved from.

Human and Nonhuman Communication

While nonhuman animals do not speak, they definitely communicate. Seagulls cry to one another when predators appear; honeybees tell each other where food is to be found by means of intricate dances; dogs indicate their readiness to mate through scents. The primates, as we saw in Chapter 5, have elaborate communication systems. Baboons, for instance, bare their teeth to threaten and smack their lips to appease. Chimpanzees, as we would expect of our close relatives, are even more communicative; they touch, hug, beg, smile, frown, glare, and so forth. Along with other animals, chimps also communicate vocally, through what is known as a *call system*. This is a repertoire of specific sounds—in the case of the chimps, about 10 to 15 different hoots, grunts, and squeals—each of which is produced in response to a particular situation.

Probably because they are in large part genetically determined, animals' calls are rigidly stereotyped; the call is always the same in form and meaning. When a chimpanzee finds a plentiful source of food, it hoots and drums. When attacked, it screams. In danger, it utters a resounding "*waaa.*" To let others know that it is in the vicinity, it produces a distinctive "pant-hoot," which can be roughly translated as "Here I am" (Goodall, 1971). Neither the call nor its meaning ever changes. Moreover, animal call systems are *closed*. That is, elements of one call cannot be combined with elements of another to produce a new message. The calls are unique, limited in number, and mutually exclusive.

Unlike call systems, human language is *open*—the number of messages that can be conveyed is virtually infinite. Indeed, a person speaking a human language easily can (and constantly does) create entirely new messages—sentences that have probably never before been spoken in the history of the human species. Thus, whereas call systems can generally convey only a very few simple meanings—danger, hostility, sexual excitement, the availability of food, and so on—language can be used to communicate a vast range of meanings, from subtle philosophical abstractions to complex technical information to delicate shades of feeling (Lancaster, 1968).

This flexibility is made possible by the *arbitrariness* of human language. Unlike animal calls, the sounds of a language have no fixed meaning. Instead, meaning emerges from the way sounds are combined into words and words arranged to make sentences in accordance with a complex set of rules (grammar). Since these vary from language to language, they must be learned (along with the corresponding vocabulary) by each individual speaker. Nevertheless, all normal humans seem able to do this very easily and for the most part unconsciously—indeed, almost automatically. This has led some theorists (most notably Chomsky) to speculate that the underlying structure of human language has some genetic basis—that our brains are "wired" for language.

Another distinctive feature of human language is that it is stimulus-free; that is, a linguistic utterance need not be evoked by an immediate situation. We do not have to turn a corner and come upon a tiger in order to say the word "tiger" or talk about "danger." We can discuss things that are not present—things experienced in the past, things that may happen in the future, even things that are not real, such as unicorns. None of this is possible in a call system, in which the dimensions of time and possibility are completely lacking. An animal cannot use calls to say "I found bananas yesterday," or "I hope I can find some tomorrow." Nor can it express anything that is untrue or merely hypothetical. Human language, however, enables us to transcend immediate experience and deal with the past and the future, the actual and the imaginary, the true and the false (Hockett, 1973). It has been said, with some justice, that humans became truly human when they became capable of telling a lie.

The Evolution of Language

When did the early humans make the transition from a closed call system to an open language? Because sounds leave no trace, researchers investigating the origins of language have to depend on very indirect evidence: studies of how children acquire language, comparisons of human and nonhuman vocalizations, guesses as to what kind of brains and vocal tracts might have accompanied fossil skulls, and of course cultural evidence.[2] The cultural evidence would seem to indicate that language was acquired long before *Homo sapiens* appeared. It is almost impossible, for example, to imagine that the elephant hunters at Torralba-Ambrona planned and executed the ambush and divided the kill with the help of nothing more than a call system. By the same

[2] In this case, studies of traditional societies do not help. Even the simplest hunting-and-gathering societies have complex, fully evolved languages.

token, much of *Homo habilis*'s scavenging, hunting, and gathering was probably cooperative. Indeed, on the basis of cultural evidence alone, it would seem a fair assumption that the beginnings of language appeared simultaneously with hunting and food sharing as part of an integrated "cooperation" complex. This would place the beginnings of language more than 2 million years ago.

The Physiology of Spoken Language

To speak, the early humans had to have more than the need. Speech requires physical mechanisms as well. First, it depends on certain structures in the brain. These structures allow us to associate incoming auditory messages with remembered messages from other sensory pathways—especially with the memory of the words that we will need to voice our thought. They also enable us to signal the muscles of the vocal apparatus to make the movements necessary to produce the appropriate sounds. Current research indicates that these operations are carried out mainly by three specific parts of the brain, all located in the cerebral cortex.

Unfortunately, as we pointed out in Chapter 6, there is no way of telling, from the internal cast of a fossil hominid braincase, whether the crucial structures and cortical connections were present. However, most anthropologists agree that early *Homo* populations spoke but that their linguistic capacities were probably less highly developed than ours—a conclusion that is suggested also by the lack of change in Oldowan and Acheulean tools over so many thousands of years.

By the time of archaic *Homo sapiens*, the cerebral cortex had reached essentially its present size and structure. Presumably, these early humans had the mental equipment needed for the further development of language. Perhaps they were not significantly inferior, in this respect, to modern humans. But how advanced was their capacity for articulate speech? Recent research has raised some interesting questions on this point.

In addition to the cerebral cortex, a second physical structure is crucial to the production of speech—the pharynx, a tunnel of muscle connecting the back of the mouth to the larynx (windpipe). In human adults the pharynx expands and contracts to give different tones to the sounds made by the vocal cords and thereby produces the sounds that constitute intelligible speech. We are the only primates, however, who make such extensive use of the pharynx. In other primates—monkeys and apes, for example—the pharynx is considerably smaller relative to body size. It is also shaped differently; it slopes upward in a broad curve rather than rising vertically as the human pharynx does to meet the back of the mouth at a right angle. These differences in shape and size appear to affect functioning, for the nonhuman primates do not move the pharynx when they speak. It is by moving the mouth that they make different sounds; the pharynx serves only as a tunnel for air. The same is true of human infants up to about the age of three months; and it may also have been true of archaic *Homo sapiens* throughout life, severely limiting their speaking abilities.

This theory is the result of work by Philip Lieberman, a linguist, and Edmund S. Crelin, an anatomist (1971). On the basis of similarities between the skulls of human infants, modern apes, and a reconstruction of the La Chapelle neandertal skull, Lieberman and Crelin estimated that the neandertals, like babies and apes, were equipped with a small, sloping pharynx. After constructing a model of the neandertal vocal tract and measuring it, they fed their figures into a computer programmed with information as to what resonances can be produced by vocal tracts of various shapes and sizes. The results indicated that neandertals would have had difficulty in clearly differentiating the vowel sounds *ah*, *ee*, and *oo*, which are basic to almost every known language. Furthermore, they would have had problems shifting quickly from one sound to another. Indeed, if Lieberman and Crelin are right, the neandertals may have talked at about one-tenth the speed of modern humans. It must be noted, though, that many anthropologists question the conclusions of this analysis, since they are based on the hypothetical reconstruction of

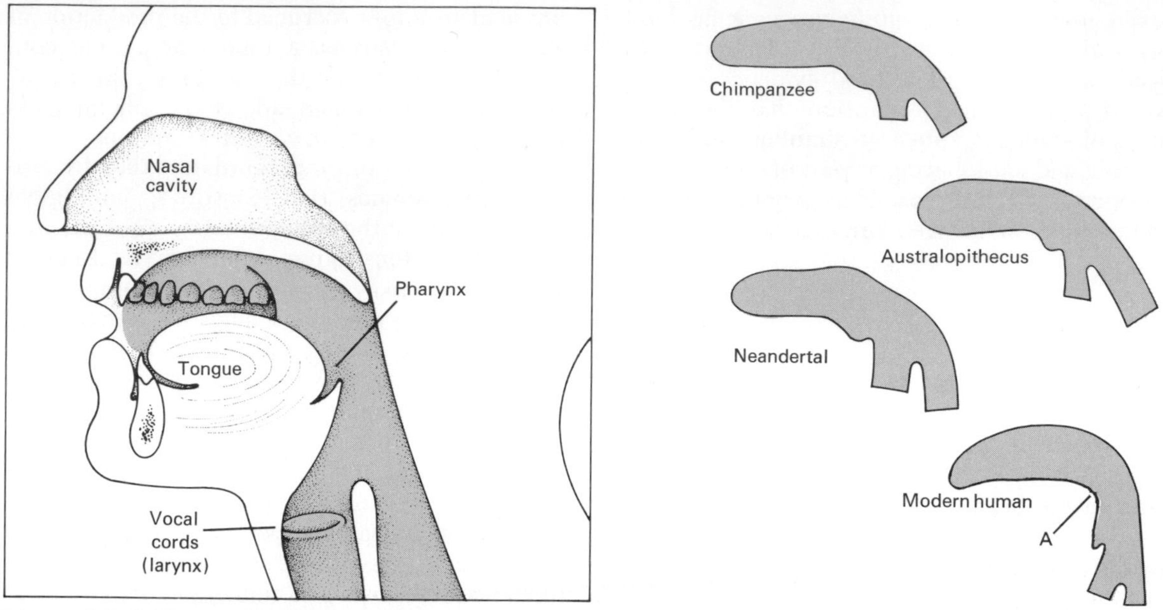

Figure 10-4. The position of the pharynx in modern humans, along with Lieberman and Crelin's models of the vocal tracts of other hominids. The vocal tract above the larynx is essentially a single, nearly straight tube in apes and early hominids—including the neandertals, if their reconstruction is correct. In modern humans, by contrast, it is sharply angled at *A*. Lieberman and Crelin suggest that, because of the shape of the neandertal pharynx, the neandertals could not have articulated the sounds of speech as rapidly and clearly as we do. (*After Lieberman, 1975*)

soft tissues (for which we have little direct evidence), and since only a single skull was studied.

The Transition from Closed to Open Communication

Given that *Homo erectus* and archaic *Homo sapiens* used language, however primitive, how did it first develop? How did the early humans make the transition from a closed call system to an open, symbolic language? Hockett and Ascher (1964) point out that a plausible way the change could have been made was through the *blending* of calls to produce new calls with more complex meanings. Presumably, such combined calls would have had a definite survival value and therefore would have been favored by natural selection, gradually becoming part of the normal human genetic endowment. As people came to regard the sounds made by their own voices as something that they could combine and manipulate, the sounds would eventually lose their association with specific situations and become instead arbitrary building blocks—the raw materials of an open and totally flexible language.

The Consequences of Language

The use of language was an indispensable part of the cultural advances that we see in *Homo erectus* and archaic *Homo sapiens.* Individuals skilled in the use of language could hunt more successfully, gather more efficiently, make more sophisticated tools, plan strategies of marriage and alliance for themselves and their relatives, resolve disputes to their personal advantage, and in general manipulate their social environment in a way that enhanced their fitness. The growth of language in turn created strong selective pressures for more agile intellect—which made possible the development of yet more elaborate language and culture. There arose, in other words, another feedback cycle: language, culture, and a brain evolved together, each reinforcing the others.

The consequences were incalculable. As people acquired the ability to communicate their knowledge and share their experiences, learning came to play an ever greater role as the shaper of human behavior. Today, our lives are rooted in language. Our social relationships are created and managed through language. Our technology and our sciences would be impossible without refined symbolic communications. Abstract thought, which underpins philosophy, mathematics, and religion, is a by-product of language. Indeed, speech directs our thoughts before we even communicate them, for we tend to frame them according to the patterns of language. Thus not only our world but also the mind that perceives it (and to some extent has made it) are the consequences of the early humans' halting progress toward the use of language.

THE APPEARANCE OF MODERN HUMANS

Contemporaries of the Neandertals

As we have emphasized, the neandertal peoples of Europe and adjacent regions were just one population of the human species. We have concentrated upon them principally because we know most about them and because their responses to the challenges of ice-age Europe illustrate the ingenuity of which archaic *Homo sapiens* was capable. From the archeological evidence, we can be sure that other populations, from China to the tip of South Africa, were also adapting culturally and physically to their particular environments.

It happens that the fossil record of the neandertals is an exceptionally rich one, largely because of their habit of living, dying, and burying their dead in rock shelters. We have relatively few remains of their contemporaries from the rest of the world. Moreover, in view of the uncertainties of dating, it is often impossible to be sure that such "contemporaries" were not in fact living a few tens of thousands of years earlier or later than the neandertals. Given the small samples of specimens, and the uncertainty of their dates, it is obviously dangerous to speak of the peoples of one region or another as being more "advanced" in the direction of modern *Homo sapiens* than their contemporaries living elsewhere. On the whole, the picture is one of physical diversity among humans of the period, paralleling the local specializations in culture and technology. Both the physical and the cultural diversity presumably reflect adaptation to local conditions and the effects of random "drift" in partially isolated populations.

Of particular interest are a series of skulls from the region immediately to the south and east of the zone inhabited by the "classic" neandertals—that is, from the Near East. The populations represented by these specimens, who were also users of tools of the prepared core Mousterian tradition, seem to have been quite as variable as the European neandertals in skull form, if not more so. Like the neandertals, they have the heavy faces and low-vaulted skulls common to archaic *Homo sapiens.* However, the features that have been interpreted as specializations of the neandertals—the very long, forward-projecting, prowlike face, broad nose, and swept-back cheekbones—are less pronounced, and often absent altogether. This has been interpreted by some as evidence that these Near Eastern populations, rather than the classic neandertals themselves, are more likely to have been directly ancestral to modern *Homo sapiens.*

The Fate of the Neandertals and the Rise of Modern *Homo sapiens*

Between 40,000 and 30,000 years ago, humans of essentially modern form appear in the fossil record. In contrast to those of the archaic populations that preceded them, their skulls are high, with a rounded forehead lacking heavy brow ridges, although cranial capacity is no greater. The face is less heavily built, with teeth that are on average smaller than those of the archaic peoples. In fact, the only noticeable difference between these people and modern humans is that, on the whole, their teeth are still somewhat larger and their skulls more rugged. The European representative of these "early modern" peoples is often called *Cro-Magnon*, after a well-known site in France.

In geological terms, the appearance of these structurally modern people is quite sudden. Almost simultaneously (that is, within a few thousand years) people of this general type appear in sites scattered from France to Indonesia to the Cape of Good Hope, occupying the whole of the previous range of the archaic peoples. Within a few thousand years more, they seem to have colonized three new continents, crossing the narrow sea barrier to New Guinea and Australia, and the Bering Strait to North America.

The Expansionist (or Replacement) Model

As with the replacement of *Homo erectus* by archaic *Homo sapiens*, there are alternative explanations to account for this change in human populations. On the one hand is the view of those who believe that evolutionary breakthroughs generally occur in small, peripheral populations. These theorists, whom we may call expansionists, suggest that only a few archaic populations—perhaps just one—evolved directly into modern *Homo sapiens*. This population then expanded rapidly in numbers and range, replacing other unevolved archaic populations. In its most extreme form, the expansionist theory suggests that the newly evolved modern populations had achieved the status of a new species, so that no interbreeding would occur with the displaced archaics.

Obviously, to replace locally adapted archaic populations so quickly and completely, the invaders would have had to possess some significant advantage. According to those who believe that the speech capability of archaic humans was limited, the change in shape of the skull, with the face shortening and becoming more "tucked under" the braincase, may have altered the relative position of mouth and larynx. This new arrangement may have permitted the "moderns" to articulate sounds more rapidly and precisely and thus to communicate information faster. Alternatively, the altered profile of the forehead may reflect a change in the organization of the frontal lobes of the brain, indicating that the human ability to scheme and persist was more fully developed among the moderns. Or it may simply have been that the invention of new toolmaking techniques—especially the fashioning of tools on blades rather than flakes and cores—gave the moderns their adaptive edge. (We discuss these new tool types more fully in Chapter 11.)

The Evolutionist Model

Diametrically opposed to the expansionist theory is the extreme evolutionist position, which states that there was no population movement or expansion involved in the replacement process. In this view, local archaic populations everywhere merely "modernized" under the influence of new selective pressures—or rather, the easing of old pressures by technological advance. According to some proponents of this view, what spread from population to population was not people, or even genes, but a cultural trait—a new technique of making tools on blades rather than flakes. Armed with these new tool kits, the blademakers no longer used their teeth and jaws as aids in toolmaking and the manipulation of new materials. Consequently, selective pressure maintaining large teeth, and the large face needed to support them, was eased, and the result was the modern skull form.

Weighing the Evidence

Our view is that it is impossible entirely to dismiss either of these theories on presently available fossil evidence, but that on the whole neither is likely to be entirely correct. As we saw, apart from a few favored areas, such as Europe, the fossil evidence is limited to a scatter of skulls, mostly rather imprecisely dated. Two regions are better documented at present—the home of the

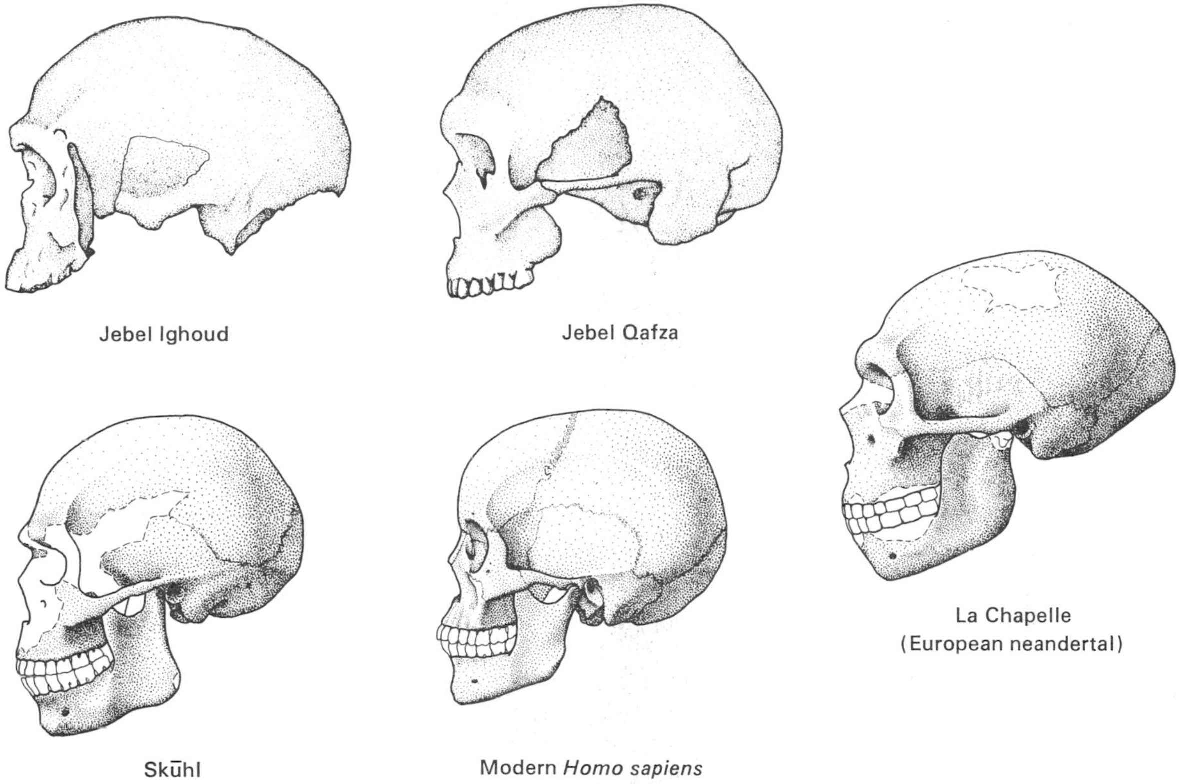

Figure 10-5. Skulls from the Near East include a number of specimens that are intermediate in form between archaic and early modern *Homo sapiens*. This suggests that modern humans may have evolved first in this region—or, more likely, in a wider area that may have included much of Asia and Africa. A reconstruction of the neandertal skull from La Chapelle-aux-Saints, France, is included for comparison. The neandertal skull is more distinctively specialized and less modern in structure. *(After Howells, 1973; Biruta Akerbergs, Robert Frank)*

classic neandertals, near the edge of the European glaciers, and the Near Eastern regions immediately to the south and east. And these two regions seem to tell different stories.

As we mentioned, the peoples who inhabited the Near East during the early part of the last glacial seem on the whole to have been less distinctively specialized, physically, than the neandertals of Europe. Starting with this relatively unspecialized archaic base, it is possible to arrange individual skulls from the region in a morphological series that effectively bridges the gap between archaic and modern (Figure 10-5). Given the uncertainties of dating, we cannot claim that this morphological series corresponds to a time series, but at least it shows that the human gene pool of the area encompassed the variability necessary to make the transition possible.

Does this mean, then, that the Near East is the home of the expansionists' breakthrough population, a true "cradle of mankind"? This has been claimed by some writers, who see the zone, rich in habitat variety, as especially conducive to rapid developments in subsistence technology that in turn would stimulate the evolution of the human intellect. But it seems altogether too great a coincidence that, if the "cradle" were so limited in area, it would be one of the few areas to have yielded an adequate human fossil record for the critical period. Much more likely, we think, the "cradle" was a more extensive area—perhaps including the whole of subtropical Asia and tropical Africa—encompassing many populations in genetic and cultural contact with one another, all evolving rapidly in the direction of modernity.

On the other hand, the evidence from the "neandertal zone," especially its western European end, seems to argue for replacement rather than evolution. Again, the details of dating are obscure (most specimens were uncovered in the days when excavation was a rough-and-ready, pick-and-shovel affair). Thus it is not possible to state, as many popular writers imply, that fully modern peoples replaced neandertals virtually overnight. Nevertheless, it is impressive that in spite of quite large samples of both archaic (neandertal) and early modern (Cro-Magnon) skulls, it is hard to point to any that are truly transitional. The archeological evidence seems to support this view. The blade tool industries of western Europe, associated with the Cro-Magnon and contemporary peoples, seem to be derived from earlier cultures of southeastern Europe and the Near East, rather than the native European Mousterian culture of the region.

Some proponents of the evolutionist model have argued that even if the evidence is compatible with a replacement scenario in some areas, such as western Europe, such a process is inherently unlikely. For one thing, they argue, hunter-gatherers are peaceable folk, lacking both the stomach and the technology for aggressive territorial expansion. Equally important, they say, two groups of hunter-gatherers are likely to be equally matched in terms of technology; in that case, if either group had an edge it would likely be the "natives," with their knowledge of local terrain and their cultural adaptations to local environmental conditions.

We believe that both points can be answered. First, it is true that the few surviving hunters and gatherers have impressed ethnographers with their gentleness. It is also true, however, that they have been thoroughly bullied, cowed, and driven into inhospitable refuges by their technologically better-equipped neighbors. Early explorers did not find the Australian aborigines, the Bushmen, or, for that matter, the Apache or Shoshone of the American West, passive peoples unskilled in the arts of warfare. It is true that most hunters and gatherers cannot take time from the food quest to go on the warpath for an extended period. But ethnographic accounts make it clear that they are by no means averse to raiding their neighbors or to spearing a trespasser at the water hole—especially if that trespasser is a stranger, a speaker of a different language, and therefore, in cultural terms, a nonperson.

As to the second point, various lines of evidence point to the conclusion that the bearers of blade tool cultures had the potential to crowd out native populations, even if overt hostility between them was rare. Surely *some* superiority—in technology or social organization or both—is implied by the fact that modern humans rapidly crossed the Timor Sea between Indonesia and Australia and the Bering Strait between Siberia and Alaska—both of which had served as barriers to human expansion for several million years. Furthermore, as we shall see, there is archeological evidence that glacial Europe supported far more people, in larger settlements, in the period of the blade cultures. The environment was the same; it was improved technology, social organization, or a combination of the two that gave the edge. Thus, even if conflict between archaic natives and modern invaders was limited to competition for scarce resources, with little overt hostility and violence, the invaders were likely to win out in the long run.

Admitting, then, that the bearers of blade tool cultures replaced archaic populations in western Europe, was this the *only* zone in which replacement rather than local evolution occurred? Again, for the same reasons as before, we believe this unlikely. More probably, there were many such populations, scattered around the inhabited world, whose first contact with the new technology came when a band of "advanced" hunter-gatherers rudely expanded its range into their territory, and who gradually gave way before the invaders.

What, exactly, in behavioral and genetic terms, does replacement involve in such a case?

The key here is the degree of difference between the two populations, native and invader, both in genetic terms and as perceived through the filter of cultural prejudice by the invading group.

In appearance, to judge from their skeletal remains, the neandertals and the invading moderns would have been more different from one another than any two groups of living humans. Even if equal in speaking ability, they would have differed in many ways. To judge from recent human behavior, relations between the two groups would have been marked by mutual contempt, repugnance, and hostility; socially, each would have regarded the other as not quite human and would have had no compunction in treating the other accordingly. On the other hand, biologically, they *were* both human members of the same species. (We do not subscribe to the view that the transition to modern *Homo sapiens* involved true speciation—the appearance of *biological* barriers to genetic exchange.) Therefore, to judge again from the behavior of modern humans, the invaders would inevitably have absorbed into their society the survivors (especially female survivors) of native groups reduced by competition and hostility. "Human" status, being socially defined, would readily have been extended to survivors who adopted the cultural standards of the invaders.

Thus, both the culture and the gene pool of the invaders would have received traits from the resident population. Selection, acting upon the new mix, would then have produced local cultures and gene pools combining the successful innovations of the invaders with the tried and tested local adaptations of the residents. This model would explain some observations about the physical and cultural attributes of the neandertal's successors in Europe. The "beaky" face of modern Europeans, especially its prominent nose, could be a link to the neandertal heritage. Similarly, the early Perigordian, one of the earliest of post-Mousterian cultures, has characteristics suggesting a mingling of elements from the native Mousterian and the invading blade culture. Such a mixture could represent the mingling of populations in the way we have suggested.

In short, our answer to the question What happened to archaic *Homo sapiens*? is a complex one. Some populations—perhaps most—evolved, by a combination of selection and gene flow, into modern *Homo sapiens*. Others, of which the neandertals are perhaps an example, were replaced by invading moderns. But even in the latter cases, replacement would have involved some cultural and genetic mingling between the groups, producing locally adapted populations of early moderns. We examine these peoples and their cultures in the next chapter.

This chapter has continued the story of human evolution by describing the earliest members of the species *Homo sapiens*. By this time, human culture has been elaborated far beyond anything seen in other species. This is not to say that processes of biological evolution came to an end; as we shall see later, they are still operating today. Rather, we have begun to investigate a phase during which changes in material culture, subsistence practices, and the organization of society were of relatively much greater importance. By the end of the period we have been discussing in this chapter, the brain had reached fully modern proportions and the dynamic element in changing human behavior had become the cultural pattern itself. It is to this that we now turn in Chapters 11 through 13.

Summary

Human fossils from about 250,000 B.P. onward are assigned to the species *Homo sapiens*. The people who lived from about 250,000 to 40,000 B.P. are known as archaic *Homo sapiens*—sufficiently advanced to belong to our species, but retaining many ancestral features of *Homo erectus*. Remains of archaic *Homo sapiens* have been found at several sites in Europe, Africa, and Java. Although the evidence is inconclusive, it is likely that many local populations of *Homo erectus* evolved, gradually and in parallel, the increased cranial capacity and more complex subsistence strategies that distinguish the first members of our species.

An important advance during this stage was the introduction of the *prepared core,* or Levallois, technique around 100,000 B.P. This was a toolmaking technique in which a core was flaked to a desired shape so that a large flake of predetermined form could be struck off. This flake became the tool. Specialized regional tool traditions, such as the *Fauresmith* in South Africa and the *Sangoan* in central Africa, also appear by this time.

The history of archaic *Homo sapiens* was profoundly affected by the *Würm glaciation,* a series of relatively rapid glacial advances and retreats that lasted from about 75,000 to 11,000 B.P. Human beings of this period had developed sufficient behavioral flexibility and resourcefulness to survive the frigid climate and exploit the great herds of the European grasslands and forests. Thus for the first time, human populations did not have to retreat south, as they had done during previous glacial episodes. The Würm transformed Europe into a variety of climatic zones, creating a far greater range of human habitats and potential resources. Under the influence of these changes, the life styles of various populations began to diverge.

One of the best-known archaic human populations is the *neandertals,* who lived in Europe and adjacent parts of the Near East during the early Würm glaciation, about 100,000 to 40,000 B.P. When neandertal fossils were first found in the nineteenth century, these people were popularly pictured as "brutish." However, although they tended to be short, stocky, heavy boned, and muscular, the neandertals were probably as agile as modern humans, and perhaps nearly as intelligent. Among the features that distinguish them from other archaic human populations are their broad, prominent nose and swept-back cheekbones.

The neandertal culture is called the *Mousterian.* Many Mousterian tools were made by the prepared core technique. The standardized flake could be refined into a great variety of specialized tools. Mousterian tools are found in five different types of assemblages, which may represent the work of different groups, or merely different tool kits for specialized activities.

Evidence from this period of a bear cult, ceremonial burials, and ritual cannibalism suggests the existence of religious beliefs among the neandertals. Religion probably arose in part as a reflection of human awe and as an effort to control life's dangers. It may also have served the social function of helping to establish accepted rules of conduct. Fossil evidence from this period suggests that archaic humans protected and cared for the aged and the handicapped. This implies that cultural contributions were becoming as important as physical strength for the welfare of the group.

It is generally assumed that *Homo erectus* and archaic *Homo sapiens* must have used some form of language. Unlike animal call systems, which are for the most part genetically based, and in which each call has a fixed form and meaning, human language is open—the number of messages that can be created is unlimited. This is possible because of the *arbitrariness* of human language—meaning derives from the combination of sounds into words and sentences according to grammatical rules. This flexibility allows discussion of the past, the future, the abstract, and the imaginary. It is likely that by the time of archaic *Homo sapiens,* the cerebral cortex had expanded sufficiently to allow the development of a fairly complex language. It is questionable, however, whether the archaic human pharynx was evolved enough to facilitate the rapid, articulate speech we use today. The beginnings of language probably set another feedback cycle in motion, creating new selective pressures for more complex brains and higher levels of cultural and linguistic development.

Between 40,000 and 30,000 B.P., humans of essentially modern form appear in the fossil record in sites across Europe, Africa, and Asia. These people quickly extended their range to include Australia and North America. Two theories have been proposed to account for this development. The *expansionist* (replacement) scenario depicts one or a few archaic populations evolving into modern *Homo sapiens* and expanding to replace less evolved groups. The *evolutionist* theory holds that archaic populations everywhere evolved modern traits under the influence of new cultural selective pressures. It is probable that both hypotheses are correct to a certain degree. In western Europe, for example, it appears that non-neandertals with different physical and cultural attributes moved into the area, eventually displacing and/or absorbing the neandertal populations. This could have happened elsewhere as well. But evolution of archaic populations into physically "modern" form may have occurred in many other regions, including the Near East.

Glossary

arbitrariness (of language) the fact that human language is made up of sounds that derive their meaning from their combination into words and sentences according to grammatical rules; the basis of the flexibility and openness of human language

archaic *Homo sapiens* humans who lived from about 250,000 to 40,000 B.P.; sufficiently advanced to be assigned to our own species, they retained certain ancestral features of *Homo erectus*

burin a chisel-edged implement used for working bone, wood, and other materials

call system a repertoire of specific sounds, each of which is elicited by a particular situation and conveys a particular meaning; the basis of vocal communication among chimpanzees and other animals

Cro-Magnon populations of early modern *Homo sapiens* who lived in western Europe

denticulate a flake tool with toothlike projections along its working edge, probably used for scraping hides or shredding plant foods; also the name of a type of Mousterian assemblage having a high proportion of such tools

Fauresmith a sophisticated form of the Acheulean tool tradition that flourished among archaic *Homo sapiens* in southern Africa

knapper a maker of stone tools

Mousterian the tool tradition associated with the neandertals, usually featuring the prepared core technique; more broadly, the culture of the neandertal peoples

neandertals populations of archaic *Homo sapiens* who lived in Europe and adjacent parts of the Near East during the early Würm glaciation, about 100,000 to 40,000 B.P.

prepared core (Levallois) technique a toolmaking technique that appeared about 100,000 B.P.; it involved flaking a core to a desired shape so that a large flake of predetermined form could be struck off; this flake became the tool

rock shelters shallow, water-formed caves in limestone cliffs where bands of archaic humans often lived

Sangoan a central African tool tradition of which the most typical products are woodworking implements

sedentism a settlement pattern in which the social group lives in a permanent, year-round community

Würm glaciation a series of relatively rapid glacial advances and retreats that lasted from about 75, 000 to 11,000 B.P.

Suggested Readings

BORDES, F. 1968
The Old Stone Age. New York: McGraw-Hill. A discussion of cultural evolution through the Upper Paleolithic with particular emphasis on tool traditions.

HOWELLS, W. W. 1973
The Evolution of the Genus Homo. Reading, Mass.: Addison-Wesley. A concise and very readable account of human paleontology.

SOLECKI, R. S. 1971
Shanidar: The First Flower People. New York: Knopf. An account of the excavation of this important neandertal site.

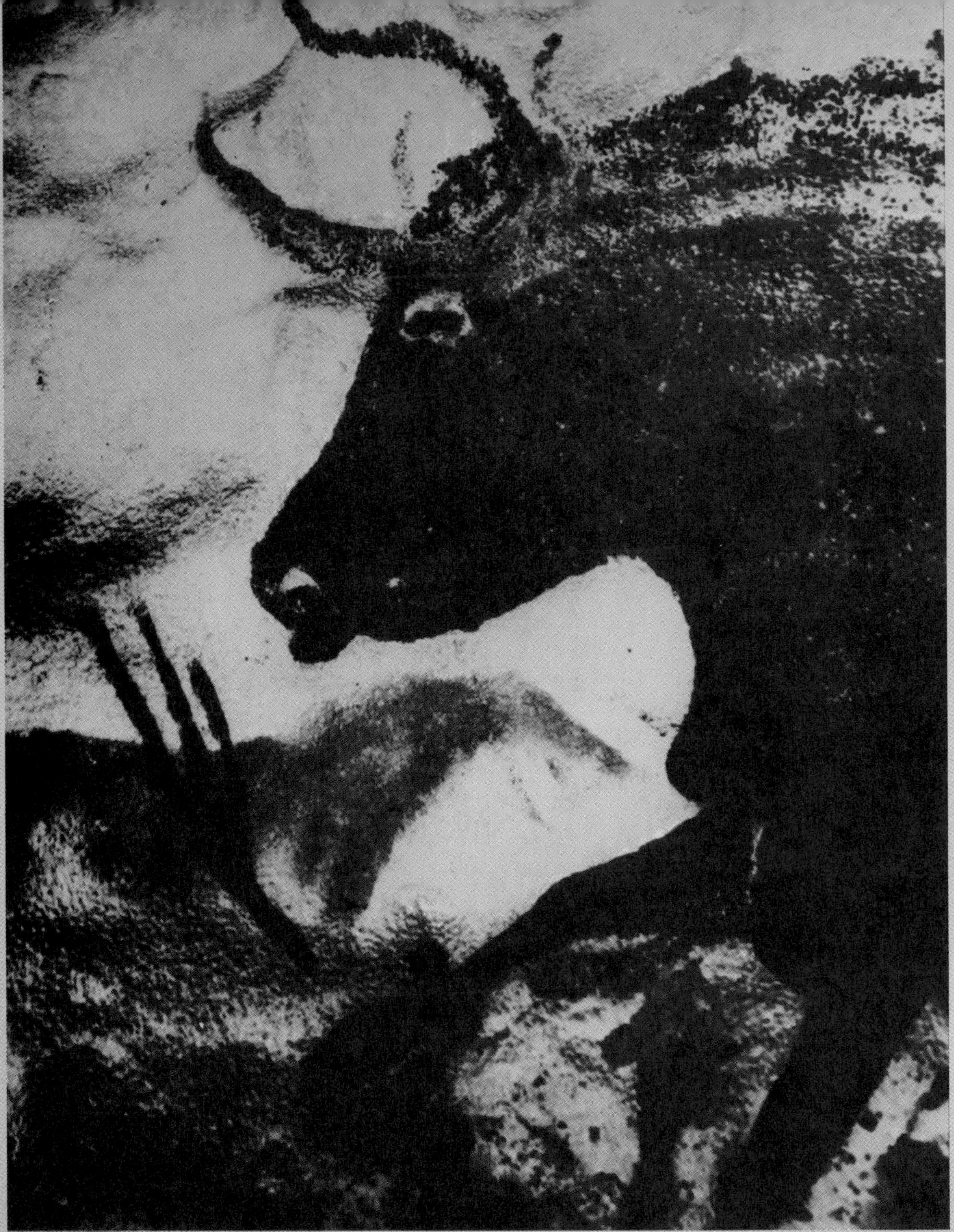

Chapter Eleven

The Evolution of Cultural Diversity

In the last two chapters, we considered the emergence, in the human lineage, of the essentials of the hunting-and-gathering way of life: tools, language, division of labor, complex social organization, and ritual. In this chapter, we will discuss advanced forms of this type of culture, and the new developments that characterize them: more permanent settlements, social boundaries, trade, the first calendars, and the earliest known works of art—as well as tools of unprecedented sophistication.

Underlying these new developments was a trend toward more proficient use of what the environment had to offer. As human populations moved into a greater number of diverse environments, they developed more specialized methods for exploiting their various resources. Although big-game hunting was widespread, each group adapted its hunting methods to the topography and the prey species of its own particular territory. Similarly, each group specialized in certain methods of small-game hunting, fishing, and gathering, depending on the available resources. The natural consequence of this territorial specialization was diversity. From region to region, groups became increasingly different from one another.

Although this pattern of specialization and diversification seems to characterize most if not all areas of the world, we will focus our discussion on Europe and North America, since these areas have been the most carefully studied by archeologists. We will first consider the stage referred to as the *Upper Paleolithic* in Europe (about 40,000–10,000 B.P.) and the *Paleo-Indian* in North America (about 24,000–8,000 B.P.). We will then turn to the *Mesolithic* stage of Europe and the *Archaic* stage of North America (both beginning around 10,000 B.P.).

The Upper Paleolithic period saw the appearance of the first known works of art. This cave painting from Lascaux, France, represents an early artistic tradition; it probably dates from between 35,000 and 17,000 B.P. *(Monkmeyer Press Photo)*

THE ADVANCED HUNTERS OF EUROPE

When we left off our account of cultural evolution in Chapter 10, humans had occupied the rich but demanding habitats of glacial Europe and were becoming increasingly skilled at hunting. In the Upper Paleolithic, this way of life developed ramifications extending far beyond basic survival strategies. We will look first at subsistence and settlement patterns and then at technology and art.

Subsistence and Settlement

During most of the Upper Paleolithic, the climate remained glacial. (In fact, the end of the Würm glaciation coincides with the end of the Upper Paleolithic.) Europe was as cold as in the time of the neandertals—and sometimes considerably colder. When the Würm reached its maximum, about 20,000 B.P., ice covered all of Scandinavia, Scotland, Wales, northern Russia, most of Ireland, northern England, and northwestern Europe. Central Europe stood between two glaciers, a northern one and an alpine one in the mountains of the south. As in the neandertals' time, different areas of Europe had different kinds of vegetation and game. And the human populations of these areas survived by becoming adept at exploiting the relatively narrow range of local resources.

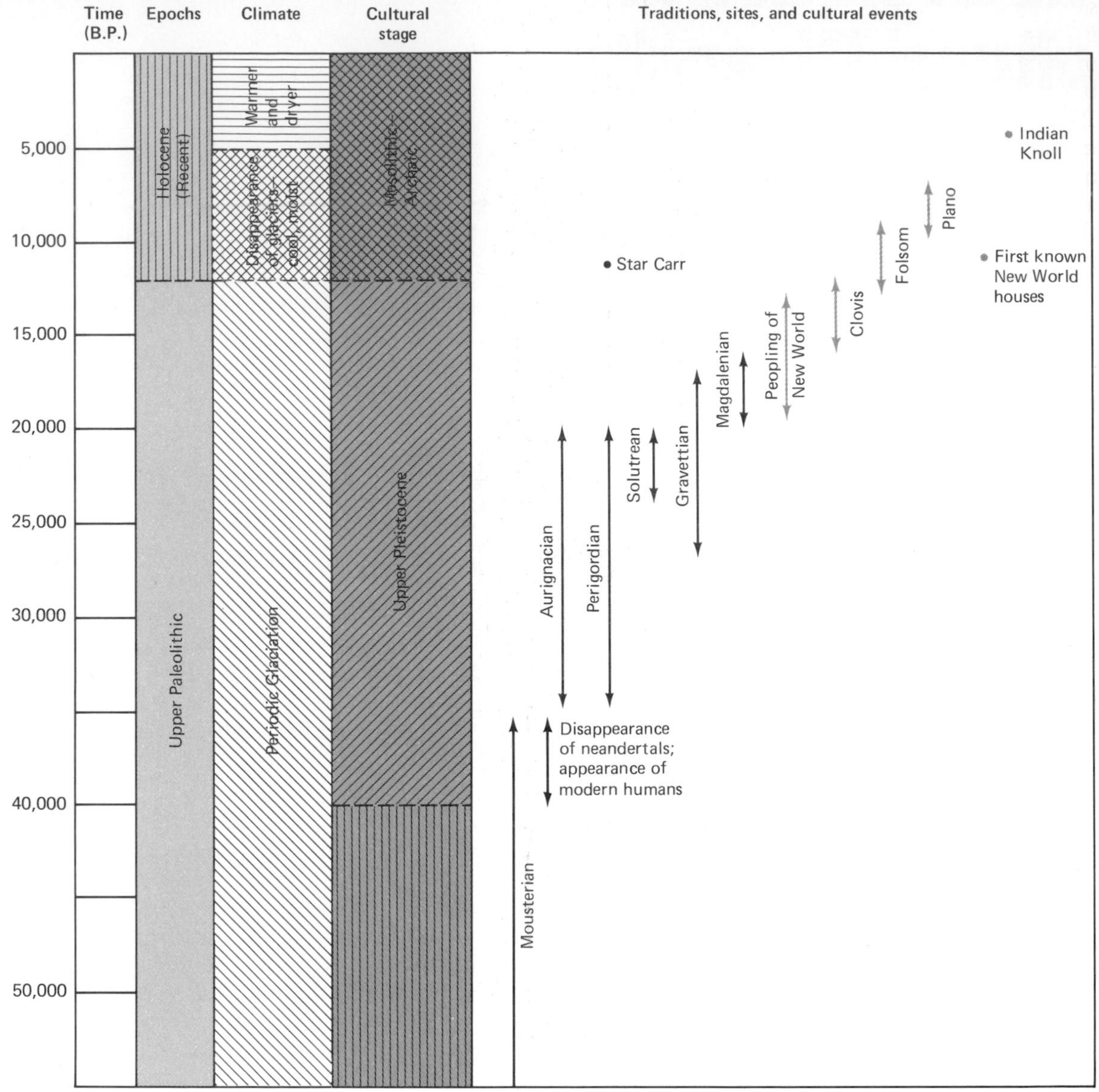

Figure 11-1. Time chart for the Upper Paleolithic and Mesolithic-Archaic stages.

Hunting

The trend toward concentrating on one or two prey species may have begun among populations of archaic *Homo sapiens*, but it became widespread among Upper Paleolithic peoples. In Mousterian sites of central and western Europe, the reindeer territory of the Würm, the bones of reindeer sometimes outnumber those of all other animals. But at some Upper Paleolithic sites of the same region, reindeer bones may account for as much as 90 to 99 percent of the animal bones (Mellars, 1973). In other areas, the pattern is the same; only the species are different. In eastern Europe and central Russia, hunters specialized in mammoth or wild horse; in southern Russia, bison; in Siberia, reindeer or horse (Butzer, 1971). Ibex, ox, and boar were also available, and in different regions may have been the favored quarry. Of course, the hunters took other available game; but they planned their tactics and their tools around the habits of their own special prey.

By specializing, the hunters became more expert. In this period we find the first evidence of two sophisticated group hunting techniques: the *jump kill* and the *surround kill.* In the jump technique, the hunters sneaked up on a herd from a downwind position, so that the animals would not pick up their scent and flee. Then they frightened the animals into a stampede. Other hunters stationed along the herd's flanks directed the stampede toward a high cliff, so that the entire herd fell to its death. At Solutré, France, over 100,000 horse skeletons were found at the bases of cliffs. Clearly, the jump technique could work extremely well. The surround kill is similar to the jump except that the herd is stampeded into a box canyon (that is, a canyon with three sides), where they trample one another or are slaughtered by waiting hunters. Both the jump and the surround almost certainly required more hunters than a single band could supply; several neighboring bands probably joined forces to stampede a herd.

Second, the Upper Paleolithic hunters used tools to make their weapons travel faster and farther. One such tool was the *atlatl,* or spear thrower, a hooked rod containing a groove into which the upper spear shaft fits. The atlatl gave the hunter a more powerful thrust and thus increased the range of the spear and the force of its impact. Eventually the hunters developed an even more efficient weapon-plus-accelerator: the bow and arrow.

The "jump" technique is a group hunting strategy in which part of the hunting group stampedes a herd of animals over a cliff and the rest of the group kills and butchers the wounded and dying animals. Killsites at the base of cliffs containing hundreds of skeletons of butchered bison, horse, and reindeer demonstrate that this technique was common among both New World and Old World Upper Paleolithic groups. *(Courtesy, American Museum of Natural History)*

Aquatic Resources

At the same time that the Upper Paleolithic peoples were becoming better hunters, they were also learning to exploit another important food resource: fish and shellfish. The first evidence of substantial fishing shows up rather suddenly at the end of the Upper Paleolithic. It is doubtful, however, that fishing began either so suddenly or so late. In fact, it probably began during the time of archaic *H. sapiens.* The only signs of fish eating during that period come from the site of Haua Fteah, on the North African shore of the Mediterranean, where mounds of shell were found buried with Mousterian tools dating from 80,000 to 70,000 B.P. (McBurney, 1960). But there are probably thousands of similar sites—all, unfortunately, under water. For the glaciers of the Würm tied up vast amounts of water, causing the sea level to drop very low. When the glaciers melted at the end of the Würm, the major coastal sites, located at the abnormally low sea level, would have been permanently flooded.

By the end of the Upper Paleolithic, however, when the people had already begun to move back with the rising sea level, we see evidence of fishing as a fully developed subsistence strategy. The sites contain not only fish bones, but also elaborate fishing gear—bone fish hooks and beautifully decorated harpoons with barbed sides. Thus while we cannot follow the progress of early *H. sapiens* in learning to fish, we know that he had mastered this skill at least by about 15,000 B.P. We know, too, from the evidence of bones found at Upper Paleolithic sites, that some populations were successfully hunting birds during this period.

Sedentism and Population

Upper Paleolithic peoples, then, were experts in taking advantage of the resources within their own ranges. Two different settlement patterns seem to have resulted from differences in subsistence strategies—seasonal migration and *sedentism* (settling down in one place). Groups that relied on seasonally migrant species, such as the reindeer, had seasonal camps: closed dwellings for fall and winter, and open-air camps for spring and summer. As the herds moved from their summer to their winter grazing lands (and vice versa), the hunters moved with them, returning again and again to the same campsites. Groups that concentrated on animals that were locally abundant throughout the year, such as the mammoth hunters of eastern Europe, stayed in one place year-round, establishing permanent open-air settlements. In addition, both types of groups probably had satellite camps, where small groups went for short periods to do special tasks.

Sedentism is surely one of the main reasons for the dramatic rise in the human population of Europe during the Upper Paleolithic. In sedentary groups, men and women are together more of the time, and therefore more pregnancies occur. There are also fewer deaths, for as we saw earlier, stable base camps give the sick a better chance of recovering. A weak infant can be kept warm by the fire; a sick or injured adult can rest and revive. Perhaps most important is the fact that in a stable base camp food can be stored, thereby evening out seasonal variation in food resources and preventing starvation when hunting is poor (Binford, 1977).

In southwestern France, for example, there are five times as many known Upper Paleolithic sites as known Mousterian ones. One authority estimates that the population of Europe in the late Pleistocene may have been ten times greater than in the Middle Pleistocene (Isaac, 1972).

Social Organization

Not only are there many more sites in the Upper Paleolithic, but some sites are much larger than the Mousterian sites. While most Mousterian camps would have housed about 25 to 30 people—a single band—many of the Upper Paleolithic sites appear to have been occupied by as many as 300 to 500 people (Mellars, 1973). What this suggests is that, like some modern hunter-gatherers, the Upper Paleolithic peoples were organized not only into bands but also into macrobands. That is, several bands that had ties to one another through mate exchange, cooperative hunting, and other communal activities eventually combined their camps into a single large camp. Initially, they may have remained together for only part of the year. Then, in time, the macroband probably became a permanent living group.

Housing

With the growth of sedentism, greater effort was invested in building sturdier shelters. In contrast to the twig huts of Terra Amata and the rock shelters of Mousterian France—both probably rather drafty arrangements—the houses con-

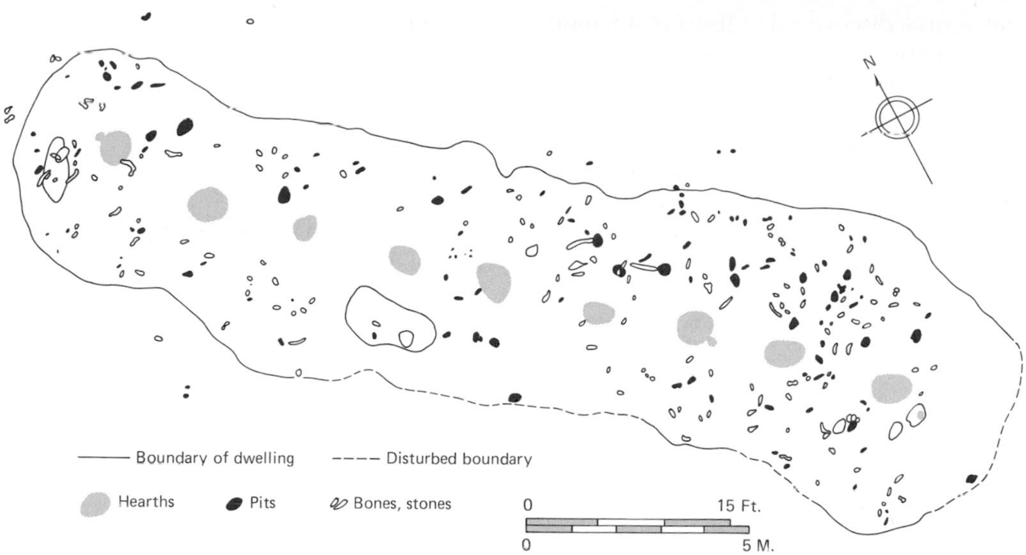

Figure 11-2. The floor plan of an Upper Paleolithic house near Kostenki in the Ukraine (USSR). The people who built this dwelling were mammoth hunters. The house was partly dug out of the ground; most likely it was covered with skins supported by bones or tusks serving as tentpoles. Presumably the many hearths under one roof belonged to different family groups. *(After Klein, 1969)*

structed by the Upper Paleolithic peoples were of solid enough construction so that their remains have survived up to the present.

In southwestern France, the people began improving the rock shelters of the Mousterian stage. In some, the floor is paved with cobbles, while stone walls seem to have been erected to shelter the openings of others. People also made pit houses—by digging a large hole in the floor of the rock shelter and erecting a roof over it. Elsewhere we find the remains of free-standing shelters. In the Dordogne Valley, there are rows of rocks that presumably served to hold down the skin walls of pyramidal tents. And in sites in northern Germany archeologists have found evidence of two kinds of skin tents; possibly, one style was for the winter, the other for the summer (Mellars, 1973).

These examples indicate that styles differed from region to region. With the growth of sedentism, local traditions of house building developed. And as groups expanded and subdivided across Europe and Russia, people with different traditions came to live in closer proximity. A fine illustration of this phenomenon is the group of prehistoric houses near the town of Kostenki in the Ukraine. Here, within a few miles of one another, were roundish roofless huts, pit houses with foundations of mammoth tusk and stone, and long wooden dwellings with hearths running down the middle and partitions to divide the space into semiprivate units. There are also some stylistic differences among the artifacts associated with the different house types (Klein, 1969). What we glimpse here is a cultural situation somewhat akin to converging ethnic neighborhoods in a large American city.

Clothing

Though it seems likely that archaic *Homo sapiens* made clothing, and that different groups probably developed their own "fashions," this is little more than an educated guess. The burial sites of the Upper Paleolithic, however, not only prove that the people wore clothing (and tell us what kind of clothing), they also provide the first real evidence of personal ornamentation. For example, in a grave discovered at the site of Sungir, in northern Russia, a hunter was buried in all his finery—a costume made of hides decorated with bone beads. And though the leather has disintegrated, the hundreds of beads lying in rows across the skeleton allow us to reconstruct the costume: a cap, a tunic, trousers, a short outer coat with an opening in front held shut by ivory pins, and a pair of mocassinlike shoes.

Other sites give evidence of other styles of burial. Thus, in the clothing as in the houses, we see the same pattern: what begins as a specialized method of mastering a particular aspect of the environment (in this case, using the skins of local animals to protect the human body against cold) is elaborated in ways that go beyond the strictly utilitarian and becomes a local tradition—part of the group's identity as a group.

Calendrics

The Upper Paleolithic peoples' mastery of their environment may have included the development of calendrics: the art of keeping track of time. Among the debris in the sites of this period, archeologists have discovered numerous animal bones into which clusters of irregular marks have been scratched. The lack of aesthetic appeal in these objects suggests that they may have served a utilitarian rather than decorative function. Alexander Marshack (1964) argues that they may have been the first notational system, with each mark representing one day and each cluster perhaps representing a lunar month. If this is true, then lunar calendrical systems were being used in Europe and Russia as early as the beginning phases of the Upper Paleolithic—25,000 years earlier than was traditionally believed.

Stone Tools

As subsistence practices became more specialized, so, naturally, did the tools. In the Upper Paleolithic stage in Europe there were many tool traditions as different as the Mousterian and the Acheulean. This wider variety resulted from a combination of advances in technology and an increase in the kinds of raw materials used. Before outlining the traditions, it would be helpful to examine these two types of changes.

Methods: The Blade

The basis of many of the Upper Paleolithic tool forms is the *blade,* a thin, parallel-sided flake whose length is usually more than twice its width. To make blades, the Upper Paleolithic knapper used two techniques—one based on the old direct percussion methods, and a new one called *punch flaking* (Figure 11-2). The knapper first flaked a core into the shape of a rough cylinder or cone with a flat top—the striking platform. The platform could be struck either directly with a hammer, or indirectly, using an intermediate tool called the *punch,* a pointed implement usually made of bone. The purpose of the punch was to direct the force of the hammer blow more precisely. With the core held between the feet or knees (or held by someone else), the knapper positioned the tip of the punch near the edge of the striking platform and hit it with the hammer. This blow removed a narrow sliver—the blade—from the side of the core. The punch was then repositioned and hit again, and another blade fell off. Blades could also be produced by attaching the punch to a piece of wood, positioning it on the striking platform, and then leaning hard on it—a variation called *pressure flaking.* Using either method, the skilled knapper could almost mass-produce his blades simply by moving the punch around the striking platform, removing blade after blade of almost uniform size and shape. It was, as Bordaz has put it, like "the careful unwinding . . . of a rolled sheet of material" (1970:51).

Blades and other flakes were the toolmaker's "blanks." To make a given tool, it was only necessary to retouch a blade or flake in the appropriate way—often by pressure flaking. The knapper placed the tip of a bone punch near the edge of the blade, pressed down at the appropriate angle, and pushed off the flakes—a method that produced a very even, flat tool surface and a sharp edge. This new technique permitted the creation of some of the most exquisite stone tools ever made, the laurel-leaf blades. These delicate

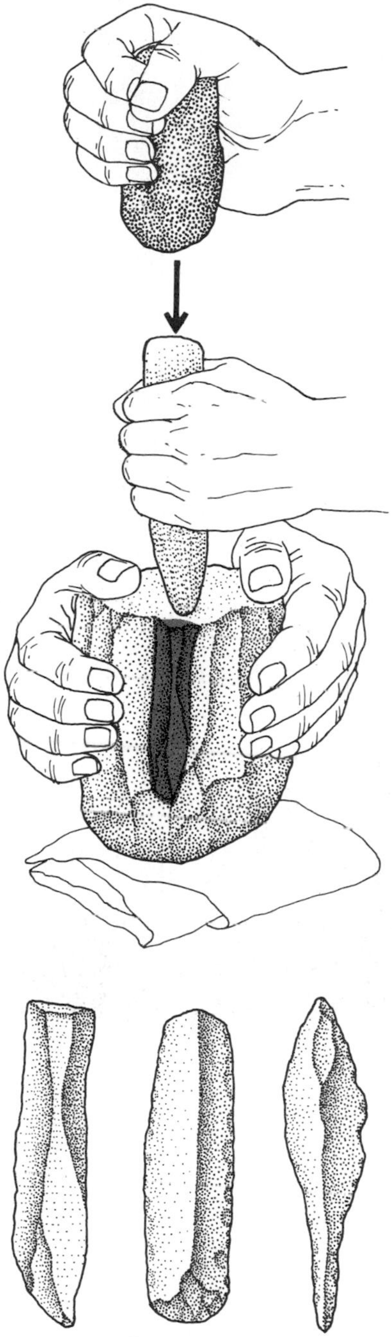

Figure 11-3. The manufacture of chipped stone tools using the blade technique increased both the efficiency and specificity of tool manufacture. More tools could be made from a single core, and the standardized blade form permitted many different kinds of tools to be made with minimal modification. (*Biruta Akerbergs*)

implements, with symmetrical overlapping flakes removed across the short axis, have an almost smooth surface. They are extremely thin—about a half-centimeter (0.2 in.) thick. Some laurel-leaf blades appear so fragile that they are thought to be ritual objects rather than projectile points or knives.

The blade technique was much more efficient than previous modes of stoneworking. The knapper could produce as much as 1,200 centimeters (40 ft.) of cutting edge from a single pound of stone, compared with about 100 centimeters (40 in.) using the techniques of the Mousterian stage. This reflects a vastly accelerated rate of change in the art of toolmaking. The Mousterian toolmaking techniques were about twenty times more efficient than the Oldowan, but this change took about 2 million years. By contrast, the twelvefold increase in efficiency from Mousterian to Upper Paleolithic took only a few thousand years (Butzer, 1971).

Bone-Working: The Burin

One of the most important tools of this stage was the *burin*, a chisel-edged blade used for cutting grooves into wood, antlers, bone, and ivory. Burins, as we saw in Chapter 10, are found in Mousterian assemblages, but it is not until the Upper Paleolithic stage that they were extensively used in toolmaking.

The importance of the burin is that it extended the range of raw materials available for tools. Bone and antler tools were produced during Mousterian times and probably earlier, but they were few in number and clumsily made. They were cut with a hammerstone, and then the final shaping was done by burning and scraping—a tedious and unsatisfactory process. In contrast, the chisel edge of the burin enabled toolmakers to

A selection of Paleolithic tools from several sites in France. Numbers 1, 6, 7, and 10 are burins, used for cutting or engraving such materials as wood and bone; 4, 5, 12, and 13 are points; 8, 9, and 11 are scrapers; 15 is a combination scraper and awl; 2 and 16 are knives; 3 is a laurel leaf blade. (*Collection, Musée de l'homme*)

shape bone, antler, and ivory into various tool forms quickly, easily, and precisely. Because bone and antler are more malleable than stone, yet more durable than wood, it is likely that bone replaced wood for many uses. Clothing and tents were easier to fashion and use with the advent of bone awls, needles, pins, and fasteners. Fishing was aided by bone and antler harpoons and fish hooks. Atlatls too were made of bone and antler.

The burin is significant not only because it opened up new raw materials for tool manufacture but also because it reflects a newly sophisticated way of thinking about tools. For the first time we see people fashioning tools to help them make other tools. Similarly, in the atlatl and the bow, we see people fashioning tools to help them *use* other tools. This is technological specialization raised to the second power. The Upper Paleolithic knappers were not just making new tools, they were working on a new toolmaking principle.

Traditions

Although the new techniques, materials, and principles produced a greater variety of tools, the tool traditions of this stage do not represent a complete departure from the Mousterian. The two earliest traditions of the Upper Paleolithic in Europe—the *Aurignacian* and the *Perigordian*—contain Mousterian-like tools, suggesting a partially shared tradition or parallel technological evolution.

Aurignacian and Perigordian assemblages date from about 35,000 to 20,000 B.P. The earliest Aurignacian sites have been found in southeastern Europe and the Near East, the earliest Perigordian ones in southwestern France and in Spain. The associated animal remains suggest that both these early Upper Paleolithic peoples hunted a wide variety of large herd animals and were not yet as specialized in their hunting as were later groups. Aurignacian tool kits contain an abundance of bone tools, including bone spearheads with a split base for insertion of a handle. Perigordian assemblages, by contrast, contain relatively few bone implements. One characteristic tool form, especially in the early phase, is a knife with a pointed blade and a curved back. The curved back is not an accidental feature; one side of the blade has been deliberately blunted to protect the user from cutting his or her hands.

The *Solutrean* tradition was rather short-lived, for reasons that are not yet known. It apparently flourished only from 24,000 to 20,000 B.P. and was restricted to southwestern France and Spain. Despite its limitations in time and distribution, this tradition is distinguished by magnificent laurel-leaf blades. Bone tools are relatively rare in this group. However, the earliest known bone needle with an eye was found in a late Solutrean assemblage. Hunters of this tradition lived during one of the coldest parts of the glaciation. Not surprisingly, reindeer constituted an important part of their diet.

Contemporary with the Solutrean and the late Aurignacian and Perigordian traditions was the *Gravettian*, which dates from about 27,000 to 17,000 B.P. This tradition seems to be limited primarily to eastern Europe. Like the Perigordian, Gravettian assemblages contain a number of backed blades. Also common are carefully worked ivory tools, a by-product of mammoth hunting. The mammoth had a spectacular pair of curling tusks, sometimes as long as 5 meters (about 16 ft.).

The *Magdalenian* tradition was the last Upper Paleolithic tradition to develop, dating from about 20,000 to 14,000 B.P. Sites are found throughout Europe and contain a greater variety of tools than any other. Included are bone needles and the first harpoons, barbed with fishlike fins. Also prominent are atlatls, sometimes decorated with carved representations of reindeer, bison, horses, fish, and (more rarely) human beings. Finally, the Magdalenian assemblages contain the first *microliths*—tiny segments of blades, about 1 to 3 centimeters (0.4 to 1.2 in.) long. These were either used alone, for fine cutting and scraping, or mounted in bone or antler to make other tools, such as arrows. Reindeer were among the specialties of this group of toolmakers. Once the climate of Europe warmed up, the tundra gave way to forest, and the reindeer became scarce, the Magdalenian tradition came to an end.

A remarkable feature of all these traditions is the standardization of the tools. In an Acheulean or even a Mousterian assemblage, tools of the same type differ greatly from one another. In an Upper Paleolithic site, on the other hand, one can collect a dozen end scrapers that are almost identical to one another. In part, this is a result of using blades as the basis for tools. Percussion flaking allowed the Upper Paleolithic knapper to manufacture uniform blades, and from these blades it was easier to make uniform tools. However, the standardization of the tools also tells us something about the mental qualities of Upper Paleolithic humans. Each tradition contained many tool types, made in many different ways. For toolmakers to master this repertoire so completely as to be able to produce the same end scraper or burin every time—and the same one as the other toolmakers of the band produced—their memories and their ability to plan and persist must have been better developed than those of their Mousterian predecessors.

It is important to note that these traditions are marked by a much greater geographical variability and a much faster rate of change than any preceding tool tradition. From hillside to hillside and from generation to generation, there is considerable diversity. Furthermore, within the individual assemblage there is remarkable variety. The Upper Paleolithic peoples were the stoneworking virtuosos of all time. No group before or since has achieved their versatility, inventiveness, and nearly total control over stone. No metal blade has ever equaled the sharpness of their microliths, and few tools created since can match the aesthetic perfection of the Solutrean laurel leaves.

The Appearance of Art

Not surprisingly, in view of the creativity of their toolmakers, the peoples of Upper Paleolithic Eu-

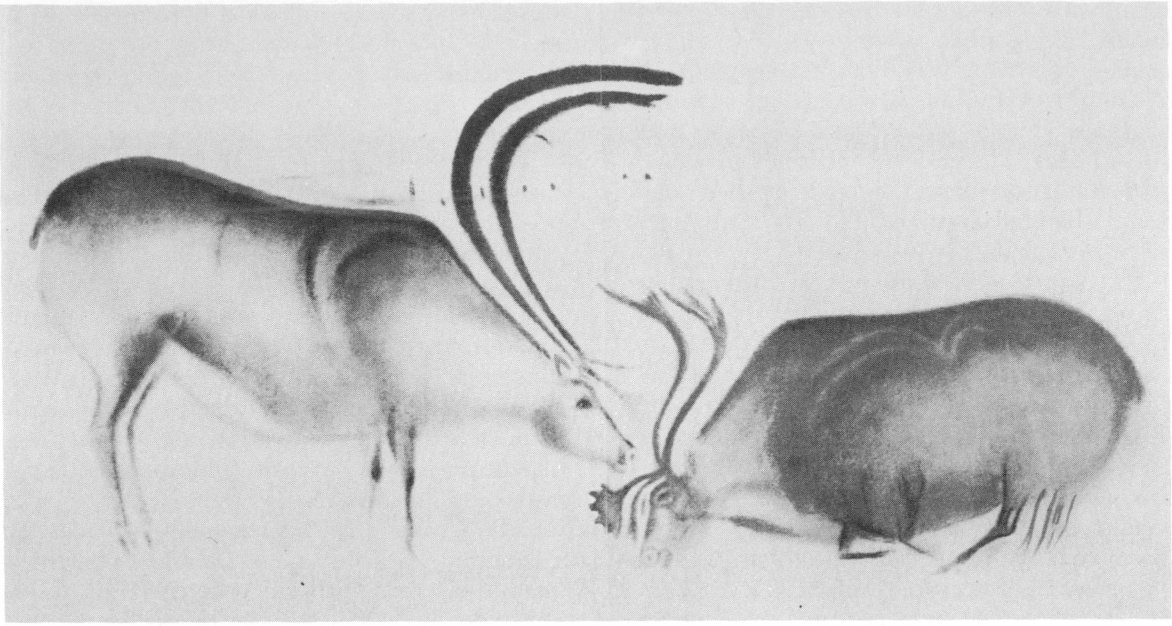

Two reindeer, painted on the wall of an Upper Paleolithic cave at Font-de-Gaume, France. The artist used several colors in rendering these remarkably fluid and graceful images. *(Courtesy, American Museum of Natural History)*

rope are the first known artists in the history of human culture. They embellished their bone and antler tools with decorative carvings; they made small sculptures out of bone and stone; and they adorned the walls of caves with painting, incision (that is, designs scratched into the walls), and bas-relief sculpture. These are the first evidence of human striving to record thoughts, feelings, and events in forms in which they could be seen, pondered, and understood by other humans, whom the artist might never know.

Since walls are less likely than tools or bones to have a datable context, cave art is harder to place in chronological sequence than any other aspect of Upper Paleolithic culture (Fritz, 1969). The most elaborate and refined art was so impressive that for ten years after the first cave paintings were discovered, archeologists refused to believe that they could be as ancient as the Upper Paleolithic. The realism of the figures—even down to the use of perspective—is striking, and their vividness is truly astounding. The walls are filled with bristling life and movement. Horses—in one case, a whole herd of horses—prance across the walls. A herd of deer swim across a river, only their heads showing above the water. A wounded bison, its entrails spilling out, bends over a human figure—presumably gored by his prey.

Behind all this vividness was considerable technical expertise. Some artists used several colors—red, yellow, brown, and black. (These were made by grinding natural pigments, such as ochre, and mixing them with animal grease.) Sometimes, instead of daubing the pigment on the walls, the artists blew it on in a powdered form—a technique that gave soft, rounded contours to the figure. They also selected their surfaces with great care, to complement the figures and add to their realism. In one cave, the painting of a wounded bison has been fitted over a large rounded lump in the wall, so that it juts forward. In addition to painting, the artists engraved the walls, cutting animal figures into the

Dating Techniques

In addition to radiocarbon and potassium-argon dating (Chapter 7), there are several other important methods of dating artifacts. One ingenious technique is *dendrochronology,* a dating method based upon the patterns of tree-ring growth. Some types of trees add one ring a year. The size of the ring depends upon climatic conditions affecting the tree during that year. If rainfall was plentiful, the ring will be thick; if it was not, the ring will be thin. By comparing the tree rings of recently felled trees with a series of increasingly older specimens found at archeological sites, dendrochronologists in the American West have formulated a "master log" of tree-ring patterns extending from the present to 7,000 B.P. If archeologists compare the tree-ring patterns of wood from prehistoric shelters, hearths, roofs, or other artifacts with the master log, they can determine the precise date at which the tree was cut down to make the object. To do so, however, they generally need the entire cross section of the log. Partial cross sections are difficult to date because we do not know if they contain the last rings added prior to the tree's death.

A second dating method is *archeomagnetism,* which is similar in principle to paleomagnetic dating (Chapter 7). This technique is based on the fact that over the centuries the North Pole has continuously shifted its position, moving up and down, north and south, east and west. Therefore at various points in the past the pole has stood in different locations, which archeologists have been able to map and date. These shifts are reflected in clay artifacts, for when clay is heated the iron particles it contains, which resemble tiny magnets, are free to move around, and align themselves with the pole. As the clay cools, they become fixed in this alignment. Thus if we know the exact position of a clay object when it was last heated, we can determine from the alignment of its iron particles what the location of the pole was at that time. By comparing this finding to an historical map of shifts in the pole, we can arrive at an approximate date for the last heating of the artifact. In this way it is possible to date hearths, kilns, and other large clay objects.

A relatively new dating method is *obsidian hydration.* Obsidian is a volcanic glass produced by the rapid cooling of molten lava. It absorbs atmospheric or soil moisture at a constant rate, creating a *hydration layer* (a layer in which the crystalline structure of the rock is saturated with water molecules) beginning at its surface. By measuring the thickness of the hydration layer of an obsidian artifact, archeologists can, in theory at least, date its manufacture. Hydration rates are influenced by such variables as atmospheric temperature, soil temperature, chemical and mineralogical composition, soil chemistry, and solar radiation. Because these factors vary geographically, hydration rates must be determined for each specific geographical region. An obsidian hydration layer does not decompose until at least 100,000 years after the creation of the fresh surface. Thus the hydration method allows us to date objects up to 100,000 years old.

Seriation is an imaginative technique that makes use of the natural popularity cycle of objects to date sites or isolated assemblages of artifacts. Usually, when a new object or style is invented, only a few people experiment with it at first. Gradually more and more people accept it, and its popularity peaks. Then begins the decline: fewer and fewer people use the object, until eventually, it becomes obsolete and disappears from use. Thus in a chronological succession of assemblages we should find examples of an artifact or style gradually increase and then gradually decrease in numbers. On this principle archeologists try to work out chronological successions.

Seriation is a three-step process. The first step divides the artifacts into various types. The next is to calculate the relative popularity of each type within each assemblage. Then the assemblages are arranged so that the frequencies of each type form a popularity curve—a curve that should also represent the chronological order of the assemblages. Unfortunately, however, the seriation method does not enable the archeologist to determine which end of the curve represents the oldest or youngest assemblages.

stone, sometimes sculpting them into bas-relief. Sometimes they also modeled the clay on the floor of a cave.

Explaining Paleolithic Art

These ancient objects and paintings stir the imagination, tantalizing the contemporary viewer with the promise of understanding people dead tens of thousands of years—if only the imagery and intentions could be understood. What moved these people to fill the walls of caves with paintings? The use of art among modern hunter-gatherers provides some possible hints. The African Bushmen, when telling stories of their own or their ancestors' exploits, paint scenes to illustrate the tale. The Australian aborigines use painting as an adjunct to myth telling. For the American Plains Indians, painting a scene was sometimes part of the necessary ritual in seeking a mystical experience. Any or all of these purposes—and many others besides—may underlie Upper Paleolithic art. As Ucko and Rosenfeld point out, "It is very possible . . . that some and perhaps many Paleolithic representations were made for reasons which still totally escape the modern observer" (1967: 238–239).

Magic Though we cannot formulate a single comprehensive interpretation for Upper Paleolithic art, there are nonetheless some striking features that suggest partial interpretations. For instance, why are some works of art found deep inside caves that seem to have been otherwise uninhabited? What brought people into these areas, sometimes through passageways that today are barely big enough for a person holding a torch to squirm through? It seems plausible that these areas were sacred and that the art there was religiously inspired. The majority of the figures are animals, some of which appear to be wounded. The artists may have been working hunting magic, killing an effigy of an animal in hopes that later they would be able to kill the animal itself. Other paintings, as one scholar has suggested, may have been connected with fertility rites. The main purpose may no longer have been to "kill" but to "make" animals—to increase their supply (Janson, 1969).

Since some of the animals are not prey but predators—cave bears, lions, and other animals feared by the hunters—it is most unlikely that the purpose of the drawing was to increase the animals' numbers. Perhaps, by drawing them, the artists were trying to gain some magical protection from them. Or perhaps they were trying to absorb some of the power of these ferocious beasts.

Ideology The most ambitious attempt to explain Paleolithic art was made by André Leroi-Gourhan (1968). From a quantitative analysis of the distributions of various types of human, animal, and geometric figures in the caves, he concluded that the drawings in any particular cave are not a random accumulation of magical symbols but a carefully laid out and highly organized system, representing a belief that nature is controlled by opposed but complementary male and female forces.

According to this theory, the mysterious geometric markings on the cave walls are either phallic or vulvar symbols. These markings are consistently associated with certain animal species, which are themselves sexual symbols. Horses, deer, and ibex, for example, are masculine; bison and oxen are feminine. Leroi-Gourhan claims that the layout of the drawings on the walls carefully segregates and opposes the two sets of symbols. In effect, the caves are like medieval cathedrals, with an elaborate and carefully plotted system of symbolic decoration, reflecting religious beliefs that persisted for centuries. Many other archeologists have found this interpretation unconvincing. Nevertheless, it is possible that male-female symbolism—probably more unconscious than deliberate—may have played a role in at least some Upper Paleolithic art.

Diversity Outside Europe

During the Upper Paleolithic period, human populations spread into almost every corner of the world that was not covered by glaciers. Since Japan was connected to the Asian mainland by a substantial landmass, people had easily and natu-

Upper Paleolithic Artifacts

These sculptures and engravings are examples of the late Upper Paleolithic artistic traditions. Like cave paintings, they are thought to have had both aesthetic and magico-religious functions. The sculpture in the bottom righthand corner, for example, is often referred to as a "Venus" or "mother-goddess" figure and is thought to have been used in fertility rites. The barbed harpoon at upper left below is a very characteristic Upper Paleolithic artifact; the carved barbs were not merely decoration, but served to keep the weapon embedded in the flesh of the prey. (*Courtesy American Museum of Natural History*)

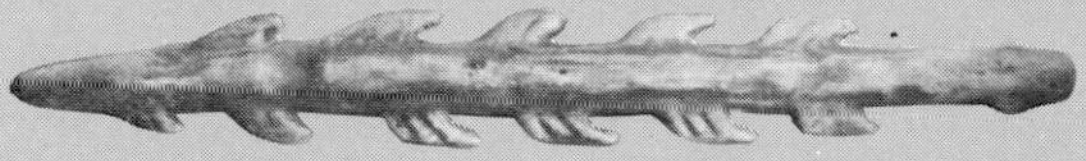

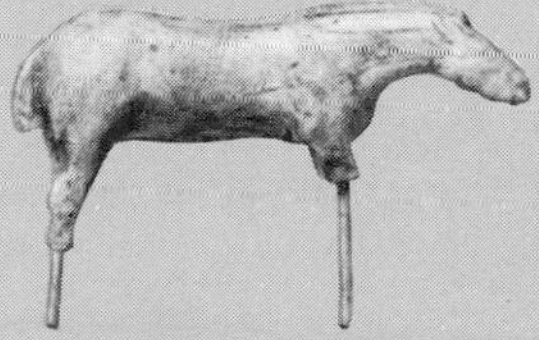

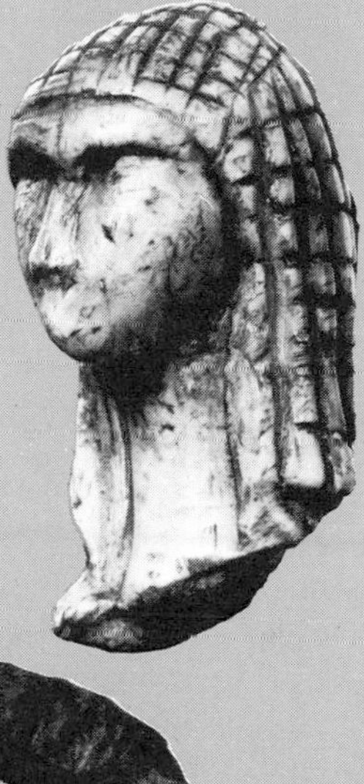

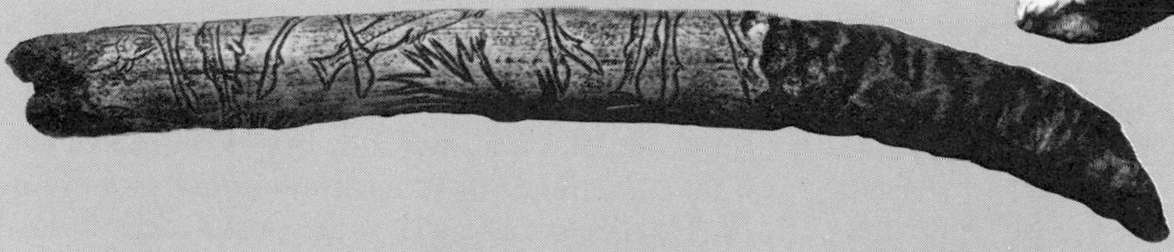

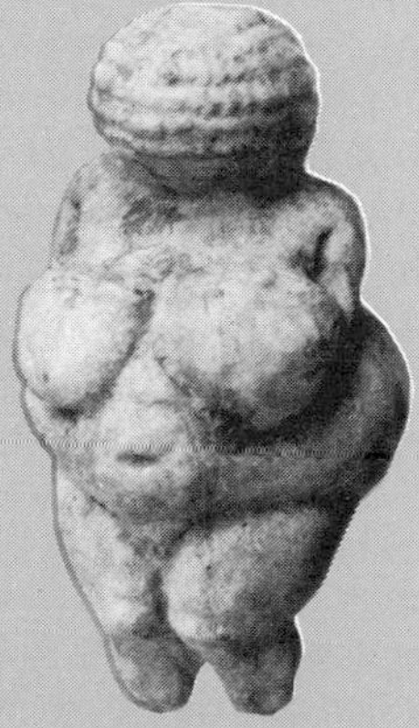

rally moved into this area. Around 30,000 B.P. other populations, crossing a strait from Southeast Asia, finally discovered and colonized Australia. At around the same time the islands of Southeast Asia received their first human inhabitants. Most significant of all, in terms of the amount of land annexed to the human territory, was the move into North and South America, which we will discuss shortly.

Interpreting the evidence from areas other than Europe and America is difficult. For some areas the record is a rich one. For others, there is enough evidence to indicate only that people actually lived there. And many areas remain largely unexplored. In short, it would be dangerous to attempt global generalizations; our knowledge of these regions is probably more a reflection of what archeologists have and have not done than of what ancient populations did or did not do. Nevertheless, in almost all of the areas where remains are plentiful enough to permit interpretation, there is unmistakable evidence of cultural diversity. In Africa, for example, there were eight different tool traditions. Like their European counterparts, they presumably grew up out of specialized subsistence strategies.

There may also be some exceptions to the rule of diversity, such as the peoples of Southeast Asia. Throughout both the Mousterian period and the Upper Paleolithic, the stone tools of this area remain much the same from region to region and are fairly crude. Essentially, they were slightly more sophisticated versions of the pebble-chopper technology. (It is possible, however, that tools made of more perishable materials, the remains of which have not come down to us, evidenced a greater degree of cultural diversity.) Unlike the Europeans, these people did not have to tailor their life styles to the exploitation of a few specific resources; their environment was rich and varied enough to permit a highly generalized subsistence pattern.

Despite such exceptions, however, the hallmark of this period, and of the Mesolithic-Archaic period that was to follow, was a multiplication of different survival strategies and cultural traditions.

THE ADVANCED HUNTERS OF THE NEW WORLD

One measure of the rapidity of population growth during the late Pleistocene is the scale of territorial expansion at this time. The human population of the earth more than doubled its range. The major addition was that of the New World, the vast continents of North and South America. To understand how the expansion to the New World took place, we must imagine the changing geography of the late Pleistocene.

The Route to the New World

As we have seen, the extensive glaciation of the Pleistocene locked up large amounts of water. As sea levels dropped, the landmass across the Bering Strait from northeastern Siberia to northwestern Alaska was reexposed. This connecting link between the Old World and the New World—called Beringia, or the Bering Plain—was definitely not a narrow bridge or isthmus, as was once thought, but an extensive piece of land. During the last glacial maximum, when sea levels dropped 140 meters (460 ft.), the area exposed was 2,000 kilometers (1,243 mi.) wide (Haag, 1973). Geological and biological evidence both suggest that Beringia emerged well before 80,000 B.P. and remained exposed until about 35,000 B.P. A warming trend occurred about then, and several subsequent times, each time flooding the land. The area was last exposed around 11,000 B.P. Soon after, it was submerged once more by the rising sea levels of the postglacial period.

The land bridge, along with the regions of Siberia and Alaska to which it was connected, was not a sterile, salty desert or an ice-covered plain, but a mosaic of tundra, marsh, and grassland that supported large herds of mammoths, reindeer, musk-oxen, horses, bison, and other animals. In fact, Beringia appears to have been a better hunting ground than present-day Alaska (Butzer, 1971). Thus a passable route—and one that had sufficient game to beckon the hunters onward—appears to have been open during much of the late Pleistocene. Even during the warm periods, when the straits were covered by sea, they were probably navigable in hide boats that the hunters could have been making by this stage. The modern hunter-gatherers who live in this region canoe across the Bering Strait with great ease.

But how did the groups disperse from Beringia into the rest of the New World, when southern Alaska, western and eastern Canada, and the northwestern United States were covered by ice

Figure 11-4. During the last glaciation, much of the northern part of this continent was covered with ice. A land bridge, however, existed at times across what is now the Bering Strait between Siberia and Alaska. The human populations that crossed this Bering Plain dispersed south via an ice-free corridor. *(After Hester, 1966, Haynes, 1973, and Jennings, 1974)*

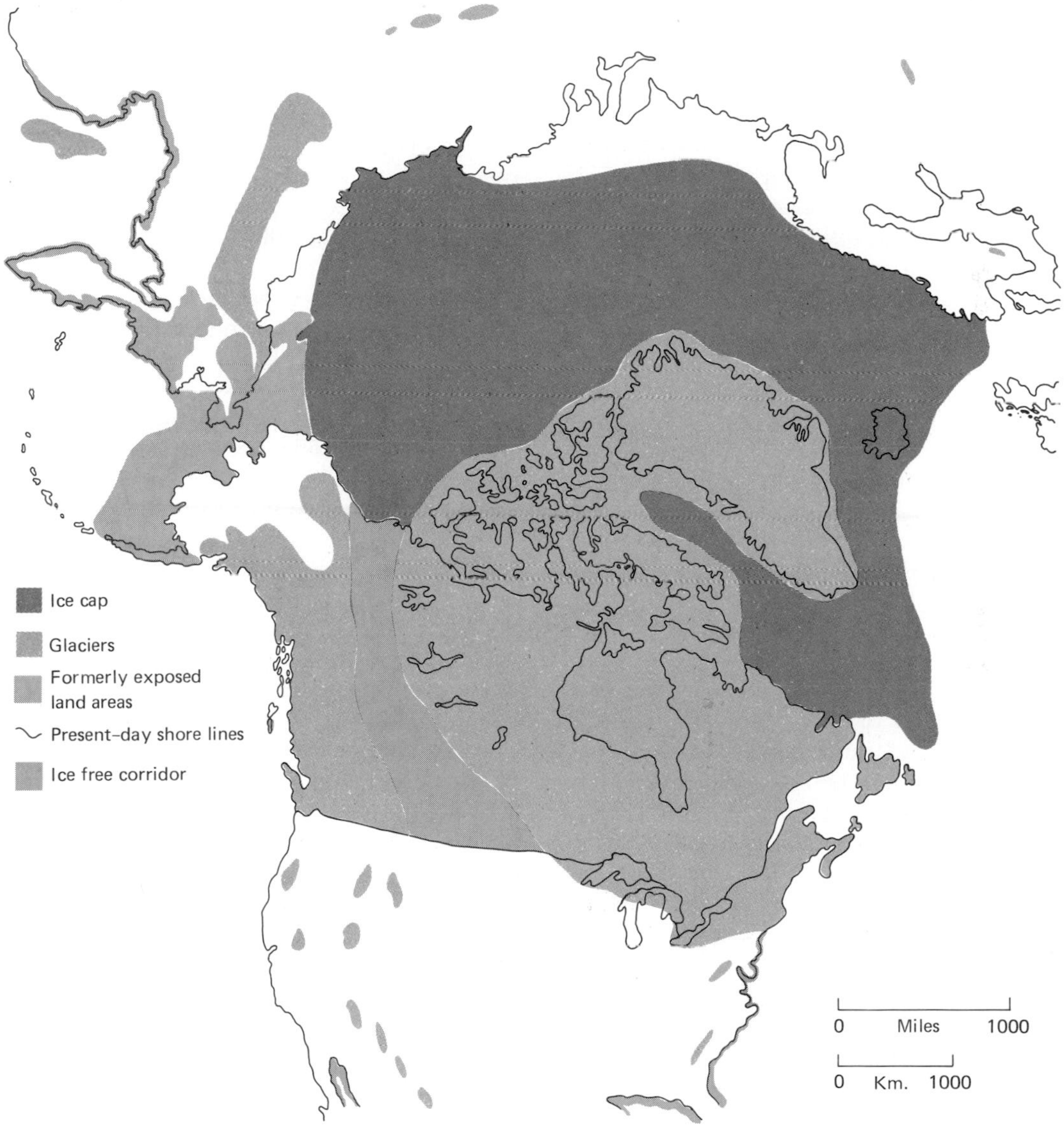

sheets? A coastal route is out of the question. Ice covered both the Pacific and the upper Atlantic coasts. It appears that the only possible route from Beringia into the rest of North America was through an ice-free corridor between the two ice sheets covering the northern part of the continent. Such a corridor, through the eastern foothill region of the Rocky Mountains, was probably open throughout much (if not all) of the late Pleistocene. During most of the period, the corridor was covered with forest-tundra and grassland that supported large herds of game on which the immigrants could feed.

Thus, both a route and a subsistence base existed for passage from Siberia, across Beringia, and down the foothills of the Rockies. Unfortunately, most of the remains the presumed immigrants left behind as they crossed into the New World lie today beneath the waters of the Bering Sea, under tons of sediment deposited by the melting of the glaciers at the end of the Pleistocene epoch. A few sites in Alaska, however, do provide evidence of their passage. Moreover, the tools of Upper Paleolithic groups in North America resemble those in Siberia—both include a bone industry and a stoneworking industry based upon the core blade tradition. The animal remains associated with the tools demonstrate that the two groups also shared the same subsistence strategy: specialized hunting of big game, including mammoths.

Dating the Arrival

Exactly when people began to arrive in the New World is a question that still stirs great debate. Archeologists have traditionally assumed that migrants did not come before about 12,000 B.P. But some archeologists now argue for an earlier date—as much as a half million years ago—on the basis of evidence from a few sites. One of these is Calico Hills, near Yermo, California, which yielded objects identified as crude scrapers, flakes, and bifaces in a stratum dated to between 500,000 and 250,000 years ago. The stratum also contained exotic materials like jasper, moss agate, and quartz, and a circle of stone thought to be a hearth.

These early "finds," however, may be explained in other ways. Many archeologists consider that, in view of their extreme crudeness and sparse numbers, the so-called artifacts could easily be geofacts—stone forms produced by such normal geological processes as weathering, erosion, glacial activity, and abrasion by water and rock. It is also possible that the "exotic" materials thought to have been carried to the site by early humans could actually be of local origin.

Similar questions have been raised about other sites that have been dated very early. For example, many North American sites contain tools of a "*preprojectile* tradition." That is, the assemblages lack projectile points such as spearheads or arrowheads, consisting instead mainly of very crude choppers and scrapers. Because of the primitive quality of the tools, such sites are thought to be well over 12,000 years old—perhaps as much as 100,000 years old. Yet almost all these sites in North America are surface finds without overlying strata to confirm the dating. Furthermore, equally crude artifacts have been found in stratified cultural assemblages spanning a range from 3,000 to 600 B.P., so crudeness does not necessarily prove great antiquity.

Nevertheless, some sites, especially in Central and South America, have yielded more convincing evidence of relatively early occupation of the New World. In the Valsequillo region near Puebla, Mexico, artifacts associated with extinct animal remains have been radiocarbon-dated to 22,000 and 24,000 B.P. (Irwin-Williams, 1968). Caves near Ayacucho, Peru, have yielded a stratified cultural sequence that is thought to extend back as far as 22,000 B.P. (MacNeish, 1973). The lowest level in this sequence contains the bones of extinct ground sloths and an assemblage of choppers and scrapers similar to the debated North American surface finds. Thus is seems quite likely that human beings were living in Central and South America as early as 24,000 B.P. And if so, they may have crossed the Bering Strait several thousand years earlier.

Mass Migration or Gradual Expansion?

How long did the occupation of the New World take, from the time of crossing to the time South

America was settled? The answer depends on whether the process is seen as a deliberate take-over of new territories or as a gradual expansion of old territories. As Americans, our thinking about the late Pleistocene immigration to the New World is apt to be shaped by our own national experience. When white settlers came to America, they came to what they knew was a New World; they spread westward purposefully and rapidly, and in a few centuries the entire continent was populated by the newcomers. It would be foolish, however, to envision the Siberian bands in the same way. They had no awareness that they were in the process of peopling a continent. And while the white settlers had political and religious reasons for striking out into remote new lands, the late Pleistocene immigrants were probably motivated by nothing more than a desire for somewhat better hunting with somewhat less competition—a desire that could probably have been satisfied by transferring the camp to the other side of the valley. Furthermore, simply in practical terms, mass migration would have been extremely difficult. These people had no horses or wagons and could not accumulate much surplus food. They survived by exploiting to the fullest what was at hand.

Thus it seems likely that the occupation of the New World was the result not of a deliberate mass migration but of a gradual territorial expansion by bands enlarging in numbers on the fringes of inhabited regions. On the basis of a given rate of population growth and a given resource requirement per person, Martin Wobst (1974) calculates that even if the initial group was as small as twenty-five people (and it could easily have been larger), it would have taken the descendants of this group only 3,000 years to expand their territory to the point where they inhabited the entire New World. In doing so, their maximum rate of expansion would have been only 5 kilometers (3 mi.) a year at the population fronts. Although such precise arithmetic should be taken with a grain of salt, the general picture is probably accurate. Groups simply ranged a bit farther in search of food than they had before and mile by mile made their way across Beringia, down a corridor between the two glacier systems of North America, and into a whole new continent—without ever conceiving of it as a whole new continent.

North America in Paleolithic Times

The terrain into which these people moved was very different from the North America that we know (Butzer, 1971). Vast tracts of land were covered by dense forests of spruce and pine. The Midwest was probably a mixture of forest with meadows and grassland; the southwestern United States, which today is desert and scrub, was also largely forest dotted with meadows. Throughout the West, there were very large lakes. These woods and lakes indicate that the Southwest was moister than it is today and able to support a large animal population. Herds of reindeer, elk, musk-oxen, mammoths, mastodons, bison, and antelope roamed across much of the country.

About 11,000 years ago, as the glaciers began to recede, all of this changed. The climate became warmer and drier, grazing animals became more scarce, and the forests thinned out. Most of our evidence of human activity dates from after the glacial recession.

The Paleo-Indian Way of Life in North America

Hunting

Like the Upper Paleolithic peoples of Europe, the North American peoples were specialized and highly expert hunters. Their hunting techniques are better documented than those of the European groups. Indeed, in some cases, we can even reconstruct the direction of the wind on the day of the hunt (Wheat, 1973). Most important, we know that these people were big-game hunters and that, like the peoples of Europe, they probably specialized in certain prey species.

The Clovis Hunters The people of the *Clovis* tradition (also called the Llano tradition) flourished throughout much of North America, from the Southwest to Nova Scotia, during the

Understanding Past Environments

To understand the cultural processes that took place in a prehistoric society, we must be able to reconstruct the environmental context in which that society existed—the climate and the plant and animal life of the area. Archeologists use several techniques to study these factors.

Perhaps the most important method is the *analysis of floral and faunal remains.* Plant and animal fossils at a prehistoric human site are our best hint as to the subsistence strategy of its inhabitants. And fossils—whether or not they are found at human sites—can reveal a great deal about ancient climates. The analysis of plant remains in sediments from the ocean floors has helped us to reconstruct global climatic conditions during prehistoric eras. Certain fauna are equally useful indicators of paleoclimate. The barren-ground caribou and the musk-ox, for example, are today found only in tundra regions and other zones with cold climates. Thus, when archeologists find caribou or musk-ox remains in sites far from the present range of these species, they infer that the area was once very cold and was covered with tundra or perhaps spruce woodland vegetation.

There are problems with such analyses, however. For one thing, if a site is located in a mountain and valley region where vertical ecological zones may be very different, data are difficult to rely on. Moreover, this approach assumes that the ecological adaptations of the various species have remained constant throughout history and prehistory—which may not always be the case. A final difficulty is that the fossils at a site may reflect only the specialization of the group that used the site, rather than the total number of species present in the region or their relative abundance. Nevertheless, despite these limitations, analysis of plant and animal remains has aided our understanding of almost every site we discuss in this book.

Palynology, the study of pollen, has proved another valuable means of reconstructing past environments. Most wind-pollinated trees and grasses produce large amounts of pollen, and pollen grains have a waxy outer coating that makes them almost indestructible. Thus grains will often be preserved as fossil pollen for long periods of time. Furthermore, since the pollen grains of various plants differ greatly in size and shape, they are usually easy to identify by genus, and often by species as well. Thus, an analysis of the prehistoric pollen grains found within or near a site gives archeologists information about the type of vegetation prevailing at the time the site was inhabited, which in turn tells us a good deal about the climate.

However, pollen analysis too has its difficulties. Pollen grains may be transported long distances by wind or streams, and thus may end up in an assemblage miles away from where they were produced. In addition, certain species may be over- or under-represented in pollen assemblages because of differences in the amount of pollen they produce, or its susceptibility to wind transport, or its resistance to decay. Environmental conditions may also affect the preservation of pollen. All these possibilities have to be taken into account in the analysis of pollen assemblages.

Soil analysis is a third method. Various characteristics of modern soils can be associated with particular conditions of temperature, rainfall, and radiation. Since we know the climatic conditions under which modern soils have been formed, we can infer what conditions were like when prehistoric soil layers were formed by matching their characteristics to those of modern soils. Soil analysis can also offer some clues about the vegetation cover of a region, which helps archeologists to understand what resources were available to the inhabitants. Much of what we know about the environment for the time periods discussed in Chapters 9, 10, and 11 is derived from soil analysis.

In certain regions much can also be discovered through *dendroclimatology:* the study of past climatic conditions by tree-ring analysis (see the box "Dating Techniques," on p. 283). What makes tree rings useful in reconstructing past environments is that the width of a tree ring is directly related to the amount of rain that fell during the year when it was formed. This fact has allowed archeologists to establish decade-by-decade rainfall maps for the American Southwest going back to 1350 B.P.

period from 14,000 to 12,000 B.P. Sites of Clovis tradition hunters are usually located near bogs or marshes; they contain artifacts made of materials whose source was as much as 160 to 320 kilometers (100 to 200 mi.) away, suggesting a large territorial range. Both site location and range size may be adaptations to the behavior of the animals that they hunted, such as the mammoth.

Mammoths, of course, are extinct, so knowledge of their behavior must come from examining fossils and drawing analogies with living species—especially the African elephant, which resembles the mammoth anatomically and inhabits a similar environment (Gorman, 1972). African elephants eat and drink enormous amounts in a day—about 45 kilograms (99 lb.) of food and 133 liters (35 gal.) of water. This means that they have to travel as much as 24 to 40 kilometers (15 to 25 mi.) a day going from feeding spot to feeding spot. If the North American mammoths ranged a comparable distance in order to find food, this would explain the large territories of the early New World hunters.

The modern elephant may also provide some insight into the hunting strategies of the Clovis peoples. When attacked, even by guns, elephants are seldom brought down at once. They charge their attacker and then flee, usually to the closest water hole or river. If mammoths also behaved in this way, it would not have been possible for Clovis hunters to stalk the herd and quickly slaughter several animals. The most feasible hunting strategy would have been to ambush an animal along the route to one of its favored feeding areas but far from water, so that after the initial attack the wounded mammoth would wear itself out traveling to the nearest water source. There the hunters could have dispatched it easily. Such a hunting strategy would help explain why the Clovis sites tend to be near bogs. In one such ancient bog, at the Union Pacific mammoth killsite in Wyoming, the crushed bones of a mammoth lie surrounded by large boulders. Apparently, the hunters stoned the animal to death once they had it trapped there. No doubt other large game was hunted in a similar way.

The Folsom and Plano Hunters The *Folsom* tradition flourished in the West between 13,000 and 9,000 B.P. Sites of the *Plano* tradition are found from the Rockies to the Atlantic and from Mexico to Canada; they date from 10,000 to 7,000 B.P. Folsom hunters specialized in the now extinct long-horned bison, which probably behaved much like modern bison. Modern bison have a very good sense of smell but poor eyesight, so hunters can easily close in on a herd as long as they approach from downwind. When frightened, the herd closes ranks and flees blindly. Folsom groups took advantage of this behavioral trait by introducing into the Paleo-Indian hunting repertoire two techniques that we have already noted in Upper Paleolithic Europe—the jump kill and the surround kill. Many of the Folsom killsites are located at the base of cliffs, over which the hunters drove whole herds. In other cases, they stampeded the bison into box canyons, arroyos (small canyons with dirt sides), or even corrals of their own making. Once trapped in these enclosures, the bison could be easily slaughtered. The Plano hunters used similar techniques with modern bison as their chief quarry. At the Plainview site in Texas, hundreds of modern bison skeletons, along with Plano tools, were excavated from the base of a cliff over which they had apparently been stampeded. At the Olsen-Chubbuck site in eastern Colorado, about 200 modern bison had been stampeded into an arroyo trap.

Campsites were evidently also selected with bison in mind. Camps were usually located on ridges overlooking bison grazing areas adjacent to water holes, so that the hunters' homes served also as their lookout stations (Judge and Dawson, 1972). Moreover, most camps were no more than a kilometer (about 1,000 yd.) from some topographical "trap" such as a cliff, an arroyo, or a box canyon.

Gathering

While many aspects of the Paleo-Indians' lives were tailored to the hunt, this does not mean that they subsisted on meat alone. On the contrary, there is reason to believe that they were as dependent on plant foods as on game. As usual, the evidence of gathering is scanty. While the heavy, durable bones of the big game have lasted through the millennia, most of the vegetable remains have long since deteriorated. Furthermore, many of these sites were excavated years ago, before the more sophisticated techniques for detecting plant life remains, such as flotation and pollen analysis, were developed. Nevertheless, there are some sites in southern Arizona and other parts of the New World that present a fairly convincing case for a Paleo-Indian hunting-*and*-gathering economy.

In the Arizona region, for example, the early sites fall into two groups: (1) Paleo-Indian killsites, where large animals were butchered, and (2) sites with ground stone tools for woodworking and for grinding and shredding plant foods. Associated faunal remains and radiocarbon dates indicate that the two types of sites were contemporary. Significantly, the two are located in different environmental zones (Duncan, 1972). The killsites are concentrated in a brush and woodland environment where game could browse. The ground stone tool sites, on the other hand, are generally situated in grasslands, an important source of plant foods. The most logical conclusion is that the two contemporary site complexes were seasonal camps within a single Paleo-Indian settlement system revolving around both hunting and gathering.

The Problem of the Extinctions

At the end of the Pleistocene epoch many animals became extinct. Although the fossil record is full of species no longer in existence, the number of animals that disappeared during this period, and the rapidity of their disappearance, constitutes a unique phenomenon. In the 2 million years prior to this period, only thirteen North American genera became extinct; in the next 17,000 years, thirty-five genera were to meet their end in North America.[1] Fully three-quarters of the mammalian genera disappeared (Briuer, 1970). Among the species that died out were almost all the Paleo-Indians' quarry. All the mammoths and mastodons, all the camels and horses, and all but one species of bison became extinct within a few thousand years of one another. The vast herds shrank and then disappeared entirely.

In the opinion of some anthropologists, these animals became extinct precisely *because* they were the quarry of the Paleo-Indians. According to this view, called the "overkill" theory, the human hunters, because of their cunning, had reached the point at which they were no longer one predator among many but a dominant force in the environment. Against this invasion of highly skilled hunters, the big-game animals of the New World—given almost no time to adapt—did not stand a chance.

Nevertheless, the overkill theory has several flaws. First, a number of species that were *not* human prey—birds, for instance—also became extinct at this time. Second, some of the extinctions seem to have occurred before humans arrived. Finally, if the species were not initially adapted to human predators, the extinctions should have become less frequent in later periods as species started to adapt to the new danger. Instead, the evidence indicates that more extinctions occurred in the later part of the period than in the earlier part.

Perhaps, then, climatic changes were to blame, since the extinctions occurred during the changeover from glacial to postglacial conditions. One theory is that with the shift from colder to warmer and from moister to drier conditions, the vegetation underwent desiccation (that is, drying up), habitats shrank, and the animals succumbed to mass starvation.

However, there are several problems with this theory too. First, since the species in question survived the general climatic changes of previous glaciations, they should not have been wiped out by similar changes at the end of the Würm. During periods of climatic stress, animals are known to migrate to more suitable regions. Such migrations had probably saved these animals during earlier warming trends and should have

[1] Although this discussion draws chiefly on evidence from North America, there were comparable extinctions in the Old World as well.

done the same this time. Second, the extinctions included animals with very diverse ecological adaptations—grazers and browsers, animals adapted to open country, to parklands, to forests. It seems highly improbable that the generalized changes could have adversely affected the food sources, habitat, or range of *all* of these various animals.

Finally, ecological studies demonstrate that desiccation rarely results in mass starvation. During such periods, smaller members of a species and those with lower growth rates—in other words, those that require less food—are likely to survive, changing the composition of that population in such a way that it becomes better adapted for the harsher conditions. Thus, the generalized change theory appears to be oversimplified. However, analyses do demonstrate that progressive reduction in size did occur in many late Pleistocene animal species, so that desiccation may have been at least a factor in the extinctions.

Rather than citing generalized climatic changes, a second group of environmental theorists believe that the fatal element was decreased *equability*—that is, a reduction in the stability of the temperature throughout the year. About 10,000 B.P., seasonal contrasts in both Europe and North America became more pronounced. Since the young are more vulnerable to extremes, mammals with long gestation periods, small litters, and a fixed birth season would have been most likely to lose entire generations (which they could not rapidly replace) and to become extinct. Larger mammals today have such characteristics, and the larger mammals of the late Pleistocene were the ones that became extinct (Briuer, 1970). In short, the available evidence suggests that decreased equability was the key factor in the late Pleistocene mammalian extinctions.

But equability was probably not the sole factor. In order to understand the extinction process, we should see it as a feedback situation in which environment and hunting practices interacted to reduce and finally eradicate certain animal populations unable to adapt quickly enough to the changing surroundings. Perhaps if the new wave of cunning human predators had not coincided with greater climatic stress, many genera might have escaped extinction.

MESOLITHIC AND ARCHAIC STAGES

About 10,000 years ago, new adaptations that mark the *Mesolithic* stage in Europe and the *Archaic* stage in North America began to appear. The most striking feature of this period is *diversification.* Whereas earlier groups specialized somewhat narrowly, the typical group of this time became more versatile, by combining *several* specialized subsistence strategies into a broad, diversified strategy. The forces behind this development were the climatic changes and the extinction of the herds at the end of the Pleistocene.

The disappearance of the mammoth and bison, along with the changes that the climate caused in the vegetation, could not have left human groups unaffected. Imagine the impact on our society if cattle and pigs gradually disappeared and the grain belt turned into forest. This would probably be enough to plunge us into a new Dark Age. But band societies were more resilient. With the catastrophic changes in their environment, the peoples of this time did abandon cave art, and their camps shrank in size; but their culture by no means collapsed. In fact, on certain fronts there were significant cultural developments: an even greater diversity of tools, more intensive foraging, and, later on, more sedentary settlements and the development of trade networks. Thus the focus of cultural evolution simply shifted. In the preceding period, the major changes were primarily in technology and art; now it appears that the subsistence strategy, the settlement pattern, and the social organization underwent the most important changes.

The Impact on Population

A shrinking food supply would have been likely to halt the growth, and perhaps even cut back the size, of human populations. It is possible that this did happen in the early Mesolithic-Archaic period. Known sites from this time are much smaller than Upper Paleolithic sites, which indicates that they had fewer occupants.

Yet smaller sites do not *necessarily* mean that the human population was smaller. It may simply mean that people lived in smaller groups. While the known Mesolithic-Archaic sites are small, they greatly outnumber those of the Upper Paleolithic stage. Moreover, there were probably many other sites that are not known. The Mesolithic peoples occupied open-air camps, which are more likely to be destroyed—and even if not destroyed, are more difficult to find—than the caves and rock shelters in which the Upper Paleolithic groups lived. The small size of the Mesolithic sites, some of which contain only a few artifacts, makes their discovery even more difficult. For these reasons, it seems safer to assume that the Mesolithic-Archaic population probably did *not* shrink. Indeed, it may even have grown, despite the postglacial environmental crises (McManamon, 1974).

Seasonal Subsistence Strategies

Individual Mesolithic-Archaic sites tend to be even more narrowly specialized than Upper Paleolithic sites. But such specialization was only a part of the adaptation to the new conditions of the postglacial period. Since the climate had become less equable, people could no longer count on an even seasonal distribution of diverse plants and animals. In one season a given hillside or riverbank might be an excellent source of food; in the next season it might be bare. Thus groups tended to spend different parts of the year at different camps and to exploit a distinct set of resources at each camp. Overall, therefore, the resource base was diversified.

The Shoshone of the Reese River valley in what is now Nevada provide an excellent example of this seasonal subsistence strategy (Thomas, 1974). By 4,500 B.P., these peoples had a summer camp and a winter camp, from which groups would leave to hunt or gather. The area they inhabited contained several zones of vegetation: the woodlands along the river, the sagebrush-grassland valley floor, the piñon-juniper forest on the mountainside, the higher-elevation sagebrush zone, and the virtually barren mountaintops. In the sagebrush-grassland area, close to water, were small habitation camps where plants were gathered and processed and small-game animals like rabbits and rodents were hunted. These were probably the summer settlements, as most plants of this zone matured then.

At the foot of the mountain were larger habitation camps, from which forays could be made into the valley floor and the forests. These were the winter camps, where the people gathered piñon nuts, worked hides, and made clothing. There were more specialized sites as well: seed-collecting camps, scattered with seed knives and grinding tools, and killsites with weapons and butchering equipment. These special-purpose sites were probably occupied for a very short time by small task groups from the summer and winter central camps. In sum, the Shoshone had a double-based seasonal settlement system, with summer and winter camps located where food was most plentiful in those seasons and smaller satellite camps devoted to special tasks. (To this day the Shoshone have the same system, although they now get around in cars rather than on foot.)

The pattern of change during the Archaic period is perhaps best documented by evidence from the eastern half of North America. Many aspects of subsistence and settlement patterns in the area have been described by Ford (1974, 1977). He found that the earliest sites all seem to have been very temporary. With time, however, there developed a trend toward more and more permanent base camps. Among the later sites there are both upland camps and ones close to rivers. Some of these were evidently occupied by people exploiting the mollusks living in the waters, to judge by the immense piles of shells found at the sites. Other camps were probably used by people exploiting the plants that grew close to the riverbanks.

There were also important changes in the nature of the food resources exploited by the Archaic peoples. At first, deer and hickory nuts seem to have been the dietary staples for groups living in the Midwest. In coastal areas, shellfish and, probably, fish were heavily exploited—at least when the sea level was such as to make them available (Braun, 1974). With time, the resource base became more diversified. For example, a greater variety of nuts were eaten. There is also evidence of an increasingly heavy reliance on seeds, and of some experimentation with their domestication.

Duncan (1972) has suggested that a common factor underlies such changes in all parts of North America: the decreasing equability of the climate at the end of the Pleistocene, mentioned previously. An initial response to increased seasonal and annual variation in the availability of resources was more movement, to be where resources were available at the time they were available. Later, there evolved a pattern focused on one or more base camps, minimizing the movement necessary to obtain seasonal resources.

Nevertheless, diversification continued. Ford suggests a reason for this continuation: population increase. With more people, boundaries would have had to be more sharply defined. Resources, however, do not respect human territorial boundaries. Hickory trees rarely produce nuts in the same locality in consecutive years; deer can range over a very wide area. One way to hedge against the possibility that the primary resource may be scarce in any given year is to broaden the subsistence base—to rely more on other food sources such as seeds or different sorts of nuts. An alternative course is to enter into relationships with neighbors, so as to have access to their surpluses when the resources of one's own area are inadequate. Interestingly, evidence of exchange among groups increases dramatically during the late Archaic period.

In short, it seems that as big game became more scarce, the people adapted by becoming more versatile. Each group exploited as fully as possible the entire range of resources available in its territory, shifting the diet from season to season. We have noted the same strategy in the Upper Paleolithic, but not to this extent. The Mesolithic-Archaic peoples were considerably more diversified than any of their ancestors in the human lineage. By perfecting this method of survival, they gained an intimate knowledge of local plants and animals. That knowledge, as the centuries passed, was to be the basis for a wholly new subsistence strategy—agriculture.

Sedentism

Intensive foraging for seasonal foods seems to have slowed the development of permanent settlements. The housing remains and large size of some of the Upper Paleolithic camps indicate that if these groups were not fully sedentary they at least established a single central base camp, from which small groups moved back and forth to short-term satellite stations for special tasks. After the retreat of the glaciers, the picture changed. Houses disappeared, and they did not reappear for some time. In southeastern Arizona, for example, there are a few dwellings that date back as early as 5,000 B.P., but not until 600 B.P. do real settlements of houses become common. The scarcity of houses and the sparsity of the tool assemblages at early Mesolithic-Archaic sites indicate that the settlements were fairly temporary and that these people led a more nomadic existence than did the people of the preceding period. Not until the late Mesolithic-Archaic stage does the base camp with satellite camps reemerge.

Trade and Social Organization

As we have seen, the hunting techniques of the Upper Paleolithic and Paleo-Indian peoples required that several bands join forces. In addition to sharing the kill, the hunting parties from the different bands probably swapped articles as well. In several sites from this period we find materials that are not of local origin and that were probably passed from band to band during hunting expeditions. Inland sites in southwestern France, for example, have yielded shells from the coast. In Russia and northern Europe, chert—flintlike stone for making tools—was exchanged over hundreds of kilometers, as was obsidian in the northeast. Likewise, at the Paleo-Indian site

Reconstructing Diets: A Case Study

Star Carr, a Mesolithic campsite radiocarbon-dated to about 11,500 B.P., is located in a low-lying area of Yorkshire, England. By using a multidisciplinary approach, J. G. D. Clark (1972), who excavated the site, was able to reconstruct the subsistence strategy of Star Carr's inhabitants—the means by which they got their food, the seasons during which they sought it, and the types of food they ate.

Among the plant remains excavated at the site were several species known to have been used as food sources by both contemporary and prehistoric Europeans. But the presence of these plants does not necessarily mean that the people of Star Carr ate them. The species in question grow naturally in the clearings of human settlements. Moreover, the open area in which these species could have thrived was not very large. Clark therefore concluded that even if such plants were consumed at Star Carr, they represented only a small percentage of the total food supply. Two marsh plants—bog beans and reeds—which were found in the area, and which European peasants have been known to eat, may also have figured in Star Carr's diet.

From faunal remains, Clark was able to identify the various animal species present at Star Carr and to estimate their populations. This in turn allowed him to calculate how much meat each species provided and hence how important each was in the diet of Star Carr's human inhabitants. For example, the scarcity of bird remains indicated that snaring or hunting birds was only a minor subsistence activity. The absence of fish remains and fishing apparatus suggested that no fishing took place at the site. The remains of mammals, on the other hand, were extremely plentiful, suggesting that the site was a hunting camp. The major prey appear to have been such hoofed animals as red deer, wild cattle, roe deer, and pig, in that order.

Clark believed that Star Carr was probably a winter hunting camp, occupied for about five months a year. He based this conclusion on the study of antler remains at the site, as well as on a knowledge of the growing and shedding periods of deer and moose antlers. The antlers of red deer and moose are fully grown throughout the winter. Moose shed their antlers in January; red deer, in April. The fact that many of the antlers found at Star Carr were fully grown and attached to the skull indicated that the site was occupied during the winter before January; the presence of some red deer antlers that had been shed suggested that the inhabitants continued to occupy the site into April.

Clark hypothesized that the site location was based on the seasonal movement of the red deer, the group's major source of food. Modern red deer populations tend to gather in low-lying areas during the winter and then migrate in spring and summer to higher ground as the vegetation begins to mature—first on the lower slopes, then on increasingly higher ones. Because Star Carr is in a low-lying area, Clark argued that its inhabitants camped there to exploit the herds of red deer concentrated in their winter quarters. Supporting evidence comes from the finding that most of the red deer skeletons at the site were those of mature deer. (Like many other animals, deer bear their young in the spring.) The preponderance of remains of fully grown male animals led Clark to speculate that to insure large herds for the following winter, the hunters avoided killing females and juveniles, concentrating instead on the stags.

Clark used archeological and faunal data to determine the territorial range of Star Carr's inhabitants—that is, the total territory they used during the winter for hunting as well as for living. First, by examining the placement of the flint artifacts at the site, Clark was able to locate four separate work areas. From this evidence he concluded that Star Carr was probably occupied by four family units—in effect, a microband similar to those found in contemporary hunting and gathering societies. Then, assuming that a family consisted of two adults and three children, he calculated the daily caloric requirement for a band of up to four family units and the amount of deer meat necessary to meet this requirement. Finally, on the basis of the density of modern red deer herds, he estimated the size of the hunting territory that Star Carr's inhabitants would have had to cover in order to procure the required daily amount of meat.

at Lindenmeier in northern Colorado, archeologists unearthed flint that came from a quarry near Amarillo, Texas, some 640 kilometers (400 mi.) away (Wilmsen, 1974).

Once large-scale hunting decreased in importance and groups began to remain year-round in tightly defined territories, such casual swapping would have become more difficult. Yet the need for exchange would have been ever greater, since the variety of resources available to the individual group from season to season decreased as territories became more restricted. The obvious solution was to meet for the express purpose of trade—in other words, to institutionalize trade. This, apparently, is what the Mesolithic-Archaic peoples did. A number of North American sites have yielded objects of distant origin. For example, at the Indian Knoll sites in Kentucky, there are seashells from Central Florida, 950 kilometers (590 mi.) away, and copper from the Lake Superior region (Winters, 1968). These materials are dated to about 4,300 B.P., when groups did not roam far from their own campsites. Clearly, they were now engaging in deliberate trade.

The export and import of valued items were not the only functions—or even the most important functions—of trade in this period. In the process of exchanging goods, information was also passed from band to band. As people met to swap goods, or as they gathered in a village where traders had arrived with bags of shell or metal, they would share gossip, hunting tips, and other bits of local wisdom. Trade, then, helped to create a collective body of knowledge that transcended the band and was shared by hundreds of bands over a wide territory. It is also likely that trade evolved primarily as a way of cementing relationships between groups. By exchanging goods, the groups formed ties to one another. They developed mutual obligations, and these feelings probably formed the basis of nonaggression treaties, spoken or unspoken.

Tools

In contrast to the elegant tool assemblages of the Upper Paleolithic, the tools of the Mesolithic-Archaic period show a combination of eclecticism and practicality. Some tools are heavily worked; others are unretouched flakes. No longer were knappers turning out elaborately formed stone shapes. In Europe, they refined a tool that first appeared in the Upper Paleolithic stage—the microlith, or blade fragment. Formed either by punch flaking from small cores or, more commonly, by fracturing a larger blade into smaller pieces, microliths were often no longer than a fingertip. A microlith is one-tenth to one-hundredth the size of a normal blade. A dozen or so microliths could be made by breaking a single blade. Thus, microliths afforded at least a tenfold increase in cutting edge per kilogram of stone. These blades were used alone or mounted in wood as arrows, sickles, or a variety of other tools serving the needs of particular communities.

While the microliths show the meticulous side of Mesolithic toolmaking, these people were not always so precise. At times they used nothing more than irregularly shaped flakes that were knocked off a core and put directly to work. Evidently Mesolithic toolmakers could be as casual, when they were in a hurry or were using less precious materials, as they were careful when making and mounting their microliths.

Another specialty of this period were ground stone tools. We have already seen ground tools in the Paleo-Indian period. In fact, occasional ground tools are found in assemblages from the Oldowan stage on. Now, however, they become quite important. Ground stone tools were made by flaking a core to the desired shape and then abrading, or grinding down, its surfaces with a rougher stone, much as we sharpen knives or polish stones today. The grinding technique could produce a smooth, rounded surface, as in a millingstone, or an extremely sharp edge, as in a stone axe or knife. Both these features were very valuable to Mesolithic-Archaic peoples.

In the Old World, where the profusion of post-Pleistocene forests gave rise to an extensive woodworking industry, we find an abundance of sharp axes and planes, which were used to cut and shape wood into various implements. Among the ground tools of the New World the mortar and pestle are especially common, providing further evidence of the importance of vegetable foods in the Archaic diet. (The peoples of the Old World probably used the mortar and pestle too, but made them out of wood.) Ground stone tools assumed an even greater importance in the next stage of cultural development, when plants were finally domesticated and agriculture became the basis of subsistence.

TRENDS IN EVOLUTION

Looking backward over our account of the Upper Paleolithic, Paleo-Indian, and Mesolithic-Archaic stages, we can see that a variety of factors combined to produce the evolutionary developments of this period. The prime mover was undoubtedly the specialized hunting of one or two prey species, which created—or reinforced—several trends. Let us briefly review the major evolutionary themes of this period.

Population, Range, and Sedentism

The strategy of prey specialization, enhanced by the new hunting techniques, was clearly successful. Thanks in large part to the sedentary life style that specialization made possible, people multiplied rapidly. Sites became much bigger and much more numerous. This population explosion was to have immense significance, both in the period in question and later. For although population growth and high population densities do not in themselves cause evolutionary change, they represent problems that people must solve, and the solutions to these problems often lead evolution down new and different paths.

The biggest problem caused by the population increase was heavy competition for food resources. The plain that one band had visited every year for springtime hunting was now being visited by three bands or six. One solution to a food-people imbalance is to kill people. The bands might begin practicing systematic infanticide, killing off every second or third of their newborn, or they might kill off some of the people who had taken to showing up in their favorite hunting grounds. Both of these variations were probably common. Another possible solution was for neighboring groups to reduce competition by exploiting somewhat different resources. Within a given area, for example, one band might specialize in following a migratory herd, while another band camped permanently beside a plain that was visited year-round by a rich diversity of herds. This solution was probably used in some regions. But the most efficient solution was to break off segments of the band and send them out into new, unexploited lands.

As the last solution was increasingly resorted to, humans came to inhabit more and more of the earth. In this period alone, as we have seen, humans entered for the first time, and rapidly populated, Australia, Japan, North America, and South America. The opening up of these new lands meant more space and more food. Consequently, it also meant that human populations could go on expanding. At the same time, territorial expansion contributed to the increasing diversity of human groups. The larger and more various the human range, the more likely it was that different groups would strike out in different cultural directions.

With prey specialization came still greater sedentism. Herd animals are generally territorial. To the extent that they migrate, the migration is between predictable seasonal feeding grounds. There are also some, like the reindeer, that disperse during the winter but every spring come together again in the same grazing area. Thus groups of people specializing in these game animals could settle down near their chosen herd, knowing that there would be enough to eat for most of the year and that if the animals departed they would return on schedule. Some groups, of course, followed the herds in their migrations and therefore were sedentary for only part of the year. But many others remained in the same camp year-round.

The growth of sedentism probably had other causes as well, including, once again, climate. The most favorable areas for intensive foraging are those that contain a variety of zones of animal and vegetable life. With the climatic changes of the early postglacial period, the mountainous areas warmed up and became more productive. And since mountainous areas have a gradient of climatic and soil conditions at increasing altitudes, they could supply a variety of different seasonal resources within a relatively small area. (The seeds that burst forth in spring, for example, might be only a few hours' walking distance from the nuts that ripened in autumn.) Thus a mountainside tract that earlier might have served as only one seasonal foraging zone—if indeed it offered any resources at all—could now offer a complete set of very diverse but closely juxtaposed foraging zones, stacked up like a layer cake. Groups in these areas, therefore, could afford to set up a central camp on the mountainside and remain there year-round rather than having to migrate seasonally between mountain and valley.

Whatever its origins, sedentism did not interfere with the intensive foraging of seasonal resources. As long as the resource base was broad and foraging skills were well developed, a sedentary band could survive by foraging. However, the group still had to send out work parties for days or even weeks to do gathering, processing, or hunting that could not be done in the immediate area of the camp.

The effects of sedentism were far-reaching. It was probably the most direct cause of the late Pleistocene population explosion. It made it practical for people to build permanent houses. And by keeping the band together at a home base for the greater part of the year, it encouraged the growth of culture in every way.

Cultural Diversity and Boundaries

Sedentism not only kept people together; it tied them to a specific piece of land. And the special qualities of this piece of land—the local stone, the local herds, the heavy rains or long dry season, the nearby river, lake, or ocean—helped shape their culture. Thus, in addition to fostering culture, sedentism fostered cultural diversity. Those settled in woodlands learned to make elaborate wooden implements. Those camped in mammoth territory used the mammoth's tusks to develop a sophisticated ivory-working industry. Those living by the sea made carvings of fish on their tools. And as each group's culture came more and more to reflect the group's environment, it became increasingly different from the cultures of other groups.

As populations continued to increase and empty lands filled up, neighboring groups no doubt came into conflict over lands and herds. The result of these conflicts was that each group's geographical boundaries became more strictly defined and people moved around less. To avoid conflict with others and to protect their own holdings from others, each group stayed within its own range.

Sharply defined boundaries would have had a psychological aspect as well. As groups quarrel with one another and the philosophy of "them versus us" is born, the individual's conscious identification with the group—his sense of "us"—is strengthened. This "territorial" mind-set probably reinforced the trend toward cultural diversity. No doubt different groups used their distinctive styles in art, tools, houses, and clothing to help define their identities (Wobst, 1975). It is certainly difficult to explain the great variety of tool traditions in this period solely in terms of adaptation to prey and geographical range. Even groups that lived in the same region and hunted the same prey often had different traditions.

Furthermore, the differences between tool traditions in this period are less a matter of function and more a matter of style than in the Mousterian stage. What this suggests is that toolmakers consciously adhered to and elaborated their own local styles, as part of their identification with the group. "Ethnicity"—the sense of difference from others—became a source of pride, something that one would want to assert by consciously stressing that difference. The same process probably underlies the development of strong and distinctive traditions in art, house forms, clothing, and language.

Trade and Social Organization

While a given group may have come to be wary of its neighbors and to think of them as "others," it would nevertheless have had continual contact with those others. The sites were simply too close together for the groups to avoid one another. Much of this contact was probably quite unfriendly. The defense of boundaries is seldom a purely symbolic matter; usually it takes the form of bloody border skirmishes. Conflict could not continue endlessly, however; eventually it would interfere with survival. Thus people had to find some means of forming alliances.

Trade was one such means. This is not to say that trade brought lasting peace. As with modern sedentary hunters, intergroup relationships probably followed an alternating pattern of trading and raiding. However, a band would think twice before poaching on the lands of a group that was their only source of copper. Trading, in other words, knitted the bands together in a network of mutual interest and mutual obligation, and thereby helped to reduce conflict.

In the Upper Paleolithic, people often lived in much larger groups than ever before. The increase in population might seem the most obvious explanation for this phenomenon: more people, larger settlements. But this explanation is not adequate. After all, we know that territorial expansion was going on during this period. To keep its numbers down, a band could easily have gone on sending out people into unexploited lands. Clearly, what occurred was not just a change in numbers, but a change in the way people organized themselves. Bands came together to form macrobands. Presumably, the need for interband cooperation in the hunt, the bonds formed through the sharing of the kill, and other mutual needs and ties brought bands together into these large settlements.

In the Mesolithic-Archaic period, people went back to single-band settlements; but eventually trade involved them once again in multiband social systems. Thus in both stages we see a far more complex social system than the simple wandering band of earlier periods. Work group, family, band, macroband, trade alliance—each of these social units would have made its own demands on the individual, transforming social life into a challenge comparable to food getting.

Intelligence and Language

All of what we have described would have had immense consequences for human intelligence. In earlier chapters we saw the increasing necessity of quick wits for survival. By the Upper Paleolithic, intelligence would have become at least as important as physical strength. For the specialized hunters of this time hunted largely with their brains. They learned very thoroughly the habits of their prey. They may have kept crude calendars to monitor the movements of the herds. They devised ingenious gadgets—the atlatl, the bow—to make their weapons fly faster and farther. And as the jump and surround techniques demonstrate, they turned the topography of the land into a hunting ally and brought down their prey primarily by trickery.

Not only the hunt but also the newly complex social organization would have favored cleverness, resourcefulness, and a good memory. The difficulties of living in the large settlements of the Upper Paleolithic were no doubt substantial. There were more names to remember, more deals to negotiate, more quarrels to settle, more conflicting demands to sort out and evaluate. Each person was caught up in many more relationships and many more kinds of relationships. In such an environment such social skills as the ability to resolve arguments, to placate people, and to win friends became increasingly valuable, and people probably began selecting mates for these qualities as well as for their food-getting abilities.

Equally important was the ability to delay gratification and to share. Undoubtedly, many a hunter went home knowing that, although a critical action on his part had ensured the success of the stampede, only a small portion of the meat was going to his family; the rest, which he had earned, would go to feed hundreds of other individuals, to some of whom he had only the most remote relationship. Yet for the group to survive, individual greed and grievance had to be suppressed.

In the latter part of the period, when the proximity of culturally diverse groups gave rise to "ethnic" consciousness, there would have been a need for skilled negotiation. The evidence of trade in this period is probably only a poor indicator of a much more substantial pattern of institutionalized interaction among groups. Someone or some few people in each group probably had to devote a substantial portion of their time to strengthening relationships with other groups—settling and resettling boundaries, agreeing to exchanges of metal and shell, and probably also negotiating mate exchanges, another form of trade that helped reduce conflict.

Thus, increasingly, there were probably individuals whose value to the group lay in their interpersonal or intergroup skills—their ability to fill the role of diplomat-trader-matchmaker. And it is likely that there were others as well whose roles were more cultural- than survival-oriented: master toolmakers, calendar-keepers, and perhaps priests.

Finally, language would have been an integral part of this feedback system. As we saw in Chapter 10, there is evidence that the neandertals had less fluent speech than we. It is possible, then, that the late Mousterian and Upper Paleolithic peoples, whose vocal anatomy was entirely modern, were the first humans capable of what we would consider rapid and precise communication. If so, this evolutionary leap would certainly have played a part in these peoples' mastery of the art of cooperation—a mastery that we can infer from the jump and surround kills, from the standardization of tools, and from the large size of the Upper Paleolithic campsites. Both in the specialized hunting economies of the Upper Paleolithic and Paleo-Indian stages and in the seasonal foraging strategies of the Mesolithic-Archaic stage, fitness was determined in large part by the ability to cooperate, both within and between bands. And, since communication was undoubtedly essential to such cooperation, these ways of life would have created selective pressures for more fluent speech.

In this summary we have given more attention to the Upper Paleolithic and Paleo-Indian subsistence strategy, with its crucial element of specialized hunting, than to the rather different strategy developed by the Mesolithic-Archaic peoples as a response to the post-Pleistocene changes in climate and food resources. If we have devoted less time to this latter response, it is not because it lacked ingenuity but because retrospectively it seems so obvious: the groups that survived were those that were able to combine a variety of specialized strategies into a regular seasonal round. Thus, while diversity *among* groups is the most striking development of the earlier period, diversity *within* groups became the hallmark of the later period.

Summary

Beginning with the Upper Paleolithic stage in Europe (40,000–10,000 B.P.) and the Paleo-Indian stage in North America (24,000–8,000 B.P.), we witness the advanced forms of the hunting-and-gathering culture. This was an age of glaciation, so the number of species available for food was restricted. By specializing, the hunters became more expert, devising two sophisticated techniques—the *jump kill* and the *surround kill*—that involved the cooperation of several neighboring bands. They also began to fish extensively.

Sedentism, or the establishment of permanent communities, increased, and it was accompanied by a dramatic rise in population. These developments led to the expansion of bands into macrobands and the construction of sturdier housing. There is also evidence of clothing and calendrics.

Stone tools became far more specialized and refined. Upper Paleolithic peoples developed two new toolmaking techniques, *punch flaking* and *pressure flaking,* that enabled the production of standardized *blades.* One of the most important Upper Paleolithic tools was the *burin,* a chisel-edged blade used for cutting grooves into wood, antler, bone, and ivory. Its development greatly extended the range of raw materials that could be made into tools.

In Europe, five distinct cultural traditions have been identified—the *Aurignacian, Perigordian, Solutrean, Gravettian,* and *Magdalenian.*

They are set apart from each other by time, geography, characteristic tool types, and artistic styles. (The Upper Paleolithic Europeans are the first known artists.) The development of different technological and artistic traditions in different regions heralded the rise of cultural diversity.

Exactly when people began to arrive in the New World is still a matter of debate. With the discovery of sites containing tools of a *preprojectile* tradition (prior to the development of spearheads and arrowheads), the once accepted date of 12,000 B.P. now seems too recent. We know very little about life in North America before this date, however.

There were three major cultural traditions of the Paleo-Indian stage— the *Clovis* (*Llano*), *Folsom*, and *Plano*. Their tools are identified by their fluted-point projectiles. The Paleo-Indians developed group hunting methods similar to those of the Upper Paleolithic Europeans, and there is reason to believe that they depended equally upon game and plant foods.

At the end of the Pleistocene, glaciation subsided, and for reasons that are still not totally clear, large numbers of mammal species became extinct. It is most likely that the loss of *equability*, or annual climatic uniformity, was the key factor behind this phenomenon.

About 10,000 years ago, adaptations to the new environment began to appear, marking the beginning of the *Mesolithic* stage in Europe and the *Archaic* stage in North America. The typical group of this time developed broad, diversified subsistence strategies. Because of increased seasonal variation, they established summer and winter camps, often with smaller special-purpose sites. The need to forage for seasonal foods slowed the formation of permanent settlements; Mesolithic-Archaic people were more nomadic than were their predecessors.

There is considerable evidence of institutionalized trade during this period. Trade became a means of providing needed resources to groups whose environments did not supply them. Trade also facilitated the development of a collective body of knowledge among hundreds of bands over wide areas. Mesolithic-Archaic tools ranged from highly precise microliths and ground stone tools to hurriedly made flakes.

A variety of factors affected the developments of the Upper Paleolithic, Paleo-Indian, and Mesolithic-Archaic societies—population increase, greater competition for food, territorial expansion of the species, and sedentism. Sedentism, by tying people to a specific piece of land, fostered cultural diversity. The creation of boundaries, the rise of trade networks, and a more complex social organization were also by-products of a sedentary way of life. None of these phenomena could have occurred without an increased reliance upon intelligence and the use of language.

Glossary

Archaic a New World cultural stage that began at the end of the Pleistocene, between 10,000 and 8,000 B.P.; characterized by the development of broad, diversified subsistence strategies based on intensive seasonal exploitation of local resources; it corresponds to the Mesolithic stage in Europe

atlatl a spear thrower first found in Upper Paleolithic contexts; its use increased the range and force of impact of the spear

Aurignacian an early Upper Paleolithic tradition of the Old World, dating from about 35,000 to 20,000 B.P.; the earliest sites have been found in southeastern Europe and the Near East; all are characterized by bone tools

blade a long, thin, parallel-sided flake; the basis of many Upper Paleolithic tool forms

Clovis (Llano) the earliest Paleo-Indian cultural tradition of North America, dating from about 14,000 to 12,000 B.P.; noted for the first appearance of fluted projectile points

equability climatic uniformity throughout the year, with relatively little change in temperature and precipitation

Folsom a cultural tradition that flourished in western North America between 13,000 and 9,000 B.P.; like the Clovis, it is characterized by fluted projectile points

Gravettian an Upper Paleolithic cultural tradition limited primarily to eastern Europe and dating from about 27,000 to 17,000 B.P.; characterized by backed blades and carefully worked ivory tools

jump kill a hunting method used by Upper Paleolithic groups, in which large herds of animals were stampeded over cliffs

Magdalenian the last Upper Paleolithic tradition to develop, dating from about 20,000 to 14,000 B.P.; found throughout Europe, it is characterized by its wide variety of tools

Mesolithic a cultural stage that began in the Old World at the end of the Pleistocene, about 10,000 B.P.; characterized by the development of broad, diversified subsistence strategies based on intensive seasonal exploitation of local resources; counterpart of the Archaic stage in the New World

microlith a tiny segment of blade, about a centimeter long, used alone for fine cutting and scraping or mounted in bone or antler to make other tools; first occurs in Magdalenian contexts

Paleo-Indian a New World cultural stage that lasted from about 24,000 to 8,000 B.P., roughly corresponding to the Upper Paleolithic in the Old World; characterized by fluted-point tools and cooperative hunting methods

Perigordian an early Upper Paleolithic tradition that flourished in southwest France and Spain from about 35,000 to 20,000 B.P.; a typical tool is a knife with pointed blade and curved back

Plano a Paleo-Indian tradition that dominated much of North America and Mexico between 10,000 and 7,000 B.P.; it includes the first evidence of housing in the New World

preprojectile tradition a primitive New World cultural tradition that preceded the development of spearheads and arrowheads; it dates back well over 12,000 years

pressure flaking a variation of punch flaking in which blades were produced by attaching the punch to a piece of wood, positioning it on the striking platform, and then applying pressure to it

punch flaking an indirect percussion technique, first used during the Upper Paleolithic, in which the knapper places an intermediate tool (the punch) between the hammer and the prepared core; it increased precision and allowed the production of thin, evenly chipped tools

Solutrean an Upper Paleolithic cultural tradition that flourished only from 24,000 to 20,000 B.P.; it is limited to southwest France and Spain and distinguished by its laurel-leaf blades

surround kill a hunting method used by Upper Paleolithic groups, in which large herds of animals were stampeded into a box canyon or corral and then killed

Upper Paleolithic a cultural stage that in Europe extended from about 40,000 to 10,000 B.P.; it is characterized by the blade tradition, refinement of toolmaking, specialized hunting, and cave art

Suggested Readings

BORDAZ, J. 1970
Tools of the Old and New Stone Age. Garden City, N.Y.: Natural History Press. A thorough discussion of the variety of tools used by early people and changes in techniques of manufacture.

BORDES, F. 1968
The Old Stone Age. New York: McGraw-Hill. A discussion of cultural evolution through the Upper Paleolithic with particular emphasis on tool traditions.

KLEIN, R. 1969
Man and Culture in the Late Pleistocene: A Case Study. New York: Chandler. A well-written discussion of archeological sites from which important evidence of Upper Paleolithic house forms has been obtained.

WILMSEN, E. N. 1974
Lindenmeier: A Pleistocene Hunting Society. New York: Harper and Row. Reconstruction of Paleo-Indian lifeways based on evidence from a site in Colorado.

MACNEISH, R. S., ED. 1973
Early Man in America. San Francisco: W. H. Freeman. Articles from *Scientific American* reporting the results of the excavations from which some of our most important information on the New World's earliest inhabitants has been obtained.

Chapter Twelve

The Emergence of Food Production

For more than 99 percent of the time humans have spent on earth, people lived by hunting and gathering. Even today, a few of us continue to live much as our foraging ancestors did thousands of years ago. The Bushmen of the Kalahari Desert, the Pygmies of the Ituri Forest, the Eskimos, aboriginal Australians, and a few Indian groups in North and South America still survive by hunting and by collecting assorted wild plants as they become available in season. In most areas of the world, however, life has not continued in this fashion. About 10,000 years ago, some people began producing food, instead of finding or hunting it. Rather than relying solely on available game or wild plants, they learned to plant and harvest crops and to bring various animal species under human control—a process called *domestication.* We refer to the stage during which these events occurred as "the emergence of food production."

During the past two decades, archeologists have given more attention to the emergence of food production than to any other phase of the human past. Archeologists in the Near East, China, Thailand, Mexico, Peru, and elsewhere have unearthed the remains of early plants and animals domesticated by humans—wheat, barley, millet, and corn; goats, sheep, and cattle. Why has all this attention been lavished on one aspect of prehistory? Over the years, we have come to realize that this stage was a complex and revolutionary period, in some ways comparable to the Industrial Revolution. At this point culture began to change rapidly, and humans began adapting to change itself as a way of life. More technological and social innovations blossomed during this stage than in all the preceding millions of years. Humans learned how to spin and weave, to fire clay and produce pottery, to construct bricks and arched masonry, to smelt and cast metals. Resources unavailable in one region were obtained through increasingly intricate systems of exchange. The first formal villages emerged, providing a new social environment, and egalitarian social organization began to give way to ranking as differences in individual prestige and social standing appeared.

Many of these trends, of course, were evident in the preceding stage of specialized foraging—manipulation of local resources, sedentism, and trade, in particular. Nevertheless, the basic way of obtaining food was still hunting and gathering. Not until reliance on food production was well advanced did people begin to reshape their environment *purposefully* on a large scale: manipulating plant and animal species to suit their own needs; controlling space, water, and other natural resources; remodeling the land to increase productivity. And it was only after societies became largely agricultural that people went on to create full-scale cities with markets, streets, temples, and palaces; an impressive array of sculpture and mural art; systems of writing, weights and measures, and mathematics; and new forms of political and social organization, which we shall discuss in Chapter 13. The food-producing revolution that began about 10,000 years ago altered human life and the relationship of human beings to the rest of the natural world

In the ancient Peruvian community of Pisac (the ruins of which can be seen in the center right), terrace farming was practiced. This was one of the many innovations by which early agriculturalists were able to increase the yield of their cultivated lands. The terraced fields at the bottom left demonstrate that the modern inhabitants of Pisac use the same methods as did their ancestors. (*Black Star*)

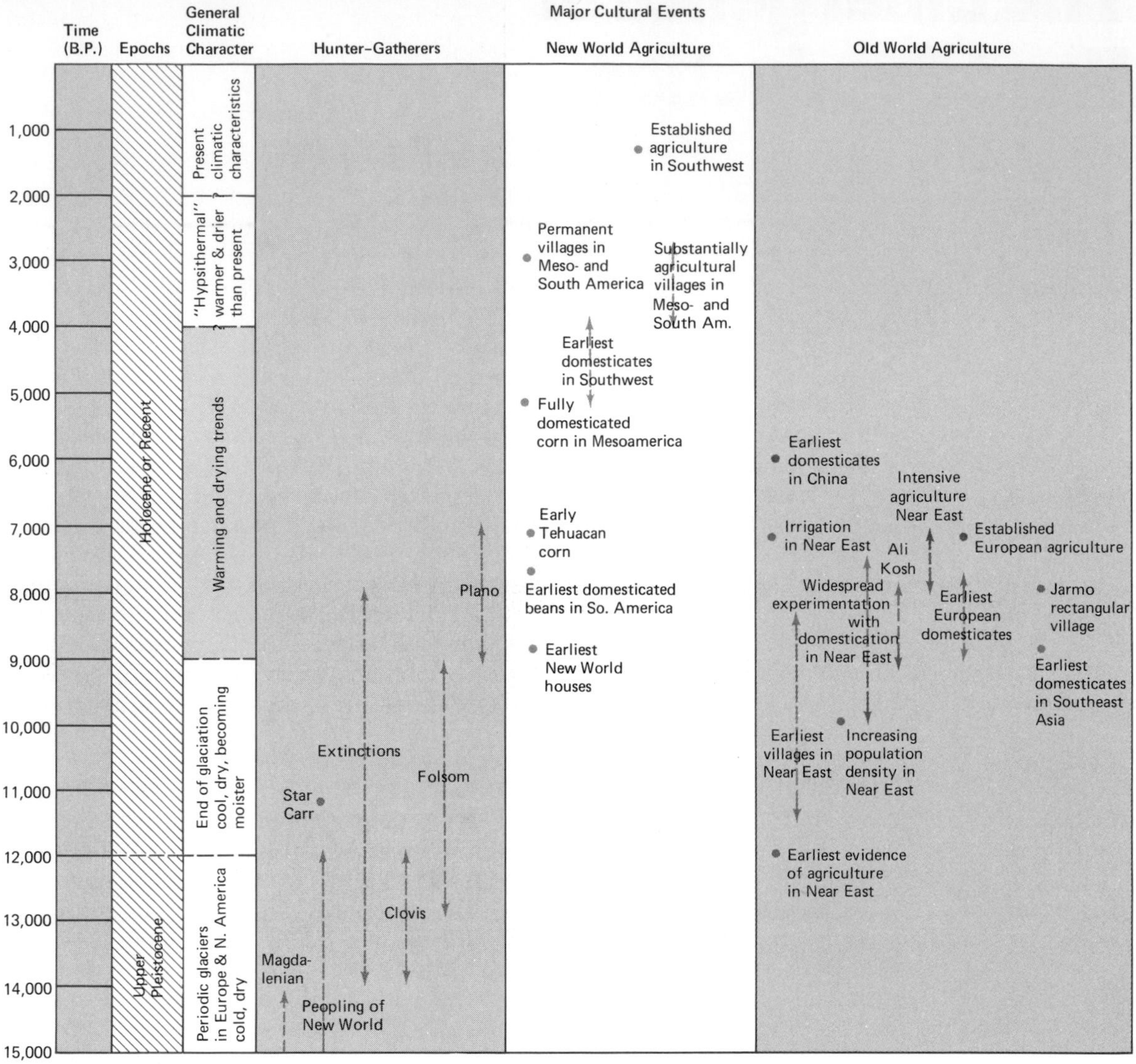

Figure 12-1. Time chart of domestication and related cultural developments.

in the most fundamental sense. In many ways we are still adjusting to the changed lifeway that began then.

THE ORIGINS OF AGRICULTURE: SPECULATION AND THEORY

Exactly how did people first begin to domesticate plants and animals? Why did they give up hunting and gathering in favor of cultivation and herding? And where did these events first take place? The answers to these questions are not as simple as was once believed.

Early theorists assumed that agriculture was a discovery that was made only once or twice, either gradually or in a brilliant flash of insight, and that it caught on and spread as more and more people recognized its benefits. For example, a few thinkers suggested that agriculture was discovered when some prehistoric individual by chance noticed that seeds sprout—perhaps when wild seeds discarded around a campsite grew into edible plants. According to this theory, groups soon began tending and harvesting these plants and deliberately spreading seeds in areas where they wanted them to grow.

However, today we know that it is not ignorance that keeps people from becoming agriculturalists. Every human group has some knowledge of the relationship between seeds and plants, and Paleolithic people undoubtedly understood it as well. Why, then, didn't agriculture develop earlier, and why didn't all foraging populations become agriculturalists? Archeologists began to wonder what social and environmental pressures encouraged some foraging groups to put their knowledge to work and start to change their subsistence strategies.

The Ecological Perspective

One of the first to note the revolutionary nature of these changes, and to view the problem from an ecological perspective, the British archeologist V. Gordon Childe (1952), attributed the change to pressures from increasing dryness in the Near East at the end of the last glaciation. Although Childe's ideas conflict with much of our more recent data, they did help to focus attention on the importance of climatic conditions and environment.

Robert J. Braidwood (1967) attempted to test Childe's ideas by investigating specific environmental zones where food production might have originated. Drawing on the results of pollen analysis carried out by a colleague, he determined that the climatic changes on which Childe's theory rested had actually been less drastic than originally believed. The drying trend did not seem severe enough to account for such a major shift in subsistence strategy. Moreover, the earliest actual evidence of domestication appeared to be associated with an environment quite different from that postulated by Childe. Braidwood found that the "nuclear zones" in which agriculture evidently developed were situated not in the lowland plains of the Near East but in the surrounding upland areas, or hilly flanks. There the wild ancestors of today's domesticates were once abundant, and dense stands of wild wheat and barley grow even today. As Near Eastern foragers settled these areas and became increasingly efficient in exploiting the specialized resources of this zone, they presumably began to experiment with and manipulate the wild plants and animals around them.

Environment, Genetics, and Society

This nuclear zone theory, however, is open to certain objections. For one thing, it assumes that human beings have an innate tendency to experiment and to accept innovations: once they learned about domestication, they adopted the practice. But in reality, few societies accept change for its own sake—especially when it concerns subsistence. A new practice or technology must satisfy some need, or confer some specific adaptive advantage. People living in an area of abundant natural resources have little need to begin exploiting new resources and not much reason to modify their already proven and productive subsistence strategies.

Moreover, the domestication of plants and animals involves certain genetic changes. Although some initial alteration may occur within a species' natural environment—the econiche to which it has become adapted—*major* changes are more likely to occur when the plant or animal has been taken to a new environment where different selective pressures are at work. Under these new conditions, it is more apt to undergo a host of random genetic changes, some of which are likely to help transform it from a wild species into a domesticate.

For these reasons, Kent Flannery (1973) believes it more probable that domestication experiments began among populations living in less bountiful, marginal areas. In such regions, human populations would have been strongly motivated to increase productivity. At the same time, wild plant forms native to nuclear zones could well have changed genetically in adaptation to the new environment. Some recent archeological finds support this conclusion, indicating that domestication in fact began not *in* but *adjacent to* the nuclear zones.

We will have occasion to discuss Flannery's hypothesis in greater detail later in this chapter. Whether we accept it or not, though, we can see that domestication was not simply a matter of planting seeds and reaping the benefits. It involved two separate but interacting processes: changes in plants and animals, and changes in human behavior. New genetic and phenotypic characteristics had to be selected for in certain plants and animals. The changes differentiated these strains from their wild ancestors and ultimately made them dependent on humans for survival. As these genetic transformations occurred, the newly modified resources became a still more important part of the human diet and were utilized in new ways by humans.

To understand these processes of change, we need to look at several related issues:

1. What changes in plants and animals are involved in domestication, and how did they come about?
2. What changes in human behavior were involved in the process?
3. How did domestication originate and spread in different parts of the world?
4. What adaptive advantages does the subsistence strategy of domestication confer? Why has it persisted and become fundamental to human survival?
5. What were its consequences?

We will consider each of these questions in turn.

CHANGES IN PLANTS AND ANIMALS

A domesticate is by definition different from its wild relative. We can see this contrast by examining one of the earliest and most important domesticated plants in the New World—corn—and a major animal domesticate from the Old World—the goat. Gathering and evaluating the evidence of such changes are central tasks for archeologists interested in this revolutionary stage.

The Changes in Corn

Archeologists and botanists are not sure what the wild ancestor of corn actually looked like. Some maintain that Indian corn—or, more properly, maize—is descended from a form of wild popcorn, now extinct (Mangelsdorf, MacNeish, and Galinat, 1964). They believe that corn, unlike wheat or other food plants, has never been found growing in its wild state. Others believe it developed from a tall, coarse grass called teosinte, the nearest relative of modern corn (Beadle, 1972). Today teosinte grows wild throughout the semiarid and subtropical zones of Mexico and Guatemala, and some Indian groups use it as "starvation food." At first glance, teosinte looks almost exactly like corn: it bears seeds on the side of the stalk, as corn does. But, unlike corn, teosinte has only seven to twelve seeds enclosed in very hard individual cases situated on a brittle stalk, or rachis (Flannery, 1973).

Our first clue to the origin of domesticated maize comes from the Tehuacán Valley in Mexico, where archeologists have found tiny, inch-

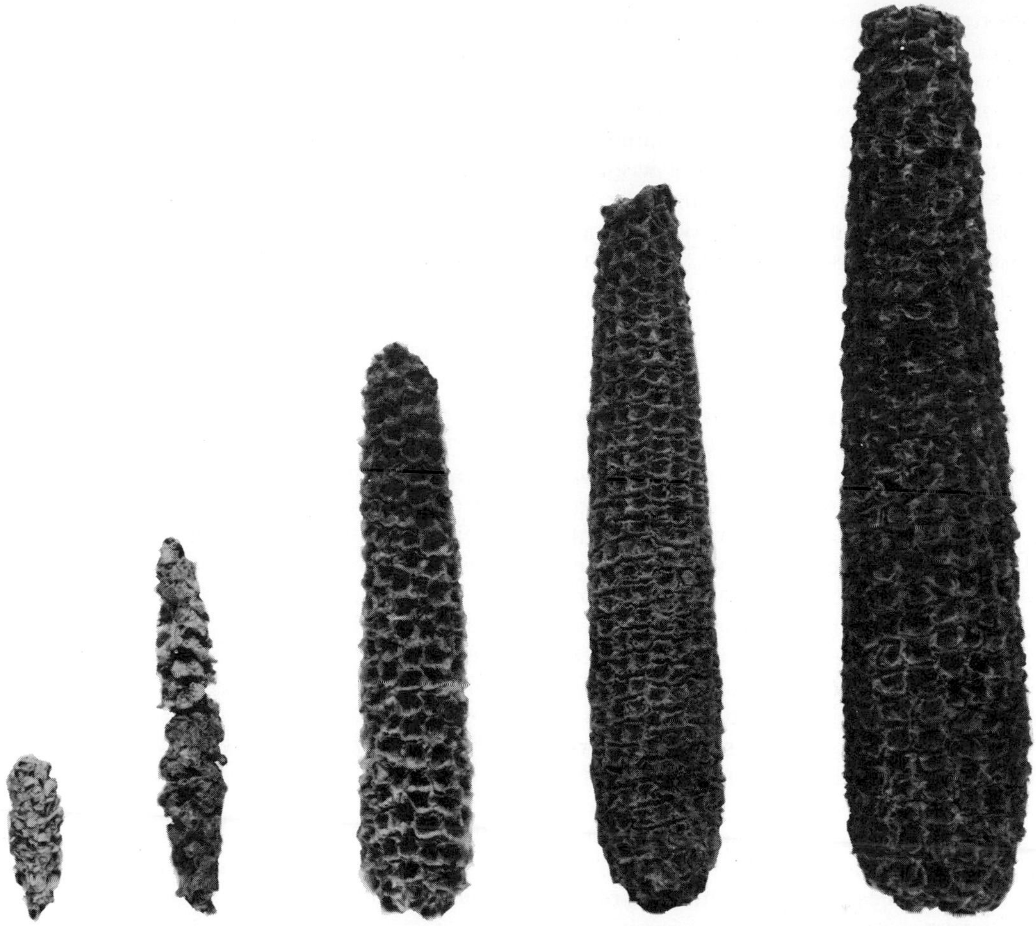

The evolution of Tehuacán corn is shown here. The earliest examples of domesticated maize (lefthand side of photo) contained many of the characteristics of their wild ancestor. This maize was a pod corn with small cobs containing only a few rows of kernels enclosed in tough husks. With years of hybridization and cultivation, the maize plant gradually became larger and sturdier. More and longer cobs and rows of kernels developed, and a single soft husk covered the entire cob rather than each kernel. The ear of Nal-tel corn at the extreme right of the photograph is an example of maize commonly grown today. *(Courtesy, R. S. Peabody Foundation for Archaeology. Photo by R. S. MacNeish and Paul Mangelsdorf)*

long cobs dated to about 7,000 B.P. We do not know for sure whether these specimens represent a type of wild maize or a transitional, semidomesticated descendant of teosinte. Whatever the case, these early forms differ greatly from corn as we know it. These short cobs were soft, with no more than eight rows of tiny kernels, each kernel sheathed in a separate protective shell, or glume. The whole ear was only partially enclosed in a few light husks, which allowed the seeds to disperse at maturity.

Modern corncobs, by contrast, are about ten times longer and have many more rows of kernels. The glumes are much smaller, and the husk system has developed to enclose and protect the entire ear. The cob is the grain-bearing axis of the corn plant, and like the rachis of domesticated wheat and barley, it has become tough and nonshattering. The structure of the cob makes corn extremely useful, since it is easy to harvest, store, and shell. Unlike wheat, corn can be easily crossed with other closely related grasses, giving rise to hybrids that may combine desirable traits of both parent strains. As a result, it has developed into an unusually vigorous plant, adaptable to a wide variety of growing conditions and purposes. Today, corn has the widest geographical range of any major crop plant.

Recognizing Plant Domesticates

This example shows that reconstructing the domestication process is often a precarious undertaking, based on deductions from circumstantial as well as primary evidence, and sometimes open to several interpretations. Most archeologists start their investigation with a general theory about how the process occurred. Then they begin their field research to collect data. The first step is to fine-comb the soil of early sites for evidence—charred seeds and the imprints of vegetable matter. Sample size is important; a single seed will hardly support any sweeping theories about domestication.

An investigator who has collected a number of specimens next faces the problems of identification and dating. Identifying the specimen is critically important. The differences between one kind of carbonized seed and another are often minute, but upon these differences hang far-reaching conclusions about the course of food production. Dating is sometimes difficult because burrowing rodents or human activities may have disturbed the position of seeds, small bones, pottery fragments, or tools, pushing them into lower strata and thereby making them seem older than they are. Even when specimens are dated by carbon-14, a range of several hundred years is given as a matter of course, since greater accuracy is not possible.

Despite the problems of distinguishing wild and domesticated specimens, botanists have been able to specify a number of identifying characteristics. Typically, the seeds and sometimes the entire plant of a domesticated species are larger than the wild form. The seed size of beans, for example, and marsh elder (an early cultivated food plant in the American Northeast) increased considerably during the course of domestication. Larger seeds or plants mean greater productivity—crops that produce a higher yield per unit area. Domesticated plants, therefore, are often more productive than wild ancestral forms.

In addition to size differences, wild and domesticated species often vary in terms of their *morphology*, that is, their shape and structure. One of the most prominent changes in cultivated vegetables and grains is the loss of natural seed dispersal mechanisms. In the case of wild beans, the brittle pods split apart when ripe, twisting into spirals and throwing the seeds in all directions. Although this mechanism is admirably suited to propagation under natural conditions, it makes harvesting difficult. In domesticated beans, fragile pods have been replaced by more flexible, nonshattering pods. In wheat, barley, and corn, the analogous development is a tougher rachis (the connective tissues holding the seedpods to the stem). The result is a crop plant that can be harvested more successfully but cannot release its seeds without human help. This characteristic is a sure sign of domestication, since without a dispersal mechanism the plants could not survive unless tended by people.

Evidence for Changes in Goats

Like plants, wild and domesticated animal species also differ in terms of size and morphology. Unfortunately, we do not always have direct evidence for some of the most important changes—more docile behavior, for example, or greater milk production. We must infer what we can from the available physical evidence, which is sometimes hard to interpret or downright mysterious. Goats provide one of the most striking examples. About 11,000 years ago Near Easterners began to keep flocks of goats as a food reserve. Under human protection and care, modifications began to occur in the anatomy of goats. One of the most obvious changes was in the shape of their horns. Ancient wild goats had smooth, scimitar-shaped horns that appear four-sided in cross section. Gradually an almond-shaped horn core evolved, as one side became flattened and the other side formed a crescent. After several more centuries of domestication, goat horns became kidney-shaped in cross-section and developed a slight corkscrew twist.

We do not fully understand why such radical changes in horn shape occurred. They do not seem adaptive, and there is no apparent reason why early breeders would have consciously selected for new horn shapes. Probably the transformations were genetically linked to some other desirable characteristic, such as high milk yield. Whatever the cause, the new forms spread rapidly among populations throughout the foothills and mountains of Iraq and Iran.

Recognizing Animal Domesticates

The archeologist investigating animal domestication faces the same problems as in the case of plants. First, there is the question of identification. For instance, is the specimen a goat or a gazelle? Often it is not easy to tell, since the two are descended from a common wild ancestor and in the earliest stages of domestication their bones look much alike.

Another problem is determining whether the specimens represent wild or domesticated populations. This too is frequently difficult. Various techniques have been developed for this purpose, but the answers they give are far from conclusive. One method sometimes tried is analysis of teeth and bone fragments to determine the age and sex ratio of herds. Some archeologists argue that if there is a high proportion of butchered immature or young male animals, there is a good chance that the herd was on its way to being domesticated. At least it suggests that some sort of selection process was going on. Herd owners tend to slaughter younger animals and surplus males, conserving females and older stock for breeding (Perkins, 1964). But population age and sex analysis is based on the assumption that selective practices were performed exclusively by domesticators, whereas it is possible that hunters also practiced selection for breeding purposes—hunting only the juveniles or males for food so that the adults or females could continue to propagate the wild herds upon which hunting groups were dependent. Thus most archeologists believe that too many factors affect age and sex ratios for them to be reliable evidence of domestication. The ratios may suggest domestication, but they do not in themselves definitely prove it.

Another criterion for differentiating between wild and domesticated animals is their size. Although a few domesticated species, such as the horse, rabbit, and various fowl, tend to be larger than their wild counterparts, the more common result of domestication is a decrease in size. Archeologists have speculated about the reasons for this development. It may simply reflect the fact that under human protection and care a larger number of smaller and weaker animals survived. Early herders may also have purposefully selected smaller, more docile animals because they were easier to handle. Bone size, however, does not always provide clear-cut evidence. There is a great range in size among both domesticated and wild species, and small bone structure may reflect other variables—such as inadequate nutrition, for example—that have nothing to do with domestication.

One of the most recent and interesting approaches to studying faunal remains is through microscopic analysis of bone sections from wild and domesticated goats, sheep, and cattle (Perkins, 1964). The studies reveal that, for reasons that are not yet understood, the crystalline microstructure of domesticates' bones differs from the microstructure of their wild counterparts. If further studies support these conclusions, microstructural bone analyses may prove another valuable tool in determining the occurrence of domestication.

Selection and Change: The Human Role

Some of the morphological changes that occurred in early plant domesticates made them more productive, easier to harvest, or easier to prepare. The outer covering of cultivated beans, for example, became softer or more permeable to water, resulting in a crop plant that is not only quicker to germinate but also cooks more evenly and is more palatable. Other transformations (such as changes in the horns of domesticated goats), though they had no apparent advantage for early producers, were doubtless genetically linked to some other desirable trait that has left no skeletal evidence behind. But why should so many traits beneficial to humans evolve in so many different animal and plant species in just a few thousand years—a very short time, by evolutionary standards? Clearly chance alone cannot account for these changes. Recent evidence from the Near East indicates that the plants that were domesticated in this area were recent arrivals; they were in the process of adjusting to new nonhuman environments. But human beings themselves played a crucial role in the process of change. What was that role?

To understand the process that took place, we must recall the discussion of natural selection in Chapter 4. We have seen that there are natural random variations in all populations. Mutations are always occurring in every species—new variations appearing in a few individuals. Most of these are not advantageous to the plant or animal, and are eliminated from the population. But a few provide survival value, and individuals with these traits form a greater and greater proportion of the species as time goes by.

Which traits will be perpetuated depends on the environment and on the constant selective pressures it brings to bear on each species. As human beings became part of the environment of certain plant and animal species, they created new selective pressures that both accelerated the pace of evolution and affected its direction. By their intervention—conscious and unconscious—they favored certain types at the expense of others. The evolution of domesticates, in other words, was the result of selection—with human beings playing the major role as selective agent.

Some of this selective activity was conscious and purposeful, but much of it was not. If a seed stalk shattered when touched, for instance, human foragers would have found it very difficult to gather seeds from plants with that genotype. They may have tried—they were not consciously selecting against this characteristic—but not as many of these seeds could have been collected. The seeds that they carried to new environments, therefore, would have been of the more harvestable varieties, with a genotype resulting in a tougher rachis. In this way, early foragers no doubt unwittingly helped to spread the strains that eventually became the earliest domesticates.

In other cases, the choice was conscious. Given a range of alternative food plants, for example, or strains of the same plant, the more productive and reliable resources would naturally have been used more frequently. It was no accident that wild barley and wheat were the first domesticates in the Near East. Both of these cereal grasses are extremely productive in the wild. In certain fertile areas even today, they grow in natural stands that are nearly as dense as a cultivated field. Using only a flint blade set in a wooden handle, botanist Jack Harlan (1967) was able to harvest about 2.7 kilograms (6 lbs.) of wild wheat in an hour. He calculated that at this rate a family of four could gather over a year's supply of wheat (approximately a metric ton, or 2,200 lbs.) during a three-week harvest. Undoubtedly, foraging groups deliberately chose these productive plants rather than plants that yielded less for the same amount of work. The high-yield resources were the ones they carried with them to new habitats. Thus, humans acted as selective agent in both conscious and unconscious ways.

Selection and Dependency

While early cultivators were deliberately concentrating on more productive resources, they were also unconsciously selecting against alternative food sources. In many instances, several resources were available at the same time, so that collectors had to decide which resources to exploit during a particular season and how best to exploit them. In the New World, for example, as maize and beans became more and more productive, people neglected other plants that had formerly been collected at the same time that corn and beans had to be planted or harvested (Flannery, 1972). The result was a change in diet—fewer wild foods and more cultivated ones. The extra time and effort spent on these resources increased the selective pressure for the more productive varieties of corn and beans, and their usefulness increased still further. In this way, the cycle of human selection and dependence on that selection accelerated.

The relationship between humans and the plant and animal species they domesticated was a mutually beneficial one. It had to be, or the genetic changes necessary for domestication would never have taken place. Clearly there was a great advantage, in terms of reproductive success, for those strains that developed characteristics valuable to human populations. It was the most useful plants whose seeds were collected and spread by migratory foragers as they traveled; it was the most productive and reliable crops that were planted and tended by early agriculturalists. Similarly, it was the strongest or most docile or most productive or most intelligent animals that were systematically fed and bred by the first herdsmen. And as the selective process favored those strains that were most valuable to humans—and thus most likely to enjoy the benefits of human intervention—it also favored an increasing *dependence* on such intervention. Domestic crop plants, as we have seen, lost their natural seed dispersal mechanisms when they became easier for people to harvest. And how long would a modern domesticated dairy cow survive, left alone in a wild environment? While humans came to depend more and more on domesticates, the domesticated plants and animals themselves were adapting to an environment in which human beings were the dominant factor.

CHANGES IN HUMAN SUBSISTENCE STRATEGIES

As we have seen, many important alterations in animals and plants resulted from the unintentional actions of people. In terms of later consequences, however, the most significant changes occurring were those in deliberate, conscious human behavior. First in small ways, but eventually in major ones, people began to take control of the propagation and growth processes of plants and animals. Without such intervention, agricultural subsistence strategies as we know them would never have been possible.

The archeological record from the time period during which these changes took place tells us little of their nature and sequence. Unfortunately, no distinctive artifacts are required to create a hybrid plant or to keep two strains of a particular plant genetically isolated. Thus we have little concrete evidence as to what people were actually doing, or when. Most of the behavioral changes in which we are interested must be inferred by projecting backward in time some of the activities in which modern food production is rooted. We believe, however, that people must have started to play an increasingly important role in (1) controlling seed dispersal, (2) developing improved strains by selective breeding, and (3) improving the growing conditions of plants and animals.

Control of Seed Dispersal and Selective Breeding

In the preceding discussion, we observed that plant domesticates have lost the ability to reseed themselves—they depend on humans for this function. People soon learned, however, that in carrying out this function they could do a great deal more than simply plant seeds. For one thing, they could alter the proportion of seed they consumed, saving more or less for planting, as conditions required. Moreover, they could store seed during periods when growing conditions were unfavorable, and plant later when better conditions returned. For example, they could wait for the spring rains or replant a crop destroyed by an unusually late frost. They could even, if conditions were unusually severe, give up completely on one year's crop and still have seed for the following year.

People also began to alter the physiology of

the plants and animals on which they relied. This manipulation followed two different lines. First, they sought to nurture more productive and reliable forms of particular plants and animals. Second, they attempted to maintain strains ideally suited to different local habitats within their growing territory. Some of this behavior was probably very simple—keeping the largest and strongest calves for breeding purposes, and sowing seeds from the plants that produced the largest and most abundant grains. But far greater sophistication must have characterized some such efforts. For example, the Pueblo Indians of the American Southwest maintain separate strains of corn resistant to different stresses that may occur in a specific growing season. Some are wind resistant, some drought resistant, some frost resistant, and so forth. In a study of farmers in highland Peru, Stephen Brush (1977) found over fifty different varieties of potato under cultivation. Each is best suited to a slightly different set of conditions—temperature, moisture, altitude, and so on—and is planted in plots where it will do best. Such practices suggest a careful monitoring of the characteristics of different strains or species over a long period of time.

Control of Growing Conditions

Finally, people began to modify the growing conditions of plants and animals. A first simple step was reducing the organisms' competitors. Weeding fields and protecting animals from predators were undoubtedly among the earliest behaviors developed. The Paiute of the Owens Valley of California—hunter-gatherers rather than agriculturalists—are known to have diverted stream waters into stands of wild plants to increase their productivity. This suggests that improving the moisture and hydrological conditions of fields was another very early and important step. The practice of wintering animals in warmer locations and bringing them in summer to locations where grasses and plants for grazing were most abundant represents still another form of environmental modification. So too does the choice of times and places for planting, discussed earlier. In addition, using animal refuse, fish, and other natural items as fertilizer, and straw, gravel, or wood as mulch enabled people to alter and improve the qualities of the soil for their crops.

The most significant changes, however, resulted from the efforts of early agriculturists to employ soil and water control methods. One of the simplest strategies, and probably one of the first to evolve, was *shifting cultivation.* This technique involves planting a field until the soil nutrients are used up and productivity starts to decline. It is then abandoned for a new field, while the old one lies fallow until its fertility is restored. This form of cultivation usually entails removal of the existing plant growth from the field to be sowed. In tropical areas, shifting cultivation is generally of the *slash-and-burn* variety. Trees are felled to allow light to reach the plot and burned to create fertilizer. Felling trees is an easier task than removing grass; extensive agriculture in grassland areas was impossible before the development of the plow to break through the heavy sod and the hard layers that often develop in the soil below many grasses.

In the beginning, farmers probably relied solely on *rainfall farming*—planting fields in locations where enough rain normally falls to sustain the growth of crops. But, in time, more dependable techniques were developed, allowing cultivation in drier areas as well. *Floodwater farming* was one of the first. It involved planting crops where they would be watered by surface runoff—on the floodplains of rivers, for example. Eventually farmers in both the Old World and the New World developed elaborate water control methods, such as irrigation and terracing. Since they require an increased investment of human labor, these innovations probably arose out of necessity, in response to scarcity. In the Near East, for instance, irrigation did not originate in fertile upland areas, where early dry farming produced high yields, but in the arid lowland steppe.

Water and soil control techniques varied greatly from one region to another, depending on topography, climate, rainfall, and soil conditions. In deciding which system to adopt, early

Modern slash-and-burn cultivation in East Africa. The jungle vegetation has been chopped down and burned to clear an area for planting. Except for the relatively modern construction of the houses, early agricultural villages in many tropical regions probably looked much like this. *(Norman Myers/Bruce Coleman, Inc.)*

agriculturalists undoubtedly weighed the costs in human labor against the final benefits. In the Valley of Oaxaca sometime after 2,500 B.P., agriculturalists were practicing *pot irrigation*, a relatively simple system that involves digging shallow wells right in the cornfield. Farmers drew water from these wells in 11-liter (3-gallon) pots and carefully watered each individual corn plant by hand. However, pot irrigation is suited only to areas where underground water is not far below the surface. When the Oaxaca Valley population expanded and moved out into the surrounding hills, they developed another form of irrigation: canals were dug to divert the water from streams into cornfields (Flannery, Kirkby, Kirkby, and Williams, 1967).

In the American Southwest, canal irrigation ranged from very simple systems, small channels barely scratched in the earth, to elaborate constructions, canals that were several meters wide and equally deep. In general, canal irrigation is a major undertaking, involving careful engineering to ensure the proper surface slope and to regulate the flow of water. Many early farming communities could not afford to invest the necessary manpower or lacked the organizational structure needed to coordinate and maintain such a complex system. In some cases, canal irrigation was simply unsuited to environmental conditions or human needs, and alternative devices were selected. Where surface slope made irrigation impractical, farmers sometimes constructed terraces, using rock fences, on hillsides and in stream channels. Terracing, by helping to hold

The ancient technique of pot irrigation is still used in many parts of the world today. In this Indian village, wells are located along the edges of the fields. Water drawn from them is dumped down shallow ditches that cut across the fields, watering the crops beside them. *(Raghubir Singh/Woodfin Camp)*

soil and rainfall, allows crops to receive more water and reduces erosion. A related technique developed at about the same time is contouring—hoeing furrows or laying rows of stone in such a way as to follow the natural contours of a hillside, at right angles to the vertical slope. Thus in times of heavy rainfall, water cannot cascade down along the furrows, washing away crops and valuable topsoil.

Initially, farm plots probably were not very different from our gardens—a great diversity of plants grew side by side. But with heavier and heavier investment in soil and water control technologies and in plows and draft animals, the practice of planting large fields with a single crop became increasingly important. This in turn led to the use of animals for harvesting—and eventually to the use of machines, such as reapers.

Agricultural Tools

With the development of agriculture came new technological advances. The most important of these involved the invention and use of specific tools for improving the food-producing effort. Ground stone axes for clearing fields, sickles for harvesting grain, grinding implements for processing it, containers and storage buildings for stockpiling surpluses—all these appear in the archeological record or become strikingly more abundant as the domestication process progresses. A few preagricultural societies made clay vessels, but the real development of pottery went hand in hand with the development of

Following the development of food production, clay containers became an important household asset. Because they kept out water and insects, they were more efficient than skin bags or baskets for the storage of agricultural surplus. In addition, the pottery made excellent cooking vessels; meat and vegetables could be boiled in them, a process that releases nutrients and may make food more palatable. The vessel shown here is typical of this early handmade (as opposed to wheel-thrown) pottery. *(Courtesy, American Museum of Natural History)*

agriculture. Pottery is not quite as portable as the skin and gut pouches, wooden containers, and baskets of hunter-gatherers; pots break more easily than baskets. Given a relatively permanent settlement, however, their greater durability and the better security from pests they provided proved extremely valuable. Equally important, they could be used for cooking. Since boiling releases important nutrients in some foods and makes many vegetable products more edible, clay pots were an important addition to agricultural production.

Pottery making also implies a new principle in human technology—various raw materials (water, clay, sand) are combined, with the aid of fire, to form a new object. Because of the nature of the raw materials, the forms that can be produced in this fashion are almost limitless. The same principle was rapidly applied to metals. These highly workable raw materials could be used to mass-produce objects in a way that stone could not, and were thus used with increasing frequency.

THE ADOPTION OF AGRICULTURE

There was no single pathway leading to the adoption of agriculture as a subsistence strategy. Rather, it was a complex series of events involving much experimentation—not always conscious or intentional—with various food crops, agricultural technologies, and forms of social organization. The process took place in many diverse localities, beginning for different reasons and following a distinct course in each case.

Halting as it was, and long as it took from the point of view of a single human lifetime, it was nevertheless dramatically rapid compared with previous developments in human social evolution. The changeover from foraging to cultivation began at widely different times in different parts of the world, but wherever it can be well documented in the archeological record, it seems to have occurred within no more than a few thousand years—indeed, within a century or two in many places. We now trace the origin and spread of agriculture as a historical process in several of these regions.

Centers of Local Innovation

In some areas, an agricultural way of life evolved directly from a hunting-and-gathering strategy. It was in these areas that domestication initially took place. Such primary centers include the Near East, Mesoamerica, South America, and Southeast Asia and China. Probably in the years ahead we will find evidence of still other primary regions.

The Near East

The earliest evidence of cultivation and herding comes from the Near East, where people had learned to extract an unusually varied fare by exploiting the resources of several closely juxtaposed environmental zones. According to the season, they hunted herd animals such as sheep, goats, and deer; collected a wide variety of small animal species such as land snails, turtles, fish, crabs, and mussels; and harvested nuts, wild lentils, and cereal grasses.

Few specimens of carbonized grain have been found from the early stages of domestication, but two developments suggest that various groups were beginning to focus on the intensive collection of wild grains. After 12,000 B.P. the storage bins, cooking facilities, and grinding implements that we would expect to find associated with heavy reliance on wild cereals began to increase rapidly. About this same time there was a shift to more permanent settlements.

Between 10,000 and 7,500 B.P., experimentation with domesticates became widespread throughout the Near East. By 9,000 B.P. the residents of Ali Kosh, a village in the Assyrian steppe, were intensively collecting wild alfalfa and tiny-seed wild legumes. And goat herders, wandering over the arid foothills, were harvesting wheat during the late winter and early spring (Hole, Flannery, and Neely, 1969). Many groups began to practice dry farming—that is, they cultivated wheat, lentils, peas, and barley without irrigation.

Between 8,500 and 8,000 B.P., the people of Ali Kosh were apparently cultivating wheat and barley more purposefully, clearing the land to plant cereal grains close to swamp margins. At the same time, they were also herding goats and sheep. As they continued to experiment, their economy became more specialized. After 8,000 B.P., there is a sharp decline in the amount of wheat and barley deposits and an increase in domestic goats and sheep, suggesting that during this time Ali Kosh became primarily a herding village, relying on nearby farming villages for grain.

Throughout the era of dry farming there is similar evidence of experimentation and general economic transition. Permanent villages became

Figure 12-2. In the Near East, early cultivators and herders exploited resources in a number of closely juxtaposed ecological zones. The high plateau probably served early herders as grazing grounds during the summer months when pastures at lower altitudes had dried up. Rich in mineral deposits, it was also a major source of copper and turquoise for prehistoric peoples. The woodland belt known as the "hilly flanks" or "nuclear zone" is the zone richest in plant and animal resources. Dense stands of wild wheat and barley grow there even today. This fertile area probably supported large numbers of preagricultural foragers who ultimately spilled over into adjacent regions. The Assyrian steppe, hot and dry during the summer, is transformed by winter rains into a natural grassland area suitable for winter grazing. Other parts of the steppe—the fertile floodplains of the area's larger rivers—are well suited to certain cereal crops. Wheat and barley have been harvested in this region probably since 9,000 B.P. The lowland alluvium or piedmont is an extremely arid region that supported few wild plant or animal resources. Food production did not come to this area until relatively late—after the development of irrigation made cultivation possible.

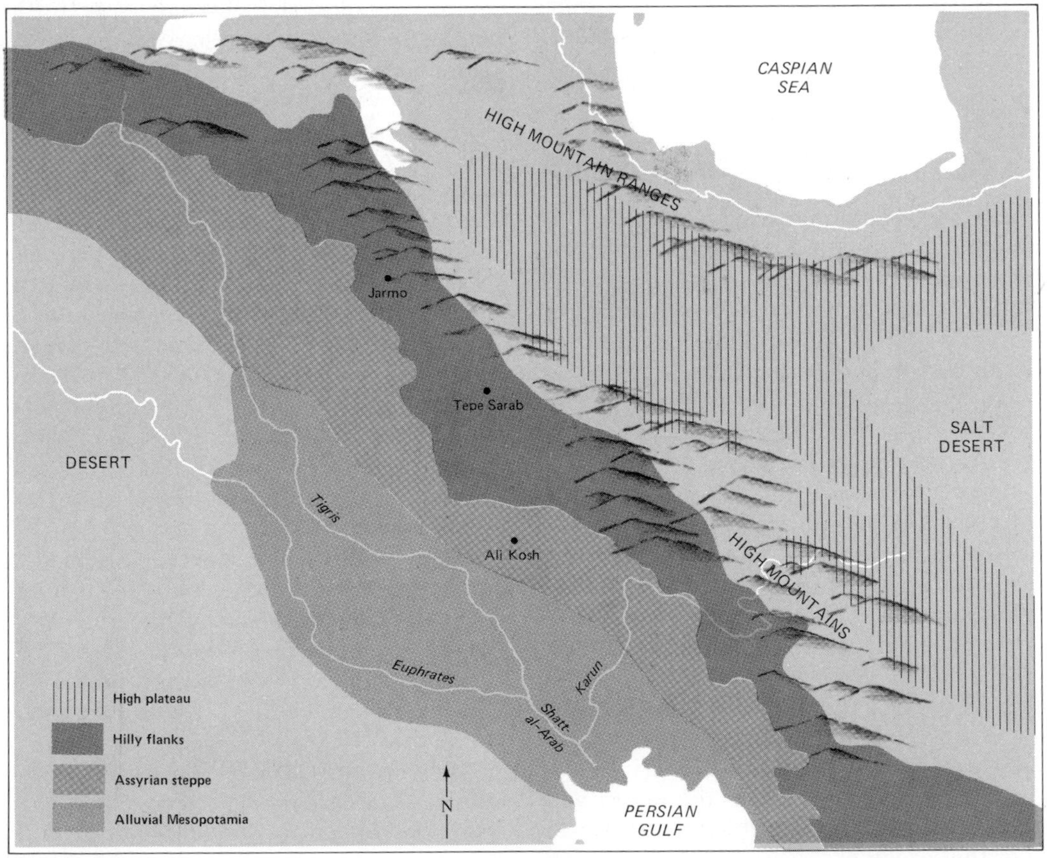

much more widespread, but temporary settlements were still common. By 8,000 B.P. the woodland valley area included sites that contrasted sharply. Jarmo, for example, was a village of about twenty-five permanent mud-walled houses with courtyards, storage pits, and ovens. Seeds of barley and emmer wheat found together with sickle blades and grindstones indicate the beginnings of cultivation and a fully sedentary life style. In contrast, Tepe Sarab, a site of the same age at a slightly higher altitude, has no houses, grain, or grindstones. However, bones of domesticated goats and sheep have been found, and their ages suggest that the settlement was occupied in later winter or early spring. Possibly it served as a seasonal camp for herders who obtained their grain from farming villages such as Jarmo. Animal and grain deposits throughout the Near East show a continuing mixture of domesticated and wild characteristics, but the focus was clearly shifting toward food production. There were few areas without farming communities by this time.

By 7,500 B.P. a fairly intensive agricultural economy had developed throughout the Near East. More domesticates were added to the basic complex of wheat and barley, goats and sheep. New strains of wheat and barley developed, and the diet was supplemented by peas and lentils (which had been domesticated earlier elsewhere), and domesticated cattle and pigs. By about 6,000 B.P., figs, olives, dates, and grapes had also come under cultivation. In some regions, simple forms of soil and water control came into use.

As technology became more sophisticated and the population grew, more and more people entered the arid lowland delta. With the development of irrigation around 7,000 B.P., crop productivity increased and larger numbers of people became concentrated on smaller areas of land. It was in this irrigated lowland area that urban life and state societies eventually emerged.

Southeast Asia and China

China and Southeast Asia were among the first regions of the world to develop agriculture. Oddly enough, the first plants to be domesticated did not include rice, the crop that today provides the economic staple for millions of Asians. In China, the first domesticate was millet, a tall, coarse cereal grass that is still grown in northern China, where it evolved. The earliest center of millet cultivation in China was the Hwang Ho River valley, a dry region that is bitterly cold in winter. However, the area offered two advantages to early food producers: the land did not have to be cleared since it lacked dense forests, and the fertile soil was soft and porous enough to be cultivated with a simple digging stick. Bushels of foxtail millet seeds stored in pits, weeding knives, hoes, and spades have been unearthed at sites dating back to 7,000 B.P. In addition, dogs and pigs, and possibly cattle, goats, and sheep were domesticated (Chang, 1970). Some of these sites were rather large villages that covered several acres and included dwellings of wattle and daub (that is, sticks and mud), constructed partially underground, with roofs supported by wooden pillars.

The origin of rice is still the biggest mystery in the development of Far Eastern agriculture. Domesticated varieties with a tough rachis and a large grain size date back to 5,000 B.P. in southern China and in the Indus River valley, on the western shoulder of the Indian subcontinent. Archeologist K. C. Chang (1970) speculates that rice was first cultivated in Southeast Asia, where it grew as a weed in yam and taro gardens. Recent archeological finds suggest that rice may well have originated in this area. Imprints of cultivated rice grains and husks have been identified in pottery fragments at Non Nok Tha in central Thailand. Rice chaff was probably mixed into the pottery clay to give it strength.

Rice, then, must have been domesticated sometime before Non Nok Tha was founded in 6,000 B.P. Earlier Southeast Asian sites, however, provide no clues as to when and where this might have happened. Rice is conspicuously absent from plant remains unearthed at Spirit Cave in Thailand. These deposits, the oldest in Southeast Asia, are dated at 8,800 B.P. and include a variety of nuts, bottle gourds, water chestnuts, cucumbers, black pepper, and a possible bean—all collected by preagricultural foragers (Gorman, 1969). There is no trace of rice, yam, or taro—the root crop staples that were to become the earliest domesticated plants in these areas.

Mesoamerica

At first glance, the differences between Old World and New World food production are striking. For one thing, in the New World, cultivation appeared at least 1,000 years later than in the Near East. Sedentary life, far from preceding the development of agriculture, was a relatively late development. In addition, New World food-producing economies were based on totally different resources. In Mesoamerica and much of South America, few animals besides the dog and the turkey were domesticated. Consequently, herding never attained the widespread importance in New World subsistence strategies that it had in the Near East. The plant domesticates, too, were different from those of the Old World. Instead of wheat and barley, the agricultural base consisted of corn, beans, squash, manioc, and a few other plants native to the Americas. Starting from different resource bases, the two areas eventually developed different technologies. Wheat agriculture, such as was practiced in the Old World, required sickles for harvesting, and threshing equipment for separating the edible part of the crop from the inedible chaff. Corn, by contrast, was picked and shelled by hand.

Between 7,000 and 10,000 years ago populations living in the southern and central highlands of Mexico were exploiting literally hundreds of plant species and hunting such small animals as the rabbit, deer, skunk, opossum, and ground squirrel. But the resources that were most heavily utilized were white-tailed deer and cottontail rabbits, as well as century plant (maguey), various cactus fruits, tree legumes, and a few wild grasses, including wild maize. The range of these focal resources cross-cut several environments. Like all other foragers, therefore, Mesoamerican hunter-gatherers were not adapted to one particular environment. Instead, their adaptation was to a few plant and animal species with a broad geographical range. This adaptive pattern is clearly reflected in the technologies of separate and distinct regions. For example, the tools, facilities, and seasonal patterns at Cueva Blanca in the Valley of Oaxaca in Mexico, a site located in a temperate woodland zone, are practically identical to those at Coxcatlan Cave, located in an arid tropical forest in the Tehuacán Valley.

Beginning at about 7,000 B.P., plant foods became increasingly important at the expense of hunting. The diet had expanded to include squash, chilies, and avocados, foods that were later domesticated. Mortars, pestles, manos, and metates—grinding implements still found in rural villages to this day—were used more intensively. Flannery suggests that at this point populations may have begun to take certain annual grasses out of their natural habitat. One of these grasses, wild maize, under the selective pressure of cultivation, underwent many favorable genetic changes.

By 7,000 B.P. populations in the Tehuacán Valley had begun to cultivate a variety of plants—squash, amaranths, and chilies, as well as maize and beans. But the corncobs found in the Coxcatlan rock shelter at Tehuacán are small and show many wild characteristics. The Coxcatlan people were still basically foragers; only about 10 percent of their diet was based on domesticates. By 5,000 B.P., however, maize had become fully domesticated. The corncobs found at Tehuacán during this period were much larger, and domesticates made up about 30 percent of the food supplies. Nor was Tehuacán the only center of domestication. In other areas of Mexico, people were experimenting with pumpkins, sunflowers, beans, and maize.

Sometime between 4,000 and 3,500 years ago, maize cultivation crossed a critical threshold: the productivity of corn became sufficient to make it worthwhile to clear away other plant resources in order to plant corn over large areas of the main river floodplains. Along with maize, the early agriculturalists also began planting beans, a source of plant protein missing in maize, and squash, rich in needed vitamin A. Together with avocados, a source of fats and oils, these domesticated resources provided a fully balanced diet.

Over the next few centuries, the highland populations became completely dependent on agriculture and full sedentism. MacNeish (1964) has found that the number of macroband settlements on river terraces increased, and some of them may have been occupied year-round. Agricultural production not only made sedentary village life *possible*, it may have made it *essential*. Increased planting and harvesting activities probably required macrobands to stay together for a longer period of each year (Flannery, 1968). By 3,000 B.P. permanent villages of wattle-and-daub houses were widespread on main river floodplains. Pottery came into use, and by 2,400 B.P. communal shrines and ceremonial centers were being built.

South America

While food production was developing in Mexico, Peruvian populations 2,500 kilometers (1,500 mi.) to the south were experimenting independently with domestication. Groups in the Andean highlands were cultivating several varieties of beans by 7,500 B.P., well before the earliest beans appeared in Mesoamerica. By about 5,500 B.P. they had domesticated the llama and alpaca, hoofed animals native to the region. These were exploited as beasts of burden and sources of meat; in addition, their hides and wool were employed to make clothing, and their dried dung may have been used for fuel. Guinea pigs were also domesticated about this time and served as a source of food and fur (Patterson, 1973). Nevertheless, except in some areas of the Andes, a herding life style apparently never became as important as it was in the Old World.

This area was also a center for domestication of the white potato and other tuberous crops, as well as quinoa, one of the few cereal grains that grows well at very high altitudes. However, we know little about the nature of early plant cultivation in the Andes because relatively little archeological work has so far been done in the highland regions. In the lowlands there has been more research, but the climate is so wet that plant remains are very poorly preserved. As a result, there are large gaps in our knowledge of early agriculture in this part of the world. Maize cultivation, in particular, remains a mystery. Was it domesticated locally or introduced from Mexico? Although the highlands lie within the natural habitat of ancestral corn, the earliest maize cobs in Peru date from 5,000 to 4,500 B.P., about 2,000 years after comparable specimens appeared in Mesoamerica. The Peruvian cobs belong to a race of corn that is closely related to a variety found in southern Mexico, suggesting that corn did in fact spread from that region.

Whatever the case, the new crop spread rapidly to the desert coast of Peru and to other parts of South America. During this period, other exchanges were taking place between the Amazon basin and tropical eastern slopes of the Andes, on the one hand, and the coastal area to the west of the Andes, on the other. Guavas, manioc, peanuts, and lima beans moved west and became firmly established on the coast.

We do not know why agriculture began in Peru. No significant increase in population occurred on the coast until 3,000 B.P.—much too late to have provided the initial stimulus for cultivation. Moreover, after domestication had begun, agriculture remained a secondary activity for a long period of time. On the coast, people continued to rely heavily on rich seafood resources and to follow a seasonal foraging pattern (Lanning, 1967). Agriculture did not begin to play a major role until at least 3,800 B.P., when more permanent settlements and ceremonial centers began to appear.

The Spread of Agriculture: Diffusion

In the past, archeologists often assumed that once subsistence strategies based on domestication were developed, the new economies invariably proved successful and so spread quickly to all corners of the earth. In fact, such diffusion was an important factor in many regions. But we now know, too, that the spread of agriculture was not a simple process. Local innovation, diffusion, and the retention of old subsistence strategies often coexisted. Northern Europe and the southwestern United States are cases in point.

Europe

After 9,000 B.P., we find evidence of all three situations in southeastern Europe. Some domesticated resources were borrowed from other areas, but people also applied the principles of domestication to native resources. Domestication of pigs and cattle probably occurred earlier here than in the Near East, suggesting that these species were domesticated locally and independently. On the other hand, cereal cultivation was already fairly well established in the Near East at this point and probably spread to Europe.

At the same time, while some populations in Greece and the Balkans were farming, making pottery, and building permanent houses from timber, wattle, and daub, others were maintaining a flourishing hunting culture. Exploiting rich river and forest resources, they were able to establish stable settlements that lasted many centuries.

By 7,000 B.P., food production had advanced up the Danube into the Hungarian plains. In addition to barley and wheat, the Danubians culti-

Figure 12-3. Dates of earliest occurrence of domesticates in several parts of the world.

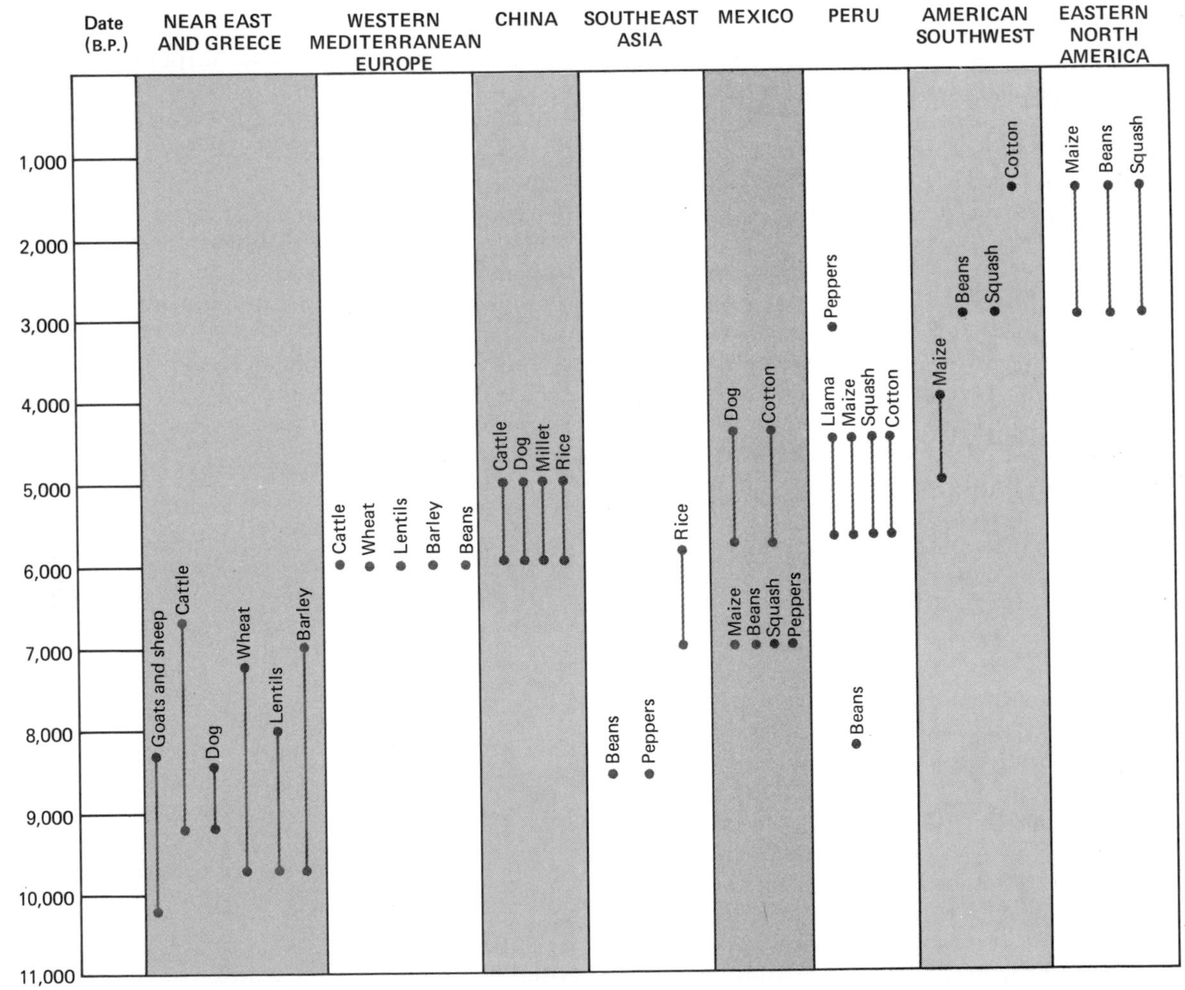

vated flax, peas, beans, and lentils. They practiced simple forms of shifting agriculture that quickly exhausted the soil and forced them to resettle often. As they moved northward, they cleared new forest areas using polished stone axes and burning the underbrush to make way for cultivated fields.

After they reached northwestern Europe, population growth forced some groups into areas with less fertile soils. Under these conditions, some cultivators began to experiment with new cereal crops, developing hybrid varieties of oats and rye better adapted to marginal conditions and the colder, damper northern climate (Butzer, 1971). Others, however, unable to grow sufficient food under these conditions, again became more dependent on hunting and gathering.

The American Southwest

The food-producing economy of the American Southwest was based almost entirely on borrowed domesticates: corn, beans, and squash. These were the basic resources of Mesoamerican agriculture. Apparently, populations of the Southwest simply adopted the crops that had already been domesticated in Mesoamerica, instead of domesticating local plants and animals. However, domesticates did not assume a major role in the subsistence strategies of southwestern groups until about 5,000 B.P.—long after they had been introduced from Mexico. Agriculture became important only after a lengthy period of local experimentation involving the development of new hybrid varieties of food crops, and after changes in population, technology, and social organization had taken place.

Corn was the first cultigen to reach the Southwest. The earliest known traces of corn appear at Bat Cave in central New Mexico and are between 4,000 and 5,000 years old. The early specimens represent primitive varieties of maize with small cobs and usually ten to twelve rows of flinty kernels. For the next millennium or so, this resource remained relatively unimportant, and gathering continued to be the major economic activity. Early sites like Bat Cave were simply seasonal camps where foragers may have sown seeds in the spring, returning to harvest the plants the following fall. There is no evidence that these crops were tended or that corn was an important part of the diet, and no cultivation technology had developed as yet, as far as we know.

By about 1,900 B.P. the picture had changed in various ways. The number and variety of domesticated resources had increased, and populations had started to develop agricultural technologies. Cultivated beans and squash were added to the diet, and by 1,300 B.P. corn had spread widely throughout the Southwest. But although many groups had begun to rely more heavily on farming, agricultural products had not yet become the primary resources. Experimentation and a flexible economy involving both agriculture and foraging were the order of the day.

Another transitional period began about 1,200 B.P. New varieties of corn, beans, and squash appeared. Some of these hybrid strains were apparently hardier and better adapted to conditions in marginal areas. Some varieties also became more productive; corn, for instance, developed a larger cob with more kernel rows. A new crop, cotton, became an important resource.

Not all parts of North America duplicate the pattern seen in the Southwest, however. In the Northeast, there was much experimentation with a variety of local plants that we now regard as weeds—ragweed, marsh elder, lamb's quarters, goosefoot. No doubt a greal deal of effort was invested in these resources, and different groups may have been heavily dependent on them in various areas at one time or another. Yet it seems that subsistence strategies based entirely on these resources either were never successfully developed, or did not last.

The Limits of Diffusion

Northern Europe and the American Southwest provide clear examples of the important part that diffusion played in the adoption of agriculture in many regions. People borrowed particular domesticates or the idea of domestication or both. It is important to realize, however, that diffusion is merely a way in which new resources, ideas, or practices can be introduced to a people; it cannot ensure their adoption. In some regions, people never did take up subsistence strategies based on domesticated resources. Other groups tried domestication but eventually rejected the practice. Even where agriculture was accepted, the rate at which it was adopted and the extent to which people came to rely on it varied greatly from group to group.

To explain this varied record, we must recognize that the practical value of agriculture to a given population depends on many factors in its environment, technology, and social organization. For example, domestication may not prove particularly useful to a group living in an environment where wild food resources are more productive than cultigens, or in an environment unsuited to cultivating a particular domesticate. The alkali content of the soil may be too high, the climate too cold or too dry. A certain plant may also fail to meet dietary requirements. Corn, for instance, is low in lysine, an essential amino acid and building block of protein. Consequently, it did not become a major staple until after beans (a rich source of lysine) and cooking technologies that enhanced the amount of protein available for digestion were also present to fill the deficiency. Finally, social organization or technology may be unsuited to domestication. Where irrigation or terracing is needed to make the land usable, cultivation is impossible unless the population is sedentary and organized enough to coordinate a complex system of farming. Thus where agriculture *was* adopted, the reasons can be understood only in the light of very specific local conditions (Flannery, 1972; Katz et al., 1974).

Other Regions—Questions and Problems

There are still a number of areas of the world and a number of domesticates about which our knowledge is incomplete. Future research and the development of new methods of investigation are certain to uncover evidence that will further enhance our understanding of the domestication process.

In 1959, George Murdock postulated, largely on the basis of ethnographic research, that there were two centers of plant domestication in Africa—one in Ethiopia and one in West Africa. West African domesticates include millet, peas, tamarind, cotton, sesame, Guinea yam, okra, and several varieties of pumpkin, gourd, and melon. Ethiopian domesticates include a number of local plants, cress, coffee, fenugreek, and castor. Thurston Shaw (1976) has observed that by the time of Christ, several African states already relied heavily on various of these domesticates. This fact indicates that the domestication process must have taken place fairly early; Murdock suggests that it probably was well under way about 5,000 years ago. Current evidence suggests that cattle may have been present in Africa by 6,000 B.P., and yams even earlier—by 7,000 to 6,000 B.P. These dates are quite consistent with the idea that domesticates might have come from adjacent Southwest Asia. Nevertheless, if Murdock's hypothesis proves correct, African farmers applied the idea of domestication to a very great variety of local plant resources.

In tropical areas of the New World, the search for domesticates is long-standing. In lowland areas, unfortunately, evidence is slight. Because of the wet climate, vegetal materials are rarely preserved. Moreover, many of the important domesticates in these areas are starchy tubers. Unlike domesticates from which seeds are taken, such as wheat, there is little of a tuber (for example, a potato) that is hard enough to stand much chance of surviving in recognizable form. As a result, most of our knowledge of domestication in these areas is indirect—based on artifacts that are presumed to have been used with particular resources.

Manioc is an example (De Boer, 1975). The roots of this highly productive crop are ground to yield a starch that can be used to make tapioca, bread, or meal. It was exploited by groups throughout frost-free areas of the New World and traded into adjacent colder climes. Evidence of the use of this resource dates to about 3,000 years ago. Graters made of thorns or chipped stone glued to a wood base were used to process manioc, and such tools are evident by about that time. But for a productive form of wild manioc to be domesticated, and for a fairly sophisticated technology for processing it to develop, a period of many years was probably required. Little is currently known of the history of this resource. Future research, in this case as in many others, will probably focus on phytoliths—microscopic silicious bodies that occur in plant species and are specific to them. Archeologists have discovered that these phytoliths can be recovered when appropriate techniques are used.

Evidence can be still more indirect. Zevallos et al. (1977) have described evidence of a village near Guayaquil, Ecuador, that was occupied by as many as 1,000 individuals about 4,800 years ago. The village was adjacent to mangrove swamps, which would have provided some of the food the people needed. But Zevallos also found indications that the villagers practiced agriculture. Some of the evidence was extremely subtle—for instance, impressions of corn kernels in pottery. While no evidence of domesticates earlier than those of highland Mesoamerica currently exists, Zevallos's data suggest that the earliest villages relying heavily on corn agriculture may well have been in tropical lowland areas. In addition to manioc and corn, peanuts, palms, avocados, cashews, chilies, herbs, and a great variety of other resources may have played a role in subsistence strategies based on domesticates in such areas.

WHY WAS AGRICULTURE ADOPTED?

Eventually, agriculture was adopted in most parts of the world—both among peoples who had developed it themselves and among those who learned it from others. The fact that so many human groups did turn to this way of life suggests that powerful and widespread forces must have operated in its favor. What is it about the process of food production that induced new populations to adopt it and led to its expansion within the populations that took it up?

The Demographic Trigger

As we have seen, the adoption of agriculture was affected by many different factors. Nevertheless, we believe there is a common theme underlying the variety of local causes and influences: population growth, and the demographic instability that must often have accompanied it.

We saw in the previous chapter that during the late Pleistocene and early post-Pleistocene epoch there emerged a marked trend toward a more sedentary life style. Increasingly, people were starting to settle down in permanent communities. This development could hardly have taken place without a growing ability to store food for future needs. The archeological record provides clear evidence of structures that appear to have been built to serve as granaries, as well as underground storage pits and the first pottery vessels. Thus food could be put away in good times for use in bad, when edible plants were scarce. Indeed, food storage made sedentism not only possible but almost inevitable. As Kent Flannery has remarked, "Where can you go with a metric ton of wheat?" (1973).

With a more stable food supply and a more sedentary way of life came an increase in human numbers. Spontaneous abortions, stillbirths, and infant mortality are generally high among hunters and gatherers, and the problems of transporting infants discourage having many children. Where life is more settled, conditions are easier for infants and mothers, and more people survive. Archeological remains in both the New World and the Old World indicate that increased sedentism is associated with marked population growth (Binford, 1968).

In many areas, such population increases probably became a source of instability, upsetting the balance between human groups and the resources on which they depended. While we cannot be sure how prehistoric peoples responded to this situation, we do know what contemporary hunter-gatherers do: they regulate the size of their populations, keeping them below the level at which they would deplete the food supply. Some societies accomplish this through infanticide— the killing of unwanted

Estimating Prehistoric Populations

Many of the theories presented in Chapters 11, 12 and 13 postulate change in population as a major cause of economic and organizational changes among prehistoric peoples. But how do archeologists estimate population for prehistoric groups? Obviously, they have no way of making a direct count. However, over the years they have developed a number of techniques that together enable them to make educated guesses as to how many people lived at a particular site or in a particular region.

Carrying Capacity

Different environments have different *carrying capacities*—that is, different levels of usable resources and therefore different potential for supporting human life. Ten acres of grassland, for example, can keep more humans alive than ten acres of desert. By studying environmental evidence, archeologists can estimate the carrying capacity of a region in a given era and hence get some idea of how many people could have lived there. However, this is a method of last resort in estimating population, since the population of the region might easily have been below its carrying capacity.

Number of Artifacts

The density of artifacts left at a site generally reflects the number of occupants. Thus, estimates of the relative population of two different sites are sometimes based on relative artifact densities: a greater density of artifacts means a larger population. However, other factors besides population—notably, the length of time a site was occupied and the way its occupants organized their work—affect artifact density. Therefore, this indicator alone is not highly reliable.

Floor Space

Living conditions are also used to estimate population. Using cross-cultural data, Raoul Naroll (1962) estimated that for the average society there is one person for every 10 square meters (107 square feet) of enclosed floor space. Using this ratio—or perhaps a different one based on a nearby group living at a site similar to the one under excavation—the archeologist can estimate population on the basis of the amount of enclosed floor space at the site.

Burial Data

The number of burials found at a site is also sometimes used to estimate how many people lived there. This does not mean that archeologists assume that prehistoric groups formally buried all their dead. Nevertheless, the existing burials often suggest what the group's burial practices were. (For example, only the rich were buried, or only the adults.) By adjusting their figures accordingly, archeologists can often estimate population on the basis of this evidence.

In most cases, these methods are used comparatively—that is, to measure the population of one region relative to that of another. Because each of the methods has its potential pitfalls, archeologists must use as many of them as possible, each serving as a check on the others, in estimating population at any given site. They must also make certain, when evaluating apparent differences in artifact density or number of burials between two regions, that these differences are not due simply to one region's having been surveyed more thoroughly than the other.

babies. Others make use of postpartum taboos—that is, prohibitions against sexual relations for some period of time after the birth of a child (commonly, until the child is weaned, which may be several years after birth). Still another method, often resorted to, involves sending excess people off to other areas where they will not tax the local subsistence base. Sometimes these migrations are more or less voluntary; in other cases they may be forced. In these and similar ways, hunter-gatherers are able to limit their numbers and so maintain equilibrium with their environment. We have little reason to doubt that post-Pleistocene peoples discovered and practiced the same solutions.

But there is another way to cope with rising population: find a way to extract more food from the same area. This strategy is called *intensification.* The introduction of agriculture represents a large and decisive step in the process of intensification, which has continued down to the present day in many parts of the world.

Evidence from the Near East suggests that occasional pressure of population on resources was indeed a major factor in the earliest known appearance of agriculture. According to Flannery (1973) and Binford (1968), an influx of colonists from areas rich in resources into more marginal areas may have disrupted the normal ecological balance in these less productive zones, already inhabited by other seminomadic groups. In such "tension zones," population excess pressured foragers to develop more effective means of food production. The result was experimentation with new subsistence strategies, leading eventually to a marked rise in the productivity of resources.

The pressure of increasing population probably took many forms. Even where population growth did not outstrip the food supply, the problems of managing a sedentary community may in themselves have created the need for new subsistence strategies. Once villages with permanent dwellings, storage facilities, wells, fish weirs, and similar fixed facilities had been built, and hereditary ownership had been established over resource areas, the residents could not lightly abandon the fruits of their labor. The people were in effect tied to one location by their investment of labor. Subsistence strategies involving migration thus became much less attractive; instead, the residents sought some more intensive means of obtaining resources without having to abandon their homes.

If the population was of sufficient size, economic specialization would have been possible—some villagers could have assumed the foraging responsibilities, traveling to areas where needed resources were available, while other residents remained working at home. The larger the community, however, the greater the area that would have had to be exploited to support it. Thus the cost in time and energy would have risen rapidly, and the efficiency of the strategy must have diminished. In such circumstances, agriculture might have been adopted as one means of sustaining greater populations within a more limited area.

The Adaptive Value of Agriculture

Population pressure, then, seems to have been a major factor in the rapid spread of food production. But no amount of population pressure would explain the persistence and growth of this strategy if it were not highly beneficial, in the long run, to the people adopting it. We must ask, therefore, what ultimate adaptive advantage (to use the evolutionary term) did agriculture give to the people adopting it? As we have seen, agriculture is not the only possible solution to the problem of demographic pressure. It differs from all the others, though, in one crucial respect: it not only fails to limit population growth but actually encourages further growth by creating a larger and more resilient subsistence base.

Archeologists once thought that the crucial adaptive advantage of agriculture was that it provided a more nutritious or better-balanced diet, so that early food producers had a better chance of survival than groups who relied solely on wild resources. Plausible as the argument sounds, however, there is no evidence to suggest that early cultivators were any better nourished than their foraging ancestors. Because they relied on a narrower range of products, early agriculturalists, in fact, may have been *less* healthy than their food-collecting ancestors. Cavities and various other health problems, relatively rare among earlier human populations, appear more frequently after the development of food production.

The Resiliency of Agriculture

Early cultivation, then, did not necessarily bring an improvement in people's diet and health. It did, however, greatly increase the stability of the subsistence base by giving people the means to even out year-to-year variation in crop size. Most of the wild resources that eventually became domesticated are characterized by high yearly yields but great year-to-year variation in crop size. Thus one may be able to collect a ton of wheat from a relatively small wild stand; but one cannot count on its being equally productive the next year, or the one after that. Once people began to produce their own food, there were a great many things they could do to increase not only the size, but also the reliability of their crop.

The major limitation on the productivity of most wild plants is the weather. For maximum yield, both temperature and moisture must be just right at certain crucial stages of the growth cycle. Most often, however, they are not. Many seedlings are destroyed by unseasonable late spring frosts; others are stunted or killed by too much or too little rainfall. But with cultivated plants, planting in carefully selected sites can do much to smooth out variations in yield from year to year. Farmers can plant in a diversity of locations to ensure that there will be some crop to harvest no matter what the weather chances to be in a given growing season. Planting in wet locations, for example, can be a hedge against a very dry year; while planting in both warmer and cooler locations provides some protection against extremes of temperature. The damage caused by unseasonable frosts can also be minimized by suitable site selection.

Human cultivators can also manipulate the time and place of planting, for their own benefit. One way to minimize the danger of too much or too little rainfall during germination is to plant parts of the crop at different times—saving some seed to plant when the rains finally arrive, if they are very late in a particular year. Humans also can control the breeding of domesticated plants—creating hybrids to combine the best features of different varieties, or preventing crossbreeding to preserve desirable pure strains once they have been found or produced. Finally, cultivation reduces the competition from other plants and the ill effects of insect and mammalian pests.

Not all of these strategies were successful all of the time. Not all were used all of the time. The important point, though, is that agriculture was intrinsically a more resilient strategy than foraging. With its adoption, human ingenuity tended increasingly to replace blind chance. Each hillside, each valley, each growing season presented unique problems; but people had a larger range of alternatives open to them in trying to find the solution. As a result, they were able to increase radically the stability of their subsistence base.

Population Growth

As we have already seen, greater stability of the subsistence base generally leads to a rise in population. So, of course, does an increase in the overall food supply. Although planting and tending crops may require a somewhat greater expenditure of human energy than traveling long distances to stands of wild crops, harvesting them, and then returning to base, it ultimately produces a larger yield. The same is true of herding, compared with hunting. In both the Near East and Mesoamerica, there is evidence of gradually increasing yields per acre as the practice of agriculture took hold. Quite naturally, the more food available, the larger the number of people that can be supported in a given area. Thus, in the Near East, population levels rose after early cultivators had developed more productive strains of barley and wheat. Likewise, in Mesoamerica there was a rise in population density after 7,000 B.P., shortly after maize had become more productive.

More people, in turn, create a greater need for more productive resources, and so more pressure for the expansion and improvement of agriculture. Thus a feedback cycle is set up that results in rapid increases in population. It has been estimated that in southwestern Iran, for example, the number of people supported by the land increased sixtyfold, "going from 0.1 persons per square kilometer in the late Paleolithic, to 1–2 persons per square kilometer under conditions of early dry farming, and up to 6 or more persons per square kilometer after irrigation appears in the archeological record" (Flannery, 1973: 75).

One result of the feedback relationship between agriculture and population is that the practice of agriculture quickly became widespread—partly through imitation, partly through competition, and partly through the increase in human numbers it had caused. Groups that adopted the practice grew at a much faster rate than those who continued to depend entirely on hunting and gathering. The advantages of an agricultural subsistence strategy must soon have become clear to many peoples as they watched their agricultural neighbors thrive. The natural result would be imitation of the successful practice, and its spread from group to group. No doubt many groups could not or would not change their way of life so drastically. Such populations may have clung successfully to their old ways for a time—indeed, as we have seen, there are hunting-and-gathering societies in several parts of the world even today. But in most places, the new strategy inevitably triumphed. Those who did not adopt it were beaten on the battlefield, crowded out in the competition for resources, or simply outbred and eventually absorbed by fast-growing agricultural populations.

TRENDS IN SOCIOPOLITICAL ORGANIZATION

For the first 2 million years of human existence, people lived in temporary seasonal camps and apparently built no permanent settlements at all. Upper Paleolithic hunters in Europe may have taken the first steps toward fully sedentary life, but it was several more millennia before settled communities became widespread—not until 10,000 B.P. in the Near East, about 6,000 B.P. in China and Europe, 4,500 B.P. in the Andes, and 3,500 B.P. in Mexico and the American Southwest. Sedentism, as we have seen, was a powerful stimulus to the development of agriculture, but the relationship was a reciprocal one. The more people came to depend upon cultivated crops, the more economical and attractive was the sedentary way of life. Permanent agricultural communities gradually became the rule rather than the exception in most parts of the world. Such sedentary and food-producing communities faced a variety of problems that had not confronted earlier groups: defense of permanent homes and fields, allocation of agricultural land among different families, scheduling of the complex array of activities involved in planting and tending crops, and the numerous problems in human interaction that must have arisen as people began to live in larger groups with the same people throughout the year.

As one might expect, patterns of sociopolitical organization changed. Modern societies of the kind we are discussing are basically egalitarian; leadership is still relatively informal and often specific to particular activities. Nevertheless, the leadership role tends to be somewhat more strictly defined than in a band. The family, rather than the whole band, is the basic producing group, and its activities are coordinated with those of other families through associations defined on the basis of kinship, age, religion, and other criteria that unite people from a number of communities. Often membership in such associations is cross-cutting: two individuals may be members of the same kin group (clan) but belong to different military groups.

Settlement Patterns: The Village

This change in social and political organization is reflected in the development of Mesopotamian and Mesoamerican villages (Flannery, 1972). The first sedentary communities in the Near East were compounds or homesteads of small circular houses. These dwellings had stone foundations

Reconstructing Prehistoric Social Organization

In the past, archeologists attempting to understand human prehistory have focused chiefly on technology and, to a lesser degree, on subsistence practices. Recently, far greater attention has been given to reconstructing the social organization of prehistoric groups and the behavior of prehistoric peoples.

In some instances, archeologists have concentrated on the organizational patterns of people who occupied specific settlements. William Longacre (1970) and James Hill (1970), for example, have investigated prehistoric Pueblo communities in northern Arizona.

By studying prehistoric Pueblo architecture and artifacts and comparing their findings to modern Pueblo society, they were able to make several inferences about the residence patterns of prehistoric Pueblo society.

During his excavation of Broken K Pueblo in the Hay Hollow Valley of Arizona, Hill noticed differences in the size and structure of the rooms, which can be put into three categories. First, there were a number of large rooms with structural features such as firepits, mealing bins, and ventilators; Hill concluded that these were *habitation rooms*. The second type of room, on the other hand, was small, with few distinctive structural features; these were presumably *storage rooms*.

Because there was an equal number of the small and large rooms, Hill inferred that each household occupied two rooms—a habitation room and a storage room. And because he could find no structural differences between individual rooms of each type, Hill hypothesized that each household unit was performing the same activities and therefore must have been self-contained and functionally independent. The third type of room Hill found had structural features indicating that it was the *kiva*, which in the prehistoric Southwest was a ceremonial room accessible only to men.

Ethnographic analysis of modern western Pueblo society supports Hill's inferences: modern pueblos do contain three types of rooms similar in size and structure to the types discovered at Broken K. Moreover, modern western Pueblo society is founded on a sexual division of labor in which separate tasks are carried out by the two different sexes in separate locations. Statistical analysis of male- and female-associated artifacts found in the different rooms of Broken K demonstrate that the sexual division of labor was also characteristic of that society.

Furthermore, by studying certain elements of design in different parts of the pueblo, Hill was able to reach a number of other conclusions regarding living patterns at Broken K. Statistical analysis of ceramics and other artifacts demonstrated that there were five basic clusters of design elements used in five different parts of the pueblo. Because the items he analyzed are ethnographically associated with female activities, because modern Pueblos pass down ceramic design elements from mother to daughter, and because modern Pueblos live in matrilocal residence units, Hill concluded that the five clusters of design elements represented five different matrilocal residence groups within the pueblo.

Jeffrey Dean (1970) and Arthur Rohn (1971) have used some of the same methods in analyzing cliff dwellings on the Colorado Plateau. Like Longacre and Hill, they were able to identify habitation, storage, communal, and ceremonial rooms. From the arrangement of the rooms, they were able to infer that the settlements were made up of a series of household units, each with one or more habitation and storage rooms clustered around a central courtyard area.

In other studies, the emphasis has been less on specific sites than on broad patterns of organizational change in a region. Deetz (1965) and Whallon (1968) have both examined shifts in post-marital residence practices—Deetz among the Arikara of South Dakota and Whallon among the Owasco, ancestors of the Iroquois. Ethnographic evidence strongly suggests that the Iroquois were matrilocal and that the Iroquois potters were women. Whallon hypothesized that matrilocality would be reflected by a high degree of stylistic homogeneity in ceramics. The styles would be homogeneous because women remained in the villages where they were born throughout their lives, and thus presumably would not be exposed to new stylistic influences. The ceramic designs proved, in fact, to be largely homogeneous, thus bearing out the hypothesis. There were changes in stylistic homogeneity through time, but Whallon argued that they reflected a decrease in the degree of matrilocality and of village autonomy.

In still other studies, attempts have been made to test broad hypotheses about human behavior and culture in general. Using ceramic collections from the Hay Hollow Valley, Mark Leone (1968) tested the hypothesis that greater dependence upon agriculture increases the social autonomy of neighboring villages. He reasoned that less communication between villages would be reflected in a rise in stylistic homogeneity, whereas more communication would be reflected in a decline in stylistic homogeneity. To measure the degree of stylistic homogeneity, Leone performed statistical tests on ceramic artifacts. His tests demonstrated a higher degree of stylistic homogeneity when people were more dependent upon agriculture, enabling him to conclude that the economic autonomy of agricultural communities resulted in greater village endogamy.

Such studies are now entering a second generation—much of the early work has been criticized, and new ways of thinking about and attacking the problem of reconstruction have been developed. For example, Stephen Plog (1977) has reexamined the ceramics that Longacre and Hill used in their studies of the Carter Ranch and Broken K pueblos. He found that some of the patterning that they discovered was the product of temporal variation in the occupation of the site rather than different but more or less contemporary design traditions, as they had inferred. Moreover, he developed evidence that some of the pottery was not made at the site at all, but traded in. These results clearly call into question the conclusion that different designs represent groups of mothers and daughters making pottery in slightly different traditions. But while Plog's research challenges the specific findings of Longacre and Hill, in a larger sense it confirms the validity of their approach; all three studies suggest that patterns of social interaction can indeed be read from the archeological record, if only we interpret that record with sufficient attention to detail.

Many archeologists have also questioned the *ethnographic model* underlying Longacre and Hill's work. Basically, they assumed that women made the pottery, and that mothers taught their daughters how to do so. Since daughters learned design techniques from their mothers and in a matrilocal residence pattern, continued to live in the same household, design traditions would be localized in the women's residence areas. Other investigators have suggested that this model is far too simple—that women making pottery would almost certainly learn techniques and absorb design influences from sources other than their own mothers.

In order to refine his model and increase the range of information that can be obtained through the study of design traditions, Longacre has undertaken a study of pottery-making techniques among the Kalinga of the Philippines. Although no results have been published as yet, his research there should greatly increase the sophistication of our ethnographic models and our ability to make inferences about past societies. Such research, carried out among living peoples to shed light on the relationship of material culture to subsistence practices and social organization, belongs to the subfield of *ethnoarcheology*. Ethnoarcheological studies are presently under way in many parts of the world. Currently, they constitute one of the most exciting areas of archeological research—and one of the most urgent, since the traditional ways of life which are their object are disappearing so rapidly.

Pueblo communities in the American Southwest were based upon a corn, beans, and squash economy. As their communities became larger and more sedentary, the Pueblos began to live in multistory cliff dwellings like the one whose ruins are pictured here, at Mesa Verde, Colorado. *(Fritz Henle/Photo Researchers)*

and room for only a few individuals. Central storage areas were probably used by the whole community. Between 11,000 and 8,500 B.P., villages of this type were widespread throughout the Near East. They reflected a social organization probably similar to that of early Near Eastern foraging groups—one based on a sexual division of labor and communal sharing rather than on the family. The houses were built not for a husband and wife and their children but for individuals; and resources were the property of the whole community. There is little evidence of social ranking, and few signs that some individuals were wealthier than others.

Nothing comparable to the compound villages has been found in Mexico. During the early stages of domestication, Mesoamerican populations were still mobile. They probably occupied a variety of sites—temporary camps for planting, hunting, and gathering. Once agriculture became firmly established, however, a new settlement pattern became widespread in both areas: a community of rectangular houses built to accommodate nuclear families. Private courtyards or patios were walled off from neighboring houses, and each home had its own food storage facilities. Variations in raw materials, luxury goods, and storage facilities from one household to another indicate that these villages were socially ranked—that is, inequalities in prestige and wealth had already appeared.

This settlement pattern reflects a form of social organization based on the individual household rather than an extended communal work group. This pattern had always been present among Mesoamerican populations, but it represented something new in the Near East. The transition occurred sometime between 9,000 and 7,500 B.P. What caused it?

The new villages had several advantages over the old compound homestead. For one thing, they were at once larger and more compact (see photograph), and therefore more easily defended. Ranking and political leadership enabled the village to grow. The earlier settlements, lacking these organizational devices, were unable to coordinate activities and keep the peace once the community had grown beyond a limited size. Moreover, where the individual household is the basic economic unit and there is opportunity for personal gain, production generally intensifies (Flannery, 1972).

As we shall see in the following chapter, the societies that subsequently developed in the Near East and Mesoamerica were based on more concentrated populations, more intensive food production, and social ranking. These developments were effectively promoted by the large, well-organized village societies that emerged late in this stage.

Trade

During this period, trade networks also became increasingly important in bringing distant resources to now sedentary groups. One of the more elaborate trade networks we know of was developed by people living in the eastern half of what is now the United States between 2,100 and 1,500 years ago. The archeologists Stuart Struever and Gail Houart (1972), who have studied these Indian sites, call the network that stretched from New York to Kansas and from Michigan to Florida the Hopewell Interaction Sphere. Through this network circulated raw materials such as obsidian from the Rockies, copper from Lake Superior, stone from the lower Allegheny Mountains, and seashells from the Gulf and south Atlantic coasts, as well as items manufactured from these materials, such as pipes, earspools (items of personal adornment, worn in the earlobe), and copper cutout figures (symbols of social standing that were worn or carried). Exchanged among groups with distinctive regional variations in subsistence items, they served as common markers of status in different cultural traditions.

The name Hopewell comes from a site in south-central Ohio, one of about twelve large sites located 65 to 290 kilometers (40 to 180 mi.) apart on major rivers in the Midwest. Of these, Hopewell is the largest. It has the greatest number of mounds, unique kinds of burial constructions, and the widest variety of artifacts and raw materials. Hopewell was probably the major receiving, manufacturing, and transaction center for the Ohio region, and perhaps beyond. Artisans and craftspeople would have worked in this center. (No doubt there were experts in various crafts at other villages as well; perhaps particular villages were already becoming known for their special skills in making one item or another.) Since someone had to oversee the manufacturing and exchange processes, there is a good chance that some central coordinating authority was located at Hopewell. Perhaps it was the headquarters of some preeminent trader who played a major role in directing the flow of resources throughout the region.

The Growth of Ranking

As we have already suggested, this period was characterized by a trend toward social ranking. Archeologists often use analyses of burial populations for studies of ranking, since the way in which people are buried closely reflects their status in life. When high-status groups exist in a community, they usually receive preferential treatment at burial. The archeologist Christopher Peebles (1971) has examined burial populations in the southeastern United States dating to around 1,000 B.P. He discovered that signs of status were similar over a wide area, and that settlements were connected through an economic and political hierarchy in which the residents of larger sites dominated those of the smaller vil-

Computers in Archeology

As the scale of archeological research has increased in recent years, so has the amount of information that the archeologist must handle. Not only more evidence, but more *categories* of evidence are being retrieved, and more kinds of analysis are being conducted on those materials. Consequently, there are many more data that must be taken into account. To help them use these data, modern archeologists have come to rely increasingly on electronic computers.

Computers can aid archeological research in a number of ways. First, they can be used simply to keep a record of what is being recovered—to store information on the kinds of evidence that have been excavated and the precise location in which they were found. In most instances, this information is fed into the computer as materials are analyzed in the laboratory. Recently, however, some archeologists have established computer terminals in the field so that the facts can be stored immediately.

Second, computers can be used to map the distribution of artifacts over large areas. Figure 1 is a map of the distribution of chipped stone artifacts using obsidian from various sources in California. These artifacts were recovered from a variety of different sites in the state. Using chemical analysis, archeologist Jonathan Erickson identified the source of the stone and then used a computer program called SYMAP to map its distribution over the state.

Finally, computers are used for a variety of typological purposes. In examining ancient artifacts, archeologists have discovered more and more different kinds of attributes that are useful in establishing date and function. However, this multiplication of different attributes can make tool analysis a bewilderingly difficult task. When confronted with a substantial collection of tools, each of which differs from some but not all of the others in perhaps twelve different characteristics, the human brain simply cannot keep all these factors in mind at the same time. Computers, on the other hand, are capable of considering the relationship among a very large number of variables simultaneously.

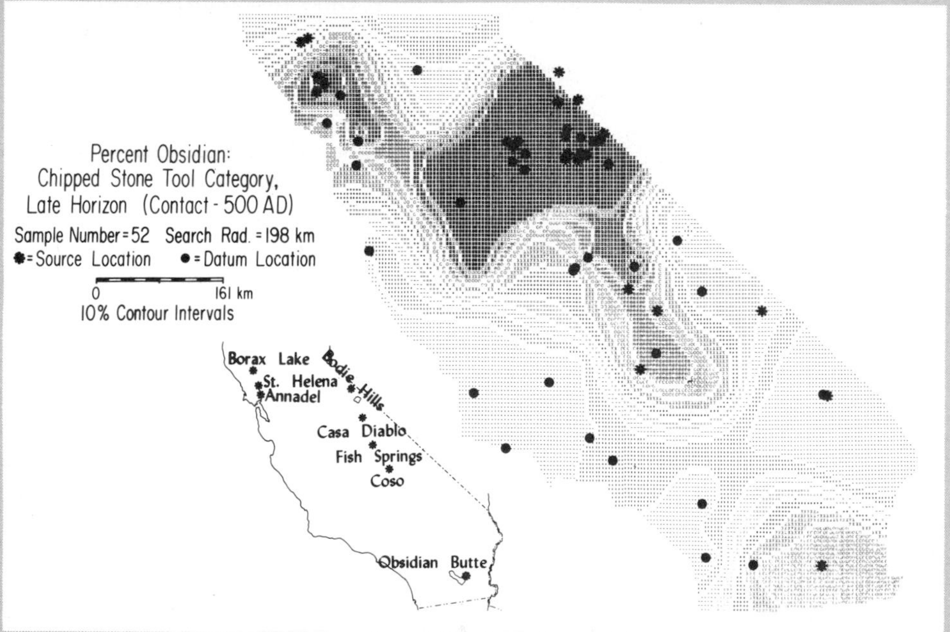

Figure 1. Distribution of obsidian chipped stone tools in California. *(Courtesy of Jonathan Erickson)*

lages. These groups were also involved in a trade network nearly as extensive as the Hopewell Interaction Sphere.

Such evidence suggests that we must regard egalitarian tribal organization, even though it still exists in some areas today, as a temporary and unstable form of organization. In the southwestern United States and northern Europe, in the Near East and Mesoamerica, tribal society was quickly replaced by new forms of organization based on the principle of ranking. In the next chapter, we turn our attention to the evolution of these new forms of social organization.

Summary

About 10,000 years ago, people began to learn to plant and harvest crops and to domesticate various animal species. The stage of the human past during which these events occurred is known as "the emergence of food production," and is of great interest to archeologists because it brought with it more social and technological innovations than had developed in the preceding millions of years of *Homo*'s existence. On the basis of archeological evidence (for example, charred seeds and imprints of vegetable matter), several theories about how and why domestication of plants and animals occurred have been set forth. One likely view is that agricultural experiments began in areas where natural productivity was low or erratic. Such efforts involved two separate but interacting processes—genetic changes in plants and animals and changes in human subsistence strategies.

Identification and dating of plant materials bearing on the history of domestication is often very difficult. Nevertheless, botanists have specified certain traits that distinguish wild from domesticated plant specimens. Domesticated seeds, and often entire plants, are generally larger than their wild counterparts, and the two types of species frequently have different sizes and structures. A sure sign of domestication is the absence of a seed dispersal mechanism. The archeologist investigating animals confronts the same problems with plants. Techniques have been developed to differentiate between wild and domesticated species—analysis of teeth and bone fragments, bone size, and microstructural analysis.

Humans played a crucial role in the rise of domesticated species. As they became part of the environment of certain plants and animals, people created new selective pressures that sped up the pace of evolution and affected its direction. When they moved to new habitats, they carried only high-yield resources, and thus acted as selective agents. The resources that these early cultivators selected became those that they depended on, and the relationship between humans and their domesticated plants and animals was mutually beneficial.

People soon began to exercise greater control over their environment. They found that they could consume or store some of the seeds they collected, instead of replanting them. They also started to alter the physiology of the plants and animals on which they depended, and to defend their fields from weeds and their animals from predators. Most significantly, the early agriculturalists began to employ soil and water control devices. They relied on techniques such as *shifting cultivation* and *rainfall farming*. Eventually, more productive methods, including *floodwater farming*, were used. Of course, these techniques varied from region to region, depending on climate, rainfall, soil, and other environmental factors.

With the development of agriculture came important technological advances. Specialized tools—axes, sickles, containers, and storage buildings—were invented to facilitate food production. The development of pottery—and later metallurgy—flourished.

The earliest evidence of cultivation and herding—dating back to about 12,000 B.P.—comes from the Near East, where wheat and barley were the first staple crops. China and Southeast Asia were also among the first areas to develop agriculture. Millet was the chief crop in early Chinese cultivation. In Mesoamerica and South America, cultivation appeared at least 1,000 years later than in the Near East. Herding never became as important in these areas as it did in the Old World. New World staple crops included maize and beans.

The spread of agriculture was not a simple process. Diffusion was a major factor in many regions, but it often coexisted with local innovation and/or older subsistence strategies. Northern Europe and the American Southwest are cases in point. In other areas, the role of diffusion was limited by environmental or social factors. There are still some parts of the world about which our knowledge of the domestication process is particularly incomplete. They include Africa and the tropical regions of the New World.

In spite of the regional differences in agricultural patterns, there seems to be a common theme underlying them—population growth and the instability that accompanied it. Sedentism is associated with marked population growth, and such increases probably upset the balance between human groups and the resources on which they depended. In some areas, infanticide, postpartum taboos, or migrations kept populations lower. With *intensification*, however, more food could be extracted from the same area to cope with a rising population.

Early cultivation did not necessarily improve people's diet and health. Its major adaptive value was that it increased the size and stability of the subsistence base. Greater productivity and reliability of food supplies led to further population growth, thus setting up a feedback cycle.

The more people came to depend upon agriculture, the more they began to settle in permanent communities. As these settlements grew, a new social organization, the *tribe*, arose. The family, rather than the whole band, became the basic producing unit.

Villages began to develop in the Near East between 11,000 and 8,500 B.P. The first villages were based on patterns of sexual division of labor and communal sharing. Later, between 9,000 and 7,500 B.P., private houses and storage facilities emerged in the Near East and Mesoamerica. During this period, trade networks became an important means of bringing distant resources to sedentary groups. This period was also characterized by a trend toward increasing social stratification.

Glossary

domestication the process of change in plants and animals making possible the planting and harvesting of crops and the bringing of various animal species under human control

floodwater farming planting crops where they can be watered by surface runoff—for example, next to shallow rivers or in seasonally flooded areas

intensification the process of investing more labor so as to extract more food from the same area

pot irrigation an early, relatively simple irrigation system that involved digging shallow wells in the fields and drawing water from them in pots

rainfall farming planting fields in locations where rainfall is generally sufficient to sustain the growth of crops

ranking the existence of differences in prestige and social standing within a society

sedentism a settlement pattern in which the social group lives in permanent, year-round communities

shifting cultivation a form of agriculture in which fields are cultivated until the soil nutrients are depleted and productivity starts to decline, and are then allowed to lie fallow until fertility is restored

slash-and-burn agriculture a tropical variety of shifting cultivation in which trees are felled to allow light to reach the field and then burned to produce fertilizer

Suggested Readings

BRAIDWOOD, R., AND WILLEY, G. 1962
Courses Toward Urban Life. Chicago: Aldine. Contains articles describing the developments leading to the emergence of food production in many areas of the world.

HEISER, C. 1973
Seed to Civilization. San Francisco: W. H. Freeman. A discussion of man's most important plant and animal domesticates and their origins.

STRUEVER, S., ED. 1971
Prehistoric Agriculture. Garden City, N.Y.: Natural History Press. An anthology of the most important theories that archeologists have developed to account for the emergence of food production.

UCKO, P. J., AND DIMBLEBY, G. W., EDS. 1969
The Domestication and Exploitation of Plants and Animals. Chicago: Aldine. A collection of theoretical and substantive articles describing recent developments in the study of food production.

Chapter Thirteen

The Rise of the State and Urban Society

The people of many cultures were still living in small farming communities well into the nineteenth and twentieth centuries. Nevertheless, the history of the last 7,000 years is essentially the history of a remarkably swift transition to an entirely new form of sociopolitical organization—the state—accompanied by an entirely new type of settlement—the city.

The rise of states and cities is often looked on as part of a still larger process—the evolution of a new form of culture that we commonly call civilization. What is civilization? To most of us, the word suggests cultural refinement—arts and letters, intellectual inquiry, elaborate codes of manners and social conduct—or perhaps the physical conveniences and creature comforts made possible by advanced technology. But these rather vague notions apply to our own society and are not particularly helpful in identifying the fundamental qualities of ancient civilizations. In one of the best-known attempts to define the concept, V. Gordon Childe (1952) has proposed that there are ten technological, social, and ideological characteristics of civilization:

Archeologists still debate whether Maya society was a true state, but there is no doubt that the Maya possessed several characteristics commonly found in emerging states, including monumental architecture and a close integration of religion and secular power. This is Temple 1 at Tikal, in modern-day Guatemala, one of the earliest and largest ceremonial centers in Mesoamerica. From such ceremonial centers the Mayan priest-bureaucrats exercised their authority over many of the society's activities. *(George Holton/Photo Researchers)*

1. Large population and settlement size (the city)
2. The accumulation of surplus wealth from intensive land use and increased productivity, and the existence of some central authority (the state) with the power to collect this surplus (taxation)
3. Public works and buildings on a monumental scale
4. Writing
5. Exact predictive sciences such as astronomy and mathematics
6. Proliferation of specialized nonagricultural occupations—craftsmen, merchants, priests, public officials, and so on
7. Division of society into different classes (social stratification)
8. Political organization based on social class and on residence within the territory, rather than on kinship (citizenship)
9. Long-distance trade networks involving the exchange of subsistence and luxury goods and services
10. Representational art reflecting sophisticated conceptualization and technique

This definition is too comprehensive to apply to all ancient civilizations (Adams, 1966). Among the Inca, for example, a civilization developed without a system of writing. Still, as a general summary of the spectacularly complex societies that we see rising in this period, the list serves quite well. All these things were happening; human societies were undergoing radical transformations.

Nevertheless, modern archeologists, rather than trying to give attention to all aspects of the early civilizations, concentrate on two specific

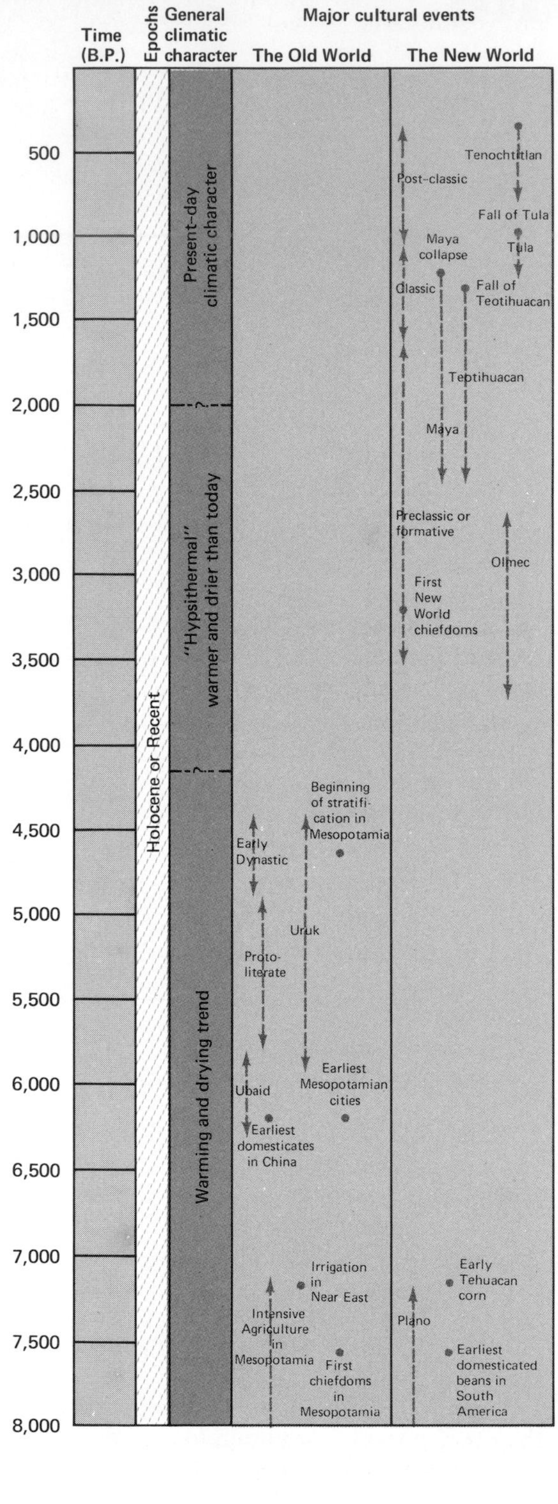

Figure 13-1. Time chart for the emergence of states and related developments.

aspects that are most central, subsuming or causing many of the other changes. These are the new settlement type—the city—and the new form of political organization—the state. Accordingly, our chapter will begin with the city, the more concrete of these two developments.

THE CITY

Cities, to be sure, are larger than villages. But at what point does a town become a city? And is size the only difference? Archeologists William Sanders and Barbara Price (1968) have defined the *city* as a community with a large population concentrated in a compact area and characterized by a high level of social stratification. *Social stratification*, an item that we have already seen in Childe's list, is the division of the members of a society into different classes, based on their wealth, power, and economic specialization. After studying numerous Mesoamerican settlements, Sanders and Price found that all settlements with population densities of 1,930 or more persons per square kilometer (5,000 persons per square mile) had a high degree of social stratification. Thus, their definition contains both a density characteristic (1,930 people per square kilometer) and an organizational characteristic (stratified society).

Stratification and population density provide the abstract framework for a definition of the city. But they do not suggest the marvelous vitality and diversity of ancient cities. Some were religious centers, some trade centers, some crafts centers, some administrative centers. Some were all of these. They swarmed with people of different occupations and different degrees of privilege: slaves, farmers, soldiers, craftsmen, priests, princes. Their avenues and alleys were lined with temples, workshops, markets, and houses and apartments by the thousands.

To get an idea of the complexity of the ancient cities, let us look closely at one of them.

Teotihuacán

Teotihuacán—the name of both a civilization and its central city—flourished between 1,800 and 1,200 B.P. The city was the most important center of religion, trade, and crafts production in all of Mesoamerica.[1] And though its inhabitants lacked certain technological aids that would seem almost indispensable in extending their influence over neighboring regions—the wheel, the sail, pack animals—they still managed to create a sizable empire.

Covering an area of 20 square kilometers (8 sq. mi.)—larger than the Rome of the Caesars—the city of Teotihuacán lay in a valley about 40 kilometers (25 mi.) northeast of where Mexico City is today. At the height of its development, in 1,500 B.P., its population probably numbered between 150,000 and 200,000 inhabitants.

To those thousands of people who journeyed to Teotihuacán year by year from the outlying farmlands, the city must have been an incomparably dazzling sight. Its streets were laid out in a grid pattern with two central axes: an east-west avenue and a north-south main street now called the Avenue of the Dead. At the center of the city, where these two roads intersected, there were two vast compounds. One was the Ciudadela, a cluster of buildings covering 16 hectares (40 acres) and including the royal palaces, a temple, and the city's administrative buildings. Opposite the Ciudadela was the Great Compound, the city's marketplace, covering fully 24 hectares (60 acres). To the north, along the Avenue of the Dead, lay the residences of the elite, numerous temples, and two gigantic religious monuments—the Pyramid of the Sun and the Pyramid of the Moon. The rest of the city consisted largely of craft workshops by the hundreds and apartment complexes by the thousands.

The architecture and layout of the city tell us a great deal about life there. In the first place, the sheer vastness of the marketplace attests to the preeminence of Teotihuacán as a trade center. To the Great Compound buyers and sellers came from all over what is now Mexico. Local farmers brought their produce; craftsmen brought their tools, pots, figurines, and gems; traders brought staples and artifacts from as far away as the realm of the Maya, 1,000 kilometers (620 mi.) to the south.

Second, the number and scale of Teotihuacán's sacred structures are evidence of its importance as a religious center—and also of the major role played by religion in this early state. For only the government could have mobilized the materials and labor necessary to build these monumental temples and pyramids. Presumably, they would only have done so to glorify the state and their gods. In fact, there is little architectural separation of religious and other royal structures. High-status residences adjoin the great temples, and one of the largest of the temples is located in the middle of the Ciudadela, the administrative center. As Rene Millon, director of the excavation at Teotihuacán, has written, "When one has walked the 'Street of the Dead' from the Ciudadela and the Great Compound . . . to the Plaza of the Moon, it is difficult to avoid the conclusion that one of the purposes its architects had in mind was to overwhelm the viewer, to impress upon him the power and the glory of the gods of Teotihuacan and their earthly representatives" (1974: 226).

The city, then, was both a great shrine and a great market. No doubt many pilgrims and traders swelled its already large population. "At its height the city must have attracted thousands of outsiders to its temples and markets every day, and tens of thousands for major festivals. These would have included pilgrims, people attracted to the marketplace, petty traders, visitors, foreign dignitaries, religious personages, and probably a predictable group of thieves and con men" (Millon, 1974: 214).

Perhaps even more central to the city's preeminence than trade or religion was its extensive crafts industry. Indeed, what made it a trade center was the fact that it produced so many trade goods. Fully a quarter of the population were families engaged in crafts. Of the workshops that have been excavated so far, 100 to 150

[1] This account is based on Adams (1966), Sanders and Marino (1970), and Millon (1974).

The Pyramid of the Sun at Teotihuacán. *(Georg Gerster/Photo Researchers)*

were devoted to ceramics, 15 to figurines, and a number of others to basalt tools, painted slate ornaments, and precious gems. In addition, there were undoubtedly a large number of workshops devoted to perishable materials that have left no trace: cloth, baskets, matting, leather goods, wooden artifacts, and precious feathers. (From the evidence of the art, feathers appear to have been highly prized as personal ornaments.)

Most important of all, however, was the production of obsidian tools. Teotihuacán's obsidian workshops probably outnumbered all the other workshops combined, and they carried the principle of craft specialization to its furthest limits. There were workshops for obsidian blades, others for obsidian knives, still others for obsidian points. Many of the obsidian craftsmen apparently worked within a walled precinct attached to the Pyramid of the Moon—a fact that suggests that this industry, so important to the economy of the city, may have been incorporated to some degree into the temple community and tightly controlled by the government.

The apartment compounds in which the craftsmen and other middle- to low-status people lived are an especially interesting feature of this metropolis. There are about 2,200 of them, ranging in size from 225 square meters—roughly the size of a modest three-room city apartment today—to 7,500 square meters, or half an acre. Each compound consists of a single walled-in rectangle containing a honeycomb of small one-story apartments. The apartments apparently did not grow by random additions. The residential rooms are carefully planned around patios, hallways, entrances, light wells, and drainage systems. Like the high-rise apartment buildings of modern cities, these compounds seem to have been deliberately designed for crowded urban life. They could house more people on a given piece of land than could separate houses. (The average compound had about sixty to one hundred residents.)

The residents of a compound formed a cohesive group. They conducted rituals together, in a small temple built within the compound. They were probably also related by common occupation and by various degrees of kinship. Preliminary research suggests that in each compound there was a core group of several families, related through the males, along with various other people who were taken on over the years because they were kinsmen, or came from the same rural village as the core family, or were simply needed as workshop apprentices.

As the apartments were clustered in the compounds, so were the compounds clustered together into barrios, or neighborhoods, of varying degrees of status. There were even tenementlike barrios on the edge of the city, where low-status people lived in especially crowded compounds. Barrio residents also tended to be employed in the same crafts. There was a merchants' barrio as well, and at least one ethnic neighborhood, the Oaxaca barrio, where families from the area of present-day Oaxaca went on for generations making their implements and designing their tombs in the style of that region.

Surrounding the city were the farms that fed Teotihuacán's elite and its thousands of craftsmen. (Some of the outlying towns had their own civic centers, modeled after Teotihuacán's—an indication of the influence of that city.) The farming communities specialized in different kinds of produce, some growing maize, others squash, beans, maguey, and other crops. A large number of the city residents—probably as many as two-thirds—were part-time farmers, living in the city only part of the year and spending the rest of the year working on the farms and bringing the produce in to the market. Why they lived in the city at all is an interesting and unresolved question. Perhaps the government forced them to do so, in order to facilitate tax collection or to retain tight control over the agricultural community.

In addition to those we have already mentioned—the royalty, the elite, the priests, the merchants, the craftsmen, and the farmers—there were people engaged in numerous other occupations: soldiers, architects, mural painters, poets, dancers, singers, and probably many more of whom we have no knowledge. Each of these occupations had its place in the hierarchy of social classes. Indeed, in all areas of life there was subdivision and specialization. Moreover, differences of status, occupation, and regional origin were probably expressed in different styles of clothing, different cult practices, and different manners. When we add to this mix the cosmopolitan element of visitors, pilgrims, and traders, with their foreign dress, language, and behavior, we can see that Teotihuacán was a true metropolis, in the modern sense of the word.

Other Ancient Cities

In Teotihuacán we can discern the basic features of the ancient city: a large collection of people concentrated in a relatively small space, occupied in specialized crafts, organized into a rigid class system, fed by an outlying agricultural belt, participating in a trade network with other cities, and governed by a supremely powerful political-religious establishment, which was glorified by massive architectural monuments. Each urban center, however, combined and expressed these basic components in a different way. For each city had its own unique physical, political, and social organization.

Thousands of miles to the south, in what is now Peru, rose the centers of the Inca empire, comparable to that of Teotihuacán in power and territory. Cuzco, the Inca capital, situated in a lone spot in the Andes, was laid out in the shape of a puma, with a fortress representing the head and a large public square situated between the front and hind legs. Cuzco's poor were not allowed to live in this artfully designed city; they were confined to an outlying squatters' area.

The control that the Inca elite exercised over the poor is even more strikingly evident in another of their centers, Huanaco Vieho, whose ruins lie just north of Lima, Peru. Huanaco Vieho was clearly an administrative center, populated by Inca officials sent out to supervise the work of the local peasants. The residential district consisted of elegant buildings clustered around a courtyard. The only evidence of the local folk are crudely made houses in an area adjacent to the center. The peasants do not appear to have had access to the finely made Inca pottery that is found in the officials' houses, nor did the officials stoop to use the locally made wares.

One interesting feature of Huanaco Vieho is a vast storage center—497 storehouses with a capacity of some 38,000 cubic meters (1.34 million cu. ft.)—situated on a hillside next to the residential area. When Craig Morris and Donald Thompson (1970) began their work at this site, they guessed that the storehouses would contain craft goods that were being redistributed to the local population. Instead they found the majority of the space was used to store food: corn in large jars and potatoes tied into bales between layers of straw. Around the storerooms were guard posts, processing rooms, checking rooms, and a building where the storage pots themselves were stored. Thus it appears that the officials living in Huanaco Vieho extracted large quantities of food from the peasants and distributed little or nothing to them in return. Census data suggest that while only about 4,000 people lived in the town itself, as many as 30,000 peasants may have contributed to their sustenance.

Another Peruvian city, Chan Chan, was the

The mountainous terrain of the Andes prevented the Incas from building huge urban centers like Teotihuacán. Instead, they controlled their empire from a series of smaller and quite specialized ceremonial, trade, and administrative centers, linked by a network of excellent roads. Machu Picchu, for example, a ceremonial center, sits isolated atop a high peak in the Andes—a weird and beautiful spectacle surrounded only by other mountain peaks jutting through the clouds. (*George Holton/Photo Researchers*)

capital of a state that eventually became the chief rival of the Inca. In Chan Chan the administrative centers consisted of courtyards containing three-sided structures, called *audencias* by Spanish-speaking archeologists, where officials held audience with citizens. Some *audencias* are arranged hierarchically: one must pass through several *audencia* courts to reach the central one. Apparently citizens had to get past, and receive the approval of, several levels of lesser authorities in order to reach the person at the top. In these curious structures we seem to see the bureaucracy of the ancient city concretized (Moseley, 1975).

The Old World too had its own diverse array of urban settlements. One region that gave rise to great cities is Mesopotamia, most of which lies in present-day Iraq. Indeed, the first cities on earth arose here. One can often spot the remains of the ancient Mesopotamian cities from miles away, for they jut upward from the flat plains of Iraq in the form of enormous mounds. These mounds were created by the building of villages on top of hamlets, towns on top of villages, cities on top of towns, and newer cities on top of older cities—so that the great capitals of Mesopotamia, which began to emerge around 6,000–5,000 B.P., sat upon layer after layer of ancient rubble. The height of these hilltop cities was often further increased by tall temples. For example, in Uruk, one of the largest of the Mesopotamian cities, archeologists unearthed the oldest known terraced pyramid, called a *ziggurat*, which once rose 15 to 21 meters (roughly 50 to 70 ft.) above the ground. The ziggurat was the economic, political, and religious center of Uruk. In it and annexed to it were crafts workshops and administrative offices.

About two thousand years after the rise of the Mesopotamian cities, urban centers began to appear in China. Between roughly 3,800 and 3,000 years ago, the Shang rulers of China established capital cities in several locations. One such city, Cheng-chou, was surrounded by an earthen wall of astounding proportions: 10 meters (33 ft.) high and 20 meters thick. So far, little excavation has been done inside the walls, but outside the walls archeologists have found many workshops,

The Shang Dynasty ruled China from about 3,800 to 3,000 B.P. In this Shang tomb, a charioteer has been buried along with his chariot and two horses. *(Courtesy, British-China Friendship Association)*

including two bronze foundries and what may have been a winery. Also located beyond the walls were a number of residences: some fine houses, probably belonging to the workshop administrators, and for the poorer citizens, clusters of circular pit houses dug into the ground and covered with conical thatched roofs (Chang, 1971).

India too had its fine cities. Mohenjo-Daro, founded on the Indus River in the northwest around 4,500 B.P. (2550 B.C.) had a population of tens of thousands, as did its sister city Harappa and possibly two other as yet unexcavated cities in the same area. Further south lay the seaport city of Lothal, complete with docks, wharves, and rows of warehouses. These sites—along with many of the smaller urban centers of ancient Africa, Greece, northern England, and the Far East—are still being excavated. The information they have yielded to date is far too extensive to be covered here, but it is clear that they have a great deal more to tell us and that we still only barely understand the way life was lived in these earliest cities.

The Process of Nucleation

Whether or not it is possible to formulate a precise and universal definition of a city, it is crucial to understand that as cities were developing there were probably more borderline cases than clear-cut examples. There is no reason why the whole complex of institutions that we have been discussing should always have appeared at exactly the same time. Certainly dense population, monumental architecture, and craft specialization are related in important ways, but they did not inevitably develop simultaneously. Moreover, during this period of time there were undoubtedly as many settlements that began to evolve urban characteristics but collapsed before the development process was completed as there were settlements that became genuine cities.

In part to avoid fruitless arguments as to whether a particular settlement was just barely a city or just barely not a city, archeologists have begun to concentrate more and more on the *process* of *nucleation* (sometimes called urbanization): the movement of people into larger centers. It is far less important to decide whether a particular settlement should be classified as a full-fledged city than to try to understand why the process of nucleation occurred and why it affected people living in different areas in different ways.

There is a second and more important reason for preferring to focus on a process—nucleation—rather than a settlement type—the city. While cities are the most visible manifestation of the changes that were occurring, these changes ultimately involved a more general change in settlement patterns—in the human use of space. For example, the very existence of a city required the organization of a "hinterland" area where productive activities were carried on at least in part to sustain those living in the city. Wright and Johnson (1975) have analyzed some of the changes that occurred in the hinterland area of one ancient Mesopotamian city, Susa, beginning about 7,000 years ago. At that time, there were only small settlements, each with no more than about a hundred inhabitants. By about 6,000 B.P. a single urban center—Susa—had appeared. Within another 500 years, there were four different kinds of settlements: small and large villages, and small and large urban centers. Eventually, Susa outstripped the other large centers and became the dominant settlement in the region.

What we see in this sequence is the replacement of a settlement pattern of more or less equally sized communities by one in which there was a marked hierarchy of settlement sizes. This pattern is characteristic of the hinterlands of virtually all early cities. It appears to reflect the distribution of activities among the individual settlements. In the case of the Susa area, for example, Wright and Johnson found evidence of increasing specialization in local production. They note that during this period the production of pottery vessels becomes progressively centralized. First, it is more and more restricted to a few villages. Second, the workshops within these villages grow larger and fewer in number over time. Moreover, the bowls themselves are made in increasingly standardized fashion. There are bowls that would have held almost exactly 0.5 liter, 0.75 liter, and 1.0 liter (1 qt.)—a pattern that suggests great regularity in the unit of measurement. This precision also implies great concern with equality in the exchange of foodstuffs, or of foodstuffs for other resources.

Such specialization means that consumers and producers no longer occupy the same settlements. It therefore becomes necessary to move more goods from the point of production to the point of consumption—food from the hinterlands to the city, for example, or pots from the workshops of one village to their potential users in other villages. The result is an enormous increase in exchange and trade, such as Rathje (1973) found associated with nucleation in the Maya

Remote Sensing: An Archeological Tool

We have said that archeological excavation is usually preceded by a search for sites that are likely to yield interesting data. In many parts of the world, remote sensing—that is, aerial or satellite photography—is becoming an increasingly important technique for locating promising archeological sites.

This method depends on a complex interaction between photographic interpretation and on-site checking. The archeologist first examines the photos of the area in which he intends to work for any unusual marks or patterns on the ground surface. He records what he finds, and then goes to the area to inspect the ground and try to determine what the observed features represent. In many cases they will prove to be modern cultural creations—a fence line, for example. Sometimes, however, they will turn out to indicate the presence of an archeological site. A feature such as a buried wall, for instance, may disrupt subsurface drainage or retain a small amount of additional heat. The result will often be a subtle change in vegetation patterns, visible to the camera's eye. Sometimes the use of infrared films, which register temperature differences directly, will enable investigators to spot such features even more easily. By studying these and similar telltale signs, archeologists are becoming skilled at recognizing "site signatures" that would seldom be easily discernible by an observer on the ground without the help of remote imagery.

An aerial view of a portion of Chaco Canyon National Monument in New Mexico. A number of important archeological features are marked. Point *A* indicates a large site called Penasco Blanco. The dish-shaped depressions around the site, marked *B*, are kivas, underground ceremonial chambers of the Pueblos. Point *C* indicates the coincidence of a modern access road and a prehistoric roadway. The prehistoric roadway continues beyond the modern one, appearing in the photograph as a deeply cut furrow (*D*); *E* indicates what may have been a footpath in prehistoric times. Before aerial photography was brought to bear on this region, the existence of many of these archeological features, in particular the prehistoric system of roadways, was entirely unsuspected. *(Courtesy of Thomas Lyons, Chaco Research Center, National Park Service)*

area of Mesoamerica. Indeed, in most areas for which good data are available, nucleation and a dramatic rise in local exchange and trade appear to go hand in hand. More exchange, in turn, means a greater interdependence among the various communities. Blanton (1975) and others have argued that the growth of such interdependence, or symbiosis, is the most basic dynamic of the nucleation process.

Exchange and settlement hierarchy thus appear to have been closely associated. Some of the larger settlements in such hierarchies owed their prominence to their role as production centers, exchange centers (markets), or both. In the Susa area, Wright and Johnson observed that some of the middle-sized communities included buildings whose walls were decorated with mosaic patterns of inlaid ceramic cones. These buildings seem to have been associated with the exchange network. There are also indications of an increasingly large bureaucracy to oversee the flow of goods. This evidence is a series of clay markers recovered from the sites: tokens, seals, and eventually tablets with writing on them. Initially, tokens were sent with shipments of goods, either in leather bags or clay cylinders. Alternatively, clay seals were affixed to jars of goods. This practice implies that someone at either end was responsible for checking to see that the transporter delivered the correct quantity of goods. Later, seals and then clay tablets were used to carry messages—records of goods sent. This means that some administrator was evidently checking on the checkers, keeping records to ensure their honesty.

Wright and Johnson argue that the existence of this additional administrative level indicates that there were already individuals whose concern was the overall flow of goods among the many communities involved in the exchange network. Such administrative complexity is, in their opinion, a distinguishing characteristic of the state in contrast to earlier forms of sociopolitical organization.

The issue of administrative complexity, however, takes us beyond the subject of settlement pattern alone. We must now begin to consider the changes in sociopolitical organization associated with the growth of cities—that is, the development of the state.

THE STATE

There are almost as many definitions of the state as there are social theorists. Still most anthropologists would agree that ancient states shared four essential characteristics:

1. Society was divided into sharply differentiated social classes
2. Membership was based on residence within the territory controlled by the state—that is, the individual was subject to the state's power simply by virtue of living within its geographical boundaries
3. One or a few individuals along with an elite group (the ruling class) monopolized political power
4. The state's apparatus was run by a bureaucracy of officials.

As with cities, one can become overly involved in attempting to decide whether a given area did or did not have state organization, or at what precise point in an evolutionary sequence it appeared, and lose sight of the processes involved in the evolution of states. Some societies acquired many of the characteristics of states, but not all. In some cases where states did evolve the characteristics appeared rapidly and relatively simultaneously, while in others evolution was slower and more disparate. For this reason, it is critical to identify the major evolutionary processes involved in the development of state organization.

State Formation Processes

What are the processes that lead toward the formation of the state? One of the first answers to this question was offered by Kent Flannery (1972). According to Flannery, any given society may be seen as a series of subsystems. Like the officers in an army, these subsystems are arranged in a hierarchy, with each subsystem controlled by the one directly above it. At the bottom of the hierarchy are the most basic, survival-oriented systems, such as crop management and herding. At the top is governmental control, or whatever decision-making institutions determine social policy. And in between are the other subsystems of the society: defense, trade, religion, education, and so forth.

Flannery argues that the differences between the state and simpler societies can be grasped by comparing their hierarchies. In the first place, the state hierarchy is much more highly *differentiated* than that of the tribe or chiefdom. Social, economic, political, and religious life are divided up into a multiplicity of subsystems—different classes, different occupations, different institutions. Second, the state hierarchy is characterized by increasing *centralization*. In contrast to simpler societies, where power is more diffuse, the state consolidates decision-making authority into a single bureaucracy, which coordinates all the subsystems of the social hierarchy and allocates rewards among them.

Not only did political leaders hold more power, they held power over more things. The state was administered by a ruling class, headed by a leader who was often an absolute monarch and a high priest as well. The state had the power to levy taxes, draft soldiers, wage war, and exact tribute. In many states a formal body of law was administered by a judicial system complete with courts, judges, and other legal specialists. Members of the government bureaucracy collected taxes, managed the budget, and administered the day-to-day affairs of state, including the coordination of increasingly complex exchange relationships. Typically, priests constituted a nearly autonomous class empowered to maintain the state religion. While these specific institutions were present to greater and lesser degrees in specific cases, there was a trend toward increased centralization of decision making.

To these two processes identified by Flannery, we should add a third. Interpersonal relations in state-organized society are characterized by increasing *stratification* (Service, 1971; Fried, 1967). As we have seen, throughout the Paleolithic era hunter-gatherers lived in small *bands*, usually consisting of several loosely allied families. In some areas, the residential groups were consolidated into larger social aggregates, or *tribes*, that were united by kinship ties, common religious traditions, shared rituals, and leadership roles (though only temporary ones). Both the band and the tribe are basically egalitarian. All families have roughly the same degree of wealth, power, and prestige. There are no institutionalized political leaders, no ruling class or elected officials. Decisions affecting the group are made by men of influence, respected either for their advanced age or for their personal accomplishments in farming, warfare, or other activities.

Chiefdoms probably appeared as early as 7,500 B.P. in the Near East and 3,000 B.P. in Mesoamerica and the Andes, after food production was well established. The chiefdom differs from the egalitarian band and tribe in several major respects. First, in the chiefdom power is institutionalized. Whereas tribal and band leaders had nothing more than *influence*, authority gained (and lost) on the basis of personal qualities, the leader of the chiefdom wields true political power, based less on his superiority as a human being than on the fact that he holds the *office* of chief. Unlike tribal or band leaders, the chief is a full-time political administrator and occupies a role that is a permanent part of the social structure. Moreover, the status of the chief is hereditary—it is ascribed at birth, not achieved through personal accomplishments. In the Near East, for example, archeologists have uncovered tiny skeletons decked out in turquoise and copper ornaments and surrounded by alabaster statues. When infants and children are buried in this manner, status inherited from their parents is strongly suggested—it could hardly have been attained by the deeds of the children.

As this example suggests, it is in the chiefdom that we see the emergence of status ranking. The office of chief was held by the leading member of an elite family. As various subsidiary offices were created, these were given to members of other families, which thereby gained in prestige. Thus a hierarchy of prestige came into being. The chiefdom, in other words, like the band and the tribe, was still fundamentally a kin-based society, but the kin groups were ranked, and individuals enjoyed prestige on the basis of this ranking.

With the rise of states, power and rank became still more absolute. Social stratification began to appear, and kinship began to play a smaller and smaller role in the definition of social groups. At first the class structure was often simple: royal family, commoners, and serfs, for example. Later, a still more complex set of increasingly self-conscious social classes are in evidence. The higher-status groups controlled more of the society's resources, and had a greater ability to command the productive activities of the lower classes. The monumental architecture of the cities was possible only because a few individuals were able to order the masses to undertake their construction. As we have seen, the multitudes often lived in huts or small apartments while the elite occupied larger houses or palaces. But perhaps the most dramatic illustration of the meaning of social stratification comes from the Maya area of Mesoamerica, where the skeletons from low-status burials consistently show more evidence of disease and malnutrition than those from high-status tombs.

A fourth process associated with the evolution of states is one that we have already discussed in the previous chapter—the *intensification* of agriculture. As we shall see shortly, a great variety of techniques for producing more food from a given area of land developed along with the early states.

Whether people were better off in the stratified and specialized urban societies than their ancestors had been in the egalitarian world of the farming community is a question that political philosophers are still debating. Regardless of the answer, however, there is no question that the processes we have been describing are evident in the development of state-organized societies in many regions. We will look at the rise of states in representative areas of the New and Old Worlds.

THE RISE OF STATES

Archeologists have given less attention to the first stages of state formation than to the early agricultural villages or the later, fully developed city-states. The reason for this neglect is partly physical. The same site may consist of layer after layer of occupation, and excavation of the upper layers is naturally much easier. In addition, later occupants of sites often constructed their build-

Figure 13-2. This drawing of the acropolis at Tikal illustrates the complex problems with which the archeologist must deal in trying to understand the archeological record of early cities. Not only is the pattern of construction of any one edifice complex, but many different kinds of buildings are ultimately superimposed one on the other as the city grows. *(From The University Museum, University of Pennsylvania)*

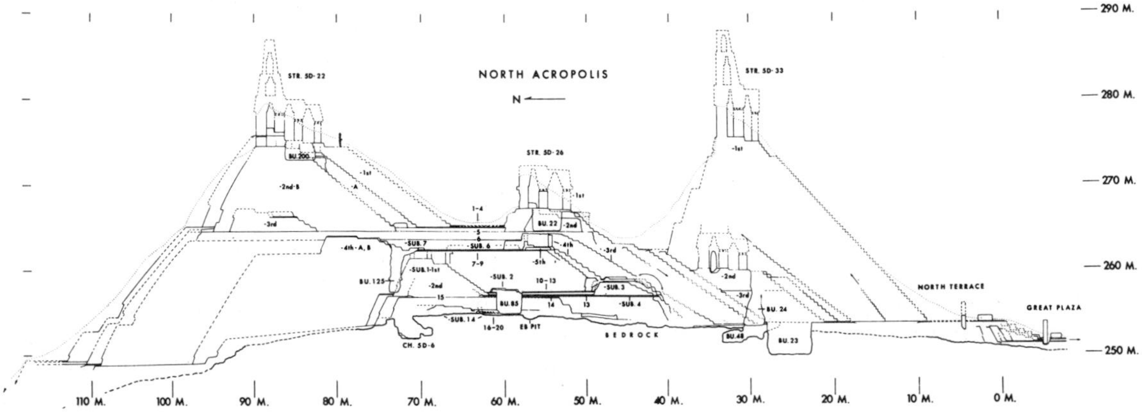

ings with secondhand materials—stones from a crumbling house, pillars from a ruined temple—thus destroying the evidence of the earlier phases of their civilization.

However, the problem is more complicated than that. State formation involves a change not only in subsistence or technology, which are relatively easy to trace, but also in social interaction—essentially, in the distribution of power. Once power is well consolidated, it becomes flamboyantly obvious. Temples and pyramids rise; high-status corpses are buried with ornaments of jade and shell, quartz and obsidian. But power in its early phases, especially before there is writing, is extremely difficult to trace. Nevertheless, recent excavations in Mesoamerica and Mesopotamia have provided enough evidence so that we can now sketch in a history of the ancient state in these two early seats of civilization.

Mesoamerica

The history of the ancient state in Mesoamerica can be divided into three stages. The first of these, which lasted from about 3,500 to 1,700 B.P., is called the *Preclassic* (or *formative*). During this stage, certain settlements grew from agricultural villages to ceremonial centers, adorned with temple-pyramids. At the same time, ranking and stratification emerged. Religion and the state were, as a rule, completely integrated by this time; full-time priest-leaders supervised both food distribution and ritual. At the end of the Preclassic stage, writing appears for the first time in Mesoamerica.

The next stage, lasting from roughly 1,700 to 1,100 B.P., is called the *Classic.* During this time, there were great increases in population and in food production. True cities arose, ten to twenty times larger than even the largest Preclassic settlements. One of these cities was Teotihuacán, which exemplifies the major characteristics of the period. With urbanism came the expansion of trade, the construction of immense ceremonial centers, and the development of a highly specialized crafts industry to decorate the ceremonial centers and to produce trade goods. The stratification system became further solidified. The state was probably ruled by a hereditary elite, headed by a monarch claiming divine power.

The third stage, the *Postclassic,* lasted from 1,100 B.P. to the arrival of the Europeans in 430 B.P. (A.D. 1520). This stage was, by and large, one of social unrest; rival states vied for territory, and militarism increased.

We will trace these changes chiefly through an examination of one major region: the Valley of Mexico. There, three different states arose in succession; each in turn flourished, ruled the valley, and was eventually destroyed.

Settlement Pattern

The valley states developed in an urban setting. From about 4,100 to 3,800 B.P., the people in this region lived in small settlements, farming the fertile soil of the valley. Near the marshy shores of lakes, they planted maize and other crops. The lakes also provided them with fish and waterfowl. Between 2,400 and 1,600 B.P., a number of larger settlements, with populations in the thousands, grew up on the lakeshore and nearby foothills. From these settlements, the first state developed.

Cuicuilco, with a population of somewhere between 1,800 and 3,800, was the largest settlement in the area. Second was the newer settlement of Teotihuacán. Over the next few centuries each of them steadily gained population, perhaps competing with one another, until at last, sometime around the birth of Christ, a volcano near Cuicuilco erupted and buried the center in lava. Its power no longer challenged, Teotihuacán grew at a spectacular pace. Population flowed in from the countryside, eventually creating the metropolis that we described earlier in the chapter. The city remained the seat of power in the valley until around 1,300 B.P., when it was sacked and burned.

There followed a period of fragmentation. Population scattered; smaller settlements competed with one another; power was much less centralized. Eventually a second state, that of the Toltecs, arose, centered in the city of Tula. But the Toltecs did not manage to amass power and population on the scale of Teotihuacán. At

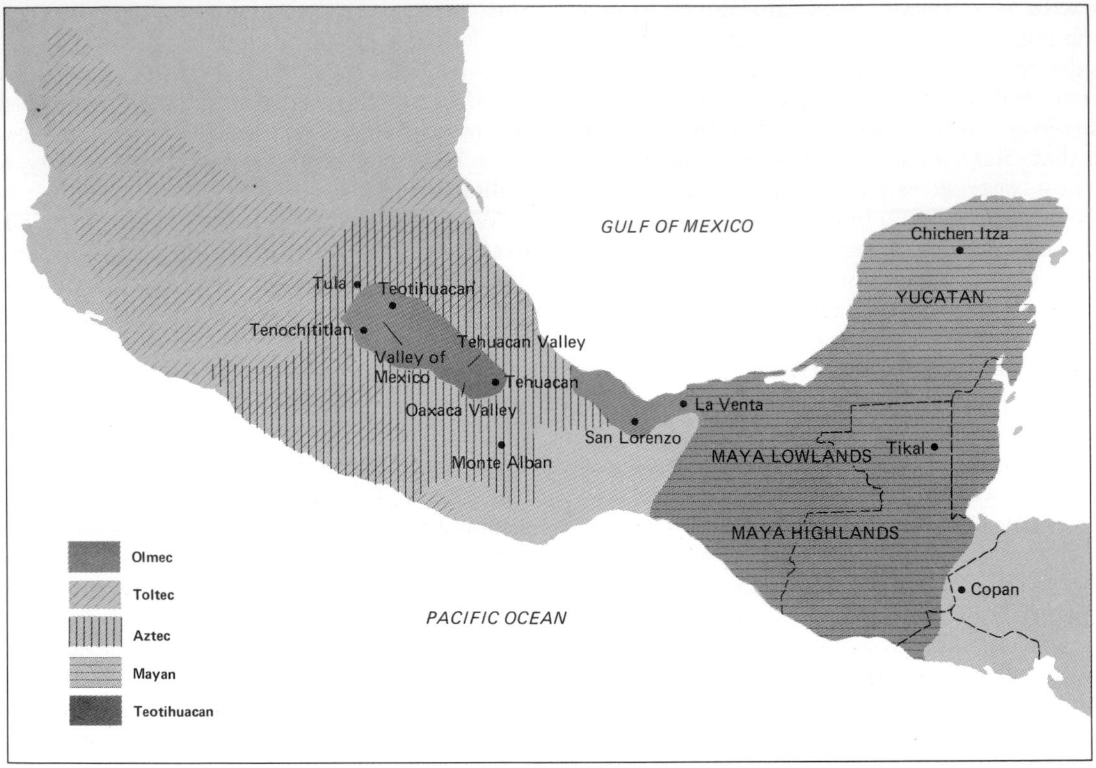

Figure 13-3. Some of the Mesoamerican societies and settlements discussed in this chapter.

maximum, Tula probably had 50,000 to 60,000 inhabitants—that is, about one-fourth to one-third of the population of Teotihuacán at its height.

Around the twelfth century, Tula fell, apparently sacked by invaders. And again, after a period of fragmentation, a new state developed: the Aztec empire, centered in the city of Tenochtitlán. Founded in 625 B.P., Tenochtitlán soon amassed a population equal to that of Teotihuacán and gained control over the valley. There is some indication, however, that its empire was shakier than Teotihuacán's. In view of its extremely short history, this is not surprising. Whereas Teotihuacán lasted almost a thousand years, Tenochtitlán had only 200 years in which to consolidate its power; in 430 B.P., Cortez and his men arrived and, assisted by Indian allies, destroyed the city.

Thus the history of the state in the Valley of Mexico is an alternation between consolidation and fragmentation. Yet despite the shifts of power, we can see in the valley states a clear overall pattern: a progression from a more theocractic to a more secular state, founded on increasing trade and social stratification.

Subsistence

The soil in the Valley of Mexico was rich, and the inhabitants devised increasingly sophisticated techniques for farming it. Lacking large field animals, the Mesoamericans never developed the plow, a great boon to agriculture in the early Old World states. They did, however, invent such highly efficient methods as canal and floodwater irrigation, terracing, and contour hoeing. By far the most original was an ingenious swamp reclamation technique invented during the Preclassic stage, perfected by the Aztecs, and still practiced in certain parts of the valley today (Armillas, 1971). Artificial island-fields called *chinampas* were created by scooping up mud from the bottom of a lake or marsh and piling it up so that it rose above the surface of the water. Around the natural island on which their city center was located, the people of Tenochtitlán created an entire constellation of chinampas, stretching for miles across Lake Texcoco. The farmers tended them in canoes, fertilizing them with human wastes, dead weeds, and nutrient-rich mud from the bottom of the lake. Thus an otherwise useless marsh was transformed into a highly productive agricultural resource.

These techniques not only yielded an ample subsistence base; they also required cooperative action and therefore brought people together in need of a leader, thus stimulating the centralization of authority.

Stratification

During the Preclassic stage, division of labor in the Valley of Mexico was rudimentary, and society was relatively egalitarian. By the Classic stage in Teotihuacán, as we have seen, society had become highly stratified. During the Postclassic stage in Tenochtitlán, the stratification system was extremely elaborate. At the top of the Aztec social ladder were the emperor and his court. Below this were the nobles. Then came the professional warriors, merchants, craftsmen, and free farmers. At the bottom of the social hierarchy were the serfs working land owned by others; the porters, who carried tribute goods from the outlying settlements back to the city; and the slaves. Precise as this class structure seems, however, there may actually have been some room for social mobility in Tenochtitlán—more, perhaps, than there had been in Teotihuacán. In Tenochtitlán, for example, even commoners could rise to high rank if they managed to accumulate great wealth or performed heroically in war (Calnek, 1976).

From other areas, we have additional evidence of marked stratification during the late Classic and Postclassic stages. Among the Maya of southern Mexico and Guatemala, for example, the monumental architecture created during these stages enables us to infer the existence of a powerful upper class. There is also abundant direct evidence of vast differences in wealth and prestige. Burials in the ceremonial centers indicate that positions in the religious hierarchy, which had once been rotated, were now held permanently—and passed down from father to son—by elite families. These families lived year-round in the ceremonial centers, where palaces were built for them. The high-status burials also contain fine luxury items, whereas rural graves often contain nothing more than skeletons. The skeletons themselves tell a story about class differences. In luxurious urban burials the adult male skeletons average about 12 centimeters (nearly 5 in.) taller than those in the poor rural burials, indicating that the Maya peasants lived shorter and much hungrier lives than the elite (Haviland, 1967). Finally, there are striking differences in housing. At Tikal, for example, residences ranged from small huts to palaces. Some of the finer houses even have huts attached—presumably as servants' quarters.

Religion and the State

During the Preclassic stage religious and secular political responsibilities were invested in the same individuals. The same was true during the Classic stage; in Teotihuacán, as we have seen, temples were the major state structures. Then, during the Postclassic stage, secular structures seem to have assumed much greater importance. This secularization is evident in the architecture of Tenochtitlán. Whereas in Teotihuacán religious and administrative buildings were to some extent combined in the same complexes, in Tenochtitlán they were separated. Furthermore, while the temples of Teotihuacán seem to dwarf the administrative buildings, the opposite is true in Tenochtitlán. The city, of course, had its great temples. The grandest, dedicated to the gods of war and rain, was a monumental twin pyramid 30 meters (98 ft.) high and 400 meters (1,300 ft.) on a side. But by far the most impressive structure in the city at the time of the Spanish invasion was the 300-room palace of the legendary emperor Montezuma.

It appears also that the temple community had no strict hierarchy of power. The palace, on the other hand, had a complex bureaucracy with

This Aztec calendar is but one example of the civilization's scientific endeavors. The Aztec year is divided into 260 days, falling within a larger 52-year time cycle. The Aztecs sacrificed humans and offered their hearts to the gods—a practice accelerated at the end of each 52-year cycle to ensure the continuity of their world. *(American Museum of Natural History)*

a rigid chain of command. Every day, for example, the leaders of the city's barrios assembled to receive the orders of the king. The orders were then passed along to lower officials, who saw to it that they were carried out.

All this is not to say that God was dead in Tenochtitlán. Religious beliefs still underpinned and legitimized the state, and daily life was still dominated by religious ceremonies, including elaborate rituals in which thousands of human beings (usually prisoners of war) were sacrificed to the gods each year. But the priests no longer exercised great influence over political affairs. These were the business of the king and his bureaucracy of officials (Blanton, 1975).

Militarism and Trade

Militarism developed slowly in the valley. There is little evidence of aggression throughout the Preclassic and much of the Classic period. Though militarism may have become important in late Teotihuacán—as indicated by murals of warriors and by signs of conflict within the city long before its fall—through most of its history it was a relatively peaceful state. With the Toltecs, however, a more military spirit invaded the valley. To increase their territory—and to bring home human victims for ritual sacrifice—the Toltecs were often at war. Toltec domination also included intensive trade, through networks even more extensive than those of Teotihuacán. After the fall of the Toltecs, the Aztecs used this same combination of intensive trade and armed force to control the valley. Through a series of huge military campaigns they eventually extended their rule over an area of 20,000 square kilometers (12,400 sq. mi.) inhabited by 5 or 6 million people. As with the Toltecs, these wars also kept them steadily supplied with sacrificial victims. But although they were continuously battling the peoples on their borders, the Aztecs did not allow this to harm their trade networks for long. Trade was in many ways the lifeblood of their state; in Tlatelolco, a sister city absorbed by Tenochtitlán, there were marketplaces larger than any in Europe at that time.

Extensive trade networks had existed in Mesoamerica long before the Aztecs, the Toltecs, or even Teotihuacán. During the Preclassic stage, trade played an important part in spreading the influence of the first great Mesoamerican civilization—that of the Olmec, who flourished along the southern Gulf coast between 3,500 and 2,500 B.P. The Olmec were part of an interaction sphere that connected them with villages from the Valley of Mexico to central Guatemala (Flannery and Schoenwetter, 1970; Pires-Ferreira, 1973). This trade, however, was probably carried on only by a relatively small number of leading families; it was casual rather than institutionalized. Moreover, it seems to have been confined to luxury goods. Aztec trade, by contrast, was highly organized. The Aztecs had a special class of long-distance traders and tribute carriers, who traveled perhaps as far as the midwestern United States to exchange and bring back goods. And although a steady flow of luxury goods poured into the city—most of the turquoise decorating the Aztec ceremonial masks, for ex-

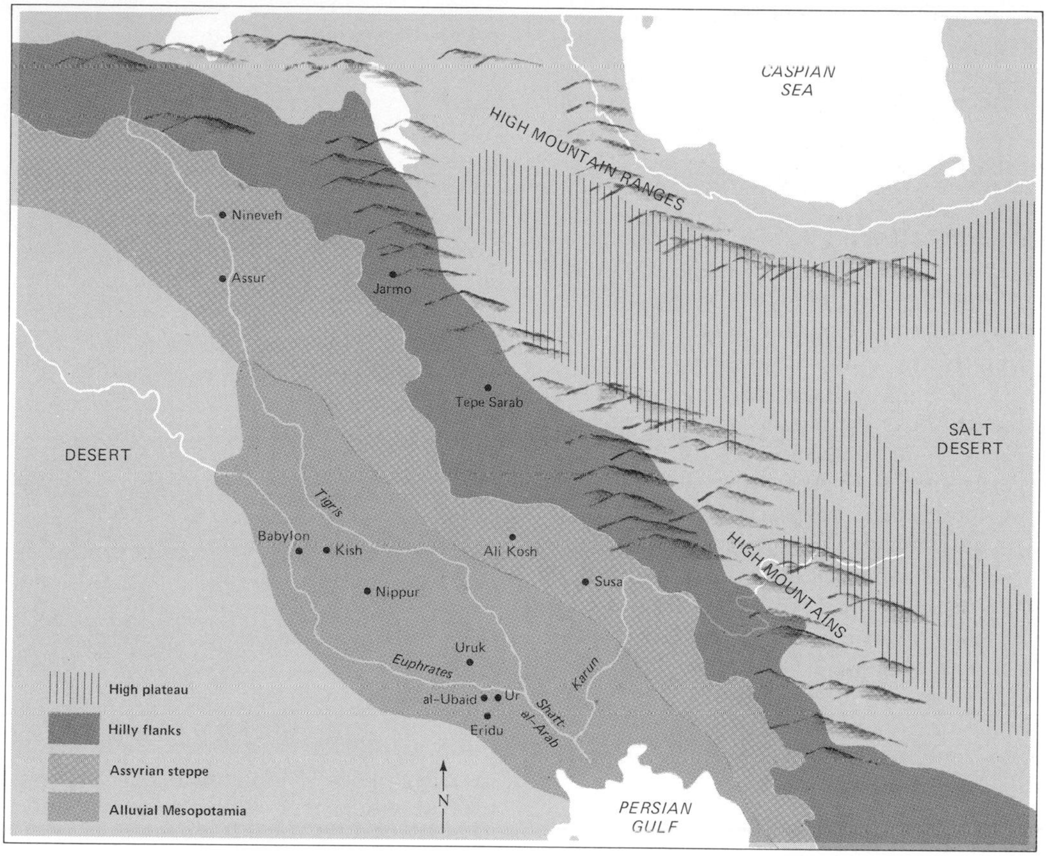

Figure 13-4. States and cities of ancient Mesopotamia.

ample, came from the vicinity of present-day Santa Fe, New Mexico—there was also substantial exchange of subsistence items, including food.

Thus the Valley of Mexico offers us a highly developed picture of the Postclassic state: a large and warlike empire, united by armed force and extensive trade, centered in a busy metropolis, and ruled by a more secular government.

Mesopotamia

Long before the Mesoamerican peoples had even begun intensive cultivation of crops, states arose in Mesopotamia, the rich floodplain fed by the Tigris, Euphrates, and Karun rivers in the Near East (Figure 13-4). The history of state formation in Mesopotamia is commonly divided into three stages: the *Ubaid* (ending 5,800 B.P.), the *Protoliterate* (5,800 to 4,900 B.P.), and the *Early Dynastic* (4,900 to 4,400 B.P.). The Ubaid phase takes its name from al' Ubaid, an early settlement of Mesopotamia. At this time people lived in small settlements centered around a temple, and priests served as ritual, political, and economic leaders. Thc Protoliterate stage, so named because it saw the appearance of an early form of writing, is characterized by the evolution of early states and craft specialization. The Early Dynastic is marked by the rise of large and powerful city-states, in constant conflict with one another.

In Mesopotamia, as in the Valley of Mexico, city and state developed together, and power passed from state to state over the course of time. Each of these states is interesting in itself. But since we cannot discuss them all, we will concentrate on one: Uruk, the largest city-state in Mesopotamia and, in its time, the largest city and state in the world.

Settlement Pattern

The evolution of the Mesopotamian civilization began on the plain between the Tigris and the Euphrates sometime between 6,000 and 5,500 B.P. During this time, the first cities grew out of clusters of farming villages and hamlets. The larger among these early communities, such as Eridu, had city centers consisting of mud-brick temples surrounded by two-story houses. Such houses were probably occupied by the elite, their servants, and their retainers (that is, live-in employees such as weavers and potters). Farther from the urban center were the houses and workshops of craftsmen. Farther still were the hovels of the peasants and farmers who provided the food to support the urbanites.

As the centuries passed and the state grew, city design remained essentially the same. However, the cities changed in other respects. In the late Protoliterate and Early Dynastic stages, they swelled in population—in some cases exceeding 40,000—and spawned huge civic and ceremonial centers. Uruk in the Early Dynastic was an enormous walled settlement with 40,000 to 100,000 inhabitants. Inside the walls were grazing fields, closely packed houses, and workshops. In the center lay the ceremonial precincts, containing temples to the god of the sky and the god of love, along with the massive ziggurat, towering above the city walls. And outside the walls, stretching for about 10 kilometers (6 mi.) in all directions, were the satellite agricultural villages, which produced food for the city.

An aerial view of the remains of Ur, one of the earliest and largest city-states in Sumeria. Dating from about 5,000 B.P., Ur covered about 375 hectares (150 acres) and contained about 25,000 people. *(Georg Gerster/Rapho/Photo Researchers)*

Subsistence

The basic crops in ancient Mesopotamia were wheat and barley. By the time the cities arose, these were being cultivated intensively. Water from the mountain streams and from the great rivers of the region was dammed, collected in reservoirs, and channeled through intricate networks of irrigation canals, to protect the crops in dry seasons and extend the amount of arable land. In addition to wheat and barley, fish from the rivers was an important part of the diet. Finally, a major factor in the feeding of Mesopotamia was the breeding of animals. Oxen and horses were used to pull the plows. Pack animals carried food from the farms to the redistribution centers. And herds of sheep, goats, and cattle provided meat, milk, and cheese in addition to hides and wool.

Early Sociopolitical Organization

The early Mesopotamian state was embedded in a society of ancient clan groups, centuries-old networks of kin who held land or practiced crafts in common. These groups also had civic duties—

to provide labor for community projects such as irrigation systems or to furnish military manpower and leadership. Thus, the clan and its leaders mediated between the state and the individual.

However, what integrated the clan groups and the society as a whole was the temple. The growing size and complexity of the society created a need for centralized management—someone to see that all the parts were coordinated. In the Ubaid and Protoliterate periods this need was probably filled by the priest, who became the early state's religious, political, and economic leader in one. Priests oversaw large irrigation projects and redistributed food surpluses from the temples, which also served as food storage centers and fish markets.

In addition, the priests supported the crafts. Stonemasons, metalworkers, carpenters, sculptors, and painters came to work on the temples. Other craftsmen turned out tools, cloth, and pottery in workshops set up within the temple precincts. The temples at Uruk, for example, maintained clothing manufacturing centers where weavers, tailors, and spinners worked. The goods they produced were then redistributed. In return for their pots, the potters were given some cloth; in return for their cloth, the weavers were given some pots. Thus the priests not only used but also coordinated specialized labor and thereby encouraged further specialization.

Trade

The temples also used the craft goods for trade. Like the Maya, the Mesopotamians lacked adequate supplies of certain very important items: timber, metal, stone for building, and stone for tools. Some things they did without. For example, whereas the Mesoamerican cities were built of stone, the Mesopotamian cities were built largely of clay bricks. But other essentials, such as copper and obsidian, they began to import as early as 7,000 B.P. Eventually, trading expeditions were organized by the temples. In time, as the temples became grander and the upper classes emerged, luxury items such as turquoise, marble, alabaster, and mother-of-pearl were brought in as well, often as tribute. Uruk in its prime had trade networks, overland and oversea, extending as far as what is now western Pakistan. And unlike Mesoamerican trade, which was carried on largely on people's backs, Mesopotamian trade was aided by the wheel, the sail, and the pack animal—all innovations of this period.

Stratification

The development of stratification in Mesopotamia was slowed by the clan groups, which followed a code of voluntary sharing. Within clans

Cuneiform, one of the earliest forms of writing, evolved in the Near East. "Cuneiform" is derived from the Latin word for "wedge," which refers to the wedge-shaped impressions of the symbols. The Sumerian tablet pictured here tells the story of "The Creation of Man." (*Courtesy, The University Museum, University of Pennsylvania*)

the richer gave to the poorer. Furthermore, clans strove to increase their prestige in the community by giving to needier clans. Thus, while there were rich and poor, there was also a constant leveling of these differences; the rich could never rise too high nor the poor fall too low.

Burials indicate that throughout the Protoliterate period status differences remained relatively slight. However, in the Early Dynastic period the Mesopotamians apparently began making up for lost time, for by about 4,400 B.P. there is evidence of a fully stratified social organization, complete with royalty and wealthy upper classes. In the city of Ur, noblewomen were buried with ribbons woven of gold in their hair. In other graves there are jewels and elegant figurines. This period also saw the rise of palaces in the cities of Eridu, Kish, Uruk, and Susa. At Susa, nearly 1,000 people, not counting slaves, lived and worked at the palace.

Actually, the great majority of the population in the Early Dynastic stage were still part of clan groups, rather than being serfs or retainers on large estates. However, the appearance of these large estates indicates the gradual shift from kinship to money as the basis of human relationships. Uruk by this time had a fairly elaborate stratification system. At the top of the social hierarchy were the royalty and the priests. Below them, in descending order, were the wealthy landowners and merchants; the bureaucrats and tradesmen; the farmers, fishermen, and sailors; and, at the very bottom, the slaves. A society that was once organized strictly by clan was now becoming organized by class.

The Secularization of the State

As the wealthy gained power, the priests lost it, and the state became increasingly secular. As Adams (1966) notes, however, the crucial factor in the separation of the role of king from that of priest was probably the militarism of the later Mesopotamian states. Traditionally, in times of crisis, a leader with extraordinary powers was chosen by the council of elders, an institution probably drawn from the clan groups. Eventually, however, an increase in the number of military expeditions and wars led to the selection of a permanent warlord to oversee the armies. From this field marshal, or five-star general, arose the office of the monarchy, which in later times became hereditary.

The king managed to displace not only the priests but the council as well. These did not disappear but became specialized institutions, the priests confining themselves to religion and the council becoming part of the king's bureaucracy.

Militarism

Militarism arose as states set out to enlarge their territories or fought to protect what they already had. The states became more defense-minded, erecting walls and other fortifications around their cities. Uruk closed itself in behind a brick wall 6 meters (20 ft.) high and 10 kilometers (6 mi.) long, studded with hundreds of watchtowers. Armor, chariots, and metal weapons came into heavy demand, stimulating the economy just as large military expenditures do in our own society.

Because of the need for security—and because more and more bodies were needed to man the army and to build the fortifications—satellite villages were drawn into the cities. In 5,000 B.P. there were hundreds of villages in Mesopotamia; by 4,400 B.P.—that is, around the end of the Early Dynastic period—only a small percentage remained (Hamblin, 1973). This interstate warring was eventually resolved by the consolidation of the states themselves. Already by about 4,800 B.P. several city-states had formed defensive alliances. After the end of the Early Dynastic, the Mesopotamian states were amassed one by one into the vast empires of the region, such as the Babylonian, the Assyrian, and the Elamite.

The basic themes of this brief sketch of the ancient Mesopotamian state should sound familiar, for they are the same ones that we saw in Mesoamerica: population increase, intensive agriculture, centralized authority, craft specialization, urbanization, trade, and stratification. Furthermore, in both areas the state grows old in much the same way: stratification becomes more rigid;

trade is extended; militarism increases; and the temple is replaced by secular structures as the seat of state power. Most of the same elements underlie the histories of other ancient states that developed in Peru, China, Egypt, Greece, Rome, and Africa.

WHY DID THE STATE EVOLVE?

It is simple to suggest, as we did earlier, that sedentism and agriculture produced the state. Yet many sedentary agricultural communities never developed state organization. Moreover, sedentism and agriculture involve a number of factors—technological, demographic, and economic. How do these factors interact to create a phenomenon such as Teotihuacán or Uruk?

Some investigators feel that it is impossible to formulate a general answer to this question. They believe that the events leading to states and cities are unique to particular times and places. Other archeologists have invested considerable time and effort in trying to identify the common elements in the birth of all (or at least most) states. We will consider several different approaches to the problem of why states arise.

Single-Cause Theories

Was there a single factor that precipitated the development of states? A number of archeologists think so, but they disagree as to what that factor is. One well-known theory is that of Karl Wittfogel (1957), who claims that the crucial factor was the construction of large-scale irrigation systems. Since these elaborate hydraulic systems required the coordination and control of large numbers of people and resources, local control, Wittfogel argues, tended to pass to an increasingly centralized ruling class—the kernel of the state.

A second important theory, that of Robert Carniero (1970), is that circumscription and warfare were the primary causes. Agricultural populations that were hemmed in either by neighboring populations or by nature (in the form of mountains, seas, or deserts) could not handle population pressure by breaking up into smaller, more dispersed settlements. Therefore they went to war to expand their territory. According to Carniero, centralized government developed to mobilize the armies and eventually to control the conquered peoples and manage the enlarged society.

Third, some anthropologists have suggested that the most important stimulus to state formation may have been trade (Rathje, 1972; Fried, 1968; Service, 1971). A number of major states grew up in areas that lacked essential raw materials. Southern Mesopotamia, as we have seen, had no wood, no building stone, and no metal; the lowland Maya had no salt, and no obsidian for making sharp-edged cutting tools. These items had to be supplied through the development of extensive trade networks. (The Maya, for example, financed and mounted long-distance trading expeditions to highland Mexico to obtain the resources they required.) The state, then, may have arisen out of the need for some centralized authority—possibly located at vital points of supply or redistribution—to control the traffic of goods.

These theories, because they focus on a single cause, have the virtue of simplicity. But that simplicity may also be a limitation. Let us take Wittfogel's theory, for example. It applies well to the states on which it was based—the early states of China. But other states, such as those of early Mesopotamia, emerged long before the appearance of complex, large-scale irrigation. Still others grew up in areas where irrigation was never very important (Adams, 1966). This is not to say that irrigation was not a major factor in the development of the state in general, but it was not necessarily the prime cause. The same might be said of warfare or trade. It is for this reason that many anthropologists prefer to think of the emergence of the state in terms of multiple causes rather than a single cause.

Multiple-Cause Theories

One of the first and still one of the most important of the multiple-cause theories was formu-

The Collapse of Maya Society

So far in this account we have concentrated on regions where conditions were such as to favor the emergence of full-fledged states. Yet the creation of a state, like the creation of a city, was not an all-or-nothing phenomenon. Although the forces that provided the impetus toward state formation were at work in many areas, local conditions often did not prove suitable for the flowering of a great state like Tenochtitlan or Uruk. There were places where nucleation, stratification, and intensive food production were well advanced, yet a viable state never came into existence, or collapsed before it could attain full development. In some instances the ecological foundations of the community were not solid enough to withstand the pressure of great population increases, including a large urban population that did not raise its own food. Among the most intriguing examples of this kind of failure is the collapse of the lowland Maya society.

A Maya ceramic figurine of a musician, from the island of Jaina. *(Lee Boltin)*

The Rise of the Maya

For years archeologists have argued over whether the lowland Maya should be considered a true state. There is no question, however, that many characteristics of state organization had already appeared in Maya society by the time of its fall.

Sedentary groups appear to have occupied the Maya areas of present-day Mexico and Guatemala by about 2,800 B.P. (Culbert, 1974). Within a few centuries, the population had increased and temple centers, the hallmark of Mayan civilization, had begun to appear throughout the forests. Already during the late Preclassic, these centers show an advanced culture. Stone temples, elaborately decorated, rose on small platforms. Jade and shells in the graves indicate that trade and social stratification were both under way. So too was the development of crafts; the ruins show the work of skilled potters, sculptors, painters, stonemasons, and architects. To administer such centers, there must have been a growing bureaucracy, headed by priests.

During the Classic period, Maya society continued its growth. Temple centers—over a hundred of them—dotted the Mayan highlands and lowlands. The people built a number of immense new temple centers, from which a glorified elite, housed in temples and palaces, ruled over the local populations. Long-distance trade networks connected the Mayan lowland settlements with the Pacific coast of Guatemala and the highlands to the north as far away as the Valley of Mexico. Obsidian, salt, volcanic stone, marine shells, and jade were imported, while feathers, chert, flint, and lime plaster were exported. As in Teotihuacan, the trade encouraged craft specialization.

The Maya were not blessed with ideal farmland. Indeed, much of their territory was dense rain forest, where fields, once cleared, soon became overgrown once again with thick foliage. Originally, it seems, the Maya probably practiced slash-and-burn agriculture, clearing a piece of land with hand tools, burning the resulting trash, and cultivating the new field for a period of two to three years. After this period, the field would be overgrown with grass, and rather than weed the grass—a slow and tedious task—the farmers would allow the field to rest for a few years while a new field (or one that had been lying fallow) was cleared and planted.

Under such shifting cultivation, the forest could support about 10 to 14 persons per square kilometer (26 to 36 persons per sq. mi.). As population rose, however, the pattern had to be modified. It is clear now (as it was not a few years ago) that by the Classic period the Maya were engaged in intensive agriculture. Through aerial photography, various types of raised fields—sometimes in the form of long ridges—have been identified. Irrigation canals have also been uncovered. And by reducing fallow cycles, allowing the fields to rest for shorter periods, the Maya grew enough food to sustain a rising population that included classes of people (primarily the elite and the craftsmen) who no longer worked the land.

During the late Classic and Postclassic stages, Maya society grew explosively. Population doubled, reaching 5 million. Building increased, and the economy accelerated. Stratification, as we have seen, became more pronounced. In the large temple centers, astronomy, writing, and mathematics flourished. A great civilization seemed to be reaching its full flower.

The Fall of the Maya

Then some time around 1,160 years ago Maya society began to collapse. The building of monumental architecture virtually ceased; production of sculpture and of the beautiful multicolored Maya pottery came to an end; the large settlements were abandoned; and in at least some areas, minor centers and hamlets were also abandoned. Adams (1973) has summarized the many factors to which archeologists, over the years, have attributed the Maya fall: hurricanes, earthquakes, invasion, disease, ecological collapse, disruption of trade, revolt by the peasants against the elite.

The archeological evidence suggests that most if not all of these problems were already present at the end of the Classic period, and therefore it is probably wisest to view the fall of Maya civilization as the result of many causes. First, as Sanders (1973) points out, soil failure—whether by erosion, depletion of nutrients, the invasion of farm areas by grass, or all of these—undoubtedly occurred, with disastrous consequences. We have already mentioned the undernourished skeletons of the rural peasants. Many people probably died of hunger and disease. And if, as is quite likely, the scarce food supplies were monopolized by the rich, peasant revolts—or at least acute political tension—may well have resulted. At the same time, there is evidence of military conflict. Militarism clearly became quite important in late Mayan civilization. Late Classic art shows scenes of combat, including large battles. Such warfare no doubt exacerbated the Maya's social and economic problems. Some populations moved, as we can tell from the abrupt transfer of pottery traditions from one region to another. Furthermore, warfare undoubtedly disturbed trade—trade that by this time was probably bringing in not just jade and obsidian but sorely needed food.

Sanders has suggested that given all these problems, people simply left, moving to the neighboring highlands. In view of the fact that Mayan culture begins to flourish in the highlands of Guatemala at about the time when lowland Maya culture is collapsing, this theory seems quite plausible. Furthermore, work by Sabloff and Rathje (1975) suggests that for those who remained in the lowlands, civilization did not really disappear in all areas. Religious government was merely replaced by secular government, and the control of trade shifted from the elite to middle-class traders. Thus it is possible that what has been called the Maya collapse was actually something less dramatic: a process of readjustment. Through emigration, person-land ratios were brought back into balance, thereby solving the subsistence problem; and the elimination of at least some of the greedy elite prevented this problem from recurring. In the process, however, the lowland Maya society as it is traditionally known—ruled by a religious elite and centered in great temple cities, with their white pyramids rising above the jungles—did in fact come to an end.

lated by Robert Adams (1966). On the basis of a comparison of the Mesopotamian and the Mesoamerican state, Adams concluded that two things were absolutely central to the ancient state: (1) agricultural surpluses, to support a nonfarming population of craftsmen and bureaucrats, and (2) stratification, to designate who would administer these surpluses. Whatever produced these, therefore, produced the state.

Adams reasoned that the agricultural surpluses resulted from many factors, but most directly from irrigation agriculture. This, then, was one cause. However, not all groups that practiced irrigation founded states. What made the difference, according to Adams, was local resource variability, backed by armed might.

With the advent of irrigation, the variability in the productive capacity of different pieces of land was vastly increased. Some lands responded extremely well to irrigation, others not so well. Whereas previously some lands might have produced 20 percent more sweet potatoes than neighboring lands, now the difference might be as great as 200 percent. From such differences, stratification was born. Some groups became much richer than neighboring groups and gradually took control over their lands. What they could not seize through economic advantage they seized through war. Thus more and more power was centralized in the richer communities, which became religious, political, and economic centers for large populations. In other words, they became states—through the combined effect of irrigation agriculture, local resource variability, and increased warfare.

Adams's model (which is outlined in Figure 13-5) provides a more comprehensive framework for understanding the origin of the state. Yet it still specifies a particular *sequence* of developments, and therefore it is still open to the criticism that this or that state did not follow precisely such a sequence. Indeed, it appears that no linear cause-and-effect theory can cover all ancient states. Because of this problem, some anthropologists have begun to experiment with a rather different kind of theory.

Circular Causation

It is possible to develop a more comprehensive and flexible model of state formation by employing the notion of circular causality rather than

Figure 13-5. Adams's model of the origin of the state.

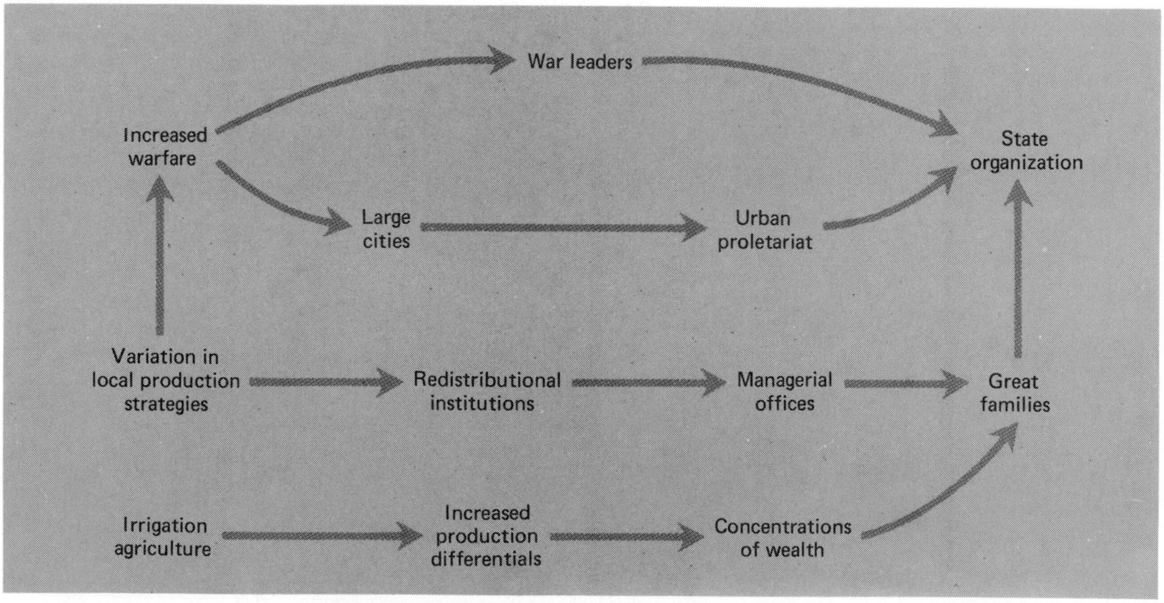

relying exclusively on a linear model. That is, instead of stressing chronological causation (X leads to Y, which in turn leads to Z), one can attempt to identify feedback cycles in which several processes, once they are set in motion, reinforce one another, ultimately producing the state. In such a model, what is important is not so much the initial stimulus, which may differ from state to state, and may even be impossible to identify in many cases. Nor is the specific order in which various institutions and attributes of the state appear the crucial factor. Instead, the emphasis is on *processes*, and the ways in which they are related to and reinforce one another.

We have already discussed the key processes themselves earlier in the chapter: intensification, nucleation, stratification, differentiation, and centralization. (The student would do well to review the definitions of these terms at this point.) We will now explore the interactions among these five processes, and attempt to construct a synthetic model for the rise of the state. This model is based on Logan and Sanders' study (1976) of the Valley of Mexico. However, because it stresses the relationship among processes rather than linear causation, it is helpful in understanding ancient states generally. For all the processes discussed are involved, to varying degrees, in the formation of all ancient states.

The Initial Stimuli: Population Increase and Intensification

Logan and Sanders argue that the initial stimulus for the formation of a state is population growth. From time to time variations in birth rates, death rates, and migration lead to population increases in some (not necessarily all) groups. To the extent that these increases place stress on available resources, the group must decide either to put up with a lower standard of living or to take some action. The actions they can take include intensification, infanticide, postpartum taboos, migration, or the breakup of the group into smaller, more dispersed settlements. Of these alternatives, only intensification leads to the state. Therefore, since states developed in relatively few areas, we can assume that in most cases population pressure among early agriculturalists was relieved by methods other than intensification.

Why did some choose intensification? This is an interesting question. Whatever method a group uses to increase the productivity of its land—whether by building canals, as the Mesopotamians did, or by reclaiming marshlands, as the Aztecs did, or by weeding fields to shorten fallow periods, as the Maya did—intensive agriculture always involves harder work than extensive agriculture. Why, then, were certain groups willing to adopt it? There are several possible answers to this question. First, some groups were forced to intensify because this was the only possible means of feeding their growing populations. If a group is hemmed in geographically, as the Incas were by the mountains or as many of the Maya were by their neighbors, and if their population increase is too great to be handled by infanticide or postpartum taboos, then they have no choice but to intensify.

Second, it is likely that many farmers simply drifted gradually into intensification. It is easy for us, with hindsight, to contrast large-scale irrigation agriculture with floodwater farming, which is so much simpler and easier, and wonder why farmers would choose the former. But in many cases there may have been no explicit choice. Digging a few shallow canals to bring water a bit further onto the floodplain was probably not a sufficiently great increase in labor that anyone thought much about it, particularly when the alternative was to leave the community—or when there was no alternative. Once the canals were built, they were relatively easy to improve—particularly since increased production could now underwrite the cost of the improvements. It is unlikely that the people involved at each step of such a process were aware of its ultimate outcome. That a few canals might eventually evolve into a complex hydraulic system was not something that the farmers who first dug them envisioned.

Finally, once states developed, they forced intensification on farmers in the areas that they conquered. When we talk about the growing influence of the Aztec or Inca state, we must try to keep in mind the concrete forms that this influence took. Many farmers were probably told that this year they had to produce, say, 20 bushels more than last year or their farms would be seized. Under such pressure, farmers find ways to increase production.

It is possible, too, that the process of intensification was sometimes triggered by forces *other* than population growth. Wright and Johnson, in their study of Susa (1975), found no evidence of population increase in this area as the state began to evolve. What they did find was evidence of a marked increase in local exchange, which they argue stimulated the rise of the state in Susa. Yet intensification, in the form of complex irrigation systems, is also soon evident in the region. Perhaps this strategy was adopted by some groups as a means of competing more successfully in an increasingly intense exchange system. Perhaps some individuals or groups simply acquired enough power to introduce intensive food production by force. Or perhaps we will eventually find evidence of population growth in nearby areas that had a secondary effect on Susa itself. In any event, it may well be that the initial stimulus for intensification is variable to some extent, so that it is not possible to find the same precipitating factor in all cases.

Of course, the strategy of intensification does not always succeed.[2] But when it does succeed, and especially when it begins to occur at a rapid rate, states result. Whether we are considering the Maya, the peoples of the Valley of Mexico, the Mesopotamians, or, for that matter, the ancient Chinese, Egyptians, or Greeks, the signs of intensive agriculture are always accompanied by signs that people are coming together into larger, more stratified communities, with centralized governments. Why should this relationship exist between intensification and the state? Probably for two reasons. First, intensification sets in motion the four other processes that we mentioned earlier: nucleation, centralization, stratification, and differentiation. Second, once these processes are under way, each of them reinforces the others.

[2] For example, 900 years ago people were building irrigation and terrace systems in many areas of the American Southwest. Two hundred years later most of these areas had been abandoned. As the farmers discovered, rainfall and other climatic factors in this region are simply too variable to support intensive agriculture. Spending a summer in the Southwest, one becomes accustomed to the fact that rain may fall in sheets in one spot while another area a kilometer away remains dry. Unfortunately, one cannot pick up a terrace system or an irrigation ditch and move it to where the rain is falling.

The Consequences of Intensification

Intensification and Nucleation The relationship between intensified production and increased settlement size (nucleation) should be obvious. After all, the stimulus for intensification is population growth, and intensification makes further population growth possible. Moreover, intensification often involves large cooperative projects, such as reclaiming swamps or building dams and canals. Nucleated settlements are not essential for such projects, but they help, since it is much easier to mobilize people and get them to cooperate when they live together.

Intensification and Stratification The relationship between intensification and stratification was already implied in our discussion of Adams's multiple-cause theory. The more intense a production system, the greater the importance of slight environmental differences. The first and second terraces of a river may be equally advantageous for dry farming. Once irrigation is introduced, however, it is less costly to be on the lower terrace. When crops are grown on a given parcel of land at five-year intervals, all of the soils in an area may be equally productive. But as fallow periods are reduced and finally eliminated, some soils will pass the endurance test and go on producing, while others, because of slight differences, will succumb to mineral depletion or erosion. In these and dozens of other ways, small differences between different tracts of land became large differences as farmers converted to intensive agriculture. And as lands differed, so did the prosperity of their owners. Thus intensification created the very rich and the very poor and the many gradations in between.

Intensification and Differentiation Intensification led to increased differentiation in at least two ways. First, farming became specialized.

Whole fields, whole farms, and eventually even whole towns were turned over to one crop because planting, irrigation, and harvesting could be handled much more efficiently if they were planned according to the needs of one kind of plant. Second, intensification spurred craft specialization. With some people spending more time in the fields, others—particularly those living on less productive land—invested their efforts in producing and marketing pottery and other tools, which they could then exchange for food coming from the more productive plots.

Intensification and Centralization While the connection between intensification and centralization is somewhat more remote than the others we have just traced, centralized decision making is ultimately a way of increasing production. The more efficient the scheduling of the use of land and labor, the less the waste and the greater the yield; and the easiest way to make scheduling efficient was to put it in the hands of one decision maker. In many early states, as we have seen, this role was assumed by the priests. Indeed, the success of intensification in these areas may be due to the fact that the priests, who already had considerable knowledge of the stars and the seasons by virtue of maintaining the ceremonial cycle, were also directing the agricultural decisions.

The Feedback Cycle

Intensification, then, stimulates nucleation, differentiation, stratification, and centralization, and it favors communities where these processes are taking place. Of equal importance is the fact that these processes encourage one another.

The Effects of Nucleation As more people come to live in a restricted area and to use its resources more and more intensively, certain essential items are bound to be exhausted. Logan and Sanders (1976) cite the example of communities in the Valley of Mexico that had (and still have) to import all their wooden objects and all their charcoal for fuel. Likewise, many Mesopo-

Figure 13-6. A circular model of state formation, based partly on the work of Logan and Sanders in the Valley of Mexico. Such models concentrate on a number of processes and the ways in which they reinforce one another through feedback cycles. The initial stimulus here is assumed to be population pressure, but it is possible that other factors may in some cases have provided the impetus toward intensification.

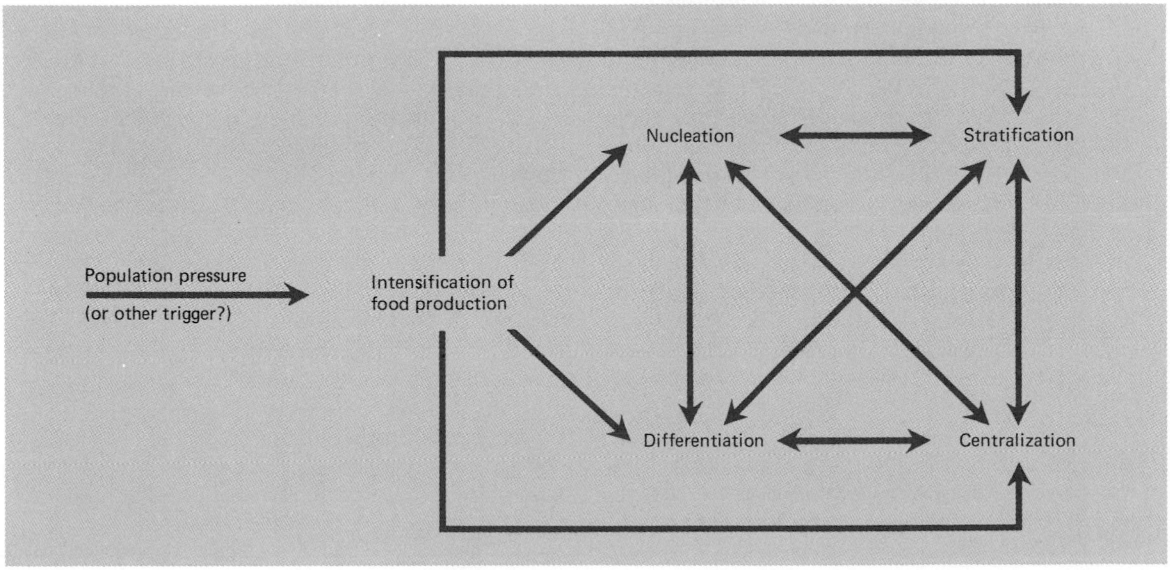

The Life and Death of Sites

So far we have assumed that the remains at a prehistoric site reflect the activities of its original inhabitants. Ideally, this ought to be the case. In practice, however, artifacts and their distribution may give only an imperfect and in some cases a highly distorted picture of their makers' way of life. For an archeological site is shaped by many factors other than the activities of the people who lived and worked there. Weathering, erosion, and other geological processes, along with plant growth, animal activity, and disturbance by later peoples all leave their marks. Archeologist Michael Shiffer (1978) refers to the changes brought about by such forces as *transformation processes*, and has studied the ways in which sites are formed by both natural and cultural processes, as well as by the behavior of the original inhabitants.

The effects of natural transformation processes are relatively straightforward. Depositional processes bury cultural remains, and erosion exposes, moves, or removes them. Animals burrow into sites and trees grow on them, displacing artifacts and modifying or destroying features of the site itself. Even the movement of herds of animals over a site can damage or destroy many of the artifacts on or near the ground surface.

Archeologists excavating ancient cities often find a succession of different levels of occupation at a single site, created as people built repeatedly on the rubble of earlier settlements or structures. These levels—each a step backward in time—are from the excavations at Nippur, in Iraq. *(Georg Gerster/Rapho/Photo Researchers)*

To a great extent, however, archeological sites are the product of human activities—both those of the original inhabitants and those of later people. In the first place, the archeologist must recognize that the people whose remains he is studying did not simply leave their tools and garbage where they used them, any more than we do. *Primary refuse*, left where it was used, is found at very early human sites, such as the campsites of *Homo erectus* bands. In later periods, however, it occurs only rarely—at Pompeii, for example, which was suddenly buried by a volcanic eruption. The deposits at most archeological sites consist primarily of *secondary refuse*, refuse that was placed in garbage pits or on a rubble mound.

Moreover, refuse does not simply remain where it was first put. Later peoples occupying the same location may dig through it to build rooms or other facilities of their own. And people do not simply remove the materials of the past; often they reuse them. There are many examples of sherds and milling stones that became part of the material for a new wall, of grinding stones resharpened to make chopping tools, of broken projectile points reshaped for use as knives or scrapers.

Much of the difficulty that archeologists encounter in attempting to interpret a site is the result of modern disruption. Many archeological sites that once existed in the eastern part of the United States have been destroyed by plowing—either because farmers did not notice them, or because the mounds stood in the way of efficient farming. While archeologists can interpret *plowzone materials* to some degree, they are naturally a poorer reflection of the past than undisturbed deposits. Other sites have been dug up or paved over for a variety of construction projects, with equally damaging consequences for the archeological record. As a result, national and state laws now require that archeological work be completed at a site before its destruction by the march of progress.

Sadly, some of the greatest devastation of sites occurs as a result of deliberate efforts to scavenge or steal artifacts from them. The prices commanded by works of ancient art on the world market have risen sharply in recent years, and many antiquities are worth a great deal of money. For some collectors and dealers, the commercial value of a few artifacts is more important than archeological knowledge. They are thus willing to buy and sell plundered works of art, although such dealing further inflates prices and so intensifies plundering.

Unfortunately, artifacts are useless to archeology once they have been removed from their context. An isolated work of ancient art may have esthetic value, but it contributes nothing to our knowledge of the past, since it is usually impossible to tell who made it, where, when, and for what purpose. Worse, those who plunder artifacts often destroy an entire site to salvage a few valuable pieces. In some parts of the world, power machinery has been used to excavate buried artifacts, thus making archeological interpretation of the site almost impossible. In Mesoamerica, entire stone temple facades, weighing tons, have been sawn up into smaller slabs, crated, and flown away from hastily cleared jungle airstrips. Stolen items are eventually smuggled to Europe or the United States in crates labeled as machinery or building supplies. They are then sold by a few unscrupulous dealers to collectors on a "no questions asked" basis (Meyer, 1973).

As a result of such activities, sites are being destroyed at an ever more rapid rate. Indeed, there are some cultures of which little or no evidence will remain within a decade or two if the present trend continues. To prevent this, many nations have passed laws prohibiting the excavation, sale, and export of artifacts. In the United States, unfortunately, such activities are illegal only on federally owned lands.

tamian communities may have run out of clay for pottery. Such problems could only be overcome through specialization. Those who had abundant clay specialized in pottery; those who had obsidian concentrated on making stone tools. Each community imported from the others to fill its needs. Thus nucleation led to differentiation.

Through the same process, nucleation reinforced stratification. For not all areas were equally endowed with resources that they could trade. Consequently, the haves and have-nots became more and more sharply divided.

Finally, nucleation, by bringing together more people in less space, increased the relative amount of conflict among them. And eventually this problem encouraged centralization in the form of institutionalized mediators and laws, to settle the conflicts (Netting, 1972).

The Effects of Differentiation Differentiation too gave rise to conflict. People playing different roles had different interests at heart. Making these interests mesh (e.g., deciding how much of my barley for how many of your pots) was not always an easy matter. Moreover, as parcels of land became increasingly differentiated—this one valuable for this agricultural asset, that one for that resource—the whole notion of property, of individual ownership, and of the right to restrict access was born and flourished. It is not incidental that some of our earliest examples of writing from Mesopotamia and China are records of disputes over land. Again, this escalation of conflict eventually led to the establishment of centralized authorities to resolve disputes.

Differentiation also affected stratification. As the uses to which pieces of land could be put were more precisely defined, the differential value of particular land parcels increased. And so, by extension, did the differential wealth of those who lived on the land.

The combination of these two elements—differentiation of property value and stratification—gave rise to another process central to state formation: war. For as different lands took on widely different values, farmers, communities, and states began casting their eyes on their neighbors' lands. The effect of war was simply to add momentum to the feedback cycle we have been discussing. Above all, war stimulated nucleation and centralization. Large settlements with powerful bureaucracies were able to put more and better-organized men in the field. Thus they were more likely to win the wars and to absorb unnucleated and decentralized peoples. At the same time, of course, the need to prepare for war and to control conquered peoples fed the power of the bureaucracies.

Finally, differentiation encouraged centralization and nucleation by another route: exchange. The more specialized the production in different communities, the greater the need for administrators to control the flow of goods from one community to the next, and the greater the importance of regional exchange centers, which often swelled into cities.

The Effects of Stratification and Centralization Stratification and centralization are somewhat more effects than causes in the developments we have been considering so far. Yet each reinforced the processes that had created them. The elite, for example, played a crucial role in furthering specialization. Without an elite, after all, there would have been no market for fine craft goods. The specialist compounds that grew up around family apartment complexes in Teotihuacán suggest that the great families of this city became sponsors of craft groups, and there is no doubt that craft specialists were supported by the temple in Mesopotamia. At the same time, the growth of the elite was a powerful stimulus to centralization. For as the elite gained increasing control over food and crafts production, they also gained control over people's lives. The welfare of the many fell into the hands of the few.

Centralization, once begun, also fed the other processes. By integrating and coordinating, the bureaucracy made complex, differentiated societies possible. It also added two more forms of specialized endeavor: management and warfare. It stimulated stratification by awarding prestige for success in these two areas. Finally, by enhancing people's sense of territoriality, centralization led to further nucleation. State after state, even into modern times, fought to sedentize the nomads, the one group of people who refused to respect territorial boundaries.

It should be clear by now that there is no single path to the state. The first processes likely to be set in motion by intensification are nucleation and differentiation, but this depends entirely on the population in question. If the environment is especially uniform, with little variability from farm to farm, differentiation (along with its natural consequence, stratification) will probably be minimal at first. If settlements are already reasonably large, the role of nucleation will be minor at first. In other words, what is constant is the *relationship* among the processes, not the sequence in which they first occur.

PRESENT AND FUTURE

Our understanding of early stratified societies will undoubtedly change drastically in coming years. Because of the vast size of the sites, their complexity, and the almost immeasurable quantity of materials that can be recovered from them, archeologists have only begun to scratch the surface of the evidence that bears on this phase of social evolution. Indeed, in some areas—perhaps many—we may even find evidence of states where none were previously thought to have existed. For example, Paolo Matthiae and Giovanni Pettineto have described their work in an area about 48 kilometers (30 mi.) from Aleppo, Syria. They found evidence of a previously unknown state, Ebla, which flourished between 4,400 and 4,200 B.P. At its peak, it controlled more than a quarter of a million people living between the Sinai peninsula and the mountains of Iran. Prior to these findings, the area was thought to have been inhabited only by nomads. These archeologists have now recovered over 15,000 clay tablets, the inscriptions on which deal with the trade relations between Ebla and nearby sites.

We can be confident, therefore, that the story of the rise of states is just beginning to be told. We will surely know a great deal more in the future than we do today.

Summary

The transition to an entirely new form of sociopolitical organization—the *state*—and an entirely new type of settlement pattern—the *city*—began about 7,000 years ago. By definition, the rise of the city involved two factors—*nucleation*, or movement toward more populous settlements, and *social stratification*, the division of the members of a society into different classes based on their wealth, power, and economic specialization. Teotihuacán, in what is now Mexico, is a notable example of an early city. It was an important center for trade, crafts, religion, and administration, and possessed the spectacular monumental architecture usually found in great ancient cities. Many other early cities had more specialized functions, serving primarily as either ceremonial, commercial, or bureaucratic centers.

The growth of cities is part of a more general change in settlement patterns. The very existence of large cities required the organization of hinterland areas, where productive activities were carried on at least in part to support urban dwellers. A hierarchy of settlements of varying sizes evolved. Different communities developed different specializations, resulting in the necessity for exchange and the creation of bonds of interdependence among them. Trade, specialization, settlement hierarchy, and administrative complexity thus grew hand in hand.

In densely populated agricultural areas where egalitarian *bands* and *tribes* were no longer adequate forms of organization, *chiefdoms* appeared. In the chiefdom, power was institutionalized. The chief often was a full-time administrator and held an office that became a permanent part of the social structure. Power derived from the office itself rather than from the personal achievements of its occupant. Although the chiefdom was essentially based on kinship ties, elites and hierarchies of prestige (status ranking) came into being.

In the state, power and rank became still more absolute. Ancient states shared four essential characteristics: (1) sharply differentiated social classes, (2) membership based upon residence within geographical boundaries, (3) political power held by an individual and/or elite, and (4) a bureaucratic administrative structure. Several processes operated to bring about the complex hierarchic subsystems that distinguish the state from earlier forms of social organization. These include *differentiation* (the proliferation of different classes, occupations, and institutions), *centralization* (coordination of the various subsystems by a single authority), *stratification, nucleation,* and *intensification* (increased food production from a given unit of land).

The history of the ancient state in Mesoamerica can be divided into three stages—the *Preclassic*, which lasted from 3,500 to 1,700 B.P., the *Classic*, which lasted from 1,700 to 1,100 B.P., and the *Postclassic*, which lasted from 1,100 B.P. to the arrival of the Europeans in 430 B.P. These stages are marked by a progression from the initial emergence of largely *theocratic* ceremonial centers and social stratification to secularization, social unrest, and militarism. In Mesopotamia, states arose much earlier, but a similar pattern is evident. The stages in that region are known as the *Ubaid* (which ended about 5,800 B.P.), the *Protoliterate* (which lasted from 5,800 to 4,900 B.P.), and the *Early Dynastic* (which lasted from 4,900 to 4,400 B.P.).

Several theories have been proposed to account for the evolution of the state. These include single-cause theories that attribute state formation to one crucial factor such as irrigation, warfare, or trade, and linear multiple-cause theories that involve various factors occurring in a specific sequence. More useful, however, is a theory of circular causation. Spurred by population increase and the intensification that sometimes resulted, the processes of nucleation, stratification, differentiation, and centralization were set in motion. Each process stimulated the others, establishing a series of positive feedback cycles. A major advantage of this theory is that it focuses on the relationships among the processes rather than on the sequence in which they occurred, which varied from state to state and from region to region.

Glossary

band an egalitarian form of social organization consisting of several loosely allied families and characterized by informal leadership

centralization the consolidation of decision-making authority into a bureaucracy that coordinates the various subsystems of the society

chiefdom a form of social organization in which power is institutionalized; unlike leaders of bands or tribes, the chief is a full-time administrator and occupies a role that is a permanent part of the social structure

chinampas artificial islands built by the Aztecs in lakes or swamps and used for farming

city a community with a large population concentrated in a compact area and characterized by a high degree of social stratification

Classic a Mesoamerican cultural stage lasting from about 1,700–1,100 B.P. and characterized by greatly increased population and food production, the development of cities and huge ceremonial centers, the growth of trade networks and craft specialization, and greater stratification

differentiation the division of a society into numerous subsystems—different classes, occupations, institutions, etc.

Early Dynastic a Mesopotamian cultural stage (4,900–4,400 B.P.) marked by the rise of large and powerful city-states that were continually in conflict with one another

nucleation the formation of large, densely populated settlements

Postclassic a Mesoamerican cultural stage lasting from about 1,100–430 B.P. and marked by social unrest, the growth of militarism, and increasing secularization of the state

Preclassic a Mesoamerican cultural stage lasting from about 3,500–1,700 B.P. and characterized by the emergence of ceremonial centers, social stratification, and writing

Protoliterate a Mesopotamian cultural stage (5,800–4,900 B.P.) characterized by the evolution of early states, craft specialization, and primitive writing

social stratification the division of the members of a society into classes differing in wealth and power

state a complex form of social organization in which societies are divided into sharply differentiated social classes (stratification), membership is based upon residence within territorial limits, an individual and/or an elite group monopolizes political power, and a bureaucracy of officials oversees administrative affairs

theocracy a state in which the official religion is a major source of political power

tribe a basically egalitarian form of social organization united by kinship ties, common traditions and rituals, and some temporary leadership roles

Ubaid a Mesopotamian cultural stage (ending 5,800 B.P.) during which people lived in small settlements centered around a temple, and priests served as ritual, political, and economic leaders

ziggurat a terraced pyramid common in Mesopotamian settlements

Suggested Readings

ADAMS, R. 1966
The Evolution of Urban Society: Early Mesopotamia and Prehispanic Mexico. Chicago: Aldine. A major theoretical treatment of state-urban origins.

CULBERT, T. L. 1974
The Lost Civilization: The Story of the Classic Maya. New York: Harper & Row. A discussion of the organization of Mayan society during the Classic period.

DAVIS, K. 1973
Cities: Their Origin, Growth and Human Impact. San Francisco: W. H. Freeman. Articles from *Scientific American* describing prehistoric and modern cities and the particular problems of life in such settlements.

SANDERS, W. T., AND PRICE, B. J. 1968
Mesoamerica: The Evolution of a Civilization. New York: Random House. A discussion of the events and processes leading to the emergence of the state in Mesoamerica.

Part Four

Variation in Modern *Homo sapiens*

Chapter Fourteen

Simple Physical Variation

Human beings, because they belong to a single species, have many more similarities than differences. Nonetheless, the degree of physical variation among individuals is very great, far greater than science can as yet tabulate, let alone explain. Humans show a high degree of *polymorphism*—that is, genetically determined variety *within* populations. In addition, the species is markedly *polytypic*—that is, there are many differences *among* populations. (See the discussion of polytypic species in Chapters 3 and 4.) And the variations we know of probably represent only a small fraction of those that actually exist.

To appreciate the degree of human variability, let us look for a moment at just one variable—hair. All human beings grow hair on their heads; but consider the range of variations on this theme. Human hair can be blond, strawberry blond, red, auburn, brown, black, and any number of shades in between. It can also be frizzy, curly, wavy, or straight. It can be coarse or fine. It can grow thickly or sparsely. It can turn gray at age twenty, forty, sixty, or not at all. It can grow thickly throughout a long lifetime, or it can fall out, starting in adolescence. It can begin thinning out at the crown of the head, or it can recede from the brow. It can do so quickly or slowly, and so on. A similar catalogue of variations could be given for human stature, weight, musculature, skin color, and the shape of the head, teeth, nose, hands, and feet—along with innumerable other, less obvious characteristics.

These variations themselves vary. Some are continuous, with a smooth gradation between extremes; others are discontinuous, dividing the species into discrete types. Some are monogenic, others polygenic. Some are purely the result of genetic variation, others of both genes and environment, others of environment alone. The most interesting differences in phenotype are those that are under genetic control, at least to some degree, and therefore subject to evolutionary processes.

Human variability has always excited interest and speculation. Aside from simple curiosity, why study it? There are, first of all, certain strictly practical reasons, such as medical need. By studying genetically determined diseases that vary strikingly from population to population—for example, Tay-Sachs disease, a fatal disorder of the nervous system found most often in Jews of Central European descent, or sickle-cell anemia, most common in people of African and Mediterranean origin—we can identify high-risk individuals and possibly develop better means of treatment and prevention. There are political reasons as well. Governments, organizations, and individuals are constantly making decisions based on their conception of the characteristics of specific groups and populations. Some of these decisions are probably well founded—for example, to set up genetic counseling programs in black communities to help prevent sickle-cell anemia. But other decisions are not so well founded, such as preventing certain populations from immigrating or voting because of a presumed population-wide mental inferiority. Only by going out and actually measuring the differences among groups

Sickled red cells in human blood. The cells are deformed because they contain hemoglobin S instead of the normal hemoglobin A. This distortion causes sickle cell anemia. Only people who are homozygous for the abnormal *S* gene suffer from this condition. The red cells of heterozygotes, though they contain both types of hemoglobin (S and A), are nearly normal in structure and function. *(Irene Piscopo Rodgers/Phillips Electronic Instruments, Inc.)*

can we test the basis for such decisions and expose cases where pseudo-scientific justifications are masking what is actually prejudice or special interest.

In addition to practical reasons, there are purely scientific reasons for studying physical variation. Without examining human polytypy and polymorphism, we can neither describe our species nor explain how it came to be what it is. For modern human polytypy is both the result of and the evidence for the evolution of our species. Furthermore, variations in modern humans—especially differences in the shape of the head and in the shape of the teeth—are analogous to differences that we see among fossil humans, and therefore they help us to interpret those observations. For instance, they help us to determine the normal range of variation within a species, to establish what sorts of variation are under genetic control, and to make educated guesses about the selective forces that may have been at work to produce or maintain such variations.

Human variation, then, merits our attention. First we shall describe the major considerations and problems involved in the study of phenotypic differences. Then we will look at a few of the simpler forms of genetic variation.

STUDYING HUMAN VARIATION

The anthropologist studying human physical variation has two tasks. The first is to *describe* variation. What traits vary, by how much, and among whom? Is the variation solely within populations, or is there also variation among populations? Even given unlimited time and funds for research, there is no danger of our running short of traits to study. Indeed, there is little chance of our ever describing all the kinds of variation within the species.

The second task is to *explain* variation. To a large extent, this means applying to particular cases our knowledge of the workings of natural selection, drift, mutation, and other evolutionary mechanisms. This, however, is anything but a straightforward matter.

Explaining Variation

The explanation of any observed pattern of variation is a process of answering a few basic questions. The first question in every case is: *How is this variation determined?* How much is attributable to genetic differences and how much to the direct action of the environment on the phenotype? This seemingly simple question is often extremely difficult to answer. In many cases (e.g., stature, weight, intelligence), the only answer we can give is that both genotype and environment play a role in producing the trait.

If we can establish that genes play an important role in the trait, the next step is to find out what forces have been acting on the genes in order to produce the variation. In the case of polymorphism, then, the second question is: *Why does this population have more than one allele at this locus?* (Or, in the case of a polygenic trait: Why does this population have alternative alleles at one or more of the loci governing this trait?) Evolutionary theory suggests three possible answers.

1. A number of neutral alleles have become established in the population—alleles that, precisely because they are neutral, are unaffected by natural selection and therefore are drifting slowly toward fixation.
2. Two or more opposing selective forces have reached a state of equilibrium, producing balanced polymorphism.
3. A selective force is in the process of replacing an old genotype with a new one—in other words, a transient polymorphism exists.

To find out which of these processes is operating, anthropologists try to find evidence of selective forces operating on the trait. This can be a difficult matter. Deviations of genotype frequencies from the predicted Hardy-Weinberg ratios will sometimes alert us that selection may be operating. However, selection can operate intensely without producing deviations large enough to be distinguishable from the effects of sampling error. Therefore, anthropologists have had to experiment with other tactics to detect selective forces—tactics that we will discuss later in this chapter.

Third, in the case of polytypy, we must ask: *What forces have caused the populations of our species to differ in this trait?* If the trait is genetically influenced, then what we are dealing with is a set of differences in gene frequency. In one population a given allele exists at high frequency; in another, at low frequency; in another, perhaps not at all. Theoretically, such differences in gene frequency among populations may be the result of genetic drift or of differential selection—that is, exposure to different intensities of selection, or different selective forces. Thus we look first for environmental factors—aspects of diet or climate, for example—that vary among different populations in ways that could cause differential selection for this trait. If no selective influences can be found, then it may be that the polytypy is due to drift. However, the possibility of hidden selective forces can never be completely ruled out.

The Interference of Culture

In seeking answers to the foregoing questions, we first try the most obvious explanation. In our species, as in any other species, polytypy is produced by the selective effects of different environments. Therefore the most logical place to look for the causes of variation is in the immediate environment of the populations in question—the climate, the food resources, the degree of exposure to sunlight, the local disease-carrying insects, and so forth. In some cases this works. But in many other cases it does not, because culture has introduced so many complications into the evolution of our species.

For one thing, culture has complicated the population structure of our species. In other species, the Mendelian population—the group of individuals that are more likely to breed with one another than with outsiders (see Chapter 3)—is usually geographically defined. A vervet monkey tends to mate with the vervet monkeys that share its patch of forest. Human beings, on the other hand, have not only geographically defined populations but also culturally defined populations—breeding groups based on identity of religion, social class, ethnicity, and so forth. These groups, cross-cutting the geographical group and one another, add up to a bewilderingly complicated breeding pattern that makes physical variation much more difficult to interpret. For example, if the inhabitants of a city were tested for some simple trait, such as ABO blood type, and the percentage of homozygotes turned out to be significantly in excess of the Hardy-Weinberg predictions, this could not safely be interpreted (as it might be in other animals) as the result of natural selection. More likely, it is the result of subdivision of the population—Italians marrying Italians, blacks marrying blacks, and so on—a pattern that, as we saw in Chapter 3, can increase the probability of homozygotes. Of course, natural selection might be operating too, but to separate this factor from the influence of subdivision of the population is very difficult.

Culture has also come to play a role in the process of selection. The basic rule of natural selection is that the genotype that confers the greatest fitness is the genotype that will thrive. In our species, however, culture rather than genotype has enabled certain populations to expand and displace other peoples. When the English settlers first set foot in North America and Australia, or the Spanish in South America, or the Arabs in East Africa, it is doubtful that their gene pools were better adapted to these environments than the genes of the natives. (If anyone had had a genetic advantage, it would have been the natives, whom natural selection had been molding to the environment for thousands of years.) But the settlers had a different and greater advantage—the cultural advantage of a sophisticated technology, including guns. Thus they were able to displace or absorb the native populations. Such cultural factors have to be taken into account when we try to interpret variations among contemporary populations. If we find green lizards living in a certain habitat, we can guess that they are green because this coloration helped their ancestors to survive in that habitat. But we cannot say that the peoples of North America are predominantly "white" because light skin proved advantageous in this environment. The light skins of the North American people are the by-product of historical processes that have to do with cultural rather than physical fitness.

Throughout human evolution, culture, like the physical environment, has imposed its own selective pressures. The deft hands and complex brain of modern *Homo sapiens* are the result of such pressures. By the same token, populations with different cultures are subject to different selective forces, no matter how similar their environments. Hunter-gatherers, for example, usually have an extremely low incidence of red-green color blindness, presumably because the ability to distinguish color—for instance, to tell red berries from green berries, or to follow a blood-trail through the grass—is indispensable to their way of life. Agriculturalists, by contrast, have a higher incidence of color blindness; but they often have adaptations that the hunter-gatherers lack, such as resistance to infectious diseases carried by animals (e.g., tuberculosis). Even in the same habitat, different subsistence patterns give rise to different sets of adaptations.

For all these reasons, human variation is more difficult to interpret than that of any other species. At every turn, we have to consider the culturally determined history of the population as well as the selective factors in its environment, past and present.

VARIATION IN BLOOD PROTEINS

At the gene level, all variation is of a similar kind. It consists of differences in the messages chemically encoded by the DNA molecules that make up the genes. These messages, as we saw in Chapter 2, are instructions for building proteins; and it is the proteins that collectively shape the organism's phenotypes.

However, not all phenotypic variation can be explained entirely as the product of variation at the gene or protein level. As noted earlier, a good deal of human variation involves traits whose inheritance is poorly understood, and that are determined by a complex interaction between the environment and the genotype of each individual. We shall look at these more complex traits in the next chapter. In this chapter we will focus on simply inherited traits. First we shall examine some variable factors in the blood. Other human tissues are probably just as variable as blood, but because it is easier to get samples of blood than of other tissues, the variations of the blood proteins are the best known.

Blood consists of two major components: *red blood cells* and *plasma*, a clear, yellowish fluid that contains various dissolved proteins, such as transferrin. Inside the red blood cells are a number of other proteins, including *hemoglobin*, the oxygen-carrying red pigment mentioned in Chapters 2 and 3. Located on the surface of the red blood cells is still another important group of variable molecules, called the *blood group substances.* Each of these three classes of substances—the plasma proteins, the proteins inside the red cells, and the blood group substances—offers interesting cases of polymorphism and polytypy. (Some examples from each group are listed in Table 14-1.) We shall concentrate on hemoglobin and one of the more familiar types of blood group substances, since the study of variation in these particular factors illustrates the difficulties of identifying selective forces in human populations.

Hemoglobin Polymorphism

The hemoglobin that makes up most of the red cell contents in normal adults is called hemoglobin A. Each molecule consists of four protein chains—two identical alpha chains, and two identical beta chains. The structure of the alpha and beta chains is determined by separate loci. Various alleles occur at both loci, but the best-known hemoglobin variants are all due to alleles at the beta locus.

Sickle-Cell Polymorphism

Among the variant hemoglobins produced by abnormal alleles at the beta locus, there are four

TABLE 14-1. Some Examples of Human Blood Proteins That Vary Within or Among Populations

PROTEIN	NATURE OF VARIATION	SELECTIVE AGENTS MAINTAINING POLYMORPHISMS
Red-cell proteins		
Hemoglobin	Some populations polymorphic	Probably malaria
Acid phosphatase	Widespread polymorphism	Unknown
Glucose-6-phosphate dehydrogenase	"Deficient" forms in many populations	Uncertain, perhaps malaria
6-phosphogluconate dehydrogenase	Polymorphism of one frequent, one rarer allele	Unknown
Phosphoglucomutase	Widespread two-allele polymorphism	Unknown
Adenylate kinase	One frequent, one rare allele in many human populations	Unknown
Serum (plasma) proteins		
Gm and inv (immunoglobulins)	Widespread polymorphism	Unknown
Haptoglobin	Polymorphism involving three common alleles	Uncertain, perhaps malaria
Transferrin	Some populations polymorphic	Uncertain, perhaps viral infection
Albumin	Some populations show low-level polymorphism	Unknown
Ceruloplasmin	Some populations polymorphic	Unknown
Blood group substances		
ABO system	Widespread polymorphism	Uncertain, perhaps disease
Rhesus system	Polymorphism	Unknown

types—C, D, E, and S—that occur in certain populations at high enough frequencies to constitute polymorphisms rather than simply random products of mutation. The best-known hemoglobin polymorphism concerns S, or sickle-cell hemoglobin. In Chapter 3 we discussed sickle-cell hemoglobin briefly as an example of balanced polymorphism, that is, polymorphism maintained by the action of natural selection. We will now look at it somewhat more closely.

Chemically, the difference between hemoglobin S and normal hemoglobin (A) is extremely slight. Protein molecules consist of long chains of chemical units called amino acids. In the case of hemoglobin, there are a total of 574 amino acids in the four chains—two alpha and two beta—that make up the molecule. Hemoglobin S differs from hemoglobin A in only one amino acid in each beta chain; in these two "links," one amino acid has been substituted for another.

This minute change has massive consequences. It greatly increases the tendency of the hemoglobin to crystallize at low oxygen pressures, producing brittle, sickle-shaped red cells. Broken cells tend to clog the smaller blood vessels, cutting off their blood supply. They also tend to rupture, resulting in a shortage of red cells, or anemia. These symptoms are far more pronounced in *SS* homozygotes, who produce no normal hemoglobin. If untreated, the homozygous condition, called *sickle-cell anemia,* usually results in an early and painful death. By contrast, the heterozygous condition, called *sickle-cell trait,* does little phenotypic harm. Sickling of cells that contain a mixture of hemoglobin A and hemoglobin S is rare, and the only consequence under normal circumstances is a mild anemia, with little effect on fitness.

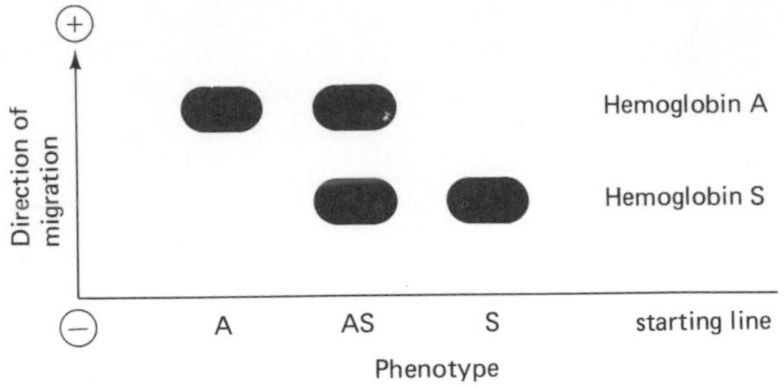

Figure 14-1. The separation of hemoglobin types by electrophoresis. The samples are applied at the starting line, and an electric current is then applied to the medium (a starch gel). The proteins "run" into the gel toward the anode (+). How far they travel depends on the structure and electrical charge of the protein molecules. The normal (A) and sickle cell anemia (S) phenotypes show their characteristic types of hemoglobin, which differ slightly in electric charge. The sickle cell heterozygote (AS) has both types of hemoglobin.

Malaria and the Sickle-Cell Gene

Despite the low fitness of sickle-cell homozygotes, the sickle-cell gene occurs at comparatively high frequencies in the populations of certain areas—especially tropical Africa, but also parts of southern Europe, Southwest Asia, and the Middle East (Figure 14-2). Why hasn't natural selection eliminated it from these populations? And why does the gene occur in these populations rather than in others?

As pointed out in Chapter 3, the answer to the first question seems to have to do with a relationship between the sickle-cell gene and malaria—or rather one form of the disease, called falciparum malaria. Sickle-cell heterozygotes have a high resistance to this disease; they are less likely to contract it, and if they do, they are less likely to die from it. This is particularly true of children who are not yet immune to the disease. The sickle-cell gene may also protect the unborn children of heterozygous mothers who contract malaria.

In the populations we are dealing with, this resistance is no small advantage. In many areas of tropical Africa, falciparum malaria is one of the leading causes of death, especially among children. Therefore, the heterozygotes' resistance constitutes a significant selective factor. While sickle-cell anemia has been removing the *S* gene by picking off the homozygotes, differential susceptibility to malaria has been preserving it by favoring the heterozygotes over *AA* homozygotes. The result is a balanced polymorphism, in which the abnormal gene survives at relatively high frequencies.

As Figure 14-2 indicates, high frequencies of the sickle-cell gene are concentrated in areas where falciparum malaria is common. The close correspondence between the distribution of the gene and that of malaria first gave geneticists the clue to this relationship and prompted clinical studies of the susceptibility of the different genotypes to malaria. These studies finally elucidated the problem.

This case, then, is a good example of the search for a direct relationship between genes and environment to solve puzzles in human variability.

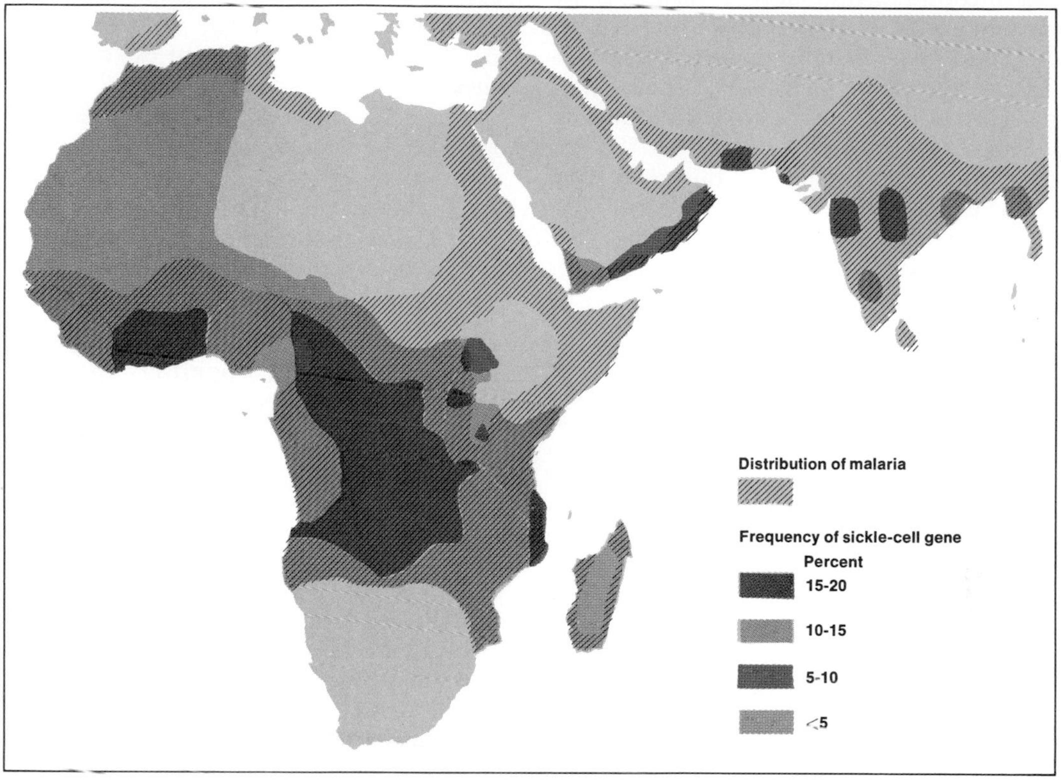

Figure 14-2. The distribution of falciparum malaria and the sickle-cell gene in Africa and western Asia. Nearly all the areas in which there is a relatively high incidence of the sickle-cell gene are also areas where malaria is common. Malaria is also widespread in eastern Asia, where the sickle-cell gene is not found, suggesting that the mutation probably originated in Africa. (*After Allison, 1961*)

Though such relationships are the first thing the anthropologist or geneticist looks for, they are seldom easy to see. For those trying to explain the stubborn survival of the *S* gene, there was no obvious connection between this gene and malaria. (Indeed, the connection is so far from obvious that biologists are still trying to figure it out.) It was simply a matter of examining variable after variable until they finally found one whose distribution was similar to that of the gene.

The Effects of Migration and Gene Flow on Sickle-Cell Distribution

While the sickle-cell case illustrates the interaction between genes and environment in producing variability, it also shows how cultural factors can complicate and obscure this interaction. If you look again at Figure 14-2, you will see that the distribution of the sickle-cell allele and of falciparum malaria in Africa and Southwest Asia are by no means a perfect match. For example, no *S* seems to occur in the heavily malarial areas of Southeast Asia. Even in the malaria-ridden West African forest belts, populations that are equally exposed to the disease show very unequal *S* gene frequencies—some high, some low. Similarly, in areas where falciparum malaria is totally absent, such as the northern United States, there are people of African and Mediterranean ancestry who carry the sickle-cell gene.

These inconsistencies can be explained if we consider migration and gene flow as well as selection. The *S* gene probably arose as a mutation somewhere in Africa, the Mediterranean, or Southwest Asia. From this point, it spread by interbreeding or was carried by migration. If this is the case, then the absence of the gene from Southeast Asia may have nothing to do with different selective forces in this area. Rather, the gene is not there because gene flow was never sufficient to establish it there.

Similarly, the surprisingly low frequencies of the sickle-cell gene among certain West African populations can be explained as a result of gene flow and cultural history. Livingstone (1958) has shown that these populations probably abandoned hunting and gathering for agriculture relatively recently. This would mean that they also encountered malaria only relatively recently, for the mosquito that carries the falciparum parasite is rare in undisturbed forests, whereas it flourishes in the garden plots of subsistence agriculturalists. These populations probably acquired the *S* gene from the invaders who introduced them to agriculture. Thus they are apparently latecomers to both the selective forces connected with the gene—sickle-cell anemia and malaria. According to Livingstone, this is why they have low *S* frequencies. Their gene pools have simply not had enough time to bring the two forces into equilibrium. In other words, they are still moving toward—but have not yet reached—a balanced polymorphism.

Finally, it is obvious that we must seek some explanation other than natural selection to account for the presence of sickle-cell genes in Newark, New Jersey, or Liverpool, England. Again, the explanation lies in cultural history. *S* genes are found in Newark not because they are advantageous there or ever have been but because most of the slaves brought to America in the eighteenth and nineteenth centuries came from West Africa, and many residents of Newark are the descendants of those West African slaves. Given enough time, selection against sickle-cell homozygotes, without a compensating advantage for the heterozygotes, should lead the gene to decline to very low frequencies in such areas. But the rate of decline is also likely to become extremely slow as the frequency of the gene approaches zero. Thus, a residue of *S* genes will persist indefinitely as part of the genetic load of these populations.

As is often the case, the distribution of the *S* allele in American populations does not represent adaptation to present environmental circumstances but a leftover adaptation to past environments. Migration in the past few centuries has simply been too recent for physical evolution to have caught up with it.

Other Variations Possibly Related to Malaria

Malaria is suspected to act as a maintaining force in many other polymorphisms besides sickle cell (see Table 14-1, third column). However, the fact that malaria is implicated in so many human polymorphisms does not mean that it is a more potent selective force than such diseases as tuberculosis or influenza. It merely reflects the fact that the malaria parasite attacks the red blood cells, and blood is easily sampled. The malaria-related polymorphisms are probably only the tip of the iceberg—representatives of a wide array of hidden disease-related genetic variations. There is some evidence that disease has also been a factor in maintaining the variety of human blood groups.

Blood Groups

Of all the forms of human variation that are under simple genetic control, perhaps the most familiar are the blood groups. Almost everybody knows that he or she is "type O, Rh positive," or "type A, Rh negative," and so on. Terms like these specify which blood factors the individual carries. As mentioned earlier, these factors are located on the surface of the red blood cells. They vary considerably within and among populations.

Blood group substances are arranged in systems. Each system includes a series of factors that are determined by alleles at one locus. For example, *A*, *B*, and *O* are the three principal alleles at the locus governing the ABO blood group system, which we discussed briefly in Chapter 2.

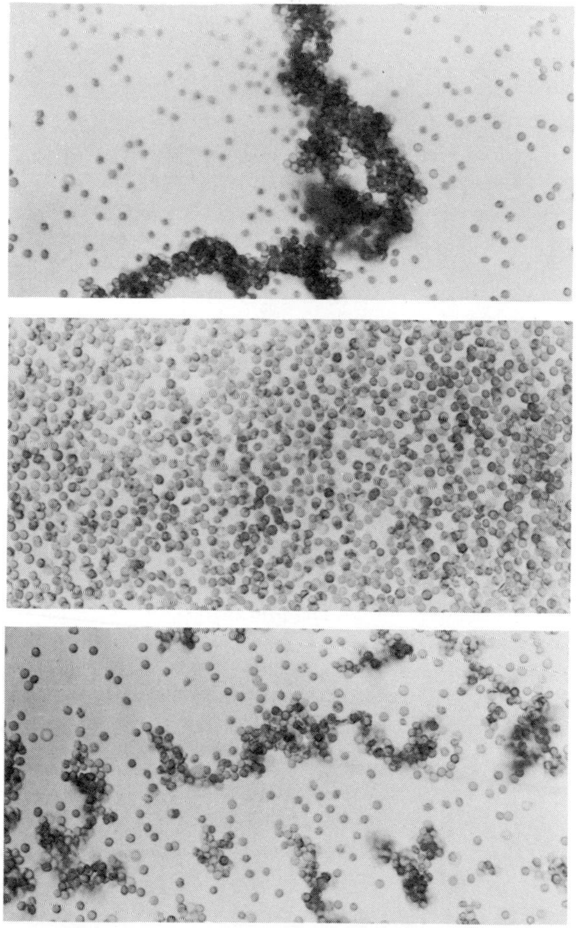

The human body makes antibodies to ABO blood group substances other than those found on its own red cells. If type A blood is transfused into an O or B individual, anti-A antibodies will attack the red cells, causing them to clump, as in these photos. Since type AB cells carry *both* A and B substances, AB individuals do not make either anti-A or anti-B, and so can receive transfusions of any blood type. Type O cells carry *neither* A nor B substances, so type O blood can safely be transfused into any recipient. *(Lester V. Bergman & Assoc., Inc.)*

Depending on which two alleles a person carries, he may be type A, B, AB, or O. Translated into biological terms, these "types" indicate which substances of the ABO system the individual carries on his red cell membranes. Type A carries a certain substance, called A. Type B carries a different substance, called B. Type AB carries both A and B. Type O carries neither. "Rh positive" and "Rh negative" are phenotypes determined by two of the many known alleles at the Rh locus. Each allele determines the presence of a particular set of factors in the Rh system.

All in all, about 15 different blood group systems are recognized in humans. Thus the blood group substances are an abundant source of variability. Indeed, there are probably more possible combinations of different blood group substances than there are human beings on earth.

The ABO system is not the simplest of the blood group systems, but because of a certain peculiarity, it is the one whose variations have been most thoroughly charted. In most of the blood group systems, people are capable of developing antibodies[1] to the blood group substances different from the ones they carry. But, in the ABO blood group system, everyone early in life makes antibodies to all the substances different from their own. (Type A blood carries antibodies to B; type B carries antibodies to A; type O carries antibodies to both A and B.) This means that if a person with type B blood is given a transfusion of type A blood (or vice versa), his antibodies will cause the donor's red cells to mass together in clumps—a reaction that can result in death. To prevent such accidents, large numbers of people all over the world have been tested for their ABO blood types. The side benefit of this testing is that researchers now have good estimates of the geographical distribution of the three major alleles of the ABO system.

The Distribution of ABO Blood Groups

As can be seen from Figure 14-3, there are very considerable differences among populations in the gene frequencies of the ABO system. A few populations have only one allele. Among pure Peruvian Indians, for example, the frequency

[1] Antibodies are proteins produced by the body in response to substances introduced from outside. They react with the foreign substances in such a way as to destroy or deactivate them.

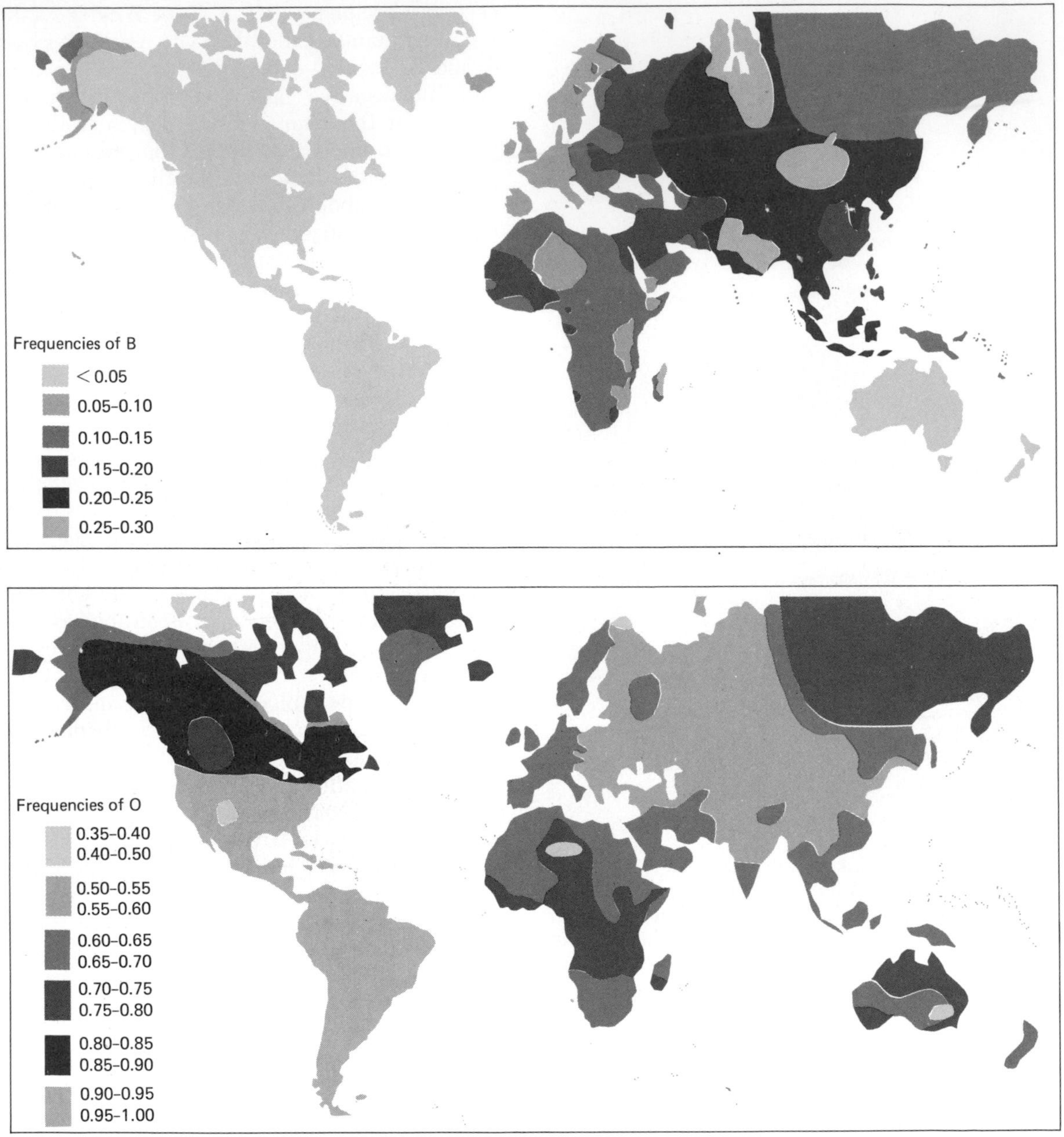

Figure 14-3. The frequencies of blood group genes *B* and *O* in human populations. The effects of population movements since 1492 have been eliminated as far as possible. Note the cline in *B* gene frequency outward from central Asia, and the apparent absence of *B* in almost all original New World populations. (*After Mourant et al., 1958*)

of *O* is close to 1.0. Other populations are more polymorphic, but each in its own way. The Tuamotuans of Polynesia, for example, have approximately equal frequencies of *A* and *O*, with no *B*, while the African Pygmies have all three genes in approximately equal frequencies. The *O* gene is most common worldwide, but certain areas have high frequencies of *A* or *B*. The *B* gene in particular shows an interesting distribution pattern—a *cline*, or slow gradient of frequency change over a geographical area. Most predominant in central Asia, *B* gradually trails off to lower and lower frequencies toward the edges of the Old World (Figure 14-3).

The frequency of the genes of the Rh system also shows pronounced variation within and among populations. Some genes are very common in some populations and virtually absent in others, whereas other genes are more evenly spread throughout the human species.

The Problem of Interpreting Blood Group Variation

It is difficult to explain the variation in human blood groups. As we have seen, genetic drift tends to eliminate variation within populations unless opposing forces are operating to maintain it. What forces, then, are responsible for maintaining the blood group polymorphisms in human populations? And why are some blood group genes common in some populations but rare or absent in others?

Certain details of blood group distribution can best be explained by reference to the immediate ancestry of the populations concerned. The ABO frequencies of white, black, and oriental Americans, for example, closely mirror those of the populations from which they were derived.

Founder effect has also been invoked to explain some peculiarities of blood group distribution. For example, it would seem logical to assume that the ancestors of the American Indians had a substantial frequency of *B*, since *B* is quite common in eastern Asia, where they originated. Yet in fact it appears that the American Indians had no *B* at all until they acquired it from the European settlers a few centuries ago. It is possible that purely by chance the *B* allele was absent from the first populations to cross the Bering Straits land bridge into the New World. Or the gene may have been lost by drift while the original population was still quite small.

However, while non-Darwinian processes may account for certain details of distribution, they cannot adequately explain the large-scale patterns of blood group variation. Given that new alleles were probably introduced into many populations through gene flow, why did these polymorphisms persist? There must have been some forces maintaining them. Or, given that the blood group differences between black and oriental Americans reflect blood group differences between Africans and Asians, why do Africans and Asians differ? Drift can account for divergence in small populations but not in entire continents of people. Furthermore, if drift alone were responsible for differences among populations, gene frequencies would be distributed more or less at random, which they are not. There are definite patterns, as we saw, for example, in the cline of the *B* allele in the Old World.

What *could* explain large-scale patterns of blood group variation, and quite adequately, is natural selection. Balanced selection could be responsible for maintaining the different blood group alleles as balanced polymorphisms, and differential selection could account for geographical variation in gene frequencies. But, of course, we cannot be certain that this is the case with blood groups until we have found the selective factors. In order to do so, biologists have adopted a number of different strategies.

ABO Blood Groups and Disease

The environmental variable that has been scrutinized most carefully in relation to blood group polymorphism is the same one that lay behind sickle-cell polymorphism—disease. One line of investigation is statistical—examining the incidence of various diseases in people of different blood groups to see whether there are any diseases to which certain blood groups are more susceptible. Some correlations have been found. Type O people, for example, are more prone to develop duodenal ulcers, whereas type A people are more susceptible to stomach cancer and pernicious anemia. It is possible, then, that these disorders (or others) have influenced the distribution of blood types, but more research must be done before we can draw such a conclusion.

The second line of investigation has to do with similarities between blood group substances and the surface proteins of certain harmful microorganisms, such as bacteria and viruses. The body will not normally manufacture antibodies to substances that it itself produces. Therefore it is theoretically at a disadvantage if it is infected by a microorganism whose surface proteins—the proteins that would normally stimulate the production of antibodies—resemble those of its own red blood cells or other tissues. The microorganism might be mistaken for "one of us" and thereby slip past the body's screening system.

For example, the surface proteins of the bacterium that causes bubonic plague are similar to blood group substances on type O cells. Therefore, type O people should, logically, be more susceptible to the disease. In light of the history of bubonic plague and the distribution of the *O* gene, this fact becomes rather interesting. Bubonic plague probably originated in Southeast Asia and spread westward. (Known as the Black Death, it hit Europe in the mid-fourteenth century, killing off an estimated quarter of the population.) Central Asia has the longest history of bubonic plague, and today it is the area with the lowest frequencies of group O blood. Possibly the disease did in fact put the *O* gene at a selective disadvantage, from which it has not yet recovered. However, since human populations are no longer prey to plague epidemics, we have no way of investigating the susceptibility of the different blood groups to the disease and thereby proving or disproving the hypothesis. Thus, as with the statistical studies, we have as yet no definite cause-and-effect relationships—only intriguing possibilities.

DIET-RELATED VARIATIONS

Disease is not the only selective factor that might underlie many forms of human physical variation. What a population eats may be as important an influence on its gene pool as what viruses and bacteria it has to contend with. Differences in diet have probably played an important role in creating variation in the digestive enzymes—those proteins that make it possible for the body to break down food chemically. Unfortunately, we know almost nothing about genetic variation in these enzymes. However, by examining two rather curious variations that seem to be related to diet—one definitely and the other possibly involving an enzyme—we can get a glimpse of the ways in which selective pressures involving nutrition may act upon gene pools.

PTC Tasting

One of the odder human polymorphisms involves the ability to taste the chemical substance phenylthiocarbamide, or PTC. To most people, PTC solutions, even at low concentrations, taste intensely bitter. However, in many populations there are people who describe PTC as tasteless except in very strong solutions. The ability to taste PTC is determined by a pair of alleles, with the "taster" condition being dominant to the "nontaster." The frequency of the nontaster gene varies from a reported high of nearly 60 percent in an Asiatic Indian population to a low of about 10 percent in some populations of South American Indians.

The selective force, if any, behind this variation remains something of a mystery. We do know that PTC is chemically close to substances that inhibit thyroid function, and that goiter, a disorder caused by thyroid malfunction, is disproportionately common among nontasters of PTC. Possibly the ability to taste PTC confers a selective advantage, in that it causes people to perceive thyroid-inhibiting substances as distasteful and hence to avoid them in food. It is not known, however, why this selective pressure was evidently relaxed in some populations, allowing the nontaster gene to reach substantial frequencies.

In itself, PTC tasting is not an important human polymorphism. Its interest is that it gives us a glimpse of what is probably a large array of biochemically controlled variations that produce selective effects by causing people to perceive particular stimuli as either pleasant or unpleasant, thus influencing their dietary preferences.

Lactase Deficiency

Another polymorphism related to diet is the ability to digest lactose, the sugar found in milk. This ability depends upon having the enzyme lactase in the lining of the small intestine. All normal human babies, like most young mammals, produce lactase and can digest milk sugar easily. So can the majority of adults in European and other "white" populations and in some African populations. But in other populations, constituting a large majority of mankind, most people cannot digest milk sugar after the age of about four years. Thereafter, little or no lactase is secreted, and drinking fresh milk in any quantity usually leads to severe cramps and flatulence.

Most geneticists who have studied the occurrence of lactase deficiency in families believe that it has a genetic basis. It may be determined by a pair of alleles—the gene for lactase production being dominant to that for lactase deficiency. In some areas, variations among populations in the frequency of lactase deficiency correlate closely with subsistence pattern. In West Africa, for example, populations of herders who drink a good deal of fresh milk and have a low incidence of lactase deficiency live side by side with farmers who drink little milk and have a high frequency of lactase deficiency.

Since lactase deficiency in adults is normal not only for most humans but also for other mammals, the nondeficient gene probably represents a fairly recent mutation. Presumably the locus involved is one of those that regulates development by switching genes at other loci on and off, thereby causing such time-dependent changes as the graying of hair. In this case, the mutant allele fails to switch off the gene for infantile lactase production. The mutation probably arose sometime in the past 10,000 years and, for obvious reasons, was strongly favored in populations that took up herding and dairying. In populations where no milk was drunk by adults, there was no advantage in prolonged lactase production, so the gene for lactase deficiency was retained.

Once again, this variation gives us a glimpse of a phenomenon that is undoubtedly widespread in the human species. The adoption of milk drinking by adults was certainly neither the only dietary change in human evolutionary history nor the most important. Early *Homo*'s crucial transition from a largely vegetarian diet to a diet involving regular meat eating probably produced considerable changes in the digestive enzymes. Likewise, the switch from the hunter-gatherer's mixed and well-balanced diet to the starchier fare of the agriculturalist must have had its impact on the digestive processes. In both cases, different groups made the transition at different times and in different environments. (In the case of agriculture, some groups never made the transition at all.) And these variations in subsistence pattern from population to population have probably resulted in substantial variation in the genetic controllers of enzyme activity.

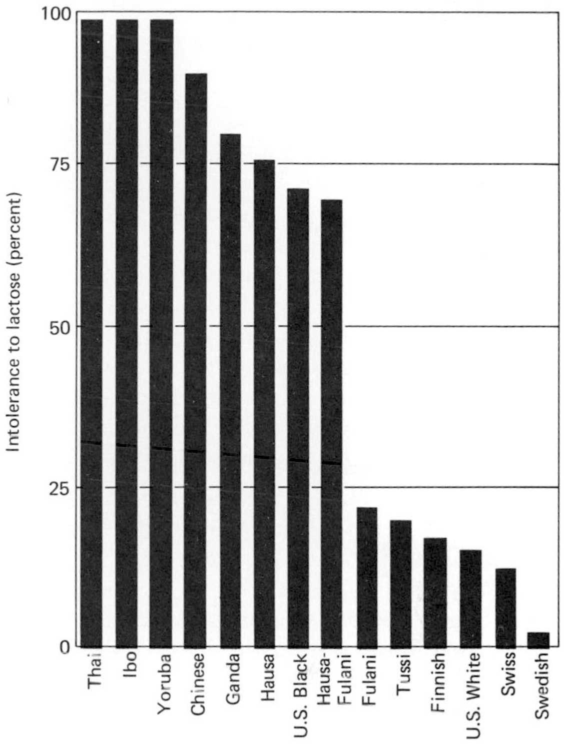

Figure 14-4. The distribution of lactose intolerance among adults in a number of human populations. *(After Kretchmer, 1972)*

THE SIGNIFICANCE OF HUMAN POLYMORPHISM

We end this brief examination of simpler genetic variations by reiterating a few important points. First, polymorphism is a widespread phenomenon. At least 30 percent of the known human structural genes—that is, genes that code for proteins—are polymorphic. Thus it is not just a poetic turn of phrase to say that every human being (with the exception of identical twins) is unique. Second, because of the difficulty of sampling, the genetically determined variation that we know about is undoubtedly only a tiny fraction of the genetic variation that exists in the species. Each of us may be even more unique than we realize. Third, the distribution of variation among modern human populations has as much to do with culture as with present-day environment.

Finally, whether cultural or physical, the causes of most genetic variation are utterly unknown to us. In order to know the causes, we must understand the selective effects of variant genotypes. But these effects are usually quite small and therefore very hard to detect. They gain their power only in the long run, over thousands or millions of years. Scientists, however, can observe them only in the short run. Hence the huge gaps in our understanding. In spite of the progress that has been made in recent decades, genetic research has only begun to unravel the significance of most human variation.

Summary

Human beings belong to a single species, so they have many more similarities than differences. Nevertheless, the degree of physical variation in modern *Homo sapiens* is very great. Humans display a high degree of *polymorphism*, or genetically determined variety within populations. Moreover, the species is decidedly *polytypic*, with many differences among populations.

Some of these variations are continuous: they appear as smooth gradients between extremes. Others are discontinuous, dividing the species into discrete types. The most interesting variations are those that are under genetic control at least to some degree, and so are subject to evolutionary processes.

To explain any patterns of variation we must often take cultural factors into account. Unlike those of most other species, human populations are defined not only geographically but also by many cross-cutting social and cultural divisions. These subdivisions of the population may have considerable effects on genotype frequencies. Cultural adaptations have also come to play a role in the process of selection, as in the case of technologically advanced settlers who have displaced native populations in many areas. Culture may also impose selective forces of its own, thus influencing biological evolution.

Some of the best known human physical variations are found in the blood proteins. A notable example involves *hemoglobin*, the red, oxygen-carrying protein found inside red blood cells. Chemically, hemoglobin S differs only slightly from normal hemoglobin. This minute difference has massive consequences, however. People who are homozygous for the hemoglobin *S* allele suffer from *sickle-cell anemia*, which can result in early death. The heterozygous condition, *sickle-cell trait*, is relatively harmless.

In spite of the low fitness of sickle-cell homozygotes, the hemoglobin *S* gene occurs quite frequently in parts of Africa and the Mediterranean countries. Its presence seems to be related to the incidence of falciparum malaria; sickle-cell heterozygotes have a high resistance to this disease, which is common in tropical areas. Thus there is a selective force operating for as well as against the abnormal gene. The result is a balanced polymorphism, in which the *S* allele survives at relatively high frequencies.

The sickle-cell phenomenon is complicated by other factors, however. The hemoglobin *S* gene seems to be absent in Southeast Asia, which is also a heavily malarial area, and conversely, the gene is present in non-malarial areas in the United States. These inconsistencies result from gene flow and migration of people.

The *blood group substances*, a set of molecules

located on the surface of the red blood cells, represent perhaps the most familiar human variation that is under simple genetic control. These substances include those that define the ABO and rhesus (Rh) blood group systems. There are substantial differences among populations in the gene frequencies of the ABO system, and this variation is hard to explain. Non-Darwinian processes (gene flow and the founder effect) can account only for certain details of this distribution. Some correlations have been found between certain blood groups and susceptibility to some diseases. However, we still cannot prove any definite cause-and-effect relationships, and so we cannot be sure what selective factors maintain this polytypic distribution.

At least two curious human variations seem to be related to diet. One is the ability to taste phenylthiocarbamide (PTC), which tastes bitter to most people, but is tasteless to large segments of certain populations. The second is the ability to digest lactose, the sugar found in milk. This ability depends upon the secretion of *lactase*, an enzyme found in the small intestine. Since most humans stop producing lactase after the age of about four years, preventing them from drinking fresh milk in any quantity, it appears that the gene for continued lactase production in adult life is a recent mutation favored among herding and dairying populations.

Human polymorphism is widespread. At least 30 percent of the known human structural genes are polymorphic. The genetic variations that we are aware of probably constitute a mere fraction of those that actually exist, and in most cases the causes remain a mystery.

Glossary

blood group substances molecules found on the surface of red blood cells; they belong to several different systems, and the molecules within each system vary considerably within and among populations

cline a gradual change in gene frequency over a geographical region

hemoglobin the oxygen-carrying protein found in red blood cells

lactase an enzyme in the small intestine that enables humans to digest milk sugar; for most of the world's population, it is present only during early childhood

plasma the fluid constituent of blood, a clear yellowish liquid that contains dissolved proteins such as transferrin

polymorphism genetically determined variety within populations

polytypic species a species in which there are recognizable genetically determined differences among populations (see Chapters 3 and 4)

sickle-cell anemia a disease occurring in people who are homozygous for the hemoglobin *S* allele, so that their red blood cells contain only the abnormal type S hemoglobin

sickle-cell trait the relatively harmless heterozygous condition in which one allele codes for hemoglobin S, the other normal hemoglobin A

Suggested Readings

HARRIS, H. 1975
Principles of Human Biochemical Genetics, 2nd rev. ed. New York: Elsevier. The discoverer of many human biochemical polymorphisms considers their biological and evolutionary significance.

RACE, R. R., AND SANGER, R. 1975
Blood Groups in Man, 6th ed. Philadelphia: Lippincott. Not only an authoritative work on a major set of human polymorphisms, but an enjoyable book for its own sake.

STERN, C. 1973
Principles of Human Genetics, 3rd ed. San Francisco: W. H. Freeman. This is an especially clear, full, and authoritative text.

Chapter Fifteen

Complex Variation and the Concept of Race

As we saw in the last chapter, the evolutionary significance of most simple human variation—variation controlled by genes at one locus, with little or no influence from the environment—is still very incompletely understood. Even more difficult to analyze are the many important forms of variation whose inheritance is polygenic—controlled by genes at several loci, or by several loci in interaction with the environment. At the gene level, these complex traits are no different from simple traits: genes code for proteins, and proteins produce phenotypic effects. The difference is that with such complex traits as skin color, facial form, or stature (to say nothing of the infinitely complicated traits of intelligence and temperament), the phenotypic effect reflects the interaction of many genes and gene products, each of which may be responsive to a different set of environmental influences. Deciphering the way in which all these factors interact with one another to produce complex variation is one of the most exacting challenges facing biologists today.

The task is made no easier by the fact that complex variation, unlike simple variation, tends to be continuously rather than discontinuously distributed within populations. No matter how many people there are in a population, with regard to ABO blood types they fall into a relatively small number of neat groups: A, B, O, and a few rarer subtypes. By contrast, even relatively obvious forms of complex variation, such as skin color, express themselves as a myriad of subtle gradations on a continuous scale. For many other forms of variation, such as intelligence, we are still uncertain what exactly we are trying to measure.

The dimensions of human variation can be seen at international gatherings such as this session of the United Nations General Assembly. Traditional "racial" classifications bring some appearance of order to this diversity, but cannot encompass the full extent of it without considerable arbitrariness and inconsistency. Nor is there any evidence that "purer," more distinct races existed in the past; indeed, the opposite is probably true. *(Courtesy, United Nations)*

Difficult as it is to study, complex variation is a tantalizing subject. Many traits of this kind are externally visible and have excited curiosity since earliest recorded times. Some of them, such as skin color and facial form, have been used to define the traditional "races" of mankind. Others, such as stature, hair color, and the size and shape of different parts of the body, form the basis for our ideas of physical beauty. Of course, from a scientific point of view, these traits are no more "basic" to the human being than are the simpler biochemical traits discussed in the last chapter. Biologically, there is no reason a person should regard his stature as a more essential part of his "self" than his ABO blood type, and having an unusually shaped nose is certainly of less consequence than having sickle-cell hemoglobin. Yet because these complex traits are externally obvious—because they are what we see when we see human beings, and what we use to tell them apart—values and attitudes have become attached to them. They have thus acquired social, psychological, and sometimes even political importance in addition to their biological significance.

We cannot describe here all the forms of complex variation in the human species. We will therefore consider a few representative categories, skin color and facial form in particular. We will then examine two issues—the usefulness of the concept of "race" and the existence of differences among populations in intelligence—

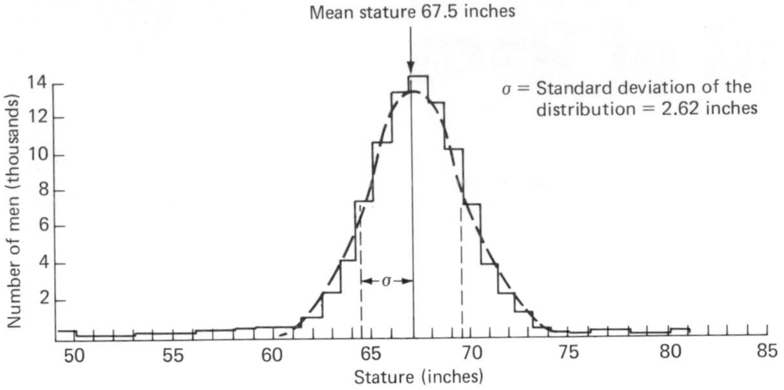

Figure 15-1. The distribution of stature among 91,163 army recruits, representing the young male population of England in 1939. The distribution of individual values plotted as a histogram closely matches a normal curve calculated from the data. *(After W. J. Martin, 1947)*

where social attitudes have been deeply implicated in the study of complex variation.

FORMS OF COMPLEX VARIATION

Many forms of complex variation show no clearcut patterns of geographical distribution. Human stature is a good example. The average stature is greater in some populations than in others. One of the most extreme contrasts is seen in central Africa. The average male among the Watusi is 177 centimeters (5 ft. 10 in.) tall, while among their neighbors, the Pygmies, the average adult male is only 144 centimeters (4 ft. 9 in.) tall. But in general the variation among populations is slight compared with the variation within populations. Other traits show marked differences among populations, and it is on these traits that we will concentrate. For such traits we can find populations with little or no phenotypic overlap. For example, the darkest-skinned Swede is not nearly so dark as the lightest-skinned Zulu. Because of this pattern of extreme geographical variability, it is these forms of variation that have served as the traditional markers for the classification of humanity into separate "races."

Human Pigmentation

The color of the human skin varies throughout the world. Almost all populations are polymorphic, and the degree of variation among populations in average skin color is considerable, ranging from very light, as in northwest Europe, to very dark, as in parts of tropical Africa, Asia, Australia, and the Pacific Islands. Human skin color is determined by the thickness of the layers of the skin and by the concentration of various pigments—especially the brown pigment, *melanin*—in these layers. The greater the melanin concentration, the darker the skin. In thin skin, when the melanin concentration is low, the blood vessels under the skin show through, giving the skin a pinkish cast. (As we saw in Chapter 3, the complete absence of melanin in the albino produces a skin color that is genuinely pink.) Modern experimenters measure the variations in skin color with an instrument called a reflectance spectrophotometer, which bounces a beam of light off the skin and measures the proportion that is reflected.

The genetic basis of skin color is still quite obscure. Clearly, pigmentation is not determined by a single pair of alleles at one locus, but how it is determined can only be guessed at. Most work on the subject has assumed that there are several genes involved, each contributing (or not contributing) a given dose of pigment, and that the sum of their contributions equals the individual's degree of pigmentation. With these assumptions, the closest fit to the distribution of skin color seen in real human populations is given by a model with about five loci, each with a single pair of alleles. However, what we know about the way in which enzymes work suggests that the situation may be somewhat more complicated, involving genes coding for enzymes that vary in their rates of activity and that influence one another, rather than independently influencing pigment production.

Possible Selective Agents Influencing Pigmentation

Variation in skin color among populations poses a second problem for anthropologists: What are the selective factors that have made some populations darker than others?

The connection between melanin production and the ultraviolet component of sunlight seems to provide a hint. In light-skinned people, exposure to ultraviolet light usually leads to increased melanin production, resulting in what we call a suntan. This fact, coupled with the fact that on the whole dark-skinned populations live (or have lived until recently) in areas exposed to a relatively high incidence of ultraviolet radiation (Figure 15-2), is strong circumstantial evidence that ultraviolet light is one selective factor determining genetic variation in skin color.

As with malaria and the sickle-cell gene, the geographical correspondence between dark skin and high incidence of ultraviolet light is not perfect. There are many exceptions—for example, the comparatively light-skinned Indians of tropical South America and the dark-skinned aborigines of Tasmania, who lived in a cool, misty climate not unlike that of northern California. However, as with sickle cell, these inconsistencies can be explained in terms of modern population movements.

Nevertheless, we are still left with the question of *how* ultraviolet light operates as a selective factor. Why would dark-skinned people be more fit in areas with high ultraviolet radiation and light-skinned people in areas with low radiation? Several different answers have been proposed. In each case, the basis for the theory is the fact that melanin in the outer layers of the skin scatters and absorbs ultraviolet radiation, preventing its penetration into the deeper layers.

One of the most obvious and painful responses to excessive exposure to ultraviolet radiation is sunburn, which irritates and destroys the skin's living layers, causing discomfort, blistering, and a risk of infection. All of these might have been selective factors in primitive human populations, favoring a "genetically" dark skin in which the melanin would protect against sunburn. This protection would be especially important in young infants, for whom sunburn can be a serious hazard.

Another potential selective agent that is influenced by exposure to ultraviolet light is skin cancer. Among "whites," tumors of the skin, especially of the exposed parts, are more frequent in sunny climates. Moreover, the "white" inhabitants of these regions have more skin tumors than their dark-skinned neighbors. However, it is questionable whether these tumors have much effect on fitness, since they are generally nonmalignant and usually occur after reproductive age.

A third possible selective agent involves an effect of ultraviolet radiation that is normally beneficial—stimulation of vitamin D production in the skin. Vitamin D is essential to the body's calcium metabolism, but too much is toxic. Possibly the melanin layer of dark-skinned peoples screens out excessive ultraviolet radiation and thus eliminates the danger of poisoning by excess vitamin D in sunny climates. It should be added, however, that there is no direct evidence that too much vitamin D is in fact a problem for light-skinned inhabitants of the tropics.

An alternative theory uses the vitamin D hypothesis to explain not why blacks are black but why whites are white. According to this theory, light skin would have a selective advantage in a climate with a low incidence of ultraviolet radiation. A deficiency of vitamin D in the growing child can lead to skeletal deformities called

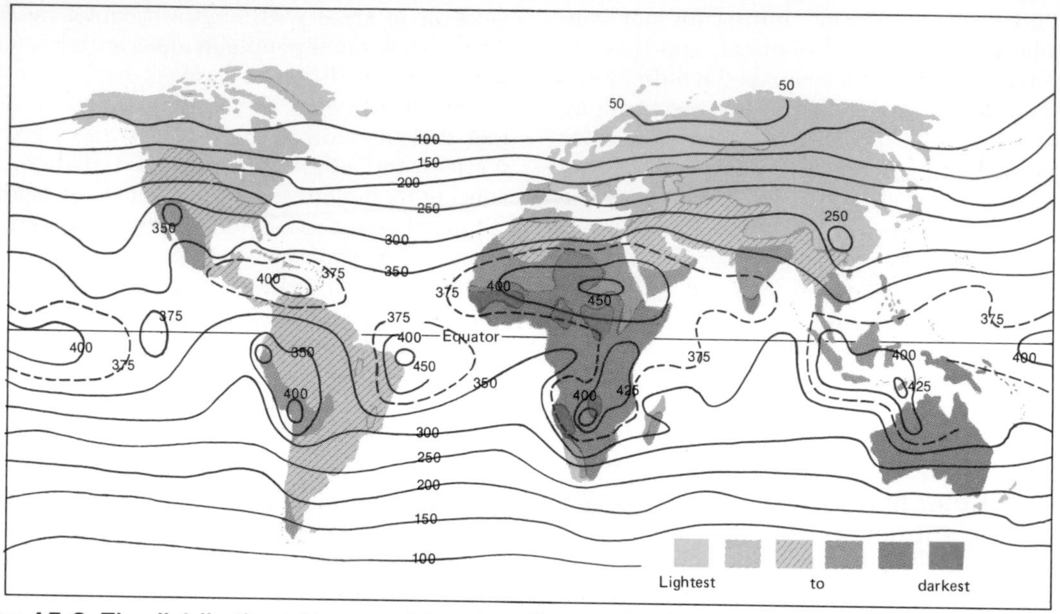

Figure 15-2. The distribution of human skin color, disregarding European and African population movements into the New World and the Pacific after 1400 A.D. Superimposed is the average distribution of ultraviolet light intensity measured in watt-seconds/sq. cm. *(After B. J. Williams, 1973)*

rickets. There is some evidence that prior to the introduction of vitamin D enriched milk, rickets occurred more frequently among black children than white children of similar socioeconomic status living in cloudy northern cities. The inference is that in areas where sunlight is weak—and especially in winter, when most of the body surface is covered—dark skins have more difficulty absorbing enough ultraviolet radiation to produce the needed amounts of vitamin D.

We need not assume that only one of these sunshine-related selective effects has contributed to the distribution of human skin color. All of them, as well as others still undefined, are probably implicated. And as with other variations, the distribution of skin color that we see today is due as much to historical events as to differential selection.

Evolution of Human Skin Color—A Hypothetical Scenario

Taking each of these various factors into account, we can suggest a tentative scenario of the evolution of human skin pigmentation and its distribution.

Judging by living African apes, the primitive condition for prehominids was probably a "white" skin with irregular pigmented blotches. Over most of the body surface, the skin was covered with a hairy coat. The naked parts of the face may or may not have been deeply pigmented; the palms of the hands and soles of the feet probably were not.

An early hominid species, presumably living somewhere in the tropics and probably in a nonforest habitat, lost its hairy coat. (We don't really know why.) Selection then favored more intense skin pigmentation to protect against sunburn, and perhaps against overproduction of vitamin D.

As people colonized the higher latitudes of the Old World, where seasonal variation in climate is more extreme, possession of a skin heavily pigmented from birth was replaced by possession of a fair skin capable of tanning. This allowed the northern peoples to change with the seasons. In summer they tanned and thus avoided sunburn;

in winter they "whitened" and thus avoided vitamin D deficiency.

Among "white" populations living in areas that remain cloudy even in summer (like Ireland), relaxed selection for the tanning response allowed the survival of mutant genotypes that tan poorly and respond to ultraviolet radiation by freckling or repeated sunburn.

During the Upper Pleistocene, America was peopled by "nontropical," light-skinned immigrants from Siberia, while Australia was colonized by "tropical," dark-skinned peoples from Southeast Asia. The fact is that in the 30,000 years or so since these movements occurred the native populations of America and Australia—that is, the American Indians and the Australian aborigines—have apparently diverged rather little in skin color from their relatives in East and Southeast Asia. The American Indians of the tropics are a little darker than those of temperate latitudes, but not much. This suggests that the selective factors that produced the original diversity in skin color have become less intense or that the process of adaptation is extremely slow or perhaps both. This, in turn, indicates that the evolution of light, tannable skin as an adaptation to seasonal climates was very ancient—perhaps much older than the species *Homo sapiens* itself.

During the past 10,000 years, population movements have altered the distribution of skin color variation. In particular, the populations of the Near East, Europe, China, and central Africa, all of which adopted agriculture, grew and expanded geographically at the expense of their hunting and gathering neighbors. Several waves of light-skinned agricultural people moved into Southeast Asia from the north, largely displacing earlier dark-skinned populations. In Africa, it was dark-skinned herders and farmers who expanded, displacing and absorbing lighter-skinned hunter-gatherers, whose remnants are represented by the modern Bushmen of the Kalahari Desert.

In the past 500 years, the situation has been further complicated by colonization. While the peopling of the New World by immigrants of diverse African, European, and Asian descent is the most obvious example of this process, other such movements should not be overlooked. Chinese, for example, migrated into Malaysia, Indonesia, and Polynesia; and Asiatic Indians into Ceylon, Malaya, and Burma.

One point should be emphasized: If our scenario is correct, the juxtaposition of very different phenotypes—blacks and whites living side by side, for example—would not have occurred before the movements of the early agriculturalists. Geographical variation in skin color would have been as gradual as variation in the ultraviolet radiation (Figure 15-2), with each population barely distinguishable from its neighbors in pigmentation. In other words, variation in skin color would have been distributed geographically as a cline—a series of small steps from one population to the next, such as we saw in the distribution of blood type B in the Old World (Chapter 14). This point is worth emphasizing, since it directly opposes the commonly held view that the "races" were at one time more distinct and "pure," until the boundaries between them were blurred by modern population movements.

Hair and Eye Color

Unlike variation in skin color, variation in the color of human hair and eyes is confined to a relatively small percentage of the human species: the populations of northwestern Europe and those derived from them. The rest of the world is uniformly dark-haired and dark-eyed, except for occasional mutants and certain blond individuals among the Australian aborigines. In the hair and eyes, as in the skin, the crucial coloring agent is melanin, and therefore the crucial genes are those that control melanin production. However, the melanin-producing genes for these three traits are independent. Although general "blondism" genes may exist—like the gene for albinism, but less extreme—black hair may nevertheless be found with the lightest skins, and blond hair, as in the case of some Australian aborigines, with the darkest skins. Similarly, blue eyes can appear with dark skins, and fair-skinned blonds can have dark eyes.

The cause of differences in hair and eye color among populations is even more obscure than in the case of skin color. It is possible, however, that variation in eye color, as in skin color, is adaptive to differing levels of sunlight. What determines the color of the eyes is the concentration of melanin in the iris, the diaphragm that widens and narrows the opening of the eye, controlling the amount of light that is allowed to penetrate to the retina. There is some evidence that eyes with a low concentration of melanin in the iris—that is, blue, green, and gray eyes—may not see as well as brown eyes under conditions of bright sunlight. It may be for this reason that populations in sunnier regions tend to be dark-eyed as well as dark-skinned and that light eyes, like light skins, are generally confined to populations—or the descendants of populations—from cloudy northern regions.

Teeth and Jaws

As we have seen in earlier chapters, a general reduction in the size of the teeth and jaws was an evolutionary trend in the genus *Homo* from its earliest history, as technology replaced anatomy in food processing. Indeed, the jaws and teeth of many modern humans, compared with those of their ancestors, are not only small but almost degenerate. Missing teeth and malocclusion (that is, "bad bite") are common. In other cases, vestigial teeth such as third molars, for which there is neither function nor jaw space, disrupt the alignment of the other teeth. C. Loring Brace (1967) has pointed out that this degeneration is most marked in populations that have had the longest exposure to the soft, mushy products of agriculture—breads and cereals that even the least dentally fit types could eat. Likewise, the largest, best-occluding teeth, with the lowest incidence of abnormalities, are found in populations that adopted agriculture only recently, such as tropical Africans, American Indians, and above all the Australian aborigines. Presumably these peoples have not yet lost the efficient teeth required for the hunter-gatherer's diet.

As the teeth diminish in size, so do the jaws, so that the lower face is, on the whole, less massive and less projecting in populations with a longer history of agriculture. Other variations in facial form, however, are thought to be connected not with diet but, like pigmentation, with climate.

Facial Form

The form of the face is a blend of many features—the forehead, nose, eyes, cheekbones, lips, and so forth. Some anthropologists have speculated that these features vary in ways that are related to the temperature and humidity of different climates. The nose, for example, takes its shape from the nasal bones, which are part of the skull, and from the cartilaginous tip. For free breathing, the best configuration would seem to be broad nasal passages, with circular, wide-open nostrils. However, in cold, dry, or dusty regions, such as Europe must have been during the ice ages, narrower nasal passages and flattened nostrils—a variation characteristic of northwestern European populations—may be better adapted. This form provides a greater surface for air to flow over and thus makes it possible for the air to be moistened, warmed, and filtered before it strikes the sensitive membranes of the upper nose.

Noses, along with the other components of the face, vary within all populations. However, some types, as we have just seen, are locally prevalent, so that there are also differences among populations. In addition, there are distinctive *sets* of facial features that are characteristic of certain populations. One of the most striking of these is the so-called Mongoloid face.

The Mongoloid Face

The Mongoloid face—the distinctive facial structure of "orientals"—has long fascinated Westerners. (If physical anthropology had been a Chinese discipline, anthropologists might be more concerned with explaining the interestingly "beaky" noses and "rounded" eyes of Europeans.) The distinctive components of the Mongoloid face are (1) high, prominent cheekbones combined with a low-bridged, nonprominent nose, which together make the face appear flat; and (2) the so-called epicanthic fold, a fold of skin covering the inner corner of the eye, which, together with a fatty eyelid, makes the eyes appear slanted. It is believed, with little experimental justification, that this facial configuration is more resistant to extreme cold than other facial types. In any case, it is found most highly developed in the coldest regions of Asia—northern China, Mongolia, and Siberia. However, some of its features, in more or less diluted

The contrasting body types of the Eskimo and the Sudanese are thought by some anthropologists to represent adaptations to different climatic conditions. It has been suggested that the short limbs and compact body of the Eskimo tend to conserve body heat, while the long, lithe build of the African, by exposing more skin surface to the air, helps to dissipate heat. *(Courtesy, American Museum of Natural History; George Rodger/Magnum)*

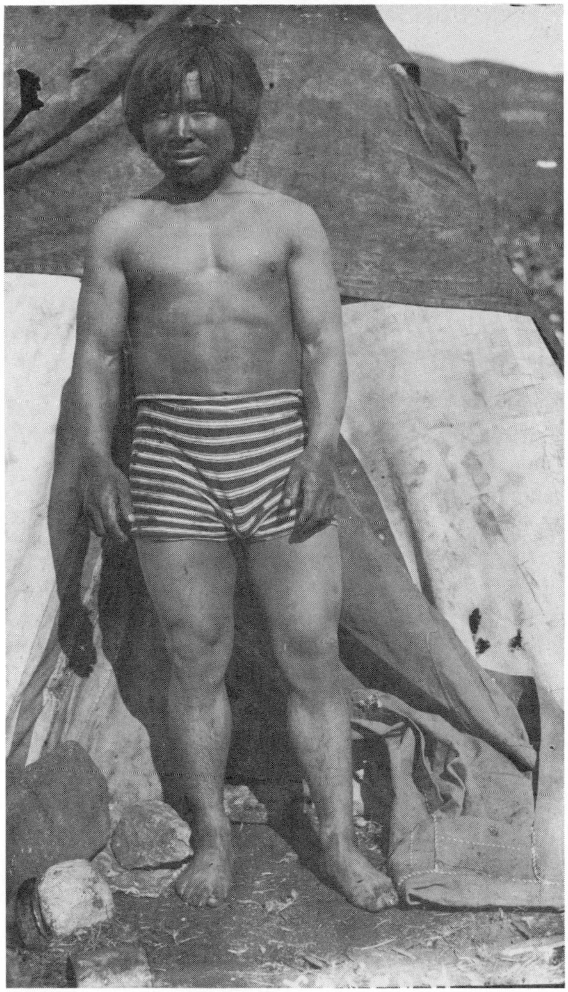

form, are seen in Southeast Asia, in Central Asia as far west as the Urals and the Himalayas, and throughout North and South America.

It seems likely that the distribution of the Mongoloid face—and, indeed, of all the forms of complex facial variation that we have discussed in this section—followed the same historical pattern that we have proposed with regard to skin color. That is, originally they were probably distributed in clines, which were later broken up by population movements. As a result, we now find sharp phenotypic distinctions where once there was simply a smooth gradient, and features in one environment that were originally adaptations to a completely different environment. For example, although the Mongoloid face may have been an adaptation to extreme cold, it is now common in tropical climates, because the peoples of northern Asia who crossed the Bering Straits land bridge and colonized America carried this facial type all the way to the extreme tip of South America, while other Asiatic populations, expanding after adopting agriculture, eventually introduced the Mongoloid face into tropical Indonesia. Likewise, the large teeth of hunter-gatherers are seen in Eskimo pipeline workers and Australian aboriginal cowboys.

THE QUESTION OF RACE

Since anthropology has been defined, on occasion, as "the study of race and culture," the reader may perhaps wonder how we have managed to discuss a good part of human physical variation without using the first of these terms. We have done this by examining the distribution of variable traits among populations as independent entities and by summarizing these distributions in geographical rather than racial terms. This approach emphasizes the continuous distribution of variation. It also allows us to consider the different, cross-cutting distribution patterns that different variants assume—skin color falling into one pattern, ABO blood groups into another, and so on.

We, and perhaps the majority of contemporary physical anthropologists, regard this as the most productive way to tackle the interpretation of human variability. However, other anthropologists have objected that something is lost in examining variation trait by trait. Genes, they argue, do not float independently of one another. They belong to populations, groups of people who share a common history, a common gene pool, and a common boundary separating them from their neighbors. According to this school of thought, the most realistic way to discuss human variation is to compare the *overall* constitution of the various populations, rather than to compare the distribution of various traits from population to population. In other words, the proponents of this view look at the same phenomena—the variable traits of the human species—but collectively rather than individually. Consequently, they see a rather different picture: one in which major divisions of humankind stand out as distinctly different entities. Such an approach tends to stress not the continuity from one area to another but rather the distinctiveness of each population.

Traditionally, the latter approach has often involved grouping populations into major divisions, or "races." Much tedious, and ultimately unproductive, discussion has been expended upon the question of whether races "really exist." We take the view that people demonstrably exist, and that some of their physical and behavioral characters can be measured. Races—like clines, populations, and gene frequencies—are abstractions from these descriptive data, used to organize the information they contain and make it easier to analyze. Insofar as the analyses can be repeated by others, such concepts have a certain reality.

The real issue with race, as with other abstractions used in classification (such as population, species, or genus), is not the reality of the concept but rather its usefulness in a particular case. In science, classification is a tool. It is not an end in itself but a means of organizing data so that scientific discussion can be precise, unambiguous, and economical. What we must consider, then, is how far the use of the term "race" and its associated concepts have enhanced our understanding of human variation.

Races as "Types"

Anthropologists of the late nineteenth and early twentieth centuries often sought to identify, in the heterogeneous population of Europe, individuals who "typified" original European strains—pure races that had supposedly existed as distinct groups before their gene pools were diluted by modern interbreeding. Each race was identified by a series of characteristics, such as head form, hair color, and facial features. The "Nordic," for example, was tall, long-headed, and blond; the "Alpine" was shorter, round-headed, and had brown or red hair. Some authors waxed quite lyrical about the personality traits they ascribed to each race.

Now that we know more about human genetics, we can see that this theory rests on some very weak assumptions. In the first place, it assumes that prehistoric populations were much less variable than modern populations. Nordics were Nordics, and Alpines were Alpines, each race showing an extremely high proportion of the typical trait complex. As we have seen, however, *there is no evidence, and no good theoretical reason for believing, that such "pure races" ever existed in Europe or elsewhere.*

Second, even if pure races had existed at one time, it would still be impossible to identify their traits by surveying modern, interbred populations. Since head form and hair color, for instance, are unrelated genetically, genetic recombination constantly gives rise to round-headed blonds and long-headed brunettes as well as to "Nordic" long-headed blonds and "Alpine" round-headed brunettes. The more independent traits that are added to the list of "identifying" characteristics, the more combinations are seen. There is no scientific reason to select any one of these combinations over the others as more typical of the supposed original strain.

Races as Major Stocks

The effort to identify pure, primal racial strains has now virtually been abandoned. Nevertheless, a somewhat broader concept of race, whereby human populations are grouped into a few "major stocks" or "great races," survived and is still accepted by some physical anthropologists today. This theory is actually much older than the "pure strains" concept. It dates back to Linnaeus's original classification of 1758. Linnaeus divided *Homo sapiens* into several groupings, defined geographically—Asian, African, European, and so forth—as well as by a few identifying traits. This classification scheme was widely adopted. Over the years the identifying traits were revised and expanded, and the geographical labels were replaced by such terms as "Negroid," "Caucasoid," and "Mongoloid," but the notion of a few major human stocks remained essentially the same.

As more peoples came within the orbit of Western science, they were shoehorned into the existing scheme. When some peoples like the Australian aborigines and the Polynesians simply would not fit, they were either dismissed as "hybrids" or assigned to new racial slots, so that in most classifications the number of races crept slowly upward.

Furthermore, as more traits were examined, it was found that many had dissimilar, cross-cutting distributions among human populations. For example, the "Caucasoid" stock was often distinguished from the "Negroid" primarily on the basis of facial features. However, many "Caucasoid" Asiatic Indians are as dark-skinned as most "Negroids," while certain "Negroid" populations, such as the Kalahari Bushmen, are confusingly light-skinned. Such discrepancies were eventually handled by subdividing the major stocks into minor stocks, according to other criteria. At the same time, however, there was no reason beyond tradition—which in science is not a good reason—to regard facial or hair form as more "basic" than other traits. All are human variations whose distribution is determined by the usual evolutionary and historical factors.

Arbitrary as it was, this system of dividing human variation into primary traits, which defined the major races, and secondary traits, which defined subraces within the major races, was nevertheless widely used. Racial classifications became very complex, with tens, often hundreds, of subraces proliferating under the race headings. Such schemes were usually too cumbersome to be used, thus violating the only real standard of value for classification—utility. They became sterile ends in themselves. The situation became more complicated as details of the worldwide distribution of such hidden biochemical traits as blood groups became known, for these traits often cross-cut traditional races still more radically. At this point, many anthropologists began to doubt the usefulness of the race concept as an organizing principle and concentrated instead upon describing the distribution of individual traits.

Races as Zoological Subspecies

For those who retained the race concept, the zoological category of subspecies seemed to offer a partial solution. In zoological classification, subspecies are groups of populations, usually geographically defined, that share obvious external characteristics (see Chapter 3). The assumption is that they share these characteristics because they constitute a major Mendelian population—a group whose members generally breed with one another rather than with outsiders. To avoid accumulating too many subspecies, zoologists have established an arbitrary threshold of difference. If 75 percent of the individuals of a population can be clearly assigned to a subspecies on the basis of a particular identifying trait, the population is sufficiently distinct to be designated as a subspecies.

Ironically, just as some anthropologists began to embrace the idea of subspecies, many zoologists were beginning to seriously question its worth. They found that as the extent of variation below the species level became better known, there were more and more traits that cross-cut "subspecies" boundaries, making these groupings seem arbitrary. The debate among zoologists on the utility of subspecies divisions still continues. However, there seems to be some agreement that the subspecies can be a useful taxonomic category *only* under the following conditions:

1. If the major subdivisions of the species are indeed major Mendelian populations—that is, if they are strongly isolated geographically, with little gene flow among them to offset the effects of drift and of different selective pressures. Groups that fit this requirement tend to show consistent rather than cross-cutting patterns of variation, since they have so little opportunity to spread their distinctive genes through exchange with other groups. (It is assumed that many such subspecies are on their way to becoming new species, provided that their isolation continues.)
2. If knowledge of the existing variation within the species is limited to a few traits, so that cross-cutting distribution is not a practical problem.

The human species has not met the second condition since the early nineteenth century. Nor do we conform to the first condition. Human populations are in constant contact with one another, and barriers to gene flow invariably prove temporary. Thus the "major races" of the human species are *not* Mendelian populations in this sense. A "Mongoloid" American Indian, for instance, is much more likely to marry a "Caucasoid" American than a "Mongoloid" Tibetan. As expected, patterns of variation cut across the boundaries of the so-called major races. The sickle-cell gene is shared by "white" Mediterraneans and "black" Africans; ABO frequencies vary enormously among so-called Mongoloid populations; the incidence of lactase deficiency among the Baganda of East Africa is three times that of their neighbors, the Watusi, but almost identical to that of the Chinese, and so on.

To sustain the subspecies idea, it must be postulated that, in the past, major subdivisions of *Homo sapiens were* Mendelian populations, separated by sharper barriers to gene flow than exist at present. Presumably, then, loss of that genetic isolation, and the process of hybridization, occurred subsequently. This hypothesis is widely accepted as fact, although it lacks support from the fossil record or from archeology. Certainly, there are some populations that show effects of hybridization. The gene frequencies of American blacks, for instance, are often intermediate between those of American whites and those of West Africans—a phenomenon that is clearly due

Human Diversity

A sample of human diversity: a Peruvian Indian, a girl from Uganda, a Mongolian woman, a Sikh from northern India, a Bavarian woman, and an Australian aborigine.

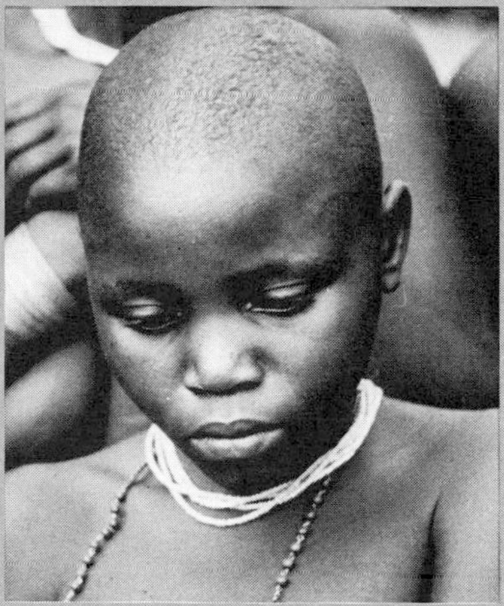

Although these people can be identified superficially with traditional "racial" categories, we can see why these categories are of dubious value in bringing order to the phenomenon of human variation. The Mongolian and the Peruvian, for example, are generally classed together as "Mongoloid," yet their differences are striking. The African and the Australian aborigine are both dark-skinned, but genetic studies reveal that, in terms of blood-group gene frequencies, the two are far apart. Many such inconsistencies can readily be found in most "racial" classifications. (*Carl Frank/Photo Researchers; George Rodger/Magnum; Paolo Koch/Rapho/Photo Researchers; Dennis Brihat/Rapho/Photo Researchers; Fritz Henle/Photo Researchers; Georg Gerster/Rapho/Photo Researchers*)

to the dual African and American ancestry of the American black population. But there is no evidence that all or even most physical intermediacy is the result of interbreeding among populations that were once highly distinct. Indeed, as we have argued with regard to such external characteristics as skin color and facial form, human variation in the past was probably *more* clinally distributed, with *fewer* sharp juxtapositions and boundaries than we see today.

The disorderly spectacle of human variation, then, does not lend itself easily to race or subspecies divisions, and the effort to retain these divisions can lead to distortions in our perception of variation, so that it looks tidier than it is. Such distortion may take the form of an unsubstantiated belief in earlier, more phenotypically distinct populations. Or, on a subtler level, it may mean disregarding traits that show cross-cutting distribution, even if, like sickle cell, they are important keys to understanding the nature of variation.

Testing Racial Classifications

In spite of these potential drawbacks, many physical anthropologists still refer to such categories as Mongoloid, Caucasoid, and Negroid—not necessarily to imply evolutionary hypotheses but because they find them useful descriptive categories. Organizing available data on human variation in this way is legitimate, and certainly does not imply that the classifier is "racist" in the pejorative sense. But once the populations are grouped into racial categories, we are faced with the question of how descriptive these categories actually are. Do the traditional racial groupings emerge as objectively defined entities if all our information on human physical variation is considered in an unbiased manner?

Multivariate Analysis

Some help with this question may come from the use of multivariate analysis, a group of statistical techniques made practicable by modern electronic computers. We cannot here describe in detail the technicalities of multivariate analysis. One form involves analyzing the differences among entities (in this case, populations) in a number of separate dimensions (in this case, frequencies of different genes or of distinctive phenotypes) and expressing the difference among the entities in terms of generalized distance: that is, distance based on all the variables taken together. Similarly, multivariate analysis can also be used to group populations pair by pair according to their overall resemblance. All variables are treated alike in this method; there is no weighting of variables because one or another is believed to be more "fundamental" or "important" in terms of human evolution.

Using these methods, Cavalli-Sforza and Edwards (1963) have produced a tree diagram, or dendrogram, based on gene frequencies for five blood groups, that depicts the degree of correspondence for these traits in fifteen human populations (Figure 15-3). In certain respects the groupings in this dendrogram agree with the traditional racial classifications. For example, the Venezuelan Indians, Eskimos, Arizona Indians, and Maoris—all traditionally regarded as Mongoloids—fall into the same grouping. Likewise, the "Negroid" members of the sample—the Tigre, Bantu, and Ghanaians—cluster together. However, there are also some decided inconsistencies with traditional racial groupings. The Koreans, whom the traditional classifiers would call typical Mongoloids, fall with the Australian aborigines. Another group of supposed Mongoloids, the South Turks, end up among the "Caucasoid" Europeans. Furthermore, the Ghurkas of Nepal (traditionally considered Mongoloid) and the Veddah of Ceylon (traditionally grouped with the Australian aborigines) fall into a rather isolated position, fairly remote from both the Mongoloid-Australoid group and the Caucasoid-Negroid group.

One point should be emphasized here. A diagram such as this in no way depicts phylogeny or evolutionary history. Below the species level, phylogeny cannot be accurately represented as a branching tree, because gene flow is usually occurring among populations. For instance, the Ghurkas' isolated position on the dendrogram may mean that these people have a unique "mix"

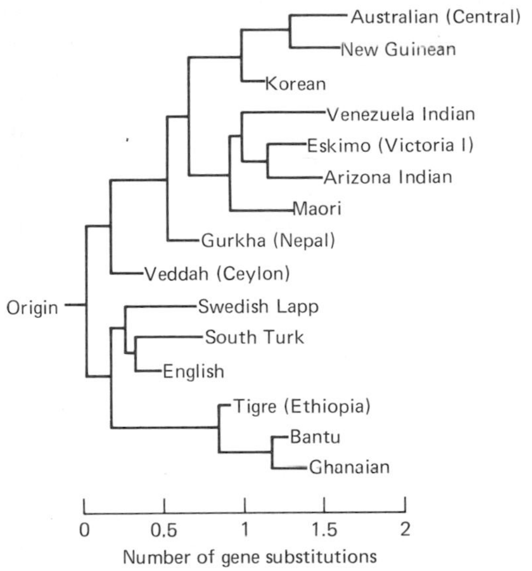

Figure 15-3. A dendrogram representing the resemblances among a group of human populations, based upon blood-group frequencies. *(After Cavalli-Sforza and Edwards, 1963)*

of blood group genes, maintained by gene flow from both India and "Mongoloid" East Asia, and perhaps further modified by drift and selection. But the diagram cannot tell us this. It expresses only resemblances and differences, some of which fit traditional race theory and some of which do not.

Our view of the concept of race, used as a means for globally classifying the populations of the human species, may be summarized thus: The concept of race conveys little or no information that could not be expressed in terms of the distribution of individual traits among populations. Furthermore, racial classification can interfere with the objective study of variation. It can create a mental set in which evolutionary theories for which there is little justification are uncritically accepted. It can also cause people to waste time finding pseudo-solutions to nonproblems—ways to make this or that population "fit"—while ignoring real problems, such as why a given variation shows the distribution that it does. Of course, it is possible that there really are major divisions of mankind, distinguishable on the basis of unbiased estimates of generalized genetic distance among populations. As yet, however, the existence of such groupings has not been satisfactorily demonstrated. And until it is, we do best to avoid "racial" classifications of all kinds.

Races as Ethnic Groups

There is one final sense in which the term "race" is used, and that is to describe sociologically defined subgroups within a complex society. Such groups may recognize one another by certain physical characteristics, and they may act essentially as Mendelian populations, but their distinctness is a function of social attitudes, not of universal biological division.

This is the normal, everyday sense of the term—and one that makes no claims to biological precision. Yet, it can still be misleading. For the term "race," no matter how it is used, always seems to imply universality, and these sociologically defined groups are very far from universal. Every society defines its "races" differently. In the United States, for instance, Asiatic Indians are regarded as "white." In Britain, they are part of an undifferentiated "coloured" population that also includes Malaysians, Chinese, and West Indians of predominantly African extraction. In racially conscious South Africa, Asiatic Indians constitute a race apart from whites, as do Bantu, Khoisan (Bushmen and Hottentots), and "Coloureds" (people of "mixed" descent).

It is probably more useful, then, to describe such subgroups as *ethnic groups* rather than as races. Unlike "race," "ethnic group" does not imply universality. What it does imply is a sociological or cultural definition, emphasizing the fact that people in "mixed" societies often use physical traits as labels or badges of membership in groups that are primarily social in function.

INTELLIGENCE

Recent years have seen the development of a bitter controversy over whether "races" differ inherently in intelligence. Generally, when the question of race and intelligence is debated, the debaters are referring to the performance of what we have called ethnic groups in the previous discussion. At the center of controversy is usually the observation that the *average* IQ of American blacks is consistently lower than that of American whites of the same age. There is no doubt that this observation is correct; it has been retested and confirmed many times. What is controversial is the implications of the observation—what it means and what, if anything, our society should do about it.

There are essentially five important questions involved:

1. What is "intelligence"?
2. Are there differences in intelligence among ethnic groups?
3. To what degree are differences in intelligence due to genetic inheritance?
4. What are the implications of these facts for educational decisions and other public policy?

The Meaning of Intelligence

What is "intelligence"? Intelligence is not a structure that one is born with, such as a kidney or an intestine. Nor is it a physiological factor, such as heart rate or blood pressure, that can be objectively measured. Rather, it is a mental construct—an idea abstracted from behavior. Because performance on intelligence tests sometimes correlates with other psychological measures—verbal ability, mathematical skill, academic achievement—some psychologists have claimed that such a factor as "general intelligence" does exist, underlying all these abilities. But since the correlation is only partial, the concept remains vague at best. In effect, intelligence can be defined only as the ability to perform on a standardized test called an intelligence test.

Vague as the concept is, the assumptions underlying intelligence tests, though not always made explicit, are fairly clear. The tests assume that the subject is familiar with the symbols and conventions of white, urbanized, middle-class, and (on American tests) American culture. At the most obvious level, this means, for example, using pictures and diagrams drawn on paper—a custom unknown in many cultures, for example, that of the Australian aborigines. At a more subtle level, the tests require familiarity with words, phrases, and usages that are the idiom of middle-class culture but that may be quite foreign to members of other subcultures, even within the same society. Of course, no one would think of giving a paper-and-pencil test to an aborigine. More dangerous, because harder to spot, are the instances in which subject A performs better on an intelligence test than subject B because subject A belongs to the same subgroup as the test's designers and scorers, whereas subject B belongs to a subgroup with different linguistic, social, and cultural habits. A commonly used test, for example, incorporates the question, "What's the thing for you to do when you have broken something that belongs to someone else?" The correct answer must include an offer to *pay* for it as well as an apology. "Feel sorry" and "Tell them I did it" are wrong answers (Kirk *et al.*, 1975). Not surprisingly, the designers of tests belong to the group that does generally score highest—the white, urban, professional class.

There is an assumption, however, that even among people belonging to the same subgroup and equally "primed" by education and cultural experiences, there will be variation in performance. This variation, presumably due to "underlying" or "native" intelligence, is what the investigator is interested in. Moreover, there is an assumption that at least part of this variation is due to genetic factors rather than to such environmental factors as nutrition. Both these assumptions can be tested and turn out to be reasonable. What is less reasonable is the belief that this true variation can be isolated from cultural effects through standardized examinations.

To get around the cultural effects, psychologists have tried two methods. One is to create "culture-free" tests—tests that contain no words or concepts that would be more familiar to one subgroup than to another. However, since there is no such thing as a culture-free test designer, there can be no such thing as a culture-free test.

It is a naive concept, and one that has never been realized. The second stratagem is to test only groups of individuals who have been carefully matched for cultural background—for example, black and white children of middle-class, professional parents. However, this too is deceptive, for even if a black child and a white child both come from families with college-educated parents, two cars, and an income of $25,000 a year, their cultural experience will still have been affected by their membership in different subgroups. The white child, for example, may, by virtue of his skin color, have received more—or less—help and encouragement from his teachers. Such factors can surely affect performance on an intelligence test.

In short, no way has yet been found to screen out the complicating effects of racial stereotyping, social class, and income level and get at the "native intelligence" that presumably lies beneath these variables.

Ethnic Differences in Intelligence

Are there differences among ethnic groups in intelligence, as we have defined it? This question, like the last one, requires a qualified answer. Even if one believes (as we do not) that it is useful to divide the human species into a number of distinct subspecies or races, it is clear that such units have not been adequately sampled by the studies that have produced the "race and intelligence" controversy. For the most part, these studies have compared samples drawn from the black and white populations of the United States. And though these populations do to a large extent behave as separate Mendelian populations, they cannot be regarded as adequately representing "Negroids" (i.e., including Africans) and "Caucasoids" (Europeans, Asiatic Indians, and so forth) as these groups are generally defined. What is being examined, then, is the difference not between "major races" but between ethnic groups within a single society. There is no reason to assume that the results of such work can be generalized to so-called races to which these groups are said to belong.

However, if we revise the question to refer not to "races," but to ethnic groups, specifically blacks and whites in the United States, the answer has to be yes. If large numbers of people of similar age, sex, and economic status are tested, the mean IQ for blacks turns out to be about 10 points lower than the mean for whites. This difference must, however, be kept in perspective. When one considers that the passengers on an average city bus probably represent an IQ spread of at least 50 points, a 10-point difference begins to look rather slight. It is certainly much smaller than the spread *within* each of the groups, and the extensive overlap between the ranges means that a sizable proportion of blacks are above the mean for whites, while a large proportion of whites are below the mean for blacks. Moreover, the difference between the means is less than that separating, say, rural and urban populations of either ethnic group.

As an object of scientific study, therefore, IQ in these two groups shows much less difference than do most of the traits with which anthropologists concern themselves. And from a strictly practical standpoint, the difference between the two *averages* is of very little significance. Americans are far from "color-coded for intelligence," as has been claimed by one biased observer of the data. An employer looking for a likely indicator of the IQ of a job applicant would find skin color a very poor predictor. Nevertheless, the differences between these two ethnic groups are statistically real and reproducible. From a scientific point of view they constitute a phenomenon to be explained.

This brings us to the question of IQ and genes—the most misunderstood question in the whole controversy.

The Heritability of Intelligence

To what extent are differences in IQ due to genetic inheritance? There are various methods of estimating the heritability of a trait—that is, the degree to which variability in that trait is due to genetic rather than environmental factors. All these methods involve testing—either of related individuals with similar genes but different en-

"Race" and IQ—A Historical Perspective*

In certain respects the current debate over "race" and IQ is simply a revival. In the first two decades of this century there were similar debates, except that the "races" in question were not blacks but rather the "white ethnics"—largely Jews, Poles, Greeks, and Italians—who streamed into the United States between 1880 and 1920. The predicament in which these groups found themselves in their adopted country in many ways parallels that of today's black and Hispanic minorities. They had high rates of unemployment and were plagued by poverty and its attendant social ills. They spoke English poorly, if at all. They lived in slums. And when given IQ tests (then a highly respected innovation), they scored significantly below the national average.

There are extensive IQ data on these immigrant groups. Many of them were tested as they arrived at Ellis Island. During World War I the Army conducted a massive intelligence-testing program on its recruits. The results of these tests were fairly consistent: the mean IQs of the later immigrant groups, those from eastern and southern Europe, were approximately 20 points below the national average—a larger gap than that between blacks and whites today.

Immigrant children being examined at Ellis Island in 1911. (*The Bettmann Archive*)

In the twenties, these test scores were analyzed by Carl Brigham, an influential Princeton psychologist and the originator of the CEEB Scholastic Aptitude Test. In his book, *A Study of American Intelligence,* Brigham noted an interesting fact: there was a strong correlation between IQ and length of residence in the United States. The IQ averages of the earlier immigrants—Germans, Irish, Swedes, English, and other northern Europeans who came to the United States in the early and middle nineteenth century—were approximately equal to the national average; it was the later arrivals, the "darker" peoples of southern and eastern Europe, who scored low. But instead of interpreting this as a sign that the tests were measuring not simply intellectual skills but familiarity with American language and culture, Brigham came to the remarkable conclusion that the IQ disparity between the two sets of ethnic groups was due to genetic differences. The more recent immigrant groups were *inherently* inferior in intelligence. Indeed, he warned that the incorporation of these groups into the United States citizenry was tainting the essentially "Nordic blood" of mainstream America and causing a nationwide decline in intelligence.

Brigham's conclusions were very much in line both with contemporary racist sentiments and with a powerful pseudoscientific movement of the day. This was the Eugenics movement, devoted to the improvement of the human gene pool. Ostensibly, the Eugenics movement was concerned with the entire human species, which was presumably threatened by genetic defects that, because of modern medicine, were no longer being removed by natural selection. However, the members of the movement were predominantly of northern European extraction, and it was the genetic protection of that "strain" that was their primary concern. The anxieties stirred up by these forces led to the passage of state laws prohibiting miscegenation (interbreeding between "races") and requiring sterilization of presumed mental defec-

* This is based chiefly on Sowell (1977).

tives. And with the help of Brigham's study, the eugenicists were instrumental in the passage of the federal Immigration Restriction Act of 1924. This law severely limited immigration by southern and eastern Europeans, favoring instead the northern and western Europeans, who presumably brought in a better class of genes.

By this time, however, a considerable number of Jews, Italians, Greeks, and Poles had already settled in this country, and over the next few decades they were gradually assimilated into the American middle classes. What happened to their IQs? In view of the current dispute over whether the black-white "IQ gap" can be closed, this is a very important question. The answer is that as the socioeconomic status of the "white ethnics" improved, so did their mean IQ scores, so that today they equal or surpass the national average. The Poles and Italians, for example, gained 20 to 25 points between the time of the World War I surveys and studies conducted in the 1970s. The phenomenon is not limited to Europeans. The mean IQs of Chinese- and Japanese-Americans, who also showed presumably inherent IQ deficiencies earlier in this century, now exceed the national average. (The Chinese-American immigrants, for example, were said to be particularly deficient in abstract reasoning—an ironic finding in view of the fact that today Chinese-Americans figure prominently among America's mathematicians and physicists.)

It is logical to assume that the IQ scores of American blacks would follow the same pattern if blacks too were relieved of the educational handicaps of poverty and discrimination. Yet the programs that might make this possible can easily be undermined by the argument that the black-white IQ gap is due to genetic factors. For the political message inherent in this argument is quite obvious: the disadvantages suffered by blacks are due not to an unjust social structure, but to genes, and therefore there is nothing the society can or need do to remedy the situation. It is for this reason that this second round of the "race and IQ" debate has been fought with such extreme bitterness. There is a very great deal at stake.

vironmental histories (for example, identical twins raised in different families) or of unrelated individuals with carefully matched environmental histories. Such studies will indicate whether it is genetic or environmental similarity that produces the greater resemblance in the trait in question. These methods have their potential pitfalls, which we cannot explore fully here, but on the whole they give results that are consistent. Such tests indicate that about 50 to 80 percent of the IQ variation *among whites* in the United States may be due to genetic factors rather than such environmental ones as nutrition, social class of parents, and education. Fewer studies have been done on American blacks, but such evidence as exists suggests a similar degree of heritability for the variation within the black population.

These estimates have created the widespread misconception that the differences in average IQ *between* American whites and blacks are genetically determined. The misunderstanding can be avoided if we keep in mind one very important point about heritability studies—namely, that the result obtained refers *only* to the population, and the environment, from which it was obtained. It cannot be regarded as an absolute value to be generalized to other populations, nor can it be applied to differences *between* populations.

A hypothetical example should bring this point home. Suppose that two farmers are keeping flocks of sheep. Farmer A has rich pasture, and the average size and weight of his sheep are greater than those of farmer B's, which graze on poor pasture. Within each farm, the environment—that is, the pasture—is uniform. Within flock A, therefore, such variation as occurs in body weight will be largely due to heredity—some animals being better fitted than others to take advantage of the rich pasture. Similarly, the variation in flock B will also be largely due to heredity—some animals being constitutionally better adapted to put on weight under conditions of semistarvation. But even if heritability of body weight *within* each flock is close to 100 percent, does this mean that the difference *between* flocks is also due largely to genetic factors? Of course it does not; the average difference in weight between the well-fed and the half-starved sheep has nothing to do with genes.

Most human geneticists suspect that ethnic differences in IQ may be analogous to this. Variation *within populations* has a comparatively high genetic component, but the small difference seen *between* populations probably does not. Differences in environment—wealth versus poverty, good nutrition versus malnutrition, familiarity versus unfamiliarity with the cultural conventions involved in intelligence tests—are probably quite sufficient to account for the observed "gap."

IQ Differences and Public Policy

Finally, what effect should these facts have on public policy? It should be obvious that even if it were found that a small difference in "IQ gene frequency" separates blacks and whites (and we have no idea which way the discrepancy would go), this would have very little relevance to policy decisions relating to education, employment, and so on. Insofar as it is desirable to "improve" the population's IQ, what is needed is to enrich the educational experience of *all* individuals—especially those who fall below the general average. In view of the large overlap between ethnic groups, those to be aided would include both blacks and whites. Similarly, since both groups show variation in the skills that are measured by IQ tests—both groups, that is, include good mathematicians and poor mathematicians, fast readers and slow readers—it would be foolish to shunt either blacks or whites as a group into special education programs. Rather, we should identify the strengths and weaknesses of individual children, regardless of ethnic group, and route them into educational programs accordingly. The same holds true for employment. To gauge a person's intellectual aptitude for a specific job on the basis of skin color is to ignore the wide range of variability within each ethnic group. Such decisions, if they are to be made wisely, must be made on an individual basis. In sum, there is no scientific reason for education or employment to be anything but color blind.

Summary

Complex polygenic traits such as skin color, facial form, stature, intelligence, and temperament are especially difficult to analyze. They tend to be continuously distributed within populations, and are often highly responsive to environmental influences. Many show no clear pattern of geographical distribution, while for others—such as skin color—we can find populations with little or no phenotypic overlap.

Human skin color varies throughout the world. It is determined by the thickness of the skin layers and by the concentration of various pigments, especially *melanin.* The genetic basis of skin color is still obscure. Among the possible selective agents that may influence pigmentation are the effects of ultraviolet rays—sunburn, skin cancer, and stimulation of vitamin D production. It is probable that different skin colors evolved from a uniform prehominid condition as adaptations to different climates. The global picture has been complicated by waves of migration in recent times, with which natural selection has not yet caught up.

Variation in hair and eye color is confined to a relatively small percentage of the human species—the populations of northwestern Europe and their descendants. The rest of the world is almost uniformly dark-haired and dark-eyed. The reason for this pattern of variation is very unclear. Teeth and jaws seem to vary according to how recently different populations have adopted agriculture. Facial form also shows variation among populations; in some cases, sets of facial features are characteristic of certain populations. The Mongoloid face is a notable example. Climatic adaptation may be a factor in such variation.

Some anthropologists have examined human

variability in terms of the overall constitution of different populations, rather than in terms of the distribution of individual traits from population to population. This approach has often involved grouping human populations into *races:* classifications based on shared physical characteristics. Several racial theories have been proposed or used, in which races are regarded as "pure strains," "major stocks," or biological subspecies. Human variation is such a complex and multifaceted phenomenon, however, that such classifications are for the most part oversimplifications of doubtful use. "Race" is often used in a sociological sense to define a segment of a population by its physical traits, but these definitions often vary from society to society. Thus such subgroups are more accurately described as *ethnic groups*, which have a primarily social significance, though physical differences are sometimes used as badges of membership.

In recent years, a major debate has arisen over the correlations between race and intelligence and their implications for society as a whole. There are many dimensions of intelligence, and it is a difficult quantity to measure fully or objectively. For one thing, the intelligence tests we use are not culture-free. Moreover, it is not clear what they measure except ability to perform on an IQ test. In the United States, blacks generally average about 10 points lower than whites on IQ tests, but from a practical standpoint, this difference is not very important. It has been suggested that test score differences indicate that intelligence is genetically transmitted, but most human geneticists suspect that while variation *within* populations may have a considerable genetic component, most variation *between* populations probably does not, and that environmental differences would account for the small gap in scores. We must thus conclude that any evaluation of a person's intellectual aptitude must be made on an individual basis.

Glossary

ethnic group a sociological or cultural division within a society, sometimes based at least partly on shared physical characteristics

melanin a brown pigment largely responsible for the colors of human skin, hair, and the iris of the eye

race a group of populations defined on the basis of shared physical characteristics; of doubtful utility in human classification

Suggested Readings

BRUES, A. M. 1977
People and Races. New York: Macmillan. An account of genetically determined variation in the human species, with emphasis on complex traits.

LOEHLIN, J., ET AL. 1975
Race Differences in Intelligence. San Francisco: W. H. Freeman. An uncommonly thorough, authoritative, and objective survey of this difficult and emotionally charged subject.

Appendix: Molecular Genetics

As we saw in the early chapters of this book, the phenotype of an organism is determined in large part by what proteins it manufactures. The instructions for the manufacture of proteins—the *genes*—are carried as long molecules of *DNA* (deoxyribonucleic acid), which are passed from cell to cell during cell division, and from parent to offspring in reproduction. In what form does DNA bear its instructions, and how are they carried out so as to produce specific proteins? Until a quarter of a century ago these questions remained unanswered. The discovery of the answers within the past few decades probably constitutes this century's greatest triumph in the biological sciences.

THE STRUCTURE OF DNA

In the early 1950s, when a number of noted scientists were trying to work out the structure of DNA, two young biochemists, James Watson and Francis Crick, decided to tackle the subject together. Imaginatively piecing together the observations of others, and bringing their own extraordinary insight and resourcefulness to bear on the problem, they solved it within two years. DNA, Watson and Crick determined, is composed of two strands which coil around one another to form a *double helix.* Each strand is a chain of *nucleotides*—molecular units consisting of a phosphate, a sugar, and a base. The base of each nucleotide is linked by a hydrogen bond to the base of the nucleotide opposite it on the other strand. Thus a model of the molecule looks something like a spiral staircase, with the paired bases forming the steps and the phosphate-sugar chains forming the sides.

A crucial aspect of DNA structure is that the pairing of the bases follows very strict rules. There are only four bases in DNA: thymine, adenine, cytosine, and guanine. And each of these bases will pair with only one of the others. Adenine will bond only with thymine, while cytosine will bond only with guanine. Because corresponding nucleotides on the two strands of a DNA molecule must always link in this way, a sequence of nucleotides on one strand always has its exact counterpart on the other. If, for example, the sequence guanine, thymine, adenine, guanine, cytosine (GTAGC) appears on one strand, the sequence cytosine, adenine, thymine, cytosine, guanine (CATCG) must be present on the other strand. In other words, the two strands are related in much the same way as a photographic positive and negative; the sequence of nucleotides on each strand precisely determines the complementary sequence on the other.

It is this structural peculiarity that allows DNA to copy itself. In the copying process, called *replication,* the two strands of the molecule come apart. As the nucleotides separate, one by one, from their "partners" on the complementary strand, they acquire new partners from the cell environment. These are then linked together, forming two new strands (Figure 1). Thus each strand of the original double helix serves as a *template,* or pattern, for the creation of a new complementary strand, and what was one molecule becomes two, *each identical to the original one.* In this way the genetic instructions, first contained only in the zygote, are copied and passed along during cell division to every cell in the organism, including those that will eventually transmit them to a new zygote.

THE GENETIC CODE

Most organisms have thousands of different proteins. To understand how molecules of DNA can contain the blueprints for so many different proteins, we must understand something of the structure of proteins. Diverse as they are, proteins are made up of only about twenty different chemical subunits called *amino acids.* These are linked together in long chains known as *polypeptide chains.* Each protein molecule consists of one or more such chains, often folded into a complex three-dimensional shape. What makes proteins so diverse is that each contains a different sequence of amino acids.

It is because both proteins and DNA are essentially linear molecules composed of relatively few subunits that DNA can carry instructions for the manufacture of proteins by means of a *genetic code.* Obviously, it would be impossible for there to be a separate "word" in the code for each and every different protein. The DNA molecule, however, need have only twenty different "words," or *codons,* one for each amino acid, with the order of the codons on the DNA helix specifying the order of the amino acids in the polypeptide chain. A codon in the genetic code consists of three consecutive bases in the chain of nucleotides on the DNA molecule. There are sixty-four codons, corresponding to the sixty-four ways in which the four different bases can be grouped in sequences of three. Each codon calls for a particular amino acid. For example, the codon TCT calls for arginine, CGA for alanine, CCT for glycine.* Hence the DNA sequence TCTCGACCT constitutes the message "add on one molecule of arginine, then one of alanine, then one of glycine" as part of the synthesis of a protein. Of course, the making of an entire protein requires a much longer message than this. A given polypeptide chain may contain hundreds or even thousands of amino acids, and the gene coding for it must contain at least three times that many bases. When we multiply this by the thousands of proteins that need to be coded for, and add in the long stretches of DNA that, for reasons not entirely clear, are never translated, we get some idea of how long the DNA strands must be. It has been estimated that nearly two

Figure 1

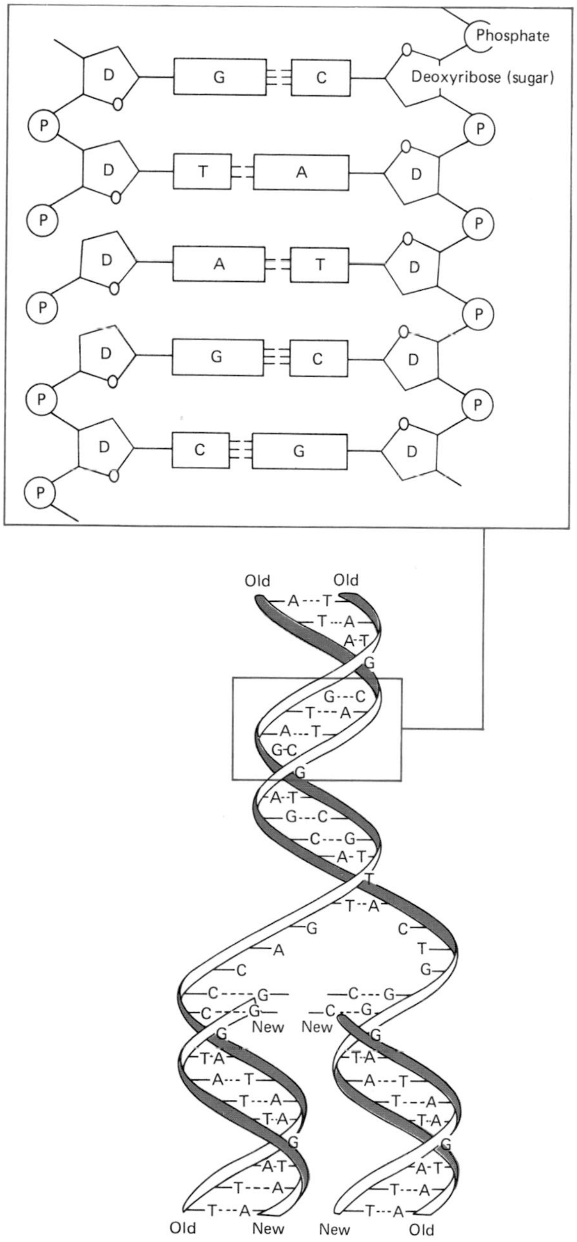

* Since there are only twenty amino acids, the code is somewhat redundant—most amino acids can be "spelled" in more than one way (that is, they can be specified by any of several different codons). The codons AUU, AUC, and AUA, for example, all code for the amino acid isoleucine. In addition, some codons seem to represent "punctuation" of the genetic message—they indicate the start or the completion of a polypeptide chain. It is a remarkable fact that all known living organisms, from viruses to human beings, use exactly the same code.

meters of DNA are packed into every cell nucleus in the human body.

TRANSCRIPTION AND TRANSLATION

How are the instructions encoded by DNA carried out? How, in other words, do cells "read" the code and assemble the specified proteins? The main actor in this process is *ribonucleic acid*, or *RNA*, a nucleic acid like DNA except that it contains a different sugar, has the base uracil in place of thymine, and forms single rather than double strands.

Transcription, the first step of protein synthesis, resembles the replication process. The DNA double helix once again "unzips," and a molecule made up of complementary nucleotides forms against the template of one of its strands. This time, however, the complementary molecule is not DNA, but a type of RNA called *messenger RNA* (*mRNA*). The mRNA makes a "negative" not of the whole molecule but only of one or a few genes. (A gene, in molecular terms, is simply the section of a DNA molecule coding for the polypeptide chain or chains of a single protein.) Having transcribed the message of these genes (Figure 2), the mRNA molecule separates from the DNA and moves out of the nucleus into the cytoplasm, the complex mixture of substances that constitutes the bulk of the cell, and that contains the amino acids needed to make proteins.

Now begins the second step of protein synthesis: *translation*, in which the genetic instructions are actually carried out. First the mRNA attaches itself to cell bodies called *ribosomes*, which apparently provide many of the enzymes necessary for protein synthesis. At the same time, floating in the cytoplasm are two other important elements: (1) the amino acids, the raw mate-

Figure 2

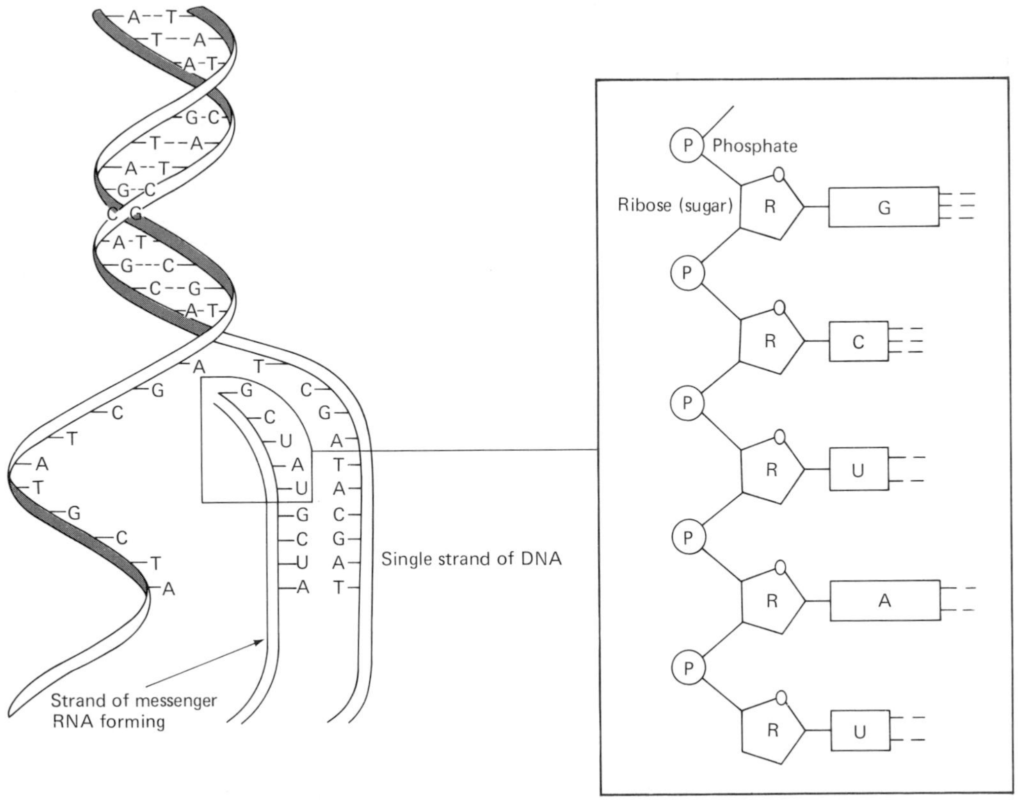

rials for the proteins, and (2) small molecules of another type of RNA, known as *transfer RNA* (*tRNA*). There are many kinds of tRNA molecules, each designed to pick up and carry a specific amino acid. At one end the tRNA molecule carries its appropriate amino acid; at the opposite end it has a triplet of bases, called an anticodon, complementary to the mRNA codon calling for that particular amino acid. As the mRNA strand passes along the ribosome, each of its successive codons is "recognized" by the anticodon of a tRNA molecule carrying an amino acid. This amino acid, held in place by the tRNA molecule, is then bonded to the one that arrived before it, and its tRNA carrier is released to go off and pick up another amino acid (Figure 3). Thus, one by one, the amino acids are attached to one another, producing a growing chain that is finally "clipped off" at the end of the gene's message. The result is a finished polypeptide chain, containing the amino acids called for by the DNA, in the order in which they were called for.

MUTATION

By understanding how the structure of the DNA molecule codes for protein synthesis, we can better understand what, at the molecular level, is involved in mutation. Many mutations are caused by an error in the replication process. A base may be left out or inserted, or one base may be substituted for another, or the order of two or more bases may be scrambled. In any case, the instructions are copied incorrectly, and therefore the proteins that are produced from them may also be incorrect.

In some cases, a mutation will have no phenotypic effect, or only a slight and harmless effect. In other cases, a mistake involving a single base may have massive consequences. For example, if a single base is inserted or left out, it can throw off the reading of the message of that entire gene. Consider, for example, the DNA sequence CCG AGT TAA. Translated into amino acids, it means: "glycine, serine, isoleucine." But if a single thymine is accidentally added to the beginning of this sequence (TCC GAG TAA A . . .), the groupings of three will be rearranged, and the message will come out "arginine, leucine, asparagine"—and so on down the strand, all the codons being misread.

The substitution of one base for another in even a single codon may also have disastrous consequences. Sickle-cell anemia, discussed in Chapters 2 and 14, provides a good example. Sickle-cell hemoglobin differs from normal hemoglobin in only two of nearly 600 amino acids that make up the four polypeptide chains of the molecule. Two of these chains have the amino acid valine at a point where the normal chain has glumatic acid. This results from the substitution of the base adenine for thymine in a single codon in the gene controlling the synthesis of this chain. The difference between adenine and thymine is literally only a few atoms! Yet even this tiny change in the DNA molecule can have enormous physiological consequences and spell the difference between life and death.

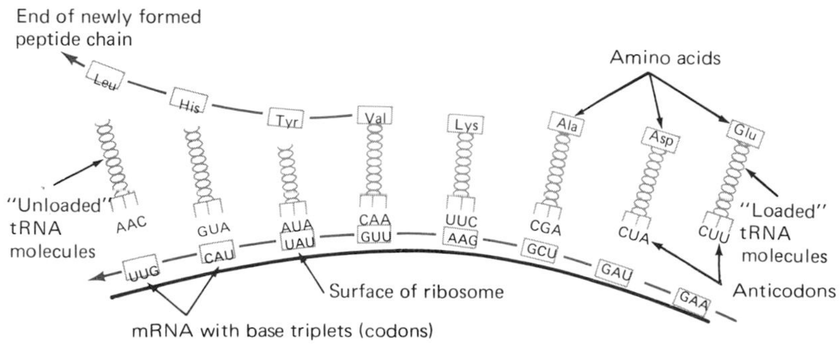

Figure 3

DNA HYBRIDIZATION TECHNIQUES

In the box on p. 78 we mentioned briefly that the DNA of different species can now be compared quite directly through *DNA hybridization techniques.* These techniques depend upon DNA's being a double molecule, its two strands linked by their complementary structure. In the laboratory, the two strands can be separated, then allowed to recombine. In hybridization techniques, DNA molecules from different species (for example, human and monkey) are broken into short lengths, separated into their constituent chains, mixed together, then allowed to recombine. Some of the recombined DNA molecules are "hybrids," with one monkey strand and one human strand. As in the recombination of two strands from the same species, such hybrids are held together by the cross-links between matching DNA sequences. If there are few such complementary sequences, "hybrid" molecules will be incompletely linked. Sensitive laboratory techniques permit us to measure the completeness of the linkage in a hybrid DNA, and hence to determine how much of the gene-set of one species corresponds to that of the other species. This is a very direct measure of genetic resemblance.

Glossary

(Numbers in roman type refer to text pages on which definitions of the following terms appear)

References

Adams, R. M.
1973 The Collapse of Maya Civilization: A Review of Previous Theories. In *The Classic Maya Collapse,* ed. T. Patrick Culbert. Albuquerque: University of New Mexico Press.
1966 *The Evolution of Urban Society: Early Mesopotamia and Prehispanic Mexico.* Chicago: Aldine.

Allison, A. C.
1961 Abnormal Hemoglobin and Erythrocyte Enzyme-Deficiency Traits. In *Genetical Variation in Human Populations,* ed. G. A. Harrison. Oxford: Pergamon Press.

Armillas, P.
1971 Gardens on Swamps. *Science* 174: 653-661.

Baker, P. T.
1969 Human Adaptation to High Altitude. *Science* 163: 1149–1156.

Beadle, G.
1972 The Mystery of Maize. *Field Museum of Natural History Bulletin* 43: 2–11.

Binford, L. R.
1968 Post-Pleistocene Adaptations. In *New Perspectives in Archeology,* ed. S. R. Binford and L. R. Binford. Chicago: Aldine.

Binford, L. R., and Binford, S. R.
1966 A Preliminary Analysis of Functional Variability in the Mousterian of Levallois Facies. *American Anthropologist* 68: 238–295.

Bordaz, J.
1970 *Tools of the Old and New Stone Age.* Garden City, N.Y.: Natural History Press.

Bordes, F.
1968 *The Old Stone Age.* New York: McGraw-Hill.

Boserup, E.
1965 *The Conditions of Agricultural Growth.* Chicago: Aldine.

Braidwood, R. J.
1967 *Prehistoric Men.* 7th ed. Glenview, Ill.: Scott, Foresman.

Brain, C. K.
1970 New Finds at the Swartkrans Australopithecine Site. *Nature* 225: 1112–1119.

Braun, D.
1974 Explanatory Models for the Evolution of Coastal Adaptation in Prehistoric New England. *American Antiquity* 1974: 582–596.

Briuer, F. L.
1970 Causes of Late Pleistocene Megafaunal Extinction: Some Hypotheses and Tests. Master's thesis, University of California at Los Angeles.

Brush, S.
1977 Farming the Edge of the Andes. *Natural History* 86: 32–41.

Butzer, K. W.
1971 *Environment and Archeology: An Ecological Approach to Prehistory.* 2d ed. Chicago: Aldine.

Calnek, E.
1976 The Internal Structure of Tenochtitlan. In *The Valley of Mexico,* ed. E. Wolf. Albuquerque: University of New Mexico Press.

Carneiro, R. L.
1970 A Theory of the Origin of the State. *Science* 169: 733–738.

Cavalli-Sforza, L. L., and Edwards, A. W. F.
1963 Analysis of Human Evolution. In *Genetics Today,* ed. S. J. Geertz, Vol. 3. Elmsford, N.Y.: Pergamon Press.

Chagnon, N. A.
1968 *Yanomamo: The Fierce People.* New York: Holt, Rinehart and Winston.

Chance, M. R. A., and Jolly, C.
1970 *Social Groups of Monkeys, Apes, and Men.* London: Jonathan Cape.

Chang, K. C.
1971 *The Archaeology of Ancient China.* New Haven: Yale University Press.
1970 The Beginnings of Agriculture in the Far East. *Antiquity* 44: 175–185.

Childe, V. G.
1952 *Man Makes Himself.* New York: New American Library.
1952 *New Light on the Most Ancient East.* London: Routledge & Kegan Paul.

Chomsky, N.
1972 *Language and Mind.* New York: Harcourt Brace Jovanovich.

Clark, J. G. D.
1972 *Star Carr: A Case Study in Bioarchaeology.* Module 10. Reading, Mass.: Addison-Wesley.

Coe, M. D.
1966 *The Maya.* New York: Praeger.
1962 *Mexico.* Mexico City: Ediciones Lara.

Coon, C.
1962 *The Origin of Races.* New York: Alfred A. Knopf.

Culbert, T. P.
1974 *The Lost Civilization: The Story of the Classic Maya.* New York: Harper & Row.

David, N.
1973 On Upper Paleolithic Society, Ecology and Technological Change: The Noaillian Case. In *The Explanation of Culture Change: Models in Prehistory,* ed. C. Renfrew. London: Duckworth.

Dean, J.
1970 Aspects of Tsegi Phase Social Organization. In *Reconstructing Prehistoric Pueblo Societies,* ed. W. Longacre. Albuquerque: University of New Mexico Press.

De Boer, W.
1975 The Archaeological Evidence for Manioc Cultivation. *American Antiquity* 40: 419–433.

Deetz, J.
1965 The Dynamics of Stylistic Change. In *Arikara Ceramics.* Illinois Studies in Anthropology, no. 4. Urbana: University of Illinois Press.

De Garmo, G. D.
1970 Big Game Hunters: An Alternative and An Hypothesis. Paper presented at Thirty-fifth Annual Meeting of the Society for American Archeology, Mexico City. Mimeographed.

Duncan, R.
1972 *The Cochise Culture.* Master's Thesis, University of California at Los Angeles.

Dyson-Hudson, N.
1973 Turkana. In *Primitive Worlds.* Washington, D.C.: National Geographic Society.

Eimerl, S., and Devore, I.
1965 *The Primates.* New York: Time-Life.

Erickson, J.
1977 Egalitarian Exchange Systems in California: A Preliminary View. In *Exchange Systems in Prehistory,* ed. T. Earle and J. Erickson. New York: Academic Press.

Flannery, K. V.
1973 The Origins of Agriculture. *Annual Review of Anthropology* 2:271–310.
1972 The Cultural Evolution of Civilizations. *Annual Review of Ecology and Systematics* 3: 399–426.
1972 The Origins of the Village as a Settlement Type in Mesoamerica and the Near East. In *Man, Settlement and Urbanism,* ed. P. J. Ucko, R. Tringham, and G. W. Dimbleby. Cambridge, Mass.: Schenckman.
1969 Origins and Ecological Effects of Early Domestication in Iran and the Near East. In *The Domestication and Exploitation of Plants and Animals,* ed. J. Ucko and G. W. Dimbleby. Chicago: Aldine.
1968 Archeological Systems Theory and Early Mesoamerica. In *Anthropological Archeology in the Americas,* ed. B. J. Meggers. Washington, D.C.: Anthropological Society of Washington.
1965 Ecology of Early Food Production in Mesopotamia. *Science* 147: 1247–1256.

Flannery, K. V., Kirkby, A. V. T., Kirkby, M. J., and Williams, A., Jr.
1967 Farming Systems and Political Growth in Ancient Oaxaca. *Science* 158: 445–454.

Flannery, K. V., and Schoenwetter, J.
1970 Climate and Man in Formative Oaxaca. *Archaeology* 23: 144–152.

Ford, R.
1977 Evolutionary Ecology and the Evolution of Human Ecosystems: A Case Study from the Midwestern U.S.A. In *Explanation of Prehistoric Change*, ed. J. Hill. Albuquerque: University of New Mexico Press.
1974 Northeastern Archaeology: Past and Future Directions. *Annual Review of Anthropology*.

Fried, M.
1968 *The Evolution of Political Society*. New York: Random House.

Fritz, M. O.
1969 Description and Explanation in Paleolithic Cave Art: A Survey of the Literature. Master's Thesis, University of Chicago.

Gardner, R. A., and Gardner, B. T.
1969 Teaching Sign Language to a Chimpanzee. *Science* 165: 664–672.

Goldstein, E., *et al.*
1972 Blueprint for Survival. *The Ecologist* 2: 2–6.

Gorman, C.
1969 Hoabinhian: A Pebble-Tool Complex with Early Plant Associations in Southeast Asia. *Science* 163: 671–673.

Gorman, F.
1972 The Clovis Hunters: An Alternate View of Their Environment and Ecology. In *Contemporary Archaeology*, ed. M. Leone. Carbondale, Ill.: Southern Illinois University Press.

Gregory, W. K.
1920 On the Structure and Relations of *Notharctus*, an American Eocene Primate. *American Museum of Natural History Memoirs*.

Haag, W. G.
1973 The Bering Strait Land Bridge. In *Early Man in America*, ed. R. S. MacNeish. San Francisco: W. H. Freeman.

Hamblin, D. J., and Editors of Time-Life Books
1973 *The First Cities*. New York: Time-Life.

Hammond, N.
1972 Obsidian Trade Routes in the Mayan Area. *Science* 178: 1092–1093.

Harlan, J. R.
1967 A Wild Wheat Harvest in Turkey. *Archeology* 20: 197–201.

Harlow, H. F., and Harlow, M. K.
1969 Effects of Various Mother-Infant Relationships on Rhesus Monkey Behavior. In *Determinants of Infant Behavior*, ed. B. M. Foss. Vol. 4. Agincourt, Ont.: Methuen.
1965 The Affectional Systems. In *Behavior of Non-Human Primates*, ed. A. M. Schrier, H. F. Harlow, and F. Stollnitz. New York: Academic Press.

Harrison, G. A.
1964 *Human Biology: An Introduction to Human Evolution, Variation, and Growth*. New York: Oxford University Press.

Haviland, W.
1967 Structure at Tikal, Guatemala: Implications for Ancient Man of Demography and Social Organization. *American Antiquity* 32: 316–325.

Hayes, H. T. P.
1977 The Pursuit of Reason. *The New York Times Magazine*, June 12, p. 21.

Hayes, K., and Hayes, C.
1951 The Intellectual Development of Home Raised Chimpanzees. *The American Philosophical Society Proceedings* 95: 105–109.

Haynes, V. C., Jr.
1973 The Calico Site: Artifacts or Geofacts? *Science* 181: 305–310.
1973 Elephant Hunting in North America. In *Early Man in America*, ed. R. S. MacNeish. San Francisco: W. H. Freeman.

Hildebrand, M.
1968 Symmetrical Gaits of Primates. *American Journal of Physical Anthropology* 26: 119–130.

Hill, J. N.
1968 Broken K. Pueblo: Patterns of Form and Function. In *New Perspectives in*

Archaeology, ed. S. R. Binford and L. R. Binford. Chicago: Aldine.

1970 Broken K Pueblo: Prehistoric Social Organization in the American Southwest. University of Arizona Anthropological Papers, no. 18. Tucson: University of Arizona Press.

1966 A Prehistoric Community in Eastern Arizona. *Southwestern Journal of Anthropology* 22: 9–30.

Hockett, C. F.

1973 *Man's Place in Nature*. New York: McGraw-Hill.

Hockett, C. F., and Ascher, R.

1964 The Human Revolution. *Current Anthropology* 5: 135–147.

Hole, F., Flannery, K. V., and Neely, J. A.

1969 *The Prehistory and Human Ecology of the Deh Luran Plain*. Memoir no. 1. Ann Arbor: University of Michigan. Museum of Anthropology.

Holloway, R. L.

1972 Australopithecine Endocasts, Brain Evolution in the Hominoidea, and a Model of Hominid Evolution. In *The Functional and Evolutionary Biology of Primates*, ed. R. Tuttle, Chicago: Aldine.

Howell, F. C., and Clark, J. D.

1963 Acheulian Hunter-Gatherers of Sub-Saharan Africa. *Viking Fund Publications in Anthropology*, no. 36.

Howells, W.

1973 *The Evolution of the Genus Homo*. Reading, Mass.: Addison-Wesley.

Hrdy, S.

1977 *The Langurs of Abu: Female and Male Strategies of Reproduction*. Cambridge: Harvard University Press.

Irwin-Williams, C.

1968 Archaeological Evidence on Early Man in Mexico. *Contributions in Anthropology*, Eastern New Mexico University 1: 39–41.

Isaac, G. L.

1972 Chronology and the Tempo of Cultural Change during the Pleistocene. In *Calibration of Hominid Evolution*, ed. W. W. Bishop, J. A. Miller, and S. Cole. Toronto: University of Toronto/Scottish Academic Press.

Janson, H. W.

1969 *History of Art*. Englewood Cliffs, N.J.: Prentice-Hall, and New York: Abrams.

Jenkins, F. A., ed.

1974 *Primate Locomotion*. New York: Academic Press.

Jennings, J. D.

1974 *Prehistory of North America*. 2d ed. New York: McGraw-Hill.

Jennings, J. D., and Norbeck, E., eds.

1974 *Prehistoric Man in the New World*. Chicago: University of Chicago Press.

Johnson, G.

1972 A Test of the Utility of Central Place Theory in Archeology. In *Man, Settlement, and Urbanism*, ed. P. J. Ucko, R. Tringham, and G. W. Dimbleby. London: Duckworth.

Jolly, A.

1972 *The Emergence of Man*. 2d ed. New York: Macmillan.

Judge, W. J., and Dawson, J.

1972 PaleoIndian Settlement Technology in New Mexico. *Science* 176: 1210–1216.

Katz, S. H., Hediger, M. L., and Valleroy, L. A.

1974 Traditional Maize Processing in the New World. *Science* 186: 765–773.

King, J. L., and Jukes, T. H.

1969 Non-Darwinian Evolution. *Science* 164: 788–798.

Kingdon, J.

1971 *East African Mammals*. Vol. 1. New York: Academic Press.

Kretchmer, N.

1972 Lactose and Lactase. *Biological Anthropology: Readings from Scientific American*. San Francisco: W. H. Freeman.

Lancaster, J. B.

1968 Primate Communication Systems and the Emergence of Human Language. In *Primates: Studies in Adaptation and Variability*, ed. P. C. Jay. New York: Holt, Rinehart and Winston.

Lanning, E. P.

1967 *Peru Before the Incas*. Englewood Cliffs, N. J.: Prentice-Hall.

Leakey, L. S. B.
1962 A New Lower Pliocene Fossil Primate from Kenya. *Annals and Magazine of Natural History* 4: 689–696.

Lee, R. B.
1969 !Kung Bushmen Subsistence: An Input-Output Analysis. In *Environment and Cultural Behavior*, ed. A. P. Vadya. Garden City, N.Y.: Natural History Press.

Leone, M. P.
1968 Neolithic Economic Autonomy and Social Distance. *Science* 162: 1150–1151.

Leroi-Gourhan, A.
1968 The Evolution of Paleolithic Art. *Scientific American* 218: 59–70.

Livingstone, R. B.
1958 Anthropological Implications of Sickle Cell Gene Distribution in West Africa. *American Anthropology* 60: 533–562.

Logan, M., and Sanders, W.
1976 The Model. In *The Valley of Mexico*, ed. E. Wolf. Albuquerque: University of New Mexico Press.

Longacre, W.
1970 Archeology as Anthropology: A Case Study. Anthropological Papers of the University of Arizona, no. 17. Tucson: University of Arizona Press.

McManamon, F.
1974 Analyzing Post-Pleistocene Adaptations. Unpublished Paper, State University of New York at Binghamton.

MacNeish, R. S.
1973 Early Man in the Andes. In *Early Man in America*, ed. R. S. MacNeish. San Francisco: W. H. Freeman.
1964 Ancient Mesoamerican Civilization. *Science* 143: 531–537.

Mangelsdorf, P. C., MacNeish, R. S., and Galinat, W. C.
1964 Domestication of Corn. *Science* 143: 538–545.

Marcus, J.
1973 Territorial Organization of the Lowland Maya. *Science* 180: 911–916.

Marshack, A.
1964 Lunar Notation on Upper Paleolithic Remains. *Science* 146: 743–745.

Marshall, L.
1965 The !Kung Bushmen of the Kalahari. In *Peoples of Africa*, ed. J. Gibbs, Jr. N.Y.: Holt, Rinehart and Winston.

Mayr, E.
1963 *Animal Species and Evolution*. Cambridge: Harvard University Press.

Mellars, P. A.
1973 The Character of the Middle-Upper Paleolithic in Southwestern France. In *The Explanation of Culture Change*, ed. C. Renfrew. London: Duckworth.

Meyer, Karl E.
1973 *The Plundered Past*. New York: Atheneum.

Millon, R., ed.
1974 *Urbanization at Teotihuacan*. Vol. 1 Austin: University of Texas Press.

Morris, C., and Thompson, D.
1970 Huanuco Viejo: An Inca Administrative Center. *American Antiquity* 35.

Moseley, M.
1974 Chan Chan: Andean Alternative of the Pre-Industrial City. *Science* 187: 219–225.

Mourant, A. E., Kopec, A. C., and Domaniewska-Sobczak, K.
1958 *The ABO Blood Groups*. Oxford, Eng.: Blackwell.

Napier, J. R., and Napier, P. H.
1967 *A Handbook of Living Primates*. New York: Academic Press.

Napier, J. R., and Walker, A. C.
1967 Vertical Clinging and Leaping: A Newly Recognized Category of Locomotor Behavior Among Primates. *Folia Primatologica* 6: 204–219.

Naroll, R.
1962 Floor Area and Settlement Population. *American Antiquity* 27: 587–589.

Netting, R.
1972 Sacred Power and Centralization. In *Population Growth: Anthropological Implications*, ed. B. Spooner. Cambridge: MIT Press.

Patterson, T. C.
1973 *America's Past: New World Archaeology*. Glenview, Ill.: Scott, Foresman.

Peebles, C. S.
1971 Moundville and Surrounding Sites:

Some Structural Considerations of Mortuary Practice 2. *American Antiquity* 36: 68–91.

Perkins, D. H.
1964 The Prehistoric Fauna from Shanidar, Iraq. *Science* 144: 1565–1566.

Pilbeam, D. R.
1972 *The Ascent of Man.* New York: Macmillan.

Pires-Ferreira, J.
1973 Formative Mesoamerican Exchange Networks. Ph.D. dissertation, University of Michigan, Ann Arbor.

Plog, S.
1976 The Inference of Prehistoric Social Organization from Ceramic Design Variability. *Michigan Discussions in Anthropology* 1: 1–47.

Premack, D.
1970 A Functional Analysis of Language. *Journal of the Experimental Analysis of Behavior* 14: 107–125.

Rathje, W. L.
1973 Models for the Mobile Maya: A Variety of Constraints. In *The Explanation of Culture Change*, ed. C. Renfrew. London: Duckworth.
1972 Praise the Gods and Pass the Metates: A Hypothesis of the Development of Lowland and Rainforest Civilizations in Mesoamerica. In *Contemporary Archeology: A Guide to Theory and Contributions*, ed. M. P. Leone. Carbondale: Southern Illinois University Press.

Redman, C. L.
1973 Methodological Frontiers. In *Research and Theory in Current Archeology.* New York: Wiley.

Rensberger, B.
1974 'Talking' Chimpanzee Asks For Names of Things Now. *The New York Times*, December 4, p. 45.

Rohn, A.
1971 *Mug House.* Washington, D.C.: National Park Service.

Rosenthal, B. E.
1977 Nim Chimpsky is a real child prodigy. *Columbia Today* 3 (Winter): 32–35.

Sabloff, J. A., and Rathje, W. L.
1975 The Rise of a Maya Merchant Class. *Scientific American* 233 (October): 72–82.

Sahlins, M. P.
1972 *Essays in Stone Age Economics.* Chicago: Aldine.

Sanders, W. T.
1973 The Cultural Ecology of the Lowland Maya: A Reevaluation. In *The Classic Maya Collapse,* ed. T. Patrick Culbert. Albuquerque: University of New Mexico Press.

Sanders, W. T., and Marino, J.
1970 *New World Prehistory: Archeology of the American Indian.* Englewood Cliffs, N.J.: Prentice-Hall.

Sanders, W. T., and Price, B. J.
1968 *Mesoamerica: The Evolution of a Civilization.* New York: Random House.

Shaw, T.
1976 Changes in African Archaeology in the Last 40 Years. In *African Studies since 1945*, ed. C. Fyte. London: Longman.

Shiffer, M.
1976 *Behavioral Archeology.* New York: Academic Press.

Simons, E. L., and Pilbeam, D. R.
1965 Preliminary Revision of the Drypothecinae (Pongidae, Anthropoidea). *Folia Primatologica* 3: 31–152.

Solecki, R.
1975 Shanidar IV, A Neandertal Flower Burial in Northern Iraq. *Science* 190: 880–881.

Sowell, T.
1977 New light on black I.Q. *The New York Times Magazine,* March 27, pp. 56–60.

Stern, C.
1973 *Principles of Human Genetics.* San Francisco: W. H. Freeman.

Struever, S.
1968 Woodland Subsistence-Settlement Systems in the Lower Illinois Valley. In *New Perspectives in Archeology*, ed. S. R. Binford and L. R. Binford. Chicago: Aldine.

Struever, S., and Houart, G. L.
1972 Hopewell Interaction Sphere Analysis. In *Social Exchange and Interaction,* ed. E. N. Wilmsen. Anthropological

Papers, no. 46. Ann Arbor: University of Michigan, Museum of Anthropology.

Tattersall, I.
1971 *Man's Ancestors: An Introduction to Primate and Human Evolution.* Levittown, N.Y.: Transatlantic.

Thomas, D. H.
1974 *Predicting The Past.* New York: Holt, Rinehart and Winston.

Toffler, A.
1970 *Future Shock.* New York: Random House.

Tringham, R.
1971 *Hunters, Fishers, and Farmers of Eastern Europe: 6000–3000 B.C.* London: Hutchinson University Library.

Tuttle, R.
1972 *The Functional and Evolutionary Biology of Primates.* Chicago: Aldine.

Ucko, P. J., and Rosenfeld, A.
1967 *Paleolithic Cave Art.* New York: McGraw-Hill.

Vadya, A. P., ed.
1969 *Environment and Cultural Behavior.* Garden City, N.Y.: Natural History Press.

Wallace, J.
In Press The Functional Interpretation of Early Hominid Dentitions. In *Early African Hominids,* ed. C. J. Jolly. London: Duckworth.

Warren, K. S.
1974 Precarious Odyssey of an Unconquered Parasite. *Natural History* 83: 46–52.

Washburn, S. L., and Hamburg, B. A.
1965 *Primate Behavior: Field Studies of Primates and Apes.* New York: Holt, Rinehart and Winston.

Whallon, R.
1968 Investigations of Late Prehistoric Social Organization in New York State. In *New Perspectives in Archaeology,* ed. S. R. Binford and L. R. Binford. Chicago: Aldine.

Wheat, J. B.
1973 A Paleo-Indian Bison Kill. In *Early Man in America,* ed. R. S. MacNeish. San Francisco: W. H. Freeman.

Williams, B. J.
1973 *Evolution and Human Origins: An Introduction to Physical Anthropology.* New York: Harper & Row.

Wilmsen, E. N.
1972 Introduction to The Study of Exchange as Social Interaction. In *Social Exchange and Interaction,* ed. E. N. Wilmsen. Anthropological papers, no. 46. Ann Arbor: University of Michigan, Museum of Anthropology.
1968 Paleo-Indian Site Utilization. In *Anthropological Archeology in the Americas,* ed. B. J. Meggers. Washington, D. C.: Anthropological Society of Washington.

Winters, H. D.
1968 Value Systems and Trade Cycles of the Late Archaic in the Midwest. In *New Perspectives in Archeology,* ed. S. R. Binford and L. R. Binford. Chicago: Aldine.

Wittfogel, K.
1957 *Oriental Despotism: A Comparative Study of Total Power.* New Haven: Yale University Press.

Wobst, H. M.
1974 Boundary Conditions for Paleolithic Social Systems: A Simulation Approach. *American Antiquity* 39: 147–178.

Wright, H. T.
1969 *Early Urban Systems in Southwestern Iran.* Ann Arbor: University of Michigan, Museum of Anthropology.

Zevallos, C., *et al.*
1977 The Sen Pablo Corn Kernel and Its Friends. *Science* 196: 385–389.

Index

(Continued from the copyright page)

from J. R. Napier and A. C. Walker, "Vertical Clinging and Leaping: Newly Recognized Category of Locomotor Behavior Among Primates." *Folia Primatologica* 6 (1967). Permission granted by S. Karger AG Basel; (d) modified from M. Hildebrand, "Symmetrical Gaits of Primates," *American Journal of Physical Anthropology* 26 (1968). Permission granted by The Wistar Press. *P. 131:* Figure, from J. R. Napier and P. H. Napier, *A Handbook of Living Primates.* Copyright © 1967 Academic Press, Inc. Reprinted by permission. *Pp. 164–165:* Figures, from I. Tattersall, *Man's Ancestors: An Introduction to Primate and Human Evolution,* Transatlantic Arts, Inc., 1971. Permission granted by the author; and from W. K. Gregory, "On the Structure and Relations of *Notharctus,* an American Eocene Primate," *American Museum of Natural History Memoirs* (1920). Reprinted by permission of the American Museum of Natural History. *P. 228:* Figure, from F. Clark Howell, University of California, Berkeley. Reprinted by permission. *P. 277:* Copyright © 1969 by Chandler Publishing Company. Redrawn from *Man and Culture in the Late Pleistocene* by Richard G. Klein by permission of Chandler Publishing Company, an Intext publisher. *P. 287:* Figure, modified from C. V. Haynes, Jr., "Elephant Hunting in North America," *Scientific American* (June 1966). Permission granted by W. H. Freeman and Company, Publishers; and J. K. Jennings, *Prehistory of North America,* 2/e, McGraw-Hill Book Co., 1974. Reprinted by permission. *P. 350:* Figure, section of the Tikal acropolis. Copyright © The University Museum, University of Pennsylvania. *P. 379:* Figure, from A. C. Allison, "Abnormal Haemoglobin and Erythrocyte Enzyme-Deficiency Traits," in *Genetical Variation in Human Populations,* ed., G. A. Harrison. Copyright © 1961 Pergamon Press, Ltd. Reprinted by permission. *P. 382:* Figure, from A. E. Mourant et al., *The Blood Groups.* Copyright © 1958 Blackwell Scientific Publications, Ltd. Reprinted by permission. *P. 385:* Figure, from N. Kretchmer, "Lactose and Lactase," *Scientific American* (October 1972). Permission granted by W. H. Freeman and Company, Publishers. *P. 390:* Figure, from W. J. Martin, *Physique of Young Adult Males,* H.M.S.O. 1947. Permission granted by Her Majesty's Stationary Office. *P. 392:* Figure, from B. J. Williams, *Evolution and Human Origins: An Introduction to Physical Anthropology.* Copyright © 1973 B. J. Williams. Reprinted by permission of Harper & Row, Publishers, Inc. *P. 401:* Figure, after L. L. Cavali-Sforza and A. W. F. Edwards, "Analysis of Human Evolution," in *Genetics Today,* ed., S. J. Geertz. Copyright © 1963 Pergamon Press, Ltd. Reprinted by permission.

About the Authors

CLIFFORD J. JOLLY was born in 1939, and raised in Leigh-on-Sea in Essex, England. He received both his B.A. with a First Class Honors Degree in 1960, and his Ph.D. in 1964 from University College, London. He began teaching at University College in 1963 and came to the United States in 1967 to teach at New York University, where he is now an Associate Professor. Dr. Jolly has published with Michael R. Chance a book entitled *Social Groups of Monkeys, Apes, and Man.* He has also edited *Early African Hominids.* His articles have been published in edited collections and in journals such as *Nature, Man, Proceedings of the Royal Society,* and *Folia Primatologica.*

JOAN ROSS ACOCELLA is coauthor, with James F. Calhoun, of *Psychology of Adjustment and Human Relationships* and is the writer of *Abnormal Psychology: Current Perspectives* (Second Edition). She has researched and written numerous articles in various areas of the social sciences.

FRED PLOG was born in New Jersey in 1944, and raised in the Southwest. He received his B.A. from Northwestern University in 1966, and his Ph.D. from the University of Chicago in 1969. Before teaching at S.U.N.Y. at Binghamton, he was an Assistant Professor of Anthropology at U.C.L.A. He is the author of *The Study of Prehistoric Change,* co-author with Paul S. Martin of *Arizona Archaeology,* and co-editor with Paul J. Bohannan of *Beyond the Frontier.* He has contributed numerous articles to a variety of journals and edited collections. At present he is conducting research on adaptive strategies of modern and prehistoric patterns in northeastern Arizona.

A Note on the Type

The text of this book is set in a face equivalent to CALEDONIA on a CRT computer composition system. CALEDONIA is a Linotype face designed by W. A. Dwiggins. It belongs to the family of printing types called "modern face" by printers—a term used to mark the change in style of type-letters that occurred about 1800. CALEDONIA borders on the general design of Scotch Modern, but is more freely drawn than that letter.

The type for this book was set by American–Stratford Graphic Services, Inc., Brattleboro, Vt. The book was printed and bound by Von Hoffmann Press, Inc., St. Louis, Mo.

The text design is by Deborah H. Payne.